Alija Izetbegović

INESCAPABLE QUESTIONS

Autobiographical Notes

Translated by
Saba Rissaluddin & Jasmina Izetbegović

The Islamic Foundation
Leicester, England

Copyright © The Islamic Foundation 2003/1423H

Published by
THE ISLAMIC FOUNDATION
Markfield Conference Centre,
Ratby Lane, Markfield, Leicestershire LE67 9SY, UK
TEL: 01530 244944   FAX: 01530 244946
E-MAIL: i.foundation@islamic-foundation.org.uk
WEBSITE: www.islamic-foundation.org.uk

Quran House, PO Box 30611, Nairobi, Kenya

PMB 3193, Kano, Nigeria

All rights reserved.
No part of this publication may be reproduced, stored in a
retrieval system, or transmitted in any form or by any means,
electronic, mechanical, photocopying, recording or otherwise,
without the prior permission of the copyright owner.

British Library Cataloguing in Publication Data
Izetbegović, Alija, 1925- , Inescapable Questions: Autobiographical Notes –
2nd ed. 1. Izetbegović, Alija, 1925- 2. Presidents – Bosnia and Herzegovina –
Biography 3. Authors, Bosnian – Biography 4. Muslims – Bosnia and
Herzegovina – Biography 5. Bosnia and Herzegovina – History – 1945-1992
6. Bosnia and Herzegovina – History – 1992-
I. Title II. Islamic Foundation
949.7'4'03'092

ISBN 0 86037 362 2 HBK
ISBN 0 86037 367 3 PBK

Designed and Typeset by T. J. Bowes
Printed by Antony Rowe Limited

The tragedy of Bosnia is an unparalleled source
of knowledge of the potential of the human species,
the worst and the best alike.

Juan Goytisolo

Contents

INESCAPABLE QUESTIONS

PART OF MY LIFE   1
An Alternative Foreword.

A SHORT HISTORY OF BOSNIA AND HERZEGOVINA   3
Based on Noel Malcolm's book by the same title.

1. YOUTH AND FIRST IMPRISONMENT   11

    Childhood and father's illness. Average schoolboy. First notions of faith and first waverings. Serbs in power. Azići – a mixed village. Draft dodger. Young Muslims. Coming of the Communists. Clash with the Communists. Communist 'equality'. Three years imprisonment with hard labour. Halida.

2. THE SARAJEVO TRIAL   25

    The Islamic Declaration. The Sixty-eight. Islam Between East and West. Reflections on great losers. Arrest, 23 March 1983. Charges and defence. Witnesses withdraw their testimonies. Sentenced to 14 years in prison. 'Verbal delict.' Belgrade intellectuals' petition. Foča Prison. In a cell with murderers. Albanians in Foča Prison.

3. FOUNDING THE PARTY AND AN ATTEMPT
   TO RESTRUCTURE YUGOSLAVIA   59

    Peace of mind, unrest in the country. Statement of the Forty. Constituent Assembly and Manifesto of the SDA: Party for Democratic Action. Travelling to America. Meeting Serb and Croat émigrés. Rally in Foča. Rally in Velika Kladuša: debates on seceding from Yugoslavia and on armaments. Zulfikarpašić and the split. First meeting with Tuđman. Victory at the polls. Member of the Presidency of Bosnia and Herzegovina. Meetings in Belgrade. Gligorov-Izetbegović Plan. Visits to Austria, Iran, Turkey, the USA, Italy. Meeting the Pope and the Serbian Orthodox Patriarch. First meeting with Milošević. The dissolution of Yugoslavia. War in Slovenia and Croatia. Zulfikarpašić and Filipović's so-called 'Historic Accord'. Responses to Alan

Cooperman. Last attempt – the Hague meeting. First SDA Congress. Sarajevo Peace Accord and the shifting of the war to Bosnia and Herzegovina.

4. WAR DIARY 109

SDS and HDZ dismember Bosnia and Herzegovina. Referendum on independence for Bosnia and Herzegovina. Cutileiro's mediation. Start of the war of aggression against Bosnia and Herzegovina. Sarajevo under siege. Cutileiro persists. Meetings in Lisbon and Brussels. Meeting with Kostić and Adžić in Skopje. 2 May – taken hostage in Sarajevo airport. State of war. Agenda of the Presidency of Bosnia and Herzegovina. Arms embargo and the arming of the Bosnia and Herzegovina Army. Concentration camps in Bosnia and Herzegovina. Speech at the OSCE Summit, Helsinki, 1992. Meeting with US President George Bush. Attempt to lift the siege of Sarajevo. London Conference. Fall of Bosanski Brod. Conference in Jeddah. First clashes with the HVO. Spring/summer 1993 – Operation Igman. How we outwitted the Chetniks. Tunnel under Sarajevo airport. Letter to President Clinton. Letter to the Security Council. Atrocities in Ahmići. Speech at the 48th Session of the UN General Assembly. Insurrection in Sarajevo and showdown. General Divjak's letter. Silajdžić's first government. Pressure on Vitez and peace with the HVO. The Washington peace and the Federation of Bosnia and Herzegovina. Dissensions in the Presidency of Bosnia and Herzegovina. Exclusion zone around Sarajevo. Operation 'Spring 94'. Goražde crisis. Speech at the 49th Session of the UN General Assembly. Crisis in the Krajina. Speech at the OSCE Summit in Budapest. Message to the people of the Krajina. Letter to President Clinton. Role of Muslim countries. Speech at the OIC Summit in Casablanca. Four-month truce. Liberation of Vlašić. No extension to the truce. Death of Minister Ljubijankić. Failure to lift the siege of Sarajevo. The Split Accord and an end to the blockade of the Krajina. Sarajevo marketplace atrocity. NATO air-strikes.

5. SREBRENICA 229

Security Council Resolution No. 819 – Srebrenica a safe area. Famine in Srebrenica. May 1995 – helicopter downed. Two meetings with Naser Orić. Start of massive attack. Letter to President Clinton. General Rupert Smith announces air-strikes – General Janvier cancels them. Disorganisation in the town and the army. Fall of the town. Exodus and massacre of civilians. Mladić moves against Žepa. Evacuation of civilians from Žepa. Letter to John Major. Letter to the UN Security Council. Report by UN General Secretary – international community acknowledges responsibility for tragedy in Srebrenica. Replies to David Harland's questions.

6. WAR AND JAW 247

Carrington's mediation. Vance-Owen Plan. Karadžić rejects the plan. Persuasion in Athens – Karadžić signs, the Serb Assembly rejects it. So-called Joint Action Plan – the West yields to Karadžić. Proclamation to the citizens of Bosnia and Herzegovina. Vance withdraws, Stoltenberg replaces him. Owen-Stoltenberg Plan. UNPROFOR's double-dealing. Pressures. Meeting on the British aircraft carrier, HMS Invincible. First Bosniac Assembly and Parliamentary Assembly of the Republic of Bosnia and Herzegovina in session. Richard Holbrooke and the American peace initiative. Tragedy on Igman. Air-strikes halted. Letters to Presidents Clinton and Chirac. Meeting with Holbrooke in Ankara and Republika Srpska. Geneva Conference and Basic Principles. Answers for Sky News. Tuđman's interview with Le Figaro. Meeting in New York. American ultimatum and cease-fire.

7. DAYTON DIARY 289

Sixteen-point peace plan. Speech at the 50th Session of the UN General Assembly. Meeting with President Clinton. Meeting with Mohammad Ali. Statement on peace. Aviation Museum at the Wright-Petterson Airbase. Talks with Milošević and Bulatović. Talks with Granić and Šušak. First part of the General Framework Agreement for Peace. Arms balance in the region. Central Bank and currency. IFOR – Multinational Implementation Force. The issue of elections. Institutions. The question of Sarajevo. Corridor to Goražde. Signing of the Agreement on Implementing the Federation. About Tuđman. Talks with US Secretary of State Christopher. Maps, maps, maps. Talks with Bildt and three European political foreign affairs directors. Zubak rebels. Talks with Shattuck. Supervision of elections. Voting of refugees and displaced persons. Talks with Antony Lake. Reservations about Project 'Delta'. Talks with Secretary William Perry. Milošević retreats – IFOR to police the entire territory of Bosnia and Herzegovina. Brčko corridor. Milošević hands over Sarajevo, but not Brčko. One-night collapse of negotiations. Milošević agrees to arbitration on Brčko. President Clinton announces peace. Initialled in Dayton, signed in Paris. Speeches. Repeal of state of war. Statement for El-Mundo. 'Civil war' – a fraud.

8. AFTER DAYTON 337

Serbs attempt to postpone the handover of Sarajevo. Letter to Admiral Smith. The storm over Father Christmas. Rome meeting. Pogorelica. Letter to Mme Agnelli. Heart attack. Message to the people of Mostar. 'Rules of the road.' Integration of Sarajevo. Serbs leave, burning Sarajevo, IFOR looks on.

Message to the Serbs. Law on amnesty. Games over Brčko. Letter to Carl Bildt. Speech in Zenica. Speech in Žuca. First signs of corruption. Speech in Gelsenkirchen. Speech in Grebak and what The New York Times' journalist heard. End of the War. Presidency of the Republic of Bosnia and Herzegovina. Speech in the 51st Session of the UN General Assembly. Arms reduction. Responses for Avaz – the balance sheet for 1996. More games over Brčko. Considering resignation. Award from the American Center for Democracy. Meeting with President Clinton. The Pope's visit to Sarajevo. Bonn Conference. The battle for a single currency. Speech at the OIC Summit in Tehran. The mistake in French protocol. Letter to President Chirac. Mitterrand and Chirac. Bernard Henry Levý. Croatia continues its dual policy. General elections, and victory. Treaty on the use of Ploce Port and Agreement on Special Relationship with Croatia. Last meeting with King Hasan. Madrid Conference. So-called 'Secret Report.' Final decision on Brčko. My testimony. Refugee returns proceeds at snail's pace. Unsuccessful presidential initiative on returns. Opposition campaign steps up. Kosovo crisis and NATO air-strikes against Yugoslavia. Speech in the Council of Europe. Silajdžić's initiative to revise the Dayton Accord. Summit of the Stability Pact for South-Eastern Europe. Klein's statement on corruption in Bosnia and Herzegovina. The New York Times' article on corruption in Bosnia and Herzegovina. Open letter to the High Representative. Report of the International Commission. New York session on the Presidency of Bosnia and Herzegovina – decision on border services. My 'rabble-rousing' speech. General Elections, April 2000, and electoral setback for the SDA. Deteriorating health. Resignation from the Presidency. Rule by foreigners.

APPENDICES 451

General Divjak's Letter. From a conversation with Sidran. Lecture to the German Association for Foreign Affairs, Bonn, 17 March 1995. Talks at the French Institute for International Relations, Paris, 30 August 1995. Two interviews for the Sarajevo weekly Dani (11 December 1994 and March 1998). Lecture at the ISESCO meeting, Riyadh, 6 December 1997. Some more important opinions and statements.

Part of My Life

An Alternative Foreword.

The following represents fragments of my life, since I have either forgotten whole sections of it, or else they belong only to me. What remains is a chronicle rather than an autobiography, an account of the events that have taken place during my lifetime, recounted as truly and sincerely as a personal account ever can be.

I am not familiar with how memoirs are written. Reading Churchill's famous work, I realised that in this type of literature, as Churchill himself says, the writer links his chronicle of military and political events 'with the threads of his own experience.' Memoirs, therefore, are always a subjective perception. They are not history, nor should history be written by those who make it or are part of it. A relatively large part of this book is composed of letters or of parts of my letters, speeches and interviews from that period.

I thought it essential to quote some of them in full or at length, since they were my immediate reactions, my rapid and at times on-the-spot comments on events as they unfolded, and as a result they are the most authentic testimony to them. It was also a way of avoiding the kind of hindsight that often appears in writings of this kind.

In brief, the following is my truth about a difficult period of our history.

Alija Izetbegović
Sarajevo, 31 March 2001

A Short History of Bosnia and Herzegovina

Based on Noel Malcolm's book by the same title.

Bosnia and Herzegovina is located in the western part of the Balkan peninsula between latitude 42.25° and 45.15°N and longitude 15.45° and 19.41°E. It borders the Republic of Croatia to the north and west, and Serbia and Montenegro to the east and south. Its surface area is 51,129 km², with a population of 4,124,256 (according to the 1991 Census) and an average population density of 81 inhabitants per km². The name Herzegovina relates chiefly to the area formed by the Neretva river basin, while Bosnia relates to the central, eastern and western regions, which form the greater part of the country.

The political borders of Bosnia and Herzegovina were determined by a series of treaties and conventions during the 18th and 19th centuries (from 1699 to 1878). At the second session of AVNOJ[1] in 1943 a decision was passed whereby the country's borders would be those of 1918, with the exception of a few minor alterations near Sutorina and in the areas of Bosansko Grahovo and Bihać.

Bosnia and Herzegovina is a European country with a long history; it has existed as a geo-political entity almost without break from the mediaeval period to the present. For the greater part of the period 1180 to 1436 it was an independent kingdom; from 1580 to 1878 it was an *eyalet* (the term for the largest territorial unit within the Ottoman Empire); from 1878 to 1918 it was a 'Crown land' within the Austro-Hungarian Empire; and from 1945 to 1992 it was one of the federal republics of Yugoslavia. Thus for 650 years out of the past 800 it has existed on the maps as an entity named Bosnia.

The earliest inhabitants of whom we have any historical details are the Illyrians. The Slavs moved in large numbers down the Balkan peninsula

[1] National Antifascist Liberation Council of Yugoslavia.

in the late 6th century, settling as far south as northern Greece. The first surviving mention of Bosnia as a distinct territory is in a politico-geographical handbook written in 958 by the Byzantine Emperor Constantine Porphyrogenitus.

In 1102 Hungarian rule was formally extended over Bosnia, but as a remote and impenetrable territory it was ruled by a *ban*, a mediaeval Bosnian ruler, whose authority became more and more independent. By the late 12th century Bosnia had become, for the first time, a more or less independent state.

Three powerful Bosnian rulers stand out in the high Middle Ages: Ban Kulin, who ruled from 1180 to 1204; Ban Stjepan (Stephen) Kotromanić (1322-53) and King Stjepan Tvrtko (1353-91). Under the second of these Bosnia expanded to include the principality of Hum (Herzegovina) and, under the third, it expanded further to the south, acquiring a large part of the Dalmatian coast.

Bosnia was cut off from the central Roman Empire until the mid 14th century, with the coming of the Franciscans. The Bosnian Church had probably fallen away from the Catholic Church as early as the 1230s, and, as it gradually became more autonomous, so the schism with Rome became ever greater.

In 1463, Bosnia came under Turkish rule. A Western commentator noted in 1595 that 'Slavonic' was the third language of the Ottoman Empire. The Sokollu family of Istanbul, which supplied a succession of grand viziers, was of Bosnian origin. During the 16th and 17th centuries there were nine such grand viziers of Bosnian origin. The Islamisation of a large part of the population under the Turks remains the most distinctive and important feature of modern Bosnian history. The Albanian priest and apostolic visitor, Peter Masarechi, drew up a report in 1624 in which he stated that there were 150,000 Catholics, 75,000 Eastern Orthodox worshippers and 450,000 Muslims in Bosnia at that time.

In the first 15 years of Ottoman control of Sarajevo (formerly known as Vrhbosna) the Turks built a mosque, a *tekke* (the lodge of a dervish order), a *musafirhan* (an inn for travellers), a *hamam* (Turkish baths), a bridge over the River Miljacka, a system of piped water and the *saraj* or governor's court that gave the city its new name. The large market in the heart of the town was also established at the outset.

It was the custom for rich men to endow lands in permanent trust to provide an income for important institutions (not only mosques and schools, but also inns, baths and bridges). This type of religious-charitable foundation is known as a *vakuf* (Arabic *waqf*); it is estimated that one third of cultivable land was owned by *vakufs* at the time of the Austro-Hungarian occupation of Bosnia in 1878.

From the 1480s onwards Orthodox priests and believers are mentioned for the first time in many parts of Bosnia. Several Orthodox monasteries are known to have been built in the 16th century (Tavna, Lomnica, Papraća, Ozren and Gostović), and the important monastery of Rmanj, in north-west Bosnia, is first mentioned in 1515.

Major wars in Bosnia occurred at least every two generations. The war from which the Ottoman Empire never really recovered was that against Austria of 1683-99. Between 1684 and 1687 the Austrians gradually occupied the whole of Hungary, driving thousands of Muslims southwards away from their lands and flooding Bosnia with refugees. By 1687, roughly 30,000 Muslims had also fled from Lika in the west. These influxes of refugees from all sides had a huge effect on the size and nature of the Bosnian population – it has been estimated that as many as 130,000 refugees found their way to Bosnia as a result of this war.

In 1737 the Bosnian Governor, Ali-paša Hećimović, defeated the Austrian army at the Battle of Banja Luka and, in the peace agreement which ensued (the Treaty of Belgrade, 1739), the northern border of modern Bosnia was established.

The next Austrian war, which began in 1788, had more serious political repercussions. Emperor Joseph II of Austria and Catherine the Great of Russia agreed to take over the Ottoman lands in the Balkans and share them between themselves. This set the pattern of geo-political interests in the Balkans that was to eventually lead to the Austrian occupation of Bosnia in 1878 and its annexation 30 years later.

The great powers of Europe, meeting at the Congress of Berlin in July 1878, decided that Bosnia and Herzegovina, although still in theory under Ottoman suzerainty, would be occupied and administered by Austria-Hungary. The Austrian occupation of Bosnia began and was completed in about three months; there was some fierce resistance, and frequent guerilla attacks, but the Austrians' total losses amounted to no more than 946 dead and 3,980 wounded.

The Austrian occupation of Bosnia produced a wave of Muslim refugees, most of them fleeing to Turkey. The Austro-Hungarian authorities issued official figures stating that 32,625 émigrés left between 1883 and 1905, with another 24,000 leaving between 1906 and 1918. However, these figures do not include those who left illegally, nor any of those who fled in the first four years (up to 1883). A total emigration of

300,000 has been claimed by some Muslim historians, but this seems improbably high.

In 1889 the Catholic Cathedral was consecrated in Sarajevo, followed by a new church of St. Anthony of Padua.

The man in charge of Bosnia from 1882 to 1903 was Benjamin Kallay, an Austrian historian and former diplomat. His Bosnian policy aimed at insulating the country from the nationalist political movements in Serbia and Croatia, and developing the idea of Bosnian nationhood as a separate and unifying factor. It was essential for his purposes that the idea of Bosnian nationhood should be first taken up by the Muslims.

In 1909, under the liberal-minded Common Minister of Finance Baron Burian (who held the post from 1903 to 1912), the Muslims were granted a system of *vakuf* administration and, in the following year, a Bosnian parliament was elected. Although it was based on a limited franchise and had no direct legislative power, it did enable the various organisations which the local communities had recently set up – the Muslim National Organisation (1906), the Serbian National Organisation (1907) and the Croatian National Society (1908) – to begin to function as real political parties. Though some prominent Muslim intellectuals 'declared' themselves as Croats or Serbs, such individual acts never undermined the general position of the Muslims, who were now firmly established as a distinct political entity.

Following the assassination of Archduke Franz Ferdinand at the end of July 1914, Austria-Hungary declared war on Serbia; the First World War had begun – it was to end in 1918 with the defeat of the Central Powers.

On 30 May 1917, the Slovenian politician Korešec and some of his colleagues issued a declaration calling for the unification of the Slovenes, Croats and Serbs in a single state. A similar proclamation was made by the Croatian Parliament on 29 October 1918. The party that quickly acquired a near-monopoly of Muslim support was the Yugoslav Muslim Organisation – founded in Sarajevo in February 1919. Its leader, Dr. Mehmed Spaho, argued that Bosnia should seek to preserve its identity as an autonomous unit within the Yugoslav State. When Yugoslav-wide elections were held in November 1920, Spaho's party won nearly all the Muslim votes in Bosnia and Herzegovina, acquiring 24 seats in the National Assembly.

In January 1929, King Alexander suspended the constitution and announced that the state would no longer be known as the Kingdom of the Serbs, Croats and Slovenes, but, instead, as Yugoslavia. The state was divided into nine *banovinas,* territorial units within the Kingdom, which cut across the old borders of the constituent elements of the Yugoslav State. Bosnia was divided into four *banovinas*: Vrbaska, which included part of Croatia; Drinska, which included a large part of Serbia; Zetska, consisting mainly of Montenegro and Primorska, which included part of the Dalmatian coast. For the first time in more than 400 years, Bosnia had been partitioned. The Bosnian Muslims were deeply unhappy: they were a minority in each of the four *banovinas.*

The Croats did not accept Alexander's Constitution; there began a political struggle between the Serbs and the Croats that would last ten years. In August 1939 the Serbian Minister, Cvetković, and the Croat leader, Maček, reached agreement on the new structure of Yugoslavia: the first point they agreed upon was the partition of Bosnia and Herzegovina; the two principal Croatian *banovinas,* Savska and Primorska (which included parts of Bosnia and Herzegovina) were merged into one, the Croatian *banovina,* and the inhabitants of the rest of Bosnia were to 'decide by plebiscite whether they would join Croatia or Serbia'.

Mehmed Spaho died in June 1939 while these negotiations were in their most critical phase. His successor, Džafer Kulenović, called for the creation of a special *banovina* for Bosnia, but his requests were ignored.

On 6 April 1941 the Germans invaded Yugoslavia, and four days later – on 10 April 1941 – they proclaimed the new 'Independent State of Croatia' (known by its Serbo-Croat initials as the NDH) incorporating the whole of Bosnia and Herzegovina. It was not an independent state, but was rather divided into two zones of German and Italian military occupation, with the dividing-line running diagonally through Bosnia from the north-west to the south-east.

The Communist Party of Yugoslavia, which staged an uprising against the Germans in 1941, had no clear ideas about what the status of the Bosnian Muslims should be. In 1936 a Communist intellectual, the Slovene Edvard Kardelj, wrote: 'We cannot speak of the Muslims as a nation, but ... as a special ethnic group,' and at the Party Congress held in 1940 Milovan Đilas, who was in charge of nationalities policy, excluded the Muslims from the list of Yugoslav nations.

There had been persecutions of minorities in the so-called Independent State of Croatia (1941-45), particularly of Serbs and Jews. In the summer and autumn of 1941 leading Muslims issued a series of public resolutions and protests against this rule of terror; such resolutions appeared in Sarajevo, Prijedor, Mostar, Banja Luka, Bijeljina and Tuzla.

In 1945 the Communists gained power in Yugoslavia. With this the majority of Muslims became reconciled to their fate: instead of absorption into Croatia or Serbia they were offered a federal solution in which Bosnia would continue to exist. What was important for them, above all, was an end to the killing. Altogether 75,000 Bosnian Muslims are thought to have died in the Second World War – 8.1% of their total population. The Communists dealt harshly with anyone who did not accept their rule. The historian Noel Malcolm quotes the estimate of 250,000 people killed in Yugoslavia by Tito's mass shootings, forced death marches and concentration camps in the period 1945-6.

The Yugoslav Federal Constitution, proclaimed in January 1946, was a direct imitation of the Soviet Constitution promulgated ten years earlier. It contained clauses proclaiming that Yugoslavia would maintain freedom of belief, but in practice things were very different. The Shari'ah courts of Islamic law were suppressed in 1946, and in 1950 the last *maktab* (elementary school) in which pupils gained a basic knowledge of the Qur'an was closed. Muslim cultural and educational societies such as 'Gajret', 'Narodna Uzdanica', 'Preporod' were also abolished. Only the official Islamic Religious Community was permitted, with two strictly supervised *madrasas* for the training of Muslim clergy. The Muslim printing-house in Sarajevo was also closed down, and the body which administered the *vakufs* was put under state control. Some of these measures, however, were covertly resisted: Islamic texts continued to circulate, children were taught in mosques, the dervish orders kept up their practices in private houses and one students' organisation – the 'Young Muslims' – resisted the campaign against Islam until several hundred of its members were imprisoned in 1949-50.

The question of what it meant to be a Muslim in Bosnia and Herzegovina – was it a religious, an ethnic or a national identity – had not disappeared, despite the belief of the Yugoslav Communist Party in the early Tito years that it would. In the 1948 Census the Muslims had three options: they could call themselves Muslim Serbs, Muslim Croats or 'Muslims, nationally undeclared'. The result was that 72,000 declared themselves as Serbs and 25,000 as Croats, but 778,000 registered as 'undeclared'. The next Census, in 1953, produced a similar result. On the 1971 Census form, for the first time, the phrase appeared 'Muslim, in the national sense.'

After Tito's death the full extent of the socialist economic system's dysfunctionality became apparent, and national tensions increased. In 1987 the annual rate of inflation in Yugoslavia rose to 120%, and in 1988 to 250%. By the end of that year, Yugoslavia's foreign debt rose to in excess of US$20 billion. The population were increasingly impoverished, which provided the ideal conditions for extreme nationalists to get to work, stirring up the politics of resentment.

On 28 June 1989, Vidovdan or St. Vitus' Day, several hundred thousand Serbs assembled at the battlefield site of Gazimestan, outside the capital of Kosovo, Priština, to celebrate the six-hundredth anniversary of the Battle of Kosovo. 'After six centuries, we are again engaged in battles and quarrels,' Slobodan Milošević told the crowd. 'They are not armed battles, but this cannot be excluded yet.' The crowd roared its approval.

The trickle of independent political parties that had started up in Yugoslavia in 1988 now became a flood. In January 1990, the Slovenian Communists walked out of the Yugoslav Communist Party Congress; both Slovenia and Croatia made arrangements for multi-party elections in the spring of 1990. These were won in Slovenia by a Liberal nationalist coalition, and in Croatia by the new Croatian nationalist party – the Croatian Democratic Union (HDZ), led by Franjo Tuđman.

In the November 1990 Elections in Bosnia and Herzegovina, the Muslim Party for Democratic Action (SDA) gained 86 seats out of the 240 in the Assembly and other Muslims, including Zulfikarpašić's Bosnian Muslim Association (MBO), gained another 13. The Serbian Democratic Party (SDS), led by Radovan Karadžić, gained 72.

By early 1991, Milošević was saying publicly that if there were any attempt to replace the federal structure of Yugoslavia with some looser, confederal arrangement, he would seek to annex whole areas of Croatia and Bosnia. On 25 June 1991 both Croatia and Slovenia declared independence. It was now necessary for Bosnia and Herzegovina to seek independence too; otherwise it would be left in a rump Yugoslavia under Serbian control. On 6 April 1992 Bosnia and Herzegovina was recognised as an independent state by the European Community. That same day the aggression against the country began.

Although the United Nations recognised Bosnia and Herzegovina on 22 May 1992 and admitted it as a member-state, the arms embargo that had been proclaimed the previous year against Yugoslavia as a whole was not lifted. It was as if nothing had changed. Serb military commanders sometimes boasted that they had enough arms and ammunition to continue the war in Bosnia and Herzegovina for another six or seven years; the embargo would have no real effect on their military capacity. But to the Bosnian defence forces it was, in the long term, a sentence of death.

Both the US and the German governments would soon press for the lifting of the embargo, but the then British Foreign Secretary, Douglas Hurd, vigorously opposed the idea, arguing that it would 'only prolong the fighting.' The embargo was not lifted, but the fighting continued, prolonged until the end of 1995. It was ended on 21 November 1995, with the Dayton Peace Accord (signed in Paris on 14 December 1995).

Chapter 1

YOUTH AND FIRST IMPRISONMENT

Childhood and father's illness. Average schoolboy. First notions of faith and first waverings. Serbs in power. Azići – a mixed village. Draft dodger. Young Muslims. Coming of the Communists. Clash with the Communists. Communist 'equality.' Three years imprisonment with hard labour. Halida.

My childhood seems very distant now, as if I were looking at the mountains on a clear day – I can see the outlines perfectly well, but not the details. Life is not short, I find it long.

I was born 75 years ago in Bosanski Šamac, in a house with a view of Bosnia's two largest rivers – the Bosna and the Sava. When I was two years old we moved to Sarajevo, where I later went to school. One day I passed the building of the school where I spent eight years of my childhood and adolescence: the First Boys' Gymnasium, or General-programme High School. It was famous, and those of us who graduated from it spoke about it with pride. It was in Sarajevo, too, that I gained my Law degree. I began by studying Agronomy, but after the third year switched to Law.

I belonged to a large family. My father had five children by my mother – three daughters and two sons. I am the older of the sons, but not the eldest, for I had two older sisters. I also had two half-brothers from my father's first marriage. His first wife died and, in about 1921, he married my mother. We have evidence that our family came from Belgrade at the end of the last century; my grandfather was born there, in a house that, as my late uncle told me, still stood until after the Second World War. It was in a spot now known as Francuska (French) Street, but was pulled down after the war. My grandfather, who served in the army in Istanbul, there married a young Turkish girl, Sedika, who was born in Iskjudar, part of Istanbul on the far side of the Bosphorus. My father understood some Turkish but, as far as I can recall, he could not speak it.

This would sometimes annoy my mother, who knew no Turkish, and hence felt excluded from these conversations.

My childhood was affected by my father's illness. He had been seriously wounded in the First World War, at the Italian front in Piava. This later turned into a kind of paralysis, so that, for the last ten years of his life, he was more or less bedridden. My late mother took great care of him, and we children helped as best we could, growing up with a good deal of freedom.

My father's family had once been very wealthy. He himself worked as a merchant in Bosanski Šamac, but his business soon failed in curious circumstances. We moved to Sarajevo, where life was much harder for us, but had some advantages too: not least that we were able to acquire an education: had we remained in Bosanski Šamac, this may not have been possible.

My late mother was a very pious woman, and I owe my commitment to religion at least partly to her. She invariably rose in time to read *Sabah* – the formal pre-dawn prayer. She would wake me, too, so I could go to the local mosque – the Hadžijska Mosque near the *Vijećnica* (Town Hall). I was reluctant to get up, naturally, being then only 12 or 14 years old, but I was always glad when returning home, especially on spring mornings. The sun would already have risen, and the old Imam Mujezinović would be in the Mosque. He always recited the wonderful *Surah al-Rahman* from the Qur'an with the second *ruku* (bowing) of the *Sabah* prayer. The Mosque amid the spring blossom, the *Sabah* morning prayer, that *Surah al-Rahman* and that *alim* – respected by everyone in the neighbourhood, form one of the beautiful images that I can still see clearly through the mists of the years that have long since passed.

In every respect I was a blend of my father and my mother: physically, I resembled my mother and her brothers more, which displeased me – I wanted to look like my father, who was a handsome, well-built man. But as for character, I was more like my father; all my mother's relatives were extroverts, open and communicative, while the Izetbegovićs were taciturn and withdrawn.

Although he had come to Sarajevo amid my mother's relatives, my father was very highly regarded by her family. When there were family or marital problems, he was a kind of judge or adjudicator in the dispute. I knew that the rest of the family listened to him, and that impressed me. As a child I was quite simply in love with my mother, and whenever she went out visiting with my father, I could not go to sleep until they came back. I would lie there awake, sometimes as late as midnight, listening out for them. I was so tired that I would fall asleep as soon as I heard the door opening and their footsteps as they entered.

I was still quite young when I freed myself from my parents' influence and began to live my life as I myself chose. Aged 15, I began to waver a little in my faith. With my companions and friends of that time I would talk about anything and everything. We read communist and atheist writings. At that time Yugoslavia was full of very powerful communist propaganda, most of it disseminated illegally by means of various brochures that circulated from hand to hand; the Communists were very effective at doing this. It was in part a reaction to the emergence of fascism in Europe – communism did not understand democracy. In Yugoslavia it was an antifascist movement, a counter-ideology, and one that was no less totalitarian. Red totalitarianism arose to confront black totalitarianism.

The Communists were particularly strong in my high school, known to have a number of teachers who covertly belonged to the communist movement. I managed to get hold of some brochures that were illegally distributed around the classrooms, and began to contemplate the problem of social justice, or rather injustice as I saw it then, and God. In communist propaganda God was on the side of injustice, since the Communists saw religion as the 'opium of the people' – a means of allaying people's unease so that they would not strive for a better life in the world of reality. It was very easy to fall for this line. I did not accept it, however; it seemed to me, if not always quite clearly, that the chief message of religion is responsibility. Its message is the same even to kings and emperors: that they should be responsible. Even if they have no fear of the police on this earth, as the police are in their hands, religion tells them that they will have to answer for the violence they commit, that there is no escaping accountability. A universe without God seemed to me to be a universe without meaning.

So after a year or two of vacillation, my faith returned, but in a different fashion. A certain firm steadiness in my faith – to the extent that it exists – derives from these doubts that arose during my youth. It was no longer merely the religion I had inherited: it was a newly-adopted faith. I never lost it again.

Later, I wrote about these quandaries and hesitations of mine, but I think that these articles were in fact a demonstration, not to others but to myself, of my faith.

At school I oscillated between being a very good and a poor pupil: I would study diligently for a while, then put my books aside completely for a time. In the fourth grade of gymnasium I was exempted from sitting the school certificate examinations, only to get poor marks at the end of the following, fifth grade. What was more curious still, was that this was in history, although I always liked history. I blamed my history teacher, not myself, for my poor marks. He was a very tall man, a Serb from Serbia proper, who spoke pure *Ekavski* – the eastern dialect, and often played practical jokes on this or that Muslim pupil. I probably thought that this was a good enough reason to blame him for my poor marks.

In the higher grades of the gymnasium, I substituted reading for all my studies. By the ages of 18 and 19, I was reading all the major works of European philosophy; I did not appreciate Hegel at that time, but was later to change my views. The works that made a particular impression on me were Bergson's *Creative Evolution*, Kant's *Critique of Pure Reason* and Spengler's two-volume *Decline of the West*.

I did not abandon school altogether, however. I graduated in summer 1943, in the middle of the Second World War. Stalingrad and El Alamein had already occurred, and the disembarkations in Sicily and Italy were about to begin. I have vivid recollections of that war, of the difficult years of danger and shortages. I remember, for example, the great famine of 1941; at home we were more often hungry than well-fed. Things improved later, thanks principally to the black-marketeers who smuggled in large quantities of food. Everything was at a standstill, only the black market was functioning – which it did ever more profitably.

Here in Sarajevo, the Ustasha, a pro-Nazi regime, were in power. After sitting my high school diploma examinations I should have enlisted in the army, but I did not do so. Instead I became a draft-dodger, and managed to remain in hiding at home throughout 1944. One day I learned that the military authorities were looking for me, and escaped to Posavina, my native region. This is a story in itself – a special experience in the nexus of the happenings of war at that time. I saw various groups in action: the Chetniks, the Ustasha, the Partisans and even us Muslims (the armed Muslim militia groups that were also actors in the events in northern Bosnia).

We also had some wonderful times during my childhood. From my mother's family we inherited a small property in the village of Azići in

Stup, not far from Sarajevo – the famous Džabijina Kula, destroyed in the recent war, a white cube of a house visible from a distance, with indigo-blue windows on all four sides. The garden had an ash-tree, the largest tree on the Sarajevo plain, and a Roman well. In summer, after classes were over, we would go out to our property. This went on for seven or eight years in a row, from 1932 to 1940. During the first few years, before my father's health collapsed, we would go with my parents. Later they would stay in Sarajevo and we would go to the property in the company of my widowed aunt, my mother's sister. Those summer days in the country were without doubt the best days of my life; the mornings were especially beautiful. During the recent war this was the front line, but this little plot of land on which I spent my childhood remained on our side of the front line, some 50 to 100 metres from the first trenches.

Azići was a very mixed village both as to religion and national affiliation. There were two Muslim families, and the rest were Orthodox or Catholic. There was also a Catholic church, destroyed in the recent war; folk festivals used to be held outside this church in summer. When I attempt to understand the causes of this recent war, the memory of Azići and that religiously mixed population always comes to my mind. As I recall it too, there was considerable mutual respect among the different groups. Whenever our neighbour Risto Berjan, an old Serb householder, walked through the village, he would always greet any woman he saw in her garden, but with his face turned away so as not to violate Muslim custom. That is how it was among the people. But in the upper strata, in the government, it was quite different.

Between the two world wars the *bans* had their official seat in the building I now use as a member of the Presidency of Bosnia and Herzegovina. From 1929 this was the (so-called) Drinska *banovina*. Sarajevo was its capital, and the *ban* was invariably a Serb. The first was one Velimir Popović, followed by Ljuba Davidović, then by ... Velimir or Ljuba, it was always a Serb from Serbia proper. I recall one other thing in this regard: almost all my elementary school teachers were Serbs. In first and second grade my teacher was old Mrs. Šušljić, a woman from Serbia, of whom I was very fond. In the third grade the teacher was Bilićar and in the fourth Krstić, again both Serbs. For a short time only we had a Muslim, Muhić. It was the same throughout Bosnia; this was a deliberate attempt to Serbianise the Muslims. We learned about King Alexander, assassinated in Marseille in 1934, when I was in the fourth grade of elementary school. When the King was killed, every house in the city had to display a black flag. The black flag remained in our house from

October to April: for six months the towns looked like black scarecrows. What is more, in some schools songs about St. Sava – the Serbian saint – were sung and the children of all faiths had to learn them. This custom was later abolished, but even then the 27th of January was always celebrated as the feast of St. Sava, the 'enlightener of people'.

More or less all the mayors of the towns, and in particular the district heads, were Serbs. This went on until the Cvetković-Maček Agreement that partitioned Bosnia, parts of the country being absorbed into the so-called Croatian *banovina* just before the Second World War. Then there came the invasion of Poland, and later the spread of war to Yugoslavia, so that the partition came to nothing.

Serbian hegemony continued under the communist regime. To begin with this was repressed by the communist, somewhat anational, mind-set, but the Serbs gradually took over power by other means – they joined the Communist Party itself. The national imbalance in Yugoslavia, or more precisely the predominance of the Serbs in all the institutions of government, led to the uprising of the Slovenes and Croats and the dissolution of Yugoslavia. The Muslims of Bosnia were divided, so that instead of being Muslims or Bosniacs, they were Muslim Serbs, who had their own cultural association 'Gajret', or Muslim Croats, with their 'Narodna Uzdanica'. This again was an attempt to divide Bosnia between the Serbs and the Croats; the attempt would later take on a bloody aspect.

A few months before the fall of Yugoslavia, I came into contact for the first time with the group known as the Young Muslims. They were, for the most part, students at the Universities of Zagreb and Belgrade, together with some pupils of the First and Second Gymnasia in Sarajevo. One group was composed of Tarik Muftić, a forestry student; Esad Karađozović, a medical student killed by the Communists in 1945; Emin Granov, an engineering student; and Husref Bašagić, a civil-engineering student who left Yugoslavia in 1951 never to return. There was also a young agronomist, Asaf Serdarević, also killed by the Communists at the end of 1944. They outlined some new ideas that were more in line with what I wanted to hear about my religion. It was all very different from what we had learned in the *maktabs*, the religious instruction we had had at school, the lectures we had attended, or the articles we read in the journals of the day. I see it as a matter of the relationship between essence and form – the *hojjas* (Islamic religious teachers or priests) were, in our view, more inclined to interpret the rituals or external forms of Islam, while neglecting the essence.

In March 1941 we tried to found a Young Muslims' association and to register it on the basis of the regulations in force at the time. We held a constituent assembly, for which a board of some kind was appointed, but in April the Germans invaded Yugoslavia and the association was never registered.

It was Islam and two points of reference of oppositional nature – antifascism and anti-communism – that determined the general focus of the Young Muslims' movement. Two systems – fascism and communism – personified by Hitler and Stalin, characterised the world order of the day. The West was visibly part of the scene, too, but these were the new trends that aspired to destroy or change the old world. As it turned out, this was nothing but an illusion; that so-called old world remained in existence, and changed itself.

When the Young Muslims' movement emerged, in the early 1940s, the Muslim world was in a very bad way. There were only a few independent Muslim countries. We regarded this as an untenable situation, and saw Islam as a living idea that must bring itself up to date while preserving its essence. We were dissatisfied with the way things were in the Muslim world, dominated as it was by foreigners, through the presence either of their militaries or their capital.

The organisation spread rapidly among the youth, particularly among gymnasium and university students. We had hundreds of supporters in almost every town in Bosnia and Herzegovina, and a strong students' group in Zagreb too. During the 1941-45 War there was a kind of unspoken non-confrontation agreement between ourselves and the authorities of the day: we avoided direct confrontation, although we were clearly the opposition. During 1944, I became less and less active, unhappy that the organisation had made a pact with El-Hidaje, the *hojjas'* association. I never wholly agreed with the *hojjas*, although there were many among them whom I respected. I was of the opinion that there should not be a special social class or order either of *hojjas* or of sheikhs, and that they were the proponents of a view of Islam that impeded both its internal and its external development. I said as much publicly, and was to some extent denounced as a result. After the war ended, we continued our activities, to the horror of the communist authorities. They tried to dissuade us and, when they failed, began arresting us in early 1946 or thereabouts.

Even as a child I wanted to be a lawyer. It was a youthful ambition of mine, a dream from my schooldays. When I left prison after 36 months, in 1949, and wanted to enrol in the Law Faculty, my maternal uncle Šukrija, himself a lawyer, dissuaded me. My father also thought that, as a former prisoner, I had no hope of succeeding in the legal profession, since the communists neither forgot nor forgave. I enrolled in Agronomy, studying for almost three years and passing 13 examinations. I was an excellent agronomy student but, as the years and the semesters went by, I increasingly lost interest, and finally transferred to Law. Nevertheless, I do not regard those three years as a waste of time: I passed exams in mathematics, geodetics, land-reclamation and even four chemistry exams: inorganic, organic, analytical and agricultural.

One interesting experience in connection with chemistry stands out in particular. While I was at school, the theory that both matter and energy are constant was still regarded as valid, although Einstein had demonstrated that it was not so. He had already published his theory on the liberation of immense energy and the loss of mass that occurred with the splitting of the atom, expressed in the famous formula $E=mc^2$, as long ago as 1905; but 35 years later we were still being taught Newtonian physics and 'living' in a Newtonian world: a logical, constant, monodirectional, rectilinear world. Einstein changed those assumptions. The universe is warped, time and space are relative and matter and energy are not constant. The atomic bomb was later to confirm that these unbelievable notions were correct, and to usher in the era of relativity. I believe that this also had a powerful impact on the spirit of the time; some widely-accepted values were also relativised. That is why I always have the feeling that I have lived in two different historical eras: my youth in one, my mature years and old age in quite another.

In April 1945, the Communists entered Sarajevo; thus began their era, which was to last 45 years. In the autumn of that year, we Young Muslims held a demonstration on the occasion of the organisation of the Muslim society 'Preporod', which the Communists wanted under their control. We made fiery anti-communist speeches. Most of the audience applauded enthusiastically and cheered us on; I and a few others were arrested on the spot.

It was obvious, following this rebellion of ours, that OZNA[1] judged it wise to keep an eye on the movement, and the next day they released us. Later, being young and foolish (I was 20 at the time), we continued meeting and they monitored everything, which enabled them to arrest us a few months later and bring us to trial. I was arrested on 1 March

[1] Odjeljenje Zaštite Naroda – the Yugoslav State Security Police.

1946 with a group of 14 like-minded people and sentenced to three years imprisonment. The sentence was not particularly severe compared with what was to come later. We were the first group of Young Muslims to be so charged and sentenced.

The Communists were to change their attitude and behaviour towards the Young Muslims movement when they became convinced that, despite persecutions, the organisation was expanding. All the signs were that the Young Muslims idea was striking a chord with the people, especially among the youth. Another group was arrested and sentenced in 1947, yet another the following year, and in 1949 the decision was taken for a final showdown. Almost a thousand people were arrested in Bosnia and Herzegovina. This was the time of the *Cominform*, when Yugoslavia clashed with Stalin. The authorities were under pressure from Stalin's accusations of laxity, of allowing anti-communist elements in the country to take hold, and were anxious to demonstrate that this was not so. They persecuted both the Cominformists (Stalin's supporters) and us at the same time, but it can be said that the Cominformists came out of the showdown much worse than we did. It is true that some of our people received death sentences at the conclusion of the trial held in summer 1949, but from the human point of view Stalin's supporters were treated far more roughly. Our people endured some very difficult experiences, but not humiliating ones, as was the case with the Cominformists. Our people were held in custody, the thinking being that we would either die out or give in, but the authorities tried to brain-wash the Cominformists, to break them ideologically.

The oldest of the four of our comrades who were sentenced to death was Hasan Biber, who was then 27; the youngest was Nusret, who was not even 20. His family appealed for mercy, writing that their Nusret was still a child. However, this did not soften the authorities' hearts. The signature of a man described by the Communists as a 'well-known humanist' was on the document rejecting the plea for mercy. This was Moša Pijade, at the time President of the Presidium. In 1914 Gavrilo Princip, a Serbian nationalist, assassinated the Austrian Archduke Franz Ferdinand in Sarajevo. Despite the fact that he had assassinated both the heir to the throne and his pregnant wife Sophia, he was not sentenced to death on the grounds that he had not yet reached the age of 21. Moša Pijade, the 'humanist', was the author of the Yugoslav Criminal Law, which permitted capital punishment of minors between the ages of 16 and 18. The victims of this legislation and practice were young people, whose only crime was that they held different opinions. The charges included terrorism, which they certainly had not committed. It is now known for a fact that the activities of the Muslims were restricted to writing, correspondence and meetings: a verbal and psychological resistance to the communist regime.

I spent three years in prison, from March 1946 to March 1949. Apart from being pretty hungry half the time, I cannot say that I was subjected to any torture.

During interrogation prior to trial I was held in the military prison in the Marshal Tito Barracks in Sarajevo, in the building next to the School of Engineering where the military court was also located. I was in a room where half the people had received death sentences and were awaiting the results of their appeals. Most of them were Chetnik fences or criminals from the time of the war. When I was sentenced to three years, they all thought it was nothing, and it was nothing compared with the others, of course. Nonetheless, out of a life of 60 or 70 years, three years is more than a thousand days and a thousand nights. I was sent to Zenica to serve my term, but did not stay there long. After two months I was transferred to the prison in Stolac, where I was held for seven months; then, as a short-term prisoner, I was sent to a construction site. There, on the building sites of Boračko Lake, I worked on the construction of the UDB[2] centre, where 'my' *udbashis*, members of the Secret Service in Tito's Yugoslavia, the people I had got to know during investigation, would later go for their holidays. I then worked for a time in Sarajevo, on the headquarters of the future Central Committee of the Communist League. Much of the plaster, bricks and concrete in that building were carried by me with my own hands. During my third year in custody I was transferred to a camp on the Hungarian border, on the Belje Estate near Beli Manastir.

One never knows what is good and what is bad for one in life. If I had not been imprisoned in 1946, which I and my people regarded as a great misfortune, I would almost certainly have been killed in 1949, as was the late Halid Kajtaz who took my post in the organisation after I was arrested. Halid was sentenced to death, and killed by firing squad in October 1949. Going to prison thus saved my life. Then there was the banishment to the Hungarian border. They wanted to punish me by sending me 400 kilometres away from my family; they did not know, however, that it would be good for me. It was a large farm, with plenty of food. There were huge piles of potatoes everywhere, which we prisoners used to bake.

---

[2] Uprava Državne Bezbjednosti – the State Security Services, or secret police.

I worked there as a woodcutter. I became very skilled at the job, and later used to reflect that, if ever I had to do physical labour to earn a living, I would become a forestry worker. Of all the labouring jobs I have done – and I have done many – this was the one that appealed to me most. I spent the whole of the winter of 1948-49 logging. We were cutting wood for fuel. It had to be hand-sawn into one-metre lengths, split and stacked. There was a daily quota that we had to meet. Since there was wood everywhere, we would make a fire and bake potatoes. Thus it was that I spent the last six months of my sentence very comfortably, contrary to what the *udbashis* had intended. When I completed my sentence, I was 24 years old and fully restored to health. My people wept for joy when they saw how well I looked: man had proposed, but God had disposed quite otherwise.

Not long after completing my sentence I married a girl I had known since I was 18. Halida was very beautiful, which could not be said of me. We had met during the war, and would get together whenever the air-raid warning sirens sounded. This happened ever more frequently, because the British aircraft that took off from airbases in Italy at ever shorter intervals, sometimes several times a day, overflew Sarajevo on their way to bomb targets in Hungary. At times they would drop their deadly loads on the city. While the people fled in panic to cellars and air-raid shelters, Halida and I would stay out on the street, sitting on a stone or the nearest bench, convinced that nothing could happen to us. The two of us were, no doubt, the only people in the city who were glad to hear those air-raid sirens.

While I was serving my three-year sentence, we continued to exchange passionate letters in which the most frequent word, other than love, was eternity – a word that people use lightly and irresponsibly. I imagine that my prison censors must have been greatly amused when they read our letters, full of fine-sounding words. But this did not bother us. We gave free rein to our feelings, which were only intensified by separation and suffering.

The first time I noticed that a woman was beautiful was when I was seven or eight. As a boy I used to accompany my mother on visits so that she would not have to return home alone. On one occasion she took me to a wedding at the home of some old *bula*[3] where the *nikkah*, the evening ceremony that forms part of a religious marriage, was to be held. The bride was very beautiful and, what is more, she was adorned

[3] The female equivalent of a hojja.

with gold threads hanging over her face. She seemed quite enchanting to me, and I could not take my eyes off her. Was it pure admiration? I recall that later I felt some uncomfortable sense of guilt because of it.

After my marriage I was more than ever surrounded by the womenfolk of the family. Apart from my wife Halida, there were soon two daughters, Lejla and Sabina, and later a series of five granddaughters: eight members of the fairer sex in the immediate family. I came to know the way women lived and the problems they faced. I was grateful to God that I was a man, and it seemed to me that I owed some kind of solidarity to women, as the less fortunate half of humanity.

My first granddaughter, Selma, was born 24 years ago. My deepest feelings are for that child; I had feelings for that little creature that I had never had before and never have had since for anyone. One fond and funny memory is connected with her. It so happened that I had to travel to Libya and stay there for two weeks. My daughter, son-in-law and little Selma, who was not yet two, had gone to the seaside and I had not seen them for two weeks. Now I had to go abroad and not see Selma for another two weeks; this was completely unacceptable. I urged my wife to agree that we should go to the coast for a day to see Selma, then come back to Sarajevo before I left for Libya. I remember how angry Halida was at the time, and with good reason: first we had to take a train, then a boat to the island where they were staying, then hitch a ride as there were no buses; all on a hot summer's day. People with a touch of madness are happy – I think I was one of them.

On my release, in 1949, I again joined the Young Muslims' Organisation through the late Hasan Biber, one of its leading members. Hasan did not immediately give me anything important to do. He asked me to write some articles for the journal *Mudžahid* that was then being covertly circulated. I saw Hasan for less than 40 days, for on 11 April he was arrested. Later I found out that, during interrogation, Hasan had been under severe pressure to admit that I was again connected with the organisation. If he had done so, I would have faced another long sentence of hard labour. He held firm, however, telling them he knew nothing about it. Others, too, said they knew nothing, which in their case was true. Hasan Biber was tried in July 1949, sentenced to death, and killed by firing squad in October. This trial was part of the whole showdown, during which there were mass arrests throughout Bosnia, beginning with a raid on the organisation in Mostar in January 1949 wherein secret files and minutes were discovered. This was followed by the arrest of a large group of our students in Zagreb and lead to a series of trials of which the Sarajevo trial in July-August 1949 was the largest and the most tragic. A little later my good friend and associate Ešref Čampara, a teacher who is still alive today, was arrested in Sarajevo and sentenced to four years hard labour. This was his second prison sentence – he had also been convicted in the 1946 trial. When I add up all the sentences from the trials held during those years, I think that the Young Muslims were sentenced to several thousand years in jail. With the 1949-51 trials the organisation was completely destroyed – all its leading members were in prison, the rest had fled or were in hiding, so that in effect the organisation no longer existed. There were merely individual members, who continued to nurture the idea within themselves. Friends would meet, but very carefully and cautiously – there was an end to organised activities.

The Communists were having a hard time organising the government as well as peoples' daily lives. They were obsessed by ever more political opponents. This was the nature of the system, from China to Yugoslavia. When I ended my prison sentence in spring 1949 – four years after the end of the war – I found Sarajevo in a very poor way. It was the same throughout the country. I clearly recall my first encounter with the city, and how appalled I was.

When I was leaving the camp on the Hungarian border, another prisoner, a political prisoner like myself who had been a tram conductor, asked me to take a letter to his wife. He explained to me that his wife worked in a greengrocer's shop in a street between the Tzar's Bridge and Baščaršija. The following day, when I returned home, I went out to look for her. I found her in the shop, and while she was reading the letter I looked around. There was nothing there except five or six crates of white turnips. It was cold, and the woman and the shopkeeper were wrapped up in blankets; there was no sign of any heating in the shop. I asked, 'What do you sell here?' 'What you see,' they replied, adding that they sometimes had a few potatoes and, when they did, a queue would immediately form. Some were 'more equal than others', however. For ordinary people, which meant the vast majority of the population, there was a little flour, sugar, oil and textiles to be bought with coupons. For the privileged few, there were the so-called ministerial stores. There were three categories of these. My wife's sister worked in one of them, designated as 'No. 3', for the third category of the privileged. The 'No. 1' stores were reserved for the top echelons of the military and political strata. There was everything in these stores, from pasteurised American milk to all kinds of chocolate; the Yugoslavs had copied this special care for the ruling caste from the Russians. In the countries of so-called 'real socialism' (the USSR and its satellite countries), there was a party personnel monopoly, which was maintained by means of the so-called nomenclature system. This was a list of the most important positions in politics, the economy and culture, which could be acquired (or lost) only with the approval of the Party Committee. The nomenclature was in fact composed of two lists – a list of the positions that could be gained only with the consent of the appropriate party organ, and a list of individuals who could be appointed to those positions. Both lists were for internal publication only. Privileges of a caste nature were linked to the nomenclature (high pay, *dashas*, separate compartments on the trains, separate schools, access to medical institutions that were closed to others, separate stores and so on), and were distributed according to rank, descending in progressively poorer quality, choice and extent. In a book entitled *Socijalne Nejednakosti u Jugoslaviji* (Social Inequality in Yugoslavia), Eva Berković described a system of similar privileges in our country (pay, villas, apartments, cars, subsidised summer resorts and so on) extending from the federal to the republic and down to municipal level. 'All public or even in-party discussion on privileges was blocked as anti-socialist and anti-state,' she wrote. It is hardly necessary to point out that the existence of the nomenclature made selection meaningless, turning it into a sheer farce for the naïve.

Sarajevo's shops were empty, yet the prisons were full – mainly of Cominformists, Young Muslims and people with wagging tongues. When they had filled all the prisons dating from the old Yugoslavia and the Ustasha regime, the Communists made a new camp in Čengić-Vila, known as 'Camp 505', holding several thousand people. Things remained unchanged until 1952. This was the justice – social and political – of the left. Until 1966, that is for 21 years, Yugoslavia was ruled by its Police Chief, Aleksandar Ranković, and it was only in 1975-78, after more than 30 years of Communist rule, that things improved a little and one could feel some very limited sense of freedom. This, however, came at the price of foreign debt equating to US$20 billion, and there was still no freedom of speech.

Chapter 2

The Sarajevo Trial

The Islamic Declaration. The Sixty-eight. Islam Between East and West. Reflections on great losers. Arrest, 23 March 1983. Charges and defence. Witnesses withdraw their testimonies. Sentenced to 14 years in prison. 'Verbal delict.' Belgrade intellectuals' petition. Foča Prison. In a cell with murderers. Albanians in Foča Prison.

I finally enrolled in the Law Faculty in 1954, graduating in November 1956 and thereby fulfilling my youthful wish.

Much of my earnings, however, came from working in the building trade. I worked for almost ten years for a construction firm, of which there were seven in Montenegro, where I was head of the site for the Perućica hydro-electricity generating plant near Nikšić. My firm built a large pressure-tunnel almost four kilometres long, the input-structure for the plant, the pipeline leading to the turbines in the hydro-electric power station in Glava Zete, the supply channel and the sealing off of the huge chasms in Nikšić plain, so that the waters of the River Zeta could be directed to the tunnel and the turbines.

At that time I tried writing some articles on Islam. Most of them were never published. In 1969 I drafted the *Islamic Declaration*, of which I published the final corrected version in 1970. This short text of some 40 pages attracted attention only after the 1983 Sarajevo trial; it was both defended and attacked with equal passion.

Although it was written in Sarajevo, the *Declaration* turned its attention to the Islamic world, not to Yugoslavia. Indeed, Yugoslavia is not even mentioned in the text. The dominant idea of the *Declaration* is that only Islam can reawaken the imagination of the Muslim masses and render them capable of being once again active participants in their own history. Western ideas are incapable of this. This message was attacked as fundamentalist, which it was, in one particular sense: it appealed to a return to the sources. It condemned authoritarian regimes, called for increased expenditure on education, and advocated a new position for women, non-violence and the rights of minorities. The *Declaration* was received in the West with considerable reservation. In my view, they could not forgive the fact that it placed Islam at the heart of the solution.

It was just before I wrote the *Declaration* that 'the Sixty-Eight' had raged like fever through the world; the Sixty-Eight being that movement of young intellectuals, imbued with socialist ideas, who rebelled against the establishment. It wanted something that was impossible to achieve at that point in history – a return to life in an ideal past. Later events – the conservative movement in the West and the religious revival world-wide – showed that the ideals of 1968 were out of joint with the times and the broad course of history. More important still, they were no longer the innocent ideals of the early 20th century, because they were already burdened with serious errors in their application.

During those years I began to work on my book *Islam između Istoka i Zapada* (Islam between East and West). Indeed, I could say that I had written it much earlier, just before my imprisonment in 1946. The manuscript remained concealed for more than 20 years. When I was arrested in 1946, my sister Azra (who died in 1997) hid it under the beams in the attic of our house. When I later found it, it was a bundle of half-decayed paper. I added some new data, re-wrote the text and sent it to a friend in Canada; finally an American publisher issued it in 1984, when I was already serving my second prison sentence of 14 years with hard labour.

My aim with that book was to consider the place of Islam in the present-day world of ideas and facts. It appeared to me that it lay somewhere between Eastern and Western thinking, just as the geographical position of the Muslim world occupies the space on the globe between East and West. I tried to show that some general ideas and some values are common to all humanity. To summarise briefly, these are the contents of the book: there are only three world-views, and more there cannot be – the religious, the materialist and the Islamic. Everything is created in pairs (Qur'an). Man is a dual being: body and soul. The body is merely the 'carrier' of the soul. That carrier has evolved, which means it has a history, but the soul has not; it was inspired by the touch of God. The first aspect of mankind is the subject of science, the second of religion, art and ethics. This is why there are two accounts and two truths about mankind. In the Western world, they are symbolised by Darwin and Michelangelo. Darwin has nothing to say about Michelangelo's man, and vice versa. Their truths are different, but not mutually exclusive. Over time they manifest themselves as the opposition of civilisation and culture. Science and technology belong within the domain of civilisation, religion and art to culture. The first is the expression of human needs (how do I live), the second of human aspirations (why do I live). This is the contradiction between utopia and drama. Utopia does not recognise the individual, drama, morality. Study and meditation are two different spiritual activities, with opposing foci: the first is outwardly oriented – towards nature, the second inwardly – towards the spirit and the Self. Every scientific method leads towards a negation of God and man, whilst all art announces religion. If there is no God, there is no Mankind either. And without Mankind humanism, human dignity and human rights are empty phrases. Civilisation knows nothing of the notion of duty, and every culture is an affirmation of the victim. Civilisation's aim is an 'earthly empire' with utopian equality, and religion's is the 'kingdom of heaven'. This is Campanella's *Civitas Solis* as against the *Civitas Dei* of St. Augustine. There is no moral order without God. Morality is merely 'another physical condition' of religion. While civilisation is evolution; history, religion and art have no true development. Every religion was pure in its origins (ur-monotheism). It becomes corrupted in the course of its history, as is the case with art and morality; hence the opposition between Jesus and the Church. Every true law is dual, and medicine is never purely science. Cavemen's drawings or the aboriginal masks from Polynesia are in essence works of art no less stirring than modern creations. The whole of human life is marked by this primary dualism, and its 'signs' may be found in every phenomenon linked with the name of man. Here too is the difference in spirit between the Old and the New Testament, between Moses and Jesus. One was a leader of the people, the other a preacher of morality. And there, too, lie their two different justices and aims: the Promised Land and the Kingdom of Heaven. These opposites are reconciled in mankind and in Islam. Islam is a synthesis, the 'third way' between these two poles that denote all that is human.

I must admit that I was afraid of experts and their reading of the book 'line by line'. I felt confident that a reader who followed the vision outlined in rough, or even hinted at, in the book would find something more in it than the pedantic, analytical mind. I was aware that my attempt at stating my vision remained understated, merely conjectural, and in places incoherent. I gave a number of familiar concepts a metaphorical rather than conventional meaning: Judaism, Christianity, Islam and so on are mere metaphors, with a general rather than a specific meaning. For example, Islam is a major metaphor for the 'third way', for every form of life, with a formula that fulfils the human person. In fact, the book was no more than testimony to a vision of the world.

I enjoyed identifying new parallels, theses and antitheses, coincidence and symmetries, but this was not the subject that interested me most deeply. There was one issue that always preoccupied me more than any other: the issue of famous losers. I regarded it then, and regard it to this day, as the deepest religious problem. It can be posited in a number of ways: whence the tragic and pathos in the Darwinian-Euclidian world? What are the great losers like, and why do we admire them so if this life is the only one we have? Were Antigone, Socrates and Jesus really losers? And if so, why are they so great in our eyes? What is the origin of our admiration for the fallen heroes that has accompanied us ever since the prehistorical *Iliad* and *The Epic of Gilgamesh*? Do not even films such as cheap Westerns exploit our innate sympathy for the victim (that is, for losers) and resistance to the calculated, to self-interest? Sympathy for the victim is not something we can find in the intellect, but only in the soul, by which I mean, essentially, that is not 'of this world'. And I say sympathy, not understanding, for this is not, and cannot be, understanding. No amount of reasoning, cogitation and sagacity can explain or justify a single case of a life sacrificed for justice and truth. Something that is very close and comprehensible to every human soul eludes explanation by all our science and philosophy. Between the act approved and the approbation there is no mediation of reflection, no apportionment of reasons *pro et con*. It may even be said that there is no time lapse. It is the instant reaction of the soul to good and justice, to something that is identical to the soul itself. In the world that atheists regard as the one and only, the tragic and tragedy are impossible. In such a world there are only incidents and misfortunes.

In this mind-set, tragedy manifests itself to us as a religious parable. In tragedy, villains fall on their feet and great and sincere souls suffer. And because there is no 'intellectual' operation to proclaim these eternal losers as mad and demented, the entire story, and in particular its tragic end, appears to us as merely the first act of a greater drama – one that only God could think up. For suffering and death – which are the end of everything to the intellect – are here merely an interval between two acts in a continuing drama. Our admiration and sympathy for the fallen hero are completely meaningless from the intellectual point of view, but for that very reason – whether we are aware of it or not – it is deeply religious. For only in such experiences do death and failure or loss have an entirely different meaning.

I dedicated many pages of *Islam between East and West* to this question, seeking to resolve it in a variety of ways, but I was never wholly satisfied with the answer. It continues to preoccupy me to this day.

The problem of the Balkans was and remains a problem of democracy. If we set aside earlier history and turn our attention to the century just ended, we shall see that during the first half of the century every country in this part of the world was under a monarchy, most of them authoritarian, and under communist rule during the second half – in this case, with the exception of Greece. In short, the Balkans have not had much luck with democracy, or rather democracy with the Balkans.

These countries, which referred to themselves as socialist, later developed in different ways. What strikes one immediately is the powerful impact of their leaders on these countries. Although they all shared the same basic ideological matrix, the actual living conditions of the ordinary people varied from country to country, depending on their leaders: Živkov, Hodža, Ceaucescu, Tito, four different men and four different regimes. This did not alter the authoritarian essence of the system, however.

On his last visit to his favourite hunting grounds in Bugojno in late 1979, Tito received Branko Mikulić and Raif Dizdarević – both prominent Bosnian communist leaders. It was not difficult to conclude from that evening's news reports which topics the two of them had raised. Sarajevo TV's main news featured Josip Broz Tito's threatening message: he literally authorised the two of them to deal as harshly as possible with 'attempts to revive clero-nationalism and pan-Islamism in Bosnia and Herzegovina.' The more indulgent atmosphere that had made itself felt from the early 1970s began to change, and heavy-handed control made its appearance once again.

Media haranguing began with an attack on Husein Đozo – a well-known Islamic *alim*. When he was taken in by the police, the official Islamic community publicly distanced itself from him. From that time on Đozo withdrew to a life of complete isolation, making silence his defence; he soon died of a heart attack.

Đozo was a friend. I had worked with him, and with his help had published articles in a volume of the Islamic calendar *Takvim*. I signed these articles with the initials L.S.B (the initials of my children Lejla,

Sabina and Bakir). They were a series of articles entitled 'Problems of the Islamic Renaissance'. Đozo and I thought alike on those issues.

Things became even worse after Tito's death in 1980. The crisis in Kosovo began, with almost daily trials of Albanians. The few critical voices from the West were negligible: the West had become used to this kind of politics from the Communists and it was important to keep Yugoslavia apart from Russia. All the indications were that political arrests could begin in Bosnia again.

Early in the morning of 23 March 1983, I was woken by someone banging on the door of my third-floor flat at Number 14, Hasana Kikića Street. When I opened the door, a group of ten or so UDB officials – members of the Yugoslavia Secret Police – burst in. 'We're from State Security,' said one. They came into the flat without taking off their shoes, and showed me their search warrant. They went through my things, looking behind everything, taking the blinds down from the windows, peering into every corner of the rooms, as though they were convinced there were explosives hidden in the flat. They were interested above all in my books and papers, all of which they piled in a heap.

The search lasted until late in the afternoon. They then ordered me to go with them to the State Security Headquarters. When we reached it, I was told that I was to be held in custody for three days. This was later extended to 30 days, and then to an indefinite period pending trial. I was transferred to the District Prison, built by the Austrians more than 100 years previously.

The interrogations lasted more than 100 days. I could say more than 100 nights, too, since night-time interrogations were very common. I spent those 100 days in a cell of four metres by two, with small barred windows looking onto the dark central well of the prison building.

Hundreds of others from throughout Bosnia had also been arrested and were being interrogated. It was obvious that the interrogators were not interested in the truth; their task was to accuse us and to prove us guilty as charged. The principal means by which they achieved this was false testimony under threat of imprisonment. Anyone who did not want to testify was threatened with being charged.

When charges were finally served, around the beginning of July, I found out, for the first time, who the people charged with me and the witnesses were. The charges were based on Articles 114 and 133 of the Criminal Law of the Socialist Federal Republic of Yugoslavia. The first related to conspiracy against the state, and the second to the famous 'verbal delict'. The charges showed that I was allocated the role of group leader, which was a pure fabrication, since there was no group. I did not even know some of the people in the dock.

They came for us in the morning of 18 July. The Sarajevo trial had begun. They took us out of our cells and lined us up in the corridor. This was the first time since our arrest that we all saw each other; all of us were pale and undernourished. Rušid was having trouble breathing. I found myself at the head of the column, where between each of us there was a policeman. We entered a half-empty courtroom through the rear door. I greeted the people in the courtroom with *Salaam* and raised my hand. Some responded. The presiding judge cautioned me loudly not to address the public. I replied that I had the right to greet my children, who were sitting in the courtroom.

We were made to form two rows on two wooden benches, with a police cordon behind us. There were ten lawyers sitting on the right. Facing them was the public prosecutor, a woman, whom I recognised from the interrogations. I did not know the judge. There was a large portrait of Josip Broz behind him.

The trial began with an argument between myself and the presiding judge. I protested against the public being prohibited from attending the trial. The only people in the courtroom with us were the judges, the prosecutor, the police, our relatives and a few selected journalists. I stated that this being the case, I would exercise the right to silence in my defence. The trial was adjourned for the judge to consult someone, probably the Central Committee. A compromise was reached by which a certain number of people would be allowed to enter on showing passes bearing their names, in other words people selected by the police.

Judge Hadžić opened the proceedings, that were to last a month:

> First we must establish that all the accused are present: Izetbegović Alija, Behmen Omer, Čengić Hasan, Kasumagić Ismet, Bičakčić Edhem, Živalj Husein, Prguda Rušid, Behmen Salih, Spahić Mustafa, Latić Džemal, Salihbegović Melika, Đurđević Derviš, Bičakčić Đula. As presiding judge, myself, Hadžić Rizah, member of the board of judges Judge Kanlić Asim, and three members of the jury of different nationalities, namely a Muslim, a Serb and a Croat. We have provided for the public prosecutor to state the charges,' said the judge by way of opening the proceedings. He then called upon the Prosecutor, Edina Rešidović, to speak.

Prosecutor: 'In early 1974, obsessed with the idea of an Islamic renaissance and the Islamisation of the Muslims, Izetbegović Alija and Behmen Omer agreed that it was essential first to shed light on this by means of texts that would be of interest to a wide circle of people, so Izetbegović wrote and published several such texts, followed by the first version of the *Islamic Declaration*, which he gave to Omer Behmen and Teufik Velagić, members of the hostile émigré community in Vienna, after which he incorporated their remarks and suggestions into the *Declaration*... He emphasised, as the principles of the Islamic movement and renaissance, that "There is no known instance in history of a genuine Islamic movement that was not at the same time a political movement. This is because Islam is a religion, but also at the same time a philosophy, a morality, an atmosphere, in a word an integral way of life... The presence of a great many laws and of a complex legislature is, as a rule, a reliable indicator that there is something rotten in that society, which needs to stop passing laws and begin to educate its people in how to behave... The Islamic movement is a coherent unity of religion and politics... Muslims are brothers... The Islamic movement should and can begin to take power as soon as it is morally and numerically strong enough not merely to replace existing un-Islamic governments, but to create a new Islamic government" – between 1974 and 1983, with the aim of creating a counter-revolutionary threat to the social order in the Socialist Federal Republic of Yugoslavia, this text of the *Declaration* was translated into Arabic, Turkish, English and German, and published in these languages with a foreword; and, with the intention of creating a group of like-minded people in the country as a counter-revolutionary threat to the social order in the manner and for the purposes set out in the *Declaration*, between 1976 and 1983 the said text was given to a large number of intellectuals to read: Đozo Husein, Kupusović Muhamed, Živalj Huso, Čengić Hasan, Mahmutćehaić Rusmir, Hadžić Mehmedalija, Salihbegović Melika and Bičakčić Edhem ... whereupon Čengić Hasan, Kasumagić Ismet, Živalj Huso and Bičakčić Edhem became members of the group...' etc., etc.

This was the opening and main substance of the charge, which amounted in all to several dozen closely-typed pages.

I was the first accused. Called to account for the charges set out, I said:

> Before stating my defence, I have three objections of a procedural nature:
>
> 1. Thirteen people are included in the charges, seven of whom have absolutely no connection with the basic subject of the charges (the creation of a group on the basis of the *Declaration*); five of the accused are not known to me at all...
>
> 2. Named passes have been issued by the court for this trial, so that only a selected audience has been invited to this courtroom instead of the public. I request that I be given a public hearing, in accordance with the law. I have nothing to hide, only the court may have. I wish to defend myself before the widest possible public, for I am innocent and will not submit my defence solely to Judge Hadžić, but to every honest man and woman in Yugoslavia and beyond, and anyone who is concealing something is clearly in the wrong...
>
> 3. My third objection relates to the conduct of the press. Even before the beginning of this trial, part of the press had proclaimed me to be a nationalist, a counter-revolutionary, an enemy of the state, and practically condemned me without trial... This is in contempt of this court, but I am not aware that the court has taken any steps to protect, if not the accused, then at least its own integrity and the law.

After stating that I was not guilty on any of the counts in the charges, I presented my defence and responded to the questions of the prosecutor, judges and lawyers. This took the whole of the first day of the trial.

These were some of the questions put by the Prosecutor, Edina Rešidović, and my answers to them:

> Rešidović: Did you state in even one single sentence that the *Islamic Declaration* does not relate to the Socialist Federal Republic of Yugoslavia?
>
> Izetbegović: No, since it was unnecessary. It is perfectly clear from the content of the text.
>
> Rešidović: Whom do you number among the seven hundred million Muslims in the world? Do you include me in that Islamic world?
>
> Izetbegović: I include people living in countries where Muslims form a majority of the population – from Morocco to Indonesia.

Rešidović: In your defence you stated that the *Islamic Declaration* advocates a modern and humane order based on Islam. What kind of a modern and humane system is it that makes no mention anywhere of non-alignment and self-management? Etc., etc.

My good friend Rušid Prguda, who had endured ten years imprisonment as a young man, could hardly sit in the dock. He was seriously ill. It would be learned later that he was already ill when arrested, and that he had been badly treated during interrogation. His lawyer, Nikola Sukno, requested that a doctor's opinion be obtained. The judge tried to avoid this, but finally yielded. The doctor confirmed that Rušid was completely unfit to stand trial, having suffered two heart attacks while under interrogation. He said that his condition was such that he could come to a tragic end at any moment. The proceedings against Rušid were set aside on the basis of medical opinion. A year after the proceedings were set aside, after three hearings in court and three stays of trial on the grounds of ill health, Rušid died.

We later received from Rušid's lawyer a written statement that the deceased had drawn up during the interrogations and that he had intended to produce during the trial. Rušid had written:

> For me this trial is rather suspicious. It is clear that it has been rigged, but I am not clear why. I have already been sentenced once before in a rigged trial to 20 years prison with hard labour, and served ten. But this was the Stalinist era, so things were even worse – when Yugoslavia had to prove itself to be communist, and found it easiest to victimise the Muslims. Attacking Bosnia was one of the ways of proving to Moscow that it was a loyal satellite and model student and practitioner of Soviet methods. I had hoped that those days were over, never to return, but those who should have been first to forget them are in fact now reminding us of them. Why is it necessary to fabricate enemies of the state, to trump up acts that no one has committed? For whom is it necessary to create new victims and new martyrs, to terrorise peaceful, innocent citizens who are conscientiously going about their duties. Are believers second-class citizens in this country?
>
> Once again the same thing is happening to the Muslims. Does this state really feel itself threatened by 12 Muslim intellectuals, university professors, lawyers, economists, poets and

imams – people who do not even know one another? Is the purpose to intimidate the Muslims? You will only embitter them. I tell you quite openly that there are justifiable reasons for bitterness even without this trial.

Omer Behmen, who spent 11 years in jail as a young man, was in a very bad way psychologically. He was not ill, but he was clearly apathetic, exhausted and pale. His hearing lasted two days. He managed to get through the first day somehow, but was still weaker on the second. At one point he began to lose his balance. It was the closed part of the trial, and there were only three people in the courtroom: my son Bakir, my daughter Sabina and Omer's wife Saliha. Suddenly Omer lost consciousness and fell down and, though they did not call upon his wife, a doctor, to help him, and worse still gave orders that no one should approach him, she came forward of her own account, splashed him with water and wiped his face. Eyes closed and head lolling, Omer vomited. His face and lips were purple. After he had regained consciousness, the judge called for a stretcher, Omer refused, and the guards took him away.

Salih Behmen's defence (he had earlier served an eight-year prison term) took only half an hour. Of the charges, he said that they 'were not worthy of comment or even of reflection, let alone of forming the basis of a properly conducted trial. They are merely a heap of lies. The charges do not even cite times and places to provide a little credibility, let alone to have any concern for the reliability of the evidence. I have prayed all my life to Allah to grant me *jannat* (Paradise), but he has once again granted me a place in history, in a repetition of the trumped-up charges of 1949. But what can I do? This is no doubt my destiny: for people to punish me for deeds I have not done, and for God to put me to the test at their hands.' One of my friends said to me of Salih, 'He is one of those people whom you cannot know without loving them.'

After hearing the other accused, the trial continued with witness testimonies, 59 of them, lasting 15 days. Almost half the witnesses changed the statements they had made to the police during the pretrial investigative proceedings, saying that they had issued them under coercion or extortion.

There were dramatic moments. One witness, Sead Seljubac, said on withdrawing the statement he had made to the investigative authorities, 'I must say here and now that my statement will be completely different from the one I made to the police.' He then denied all the statements he had given during the investigation against Čengić, Spahić and Latić.

The Prosecutor, Rešidović, was furious. She announced that criminal proceedings would be initiated against Seljubac for making false statements. She meant by this, of course, the statements he had made in court. The threat was broadcast on Sarajevo television that same evening, and in the daily newspaper *Oslobođenje* the following day, with the added detail that the accused could be sentenced to five years in prison for such an offence. The aim was to intimidate the witnesses whose testimony was still to be heard in court. Seljubac was subjected to special police treatment the whole of the following night and day.

Two days later, Presiding Judge Hadžić announced that Seljubac had appeared in court and wanted to testify again, which the court accepted, of course. This time Seljubac acknowledged as his all the statements in the accusatory deposition made during the investigatory proceedings. Asked by the presiding judge what were his reasons for testifying again, Seljubac replied that two days prior to his first appearance as a witness he had been subjected to pressure by Nedžad Latić, brother of the accused Latić, and Nusret Čančar. Čančar had allegedly told him that Nedžad was in such a state of mind that he was ready to kill any witness who made false statements against his brother. Following this Seljubac had had a meeting with Nedžad and promised to change his testimony. 'After I made my first deposition, I realised I had done wrong. I decided to put things right, and went that evening to the Ministry of the Interior, after deciding to make a fresh statement. I was not influenced by what was written in the press about my being charged with perjury.' No one believed his story.

However, the real storm was yet to come. Nermina Jašarević, the key prosecution witness – or so she was thought to be – was to appear in court. That day, when Seljubac testified for the second time and Nermina Jašarević for the first, was a turning point in the entire trial. With the denial of the depositions made in the pre-trial proceedings, the trial began to turn into a farce. The court tried to turn things around by exerting all possible pressure on Seljubac and Nermina. Since things had gone only so-so with Seljubac, it was essential that Nermina repeat her original deposition and reinforce the charges.

Special preparations were made for the day when Seljubac and Nermina would appear. The courts, which were ordinarily half empty, had been carefully packed with strangers. The presiding judge went to the room where the witnesses were waiting and drew their attention to the presence of foreign journalists, and pointed out that it had been very unpleasant on previous days to listen to witnesses' accounts of being put under pressure, beaten and so on; accounts which 'blackened the name of Yugoslavia abroad.' The security police had 'cleared' the street where the court was located of passers-by and parked cars. The prosecutor and members of the board of judges addressed the witnesses and the accused alike much more politely than usual.

Before Nermina began testifying, the presiding judge warned her that she must tell only the truth, since perjury was a criminal offence. He also told her what the sentence was – up to five years in jail. Nermina replied with a question: 'Will the court protect me if I tell the truth?' On receiving an affirmative answer, she said, to the horror of the prosecutor, the court and everyone present, 'Everything that I signed as my deposition during the investigative procedure was false.' Nermina then explained that she had been subjected to pressure when making her deposition. The investigation officers had persistently demanded that she repeat certain phrases, until she had no longer had the strength to refuse. She had been questioned several times, and finally a transcript was made. She said that they had spent six days in the police station forcing her to learn by heart the deposition she had made during the pre-trial proceedings. Two days earlier she had been summoned twice by the police and warned that she must repeat everything in court she had said during questioning. Finally she said, 'I have told you the truth. I would rather spend five years in jail than live a single day in the knowledge that I was responsible for telling lies that sent these people to jail. If you want, I can be sentenced at once together with them!' There was complete silence in court. The judge was also silent for a while, and then told the witness she could stand down.

There were also some amusing scenes during the witnesses' testimonies. One witness, Enver Pašalić, better known as *Hojja* Pašo, a wise man, pretended to be both deaf and stupid in court. He spent two hours making a fool of the judge by giving answers that had absolutely nothing to do with the questions. In vain the judge tried to bring him back to the point; he simply went on talking, going into the minutest detail on matters that were quite meaningless. Time went by, the public in the courtroom were highly amused, and the judge became more and more irritable.

When the judge observed that he was not saying the same in court as he had to the police, Pašalić replied that he was saying the same things, but that the transcript perhaps read differently, since he had been questioned several times and, he said, 'I cannot say that I said the things that do not coincide with what I am saying now.' Seeing that there was nothing useful to be gained from this witness, and that it was simply a waste of time going on with him, the judge looked around the courtroom as if seeking assistance, obviously not knowing what to do, and then told him he could stand down with the words 'Come on, brother, don't let me see you here again.' At these words, *Hojja* Pašo turned to the court and apologised, and then turned back to us, giving the Muslim parting greeting *allahimanet*, his hand raised in the old Bosnian way. Everyone in the courtroom burst out laughing, with the exception, of course, of the judge and the prosecutor.

Fifty-six of the fifty-nine witnesses had been questioned for the prosecution and three for the defence. Of those, 23 were irrelevant both for the prosecution and the defence, and the verdict does not even mention them. Of the remaining 36, 15 stood by the statements they had made in the pre-trial proceedings, statements that favoured the prosecution, and 21 to a greater or lesser extent changed the depositions they had made earlier during questioning, or retracted them completely.

It is understandable that the accused should alter their statements, and in fact it happens quite frequently. Indeed, the legislation of every civilised country tacitly recognises the right of an accused to do so (the so-called 'right to lie' of the accused). The position of witnesses, however, is quite different. A witness is required to tell the truth both when questioned during investigations and in court, and if he commits perjury he faces a prison sentence. Why then did 21 witnesses alter their statements and risk criminal prosecution?

The witnesses gave various answers to this question from the court and the defence. Most of them explained that, after oral questioning lasting for hours, the investigation officer had drawn up a transcript which they could not recognise as their own statement, and had given it to them to sign. After their refusing to sign the transcript as it stood, an exhausting process of persuasion, pressure and threats would begin. All this was done in the spectral silence of pre-trial custody in Sarajevo Prison, where, as one witness described it in court, all that could be heard was the occasional opening or closing of the metal doors, and the stomp of the wardens' footsteps in the passageways. One witness, Enes Karić, recounted that his statements about commonplace events had been turned by the investigative officer into 'an explosive deposition.' Asked to explain what he meant, he gave an example: 'My words

"Čengić told me we would meet outside the cinema" would be noted down by the investigative officer as "Čengić arranged a meeting with me outside the cinema".' Naturally, the implication was that this was an illegal political meeting. Or the words 'I told him I had been in Turkey' became, in the investigation officer's version, 'I submitted a report to him about my trip to Turkey,' and so on. As Karić explained: 'The investigation officer persistently tried to convince me that this was the same, and that I should sign the transcript. After nine hours of persuasion and pressure, I signed the transcript, because I had no choice, but with the intention of stating in court the circumstances under which I had signed the deposition and what was actually true in the deposition.'

Another witness, Hilmija Áerimović, said that his interview with the investigation officer had lasted 40 hours, with brief pauses, in order to draw up a deposition of one typed page. Yet another, Vahid Kozarić, was interviewed for three days without being permitted to return home (in effect, therefore, he was deprived of his freedom). On the third day he had a heart attack and was taken to hospital, where he remained for 20 days. After his release from hospital he was again taken to the police station, where he signed the deposition which the investigative officer had insisted upon during the three days of his interview. Two witnesses, Mehmed Arapčić and Hamzalija Hujdur, who had been interviewed during the course of the pre-trial investigations, did not appear in court. Both had suffered nervous breakdowns and at the time of the trial were undergoing psychiatric treatment, so counsel for the prosecution waived the right to question them during the main hearing. Rešid Hafizović, when giving his evidence, said that the investigation officer had pulled a gun on him. After he refused to sign the deposition of his interview, the officer told him that he would not leave the building until he signed, no matter how long it took. Hafizović replied that he was not a prisoner but a free citizen, and made for the door. It was then that the officer pulled a gun on him and told him to stop at once, because he would not even be able to take three steps. Rašid Brčić, another witness, said that he was questioned for five days, for nine hours each day, and that he was exposed to extremely insulting treatment during questioning. Mustafa Spahić, one of the accused (and condemned), recounted at a session of the Supreme Court on 14 March 1984 that the investigation officers had offered him a choice: either to sign an accusatory deposition against one of the three first accused (he could choose for himself which one), and to go home, or to be accused himself. He gave the names of the two investigation officers and the date on which this occurred. After refusing, he was accused, and sentenced to five years in jail.

None of this, as it was described during the trial, troubled the judge in the least. Furthermore, in the verdict the court was to issue, every testimony before the court, without exception, that differed from the deposition was rejected, and the statements made in the deposition were accepted. The possibility of accepting depositions made during the pre-trial investigatory proceedings and not statements made during the trial had been granted to the court by the legislature as an exception, but the court had turned it into the rule. This was not the only example of the application of legal exceptions during these court proceedings. It was the rule for pre-trial investigations to be conducted by an investigating judge, and the exception for them to be entrusted to the police. The exception was applied. It was the rule for defence counsel to be present during questioning of the accused and witnesses, and only as an exception could counsel be deprived of this right. Again, it was the exception that was applied. By thus turning three exceptions in a row into the rule, the government authorities and the court turned these legal proceedings into a caricature, making a mockery of both the letter and the spirit of the law.

The way in which the courts explained their 100% preference for the statements made by witnesses during pre-trial questioning was characteristic. Thus the Court of First Instance said: 'The court accepted what the said witnesses stated during pre-trial proceedings because the explanations given by them during the main hearing, in relation to the changes to their statements, were unacceptable and illogical… These witnesses had given their statements without suggestions from anyone, and what they stated was clearly dictated in the deposition, which they had signed after reading' (p. 153 of the verdict of Sarajevo County Court). The court did not explain why it believed that this had been 'without suggestions from anyone or indeed pressure,' although almost every witness asserted the contrary.

Then there is the statement from the Supreme Court of Bosnia and Herzegovina: 'The explanations given by witnesses about the alterations to their statements amount to the assertion that the statements were made when they were in a particular psychological condition, under threat, or that the investigation authorities had wrongly entered in the deposition what they had in fact said… Accordingly, the judgment that the explanations given by witnesses for altering their statements amount to unfounded suspicions about the work of the investigation authorities is correct...' (pp. 38 and 39 of the verdict). And the Federal Court: 'In regard to the assertion that the statements by witnesses were made under coercion or extortion, that is contrary to Article 228 of the Law on Criminal Procedures, there is no evidence in support of this in the records, nor was any evidence produced upon request' (p. 26).

One of the charges against the third accused, Hasan Čengić, was that he had said that 'a Muslim may not receive blood from a non-Muslim, nor may he give blood to one.' Čengić persistently denied that he had ever said any such thing. Quite by chance, however, it was to be established during the main hearing that Čengić was a voluntary blood donor and was in possession of a donor card. Prosecution witness Enver Pašalić, while giving evidence in court on 6 August, said that he was surprised to read this accusation against Čengić in *Oslobođenje*, since he knew that Hasan Čengić was a frequent blood donor in the *Madrasa*. This testimony sent a shockwave through the courtroom, and we all believed that there could have been no better refutation of the charge. But the court did not share this view, and in the verdicts of all three courts voluntary blood donors were condemned as people who were opposed to giving blood to anyone other than a Muslim (though everyone who gave blood knew – as did Hasan Čengić – that as a rule the recipient of blood is not known).

When pronouncing sentence, the Sarajevo County Court was to state that 'in the view of this court, there were no mitigating circumstances for the accused' (p. 178 of the verdict). Courts try war criminals, murderers, highway robbers and all manner of violent criminals, and almost always find some mitigating circumstance or other for the benefit of the accused. The most prominent legal authorities world-wide even hold the view that there is no criminal for whom at least one mitigating circumstance could not be found, and if the court does not find it, the court is responsible for this failure, not the person being tried. Those being tried in this court included two poets accused for their words; almost all the accused were family men and women, some of them were over 60 and five were under 30. Eight were facing trial for the first time, one had received significant recognition from the organisation where he worked for his professional contribution, for two of the accused doctors found bad health conditions, and so on. All these facts, which, according to any law and for any court, would constitute mitigating circumstances, were not regarded as such by the Sarajevo County Court in this trial. Even the Supreme Court of Bosnia and Herzegovina, not known for its objectivity, would find when hearing the accuseds' appeals that the

County Court had gone too far (p. 71 of the verdict of the Supreme Court of Bosnia and Herzegovina).

But what could one expect of judges, prosecution and investigation officers who had begun their legal expertise with the Marxist definition that 'justice is the will of the ruling classes transformed into law,' a formula that is cynically contrary to the very notion of justice?

It was the same throughout the communist world. When the famous anti-Stalinist film *Penitence*, directed by Tengiz Abduladze, was screened in Tbilisi, Georgia, an opinion poll was conducted in the city. The public were for the most part delighted with the film, but there were exceptions. And who were they? Abduladze responded to that question in an interview he gave. 'They were mostly lawyers and judges aged between 60 and 70. And was it not precisely they who were the bullies and torturers?'

There is violence and injustice in all societies. The specific nature of communist oppression was its lawlessness, disguised under the cloak of law and reform. This hypocrisy created widespread confusion. Some people live and die under such systems without ever knowing what was false and what was true. Naïvely believing the press, the authorities, official pronouncements, they live in perpetual delusion, unintentionally and unconsciously supporting falsehood and injustice. Such people can often be heard, to one's horror, giving this naïve explanation: 'Well, that's what the newspapers say.' Dictatorships and the uninformed, stultified masses go hand in hand, each feeding the other.

The almost one-month long trial was coming to an end. Unlike the judge, who behaved like a 'contractor', the prosecutor threw herself into her work with passion and emotion. In her summing-up, she acknowledged that the witnesses had changed their statements in court, but that in her view this was unimportant, since when making their statements to the police they had been warned that they must tell the truth. 'For this reason their statements made during pre-trial proceedings are regarded as accurate,' stated Prosecutor Rešidović, with typical Stalinist logic.

Ending her summing-up, the prosecutor concluded that there was a convergence of two criminal acts in the case of the first six accused: associating with the purpose of imperilling the social order and counter-revolutionary activities; while the other six were guilty of 'verbal delict' as defined in Article 133 of the Criminal Law. She called upon the court to find all the accused guilty and to pronounce the sentences prescribed by law. Her explanation was as follows:

> *The Islamic Declaration* is an attack upon the values of our social order. In it there lie abstract danger, written and verbal delict, the consciousness of counter-revolutionary activities. These latter actions have some similarities to enemy propaganda. But this is a case of incessant activities and intensive propaganda, which shade into counter-revolutionary activities.

I argued with the prosecutor, even though I was aware that it was pointless. We had already been condemned. In my own summing-up, I said:

> I love Yugoslavia, but not its government... I bestow all my love on freedom, and there is nothing left over for the authorities. I am not being tried for having violated the laws of this land, for I have not done so. I am being tried for having transgressed some unwritten rules by which individual power-holders in our midst impose their own standards of the prohibited and the permissible, without regard for the Constitution and the Law. By all appearances, I have gravely transgressed those unwritten rules.
>
> I therefore state: I am a Muslim and so shall I remain. I consider myself to be a fighter for the cause of Islam in the world, and shall so feel to the end of my days. For Islam for me has been another name for all that is fine and noble, a name for the promise or hope of a better future for the Muslim peoples of the world, for their life in dignity and freedom, in a word for everything that in my belief is worth living for.

Omer Behmen uttered only two sentences: 'From me, *halal*[1] to all who have taken part in this – investigation officers and witnesses alike,' and then, turning towards Prosecutor Rešidović, he continued, 'And there were some really below-the-belt blows'. The others, too, made their own summings-up. No one either requested leniency or expressed repentance.

20 August was the date when the verdict was to be issued. I was mentally prepared for this moment. The judge told us to rise. The camera lights were turned full on my face. And then came this: '...and are hereby sentenced as follows: the accused Izetbegović Alija to a prison term of fourteen years...' and so on. My heart was pounding, but I held my head

---
[1] Forgiveness - from the Arabic *halal*, permitted.

high and put on an unconcerned air. The camera was there to record my shock, but all it recorded was my looking up at the ceiling. The judge read out the other sentences: fifteen, ten, eight, a total of 90 years imprisonment, ending: 'In conformity with the positive laws of the land, this society will uncompromisingly resist all attacks against brotherhood, unity and all the other achievements of this society.' Applause broke out behind me from an audience brought there especially for the occasion.

When I read the notes by Frida Vidgorova from the trial of the poet Josif Brodski (USSR, 1964), winner of the 1987 Nobel Prize for Literature, the whole time I was saying to myself, 'My God, it's exactly the same from Berlin and Sarajevo to Moscow and Vladivostok – malevolent and unfeeling judges, an uninterested and mentally absent jury, a bespoke public.' This is part of the description: '...Saveljeva, a gloomy woman of about forty, looking more like a housekeeper exasperated by the night-time scandals of drunkards than a dispenser of justice. To her right and left were languishing the jurors, barely grasping what was happening, and gazing dubiously at the door behind which the young people were clamouring. The police had formed a cordon on the steps, on the pretext that there was not enough room in the courtroom...' Just like Sarajevo in 1983.

The day after the sentences were pronounced, the *Oslobođenje* headline was 'Enemies 90 years jail.' I finally obtained a newspaper, after having been hermetically sealed off from the world ever since my arrest. My only link with the outside world were my children's letters. In one, Bakir wrote that little Jasmina was born during the trial. She was five when I saw her for the first time.

There is no rational explanation for the regime's behaving so rigorously. Was it a desperate move on the part of a government that was already in decline? Strong regimes do not condemn people for the spoken word; weak ones are afraid, and resort to violence in an attempt to prolong their existence.

As for the public, it often regards political prisoners as guilty for its own selfish reasons. It is a kind of defence mechanism. People cannot come to terms with the fact that they are living in a society where they do not have the protection of law and order. Then they are faced with the question of how it is that they can remain silent. Is it because it is easier for them to believe that the convicted person is guilty, that in any case he must have broken the law, because if not why would he be imprisoned and convicted? For if an innocent man is convicted in disregard of the law, then the person reflecting on this does not feel safe any longer, and people instinctively reject this in self-defence. The harsher the sentence, the more easily this conclusion is reached and accepted. In the absence of evidence, a severe sentence is itself evidence of guilt. For, as the man in the street reasons, if he wasn't guilty, he'd have got two or three years, not fifteen. Without clear and explicit proof of guilt, a lenient sentence of itself arouses suspicions, and indicates that even the authorities are unsure of themselves. In the case of a harsh sentence, that kind of doubt is dispelled. So the innocent man receives twice the sentence. This is an old trick that the Nazis, too, used to use, not in length of sentence but in the cruel harshness of punishment in concentration camps. 'Surely they wouldn't be so harsh with them if they weren't traitors' – this is probably how the average German rationalised things.

But things take their own course in this world, the communist regimes were manifestly weakening and wearing out, in the Soviet Union, Romania, Czechoslovakia, Poland and Yugoslavia alike. A process that ran in parallel with our prison sentences.

After the sentences were pronounced, and indeed the whole time we were in prison, petitions kept arriving from within the country and abroad, protesting against the trial and calling for our release. Twenty of Belgrade's best-known intellectuals (12 of them academics) wrote in their petition of 6 July 1986 to the Presidency of Yugoslavia:

> Between 18 July and 19 August 1983, 12 Muslim intellectuals were on trial in Sarajevo. The trial will remain known in the history of modern Yugoslav judicature as an archetype of exemplary punishment for word and thought. The Court of First Instance pronounced draconic sentences for offences of opinion, of a kind unusual even in our circumstances: three of the accused received sentences of 5 years imprisonment each, two of 6, one of 6 years and 6 months, one of 7, two of 10 each, one of 14 and one of 15 years. The Supreme Court of Bosnia and Herzegovina pronounced significantly more lenient sentences, ranging from 3 years and 6 months to 12 years, and the Federal Court, with further reductions to the scope of the charges, pronounced sentences of between 2 years and 8 months and 9 years imprisonment.

A further petition by the same group of Belgrade intellectuals, four months later (4 October 1986), claimed that the trial was unlawful and rigged, and demanded our immediate release.

The principal charge in the Court of First Instance in Sarajevo related primarily to the serious criminal act of association for hostile purposes (Article 136 relating to Article 114 of the Criminal Law of the Socialist Federal Republic of Yugoslavia), to which was added the so-called offence of opinion – enemy propaganda as defined in Article 133 para. 1 of the Criminal Law of the Socialist Federal Republic of Yugoslavia. Taking these serious charges as proven, the Sarajevo County Court pronounced the maximum sentence of 15 years in one case, and somewhat shorter sentences of from 5 to 14 years in the other cases.

In its verdict of 31 October 1985 the Federal Court dismissed as unfounded and unproven the principal charge of forming a hostile group for the purposes of endangering the social order by counter-revolutionary activities, and reduced the remaining charges to some texts and alleged verbal statements, qualified as the significantly milder criminal act of hostile propaganda. For all that, the sentences remained draconian. Although, after all reductions, sentences for such acts are usually of the order of one or two years in prison, Alija Izetbegović was sentenced by the Federal Court to nine years' imprisonment, Omer Behmen to eight, Ismet Kasumagić to seven, Hasan Čengić to six and Salih Behmen to four.

We take this opportunity once again to call your attention to the illegality of the entire proceedings and the arbitrariness and injustice of the sentences. Doubts and suspicions are aroused above all by the fact that at the main hearing, out of 36 witnesses on whose statements the verdict was based, 21 to a greater or lesser extent changed the statements they had given during the investigative proceedings or repudiated them entirely. The reasons for this unusual behaviour on the part of witnesses were heard during the main hearing: the statements they had given during the investigative proceedings from which the defence was barred without any written decision or explanation, were made under duress by subjecting them to lengthy and exhausting ill-treatment, serious threats, and at times even rough handling. Not one of those summoned to interview by the State Security Services knew whether he would be a witness or be charged in the forthcoming trial, and many of them were deprived of their travel documents as further pressure and blackmail. The best evidence of this is the case of Mustafa Spahić, who was originally intended as a witness in this trial. At the session of the Supreme Court of Bosnia and Herzegovina held on 14 March 1984 he recounted that the investigation officer had presented him with a choice: to sign an accusatory statement against one of the three first accused, of his own choice, and then to go home, or to be himself charged. He was told that the minimum sentence at the forthcoming trial would be five years. At the session of the Supreme Court Spahić named the two investigation officers concerned and the date on which this occurred. After he refused to testify, Spahić was charged and sentenced to five years' imprisonment.

All of this supports us in our conviction that the charges based on such testimony from the investigative proceedings were pure fabrication and that the court should have treated the statements given during the main hearing as reliable evidence. However, the court did not wish to trust what it directly heard and saw, but put its faith in statements issued under duress during the investigative proceedings, given without the presence of defence counsel. And it did so with astonishing persistency even when material evidence disproved individual charges based on such statements. Thus, for example, Hasan Čengić was charged with having said that 'a Muslim may not receive blood from an unbeliever nor donate blood to one.' At the main hearing, however, it was established that Čengić was a voluntary blood donor and that he had a donor card to prove it. What is more, he had organised a blood donation action in the *madrasa*.

This and similar facts lead us to the conclusion that the sentences are not based on valid reasons and that the entire trial was rigged.

The Board is also acquainted with the proposal of the first accused, A. Izetbegović, to raise a claim for the protection of legality against the verdict of the Federal Court, and shares his view that this trial of Muslim intellectuals was the victory of the irrational politics of autocracy over justice, reason and truth. Now, however, it is not only justice that is trampled upon. After three and a half years spent in prison in appalling, and often unbearable conditions, not only the health but the very lives of Alija Izetbegović, Omer Behmen, Hasan Čengić, Ismet Kasumagić and Salih Behmen are threatened. We therefore urge you once again, for the sake of preventing this most severe and tragic of consequences, to enable them to be released.

Every petition and appeal went unanswered.

In November 1983, I was transferred to Foča to be held in detention for 14 years, and put in section S-20. This was known as the murderer's section, since the majority of convicts in that section were responsible for one or more such crimes.

In fact, the premises consisted of several rooms with a large central area as a living room, and four dormitories, two to the right and two to the left, together with sanitary facilities. This constituted one prison section. There were between 80 and 100 of us. This included one man who had three murders on his conscience, who had been sentenced to death, and then had the sentence commuted to 20 years in jail. It may sound paradoxical, but it was my good fortune to be sent to that section. Some of my comrades from the trial were in a worse position, with petty thieves and small-time criminals, which is a great misfortune in prison. These are people with no character, while murderers are a different type altogether.

I cannot say that I was subjected to ill-treatment in jail, although hard labour is in itself both physical and mental torture. One fact exacerbated my situation. Political prisoners are held together with other convicts. This was not generally known to the public, since the Communists who were held as political prisoners in the old Yugoslavia were held separately and had favourable treatment. When they came to power, however, the Communists abolished these privileges in the case of their own political opponents. What is more, the position of political prisoners in communist Yugoslavia was even worse. Almost every convict other than political prisoners had the right to visits outside the prison, to leave of absence and to annual family leave. For almost six years, I was not allowed outside the prison walls, though during that time my 'colleagues' who had been convicted of theft, commercial crime, highway robbery and such like had been allowed home several times on leave or vacation.

I retained some hope until the verdict of the Supreme Court of Bosnia and Herzegovina. At first I could not believe that I could die in jail because of something I had written – whatever I might have said. But when the Supreme Court in effect confirmed the sentence, a year later,

I realised that the devil had had the last laugh and that they were really serious. What could I do? I sighed deeply and set out on that long road of which the end is not to be seen. I felt as though I were sentenced to life imprisonment. I did not sink into despair, however, and at times I was even cheerful. I am no hero, it was just a question of a certain consistency. You say certain things all your life, you think it and believe it, and then comes the moment of truth. One of the teachings of Islam (many regard it as the most important) is that one must accept everything that happens to one as the will of God. To tell the truth, I had not thought about it much before, but when I was faced with the prospect of spending the rest of my life in jail and dying among convicts, I reminded myself of the bottom line: of a touch of consistency. I remained of sound mind, and the doctors said I was physically sound too. On the whole, I can thank my faith for this, and one other thing: the loyalty and moral support of my children.

I often wondered, particularly during the first few days after the verdict, whether I would have the courage to withstand what lay ahead. The years went by and I did not notice in myself any lessening of the will to live, but more and more frequently I caught myself thinking that I was fairly old and that death could not be far off. That thought brought me relief. I kept it to myself like some great secret.

I also reflected that perhaps this great misfortune was sparing me from hundreds of small misfortunes that would have consumed me each day, slowly but surely. Maybe…

At other times I would try to penetrate into some great mystery. I would tirelessly reflect on some issue, certain that I was close to reaching some truth that was eluding me, but that was there, just within reach. If I had been a painter I am sure that at those times, sensing the powerlessness of words, I would have painted those incomprehensible images that I would stand and gaze at, baffled but full of questions. At those times, I think, I understood modern art in a way that no one else, except its creator, can do so.

At one time, after the investigative proceedings and the trial were over and I had adjusted a little to my new living quarters, I began to make notes: reflections on life and destiny, religion and politics, on the books I had read and their authors, and on all the things that come to a prisoner's mind during more than two thousand long days and nights. These notes turned into 13 volumes of the size known in the trade as A5, written in tiny and deliberately illegible script. One fellow inmate smuggled these volumes out in a chess-set box. They then lay dormant for more than ten years, before being issued in 1999 by the Sarajevo publishing house *Svjetlost* as a book entitled *Moj Bijeg u Slobodu* – My Escape to Freedom.

My courage in facing reality diminished as the days passed. The worst time was the early evenings, when I would struggle against the onset of melancholy. I must have written unguardedly about this to my daughter Sabina, for one day I received the following letter from her:

> I don't know if you have felt this before, but with me that feeling always manifests itself as darkness falls. I have to be very involved with something to repress it at least a little. Sometimes the sadness is mingled with a sense of fear and physical weakness. I know that it was always hard for me in a way to get ready when I had to go out at that time. But as soon as I was out, and as soon as darkness had fallen, it would pass. It seems to me that all my fears, uncertainties and sorrows came together in that feeling, and I reflected that it is the state of mind in which people decide to resort to alcohol or drugs to get through it. I'm telling you this because I want you to know that I too know that feeling, at least in part, and that I can imagine how you feel. Prison must make it harder, just as in my case the sense of freedom in this house makes it easier for me to get through that part of the day. Perhaps the best thing would be for you to try to do something entertaining when it comes on you, read something light if you can, do a crossword or watch TV. I know for sure that it is not a good thing to think or to give in to those feelings at such moments. It would only be even harder for you.
>
> You see, I'm pontificating again, but I wanted to make it easier for you somehow. In fact, what I'd like best of all at such times is for us to sit together at my place and drink coffee. But at least you should know that I am always thinking about you, and especially in the early evening.

You can be a professor or a famous philosopher in prison, and it will do nothing to make your life easier. Among prisoners it is more important to be a lawyer. As it happened, I was the only lawyer in the section. My fellow-sufferers used to ask me to write all kinds of requests, petitions and appeals on their behalf. They would tell me about their cases, confessing to me in effect. This was an interesting experience. I knew each individual case, and thought a great deal about them. Dare I say that some murderers were good people? Many of the convicts had killed for some human reason that, even if it could not be justified, could be understood. One of my fellow inmates in Foča was a young man who had killed someone while defending his father. He had been working in the house one day when he was told that his father was being beaten up in the local eating-house. He rushed over and found his elderly father under the table being beaten up by some village thug, pulled out a knife and killed the man. I think I would have done the same. Another person I shared a prison-room with for almost three years was Junuz Kečo, a quiet, unhappy man, about whose fate Abdulah Sidran wrote a moving screenplay for the film *Kuduz*.

One prisoner was serving a 20 year sentence for having killed his unfaithful wife and her mother who was protecting her. He was sentenced to death, and went through a very difficult time for almost a year as all the courts, one after another, confirmed the death sentence. It was only thanks to a last-minute commutation that he survived. He told me that he had cried like a baby when they told him his life had been spared.

The literature of the late 19th century shows a certain understanding for criminal offenders and sinners. 'Be whatever you want, but be it to the limit,' says Ibsen's *Brand*. In certain extreme situations, an offender seems to us to be a free man who is acting according to his own laws, while the righteous man is a slave to rules. Behaviour according to some code that does not derive from the soul appears repugnant to us. In that choice, our sympathy goes out spontaneously to the free man.

Most people do wrong in their own interest (power, wealth, glory, love or whatever it may be). But there is also evil for its own sake, evil that is its own end. And this is pure hell. I have also, unfortunately, had the opportunity to know such evil and the people who commit it.

One of the prisoners had killed a man out of sheer envy. This was noted in the verdict. He was sentenced to 20 years, saved from capital punishment only by a psychiatrist's report that he was of very low intelligence. Not mentally disturbed, for he was perfectly normal, but mentally handicapped. For no reason whatsoever he surreptiously threw a book belonging to a prisoner friend of mine, with whom I sometimes used to 'philosophise', out of the window into the prohibited area from where it was impossible to rescue it. The man went to the WC, leaving the book on the window ledge. When he came back, the book had gone. He discovered later from another prisoner what had happened. Compared with these villains, thieves appear to be perfectly normal and acceptable people: they steal because they need what you have. They have some kind of humanly understandable motive. My friend who lost his book told me, 'I know that you believe in God. I'm not sure if God exists, but I am absolutely certain that Satan does.'

There were numerous Albanians in Foča Prison, convicted of involvement in the resistance movement against the Serbian regime that had abolished Kosovo's autonomy. We were on friendly terms with the Albanians, but we did not mix much. They used to exercise in the central area of the prison grounds and we in a separate area at the far side. This unwritten rule of the prison regime was respected by all, prisoners and wardens alike. The Albanians were taciturn, conspiratorial and extremely serious. At times they would go too far, and go on strike. They wanted to read Marxist literature that other Marxists, the prison governor and others, would not allow them to read. The Prison Board employed an Albanian policeman whose duties included acting as censor for 'irredentists'.

We served our sentences differently – avoiding direct confrontation with the administration, but behaving with dignity. I think we must have been the most honest and decent prisoners incarcerated in Foča and Zenica. The prisoners trusted us. This was the reason that the Albanians were not afraid, one day, to propose to us political negotiations on their movement for 'national and social liberation,' as they put it. They also proposed the composition of the delegation, and that talks should be held during exercise one non-working Saturday, when the prison grounds were packed with prisoners and we could mingle as we walked without being noticed. We agreed to talks, not without some jokes at the expense of both 'negotiating parties'.

On our side there were myself and two of my comrades, Džemal and Edhem. The Albanians asked us what we thought of their movement. 'The Albanians are a Muslim people, and that is the main reason for our supporting your struggle for freedom,' I answered. They were a little flustered by this. The leader of their 'delegation' responded that there were 'some mistaken views' in my answer since, in his view, religion had played a negative role in the history of the Albanian people, and had been in the service of the occupying powers. 'We have outgrown religion, it is not needed by our people in their struggle for freedom,' the 'comrade' ended. 'Then you must be the only people in the world who can live without religion,' I answered, 'but our impression is that the majority of the Albanian people do not share your view.' 'It is only Marxism-Leninism that has brought progress to our people,' he said self-confidently. 'Fine, you go your way, that's your business, and as far as we are concerned, we shall continue to support the legitimate claims of the Albanian people for equality and freedom.' And thus the talks ended, but we remained good friends thereafter.

After the Supreme Court of Bosnia and Herzegovina had, for the most part, rejected our appeals (my sentence was reduced, in a symbolic gesture, from 14 to 12 years), we could still apply to the Federal Court in Belgrade for an Extraordinary Judicial Review of the verdict. I took advantage of that possibility.

In the application, which was 30 pages long, I produced evidence to show that the charges were false and that this had led the court into serious procedural breaches of the law. I wrote:

> Unlawful verdicts of the court are generally the result of errors or illegality in the proceedings that led to the verdict. In this case, the reverse is true. The false basis of the charges – concerning the nature and purposes of the *Islamic Declaration* – of which the falsity was blatantly clear from the very first day of the investigative proceedings... led certain investigative authorities and the court into gross breaches of the law, and into overt falsifications. It may sound paradoxical, but I assert that if I had really been guilty, I would have been given a fair trial. I did not receive a fair trial, because I was innocent. If I had really been guilty, the investigation would have been conducted by an investigating judge, and not by the police; defence counsel would have been allowed access to the accused from the very first hearings, as the law requires (such access was not allowed until the charges were actually filed); interviews with both the accused and witnesses would have been conducted in the presence of defence counsel, also required by the law; illegal methods would not have been applied to witnesses and their statements would not have been misrepresented; it would not have been necessary for the press to create a sense of psychosis by means of an unprecedented campaign and to persuade the public, even while the investigation was still being conducted, of the guilt of the accused; and, of course, we would not have been tried in secret. None of this would have been necessary, but it was necessary to find guilt where there was none, and to conceal the truth of the case from the public.

The world press, international human rights organisations and the free element of the Yugoslav press had already written extensively about the fact that the trial was rigged. This had created an environment for the verdict to be altered, but it took almost three years. The verdict of the Federal Court did not substantially reduce my sentence, but it did alter the nature of the offence, leaving only 'verbal delict' as defined in Article 133 of the Criminal Law. This is the famous Article that reads, to cite its essence in a free interpretation: 'Anyone who insults or attacks the state order in word, writing or images shall receive a prison sentence of up to ten years.' The final verdict was a sentence of nine years with hard labour. In effect, I served five years and eight months of this all because of some writings, words, statements – in short, because of my beliefs.

We learned at school that the history of mankind began, that man became a 'historical animal' when he learned to write. But man became the human species when he learned to speak, to say what he thought. And then came others who forbade him to speak, thinking up the infamous 'verbal delict', offences of the word, and returned him to the obscurity whence he had emerged.

From a historical perspective, the 'credit' for the institution of 'verbal delict', in the modern sense of the term, belongs to the first socialist state in the world – the USSR. In a proposal to amend the Criminal Law of the Soviet Socialist Federal Republic of Russia, in May 1922, Lenin cited enemy propaganda as one of six new criminal acts for which the death sentence could be pronounced. The explanation Lenin gave for this proposal was as follows: 'The basic meaning is, I hope, clear; the widest possible definition must be given, since it is only the revolutionary consciousness that will determine a narrower or broader application in practice' (from a letter to the Commissar of Justice, Dmitri Kurski).

During a public lecture in Sarajevo in 1994, a member of the public asked me about censorship. 'Mr. President, do you know what is being written, this is war-time after all. Why do you allow it? Why do you not introduce censorship?' I replied that after all I had gone through, I would never be in favour of such prohibitions. This is not only a matter of principle, but also an issue of productivity. I believe that prohibitions and force achieve nothing when persuading people is in question. I recalled that the Qur'an itself makes this point in one of its most sublime and at the same time most concise of sentences, which in Arabic reads *La ikraha fi'l din* – there is no compulsion in religion. If this is interpreted a little more widely, one has 'in beliefs, in what people think, there can be no coercion'. It would have suited the Communists if it were possible to put a stop to ideas with threats, beatings, the police and prisons, since these were the methods, more than any others, that they used. The experience of the communist system, and its defeat, have demonstrated for good – in a kind of historical experiment – that it is not possible.

One can get a sense of the atmosphere at home – alternating hopes and disappointments – from some of the letters I received from my children.

Sabina, 30 June 1985:

> It's not true that time heals everything. The anger and pain that I feel grow greater every day, and the more time passes since the trial the more I think about it, and feel as though I couldn't bear it today the way I did then. I write to you about commonplace, everyday things above all because I can't write to you about my own daily, ordinary thoughts and feelings about everything we've endured and are still enduring, and that I can't accept must still go on. I'm confiding in you so that you know everything. At the same time, I must say that never, not for a single moment, did I think or believe that there was even a shred of human justice in the name of which all this was done. I hope that there will be some in the decision of the Federal Court.

Sabina, 3 September 1985:

> This morning I went to the Ministry of the Interior to ask for my passport back. In fact, I'd already been there for this purpose countless times, but before going to the seaside I had filled in some form that they gave me there, so this time I was hoping for something. But once again it was just a waste of time, because they told me that my application had been turned down, and that I would soon receive a written decision – an explanation that explained nothing about the reasons for my passport being confiscated. Why I of all people can't have a passport I don't know, and I'd be really interested to know what reasons they had in mind when they made this decision. I'd even agree to still being without a passport, just to know the reasons. But it seems that I'll still be without either a passport or the 'reasons'.

Sabina, 30 September 1985:

> One of our daily events is now to speculate about and wait in anticipation for the decision of the Federal Court, and for days now, every time the telephone rings, we are on tenterhooks. But nothing new has arisen yet. Attorney Orhan called from

Belgrade to say that the verdict hasn't been pronounced yet. How much longer will this last? And yet I have the feeling that something has given way, and that we'll soon have some news. What I don't like, though, is that the optimism I've felt until now has dwindled, and I feel more fearful than hopeful. But hope is our only possible way of life, so I mustn't let it go.

Sabina, 16 October 1985:

I think about you all the time: today you should be getting the letter I wrote to you about the decision of the Federal Court. If we could just be with you, even for five minutes. However much you tell us you are prepared for anything, I know that it won't be easy for you. This is the final verdict, however, and the conjecture is over. I don't know how disappointed you will be. For us it was a huge disappointment.

Bakir, 14 December 1985:

Dear Daddy, I think you've received Sabina's letter where she tells you that your sentence has been reduced to nine years. It's worse than we'd hoped, but that's that. Don't fret.

We were very disappointed. God knows how it will be for you when you find out (perhaps at this moment). I thought up some words to calm you, and as I did so I calmed myself down a little too. You and I believe in destiny, which means that the date you come out of jail is already 'written'. Numbers like 14, 12 and 9 are only numbers, and not worth worrying over. You said it so well at the end of your book: the greatness of a man lies in 'a soul that measures itself against time'. In that regard, maybe you have a chance to live a true life, maybe you're in the right place, while we are left on the margins, or at best are mere onlookers.

Don't lose your nerve and begin to doubt this.

The verdict of the Federal Court finds you guilty under Article 133 (probably there won't be any misleading news again, since the verdict is in Sarajevo). There is still hope in a revision of this Article, in your being granted a pardon, or in some amelioration of the conditions in which political prisoners are held (we must step up the pressure for this, on our side above all, I mean the family).

Lejla, 24 April 1988:

> Dear Daddy, these visits pass by in a flash and it seems we don't even begin to say what we want to. These are long years that these 'locusts have eaten', as Pekić puts it. But I cherish the persistent memory of our last conversation and meeting outside the mini-market, if you recall, before you left. I shall try somehow to connect that moment and the long wait that followed. But I know that we shall always divide life into life before and life after. As for this present moment, I think that we shall 'accidentally bypass it'.

With the exception of swear-words, the two words most often heard in the prison were pardon and amnesty. After family visits, prisoners would always bring 'reliable' evidence about an amnesty that was about to be announced, but which never actually came about. I, too, secretly hoped for some kind of amnesty or pardon. Surely I would not actually serve nine years hard labour…

One morning, it was 1 February 1987, I was unexpectedly summoned to a special visit. I made my way in a worried state of mind to the building for the meeting. Something terrible has happened, I kept thinking. In the visiting quarters I found my two daughters, Lejla and Sabina. It was as if they were reading my mind. They greeted me with smiles, wanting to let me know at once that they were not bringing bad news. Then they told me that they had had a message from a 'senior position' saying that I should draw up a plea for pardon, and that I would be released. The message had been conveyed to them by Lejla's school classmate Zdravko Đuričić, Secretary of the State Commission for Pardons, and ostensibly came from Nikola Stojanović, a senior party official and Chair of the Commission. Zdravko Đuričić, whom I met many years later, was a good, well-intentioned man, who advised them that the plea should contain some words of remorse and something nice about the regime. My daughters had even brought me a petition written in that spirit. I read it, but did not sign it. My prison sentence continued: I had another five years yet to serve.

On my birthday, 8 August 1988, I wrote in my notes (published in 1999 with the title *My Escape to Freedom – Notes from Prison*): 'Today is 8 August 1988. I have lived for 63 years. I have already been in prison for five and a half. There is less than half my sentence still to go – three and a half. While there are turbulent events outside, I can only look on. Even that is something. The spectacle is extremely exciting and disturbing,' (p.345).

Things gained momentum rapidly, however, and I was not to remain a mere onlooker. I was to stay in jail less than four months more. On 25 November 1988, between three and four in the afternoon, I was called to the Prison Board. There the Commander of the Guard, Malko Koroman, in formal uniform and adopting a formal voice, read out to me the decision of the Presidency of Yugoslavia to release me from serving the remainder of my prison sentence. It was the two thousand and seventy-fifth day of my imprisonment. The years the 'locusts had eaten' were behind me.

On gaining my freedom, I gave many interviews in which I spoke about the trial. In 1990, when I was victorious at the polls, the most frequent question was whether there would be reprisals against the Communists for what they had done to me and my friends. I replied that there would be no reprisals: and there were not. All those who took part in the trial – the investigation officers, the prosecutor and the judges – continued to live their lives normally and to do their jobs, and some even retained the same posts as before. As a politician, I forgave them. As a man, I did not.

Chapter 3

FOUNDING THE PARTY AND AN ATTEMPT
TO RESTRUCTURE YUGOSLAVIA

Peace of mind, unrest in the country. Statement of the Forty. Constituent Assembly and Manifesto of the SDA: Party for Democratic Action. Travelling to America. Meeting Serb and Croat émigrés. Rally in Foča. Rally in Velika Kladuša: debates on seceding from Yugoslavia and on armaments. Zulfikarpašić and the split. First meeting with Tuđman. Victory at the polls. Member of the Presidency of Bosnia and Herzegovina. Meetings in Belgrade. Gligorov-Izetbegović Plan. Visits to Austria, Iran, Turkey, the USA, Italy. Meeting the Pope and the Serbian Orthodox Patriarch. First meeting with Milošević. The dissolution of Yugoslavia. War in Slovenia and Croatia. Zulfikarpašić and Filipović's so-called 'Historic Accord'. Responses to Alan Cooperman. Last attempt – the Hague meeting. First SDA Congress. Sarajevo Peace Accord and the shifting of the war to Bosnia and Herzegovina.

A new era of my life had conclusively begun with my arrest in 1983. There followed six years in prison, a year of rest, and then almost ten years as a member of the Presidency of Bosnia and Herzegovina. The year that separated prison and the Presidency was a year of relative peace and repose. When you have spent six years in jail, everything that happens to you afterwards is wonderful. And so it was for me. I read, travelled, walked and was surrounded by the care and attention of my children. What was also important, I felt a complete peace of mind.

Peace in our Republic of Bosnia and Herzegovina, on the other hand, was becoming ever more unstable. In the previous few years the country had been shaken by two scandals. The first was in the northwestern border region of Bosnia known as Bosanska Krajina: the Agrokomerc Affair, so-called after the giant company that had developed in a region of Bosnia and Herzegovina with a large Muslim majority population. The crisis developed in the company so fast that it was obvious it had been planned, with a threatening political background. The 'suicides' of some of the main players in the affair soon began, the journalist who had exposed it was also killed or died suddenly and the investigation procedure and the trial of the alleged guilty parties were confused and questionable.

Not long after this, another new scandal in Bosnia and Herzegovina was exposed – the exposure again coming from Belgrade – this time concerning the villas in Neum belonging to Bosnian Communist leaders. Neum is the small but very lovely part of the Adriatic coast belonging to Bosnia and Herzegovina. People were shocked by the luxury in which the Republic's leaders had been living.

New forces were emerging on the political stage in Yugoslavia, forces that we then called democratic. At that time Belgrade was a much more open city than Zagreb, and more open especially than Sarajevo. In the capital city of the Socialist Federal Republic of Yugoslavia the communist regime was being openly attacked on public platforms and in the editorials of certain newspapers, and demands were being made for the pluralisation of political life. These demands were tinged, in Belgrade, with nationalist tones, sometimes disguised as Serbian royalism, and sometimes openly Chetnik.[1] The voices calling for changes to the communist system were even louder in Slovenia than in Belgrade. Two publications began to appear in Ljubljana: *Mladina*, a magazine that shocked even the most democratic at that time, and the periodical *Delo*, which published serious critical articles by the most renowned of Yugoslav democrats and dissidents. The Slovenian Socialist League launched new, liberal ideas that had absolutely nothing to do with the regime of a state in which the Communist Party was in power. In both Ljubljana and Belgrade numerous articles and books were published on the crimes committed by the Yugoslav communists against their own people. The press in both these cities wrote about our 1983 trial, and every time such an article appeared in either Belgrade or Ljubljana, the newspaper would sell out within minutes.

The question of the national institutions of the Yugoslav Muslims was very topical at that time. One polemic that took place showed how 'inarticulately' this delicate issue was discussed. The Belgrade magazine *Intervju* published two different views: that of Professor Hamdija Ćem-

---

[1] Chetniks – the military element of the Greater-Serbia Organisation that committed genocide against the Muslims in Bosnia and the Sandžak during the Second World War.

erlic (*Intervju*, 4 December and 18 December 1987), and Dr. Sulejman Grozdanić (*Intervju*, 31 December 1987). Ćemerlic's view was that: 'Every nation has institutions for the development of its own identity. The Muslims have none. Such are the circumstances! Politics has taken the view that they are not required, and there things have remained... This is why a comprehensive national institution should be formed that would deal solely with national issues within the Muslim community... unfortunately the Islamic Religious Community, or rather its Supreme Council, is the only institutional representative of the Muslims in our country.' Dr. Grozdanić's view was: 'This is certainly not a new issue. It was particularly topical during the 1960s. I recall that my humble self then represented the view, independent of "politics", that we did not need them. Quite the contrary... I mean that advocating national institutions is often based on theoretical premises of a definition of national identity, which gives them absolute value while ignoring the real and actual state of affairs... Is it necessary for everything to be the same everywhere and always on the basis of some absolutised theory... Must every nation, everywhere and always, have its own exclusive institutions?' Dr. Grozdanić responded to his own question that it need not, continuing his explanation: 'And the social and historical reality here in Bosnia and Herzegovina imposed the very solution achieved here, known as – common living. My view is that the Muslims do not need separate national institutions. They already have them in a new, unconventional and perhaps "unhistorical", certainly extra-theoretical sense, which beyond any doubt represents a new, more modern, more revolutionary and more humane model of understanding national identity than the historical one that, *nolens-volens*, presupposed or at least stipulated possible parochialism, restriction, separation, disunity... The Muslims, then, have their national institutions, but they are common institutions, the national institutions of the three peoples and all others of Bosnia and Herzegovina equally... Ergo, the Muslims have their own flag, their own coat of arms, their social and political, scientific, cultural, educational and artistic institutions, but they are not only theirs, they are common not only to them but also to the Serbs and Croats and all other members of the other peoples and nations in Bosnia and Herzegovina.' Thus was Dr. Grozdanić's explanation.

Bosnia and Herzegovina represented the hardest-line core of Yugoslav totalitarianism, but even Bosnia could not remain immune to the events surrounding it. It was then under the omnipotent rule of Branko Mikulić, a Bosnian Croat, who advocated the equality of Bosnia with the other entities of the Yugoslav Federation. Unfortunately, his political orientation was not democratic. Mikulić advanced to the position of Federal Prime Minister, while retaining power in Bosnia and Herzegovina. The youth press in Sarajevo promoted the Bosnian line, and little by little began to take a critical stance towards the undemocratic conduct of the Communist Party of the day in Bosnia and Herzegovina.

News began to reach us from the more liberal sector of the press about the appearance of Chetnik songs and symbols in Belgrade, the Sandžak, Montenegro and Herzegovina. Posters of Dražo Mihailović[2] were put up in Terazije, Belgrade's main avenue, and long-bearded youths wearing the Serb military cap sang Chetnik songs. Particularly worrying was the fact that there was absolutely no meaningful reaction from the authorities to these spectacles. The Belgrade *Književne Novine* (Literary News) launched a debate about Jasenovac and the thesis that the 'Croats are a genocidal nation.' The Croatian press reacted angrily to this. The heavyweight weekly *Danas*, published in Zagreb, in the Krležian spirit, showed critical audacity, but also retained level-headed views. The Slovenians continued to be the most vociferous. On the grounds of some statements made by Slovene youth, Belgrade accused the Slovenians of anti-Yugoslav activities. The reaction from the Sarajevo political leadership and the pro-regime press to these events in Serbia and Slovenia was as sharp towards the revival of Chetnik-dom from Francuska 7 (the headquarters of the Writers' Association of the Federal Republic of Serbia) as it was to Slovene secessionism and 'counter-revolutionary activities'.

The so-called 'Irredenta'[3] erupted in Kosovo. A state of emergency had already been proclaimed there, in 1988, because of the uprising of the Albanians in this formerly autonomous region of the Yugoslav Federation. Serb nationalist forces from Serbia proper were calling for a revision of the 1974 Constitution of the Socialist Federal Republic of Yugoslavia, which accorded the regions Kosovo and Vojvodina a high degree of autonomy. There were trials week after week of young Kosovan 'irredentists', who received severe jail sentences. I had come to know some of them in Foča Prison.

I never believed that such a rigid form of communism could last for long, but I must also admit that I did not foresee its collapse in 1989-1990. I believed, rather, that we would see some kind of internal relax-

---

[2] A Second World War Chetnik leader.
[3] The Serbian name for the Albanian independence movement in Kosovo.

ation that would enable other political options to emerge, some kind of competition under communist rule. Events proved me wrong. It is of the nature of the communist system to be all or nothing – there is no happy medium. Communism and liberty are mutually incompatible – either communism destroys liberty, or liberty, communism. In the mid 20th century, communism destroyed freedom. At the end of the century we were seeing the film run in reverse.

The fall of the Berlin Wall in November 1989 had a domino effect in the communist world. Every communist government behaved as though stricken with paralysis, incapable of doing anything. In Yugoslavia this widespread condition was additionally burdened with ethnic tensions, which have always been present, but which gathered particular momentum at this time.

Yugoslavia was anyway suffering from two maladies that would be the cause of its downfall: the inefficient socialist economy, which was so run that it was always lagging behind the developed capitalist world, and Serbian hegemony, which had been built into the system from the very start. The Serbs were the dominant nation, taking over every major position while the other peoples – the Croats, Slovenes, Montenegrins, Macedonians and Muslims, felt repressed.

Serb domination was particularly marked in the most sensitive areas. In the Ministry of National Defence of Bosnia and Herzegovina, for example, there were 28 active officers before the war, of whom 63.2% were Serbs, 10.5% Yugoslavs, 7.9% Muslims, 5.3% Montenegrins and so on. In the Federal Secretariat for Internal Affairs all nine senior-level civil servants from Bosnia and Herzegovina were Serbs (quoted from M. Bojić, *Historija Bosne i Bošnjaka* – History of Bosnia and the Bosniacs, p. 301).

I was not happy about this. I was emotionally linked to Yugoslavia, and perhaps, as a Muslim, I felt instinctively that the dissolution of Yugoslavia would not be to our advantage. Although the largest concentration of Muslims was in Bosnia, there were also Muslims in Serbia, Montenegro, Macedonia, Kosovo and Croatia. In my summing-up at the 1983 trial, I said that I loved Yugoslavia, but that I did not like its government. I continued to believe that it would be possible to reconstruct Yugoslavia as a democratic state, with the introduction of a market economy and constraints on Serbian hegemony. The latter would have been achieved by a gradual increase in the autonomy of the six republics constituting Yugoslavia.

The religious sentiments of the Muslim people were systematically repressed and stifled for over 40 years of Yugoslav communist rule.

Although in this regard the situation in Yugoslavia was incomparably better than in other communist countries, it could not be said that we enjoyed religious freedom. It was a kind of restricted-dose, a controlled freedom. The events that followed showed that these religious sentiments had not been extinguished. Beneath a thick layer of ash, the embers were still flickering and would later burst into flame.

If the country was to undergo democratic reconstruction, it was necessary to establish democratic parties. Political parties are not without faults, but the world has yet to think up anything better.

We needed a pro-Bosnian and pro-Muslim political organisation that would bring together our people living in a broad band of territory from Novi Pazar to Cazin, mingled with Serbs and Croats. If Yugoslavia were to break up, it would be harder for us than for the Serbs and Croats, but if these fateful issues were to be decided without us, it would be even harder. At first I thought of reviving the Yugoslav Muslim Organisation (YMO), which had dominated the life of the Muslims of Bosnia and Herzegovina between the two World Wars, but which had ceased to exist in 1941, with the fall of Yugoslavia. It was the leading organisation of the Muslim people, and was headed by a great man, Mehmed Spaho. Spaho died – or, as some accounts have it, was killed – shortly before the outbreak of the Second World War, and after his death the shameful Cvetković-Maček pact on the partition of Bosnia was signed. This great man did not, however, create a great organisation. Spaho's YMO fell apart as soon as it felt the first winds of the war that swept over Yugoslavia in 1941. When I decided to found this party, I conceived it as different from the YMO, so that it would be able to withstand the trials that, with time, it would have to face.

I had spoken to my friends in jail about my intentions. I saw it as a Muslim party. I was sure that it would have no difficulty in bringing together the Muslim people in Yugoslavia, and that just a clear appeal to them would do. Part of that vision was later to become reality almost exactly as I had envisaged it; as though the people had been waiting years for just this. The business of forming a political party – later to be called the Party for Democratic Action (SDA – Stranka Demokratske Akcije) – began in November 1989, exactly a year after my release from prison, and the Party was victorious in the November 1990 elections, a year after the first steps were taken to found it. From the very start I was the 'leader', though I never knew why. I thought to myself, 'if I'm the best, then what are the rest like?' But perhaps leaders do not have to be the best. To be leaders, they must also have some major failings, and I certainly had plenty.

Whenever I thought about forming a political party, I always imagined that I must make a start with Professor Muhamed Filipović, at the time the most prominent Muslim intellectual. I said to myself: 'you need Filipović and a hundred intellectuals, and then the task is half done.' As it was, events took a different path. I spoke with Filipović, who had then formed the Committee for the Protection of the National and Religious Rights of the Bosnian Muslims – this was January 1990 – and he politely turned me down, giving as his reasons: 'it's not yet the time for this.' And it was not the time. The law prohibiting all political activity other than under the auspices of the Communist League was still in force. Any other political activity could always be construed as activities against the state or at least as 'verbal delict', which could lead to a ten-year prison sentence.

I took the risk. I never know if this is true courage, but I have always liked to take a bit of a risk. It was the same in 1946, when I became involved in the banned Young Muslims Organisation, earning myself in the process that three-year custodial sentence.

I went to Zagreb to raise interest in my ideas among my acquaintances. There was a large group of prominent Muslims there, centred on the Zagreb Islamic Cultural Centre, and headed by Salem Šabić and Dr. Šemsudin Tanković. I knew both of them from earlier days. Šabić deserved most of the credit for the construction of the monumental Zagreb Mosque, the largest and most beautiful of its kind built under communist Yugoslavia, and Šemsudin Tanković was a prominent Professor in the then Faculty of Economics. About 15 invitees came to the meeting organised by Šabić in the Annex to the Mosque. We quickly reached agreement in principle on the formation of a party from 'Muslim cultural circles' – later the SDA.

In addition to wanting to bring together the Muslim people of Bosnia and Herzegovina and coordinate them politically, the party aspired to be the party of all the Muslims of Yugoslavia, which meant also in Serbia, Montenegro, Kosovo and Macedonia. The Party was first formed throughout Yugoslavia, wherever there was a Muslim population, and later abroad: in Europe, America and Australia. It became in a sense the movement of the Bosniac Muslim people world-wide.

The situation altered abruptly in Yugoslavia under the impact of the general crisis of the socialist system, especially after the fall of the Berlin Wall. The weakening of the regime, and the general political thaw associated with it, gathered pace. Things that had previously taken years now happened in just a few months.

With the first days of spring – more precisely, on 27 March 1990 – I called a press conference, in one of the conference rooms of the Holiday Inn in Sarajevo, to announce the founding of the political party. One could feel in the air that people were nervous about the regime's reaction. I sat at the table, greeted the numerous journalists, and read out, in a voice that betrayed my agitation, the *Public Statement* signed by 40 citizens, founders of the Party for Democratic Action, better known as the *Statement of the Forty*. In my opening words I emphasised that the announcement, although written in programmatic form, was not the Party's formal manifesto. Its primary objective was to inform the public.

The *Statement* read as follows:

> We the undersigned,
>
> faced with the social crisis in Yugoslavia, which is not only economic but also political and moral, concerned to preserve Yugoslavia as a community of peoples and nations, and wishing to see the unimpeded continuation of the democratic processes aimed at the creation of a modern state characterised by freedom and the rule of law, desirous of supporting these developments and fulfilling in such a community not only the interests common to all its citizens, but also and particularly those that we have as citizens belonging to the Muslim cultural and historical community, have resolved to launch an initiative to form the PARTY FOR DEMOCRATIC ACTION, and with this aim hereby announce the 16 programmatic principles of our political activities:
>
> I.
>
> The Party for Democratic Action is a political alliance of the citizens of Yugoslavia who belong to the Muslim cultural and historical community, and of other citizens of Yugoslavia who support the programme and aims of the Party.
>
> II.
>
> The Party for Democratic Action (SDA) will strive, within the framework of democratic contest – which it advocates – to implement its programme and aims by attracting voters,

participating in elections and participating in the representative bodies and organs of government in proportion to the results it achieves in free elections.

III.

Democracy is one of the basic determinants of our Party. Since this term is subject to diverse and often contradictory understandings and interpretations, we emphasise that by democracy we mean government by the people, regulated by the rule of just laws. These are laws centred on man as a free individual, that unreservedly and without any limitations affirm the rights, freedoms and equality of people and of citizens regardless of religion, nation, race, language, sex, social status or political convictions.

By human rights, both in extent and content, we mean those that are set forth and defined by relevant documents of the United Nations, namely the Universal Declaration of Human Rights, the International Covenant on Civil and Political Rights and the International Covenant on Economic, Social and Cultural Rights. Since our country has accepted and ratified these instruments, the SDA will advocate their consistent application in their entirety in the legislation and practice of this country.

IV.

We call for democratic government, and for this to come about, it must be possible to dismiss government. This requires the abolition of one-party monopoly and its outcome – the party state. This process has however only just begun, and in the greater part of the country has gone no further than formal proclamations.

The country should be governed by representatives of the people, from all strata and sectors, directly elected in general, free elections by secret ballot, and assembled in representative bodies. We believe that the federal parliament (assembly) should be composed of two houses with equal rights: a citizens' council (instead of the present federal council) and a peoples' council. Decisions would, as a rule, be adopted in the first by majority vote, and in the second by consensus.

Government should ensure the independence of the judiciary by means of the constitution, laws and organisation. Judges should be elected by the representative bodies at a level no lower than that of the Republics, and the current so-called tenure review of judges should be replaced constitutionally by the same permanent judicial office that exists in the majority of civilised countries.

V.

Defining democracy primarily, not as the rule of majority, but as the rule of law, we wish to stress our commitment to the principle of the full equality before the law of peoples both large and small, and to the rights of religious and national minorities; to this end we reject all forms of outvoting.

Majority rule without the mediation of law inevitably transforms itself into the tyranny of the majority, and the tyranny of the majority is as much a tyranny as any other.

VI.

We advocate the maintenance of Yugoslavia as a free community of nations, as a federal state within its existing federal borders. In this regard we support the slogan 'Helsinki for Yugoslavia'. In our judgement any demands for the revision of the country's internal borders would lead to a dramatic worsening of relations between its peoples and to potential conflicts of which the consequences are impossible to predict. In this regard, the members of nations living in a federal entity that is not their mother entity have all the rights that they enjoy in their mother entity, and we regard any restrictions to these rights as illegitimate.

VII.

Faced with the disregard of the national distinctiveness of the Muslims of Bosnia and Herzegovina and of their usurpation on this basis, and rejecting these aspirations as contrary not only to historical facts, but also to the clearly expressed will of this people, we proclaim that the Muslims of Bosnia and Herzegovina, both those living in Bosnia and Herzegovina itself and those living beyond its borders, are an indigenous Bosnian people and, accordingly, form one of the six historical peoples of Yugoslavia, with their own historical name, their own land, their own history, their own culture, their own religion, their own poets and writers, in short their own past and their own future. The SDA will therefore revive the national consciousness of the Muslims of Bosnia and Herzegovina and insist on respect for the fact of their national identity, with all the legal and political consequences this entails.

While emphasising the right of the Muslims of Bosnia and Herzegovina to live in this land under the national name and as an indigenous people, we recognise this right equally and without any restrictions or limitations for the Serbs and the Croats, as well as for all the other peoples and nations of Bosnia and Herzegovina.

In this regard, we state our particular interest in the preservation of Bosnia and Herzegovina as the common state of Muslims, Serbs and Croats. To this end the SDA will resolutely resist any attempts to destabilise, partition or encroach upon Bosnia and Herzegovina, regardless of the origins of these or similar ideas.

VIII.

Another of our interests of this kind concerns the region of Kosovo. We regard this as a conflict between peoples that cannot be resolved by repression. We see dialogue as the only solution, but dialogue can be successful only if conducted by genuine representatives of the people. We therefore call for democracy for the Albanian people. We support and believe in the Yugoslav option for a resolution of the crisis in Kosovo, in which we are encouraged by the knowledge that there are still influential Albanians who share this conviction. In this spirit, we support as the basis for a resolution the declaration 'For democracy – against violence,' drawn up and issued in January 1990 jointly by the Regional Committee for the Protection of Human Rights and Freedoms, the Association of Philosophers and Sociologists of Kosovo and the Kosovo branch of the Association for a Yugoslav Democratic Initiative (UJDI).

IX.

Bearing in mind that Muslim circles in Yugoslavia have begun, as the result of a series of unfavourable historical circumstances, to fall behind in development and education, the SDA believes its primary task is to inquire into and eliminate the causes of this situation, and to initiate and support all measures aimed at the development of education and schooling at all levels. This relates particularly to elementary school education, which must be compulsory, free of charge and as comprehensive as possible. The SDA will accordingly call for fundamental reforms to the school system and a review of curricula, in order to eliminate all the ideological dogmas and prejudices that have arisen during the period of political and mental monopoly.

X.

Regarding freedom of religion as a fundamental human right and convinced of the powerful moral potential of religious teachings, we advocate:

– full freedom of action of all religions in Yugoslavia, the full autonomy of their religious communities and strict respect for that autonomy.

– the freedom to erect religious buildings in accordance with the demands and needs of believers and their communities. To this end we shall call for a review of urban planning programmes, which are wholly 'anti-religious' in concept, since as a rule there is no provision for religious buildings in newly-constructed housing estates and settlements.

– access to the information media (TV, radio and so on) for religious communities and their adherents, for which there are both principled (the principle of equality of citizens) and practical reasons (the equal contribution of believers in financing the media).

– recognition of the major religious festivals as days off for the relevant category of believers, and where a single religion is in a majority, as state holidays also. In the case of Bosnia these would be the two *Eids* and the Orthodox and Catholic Christmas.

– the provision of meals in the army, in hospitals and in prisons in accordance with the religious prescriptions of citizens who so request for religious reasons.

XI.

The SDA supports the programme of economic reform adopted in December 1989, but regards it as merely the first stage in the reconstruction of the national economy. We believe that at least another two radical changes are indispensable:

First, the widespread denationalisation of commercial firms, beginning with the smaller and proceeding to the larger. Only activities of common social concern (the PTT, the railways, mines, air traffic, etc.) should remain in social (public, state) ownership, together with those that, by their nature, are not market activities. We underline that we do not see private ownership solely as a factor of economic efficiency, but also as a guarantee of the basic freedom of citizens.

Second, to restore to agriculture the dignity and meaning that belongs to it in a country such as ours, for this is a great opportunity for it. It is necessary to protect cultivable land by law, since this land is currently exposed to relentless degradation, and to abolish maximum limits on land-holdings, reduce taxation and provide rural incentives for modern market production – in particular by guaranteeing sales – in which the experience of certain Western countries should be emulated.

We believe that the aforesaid measures will encourage a large number of our workers to return from abroad, bringing to the country not only their capital, but also the work habits they have acquired, which in the long term would make possible the employment of a large number of those who are currently unemployed.

XII.

Structural changes to the economy and property ownership must not be permitted to endanger rights acquired, nor the positive functions of the welfare state, which must be retained and promoted. This relates in particular to minimum levels of free health care, the minimum living standard for the unemployed, the elderly and the sick, free elementary and secondary education, measures to protect mothers and children and so on; with the proviso that the institutions through which these are provided should be efficiently organised and freed from the burden of excessive interference and bureaucracy, the maintenance of which absorbs a large part of the resources intended for these fundamental purposes.

We shall call for special measures for working wives and mothers. We believe that one solution could be the introduction of differentials in working hours (fewer working days in the week, fewer working hours in the day and such like), depending on family circumstances and the number of children a working woman has.

XIII.

The SDA accords particular significance to the preservation of the moral and ethical values of the family, as the most important factor in the upbringing of the individual and the creation of social cohesion within every community. As a result our endeavours will be directed against all forms of pseudoculture in the shape of pulp literature, pornography, etc. The people should be offered true freedom in place of false freedom and true culture in place of pseudoculture.

Our interest in the prevention of so-called dependency diseases (alcoholism, nicotine addiction, drug addiction and so on) is related to the above. This would be achieved by educational activities and restrictive measures (taxes, bans on advertising, zones and periods of partial prohibition, etc.) based on experience gained elsewhere in the world.

XIV.

We advocate amendments to the criminal legislation (material and procedural) and its harmonisation with the human rights and provisions of the international conventions accepted and ratified by Yugoslavia. Articles 114, 133 and 157 of the Criminal Law should be abolished altogether, and political activities by citizens should be regarded as criminal only if they advocate violence. Under the same conditions (the absence of the element of violence), we call for the release of all political prisoners and the free return of political refugees to the country, as provided by Article 13 of the United Nations' Universal Declaration on Human Rights.

XV.

We support the development of an environmental culture and all measures and activities for the protection of the environment. Members of the SDA should be active members of the environmental movement in their own region and support its activities and endeavours.

XVI.

The aims set out in this Statement, which have common and universal significance, will be achieved in cooperation with other democratic forces in the country. In this regard, the SDA regards itself as an integral part of the democratic front formed by various democratic parties, movements, associations and groups, together with the numerous human rights committees in Yugoslavia. The SDA will not collaborate with parties that are working for the dissolution of Yugoslavia or its retailoring, or that advocate chauvinism and intolerance.

We associate ourselves with the statement of representatives of the democratic movements of Otočec dated 8 October 1989 and regard this Statement as our own.

We believe in the democratic path to achieving changes to the social, political and economic nature of the country without hatred and revanchism.

The signatures of the 'forty' followed:

Alija Izetbegović, graduate lawyer, of Sarajevo; Muhamed Čengić, graduate mechanical engineer, of Sarajevo; Dr. Maid Hadžiomeragić, dentist, of Sarajevo; Dr. Muhamed Huković, teacher, of Sarajevo; Edah Bećirbegović, attorney, of Sarajevo; Dr. Šačir Čerimović, medical doctor, of Sarajevo; Salem Šabić, businessman, of Zagreb; Prof. Dr. Sulejman Mašović, Faculty of Special Education, Zagreb; Prof. Dr. Fehim Nametak, research worker, of Sarajevo; Salih Karavdić, attorney, of Sarajevo; Fahira Fejzić, journalist, of Sarajevo; Dr. Šaćir Čengić, medical doctor, of Sarajevo; Edhem Traljić, graduate lawyer, of Sarajevo; Džemaludin Latić, writer, of Sarajevo; Omer Pobrić, musician, of Sarajevo; Dr. Sead Šestić, research worker, of Sarajevo; Dr. Tarik Muftić, medical doctor, of Mostar; Safet Isović, performing artist, of Sarajevo; Dr. Šemso Tanković, assistant lecturer at the Faculty of Economics, of Zagreb; Mirsad Veladžić, M.Tech, of Velika Kladuša; Dr. Kemal Bičakčić, medical doctor, of Sarajevo; Abdulah Skaka, artisan, of Sarajevo; Omer Behmen, graduate civil engineer, of Sarajevo; Šefko Omerbašić, chief imam, of Zagreb; Dr. Mustafa Cerić, assistant lecturer, Islamic Theological Faculty, of Sarajevo; Dr. Sulejman Čamdžić, research worker, of Zagreb; Prof. Dr. Lamija Hadžiosmanović, Faculty of Philosophy, of Sarajevo; Dr. Halid Čaušević, graduate lawyer, of Sarajevo; Kemal Nanić, graduate civil engineer, of Zagreb; Bakir Sadović, student, of Sarajevo; Faris Nanić, student, of Zagreb; Nordin Smajlović, student, of Zagreb; Husein Huskić, M. Eng, of Maribor; Mirsad Srebreniković, graduate lawyer, of Zagreb; Nedžad Džumhur, graduate technologist, of Banja Luka; Fehim Nuhbegović, businessman, of Zagreb; Đulko Zunić, businessan, of Zagreb; Prof.

Dr. Almasa Šaćirbegović, Veterinary Faculty, of Sarajevo; Prof. Ahmed Bračković, Faculty of Economics, of Sarajevo.

After I had read out the Statement, a journalist from the Belgrade newspaper *Borba* asked me, 'Mr. Izetbegović, if you gain power, will you take revenge on those who sent you to jail?' I replied that there would be no revenge, and that it was so written in the Statement I had just read out. 'There will be many much more important existential issues to deal with,' I replied after a short pause. Then Džemaludin Latić, who was sitting in the audience and who had for some months been conducting a major media campaign for a review of our trial, rose to his feet and said, 'Mr. Izetbegović, that is only your opinion, and not all of those convicted in the same trial can agree with it. As far as I am concerned, I shall call for a review of our trial. I shall demand that those who ordered it be brought to justice, which does not necessarily mean that they will go to jail.' The Statement produced a tumultuous reaction among the public. It was the first time since the communist system had existed in Bosnia and Herzegovina that a political force not belonging to the communist school of thought had come out in public.

We learned later from information that reached our headquarters that the authorities had been hesitant about whether or not to prevent us from so doing. The news even came that preparations were being made to arrest all 40 signatories. It was obvious that the authorities were not sufficiently powerful to do so; for perhaps the first time in their history, the Communists were unable to act. They gave vent to their displeasure in their captive media, and criticised us, but that was all.

In April, believing it could convince the public that I had a 'bad past', *Oslobođenje* began publishing a *feuilleton* on my 1983 trial. The journalist chosen retained the same style and the same manner of trumped-up charges as she had seven years earlier when reporting on the trial. The Communists were sure they would be victorious at the polls and that 'working people and citizens,' when reminded of the 'reactionary plans of former convicts and incorrigible fanatics,' would show them where they belonged – in the political back seat.

In reacting to the *feuilleton*, I decided to make use of the opportunity to promote my own views. I included a quotation from my summing-up at the 1983 trial prior to pronouncement of the verdict: 'I love Yugoslavia, but not its government…'

Two months later, on 26 May 1990, the Constituent Assembly of the SDA was held, once again in the Holiday Inn. The hall was packed. Fear had given way to defiance and resolution. I recognised people from all parts of Bosnia and Herzegovina, and Yugoslavia as a whole. Adil Zulfikarpašić had even come from Switzerland.

Zulfikarpašić was the best-known Bosniac émigré. He lived in Zurich, where he had founded the Bosniac Institute. Together with Teufik Velagić – a prominent member of the Party, and also a political émigré – who lived in Vienna, he was a signatory to the 1976 London Declaration, known as the proclamation of the Democratic Alternative, also signed by a number of prominent émigré Serb and Croat democrats. I had come to know Zulfikarpašić in the summer of 1989. Our first conversations indicated that we had somewhat differing views. He wanted to eliminate the Muslim and emphasise only the national, Bosniac nature of the party. I suggested that he come to Bosnia and that we work on the issue, but he was not yet ready to do so. It was only on the eve of the Constituent Assembly that he appeared in Sarajevo. It was Friday. The media and the people gave him a ceremonial welcome. Zulfikarpašić's objections were without foundation, for to a large extent I respected his proposals on 'Bosniac-hood'. I included in the text of the Declaration a sentence in which our strategy was quite clear. I wrote that we were 'one of the Bosnian peoples, with its own language, culture and tradition…' The designation Muslim for a nation was obviously inadequate, but we had to retain it. If we had not, it would have given rise to confusion among the people ahead of the population census planned for the end of that year.[4] While the speaker read out the Programmatic Declaration, Zulfikarpašić frowned, but did not react.

I began my speech at the Constituent Assembly with the *bismillah*.[5] I did so for two reasons: first, I was quite sincerely appealing to the Almighty for help, and second, it was a mark of religious freedom and a clear signal of disobedience to the regime. Until that time, it was unimaginable to utter any kind of religious phrase on a public platform. I continued my speech with a story of freedom. I said that the previous year, after the fall of the Berlin Wall and the collapse of the communist system, the era of freedom had dawned for millions of people over a huge area of the globe. I compared the significance of those occurrences

---

[4] In the 1991 Census, in Yugoslavia as a whole, 2,289,722 persons declared themselves as 'Muslim' by nationality, of whom 1,905,869 were in Bosnia.

[5] *Bismillahir-rahmanir-rahim*: In the name of God, the Benevolent, the Merciful.

with great historical events such as the fall of Byzantium, the discovery of America or the French Revolution two centuries earlier:

> I do not claim the right to speak on behalf of the Muslim people, for no one has authorised me to do so, but I am sure that I am rightly interpreting their deepest sentiments when I say that they will not permit Bosnia to be dismembered. The shameful Cvetković-Maček Agreement on the partition of this country is a dead letter. The guarantee of this is the force at work in this hall today...

Reviewing the communist order, now in total collapse, I concluded:

> The giant attempt to create 'heaven on earth' without God and man, indeed even against God and man, has ended in total failure.

The audience interrupted me with applause. Some people were in tears. It was clear that a new page of our history had been turned.

Our guests of honour were sitting in the first few rows, among them Jože Pučnik, Chair of the Slovene DEMOS; Dalibor Brozović, representing the Croatian HDZ; Dražen Budiša, Chair of the HSLS (Croatian Social Liberal Party) from Zagreb; Dr. Fuad Muhić, the most eloquent ideologist of the communist elite in Sarajevo; the late Vladimir Srebrov, a misfortunate poet and victim; Rasim Kadić, Chair of the Socialist Youth; and so on. Somewhere in the hall I noticed the Priest Fra Ferdo Vlašić, a good man from Duvno (Tomislavgrad), who had been in jail with me in Foča. They all made speeches in which they expressed support for the formation of the party and wished it every success. The meeting proceeded as planned until the moment when Dr. Brozović took the floor, saying that 'Croatia would be defended right up to the Drina.' Scattered applause broke out. Later Srebrov took the floor to censure what Brozović had said, but he began also to challenge the call for the Bosnian language. He spoke disconnectedly. The hall wisely refrained from responding to either statement.

There was a brief report covering the Assembly on TV Sarajevo's main evening news. We were described as a group of former prisoners, failed university professors and political discontents. This was the only damage the authorities of the day were able to do to us.

TV Sarajevo quoted my opening words:

> Ahead of us is a new concord of the peoples of Bosnia and Herzegovina and the peoples of Yugoslavia on the kind of

Bosnia and Herzegovina and the kind of Yugoslavia we want. Agreements of this kind can be brought about only by genuine representatives of the peoples, and who those genuine representatives are can be determined only by the people themselves in free elections. Whatever path we take, therefore, we always come up against that magic word 'freedom'. The battle for Yugoslavia will be won or lost right here, in Bosnia.

The Assembly carried the Programme Declaration by vote, and elected the Party's leadership. I was elected as President, and Adil Zulfikarpašić as one of the three Vice-presidents.

A quiet fever ruled among the people. Like a snowball gathering momentum, the party grew at a rate that no one could have foreseen. Regional and local organisations of the SDA burgeoned throughout the country. The first should have been founded in Banja Luka in early June, but it was prevented by the police, and a meeting of about 20,000 people was finally held on 8 July in the big square outside the *Boska* department store. Dr. Hamza Mujagić, from Banja Luka, was elected as Chair of the branch. The meeting was greeted by a representative of the Democratic Party from Belgrade, and there were special greetings for Academician Muhamed Filipović, who was born in Banja Luka. His observation that the time of political conformism was over was particularly noted.

The election campaign was at its height at the end of August when I went to America, accompanied by the poet Džemaludin Latić, at the invitation of the SDA there. After many decades, I met there, close to Niagara Falls, my classmate from my days at the gymnasium high school, Hasan Karačić, whose surname was pronounced Karachi in America. He had by no means been a good pupil, but he was a good and likeable man, a restless spirit. Hating the communist regime, he had emigrated to Canada, where he had started a paint and lacquer factory, built a fine house not far from the Niagara Falls, and married a Turkish girl, with whom he had two daughters and a son. But Hasan was now virtually confined to bed, after surviving a stroke. He carried a stick, spoke with difficulty, and wept a good deal. He was as happy as a child to see me. He was exceptionally well-regarded and well-liked by American Muslims. We were soon joined at Hasan's place by Dr. Nedžib Šaćirbegović, who was in charge of our ten-day trip. We visited with him the Bosniacs of Toronto, Washington, Chicago and the later-to-be-famous Dayton, a town that will be remembered for quite different reasons and often mentioned in this book.

During the course of our meetings in America we discovered more or less the same dilemmas and desires of our people as at home. They felt themselves to be Muslims in the national sense (the term Bosniac had yet to appear on the scene), loyally celebrated state and religious holidays and festivals, steered clear of the Ustasha and Chetnik émigrés, for the most part worked as labourers in lower-grade jobs, read little, but organised a lot of concerts of newly-composed music. A few individuals, however, had succeeded in making their mark in American society: Nedžib worked as a specialist doctor in the Washington Clinic, Ilijas Zenkić, from the Krajina region, had made an important political career for himself; Safet Ćatović, a young Muslim from Plana near Bileća, after serving a long prison sentence and emigrating to America, had become a prominent pedagogue; Dr. Edib Korkut had become a member of a team of some Nobel Prize winner. The best known among them was Dr. Ćamil Avdić, who had founded the Islamic Centre in Chicago and written some important papers on Bosnian cultural history. Nedžib had arranged some important meetings for us in Washington, first at the Yugoslav Embassy, and then with the Serb and Croat émigré communities.

The Yugoslav Embassy in Washington was led at that time by Dževad Mujezinović, a Muslim from Bosnia. He organised a press conference for us in the embassy. The conference proceeded quietly until some Belgrade journalist began pressing us with questions about Kosovo. He wanted at all costs to make me either come out in support of the 'Albanian Irredenta,' as the Kosovo demonstrators were called, or censure them. Ambassador Mujezinović interrupted his questions: 'Ask about Bosnia, but if you really want an answer, no one can support the use of violence against any people,' he told the journalist bluntly.

I received from Mujezinović some facts about the inferior position of Bosniacs in the then Yugoslav diplomatic service. Of about 1,770 employees in the Ministry of Foreign Affairs of Yugoslavia, there were only 23 Bosniacs, or less than 1.5%. At that time Bosniacs constituted more than 8% of Yugoslavia's population.

Mujezinović originated from Cazin. As a war orphan, he had spent his life in Belgrade, but always remained attached to Bosnia and his Krajina region. He was a true Bosnian patriot. He had been appointed as a minister in Ante Marković's first Federal government, but was soon sent to Washington, so that Marković's government was left without a single Muslim.

The following day we had talks with the Serb émigré community, of whom the most active was Mihajlo Mihajlov, a well-known dissident from Zadar, whom the Communists had sentenced to a long term in prison for the infamous 'verbal delict'. We were guests in the home of some Serb from Banja Luka. Naturally, we talked about Milošević, his rally in Kosovo Polje and the introduction of martial law in Kosovo. To my surprise, those present did not support Milošević. And even during the most difficult years, the Serb Democrats did not alter their views. Mihajlov later visited us in Sarajevo during the siege. 'Are you going to see the Croats now?' they asked at the end of our talks. 'Go ahead. You won't be able to convince them about anything; for them Bosnia was and remains ancient Croat land, and you Muslims are their 'flowers',' they said almost as one, and laughed.

The hotel in which we met the Croats was full of people and smoke. Whenever Džemal and I mentioned the Bosnian Muslims as a distinct people, or the Bosnian language, the Croats would start heckling, and interrupt us. They launched into their tirade: they spoke about Bosnia as an integral part of independent Croatia, said we were Croats 'of the Islamic faith', and talked of Serb aims and Serbs as Chetniks. As far as we could, we emphasised the proximity of our and the Croat peoples, the fact that we were familiar with each other, the absence of any historical traumas between us and the Croats, but we failed to halt them in their encroachments on us and Bosnia. At one point, a tall, elderly man came up to my table, shook my hand, and said out loud: 'Mr. Izetbegović, allow me to express my deep respects for you and to say that I support your views. That is the way to go ahead.' It was the late Dr. Branko Pešelj, a signatory of the Democratic Alternative for Yugoslavia, an anti-fascist and anti-communist, leader of the Croatian Peasants' Party in exile.

Another émigré then spoke up, Nijaz Baltak Daidža, a 'Croat of the Islamic faith,' as he introduced himself. He turned to the audience and said: 'Why are you attacking these people. They are more religiously than nationally inclined intellectuals. Let them be, they will come to the right answers. And I should like to ask you, Mr. Izetbegović: have you made military preparations to confront the Chetniks? You haven't! Well, let me tell you, they will again slaughter you by the Drina, no matter how much you may talk about the Bogumils and tolerance. They'll butcher our people, whatever we call them here!'

When the war broke out in Croatia, Nijaz Baltak, Mate Šarlija or, simply, Daidža, became a general in the Croatian Army, fought against the Chetniks in Bosnia, and was wounded on Igman. Džemal told me that when he arrived in Bosnia, he called him and asked him mockingly about the Bogumils, reminding him of his words of warning spoken in that Washington hotel.

The following day we were received at the South-East Europe Desk of the US State Department and the Centre for World Democratic Development. 'Alija, say *Bismillah*,' urged Džemal as we entered the State Department. The years that were to come demonstrated that our talks at the heart of the US administration had an importance far greater than we could have imagined at that time.

We spent our last day in America in Dayton, a town that would become part of the history of Bosnia and Herzegovina. We were invited as guests to the annual meeting of North American Muslims. My book *Islam Between East and West*, translated into English while I had been in jail, was well-known in Muslim circles in America. When we entered the hall, it was already packed. Entire families had come; there were children running about noisily. 'You can see that we're among Muslims,' said Džemal, entranced by this 'Muslim vitality'. He had been surprised to see, everywhere else, how pre-planned, disciplined, punctual and somewhat depressing everything had been.

I cannot remember all the meetings, but those in Novi Pazar, Foča and Velika Kladuša were the most impressive, with the largest number of people attending. Prior to Foča I went to Zagreb, Bihać, Zvornik, Goražde, Tuzla and Tetovo. The focal event of the meeting in Foča, held on 25 August 1990, was the *janaza*, burial, of Muslims killed during the Second World War. Although more Muslims had been killed, proportionately, in that war than any other people, the killing-fields where they had died had not been marked. Foča had been one such huge killing-field. The atheist regime had never permitted the erection of a religious memorial to these innocent victims. The meeting was convened under the title 'Foča must never happen again.' I appealed to the 100,000 or so Muslims who had gathered there for peace and forgiveness. I said that on that day the Muslims were passing an historical test. I rejected the notion of the collective responsibility of the Serbs for the atrocities committed by the Chetniks against the Muslims. 'For us, seeing it from the perspective of Foča, there are only two nations – the murderers, and the innocent victims,' I said, attempting to quell any national euphoria. Boys and girls threw flowers from the bridge where, almost 50 years earlier, the Muslims had been killed. I also proposed that we lay flowers on the graves of innocent Serb victims. The people agreed. Unfortunately, this was vain idealism. In 1992, the horrors of Foča happened again, in even worse form. The population was killed and forced to flee, and all the mosques were destroyed, among them the world-famous Aladža, built in the 16th century. Was there any point in those attempts at reconciliation? Even today, I think there was. Attempts of that kind are never pointless.

In Velika Kladuša, where almost 2,000 people had assembled, I went a step further:

> Bosnia and Herzegovina as a civil republic, that is the conclusive option of the Muslim people: not Islamic, and not socialist either, but civil; but for this we need the Serbs and Croats to accept it too…
>
> If Slovenia and Croatia carry out their threat to separate from Yugoslavia, Bosnia will not remain in a rump Yugoslavia. Bosnia will not agree to remain in and be part of Greater Serbia… If need be, the Muslims will take up arms in defence of Bosnia.

This was the first time I spoke publicly of separating from Yugoslavia and of taking up arms. It was 15 September 1990.

The Muslim nation was thereby, at least in part, prepared for the events that were to follow. Although lacking sufficient arms, it was organised.

Just before the war broke out – I think it was in March 1992 – I had talks with the head of KOS,[6] General Vasiljević. He said that we were acquiring arms, which I denied, of course. He claimed to have evidence, and offered to show it to me. It seemed that someone working for the SDA was also working for him. When we entered the 'Maršalka' (Marshal Tito) Barracks, in May 1992, we found some of our papers there. Vasiljević did, however, tell me this: 'Mr. Izetbegović, we've never been afraid of arms. Twenty like-minded people who organise themselves, that worries us. But depots full of arms, not at all.' We had brought those 20 people together – and not just 20, but a thousand times 20, in all parts of Bosnia and Herzegovina. And it was this, in fact, that ensured the country's defence.

---

[6] The Yugoslav Counter-intelligence Service.

During the 1990 campaign I gave a great many speeches, sometimes two a day. I wrote them myself. Only in one case – the Mostar meeting held in July in the stadium below Bijeli Brijeg – did I ask a friend to write my speech for me. It was a good speech, but they were not my words. I was completely unconvincing, and the applause was half-hearted. Halfway through the speech, I folded the paper and went on speaking off the cuff. The impact was markedly better after that.

Given the number of meetings, I could no longer think up what to say in my speeches. It was quite usual for me not to know what I was going to say until I was called to take the floor, and then, walking up to the rostrum, I would try to formulate a few well-thought-out sentences in my mind. I would slow my pace, and choose the longest way round to the rostrum, to give myself a few more seconds. There were cases when I prepared my speech *en route*, but this was not a success when I was being driven in a large car full of talkative people. In those cases, I let my instincts take over.

We took the design of the SDA banner from an old album in which there was a picture with a caption saying that it was the flag of the Spanish Muslims. Nothing could be more logical than for us, as European Muslims, to adopt that flag. People accepted it warmly, and later used it to cover the *tabut*, coffins, of fallen soldiers. When we proclaimed the independence of the state, a new Bosnian flag was designed: fleurs-de-lis on a white background. I do not know if we could have found any more innocent symbol of our identity than the crescent and flowers.

Zulfikarpašić was angered, however, by the flag and some chants by the audience. The Saudi Arabian flag, with its embroidered lettering and sword, was allegedly seen at the Kladuša meeting. It is true that the décor was too pronouncedly religious for a political gathering. But I do not think that this was the real reason for what happened. The SDA was in fact a movement, and different wings were developing within it. The chief problem arose with the group centred around Zulfikarpašić. It was evident from day one that we were not an ideologically and politically unified group. In the case of Zulfikarpašić, there was also the problem of his personality and opinion of himself. He regarded himself as the leader of the Muslim nation. The November Elections were to show that he was deluding himself completely. As time passed, it seemed to him that my popularity was growing at the expense of his. We had a series of acrimonious discussions on the matter. I concluded from one of these, in Velika Kladuša, that he was preparing for a schism within the party. I tried to dissuade him, since the people were experiencing a kind of liberation with us.

On 18 September, three days after the huge Kladuša meeting, I was sitting in the party headquarters preparing for a meeting to be held that evening in Ilidža, when a group of people burst in without knocking and informed me that Zulfikarpašić and Filipović had just held a press conference. They had announced that they were taking over control of the party. Their reasoning being that the party was becoming rightist, that I was leading the party into fundamentalism while they wanted to lead the people into Europe, and so on. It was a classic political *coup*, since the two of them had decided to take over power in the SDA without reference to the party's official bodies. The people were deeply depressed by the news. Articles appeared in the newspapers with the headline *The Day Bosnia Wept*.

It was very soon to become clear that the *coup* had failed. At the large SDA meeting held that evening in the sports hall in Ilidža, Filipović was not allowed to enter, and I was carried in shoulder-high. The people were with us. This was confirmed by the series of meetings that followed, both theirs and ours. Finally, the November Elections showed precisely how things stood. I beat Zulfikarpašić in the Presidential Elections by ten to one.

The name of one man was ever more frequently mentioned in the Yugoslav crisis, the tempo of which was constantly accelerating. This was Dr. Franjo Tuđman, the then Chair of the HDZ and future President of the Republic of Croatia. I had heard of Franjo Tuđman while I was still in prison, but the wider public came to know more of him in 1989, when he formed the party known as the Croatian Democratic Community, better known by the initials of its Croatian-language title, HDZ. Franjo Tuđman was spoken of in Bosnia with mixed feelings; I decided to get to know him better. My defence counsel from the 1983 trial and good friend, the Zagreb attorney Nikola Muslim, offered to introduce me to Stipe Mesić, one of the founders of the HDZ, who would take me to meet Tuđman.

I reached Zagreb by the morning train in, I think, February 1990. Attorney Muslim, who had come to meet me at Zagreb railway station, took me to a building in the centre of the city, where a design company was located on the third floor. The Director of the company was Stipe Mesić. So began a friendship that has lasted to this day. Mesić was later a member of the Presidency of Yugoslavia, and during 1991 we frequently met there. As I am writing this, Mesić is serving his five-year term as President of the Republic of Croatia.

We set off by tram to the meeting with Tuđman, and got off not far from a flyover. From the tram stop one could see a nondescript wooden shack, which was the HDZ Headquarters. We went into the premises, which were humming with activity. After a brief wait, I was received by Tuđman. So began discords and disagreements that were to last for years.

Tuđman invited me to lunch in a Zagreb restaurant. He drove us there himself. During our conversation, obviously wanting to make himself quite clear, he said to me these very words: 'Mr. Izetbegović, don't create some Muslim party, it's quite wrong, for the Croats and the Muslims in Bosnia and Herzegovina are one people. The Muslims are Croats and that's what they feel themselves to be.' I said that he was deluding himself, that the Muslims felt themselves to be Muslims, that they liked and respected the Croats very much, but that they were not Croats, and so on. He produced some historical arguments in his favour, to which I granted that with his doctorate in history he knew history better than I, but that I knew present-day Bosnia better than he. He said that the HDZ in Bosnia and Herzegovina would gain all the Croat and Muslim votes and that it would get 70% of the votes. I replied that the HDZ would not get 70% but 17% of the votes. And indeed, in the November 1990 Elections, the HDZ did get 17% of the votes, which had not been difficult to predict. As a matter of fact, the elections were a mere population census.

The elections were held on 18 November 1990. The SDA captured 86 of the 240 parliamentary seats of the Republic of Bosnia and Herzegovina, and of the seven-member Presidency, three were SDA candidates. The candidate who gained the most votes in the Presidential Elections was Fikret Abdić – something over a million. I gained 870,000. Abdić had been helped by his reputation as a victim of the trial of the so-called Agrokomerc 'Bill of Exchange Affair' of 1986-87. He boosted that popularity by joining the political party, which was on the ascendant – he joined in September, two months before the elections. He also had a reputation, and gained votes, among a certain number of Croats and Serbs, as some analyses indicated.

Abdić's name was later to be associated with the mutiny in western Bosnia in September 1993, which caused enormous damage to Bosnia and Herzegovina and to the Muslim people. Through Abdić, Karadžić's Serbs were able to achieve one of their strategic objectives, to incite conflict within the Bosniac corpus. It would be premature to pass judgement on all the reasons for Abdić's embarking on this adventure, which ended unhappily for him. There are various interpretations of the event, starting with the fact that he had always been in a sense their man. I have no evidence of this, although some things that gave rise to suspicion could be observed here even in the very early days of the war. He found it extremely easy to establish contact with General Mladić, communicating with him by telephone without difficulty during the shelling of the city. It is known that he traded with the JNA during the war. Huge supplies of food and fuel went through Agrokomerc.

The transfer of power itself was carried out properly with the departing communist team, and was even accompanied by a certain ceremonial spirit. At the constituent session of the Presidency of Bosnia and Herzegovina, I was elected as President, on the basis of an agreement reached earlier between the victorious parties.

There then followed the appointment of government. This was an arduous business, in which there were hints of future discord and conflict. It seemed to me then that we should form a joint government, since it was obvious that the SDS had gained the votes of Serbs, the HDZ of Croats, and the SDA of Bosniacs. A joint government, so I believed, should be the framework for national harmony and reconciliation. The future was to show that I was wrong, but I still believe that we had to make the attempt. If we had taken another route, I am sure that war would have broken out as early as 1991, and critics would have interpreted the conflict that arose later as self-serving parties destroying a third by means of a coalition behind their backs. On the contrary, I tried to achieve a national consensus for Bosnia and Herzegovina.

The government that was formed after two months functioned poorly. It was clear that the parties had divergent, and in some cases opposing, views on what Bosnia and Herzegovina was and should be. It emerged that the SDS and the HDZ were merely extensions of their parent parties in neighbouring Serbia and Croatia. There began serious outside interference in the internal affairs of Bosnia and Herzegovina. The guilt for the schism within Bosnia and Herzegovina lies above all with the SDS, of course.

In a situation that presaged no good, the SDA issued a Proclamation to all SDA members, the Muslim people and the citizens of Bosnia and Herzegovina. A few days after the Proclamation, the Belgrade newspaper *Borba* asked me for a more detailed explanation. In an interview I gave the newspaper, I stated: 'The key point of the Proclamation is a call to the

Muslims not to be drawn into division, and if a state of emergency should arise, to protect their Serb and Croat and other neighbours. We respect the Serbian people and live in harmony, as we do with the Croats, but the destiny of Bosnia is determined more by Serb-Muslim than by Serb-Croat relations, for the simple reason that the Serbs are more numerous here than the Croats... The truth is, it is not in our hands whether a state of emergency will arise, it is others who are stirring this up outside Bosnia' (*Borba*, Belgrade, 9-10 February 1991).

I began to go to the sessions of the extended Presidency of Yugoslavia in Belgrade from early January 1991. These were meetings at which there were attempts to resolve the crisis that was threatening to lead to the dissolution of Yugoslavia. On my departure for the first session of the Presidency of the Socialist Federal Republic of Yugoslavia, in January 1991, I told journalists:

> At the last session of the Presidency of the Republic of Bosnia and Herzegovina we established our initial standpoint on the future of Yugoslavia. We agreed that we are for Yugoslavia, but also for Bosnia and Herzegovina as a sovereign state within Yugoslavia, sovereign, of course, to the extent possible within future integration. Yugoslavia should be a democratic country, in which the Republics, peoples and nations will be on an equal footing. We also committed ourselves to a free market, the free movement of goods, people, capital and the labour force. The dilemma of whether to opt for a federation or a confederation is a false one; democracy is the essential. This is our initial position in future negotiations.

Commonplace ideas at first glance, but for the Yugoslavia of that day, 'revolutionary' ideas.

I cannot say that the first session of the Yugoslav Presidency left a particular impression on me. While the political crisis was being debated, I followed the discussions with close interest, but I remember that I was very bored when the time came to deal with issues of a routine character. At one point I dozed off. When I returned, I recounted it to my children. They were curious to know how my first attendance at a session of the Presidency of Yugoslavia had gone, the same Presidency that had released me from jail two years earlier.

The extended Presidency of Yugoslavia was composed of a regular complement of eight members, increased by the presidents of the republic presidencies. It was also normally attended by the Federal Prime

Minister, Ante Marković, and the Minister of National Defence, General Veljko Kadijević.

It was not my first meeting with the majority of these people. I already knew Prime Minister Ante Marković well. He was a likeable and intelligent man, who was trying to reconstruct Yugoslavia, differing in this from the majority of his fellow Croats. I had also already met Slobodan Milošević, Franjo Tuđman and Kiro Gligorov on several occasions. It was, however, my first encounter with General Kadijević. He was a highly-trained officer, a Yugoslav by conviction, unlike his deputy Adžić, who was beyond any doubt a Serb chauvinist. Kadijević tried to preserve Yugoslavia. At this first meeting of ours we agreed that I would go to see him at GHQ. I did not take back with me a negative impression of him. He defended the Yugoslav cause, and there we were in agreement, but I asserted that the state must be reconstructed, and on this we did not agree. Kadijević was obviously afraid to touch the existing structure, which was very fragile.

Serb hegemony was built into the foundations of Yugoslavia from the very start. If all its peoples were not on an equal footing, Yugoslavia could not survive, but for the Serbs the very mention of an equal footing was like an insult. They believed that they had created Yugoslavia, and that it was theirs alone. To this fundamental cause of the dissolution of Yugoslavia must be added the inefficient economic system, based on so-called social ownership, which was in fact 'ownership without an owner'. The country was economically backward, and suffered from a huge foreign debt. Chaos broke out when inflation ran out of control.

During the next few months I visited several countries and met some important people. Things, however, did not get off to the best of starts.

On 25 March 1991 I was invited to the Conference on Minorities in Vienna, held on the ship *Mozart*, on the Danube. It was my first official visit to a foreign country. I was received by the then President of the Republic of Austria, Kurt Waldheim.

Waldheim had survived a serious crisis caused by his alleged Nazi past. My meeting him was politically risky, but protocol so decreed. Nevertheless, this visit was an important step for the infant Bosnian diplomacy. We achieved a high degree of friendship and understanding with Austria during the following years. The country's Foreign Minister at that time, Alois Mock, was one of the chief advocates of the Bosnian cause worldwide. When the war came to an end, I presented him with the Honourable Order of the *Zmaj od Bosne*, the Dragon of Bosnia, which the war

Presidency of Bosnia and Herzegovina had conferred upon him. There followed visits to Iran and Turkey, two countries whose relations with the West were diametrically opposite.

In Iran, whose military consignments were to play an important role during the war in Bosnia's defence against aggression, an exceptional welcome had been prepared for me. On that May day in 1991 large units of the three Iranian military services – the army, navy and airforce – had been deployed at Tehran airport, with a long line of more than 50 diplomatic representatives and other officials standing there in the hot midday sun. I was caught somewhat unawares, and I am not sure if I coped as best I could have. I was then taken to a super-luxury two-floor suite in a hotel in the northern part of Tehran. The living room was about 20 metres long. The western wall was entirely glass, and the sun beat mercilessly into the suite. All the air conditioners were working, humming unpleasantly, but to little avail. The temperature in the room was 28 degrees centigrade. In the distance one could see the well-known Evin Prison, surrounded by high walls. From our vantage-point on the seventeenth floor, one could clearly see the huge prison yard, crossed from time to time by a human figure. I thought to myself that perhaps someone was being hanged that very day. Iranian laws on murder and drugs are very strict. With those thoughts, and in that hot room, I tried to get to sleep. I succeeded only just before dawn, when the suite cooled down a little.

In the morning Minister Velayati came for me, to accompany me on the visits planned for that day. As is usual, he asked me how I was and whether I had slept well. I replied honestly that I had not, and told him part of the story. When we returned to the hotel later that afternoon, one of the security guards told me that he would come for me in an hour to take me to another hotel. I was transferred to the Hilton, to a smaller suite, where everything was on a human scale.

In Turkey I met Turgut Özal, a great friend of Bosnia. Özal was the popular Turkish President, known for his economic reforms. When I asked him what the secret was, he replied, 'President Izetbegović, remember one word – bank. You have to begin by setting the banks in order.' That was the year when Turkey held the presidency of the Organisation of the Islamic Conference (OIC), and it was in our interests for Bosnia to be on closer terms with that organisation. It was said of President Özal that he had distant Bosniac origins, his forefathers having allegedly lived in Jajce. I did not check this out with him, but he was surprised when I said that I had some Turkish blood.

At the end of July I visited the United States. I had talks there with four US Senators, the most remarkable of whom without doubt was Bob Dole. I was received on behalf of the State Department by Deputy Secretary of State Lawrence Eagleburger. I noted that the Bush Administration had no understanding of the Yugoslav crisis, and said as much to the press on leaving the meeting. I read later that as early as 1990 the CIA had formed the judgement that Yugoslavia could not survive. Roy Gutman analyses the reasons for the 'hands-off' US policy towards Yugoslavia in his book *A Witness to Genocide*. He writes:

> Personalities also made a difference. In addition to Eagleburger, who returned to government service under the Bush administration as deputy secretary of state, another old Yugoslav hand, Brent Scowcroft, became national security adviser. Scowcroft had been an air attaché in Belgrade in the early 1960s; later at Columbia University he wrote his doctoral thesis on foreign aid to Yugoslavia. While out of government during the Reagan administration, both continued their relationship with Serb and Yugoslav leaders. Eagleburger joined the board of Yugo America, the U.S. branch of the Serbia-based car manufacturer, and served as president of Henry Kissinger Associates, which had contracts with Yugo America and other Yugoslav state-owned enterprises. Scowcroft was vice president. Both spoke Serbo-Croatian, reportedly to each other on occasion, and both, according to official sources, came down on the side of the State Department in the Bush administration internal debate.[7]

In Rome, on 28 August, I attended an Extraordinary Session of the European Community Ministers, at which a Declaration on Yugoslavia was adopted. I then visited the Pope, and a few days before that visited the leader of the Serbian Orthodox Church, Patriarch Pavle, in Belgrade. The Pope, for whom I nurtured a deep and genuine respect, appeared older than I had expected, and Patriarch Pavle, a frail man of a very advanced age, looked as though he had just stepped down from one of the frescoes that decorate the walls of mediaeval Orthodox churches and monasteries. On the occasion of my meeting with the Patriarch, I said that the Muslims would never raise a hand against the Serbs. Bishop Irinej of Backa's comment on this was, 'I sought a similar statement that

---

[7] Gutman, Roy, *A Witness to Genocide*, pp. xxiv-xxv, Macmillan Publishing Co., New York, 1993.

the Serbs would never attack the Muslims from Radovan Karadžić. I never heard one.'

On my return from Rome, a journalist asked me, 'Since you have spoken within a short space of time with both Patriarch Pavle and the Pope, what is your view of Serb-Croat relations?' I responded that I was certain the religious leaders were committed to peace, but that unfortunately they had little influence on the course of events in our part of the world.

After it had become clear that the state presidency was unable to resolve the political crisis, someone proposed that the presidents of the six republics attempt to do so. Meetings were convened at intervals of a few days each. The whole of spring 1991 was marked by these meetings, alternating between Ljubljana, Zagreb, Sarajevo and so on. But wherever Milošević and Tuđman were present, nothing could be done. It was a tragic moment. There is no doubt that subjective, human factors made a major contribution to events in Yugoslavia turning out as they did. Objectively it would have been possible to take another route, and still achieve the essential aims of the Croat, Muslim, Serb and all other nations in former Yugoslavia. The character traits of some of the personalities who headed Yugoslavia and the republics at that time, or held other key positions, meant that every agreement was condemned in advance to failure.

The conduct of the great powers as regards Bosnia and the former Yugoslavia, too, demonstrated that nothing was essentially preordained and that much depended on the people who formed or implemented policy. America under Bush was not the same as America under Clinton; Britain under Major was not the same as Britain under Blair. It was the same with France under Mitterrand and under Chirac. We had learned the erroneous theory that politics, defined by interests and by teams of people, was rational and predictable, and that it depended but little on personalities. It was to become clear that this was not quite accurate. The fate of Yugoslavia, and its dissolution, were not an inevitability; and dissolution itself, when it came about, could have developed quite differently. What did happen was determined by the personalities of Milošević and Tuđman, but nor were they by any means a historical necessity. We Bosniacs had the misfortune that at a critical time an unlucky constellation of personalities held key positions: Bush, Major, Mitterrand, Milošević, Tuđman, Ghali, Akashi, Janvier and so on. For us Bosnians, all these people and their policies were a 'given quantity', an objective fact, over which we had little influence. For us, they were part of the imperatives facing us.

The first meeting of the state delegations of Bosnia and Herzegovina and Croatia was held in Sarajevo on 22 January 1991. This was immediately after the Decree of the Presidency of the Socialist Federal Republic of Yugoslavia on the disarmament of illegal and paramilitary units in Yugoslavia. Dr. Tuđman's press conference was entirely dedicated to this. On this, as on other issues concerning Yugoslavia, our views were much more moderate than the Croats'. Apart from myself and Tuđman, the delegations included on our side Fikret Abdić, Franjo Boras, Ejup Ganić, Stjepan Kljuić, Nikola Koljević, Biljana Plavšić, Bogić Bogićević, Momčilo Krajišnik and Jure Pelivan, and on their side Stipe Mesić, Žarko Domljan and Hrvoje Šarinić. All these names would long be mentioned, in one way or another, during the aggression by the JNA against Croatia and Bosnia and Herzegovina.

The following day our delegation travelled to Belgrade. Milošević's delegation was composed of quite unknown people, few of whom I remember today. The main topic was again the JNA. We accepted a single Yugoslav Army, but one that was balanced as to personnel and depoliticised. The latter met with a chilly reception. During the meeting, Slobodan Milošević was the principal speaker for the Serb side on every issue.

The negotiations with the Montenegrin delegation that were held a few days later were not difficult. We were in agreement that as smaller republics we must not be of inferior status in any future Yugoslavia. Momir Bulatović and Svetozar Marović were sitting opposite Krajišnik, Bogićević and myself. Although Bulatović was the leader, I noticed that Marović was much the more eloquent and shrewd of the two. The impression was that Bulatović did not think as he spoke, but merely declaimed views that he had learned in advance. He set them out in long, monotonous sentences in the style typical of communist politicians. He spoke in the same way at the press conference, too. I said in my speech that human and national rights were not respected in Yugoslavia. It was clear that the Montenegrins did not agree with this harsh assessment.

The following day, 26 January, I met Milan Kučan, President of Slovenia, in Sarajevo. Kučan enjoyed an exceptionally good reputation. He spoke quietly and wisely. If I had not known him already, I would never have said that he had been in the Communist Party. Our discussions were cordial. Kučan wanted to help us, and to alleviate things between us and the intransigent positions taken by Croatia and Serbia. After the session with the Slovene delegation I said that Bosnia and Herzegovina had the strongest motives and was the most called-upon to offer a new concept of negotiations on Yugoslavia.

But the incident, or affair, over General Martin Špegelj then occurred. The Croatian government was accused of illegally procuring arms. Karadžić exultantly called on the Presidency of the SFRY to prove 'that it was not dead.' He called for armed action.

It was in this atmosphere that talks were held with the Macedonian delegation on 29 January. We were closest of all to the Macedonian position. Gligorov and I gave almost identical press statements. We advocated the preservation of Yugoslavia, but structured fundamentally differently.

The following session of the Presidency of the SFRY, on 31 January, lasted eight hours. Waiting for me on the table were papers from Ante Marković amounting to more than 100 typed pages. Most of the time was spent discussing this material. At the next, stormy session, there was a debate on the letter that the JNA Political Administration had sent to all its units. Whenever I returned to Sarajevo from Belgrade, there would be journalists at Sarajevo airport waiting for me to give a statement. One of them pertinently noted that each time I returned from Belgrade I was less optimistic.

At the height of these talks I agreed to go to Bihać to speak at a meeting organised by the Patriotic League of Bosnia and Herzegovina. The questions put to me at this meeting were of a more military than political nature. One such was: will the JNA conduct a military *coup* in Yugoslavia? I rejected the possibility, but – I must admit – not wholly sincerely. I saw before my eyes Jović, Adžić and Kostić. I knew within myself that one could expect any kind of evil from them. And indeed, it was not long before I saw recordings of a session in Belgrade where Jović was persuading Bogićević, the Representative of Bosnia and Herzegovina, to vote for the proclamation of a state of emergency, which meant in effect martial law. As is well-known, Bogić stood firm and the demands of the military were defeated by one vote.

The session of all the presidents of the republics, held in Sarajevo on 22 February 1991, was dubbed the Yu-Summit by the media. During the session, I presented a proposal for an asymmetric federation. Some referred to this as a graded federation. My proposal was for Serbia and Montenegro in a classic federation, Slovenia and Croatia in a confederation with the first two, and Bosnia and Herzegovina and Macedonia in equal proximity or distance from all. Many years later, at the Summit of the Stability Pact for South-Eastern Europe, held in Sarajevo in the summer of 1999, one journalist compared this plan with the notion of the pact, holding the view that the plans shared a common point of reference for the way in which relations between the states of south-eastern Europe should be determined. 'If the idea of a graded federation had been proposed by someone from Europe, with NATO behind him, as is the case with Joschka Fischer as the brains behind the Stability Pact, would it have been successful?' he asked.

In March 1991 a further three so-called Yu-Summits were held, the first in Split, the second in Kranj, and the last in the Villa Biljana in Ohrid. None of these produced anything new or better. After the Kranj meeting, I avoided journalists, for fear of adding fuel to the fire with some statement or other. The atmosphere of intolerance had now reached a peak. I suggested that Milošević expound his position to the Slovenian Assembly, and Kučan his to the Serbian Assembly. While I was making this proposal, *Tanjug* reported on 25 March that 'the two republic presidents, Slobodan Milošević and Dr. Franjo Tuđman, have met at the border crossing between their two states.' I later learned that the main topic of the talks was the partition of Bosnia and Herzegovina. Those secret talks in Karađorđevo were to go down in history.

Thus the first round of talks in an attempt to save Yugoslavia ended in failure.

I remember the next meeting of the leadership, or Summit of the Six – as journalists pretentiously dubbed it – for the attempt to dismiss Ante Marković, Prime Minister of the Yugoslav Government, and to contest Stipe Mesić's taking over the function of President of Yugoslavia. It was then, too, that Kiro Gligorov and I made our last attempt to find a solution.

At the meeting of the 'Six', the six presidents, in Stojčevac near Sarajevo on 6 June, Kiro Gligorov, President of Macedonia, and I issued our Platform Statement on the structure of the former Yugoslavia. Instead of a federal state, we proposed a Yugoslavia transformed into a federation of states. Janez Drnovšek, the Slovene Representative, was the first to express public support for our proposal, and Milošević's adviser gave a statement to Reuters saying that this was 'a step forward.' The proposal was widely viewed as the last chance to find a way out of the crisis. At its session two days later, the European Community hailed the proposal (the 8 June 1991 Declaration on Yugoslavia).

One of the decisions made at the Stojčevac meeting was to hold a meeting of the three Presidents, Tuđman, Milošević and Izetbegović, as soon as possible. This was justified by saying that 'worsening intercommunity relations are the basis of the crisis, which are breaking apart in the individual republics in particular.' This meeting was held in Split on 12 June. The talks lasted for hours. Milošević and Tuđman had evidently come prepared. They were trying to direct the talks towards a tripartite partition of Bosnia. I responded with proposals for the re-construction of Yugoslavia on the basis of the Gligorov-Izetbegović platform. It was a long dialogue of the deaf, looking like a game of chess in which I was playing against the two of them, and with one chessman fewer. I managed to bring the game to a draw. After my return to Sarajevo airport, asked about speculations on the partition of Bosnia and Herzegovina, I responded to *Oslobođenje*: 'For me this is non-negotiable.'

The Split talks demonstrated the new political reality in Yugoslavia. Unlike the old Yugoslavia, in which only two sides were relevant, the Serbs and the Croats, the Bosniacs had now emerged as a factor without which no decisions could be reached. And my personal mission in these talks was to try to identify the points of contact between Tuđman and Milošević. I was to negotiate once more with the two of them, in Belgrade, on 19 June. The basis of these talks was mine and Gligorov's platform for the resolution of the crisis in Yugoslavia. I have to say that Milošević was closer to accepting it. Tuđman almost directly rejected it, referring to the Croat Referendum when Croats had opted for independence. James Baker, US Secretary of State, who came to Belgrade on 23 June in an attempt to save the Ante Marković Government, also supported the platform. In a meeting with Baker I said that Yugoslavia was on the brink of war, and that the involvement of America could prevent it. America remained on the sidelines. This was the end of talks on Yugoslavia. Milošević was to try to revive them at the end of August, in restricted form, inviting Bulatović, Gligorov and myself only. I refused to go to talks in which Slovenia and Croatia were not taking part.

In an interview I gave many years later for the Podgorica newspaper *Vijesti* (2 January 1998), the journalist Ljubiša Mitrović asked me this question:

> Mitrović: Mr. Izetbegović, after the 'Socialist Federal Republic of Yugoslavia battle', a lot of people have excellent hindsight. The price of dissolution was horribly high. You and the Presi-

dent of Macedonia offered a timely concept for a way out without bloodletting. Was there really no chance for your concept to succeed, and is there any chance that it might be revived one day in a new shape?

Izetbegović: I regret that the attempt you refer to failed, although regrets of this kind are probably pointless… All the forces, all the quantities that determined the course of events during those critical days in the Balkans were givens: the vacillating world, the flare-up of nationalisms, the incompetence of politicians both here and abroad, Milošević and Tuđman and their aims, and mine too, of course, if you will, all this was there and the result was inevitable too. As for the second part of your question, I regard cooperation of any kind as welcome, but a project of this kind, or similar, is obviously now out of the question.

On 17 June 1991 war broke out in Slovenia, and with it the departure of Slovenia from Yugoslavia. Shortly after that the war between the JNA and Croatia broke out, culminating in the siege of Vukovar and the shelling of Dubrovnik. We announced that we would not remain in a Yugoslavia without Slovenia and Croatia, since it was no longer Yugoslavia but Greater Serbia. At the end of October 1991, Karadžić made his famous threatening speech: 'Don't think that you won't lead Bosnia and Herzegovina into hell, and the Muslim people into extinction perhaps.' This was in front of the TV cameras at a session of the state parliament. I responded to this threat with the words: 'Karadžić's statement and message are the best possible explanation for our perhaps not remaining within Yugoslavia. The kind of Yugoslavia that Mr. Karadžić wants is one that is not wanted by anyone else. Anyone but the Serb people' (report by RTV Sarajevo).

The destruction of Bosnia and Herzegovina was taking place almost unimpeded out in the field. In spring 1991 the SDS had already formed the Serb Autonomous Regions, the infamous SAOs, which meant the direct demolition of the Republic. The JNA was arming them. It can be seen from a report from the Second Military Sector, dated 20 March 1992, that the army had distributed 51,900 light weapons to the Serbs in Bosnia. To this should be added a further 17,300 firearms that the SDS had distributed through its own channels.

We were faced with the dilemma whether or not to oppose the creation of this new situation on the ground by force, but our assessment was that we could not. The conflict was deferred month after month. Objectively, it could have begun in the summer of 1991, at the time of the Croat-Serb War, but we did everything we could to avoid it. In Sarajevo itself there were eight JNA barracks, some large and some small, at that time. Sarajevo was full of the military, a regular fortress of the Yugoslav Army, and it was impossible to try anything.

Despite this, during the summer of 1991 we made two courageous moves. First the SDA constituted the National Defence Council, from which the Patriotic League would later emerge, itself to develop into the Army of Bosnia and Herzegovina. This was on 10 June 1991, after a meeting in the police centre, attended by about 400 representatives from all over Bosnia and Herzegovina. The Yugoslav Army knew about the meeting, and let it pass, not feeling sufficiently strong to react. It was later, from talks with the head of KOS in March 1992, that I discovered they had known about it.

The second move was our decision not to draft recruits from Bosnia and Herzegovina into the JNA. This was in 1991, at the height of the war in Croatia, when I heard the disturbing news that General Nikola Uzelac, Commanding Officer of the Army Corps in Banja Luka, was drafting our young men and sending them to the front. I called upon the Presidency of the Republic of Bosnia and Herzegovina to pass a decision declaring that our young men should not respond to the call-up. The decision was passed by majority vote (the Serb members of the Presidency voting against it).

News of the bloody conflicts in Croatia continued to pour in. After one such horrifying spectacle from the Vukovar battlefield, without much reflection I asked RTV Sarajevo to give me air-time. On the way to the TV Centre, still agitated, I tried to form a few coherent sentences in my head. This was late in the afternoon of 6 October 1991. Speaking primarily for the general public in Bosnia and Herzegovina, I said: 'I wish everyone to know that Bosnia and Herzegovina does not wish to be part of this senseless deed... It is your right, as citizens of Bosnia and Herzegovina, not to respond to the call-up nor to any call to take part in a civil war. You are not obliged, remember, nothing requires you to raise a hand one against another, to fire on one another... I know that this needs a certain courage. I am aware of the risks that I personally am exposed to, in summoning you to peace. Today, unfortunately, the time has come when we need more courage to preserve peace than to descend into war. Remember, this is not your war. Let those make war who want to. We do not want that war. Help us to work with you to preserve peace in Bosnia.'

The Croatian media hailed these words of mine as an act of courage. I was, of course, governed primarily by the interests of our young men not to go to war and be killed for a cause that was, to say the least, dubious. I think that by doing what I did, objectively speaking I helped Croatia, because otherwise it would have meant at least 20,000 additional troops at the battlefront fighting on the JNA side. When it suited the Croatian regime, however, they inverted my meaning, saying, 'For Izetbegović, our struggle for freedom was not his war.' At the Presidency sessions in autumn and winter 1991, we extended the decree by which our young men would not respond to the call-up on military service, and indeed they did not respond.

Everything possible was done in Bosnia to preserve peace; desperate attempts, one could say...

I was preparing to travel to America when Adil Zulfikarpašić and Muhamed Filipović, for the first time since the split in October 1990, asked to see me. We met in my office in the Presidency building on 27 July 1991, just before my departure. They set out a plan for an agreement with the Serbs which, in their view, could ensure that Bosnia would not get drawn into the war that had already erupted in Croatia. I supported their initiative, believing that any attempt to preserve the peace was welcome.

Zulfikarpašić and Filipović had held talks with Karadžić, Koljević and Krajišnik in Sarajevo in mid July, following which they had gone to Belgrade for extended talks with Milošević. There they also had talks with Vuk Drašković, and the newspapers also spoke of a meeting with Milovan Đilas. When the draft of the agreement, which its protagonists had immediately and pretentiously dubbed 'historic', was on the table, however, it was clear that its end result would be the creation of a rump Yugoslavia. In their desire to preserve the peace in Bosnia at all costs, Zulfikarpašić and Filipović had caved in to the threats by Karadžić and Milošević. But it was very questionable if peace and the integrity of Bosnia could have been preserved: for there were still the Croats, and Croatia, and their plans and differences of opinion. Although Zulfikarpašić and Filipović stressed that the agreement was also open to the Croat people, if they so desired, the Croats read it correctly and reacted angrily.

Stjepan Kljuić, who was then heading the HDZ, gave a statement to the effect that the agreement was a deal between two of the peoples behind the back of the third, and that peace could not be preserved in this way. Ivo Komšić, then Vice-president of the SDP, described the agreement as treasonable, and said it meant handing Bosnia over to Greater Serbia (*Oslobođenje*, 4 August 1991). The same day I gave a press conference at which I said: 'There can be no peace, no stable Bosnia and Herzegovina, without the assent of all three peoples, nor can there be Yugoslavia, as we see, without Serbia and Croatia. The constitutional framework that is proposed in this "historic agreement", however, provides for a federation of the old kind, with its nucleus formed by Serbia and Montenegro and, in the view of the agreement's sponsors, Bosnia and Herzegovina.'

In an interview with the Belgrade newspaper *Borba* I said: 'We are holding a firm course – Bosnia and Herzegovina is veering neither to one side nor the other. This is a constant, as clear as mathematics… for we would automatically call into question our major interest, which is Bosnia and Herzegovina. It is curious that the creators of the agreement did not see this. They probably judged that Milošević has won and that we have to incline towards him. I personally do not see it that way…' (*Borba*, Belgrade, 16 August 1991). The prominent journalist Stojan Cerović wrote of the agreement:

> Between fear and pride, Zulfikarpašić has proposed an agreement that diminishes fear but hurts pride. His words: 'I trust Milošević' shocked the Croats, scandalised Bosnia and made much of Serbia laugh. Not a single Serb nationalist worthy of the name will take this seriously. It will certainly look to them as though Zulfikarpašić is offering Bosnia to them on a plate. Milošević himself could barely wait to bring about what he saw as a major victory, and invited the Bosnians and Montenegrins. He got it wrong. Not one of the Muslims came, and Izetbegović decisively rejected a rump Yugoslavia. For now, he has opted for both pride and fear… (*Vreme*, Belgrade, 22 August 1991).

Exactly nine years after these events, I was visited by the American journalist Alan Cooperman, a correspondent for several American newspapers and author of a book on the Bosnian War, who asked me for an interview on the events of 1991-1992. The 19 July 2000 interview proceeded thus:

> Cooperman: Mr. President, the focus of my research is the SDA strategy in the period 1991-1992, before the outbreak of war in Bosnia. It takes in the negotiations and attempts to avoid

war, and also the military preparations in the event of the failure of negotiations. My specific questions related to the Belgrade Agreement and the Cutileiro Plan. Did you authorise Zulfikarpašić and Filipović to negotiate on your behalf in Belgrade?

Izetbegović: They were negotiating primarily on their own behalf, that is on behalf of their party at that time, the MBO. Before going to Belgrade they came to my office, and informed me of their idea to hold talks with the Serbs. I welcomed the idea, and told them they could negotiate on my behalf as well.

Cooperman: Immediately after their return from Belgrade, did you support the agreement?

Izetbegović: On the basis of the initial press reports, yes, but when I had read the agreement, I saw that it was unacceptable. That same evening, on Zulfikarpašić's and Filipović's return from Belgrade, we all gave statements on RTV Sarajevo: I quite explicitly rejected the plan.

Cooperman: Were you dissatisfied with certain details of the agreement or with the general principle of Bosnia's remaining within Yugoslavia?

Izetbegović: I was always in favour of Bosnia's remaining within Yugoslavia, but not in a rump Yugoslavia. I could see, once I had familiarised myself with the Belgrade Agreement, that it clearly entailed not Yugoslavia but a rump Yugoslavia, composed of Serbia, Montenegro, Bosnia and Herzegovina, and possibly Macedonia, without Slovenia and Croatia. It is true that the agreement included a provision that it remained open to others, but the Croats had immediately come out unequivocally against the Agreement, regarding it as an agreement between two against a third.

Cooperman: Were you personally in favour of the agreement, but hard-liners within the SDA against it?

Izetbegović: I think I have just responded to that question. The SDA had already determined its strategy: any Yugoslavia that would comprise both Serbia and Croatia was acceptable. No Yugoslavia that excluded either one of them was acceptable. In line with that strategy, I had to reject the plan.

Cooperman: Why did it twice appear that you had accepted the Cutileiro Plan in February and March 1992, only on both occasions to reject it thereafter?

Izetbegović: You have to bear in mind two facts: first, the whole time we were negotiating under the threat of aggression, and second, we were not on an equal footing in the negotiations. The Serbs were negotiating from a position of strength, because they had an army behind them, the JNA, that was the fourth largest military force in Europe – both in manpower and equipment. In such a situation we could not adopt a firm and resolute position, but had to act tactically in such a way as to find some kind of a solution and avoid conflict, and to gain time. Nothing was signed at either the Lisbon talks (21 and 22 February 1992) or the Brussels talks (7 and 8 March 1992). There was only my statement that I supported the negotiating process and that I hoped for a positive outcome. It was not I who rejected the Cutileiro Plan, but the Serbs. They did so immediately after the Brussels talks, and then confirmed their rejection of it at the next session of their national assembly, on 11 March 1992. Meanwhile, between the Lisbon and the Brussels talks, we had held a Referendum on Independence (29 February and 1 March 1992).

Cooperman: What did you expect to happen if Bosnia proclaimed independence?

Izetbegović: I expected the international community to recognise Bosnia's independence following the referendum, and to come to the defence of the state it had recognised.

Cooperman: Did you believe in Karadžić's threat of bloody war to the point of extinction if Bosnia proclaimed independence prior to reaching agreement on the political and territorial reorganisation of Bosnia along ethnic lines?

Izetbegović: I did not believe it would come to a genocidal war. I thought there were two possibilities: (1) that the Serbs would accept the independence of Bosnia as a *fait accompli*, or (2) that they would go for a *coup d'etat* in Bosnia (that they would arrest me and the SDA leadership). If they did not want to accept the independence of Bosnia, the second would have been a logical and reasonable step. Instead, they chose aggression.

Cooperman: What preparations did you make in case war broke out?

Izetbegović: Some light weapons were amassed, and we reckoned on the police force, too. These forces could have defended the towns and cities, and this is what they did, when the attacks came.

Cooperman: Did you reject the plan on the assumption that Western diplomatic and military intervention would prevent Serb aggression?

Izetbegović: As I have just said, the Serbs rejected the plan, feeling themselves to be in a position of strength. As far as I am concerned, I did believe that the West would defend Bosnia both politically and militarily when it recognised the country's independence.

Cooperman: Did anyone, including Ambassador Zimmermann, suggest something of this kind to you?

Izetbegović: No Western diplomat, including Mr. Zimmermann, either suggested or promised anything of this kind to me.

Cooperman: If you had been able to see things from this perspective, knowing everything that happened, would you have done anything differently either politically or militarily?

Izetbegović: To this day I believe that I had no choice. Seen with hindsight, it seems that the only way to avoid war would have been to accept Bosnia's becoming part of a rump Yugoslavia, or in fact of Greater Serbia. In that case Bosnia would now be ruled by Milošević and Karadžić. No one can say what would have happened then. We can only guess, on the basis of what we have seen in Kosovo and now in Montenegro. That is why I believe that there was no choice, and that the independence of Bosnia was the only dignified way out.

Cooperman: With hindsight again, was there any solution that would have appeased the Serbs, averted the war and at the same time been acceptable to you?

Izetbegović: There was the plan to reconstruct Yugoslavia, drawn up in summer 1991 by the Macedonian President Gligorov and myself (the Gligorov-Izetbegović Plan). The plan provided for the decentralisation of Yugoslavia and greater autonomy for the republics. It suited us, for Bosnia would have remained intact within its then borders. It should have suited the Serbs too, since it guaranteed the survival of Yugoslavia, which was their overriding interest. Milošević gave his conditional assent to the plan (he had some objections in regard to the position of the army), but Tuđman rejected it. That plan could have averted war, while guaranteeing the basic rights of all the peoples in the Yugoslavia of that time. Unfortunately, there was insufficient political wisdom and courage to accept the plan. The war came, and everyone has paid the price.

The assessment I gave Alan Cooperman was in one regard only partly accurate, however. I have thought about this a great deal of late. If, out of indecision or fear of Karadžić's threats, we had not held the referendum and proclaimed independence, Bosnia would have been faced with two possibilities, one worse than the other: either to remain intact in a rump Yugoslavia (with Serbia and Montenegro), or to be partitioned between Serbia and Croatia. This second and more tragic alternative was the more likely, I even now believe the only realistic one. Tuđman would never have agreed to be left without his piece of the Bosnian cake, nor would the Bosnian Croats have agreed to come under Serb governance. And partition could not have been effected by peaceful means. There would have been war between Croatia and Serbia, and Bosnia would have been the battleground on which it was fought. The war would have been accompanied by massacres of civilians, ethnic cleansing of territories, waves of refugees and destruction. The Bosniacs would have been exploited as cannon fodder by both its warring neighbours. One thing is sure: in such a war, Bosnia would have ceased to be, and the Bosniacs as a people would have been annihilated.

The last year of peace was drawing to a close. Behind us was a fine and fruitful autumn. Snow had fallen early, in September, followed by a long, sunny Indian summer, or Michaelmas summer, as we call it here. This is the most beautiful time of year in Bosnia. Autumn reveals all the magnificence of the Bosnian forests that the people have so often sung about in their folk-songs. But this autumn these beautiful forests were a source of fear and unease. Serb paramilitary units that had already been fighting in Croatia – calling themselves Chetniks, an old and mythical name – were appearing ever more frequently. Almost invariably drunk, with long, unkempt beards and wearing the black or fur cap with the skull and cross-bones, they would sing songs full of hatred of the Muslims and Croats. At that time they were razing Vukovar and bombarding Dubrovnik.

Meanwhile, the world made one last effort to return peace to the region, or at least to prevent the eruption of war, but it was a sluggish and indecisive attempt.

The Conference on Yugoslavia, held in early November in the Hague, reminded me of the unproductive meetings of the six presidents of the republics at the beginning of the year. I suggested that the European Community send a goodwill mission to Bosnia and requested a peace-keeping contingent of 'blue helmets'. Cyrus Vance, the UN Secretary-General's Envoy, accepted the idea in principle on his visit to Sarajevo in November.

Some called upon the Party for Democratic Action to adopt a more resolute, even peremptory policy towards the JNA, the SDS and even the international community. I responded that it was impossible to drive fast along the steep, winding roads of Bosnia. I kept the radical elements in check, out of fear that we might provoke a clash with the JNA. I would say, though at times without conviction, 'Peace in Bosnia is not merely possible. It is essential. I cannot think of it in any other way.' It was in such circumstances that the first SDA Congress was held.

The congress was convened on 1 December, and lasted three days. It was attended by about 600 delegates, and the same number again of guests. It was clear from the speeches that Bosnia was 'at the doors of hell'. I made this the subject of my speech at the first plenary session of congress; I think that the speech illustrates the situation we were in:

Speech at the First SDA Congress

> These are truly unusual circumstances and an unusual moment in time – unusual, unfortunately, in the negative sense. Bosnia and Herzegovina and its citizens, and thereby the Muslim people too, are undergoing the most dramatic moments in the past hundred years of the country's history. It is a matter of war and peace.
>
> Bosnia has known both war and peace in the past. What makes the current situation exceptional is that the war we are threatened with would be no ordinary war. It would be total war, and many of the chief actors in the events taking place are not aware of this, or pretend to be unaware. The Army is strolling around the length and breadth of Bosnia, as though everything was just so, and some irresponsible cartographers, wholly unaware that they are sitting on a powder-keg, are drawing new maps and partitioning Bosnia. It is as if the borders of Bosnia, 300 years old and more, created by the political shifts of tectonic forces during a long and turbulent

history, were not to their taste, as if they were merely administrative, arbitrary and as if the ones they are now drawing in smoke-filled party offices are the true, historical borders. But if powder-kegs explode, everything will vanish in a cloud of smoke and disgrace: the cartographers and the generals, and all the parties and their leaders, all the laws and institutions, and the greater part of everything that has been built up in this region by the painstaking labours of dozens of generations. Because they have the misfortune to be indestructible, all that will be left is three bloodied and defeated peoples, half-crazed and degraded to the limits of barbarism. Confronted with this bleak picture, our party has opted for peace and the avoidance of every risk of conflict. And the greater the danger, the more, and the more resolutely, will we opt for peace… We need to do everything to avoid conflict, for if it should come to this – since it will be no ordinary, limited conflict – everything becomes meaningless. We have fully understood this. Others must understand it too. Our option for peace is more, therefore, than the ordinary love of peace. It is a sense of responsibility in the finest sense of the word.

The SDA has the right to its own specific aims and interests. But in striving for peace in Bosnia and Herzegovina, it represents equally all the citizens and peoples of the Republic, for the maintenance of peace and the avoidance of conflict is supremely in the interests of each and everyone in this country. Our advocacy of the survival of Yugoslavia, in the early days, was motivated by this interest: the survival, that is, of a particular form of state community now and to come. It seemed to us that this was the only way to find a way out of the crisis by political means and for everyone to obtain something, if we could not all have everything we wanted. We believed that every other route, in which secession and a 'rump Yugoslavia' were mutually linked and interdependent, led to violence and conflict. Unfortunately, we were not deluding ourselves. We continue to believe, though it is now somewhat utopian, that some form of community of the nations (republics) that formed Yugoslavia is both desirable and possible. This is why we accepted without reservation the Hague document, that opened up such a possibility… Those who did not want to revive any kind of Yugoslavia either now or in the future, either in the old or the new European bases, rejected the 'Hague paper'. They were the Slovenes and the Serbs. Unlike the usual pattern, the

Slovenes did so this time quite openly, the Serbs covertly. The Slovenes rejected the idea of any kind of new Yugoslavia in favour of independence. The Serbs rejected the proffered Yugoslavia in favour of 'Yugoslavia'. Their Yugoslavia, of course, was not Yugoslavia at all, and that was the primary reason for its being unacceptable to us. The second and more important reason was that the future structure offered to us (formulated in the so-called Belgrade initiative) was not democratic. We could live with anyone, in any kind of community, on condition that it is a democratic one, but democracy in this region, to all appearances, will be reached only through a long process in a rather distant future.

In such a situation, a sovereign Bosnia and Herzegovina in a free union was for us the only guarantee of our living in dignity and freedom. This is true not only for the Muslim nation, but also for the Serbs and the Croats. Given the population structure, such a Bosnia and Herzegovina must have a special relationship with Serbia on the one hand, and Croatia on the other, regardless of whether these two republics (states) have themselves any kind of mutual connection. We believe that this could be resolved. The Serbs must not have the feeling that they are cut off from Serbia by state borders, nor the Croats from Croatia. This would mean that the Serbs would not need passports at the Drina nor the Croats at the Una.

Serbia and Croatia are nation-states. Bosnia and Herzegovina is not, and can therefore only be a civil republic. For it is not Serbs, Croats and Muslims who live in Bosnia and Herzegovina, but a national blend of these peoples, and others too, of course, in smaller numbers. Anyone who talks of national self-determination (in the ethnic sense) must explain how this principle, which is in itself not in dispute, can be applied to such a mixed population as we have, not only here in Sarajevo for example, but also throughout Bosnia and Herzegovina. In Bosnia and Herzegovina the real question is not how to achieve national self-determination, but how to achieve the self-determination of a population of mixed nationalities. There is an answer to that – the historical formula of Bosnia as a multi-confessional, multi-national, multi-cultural community. Why spoil something that has been created by a confluence of historical circumstances and which has functioned well, and in addition which represents a humane, democratic and – if you will – European solution? Why change it, even if it were possible to do so? And especially if it is impossible without violence and bloodshed, and if the alternative on offer is a retrograde concept of national autocracy?

I therefore invite our Serb and Croat fellow citizens, and our Serb and Croat neighbours, and their leaders, to seek a fitting way out of this situation, one based on equity and reason, so that our peoples may be spared the suffering that we have been witness to these days.

Let no one try to subjugate us, for we cannot be subjugated, nor to deprive us of our rights, for one day we shall regain those rights. We neither love life more than others nor fear death more than others, and our wounds pain us equally.

We have proclaimed our neutrality in this war, for it is a dirty fratricidal war in which we cannot and do not need to soil our hands. We have refused to send our young men to the military, for this is not a war for freedom. In so doing we have saved the lives and souls of many of our people: their lives, because they have not been killed, and their souls, because they have not killed. We have so acted as to be neither executioners nor victims. This stance of ours has gained the recognition and support of all people of good will. It has immeasurably enhanced the reputation of Bosnia in the world. At a time when you are justifiably ashamed of some of the events taking place in this region, you can say with pride, if you are in a foreign country, that you are from Bosnia. Out there, that means that you are for peace, democracy and human rights.

I shall end this brief speech by addressing the Muslim people. Like us today, a small nation once found itself faced with the same dramatic choice: to bow its head, or to hold it proudly aloft – to be slaves, or to remain free people. The poet of that nation responded with these famous words, with which I shall conclude my speech: 'I swear to God Almighty that we shall not be slaves!'

The speech had significant repercussions in the country, and to some extent abroad as well. During the war my warnings were often quoted, particularly the one where I said that if it came to war 'everything would vanish in a cloud of smoke and disgrace' and that all that would be left would be 'three bloodied and defeated peoples.' At the Geneva talks, in late 1993, a diplomat quoted them, calling them prophetic. I had no reason to be glad about this.

At the press conference that followed the congress I expected more questions about how to safeguard peace in the country. However, the questions related more to personnel matters and the alleged clash between two wings within the SDA – the civil and the religious. I replied that there were only two theologians on the Party's Governing Board of more than 100 members. One must bear in mind that the majority of the journalists were from the 'communist school of journalism', where students were selected, and in particular employed as journalists, on the basis of their loyalty to the communist idea. They showed animosity to anything that was religious. Then again, instead of focusing on the peace campaign, the media paid more attention in its reporting from the first SDA Congress to the clash with Fikret Abdić.

Abdić was a member of the Presidency of Bosnia and Herzegovina. He had previously been general manager of Agrokomerc, and had the charisma of a victim of a rigged trial. He was more experienced than I in politics. He knew many of the managers of state enterprises and the prominent politicians of the day. I had not had a personal confrontation with him, but other congress delegates had criticised him. In winding up the congress, I said:

> On this occasion we are bound to remember the Muslim nation, which is showing enormous *sabr*.[8] This nation is a discovery for us and for the world alike. I invite you to applaud this nation.

Everyone rose to their feet and clapped, except Fikret Abdić. The following day the front page of every newspaper had a photo of Abdić sitting while everyone else gave a standing ovation. The caption was 'Get up, babo!'[9]

'Babo' rose, but only two years later, when he staged an insurrection against the legal Bosnian government and proclaimed the autonomy of the Krajina region of north-western Bosnia. Although he was supported by Milošević, Karadžić and Tuđman, the plan was both militarily and politically defeated.

The war in Croatia was continuing, meanwhile, and indeed escalating. 12 cease-fires were signed and then broken. Success finally came with the thirteenth cease-fire, signed by Cyrus Vance and Croat representatives in Sarajevo on 2 January 1992. A force of 'blue helmets' came to Croatia and established the UNPA Zone. There was a touch of irony about the fact of the truce, which had the effect of shifting the war and

---

[8] The Arabic word for a quality encompassing patience, endurance and stoicism.
[9] Babo – the vocative form of the Persian baba, father.

all its accompanying misfortunes to Bosnia and Herzegovina, as it was signed in Sarajevo, in the Bosnia and Herzegovina Presidency building. It was with this piece of news that we embarked upon the new year 1992, the most tragic of all in the long history of Bosnia and Herzegovina.

Chapter 4

War Diary

SDS and HDZ dismember Bosnia and Herzegovina. Referendum on independence for Bosnia and Herzegovina. Cutileiro's mediation. Start of the war of aggression against Bosnia and Herzegovina. Sarajevo under siege. Cutileiro persists. Meetings in Lisbon and Brussels. Meeting with Kostić and Adžić in Skopje. 2 May – taken hostage in Sarajevo airport. State of war. Agenda of the Presidency of Bosnia and Herzegovina. Arms embargo and the arming of the Bosnia and Herzegovina Army. Concentration camps in Bosnia and Herzegovina. Speech at the OSCE Summit, Helsinki, 1992. Meeting with US President George Bush. Attempt to lift the siege of Sarajevo. London Conference. Fall of Bosanski Brod. Conference in Jeddah. First clashes with the HVO. Spring/summer 1993 – Operation Igman. How we outwitted the Chetniks. Tunnel under Sarajevo airport. Letter to President Clinton. Letter to the Security Council. Atrocities in Ahmići. Speech at the 48th Session of the UN General Assembly. Insurrection in Sarajevo and showdown. General Divjak's letter. Silajdžić's first government. Pressure on Vitez and peace with the HVO. The Washington peace and the Federation of Bosnia and Herzegovina. Dissensions in the Presidency of Bosnia and Herzegovina. Exclusion zone around Sarajevo. Operation 'Spring 94'. Goražde crisis. Speech at the 49th Session of the UN General Assembly. Crisis in the Krajina. Speech at the OSCE Summit in Budapest. Message to the people of the Krajina. Letter to President Clinton. Role of Muslim countries. Speech at the OIC Summit in Casablanca. Four-month truce. Liberation of Vlašić. No extension to the truce. Death of Minister Ljubijankić. Failure to lift the siege of Sarajevo. The Split Accord and an end to the blockade of the Krajina. Sarajevo marketplace atrocity. NATO air-strikes.

INESCAPABLE QUESTIONS

History stepped up the pace in this part of the world. 'It was a time when hours were compressed into minutes, days into hours, months and years into days; is absolutely certain that never in recent history have so many unavoidable questions and quandaries about the world we live in been as concentrated as here in Bosnia' (Kasim Begić).[1] Dramatic events followed one another at the pace of an action movie.

The Serbian Democratic Party (SDS) began to dismember Bosnia and Herzegovina with the creation of the so-called Serb Autonomous Areas (SAO), which did not recognise the authority of the Government in Sarajevo. The first to be formed was the Krajina SAO, with its headquarters in Banja Luka, on 16 September 1991, followed by the Herzegovina and the Romanija SAO, with its headquarters in Sarajevo. On 9 January 1992, the self-styled Serbian National Assembly proclaimed the self-styled Republic of the Serbian Nation of Bosnia and Herzegovina. On 26 October 1991, the SDS passed a Resolution on arming the Serb population of Bosnia and Herzegovina, and in November 1991 Bosnian patriots stopped a convoy with 400 submachine guns destined for Serbs in Sarajevo. It was known as the 'Banana Convoy', since the contents were stated on the bills of lading as bananas.

On 12 November 1991 the HDZ formed the Croatian Community of Bosnian Posavina, with eight municipalities, and immediately after that, on 18 November, the Croatian Community of Herceg-Bosna, with 30 municipalities, 'as the political, economic and cultural community of the Croats in Bosnia and Herzegovina.'

With their proclamation in August 1993 of the Croatian Republic of Herceg-Bosna (CRHB), Croat extremists would later follow in the footsteps of the self-styled Serbian National Assembly's 9 January 1992 proclamation of the so-called Republic of the Serbian Nation in Bosnia and Herzegovina (RS). These two projects, RS and CRHB, were identical in their ambitions to dismember Bosnia and Herzegovina.

On 2 January 1992 I was present at the signing of the cease-fire between Croatia and the JNA that Cyrus Vance, the UN Secretary-General's Envoy, had brought about. After the meeting, Vance delivered a statement in which he said that he believed the conflict would not spread to Bosnia and Herzegovina. Observers, but not blue helmets, would be sent to Bosnia and Herzegovina. The plan to create so-called UNPA zones in Croatia (zones under the protection of the UN) pro-

[1] Kasim Begić, *Bosna i Hercegovina od Vanceove Misije do Dejtonskog Sporazuma* (Bosnia and Herzegovina from the Vance Mission to the Dayton Accord).

vided for JNA troops, and all other troops under the JNA's patronage, to withdraw from Croatia. Where would they go? To Bosnia and Herzegovina, of course.

In making its preparations for independence, the Government of Bosnia and Herzegovina declared on 8 January 1992 that it accepted the UN Charter, the Helsinki Final Act, the Charter of Paris, the Universal Declaration on Human Rights, the International Covenant on Civil and Political Rights and all other international instruments guaranteeing human rights and freedoms, as well as the commitments assumed by the former Socialist Federal Republic of Yugoslavia in the field of arms control.

On 15 January 1992 the 'twelve' recognised the independence of Slovenia and Croatia, but made the independence of Bosnia and Herzegovina and of Macedonia contingent upon a referendum. The finding of the Badinter Arbitration Commission (composed of the presiding judges of the constitutional courts of France, Spain, Germany, Italy and Belgium) was that Yugoslavia was in the process of dissolution.

At its session on 14 January 1992 the Parliamentary Assembly of Bosnia and Herzegovina passed a Resolution on the sovereignty of Bosnia and Herzegovina. The validity of the Resolution was contested by the Serbian community in Bosnia and Herzegovina. On 25 January 1992, at the proposal of the Presidency of Bosnia and Herzegovina, the Parliamentary Assembly of the Republic of Bosnia and Herzegovina passed a decision to hold a referendum on the independence of Bosnia and Herzegovina. The SDS and SPO Deputies walked out of the session before the vote was held. The referendum question read: 'Are you for a sovereign and independent Bosnia and Herzegovina, a state of citizens and peoples of Bosnia and Herzegovina – Muslims, Serbs, Croats and members of other nations living in the country – with equal rights?' After the vote on the decision to announce a referendum was carried, I gave a statement to *Oslobođenje*:

> [The SDS] blocked the adoption of the new constitution submitted by the Constitutional Drafting Commission, and rejected the concept of a civil constitution submitted by liberal and independent intellectuals, yet continually accuse us of wanting a 'Muslim republic'. The fact is, however, that it is they – with their proposal to partition Bosnia and Herzegovina into three, a Serb, a Croat and a Muslim Bosnia – who are offering and indeed forcing this upon us. Our stance is known: we do not accept this.

During the run-up to the referendum, the news came that at a meeting held in Livno the Croats (more exactly, the leading Croatian party, the HDZ) had made the referendum conditional on a change to the referendum question. They called for the word 'citizens' to be removed, and to make other changes that would promote the various peoples or nations as sovereign in the areas where they formed a majority. Of course, this called into question not only the holding of the referendum on the date fixed, but also the very meaning of the referendum. I called on everyone to stand firm and not to allow any alterations to be made.

The confused situation provoked by the 'Livno question' continued during the entire remaining 20 days of the run-up to the referendum. The end of February was drawing near, and the HDZ stuck stubbornly to its demands. On the first day of the referendum (29 February) came the news that the polling stations in areas with a majority Croat population were half empty. By good fortune, it was a two-day referendum. On the second day, 1 March, particularly in the afternoon, the Croats flocked to the polling stations. We later learned that Tuđman had given them the go-ahead for the referendum, but that he had also been behind the earlier procrastination. On the second day, he had come to the conclusion that his obstinacy could lead to a Greater Serbia along several hundred kilometres of the southern and eastern borders, and so he had yielded at the last minute.

When the votes were counted, they showed that 63.4% of the total electorate of 3,253,847 had taken part in the referendum, and that more than 99% of those who had done so had circled the answer 'Yes.' The fate of Bosnia and Herzegovina was decided, but only in the formal, legal sense. The true fate of Bosnia would be determined on the battlefield, but no military victory could change what was achieved by that referendum.

On 6 April 1992 the European Community recognised Bosnia and Herzegovina, and the following day the United States of America also did so. Our application for recognition read as follows:

> 1. The Presidency and Government of the Socialist Republic of Bosnia and Herzegovina, on behalf of the said Socialist Republic of Bosnia and Herzegovina, express the wish that Bosnia and Herzegovina be recognised as an independent state, and request the European Community and its member states to so recognise the country by means of the procedures and within the terms laid down in the Brussels Declaration on Yugoslavia.

2. Bosnia and Herzegovina declares that it accepts all the commitments comprised in the 'Directives for the recognition of new states in Eastern Europe and the Soviet Union' adopted by the Council of Foreign Ministers in Brussels on 16 December 1991.

3. Bosnia and Herzegovina accepts the Draft Hague Convention, including the second chapter relating to human rights and the rights of national and ethnic groups discussed within the context of the Conference on Yugoslavia. In this regard, Bosnia and Herzegovina will continue to advocate the formation of a new community that will enable all its members to enjoy prosperity.

4. Disputes between the Yugoslav republics should be resolved by peaceful means. We appreciate and support the efforts of the UN Secretary-General and the European Community and express our support for the continuation of the Conference on Yugoslavia.

We emphasise in particular that Bosnia and Herzegovina has no territorial aspirations towards any neighbouring state, nor will it have any as an independent state, and that it will not conduct any hostile propaganda activities against any neighbouring state, including the use of titles that would imply any such territorial pretensions.

We therefore propose that the European Community and its member states recognise the sovereignty and independence of Bosnia and Herzegovina.

Before all these events, however, came the unsuccessful Cutileiro mediation efforts.

At the beginning of 1992 the Chair of the Conference on Yugoslavia, Lord Carrington, announced an EC mediation mission for Bosnia and Herzegovina. The first talks were held on 13 and 14 February in the presence of all the political parties represented in parliament at that time. Our delegation was composed of Dr. Rusmir Mahmutćehaić, Dr. Naim Kadić and myself.

The first meetings showed that there were three divergent views on the future of Bosnia and Herzegovina. Prof. Kasim Begić summarises these as follows: '...For the SDS the talks were an attempt to legitimise the Serb plebiscite and partition of Bosnia and Herzegovina, for the HDZ, the issue was how to get the Livno question officially adopted for the referendum, and for the SDA, how to ease political tensions prior to the referendum on the sovereignty of Bosnia and Herzegovina, with special legal and institutional protection and guarantees of national equality.'

The SDS leader announced that the Serbs and Croats did not accept a Greater Bosnia and Herzegovina. Greater Bosnia and Herzegovina, to him, was the whole of Bosnia and Herzegovina within its present borders. This meant that he was calling for the dismemberment of Bosnia and Herzegovina. Boban, President of the HDZ, said that only 'nations could be sovereign.' Referring to the views of the Badinter Commission, I announced that 'the nation is sovereign, but not the nation in the ethnic, but rather in the European sense, the nation as citizens of a single state...' I also said that we did not know what this Greater Bosnia and Herzegovina was. 'Bosnia has existed within these same borders for more than 300 years, neither greater nor smaller, but just as she is. And we would not wish to wake up one morning in a partitioned Bosnia, for a partitioned Bosnia means a Bosnia in conflict, a Bosnia at war.'[2]

The negotiations continued in Lisbon on 21 and 22 February, with Dr. Haris Silajdžić joining our delegation on this occasion. The good side of the Lisbon talks was that they confirmed the survival of Bosnia and Herzegovina in its present borders. The downside was the mention of several possible entities. Although there was no final agreement nor was anything signed in Lisbon, the SDS was quick to give its own interpretation of what had been 'agreed'. It proclaimed the illegal Serb assembly to be the supreme body of its 'entity', and Karadžić announced that 'after the Lisbon agreement, it is clear that there will be three Bosnia and Herzegovinas: the Serb, the Croat and the Muslim.'

The Lisbon talks were held under the menacing shadow of the war that had been hovering over Bosnia and Herzegovina, and that was to erupt in less than two months. There followed further talks in Sarajevo on 28 February, in Brussels on 7 and 8 March and again in Sarajevo on 18 March. I tried my utmost to save both Bosnia and peace, but was it even possible any longer? The day was drawing closer when the choice would have to be made, one way or the other.

The Brussels Document was a European proposal, in which everyone obtained something and lost something. On my return from Brussels I delivered a statement saying that the Muslims would not be satisfied because the proposal provided for national (or 'ethnic') regions, the Serbs because it provided for an independent and integral Bosnia and Her-

[2] K. Begić, op.cit., p. 85.

zegovina, citizens because it provided for national cantons and the nationalists because to some extent it affirmed the civil principle. Nor was I satisfied with the 'European proposal', but I was for reaching a compromise in order to avoid the outbreak of war, of which the menacing signs could be seen everywhere.

The agreements reached in Brussels and Sarajevo immediately eased the tensions, but only temporarily. After the Sarajevo meeting, the Sarajevo newspaper *Oslobođenje* carried an article reading:

> In an atmosphere where feelings are running high, full of tensions, mutual distrust and totally opposing views on the future of Bosnia and Herzegovina, it is possible that the latest agreements will bring an end to the agony in which we all find ourselves. Whether this is short-term, and how long it will last, we shall soon see. (*Oslobođenje*, 19 March 1992)

But the time for peace was fast running out, and war was just a month away.

On 11 March the self-styled assembly of the Serbian people rejected the Brussels arrangement. The only two acceptable options, for this assembly, were to remain in Yugoslavia or to restructure Bosnia and Herzegovina as a confederation of three national republics. Europe did not react to this as might have been expected. It had begun to turn a blind eye to Serb threats; it was the start of what can be called its disgraceful silence. Serb extremists were much encouraged.

It can be seen from the statement proposed by the EC that violence had already broken out in Bosnia. The statement read:

> The leaders of the three main parliamentary parties formally undertake to do all that lies within their power to reduce the level of violence in Bosnia and Herzegovina and appeal urgently to all in Bosnia and Herzegovina, regardless of ethnic origin or political circumstance, to refrain from violence, incitement to violence and all other military or political actions that could pose a threat to the agreements already reached by the three parties, or cast doubts upon the successful outcome of talks. They are firmly convinced that a peaceful situation will facilitate their coming to an agreement, accelerate the negotiations and make it possible to draft a new constitution acceptable to all, in the shortest possible time.

The outbreak of war was already just days away, soon it would be only hours.

The war of aggression against Bosnia and Herzegovina began on 1 April with the attack by paramilitary units from Serbia on Bijeljina. Many, however, consider that the war in Bosnia began when, without any prior warning, reservists and volunteer troops from Serbia and Montenegro, formally part of the Titograd and Užice JNA Corps, invaded Bosnia in a war-mongering, looting frame of mind. Another date that can be taken as the start of the war is the destruction of the Croat village of Ravno in the first days of October 1991. The first casualties, however, came much earlier. In September 1991, almost seven months before the date on which the war is usually reckoned to have begun, a burst of gunfire from the woods along the Kravica-Bratunac road mortally wounded Nedžad Hodžić and Džemo Jusić. The murder of these two unarmed civilians was a dire warning of what was ahead of us in Podrinje.

In his *Historija Bosne i Bošnjaka* (History of Bosnia and the Bosniacs), Mehmedalija Bojić writes of that period: 'In the summer of 1991 the armed forces of the JNA in Bosnia were vastly increased. First, two army corps invaded Bosnian territory (the Užice and Podgorica Corps) with reservists and volunteers from Serbia and Montenegro. Then another two army corps (the Fourteenth Slovenian and the Tenth Zagreb) were relocated to Bosnia and Herzegovina. Significant air forces were also transferred from Slovenia and Croatia (the Fifth Air Force and the Anti Aircraft Defence). All these military forces concentrated in regions where there were already three corps. With the escalation of the war in Croatia, and an economic blockade on all sides, the Republic of Bosnia and Herzegovina was faced with total destruction' (Bojić, p. 318).

Cutileiro prolonged his mission for a while longer, hoping for the impossible. A meeting was fixed for 10 April in Sarajevo, with another 20 days later in Lisbon. The war was already under way, Sarajevo was cut off and was being heavily shelled. Meanwhile, news came that on 5 and 6 April, Karadžić and Boban had met to talk about a 'bilateral agreement on a cease-fire and the partition of Bosnia.' This news was commented on by the *Washington Post* of 11 April in a report that said the two had met on behalf of Milošević and Tuđman, that the meeting reminded one of the Stalin-Hitler Pact just prior to the invasion of Poland in 1939 and that Yugoslavia and Croatia were 'gangster states'. It was in this atmosphere that I travelled to Lisbon on 29 April for more fruitless talks being mediated by Cutileiro.

I took off from Sarajevo airport, which was already under the control of the Bosnian Serb military, in an aircraft loaned by the European Union's Monitoring Mission. I reached the airport, some ten kilometres from the city, under heavy UNPROFOR security escort.

It was a fine summer's day in Lisbon, but I was in the grip of a deathly mood. The negotiations produced no results whatsoever, and on 2 May we set off on the return journey home. We flew over Italy and the Adriatic sea in blessed ignorance of what was happening in Sarajevo. But on the streets of Sarajevo, that day, a real war was being waged with the remnants of the Yugoslav Army, which was more and more under the influence of the Serb nationalist leadership headed by Karadžić.

The pilot touched down in Rome to refuel. He held a telephone conversation of some kind with the base in Sarajevo, and received permission to land. When we were about half way over the Adriatic sea, the stewardess who was occupying the co-pilot's seat came up to me and told me that we could not land at Sarajevo airport, but must choose between Belgrade and Zagreb. Naturally enough, I opted for Zagreb. We all sat in worried silence as we felt the aircraft veering northwards. Incomprehensible voices speaking in English reached us from the cockpit, and then the stewardess came up to us again and told us that we could land in Sarajevo but that it would be on our own responsibility. I accepted without hesitation.

It was cloudy over Bosnia, but the visibility was good. We landed in the early evening. I noticed at once, through the aircraft window, that my UNPROFOR escort was nowhere to be seen. There were some uniformed figures, but they were not 'blue helmets'. They were in fact JNA troops, but as would soon become clear, they were completely under the control of Karadžić's Serbs. We were told that we must go to the airport manager's office. The behaviour of the soldiers was enough to tell me at once that we were prisoners.

With me were Zlatko Lagumdžija, as a member of the delegation, and Nurudin Imamović, acting as an escort. My personal situation was greatly exacerbated by the fact that my daughter Sabina was travelling with us as interpreter. They told us we were going to Lukavica for talks. I refused, at which they threatened to use force. They did not seem to know quite how to handle things. They went in and out of the office, obviously for consultations. At one point the telephone on the table rang. The only other person in the office at the time was a soldier. Without hesitation, Sabina picked up the receiver and I heard her manage to tell the person on the other end of the line, a woman wanting some flight information, that President Izetbegović and his delegation were being held captive in the airport building. The soldier did not react, either he did not want to, did not dare to, or simply did not know what to do, and at least someone knew about our fate.

The telephone soon rang again. This time I myself reached for the receiver. I recognised on the other end of the line the voice of Senad Hadžifejzović, of Sarajevo Television, asking me what was going on. I said that we had been taken captive, and that we were to be transferred to Lukavica. As was later to become clear, this telephone call and certain other circumstances saved our lives. The whole world soon knew that the President of an independent country was being held prisoner by paramilitary units, in a country, at that, where UN troops were charged with keeping peace and order.

We set off for Lukavica, a few kilometres from the airport, in three cars, escorted by two tanks making a huge amount of noise and dust. Everyone behaved towards us as though we were prisoners. We spent the night in the barracks. A bedroom of sorts was improvised for me in the garrison commander's office; the others were taken to another room. A woman in uniform, who introduced herself as a doctor, came for Sabina.

I can recall only a few nights in my life when I have not slept at all. One of them was that night in Lukavica. It was partly out of concern for Sabina, and partly because of the thunder of artillery and rocket-launchers in the barrack grounds belching fire at Sarajevo almost without break. There was an old military clock on the wall opposite my bed. I watched as the hands showed midnight, one o'clock, two, three. And then dawn began to break, but still I did not get even a moment's sleep.

After Sarajevo Television reported what had happened to us, interventions followed. The entire morning was taken up with telephone conversations and visits. The long hours ticked by. By afternoon there was still no result.

The event that had had a major impact on the whole affair was this: a day earlier, 2 May, while we were in Lisbon and on our way home, a decisive battle was being fought in Sarajevo between armed civilians and the Yugoslav Army. JNA troops stationed near the Military Hospital, in Skenderija and in the JNA Centre, had that morning launched a coordinated attack with the aim of seizing the Presidency building. They came up against unexpected resistance on all sides, however, and withdrew to barracks in the early evening. One group of our men surrounded the Second Army command in Bistrik and its commander, General Kukanjac, the entire general staff and several hundred officers and men with their equipment.

My son Bakir, as soon as he learned that I had been taken prisoner on 2 May, went into action. He made his rounds of all the officials he could, more or less unsuccessfully. Finally he suggested to someone in the Presidency that he should talk to General Kukanjac, who was also being held prisoner in his Command Headquarters in Bistrik. An exchange was agreed. Lagumdžija, Sabina, I and the others left Lukavica on 3 May at about five, in an UNPROFOR APC. Through the small windows of the APC I could see destroyed vehicles and tanks, the aftermath of the previous day's battle. On Skenderija Bridge, on the far side of the river, stood a burned-out tram. We drove through a completely deserted part of the city on the left bank of the Miljacka. We then halted outside the barracks in Bistrik. At the entrance to the building, which resembled a fortress, there was an enormous tank almost completely blocking the wide entrance. I got out of the APC. There was complete silence, that beautiful May afternoon. There was nothing, absolutely nothing, to remind one of the confrontation that had loomed. I learned later that we had our marksmen positioned on the roofs of the neighbouring houses, holding the barracks under siege.

In the barrack grounds we found a large group of officers and men ready to move off. And set off they did, but the convoy of the Yugoslav Army was attacked ten minutes later in Dobrovoljačka Street. Five officers were killed, four injured, and 160 taken prisoner (the prisoners comprised of 126 soldiers, 30 officers and four civilians). The following day, after UNPROFOR intervention, they were all released and joined their units under the Pale command. A number of them went home.

I and those with me left the APC on Skenderija Bridge, on the line along which Sarajevo was already divided, and went to the Presidency. There I was welcomed as if I had returned from the dead.

Seven years later an *Avaz* reader asked me about the significance of the events of 2 May.

> Reader from Sarajevo: This question is one I raised two weeks ago. I received no answer, so I am repeating it. It is to do with 2 May 1992, when the showdown with the JNA took place in Sarajevo, and you were held prisoner in Lukavica. Some say that on that day Sarajevo was saved, but also your life and the life of Bosnia. What is your view of this?
>
> Izetbegović: I would say that it was the day we conquered our fear of the Chetniks. We do not have that fear any more, we are

not afraid of them any more, but we suffered for decades from that complex, which was a fatal one. Then we held our heads up high and resisted. We realised what we could do if we stood up and did the right thing. This is perhaps merely a moral and psychological factor, but it was of crucial importance for the future. In Sarajevo, on 2 May 1992 (and later in Tuzla, on 15 May 1992), it became clear that some psychological shackles can be broken. In my view, this was the most significant factor of the day you are asking me about.

Three days before Lisbon, on 26 April 1992, I flew to Skopje for talks with Branko Kostić, a member of the political body then regarded as the supreme command, and General Blagoje Adžić, Acting Chief of General Staff of the JNA. I travelled from the Presidency to Sarajevo airport under UNPROFOR protection, but, because of some hold-up, the journey took more than an hour, while the distance between war-besieged Sarajevo and peaceful Skopje took only 40 minutes.

It was a sunny late April day in Skopje, and we sat in a garden, but the atmosphere was tense and gloomy. I already knew Kostić and Adžić from meetings of the extended Presidency of Yugoslavia. We barely concealed our mutual animosity. More unpropitious interlocuters than the three of us would have been hard to find. The Macedonian President Kiro Gligorov – a likeable and good friend, who was there in the role of host – tried to mediate, but the positions of the three of us were far apart and our personal relationships poor – the whole thing was ordained to fail. After the talks, which lasted more than three hours, I said to the assembled journalists:

> A process has begun that will lead, ultimately, either to the departure of the JNA from Bosnia, or to its radical transformation, which will end in its becoming the Bosnian Army, the armed forces of Bosnia and Herzegovina. We do not need any confrontation with the army. We have issued a call for a cease-fire, which has been accepted. Unhappily, however, it remains a mere proclamation. The goodwill expressed in the statements issued by the army command during the Skoplje talks must be put to the test of specific behaviour, above all in relation to the agreed removal of roadblocks and the opening of Sarajevo airport. As for the future Bosnian Army, we see it as smaller in numbers, nationally balanced, and with some of the equipment currently in the possession of the JNA.

On that occasion I said nothing about Adžić's most important statement. When I proposed that a number of Muslim generals be appointed as commanding officers in Bosnia and Herzegovina, Adžić looked thoughtful for a moment, avoiding an answer. 'Do it if you want to save the country,' I said. Adžić replied: 'Mr. Izetbegović, you know that the army is overwhelmingly Serb. It would be unrealistic for any of its commanding officers to be Muslim generals.' Adžić was militarily blunt and sincere, unlike Kostić who was trying to act the politician. He tried to sweep under the carpet the collusion between the JNA and paramilitary Serb units and the atrocities committed by the army in Croatia and Bosnia. He replied to a journalist's question thus:

> To all appearances, given the question, we have different information about the conduct of the army in Bosnia. Our information is that the army has behaved fairly neutrally in Bosnia…

I must admit that as I boarded the aircraft I wondered if I would get back to Sarajevo safe and sound – because it was now a case of open war. This was the only conclusion I could draw from the Skopje meeting. And yet it took us 70 days to accept that what was happening was war, that there was no going back and that it would go on for some time. The Presidency of Bosnia and Herzegovina proclaimed a state of war only on 20 June 1992. Until then, we were in the grip of some crazy hope that a miracle would happen to end the senseless bloodshed.

Six days after the proclamation, the Presidency adopted its famous platform. This brief but dense text defined itself as 'a call to all citizens and all the peoples of Bosnia and Herzegovina to become active members of the patriotic front against the aggression.' It listed the principles by which the Presidency would operate in conditions of war: a parliamentary civil democracy, a market economy, party pluralism, human rights and freedoms, the internationally recognised borders of Bosnia and Herzegovina, the constituent status of the peoples on the principles of parity and consensus, and the politics of European orientation.

The platform saw the way out of the war in negotiations that would lead to a just peace:

> Every war throughout history has ended in peace. The sooner peace takes over from war the less will be the destruction and the fewer the human casualties. For this reason the Presidency is for negotiations leading to peace.

But also:

> Bosnia and Herzegovina will not agree to negotiations based on the creation of ethnically pure territories, or the regional partition of Bosnia and Herzegovina into exclusively ethnic areas. Nor will Bosnia and Herzegovina ever agree to any kind of territorial and demographic changes and privileges brought about by war and the use of force.

The ideals of this exalted declaration would come into conflict with the brutal use of force on the ground and with a world that was more indifferent than favourably inclined. Force was not victorious, but neither were ideals.

Our intention to achieve the objectives of the platform was sincere. The composition of the government that had been appointed only some ten days earlier (on 15 June 1992) bore witness to this. It was a typical 'government of national unity', since every nation and every then relevant political tendency in Bosnia and Herzegovina was represented in it. This is how it looked:

Prime Minister:	Jure Pelivan
Deputy Prime Minister:	Hakija Turajlić (for the Economy)
Deputy Prime Minister:	Dr Miodrag Simović (for Home Affairs)
Deputy Prime Minister:	Dr Zlatko Lagumdžija (for Social Affairs)

Ministers:
Foreign Affairs:	Dr Haris Silajdžić
Interior:	Jusuf Pušina
National Defence:	Jerko Doko
Justice and Administration of State:	Ranko Nikolić
Finance:	Dr Žarko Primorac
Energy and Industry:	Dr Rusmir Mahmutćehaić
Supplies and Commerce:	Alija Delimustafić
Agriculture:	Radovan Mirković
Forestry and Timber Industry:	Dr Hasan Muratović
Traffic and Communications:	Tomislav Krstičević
Reconstruction:	Uglješa Uzelac
Town Planning, Construction and Environment:	Dr Munir Jahić
Health:	Dr Mustafa Beganović

Education, Science and Culture:	Dr Nikola Kovač
Employment and Social Policy:	Martin Raguž
Religion:	Dr Milenko Brkić

The task of the government could be fairly simply defined: to resolve the existential issues of a country that was under attack.

When a nation suffers the misfortune known as war, one question is inevitable: could it have been avoided? The answer in this case is: until Slovenia and Croatia left, it could have been avoided; after that, it could not.

This second response is only partly accurate. Even after the departure of these two republics from the former common state, peace could have been preserved, but only on condition of capitulation. For Bosnia and the Bosniac people, this would have meant becoming part of Greater Serbia and accepting the supreme and irrevocable authority of Karadžić and Milošević. And slavery is the worst of all outcomes, worse than war.

According to certain data, during the 43 months of war, and along a front of 1,200 kilometres, the Army of the Republic of Bosnia and Herzegovina undertook more than 3,000 defensive and offensive operations. Some of these were brilliant victories, some were tragic defeats. The final balance of these largely unequal battles was indeterminate. The war in Bosnia and for Bosnia ended without victors and vanquished. The peace with which this terrible war was ended was a reflection of this 'drawn match'.

Given the conditions in which it arose and developed, the creation and equipping of the Bosnian Army is regarded as a minor miracle. By any normal military logic, it should have been nipped in the bud, and Bosnia and Herzegovina occupied, in the very first months of the war.

The army was from the start composed of a number of shakily linked but courageous groups, most of them at military company level, but by the end of the war it had 96 brigades in six corps. The statistics are not reliable, but according to data collated by Military Headquarters, there were about 186,000 troops registered in the defence of Bosnia in August 1992, of which about half were registered as soldiers in the Army of Bosnia and Herzegovina. The other 50% were regular and reserve police, or volunteers, who were taking part in the defence of their streets and villages, armed or unarmed, under the auspices of the Patriotic League, the Green Berets and other organisations.

At that time only every fifth soldier had a rifle. By the end of the year the Army had about 40,000 firearms of various types (including the police with about 18,000), 231 rocket launchers, one 130mm cannon, ten 76mm cannons and 21 howitzers. By way of comparison, the RS Army and the JNA then had 1,062 howitzers in Bosnia.

In the second half of 1993, the Army formally numbered some 207,000 troops, but not all of them were organised or regularly took part in battle. That year we had 33 artillery pieces, 36 howitzers, 1,000 rocket launchers and 66 anti-armour weapons. About 60,000 troops had rifles and light machine guns, that is every third man. By the end of 1994, there were 227,000 members of the armed forces, with more than 80,000 rifles and light machine guns. We then had 42 artillery pieces, 60 howitzers, 125 rocket launchers of various kinds and 115 anti-armour weapons.

We acquired our arms in three ways: by capturing them from enemy forces, by manufacturing them in our own factories and even in small workshops, and by importing them from abroad, sometimes 'over the seven mountains and the seven seas,' as the folk saying goes. The arming of the Bosnian Army is a moving story of human courage, determination and resourcefulness on an invisible battlefront for the survival of Bosnia.

During the war 65 military plants were working for the Bosnian Army, and as early as 1992 every single small craft workshop in Sarajevo was doing the same. When I went to Breza in 1993, itself completely surrounded, they proudly showed me a rifle hanging on the wall, produced by their own mechanics and craftsmen. The Zenica Steelworks and many of the factories in Tešanj were military plants by that time. Those in Novi Travnik, Bugojno and Goražde had been from the very start. Every peacetime clothing and footwear factory was producing uniforms and boots for the military. The very last reserve stocks of production materials intended for peacetime needs were used up. As for the procurement of arms 'over the seven mountains and the seven seas,' despite the embargo and countless obstacles, a whole book could be written on that subject.

Although the situation with regard to arms and equipment gradually improved, it was only just before the end of the war that the Bosnian Army reached an equipment level that would have enabled it to launch combat operations of greater extent. But even then it did not have sufficient artillery, tanks and APCs.

I described the situation in responding to a question from the German newspaper *Stern* (5 November 1994):

> From the beginning of the war two processes have been running concurrently: we are becoming stronger every day, and they are becoming weaker. These processes do not keep exact pace with each other, but the general trend is as I have just described it. Our infantry has been superior to theirs for a long time now. Or to put it another way, our handicap is in our lack of heavy weapons, of artillery, to be precise, and theirs is their infantry. There are still more unpleasant surprises to come, both for us and for them, but the overall picture is that we have established a balance of power and taken the initiative. The balance is strategic, the initiatives are thus far purely tactical. How can the successes we had in Bihać, Kupres or Sarajevo be explained? There are many factors, but the most important, the moral factor, is not susceptible to analysis. Even we are sometimes surprised and taken aback. What we are dealing with is a unanimous resolve of our people to survive, of a people that had been condemned to extinction.

In fact, an interesting combination of 'oriental' and 'occidental' factors made the defence of Bosnia possible. The West maintained a no-flight zone, a very important ban on flights by military aircraft over Bosnia, and kept us fed through UNHCR with the protection of UNPROFOR. Islamic countries provided us with arms. The combination of these facts was a powerful support to our resistance. But over and above that, our will to defend ourselves, the courage and inventiveness of our people, played a key role in the defence.

In September 1991, the United Nations Security Council passed a Resolution imposing an arms embargo on the whole of the former Yugoslavia. The embargo had the effect of depriving only the Bosnian Army of the means of arming itself. The Serbs already had more arms than they knew what to do with – they had been stockpiling them for 40 years, and the Yugoslav Army was regarded as the fourth best equipped army in Europe at that time. This was the result of foreign aid, which itself was motivated by the wish to neutralise Soviet influence. In his memoirs, Lord Owen notes that 'Western aid and loans financed the absurdly large Yugoslav army long after any remote threat of Soviet invasion had gone.'[3]

[3] David Owen: *Balkan Odyssey*, p. 36

True, on 12 May 1994 the US Senate declared a unilateral lifting of the arms embargo on Bosnia and Herzegovina, followed by the House of Representatives on 9 June; but President Clinton, under pressure from European allies, in particular from Britain and its Foreign Secretary Douglas Hurd, vetoed the decision. The Russians claimed that as soon as the lifting of the embargo was announced the Serbs would simultaneously attack the positions of the Bosnia and Herzegovina Army and the HVO[4] and attempt to occupy the Podrinje enclaves.[5]

Despite the arms embargo, by mid 1993 we had succeeded in bringing into the country 30,000 rifles and machine guns, 20,000,000 bullets, 37,000 grenades, 46,000 anti-tank missiles, 20,000 uniforms and 120,000 pairs of boots (data which I gave on RTVBiH in August 1993).

The need for arms led us into all kinds of adventures. During a visit to Brussels, of which I forget the date, I was told that some people were offering to procure arms for us that would enable us to target effectively the Karadžić troops holding Sarajevo under siege. They would supply us with two special armoured helicopters and the appropriate missiles. The offer was very attractive to us, being caught in a trap for more than 500 days, under constant exposure to random fire from rocket launchers and snipers. We could see no end to our troubles.

When I received them, these people, who were strangers to me, offered to land the helicopters with their precision missiles on Igman and in the Zenica Stadium on a given night. They were two inoffensive looking men, who did not introduce themselves, but merely said that they were of South African origin and that they worked all over the world.

They laid down two conditions: first, they wanted cash, to be delivered the moment our people confirmed that the helicopters had landed at the agreed sites. And second, one of our people would be taken by them and held hostage in a secret location prior to delivery, as a guarantee that we would not try to trick them. They suggested that the entire business be conducted in one of our European embassies, and that the hostage be the chargé d'affaires of that embassy. After haggling for a long time, we accepted the first condition and rejected the second. They then asked for the money to be brought and handed over the moment our people confirmed that the consignment had reached its destination.

Along with the drugs mafia, arms dealers are among the most unscrupulous, and also the most dangerous of people. They earn their money in

---

[4] 'Croat Defence Council,' the military force of the Bosnian Croats.
[5] Srebrenica, Žepa and Goražde, the so-called UN 'safe areas'.

haram business, and are ready to do anything. But if you need arms, you can only buy them from such people. We sent a message to our connections in Istanbul to procure the cash the dealers wanted, and to courier it to our embassy in that European city.

The dealers arrived at the agreed time. They said that the operation was ready, and that the helicopters would be taking off from a base in Italy and should be over their destination in Bosnia at around midnight.

Our chargé d'affaires and courier were sitting with the money in one corner of the room, the dealers in another. I don't know who was more afraid of whom just then: we of them, or they of us. Our people, naturally, were afraid that the dealers would stage a classic gangster hold-up and seize the money, so they were at the ready with pistols cocked. Just in case, the dealers had been warned that there were security guards in the corridors and at the entrance to the embassy. The dealers were constantly in touch with someone by mobile phone.

One of those who was involved in this action on our side later told me: 'Eleven o'clock struck, then midnight, then one, two, and three o'clock. We were staring fixedly at one another, watching each other's every move. Around dawn, they asked for permission to leave to check up on something. They said that "something was wrong".' They left, and never returned.

It is still not known whether they were really arms dealers, whose operation had failed as a result of some unforeseen circumstances, or conmen trying to get their hands on some easy money. General Delić in Zenica and a group of officers on Igman had even been standing around burning fires, awaiting for some miracle from the skies. The miracle did not happen. And I too had a sleepless night, because I had remained on duty by the telephone the whole time.

In its early stages the war in Bosnia was not a classic war, if by this is meant a conflict between two armies. It was an attack by a powerful military machine on an unarmed people. The aim was to create Greater Serbia.

The preparations to achieve the Greater Serbia idea began in the mid-19th century with Ilija Garašanin's *Načertanije*, and culminated at the end of the 20th with the *Memorandum* of the Serbian Academy of Sciences and Arts (SANU) in September 1986. The person who was to bring the idea into reality was Slobodan Milošević, with the 'Serbianised' JNA and Serb paramilitary units in Bosnia and Herzegovina, Serbia and Montenegro.

After the nationalists came to power in Croatia, it was clear to Milošević that he could not take the whole of Bosnia and Herzegovina. He was ready to reach agreement on the partition of Bosnia between Serbia and Croatia. Tuđman and Milošević held their first talks on the subject in Karađorđevo on 25 March 1991, and continued to do so until the end of the war in Bosnia and Herzegovina. The Karađorđevo Agreement envisaged that the Muslims would be left with part of Bosnia that would act as a buffer zone between Croatia and Yugoslavia. This would include part of Sarajevo and central Bosnia, but none of the Podrinje region, where the Bosniacs were in an absolute majority. Naturally, Muslim Bosnia would have no access to the sea, nor to the Sava, Drina or Una rivers.

The attack on Sarajevo began with the setting up of a large number of barricades on 4 April 1992, and with an armed assault on the Police Academy in Vraca on 5 April, when we suffered our first casualties. It was the second day of *Eid*. By this time, the JNA and paramilitary units had already surrounded Sarajevo, under the pretext of conducting military exercises at the end of 1991 and in early 1992. Zvornik was attacked on 8 April by JNA troops and paramilitary units from Serbia, Montenegro and Bosnia and Herzegovina. The resistance mounted by our defence in Kula-Grad above Zvornik was broken only on 28 April 1992. There followed the occupation of Brčko in northern Bosnia, and the attack on Prijedor and Kozarac in western Bosnia. These two towns were occupied on 29 April 1992 by the JNA's Fifth Corps. Estimates are that more than 800 people were killed that day, and 1,200 civilians were taken prisoner and transferred to camps.

On 15 May 1992, Bosnian patriots halted a JNA convoy in Brčkanska Malta. With this events took a new course in the wider Tuzla region. The arms that were confiscated had a crucial impact in raising morale among our troops and strengthening their resolve to defend the area.

In a joint coordinated action by the Croat Defence Council (HVO), the Territorial Defence and Bosnian police troops, the JNA troops were forced back out of Mostar in early June 1992. The city of Mostar was liberated, together with a wide surrounding area, and stable lines of a more solid defence were established towards Prenj, Velež and Nevesinje, which did not change to any significant extent all through the war.

In May and June 1992, concentration camps began to sprout like sinister mushrooms throughout Bosnia. The victims were mainly Muslim civilians, both men and women. UNPROFOR knew about these camps. It was only by turning two blind eyes to them that they could not have seen them.

The camps in Keraterm and Omarska, of which the images were seen throughout the world, were ominously reminiscent of the Nazi camps of half a century earlier. The world had sworn that such things would never happen again anywhere. But happen again they did, and in the very heart of Europe. Artists, journalists and ordinary people reacted.[6] Politicians, for the most part, said nothing. It was to be demonstrated – not for the first time – that politicians are not the conscience of a nation (there are exceptions, of course: the former Prime Minister of Great Britain, Margaret Thatcher, cancelled a visit to Zagreb, where she was to have received a decoration, in protest against the involvement of Croatia in the war in Bosnia).

On 13 July 1992 the State Commission for the Exchange of Prisoners submitted to UNPROFOR commander General Lewis McKenzie a list of 42 camps that had by then been registered in Bosnia and Herzegovina. McKenzie publicly denied the existence of camps, and instead of forwarding the letter giving details of the camps to the United Nations, he held on to it.

On 8 August 1992 the Sarajevo daily *Oslobođenje* published a list of 94 concentration camps in Bosnia and Herzegovina and the famous photograph taken in Omarska Camp, broadcast by CNN. It was only then that the world, albeit unwillingly, began to face up to the horrific truth.

After Bosnia and Herzegovina was recognised, its borders became state borders. The first Helsinki principle, on the unalterability of existing state borders by force, was in our favour in this regard.

On 9 July 1992 I took part in the OSCE Summit in Helsinki. The presidents and prime ministers of European countries, the US President and the Prime Minister of Canada were also present. I made use of the occasion to inform the world of what was going on in Bosnia and Herzegovina.

Speech At The OSCE Meeting
(Helsinki, 9 July 1992)

It is a great honour for me to be able to address this historic meeting in the name of the citizens and peoples of Bosnia and

---

[6] A young man even burned himself to death in London's Parliament Square on 29 April 1993 as a sign of protest against the violence in Bosnia.

Herzegovina. Bosnia and Herzegovina is joining this great community of peoples and countries, thus becoming part of the process of building a new Europe and a new world order, of which the foundations were laid here in Helsinki.

I should like to take this opportunity to affirm Bosnia and Herzegovina's adherence to the democratic principles and human rights set out in the documents of the European Conference on Security and Cooperation, and above all in the Helsinki Final Act and the Paris Charter.

Bosnia and Herzegovina undertakes to observe the policy of mutual security, including the Agreement on Nuclear Arms Limitation, together with other instruments in this domain. It is our constant aspiration to become, one day, a demilitarised country. We also commit ourselves to take an active part in seeking a political solution to the Yugoslav crisis through the European Community's Conference on Yugoslavia under the mandate of the OSCE. We shall honour the commitments arising from that Conference as they relate to the crisis in Bosnia and Herzegovina. Bosnia and Herzegovina will respect the independence, territorial integrity and borders of all its neighbouring states, as laid down by the UN Charter and the basic documents of the OSCE. Bosnia and Herzegovina will continue to build democratic institutions and contribute to the process of European security and cooperation. Unfortunately, at present her ability to do so is severely restricted.

From the very moment of being recognised as an independent state by the European Community, Bosnia has been the victim of aggression by Serbia, Montenegro and the Yugoslav Army. The aggression intensified when Bosnia and Herzegovina became a member of the OSCE, and became even fiercer and more brutal when she was admitted to membership of the United Nations.

Bosnia and Herzegovina has been rendered incapable of providing her citizens with the benefits of freedom, independence and international recognition.

Bosnia did not merely come into being after the dissolution of Yugoslavia. She was already an independent European kingdom six centuries ago. She straddled the boundary between the Greek and the Latin churches, with their different spiritual orientations, and was recognised then by her neighbouring states, including the Holy See and its leader.

Then followed centuries of turbulent history, of which the result was Bosnia and Herzegovina as a multi-national, multi-religious and multi-cultural entity. It is with pride that we highlight this aspect of Bosnia and Herzegovina, and with justification that we say to foreigners that we are a corner of Europe in the Balkans. But all this has now been called into question.

Bosnia has become the battleground of genocide. She is now a country of concentration camps. Schools and sports stadiums have become torture chambers and sites of mass murders. You have seen on your television screens the images of the massacre in Sarajevo. But you have not seen the seven children killed by a shell a few days ago in the suburbs of Sarajevo as they picked cherries. You have not seen the mass graves in other parts of Bosnia and Herzegovina. Even we do not know exactly what is happening there, for entire regions are cut off and all the telecommunications and television links with Sarajevo have been destroyed.

Not a single international humanitarian organisation or reporter has been allowed to visit the occupied areas where, according to the deeply disturbing and moving accounts of surviving refugees, mass expulsions and murders are being carried out. Permit me to mention only the town of Prijedor, from which 13 truck-loads of corpses were removed for burial in mass graves.

What we do know for sure is that Bosnia and Herzegovina is being treacherously attacked by Serbia and Montenegro, and that the aggressor forces have not withdrawn from Bosnia despite all the Resolutions adopted by the UN Security Council, the demands of the European Community and the promises issuing from Belgrade. An unprecedented sleight of hand has taken place: the army has merely changed its name, being no longer the Yugoslav but now the Serbian Army. Some 80,000 troops have remained in Bosnia and Herzegovina, along with more than 600 tanks, a huge quantity of heavy weapons and equipment and 50 fighter aircraft. It is still, to this day, one of the most heavily armed forces in Europe.

It was this force, in complicity with the plan for the ethnic cleansing of Bosnia, that swept down upon the innocent Bosnians and Herzegovinians. For our part, we had not prepared ourselves for war, but for peace. The result is that our towns and cities are occupied, under siege and destroyed, our villages burned out, our population displaced. One in three of the inhabitants of Bosnia and Herzegovina have been forced to leave hearth and home and join the millions-strong refugee columns.

Dear presidents, prime ministers and friends, it is not only Bosnia that is being defended in Bosnia. It is Europe that is being defended in Bosnia. The Helsinki Final Act, the Paris Charter and the other instruments that Europe has sworn to uphold are being defended in Bosnia. If Bosnia is not saved, then these charters, acts and instruments are meaningless.

We are trying, out of some kind of mad hope, to preserve the vision of a civil and cosmopolitan Bosnia and Herzegovina. But this will be impossible without international support. We are immeasurably grateful for the humanitarian aid that you are sending us. But this cannot save Bosnia from aggression. Aggression and its aftermath cannot be eliminated by charitable hand-outs: this is the message that I bring you from the citizens of my country.

During the Summit our delegation was received by US President George Bush. We informed him of the seriousness of the situation in Bosnia. I did not gain the impression that he was willing to do anything significant to halt the aggression. At that time, and for a long time thereafter, America regarded Bosnia as a European problem and was of the view that we should properly be addressing ourselves to European governments.

The war divided families, father on one side, son on another; husband on the side of the defence, wife on the attack; or vice versa. Life in Sarajevo under siege was told in moving stories. One of the saddest was recounted by the journalist Šefko Hodžić. The story was published in the Sarajevo daily *Oslobođenje* on 29 July 1992 with the title 'Drama on the Grbavica Road'. When the attack came, the husband was on our side and the wife on the opposing side of the divided city, while their baby, only a month and a half old, was with the father and their two daughters of eight and ten were with their mother. It was agreed that the children would be exchanged. A temporary cease-fire was agreed through UNPROFOR so the exchange could take place. The place where it was to happen was Trg Heroja, Heroes' Square, in the western part of the city. This is how Hodžić describes this moving family drama:

We followed this unusual exchange. Peko,[7] with the baby in his arms, reached the corner of the building where it had been agreed that the exchange would take place, and waited. He looked right and left, but in that open space between our and the Chetniks' positions there was no one except himself and the baby. And then a man appeared with one of Peko's daughters, aged about ten.

Peko handed the baby over to the man, and then something strange occurred. He and the little girl stood still, making no move to go back. We realised what was going on. His daughter had changed her mind and didn't want to go with Dad. She wanted to go back where she'd come from. It was obvious her father was unable to persuade her. And he didn't have much time to try.

Then the man, a stranger to Peko, reappeared, having already handed the baby to someone, and took Peko's daughter in his arms. Peko stood as if rooted to the spot, right there, in that open, exposed space, not knowing what to do while his daughter was leaving…

Then there followed a new act in the drama. From the direction of the 'Željo' football stadium Peko's wife appeared with their other daughter. Now they were all running towards one another, Peko from one direction, his wife and their other daughter from another and the daughter who 'wanted to stay with Mum' from a third. They finally met on a lawn between the houses where our positions were to the right and the Chetniks' to the left, and all fell together in a single, despairing hug. For the first time in more than two months, the whole family was together.

But their moment of happiness lasted only a few minutes. They talked, and wept, and smiled, and embraced one another, and then all hugged together again. But finally, they had to separate.

The mother took one of the little girls off towards Grbavica, while Peko ran towards our positions with the other. While father and daughter were running, the front line on the Square was on full alert, the troops with their fingers on the trigger. They were protecting the father and the little girl who

---

[7] Peko Stanić was killed in the war as a soldier of the Bosnian Army in January 1994. His wife and children are now living in America.

had agreed to go with Dad. (Šefko Hodžić, *Vitezovi i Huni* [Knights and Huns], p. 54)

Three unsuccessful attempts were launched to lift the siege of Sarajevo, which had been completely surrounded and cut off since April. The first was made on 3 May from the Visoko direction. The action failed, for lack of basic resources and personnel, and also because of inadequate intelligence about the aggressor forces along the line of the attempted breakthrough. The second attempt, named *Jug-92*, utilising about 6,000 troops, was conducted both from outside and within the city. It produced only the most minor results. The third effort was attempted at the end of the year, under the code-name *Koverat*. Once again, this showed that there was a wide gap between what we wanted and what it was possible to achieve. Further attempts were also to demonstrate that lifting the siege of Sarajevo was an extremely difficult task; these attempts included an operation by combined forces of the Bosnian Army in June 1995. The siege was to be lifted only in autumn 1995 after air strikes by NATO forces.

Until then, it was hell in Sarajevo. There was no water, electricity, gas or food; but there was an unprecedented level of human solidarity, which probably only manifests itself at times of suffering and that later, when things return to normal, is remembered with nostalgia. It is estimated that during the more than 42 months of the siege, over 10,000 people were killed by shells or sniper bullets, of whom 1,300 were children, and more than 70,000 people injured.

The Presidency building was a particular target. All kinds of missiles were fired at it, everything the Chetniks could lay their hands on, from artillery and mortar shells to guided missiles. 57 people were killed in and around the building during the siege. Two girls – Emira Huseinović and Svjetlana Gavrić – were killed by sniper bullets while working in their offices. One of them was hit in the head, stood up for a moment and asked her colleagues, 'What's happening?' and fell dead. Towards the end of the war they tried to target us with modified flying bombs on which they had fixed reactor engines. They hit the neighbouring building of the Railway Directorate and the City Dispensary.

One of the fiercest attacks on the city came during the night of 28 to 29 May 1992. Ratko Mladić was personally in charge of the firing, which lasted for many hours and was targeted at the Parliament and Presidency buildings and at the residential area of Velešići. 'Fire at Velušići, there aren't many Serbs living there,' he ordered brusquely, overheard by both ourselves and UNPROFOR. He did not know exactly what Velešići was called, but he did know that not many Serbs lived there. Nevertheless, he was ready even for some of them to be killed if it meant also killing a lot of Muslims. That evening I had moved across to the neighbouring building, where the City Assembly was housed, to visit Bakir, who was on duty there. No sooner had we entered than a shell hit the building. It was probably a howitzer shell, since the building shook to its foundations, and some people were knocked over. We hurried into the basement, where part of the city defence headquarters was located. We spent the next few hours under heavy fire. Shells land unexpectedly, but you can hear the missiles fired from multi-barrelled rocket-launchers as they approach. The nearest hit was to a basement wall about ten metres away from us. The dust and the acrid smell of burned explosives began to choke us. The shelling stopped just before dawn. We went outside. The traffic lights in Skenderija, which were still working, could be seen through the hole in the basement wall. There were fires blazing all around. The streets were littered with broken bricks, plaster and glass. Whole windows had been blown out of the walls, and there were huge branches, knocked off the trees, lying in the park and on the street outside the Presidency building. My car, which was parked outside the building, had been crushed by one of these branches. In the morning I learned that the house in which I had lived until war broke out had been hit several times during the night, that the roof over my flat had burned out, and that both my daughters' flats had been hit. By good fortune, no one was hurt, because they had all been sheltering in the basement.

A CNN correspondent who was in the city on 2 June reported to his viewers: 'You always think it can't get worse in Sarajevo. But it can. The city is shaking, crackling and hissing with agony, as though it wanted to climb those hills.' The Spanish writer Juan Goytisolo was to find the same picture a year later. In his *Sarajevo Notebooks*, Goytisolo writes: 'On "hot" nights and days there are not enough places in the hospitals, not enough places in the morgues – the corpses have to be laid out on the tiles – and not enough places in the graveyards. Since funerals are a favourite target of the snipers, they have to be improvised in the least exposed places (the park on the Kovači slope) or dusk taken advantage of so as to bury the victims secretly.' Goytisolo ends by saying: 'No one can remain unmoved after landing in the hell that is Sarajevo.'

Although, with the help of SDS paramilitary troops, the aggressor forces had partly occupied Goražde right at the start of the war, thanks to the good organisation and determination of the Territorial Defence Forces of Bosnia and Herzegovina, the town was liberated in battles that took place between 15 and 28 August 1992.

It was during the battle for Goražde, on 26 August 1992, that the London Conference on the Yugoslav crisis was held, with about 40 participants, including UN Secretary-General Boutros Ghali and the British Prime Minister John Major. I addressed the Conference.

Extracts From Speech At The London Conference
(26 August 1992)

I come from Bosnia and Herzegovina, the newest member state of the United Nations, a country that has become the victim of brutal aggression. I bring you greetings from its citizens, gratitude for what you have done for our country, and reproaches for what you have failed to do.

And what you have failed to do for Bosnia and Herzegovina, you have failed to do for yourselves. For in Bosnia, in an unequal fight, we are attempting to defend an eminently European principle of life and of relations between people and between social and national groups. This is the principle of diversity and mutual tolerance, an example of which Bosnia and Herzegovina has always represented, despite all the historical trials and tribulations it has passed through, and which it is striving with utopian resolution to retain.

In the view of the power-holders in Belgrade, whose representatives are in this hall today, after the dissolution of Yugoslavia Bosnia and Herzegovina should have remained within a diminished Yugoslavia (or Greater Serbia, as the world usually calls it) together with Serbia and Montenegro. In the referendum we held, the people overwhelmingly rejected this. The will of the people was recognised by Europe, and then by the majority of the civilized world. But this will was neither recognised nor accepted by the Belgrade regime.

Reprisals followed, and attempts to impose their preferred solution by brute force. The machinery of one of the most highly equipped armies in Europe was set in motion against the newly-created state and its unarmed people. More than 2,400 armoured combat vehicles, more than 1,800 artillery pieces of various calibres, the JNA's airforce and missile systems, and more than 100,000 JNA troops, joined by the same number of irregular party troops of the SDS, swept down on the young, defenceless, unprotected state. More than half the country was rapidly occupied. With a few hurriedly-acquired light weapons, the people put up a resistance, and continue to resist, in Sarajevo, Goražde, Srebrenica, Bosanski Brod, Brčko, Jajce, parts of Herzegovina and central Bosnia, the Cazin border region, and relatively broad zones in the valleys of the Rivers Bosna and Neretva. This is an important, mainly urban and industrial part of Bosnia.

Gentlemen, this is no ordinary war, nor is the conquest and occupation launched by Serbia any ordinary military occupation. It is a genocidal war against a civilian population and their religious, national and cultural values. Cities have been ravaged, the undesirable population has been killed and expelled. Like sinister mushrooms, concentration camps are sprouting all over Bosnia and Herzegovina, in which men and women are being killed or are dying slowly of starvation and torture. There are no sufficiently ugly words in the languages of civilised countries to name and describe the atrocities being committed…

Now we are being asked to negotiate, as though nothing had happened. As though no cities had been ravaged, no one killed or expelled, no mistrust and hatred had been sown.

Negotiations can be conducted, but the first talks must be on putting a stop to the aggression and the elimination of its consequences, and then of the future structure of Bosnia and Herzegovina.

Putting a stop to the aggression and eliminating its consequences include:

– an immediate cease-fire;

– the withdrawal of the JNA and the paramilitaries connected with it from the territory of Bosnia and Herzegovina in accordance with UN Security Council Resolution 752;

– the return to their homes and villages of those who have been forced to leave;

– the return of looted property and reparations for war damage;

– determining where the responsibility for war crimes lies…

Our government has prepared a study on the future constitutional order of Bosnia and Herzegovina. I shall not go into detail about this here. I should like simply to cite two fundamental principles on which the future constitution of the country will be based:

1. Bosnia and Herzegovina will be a democratic, secular state, based on the sovereignty of its citizens and equality before the law of its nations.

2. It will be a decentralised state, with wide regional and local self-administration...

Reject the plan to partition Bosnia and Herzegovina, and quell the aspirations of this kind. If you do not, instead of being punished the aggressor will be rewarded, and the two-million-strong Muslim people will remain without a homeland. In this case, its worse portion would turn to crime, and its better to revenge. The latter would seek to avenge itself on the savage aggressor and the indifference of the world. And this could last for years.

Finally, Bosnia and Herzegovina is a European country, and its people a European people. But the evil that has befallen us has not come from Asia, it too is of European origin. Two evils have united in the aggressor: fascism (racism and extremist nationalism) and bolshevism (the total lack of any sense of justice and law). Both are European products.

You cannot allow Bosnia and Herzegovina to die under the boot of these two evils, and then go to your meetings and speak of the new world and new European order. Europe is being both defended and built, and perhaps buried, in Bosnia.

The conference ended with the adoption of the Declaration on Bosnia and Herzegovina, calling for an end to all the fighting, affirming the integrity of Bosnia and Herzegovina and providing for the return of refugees to their homes, respect for human rights and the deployment of international observer groups on the borders between Bosnia and Herzegovina and Serbia. The Declaration remained a mere dead letter, and the aggression continued.

At the beginning of October 1992 I was in Zagreb, where the news reached me that Bosanski Brod was about to fall. Tales were circulating to the effect that the Croatian Army was retreating from the town and putting up no resistance. These accounts were accompanied by rumours of a secret agreement between Tuđman and Milošević to hand over the Posavina. I did not want to believe these stories, and decided to check them out.

On 5 October I took a circuitous route out of Zagreb towards Brod. The motorway that would have taken me there in two or three hours had already long since been closed as the result of hostilities. I reached Slavonski Brod at dusk. The political leadership of Slavonski Brod and Bosanski Brod was waiting for me there. Everything was gloomy: the weather, the people, and the atmosphere. It was decided that I would return that same evening to Zagreb and request President Tuđman to send reinforcements. Over the telephone I arranged a meeting for eight o'clock in the morning in Zagreb.

I travelled all night, and was back in Zagreb before dawn. I remember Tuđman staring at my crumpled, tie-less attire. He said that Bosanski Brod would not fall, and agreed to send reinforcements of 1,000 troops immediately. I left feeling encouraged, and travelled to Split, for a meeting with the then leader of the Bosnian Croats, Mate Boban. The moment I arrived, late in the afternoon, Boban informed me that Bosanski Brod had fallen that morning. His reaction to my horror at this news was: 'You needn't feel any regrets, they're not worth it, we'll get Bosanski Brod back one day.' This 'they're not worth it' related to the Croats of that region, who did not belong to Boban's HDZ party and who, unlike Boban, regarded Bosnia and Herzegovina as their homeland.

Almost eight years later, the Croat commander of the region, General Petar Stipetić, delivered a statement to the *Nacional* newspaper in March 2000, which read:

> We were immensely surprised when we lost Bosanski Brod on 6 October 1992. We did not lose it as a result of pressure from and attacks by a more powerful opponent, which we could have accepted, but for reasons which are wholly unclear to me. The troops that should have defended the area around Bosanski Brod were withdrawn without my knowledge, and the Serbian troops simply walked in. To this day I have not been able to find out who was behind this, but I am certain that the background was an agreement between Mate Boban and Radovan Karadžić in summer 1992 when they met in Graz.

After consolidating the situation around Bosanski Brod, the Serbs moved on Gradačac, but were forced back in battles fought from 22 to 25 October. It was during this battle that the famous episode took place in which our forces decoyed and destroyed a JNA armoured train and confiscated a significant quantity of arms and equipment.

The events surrounding the fall of Bosanski Brod showed that there were serious rifts in the relations between the Bosnian Army and the Croat Defence Council (HVO). The HVO held different views on the future of Bosnia and Herzegovina, more precisely they wanted to create their own integral territory in Bosnia and then to merge it with Croatia; disagreements grew more frequent and turned into open conflict.

The first clashes came as early as June 1992, in the Lašvanska Valley, and in October 1992 in Prozor, where HVO troops attacked the town from 23 to 25 October and massacred civilians. I dictated a letter to Tuđman:

> Mr. President, the latest events in Bosnia and Herzegovina compel me to address this letter to you.
>
> HVO troops have deliberately provoked clashes in Novi Travnik, Vitez and Prozor. There have been casualties – both dead and wounded – in the course of these clashes. All roads through western Herzegovina are closed even to humanitarian aid. At the same time, a propaganda war is being waged in the Croatian media against Bosnia and Herzegovina and its legitimate government. News has been concocted, and then persistently repeated, of an alleged coup d'état in Bosnia and Herzegovina; there are speculations about changes in government and the battle, being waged by the Army of Bosnia and Herzegovina on extremely unequal terms against the Chetniks, is stubbornly ignored. Our people, who have been under fierce physical attack from the Chetniks, are now, it seems, to have their morale undermined and to be left without hope. It also seems that the Croatian media have taken this latter task upon themselves.
>
> The truth, as you well know, is that there has been no coup d'état of any kind in Sarajevo.
>
> It is also true – as the whole world apart from Croatian TV knows – that the Army of Bosnia and Herzegovina has been fighting bravely in Goražde, Sarajevo, Konjić, Jajce, Gradačac, Žepa, Maglaj, Višegrad, Brćko and elsewhere. Why is this ignored, and a sense of hopelessness disseminated instead?
>
> It is further true that tanks fired on Prozor and entered the town, and that these were not the tanks of the Army of Bosnia and Herzegovina.

Military supplies that are vital for the resistance to the Chetnik invasion of Bosnia and Herzegovina are being held up in Zagreb and Grude. The consequences are clear to see.

Talks are being held in Geneva on the future structure of Bosnia and Herzegovina. Simultaneous with this, a political *fait accompli* is being brought about by the use of force, which makes the London and Geneva talks irrelevant.

The HVO has gone beyond the limits of legitimate defence against the Chetniks and has embarked on the systematic destruction of the legitimate civil authorities and the establishment of parastate institutions.

The impression is inescapable that there is a desire to exploit the difficult situation in which Bosnia and Herzegovina finds itself, perhaps the most difficult in its entire history, in order to impose an outcome that is contrary to the will of the majority of its citizens.

What reasonable person among the general public could believe that, while waging this tough fight against the Chetniks, we have also opened up a front against the HVO? Does not this rather resemble the Chetnik accounts of our shelling ourselves in Sarajevo?

Bosnia and Herzegovina will never agree to a partition on purely ethnic grounds, and will not accept any solution imposed by force. The country has sufficient strength and sufficient friends abroad to defend itself.

Prominent among these friends of Bosnia and Herzegovina were Croatia and the Croatian people. My country will continue, despite everything, to believe in this friendship, and to behave accordingly.

Mr. President, please use your influence to eliminate the obstacles in our way, so that our relations may develop in conformity with the Agreement on Friendly Relations and Cooperation between our two countries.

There was no reply, or to be more precise, none came for several months.

At the end of January 1993, Tuđman and I exchanged sharply-worded open letters. It was not difficult to see from these how far the situation on the ground and relations between the two countries had deteriorated in the meantime. Tuđman wrote in his open letter dated 27 January 1993:

> The deplorable events taking place these days, in which Muslim extremists in central Bosnia are carrying out organised, criminal and brutal attacks on Croat residential areas, firing on civilians and defenders alike, compel me to address this letter to you.
>
> Last night, as you are surely well aware, 35 HVO soldiers were killed defending their villages in the Busovača area against invasion by Muslim troops. In addition, these troops burned several Croat villages. The event has deeply disturbed the leadership of the Croat people in Bosnia and Herzegovina, who have turned to Croatia for help, and to the world as a whole likewise.
>
> For this reason, deeply concerned, I appeal to you to put a stop to this brutal aggression, which could lead to the most serious worsening of relations between Muslims and Croats in Bosnia and Herzegovina, who have been together putting up a resistance to their common enemy in much of your country over the past months. If this aggression is not halted, it will also worsen the relations between our two states, and wholly incapacitate the flow of humanitarian aid on which many are living in Bosnia and Herzegovina.
>
> The citizens of Croatia ask themselves whether the aggression against Croats in Bosnia and Herzegovina is the response to all that Croatia is doing to assist your countrymen:
>
> – to protect and care for half a million refugees;
>
> – to organise, support and deliver huge amounts of humanitarian aid;
>
> – to enable many of the civil service sectors of your state to function in Croat towns;
>
> – by way of overall support for the defence against the Serbian aggressors;
>
> – in contributing to the search for the most just solution possible for the final structure of Bosnia and Herzegovina and the establishment of peace as soon as possible, within the framework of the Geneva talks.
>
> I take this opportunity to address the Croat and Muslim peoples in Bosnia and Herzegovina direct, calling upon them

to bring to an end their mutual hostilities and to cooperate fully in the defence of their common aggressor, and in the search for a solution enabling them to live in harmony as constituent peoples on a fully equal footing in Bosnia and Herzegovina.

I hope that your urgent and decisive order to the Muslim troops to halt their aggression against the Croats of Bosnia and Herzegovina will enable Croats and Muslims in Bosnia and Herzegovina to become a force of defence against the Serbo-Montenegrin and Yugo-Communist aggressor. This is also a minimal prerequisite for maintaining the willingness among the Croatian general public to continue to make enormous sacrifices in caring for refugees and offering overall assistance to Bosnia and Herzegovina.

I replied the following day:

I write in response to your letter of 27 January, relating to the latest clashes between the Army of Bosnia and Herzegovina troops and the HVO in central Bosnia.

I have tried, as far as it lay within my power, to learn the truth about the occasion for these latest clashes, which are deeply to be regretted.

I fear that you have relied on only a single source of information and have regarded it as sufficient. I have been in constant contact with three sources: responsible officers in the Army of Bosnia and Herzegovina, the HVO and UNPROFOR (that is, EC monitors). Reports from the Army of Bosnia and Herzegovina and the HVO, as you may suppose, have been contradictory. The facts that I have learned from UNPROFOR and EC representatives, however, have clearly confirmed that the latest clashes in Gornji Vakuf and Busovača were provoked by HVO troops in an attempt to carry out the orders of the Minister of Defence, Božo Raić, to bring units of the Army of Bosnia and Herzegovina under the command of the HVO in Herzegovina and central Bosnia. The Army of Bosnia and Herzegovina's troops mounted a resistance to this, and there were casualties. No single item of information has confirmed that there was violence of any kind against the Croat civilian population, let alone those of the kind that Croatian TV and some Zagreb newspapers are trying to convince the Croatian general public, took place.

A deeper reason for the conflict in central Bosnia, however, is the attempt by some people from the HVO to persist in the establishment of a form of state entity within the state of Bosnia and Herzegovina. This is the true cause of the tensions and growing distrust between the two peoples, and we must face up to this fact.

In Geneva, Mr. Boban signed a document on nine principles from which, despite all the deficiencies of the document, it is at least clear that Bosnia and Herzegovina is a sovereign state and that there will be provinces within it, but that these provinces will be neither states nor nationally defined areas belonging only to a single people. The day before yesterday I offered Mr. Boban the text of a joint statement in which we call for an end to the conflict in central Bosnia. Among other things, the text specified the equal status of the peoples in the future proposed provinces of Mostar and Travnik, and was wholly in conformity with the documents put forward in Geneva.

This was a statement that would have eliminated certain disagreements and would certainly have contributed to a normalisation of the situation, but Mr. Boban refused to sign it, and limited it solely to an appeal to end the hostilities. The only explanation I can find for this is that Mr. Boban has not given up his ambition to create an exclusively Croat national area in central Bosnia, where, as you well know, the Muslim and Croat populations are almost equal in number, for which reason this area cannot be solely Croat. I am enclosing a copy of the unsigned statement with this letter, so that you may judge for yourself.

Because of some of the assertions in your letter I take the liberty of asking you, Mr. President, whether you are acquainted with the following:

– that the insignia of the state of Bosnia and Herzegovina have long since been 'expelled' from the territory under HVO control;

– that TV transmitters in these areas have been realigned so that they cannot receive the programmes of TVBiH;

– that in a series of municipalities in Herzegovina and central Bosnia the legal authorities have been broken up by the unilateral action of the HVO;

– that the humanitarian aid reaching Bosnia and Herzegovina is constantly being held up and inequitably distributed. A Turkish ship with 4,500 tonnes of food has, just recently, been literally sold off by the HVO; the HVO has, without authorisation, taken from a Turkish oil-tanker, laden with fuel supplied thanks to the voluntary donations of the Turkish people, 1,000 tonnes of fuel in addition to the quota we allocated it, resulting in the corps of the Army of Bosnia and Herzegovina in Mostar receiving nothing at all; two directors of IGASSA, Ghalib as-Sufi and Abu-Hasan Ali, were kidnapped in Busovača at the end of December 1992 and have been held prisoner in Mostar for more than a month now. Money and goods to the value of more than half a million DM has been taken from them. In the current issue of *Slobodna Dalmacija*, there is an open letter from Mrs. Marija Wernle-Matić, Secretary of the Association for Humanitarian Aid in Zurich, who speaks of widespread confiscations of humanitarian aid on the roads crossing Herzegovina. Please find the time to read this article. It will make many things clearer to you.

– that the confiscation of equipment vital to the resistance against the Chetnik aggressor be stopped. As you know, in November 1992 we made a gift to the Croatian Army of half the consignment of this equipment, with a value of at least ten million US dollars, but despite this the other half did not reach its destinations in Bosnia intact. A significant proportion was halted and seized in Grude. If this had not happened, Sarajevo and many other places in Bosnia would already have been liberated, and our refugees could have returned to their homes;

– that in early December 1992 an attack was carried out by HVO troops on Prozor. The town was shelled for two days, 22 soldiers and civilians were killed, and the Army of Bosnia and Herzegovina and the surrounding Muslim villages were disarmed.

After they were disarmed, 74 Muslim houses were blown up. I am enclosing a list of the owners of these houses by first name and surname with this letter. I take the liberty of proposing that the two of us visit this town and see for ourselves what really happened there.

The disagreements reached a peak in mid January, when the order was given to bring the Army of Bosnia and Herzegovina under the command of the HVO in an as yet undefined province with a Croat majority. There followed a series of clashes, of which the most severe was in Gornji Vakuf, which was also pounded by heavy artillery for days; all humanitarian aid for the civilian population of Bosnia and Herzegovina was halted, hundreds of vehicles owned by Muslims who happened to be on the roads in Herzegovina at the time of the escalation of the conflict were confiscated, and so on, and so on... I must state with regret that an unprecedented campaign against Bosnia and Herzegovina is being conducted in the Croatian media. Such a campaign is not required by those who have the facts at their disposal and on whose side is the truth.

Bosnia and Herzegovina opted for an alliance with Croatia at a time when it would have been much more painless to join the more powerful side and remain in Yugoslavia. This was not a calculated choice, but a matter of principle and consistency. I remind you that we refused to send our young men to the JNA when it was ravaging Croatia, and indeed that a large number of volunteers joined the Croat struggle for sovereignty and freedom, and were killed doing so. We expected reprisals from the Yugoslav Army for this choice, and this was what happened. We did not expect refugees from Bosnia and Herzegovina to be declared undesirable in Croatia, and the poorly armed Army of Bosnia and Herzegovina to be proclaimed an aggressor in its own country.

In conclusion, I associate myself with your appeal to the Croat and Muslim peoples to cease their mutual hostilities and bring about true cooperation in the defence against their common aggressor and in the search for a solution enabling the two peoples to live in harmony on an equal footing in Bosnia and Herzegovina.

Enclosed with this letter was the list (with first names and surnames) of the owners of the houses razed and burned by HVO troops in the town of Prozor and the villages of Memići and Blace.

The open letter from Mrs. Marija Wernle-Matić that I referred to in my response to Tuđman was addressed to Mate Boban, leader of the rebel Croats. This letter, published in *Slobodna Dalmacija* on 28 January 1993, p. 33, read as follows:

> I am Marija Matić, married name Wernle, born on 2 February 1942 in Vijaka, Vareš municipality, of the Catholic faith. I have

been living in Switzerland since 1964, and have been a Swiss citizen since 1967. My current position is Secretary to the Association for Humanitarian Aid to Bosnia and Herzegovina.

I feel compelled by a sense of great bitterness to write this letter. My journey to Bosnia, which began on 18 October 1992 and was forcibly halted by the closing of the Bosnian borders so that I remained in Split until 4 November 1992, finally entering Bosnia on 4 November 1992, convinced me that the Catholic Croats of Herzegovina and Bosnia are confiscating whatever the fancy takes them from the humanitarian aid intended for the people of Bosnia and Herzegovina, and selling a large part of the confiscated goods in shops for foreign currency. I shall mention just three places where large-scale confiscations are taking place: Tomislavgrad, Grude and Kiseljak.

In Žepče, Branko Marković removed from my care a truck full of clothing, in a convoy which I had personally accompanied, but which because of the closure of the borders already referred to had had to proceed, truck by truck, from Split, so that on arrival in Žepče I had to go from office to office for a week, talking to people in authority from the HDZ who, unfortunately, were not willing to meet my requests to return the goods taken from me, with the consequent loss of one-third. In the same place I saw the shop where the wool that had been taken from me (100 kg) was being sold. The *Caritas* Pharmacy is selling humanitarian aid: baby food, articles of personal hygiene – for example, toothbrushes, being sold for 4 German marks each. In November 1992 the women of Berne sent four articulated trucks (more than 100 tonnes) of new children's clothing, food and articles of personal hygiene. The consignment went missing somewhere between Split and Travnik, which means that it never reached its destination. Those consignments that do reach their destination frequently look as though they have been gone over by wild animals, and of course there is always a proportion of the goods missing.

When I saw what was on sale in the shops in Kiseljak, it would have been better for my health if I had not seen it. I have witnesses to testify that HVO troops take people of Arab or Bosnian Muslim origin prisoner and take them to the HVO Barracks in Kiseljak. There they are stripped of everything they are carrying with them, and this is followed by the excuse that the theft was carried out by some gang or other. It is very interesting that these gangs take their victims to the HVO Barracks.

The latest consignment from our Association, which had the proper accompanying documentation, was forcibly removed from a bus on the regular Lucerne-Travnik line on 17 January 1993 between Metković and Mostar. The consignment consisted of 113 women's warm winter coats, 31 down-quilted jackets, 65 track suits, 6 suits, a housecoat, a green jacket, seven boxes in all sponsored by the Swiss insurance company Fortuna. The consignment was intended for the rehabilitation centre in the Zenica Steelworks Clinic. Five large packages of various medicines and two of various other goods, sent by a number of Swiss pharmacies care of the bus driver, were also confiscated.

Another consignment, transported by truck, was stopped in Grude at the same time. This consisted of 20 packages of bandages and five of special medicines with the reference 921130/1223 Mediswisa and 8005/16 IVG, Neuhausen on the accompanying papers, intended for the Health Centre in Lukavac.

Two Centrotrans buses from Zenica were prevented from going any further than Busovača, and the passengers were compelled to continue their journey on foot. This was just one of many such events.

I appeal to you, in the name of God, in whom we both believe, in the name of the Church that we attend, in the name of the people we love and for whom we are fighting, in the name of the country we love and wish to liberate from atrocities, to do all that is in your power to prevent these ugly and evil deeds from taking place any more. Free our wretched and long-suffering people from these troubles and tribulations, for you know better than I do that the people are almost at the end of their tether. Let no individuals become wealthy at the expense of those most at risk in Bosnia and Herzegovina. (Marija Wernle-Matić).

Although the aggressor killed Serbs and Croats, Jews, Roms, Slovenes and Albanians, the largest number of victims was among the Muslim population. It was clear that a genocidal war was being waged against the Bosnian Muslims, and that fact sent shockwaves through the general public in Muslim countries. It became obvious that the catch-phrase 'the new world order', so often repeated at that time, was mere hypocrisy, for the new world order clearly had double standards right from the start. For the Bosnian Muslims, although they are an indigenous European people, a different standard applied than for Westerners. After the collapse of the Soviet communist empire, some of the republics of the Soviet Union had declared themselves to be independent states, but nowhere did such a tragedy occur as in Bosnia. The Western military alliance would not have permitted the genocide of a Christian people. I believe many Muslims the world over thought like this. What was to be done? The answer was an extraordinary meeting of the Organisation of the Islamic Conference (OIC) in Jeddah, convened in early December 1992.

I took off from Sarajevo in a UNHCR aircraft. In Zagreb another aircraft was waiting for me belonging to Shaikh Qasim, Sultan of Sharjah, a good-hearted and highly educated man and a great friend of Bosnia. Sharjah is one of the emirates forming the United Arab Emirates (UAE).

On the way to Jeddah we landed in Tirana, where we were joined by Sali Berisha, then President of Albania. As we were flying over Albania, we were amazed by both the beauty and the poverty of that country: green meadows and hills along the sea coast were intersected by narrow cobbled roads. The aircraft landed at a poor, run-down airport, surrounded on all sides by grey concrete bunkers – hundreds of them – built by the regime of Enver Hoxha. President Berisha, a medical doctor educated in America, was fully aware of the state of collapse to which Enver's communism had led his beautiful country. When I asked him about the economic situation in Albania, he replied that it looked like a heavily-trodden path in which it was almost impossible to plant anything.

We were welcomed at Jeddah International Airport by Prince Salman. Tall, in traditional Arab costume, with an aquiline, typically Semitic nose, a large frame and hoarse voice, the Prince showed the most natural modesty and dignity. 'President, we have called this extraordinary session so that together we can do as much as possible for your people! We shall not stand by indifferently looking on as Muslims suffer!' he said during our brief wait in the airport's VIP lounge.

In Qasra'l-mu'tamar, the Palace where important gatherings are held, the Conference was opened the following day by the sovereign ruler of Saudi Arabia, King Fahd, Guardian and Servant of the Two Harams, as his official title states. He spoke fluently and boldly, appealing to international rights and charters, to the religious obligations of every Muslim and every member of the OIC, and highlighted the sufferings of the Muslims in Bosnia.

As the old diplomatic custom goes, the Conference had two tracks: the official, and the behind-the-scenes. The Egyptian Foreign Minister, Amr Musa, the Pakistan Minister Muhammed Sattar, the Iranian Foreign Minister Ali Akbar Velayeti and, of course, Prince Salman set the tone for the two-day meeting. I learned that in Ankara the Turkish President Turgut Özal was following live all the proceedings in Jeddah. In the evening of the first day's work, a draft resolution made its appearance, prior to its intended adoption the following day. The draft was too bland and general, without specific commitments and deadlines. Silajd•ić and Šaćirbegović were nervously pacing around the hotel room, disappointed by the 'billion Muslims'. All at once the telephone rang: Velayati was calling.

The following day the draft was substantially reworked. We were satisfied with the result, and looked forward to its adoption. We then learned that Lord Owen, international mediator in the talks on Bosnia and Herzegovina, obviously dissatisfied with the new version of the Resolution, had angrily left the Conference early.

In the Resolution, the Muslim countries called on the United Nations to lift the arms embargo against Bosnia and Herzegovina. If the embargo was not lifted by 1 February the following year, the Muslim countries would cease to honour it. I recommended to the journalist reporting from the conference that he refrain from raising the hopes of our people in his reports for Radio-Television Bosnia and Herzegovina. I knew the situation both within and outside Bosnia too well.

Prior to our return our hosts organised our visit to Makkah to perform *umra*, the lesser pilgrimage. We donned the *ihram* and set off for Makkah. Any notions one may have of the Haram al-Sharif and the Ka'bah gleaned from seeing them in photographs or reading accounts of them vanish the moment one sees them in reality. I glimpsed the Ka'bah from the street, through a forest of columns. We went to the colonnade near the Zamzam Spring. Some pilgrims recognised me, and began to chant 'Bosnia, Bosnia'. I sat in a corner and prayed two *rakats*, looking at the impressively tall Ka'bah. 'God, please help my people in their misery and isolation, living far from their centre,' I prayed in my thoughts, and then began to perform the ritual to the instructions of an Arab guide who dispersed the astonished pilgrims ahead of us to clear the way for our group. 'Bosnia, Bosnia, may Allah help our brothers from Bosnia,' chanted the tearful Muslims, who had come here from every corner of the world.

The following day we flew back home. Seeing us off in the airport lounge in Jeddah, Prince Salman came up to me and said almost in a whisper, 'President, permit me to say that Al Gore called me from America just before we left for the airport, and told me that America is reconsidering its position on the embargo on the supply of arms to Bosnia and Herzegovina.'

Bill Clinton, then Governor of Arkansas, had just won the presidential elections and was preparing to take over the leadership of the greatest world power. Al Gore was his Deputy. I concluded that the Americans had been monitoring the Conference closely and that it would have an influence on the course of events in Bosnia and Herzegovina. This was to prove correct, at least to some extent.

During the first half of June the Serbs cut off Goražde completely. There was a real danger that they would occupy the town. UNPROFOR turned a blind eye, or rather closed its eyes to the danger altogether. To alleviate the position of those defending Goražde, troops from the 1st Corps carried out several offensive actions in the Igman, Treskavica and Bjelašnica region during the spring and summer of 1993.

The fighting with Serb forces from the end of April 1993 to February 1994 was conducted in parallel with the battle the Bosnian Army was fighting against the Croatian Army and the HVO. Bearing in mind that a third front had opened up against the Bosnia and Herzegovina Army with the proclamation in Krajina of the so-called Autonomous Region of Western Bosnia, 1993 was clearly an exceptionally difficult year both for Bosnia and for the Bosniacs. In these difficult conditions, certain events were crucial: the battle in Karuše from 19 to 22 March 1993, the fighting on the Tešanj-Maglaj stretch from 24 to 29 May 1993, and the battle for the defence of Olovo which lasted throughout the autumn months of 1993.

The conflict with the HVO was to last almost a year. Widespread attacks by the HVO began with the storming of the command headquarters of the 4th Corps of the Bosnia and Herzegovina Army in western Mostar. The attack began in the early morning of Sunday 9 May 1993, and was carried out by the joint forces of Mladen Naletilić Tuta and Juka Prazina, who had just deserted from the Bosnian Army. Despite serious resistance, the enemy forces occupied the building in the afternoon. The defenders tried to break out, but most of them were apprehended and taken to camps, and to this day nothing has been learned of the fate of 12 combatants who surrendered to the HVO forces. Despite this initial failure, this was the beginning of the heroic defence of Mostar led by Safet Orucević, Mayor of the city.

On 16 May I sent a message to the citizens of the Republic of Bosnia and Herzegovina concerning the Croat aggression. The message read:

> Dear fellow citizens, I am addressing you as a citizen of this long-suffering country, speaking to you above all as people, as individuals with names and surnames, believing in the sense of justice, a trait of ordinary, normal people.
>
> Three days ago an agreement was signed on the cessation of hostilities between the Army of Bosnia and Herzegovina and troops of the Croat Defence Council in Herzegovina and central Bosnia. The fighting should have ceased, the armies should have withdrawn to barracks and civilian prisoners should have returned to their homes. As you know, however, all this is taking place very slowly and painfully. That is why I am addressing you now. While we are trying painfully to quench the fires of war and at the same time asking ourselves, anxiously and hopefully, what the future holds for us – a calming of tensions, at last, or another round of evil – some elementary and inescapable questions must be asked:
>
> Why did these conflicts break out, who is so persistently goading them on and why?
>
> Who is the mastermind who has succeeded in poisoning relations between two friendly peoples?
>
> Is not someone attempting to build his statelet on the basis of this shared misfortune of ours?
>
> What is the purpose of all this horror, when it is absolutely clear that not a single problem faced by the Croat people in Bosnia and Herzegovina, either now or in the past, in our long history of common living, has been caused or provoked by the Muslims?
>
> The Muslims have never usurped or seized Croatian land, have never sought to obliterate the things that are sacred to Croats, have never nurtured any feelings of hatred towards Croats. Nor vice versa. So where has all this evil sprung from? Try to answer these questions honestly and fairly.

Your unbiased conduct can contribute to putting an end, at last, to this misfortune. Demand of your leaders that they discuss this conflict, that has evidently been staged on someone else's account, and that they do so in peace, like civilised people. Call upon them to honour what has been agreed, to tell the truth and to condemn evil.

History will never forgive anyone anything. It will never give pardon for crimes to anyone. The people will punish and history will heap ignominy on those who commit them, and above all on those who conceived and ordered them.

Between 24 and 30 June 1993 HVO troops forced both the military and civil authorities to leave Žepče. A large number of both civilians and members of the Territorial Defence of Bosnia and Herzegovina were taken prisoner.

At the very time that this was going on in Žepče, on 25 June, I received Tuđman's letter in which he accused the Bosnian Army of instigating the fighting and of expelling Croats in central Bosnia. I proposed that we leave it to independent investigators to determine the truth and that we invite European Community monitors and UN-PROFOR to establish the facts:

> The Presidency of the Republic of Bosnia and Herzegovina has received and considered your letter of 25 June 1993.
>
> We share your concern at the tragic situation in central Bosnia, and condemn all crimes against the civilian population, regardless of who committed them.
>
> We must point out, however, that these regrettable events are the result of the policy of attempting to destroy Bosnia and Herzegovina, the dangers of which we have been drawing attention to for months now. The constant stopping of convoys with food for the hungry population, preventing the inflow of the means of defence and organising parastate institutions in the regions under HVO control, have caused bad blood between Croats and Muslims and threaten to prolong the conflict.
>
> Ethnic cleansing in Prozor, the atrocities in Ahmići, and the attack on Mostar – which are the means of spreading terror and in which the remaining three mosques (in Balinovac, Pijesak and Podhum) were deliberately destroyed – were planned, begun and executed by the HVO. Since the Army of Bosnia and Herzegovina did not respond in kind to the ethnic

cleansing in Mostar, Čapljina and Stolac, the HVO planned the action to effect a mass movement of the Croat population from central Bosnia. This was intended to prove that common living is impossible, and that the ethnic partition of Bosnia is an inevitability.

We do not deny that there have been instances of violence and illegal conduct on the part of units of the Army of Bosnia and Herzegovina also, but we condemn and are prosecuting these cases. Our policy is not the emigration of the Croat or any other population from their homes. We continue to believe in the common living of the peoples of this region. Similarly, so-called 'humane resettlement' is, for us, extremely inhumane.

Given the disagreements and contradictory information on the causes and perpetrators of the conflict, which your letter also demonstrates, we have called upon EC monitors and UN-PROFOR representatives to report to us their findings in the field. We suggest that you too request such reports. We are in agreement that the general public in our country, in your country and abroad should be informed of the findings of these neutral rapporteurs.

We also propose an urgent meeting of representatives of our two countries' governments to seek a way to end the conflict, eliminate its causes and resolve all contested issues.

The Presidency of the Republic of Bosnia and Herzegovina once again expresses its readiness to develop friendly relations and cooperation between the Republic of Bosnia and Herzegovina and the Republic of Croatia on the basis of equity and in the spirit of the agreements thus far signed between the two countries.

Tuđman did not reply to this letter.

In the first half of June 1993, Travnik came under attack, but was successfully defended, and remained free until the end of the war. This was of major importance for the defence of central Bosnia. In confrontations with the HVO lasting from 17 to 28 July 1993, the Army of Bosnia and Herzegovina defended Bugojno, which was crucial in preventing the rebel Croats from turning their aspiration to create a Croat state in Bosnia and Herzegovina into reality.

At the end of July 1993, the Serbs launched a powerful offensive with the aim of surrounding the whole of Sarajevo. The action was part of a broader plan. On 27 May they had taken Grebak, thereby cutting Goražde off completely, and on 12 July they had seized Rogoj and moved on towards Igman. The race against time continued, for simultaneously we were completing the digging of the tunnel under Sarajevo airport that was to form a way out of the city.

The Sarajevo tunnel, in fact a meandering underground passage some 700 metres long passing beneath the runway, was dug over a period of five months in the first half of 1993. There can be no more pitiful object in the history of construction than this tunnel that played such a significant role in the life of the city. It is estimated that during 30 months of the war more than a 100,000 tonnes of arms, ammunition, food and medicines entered besieged Sarajevo through this tunnel. From the end of 1994 onwards it was also the conduit for 10-15 megawatts of electricity generated in the power plant on the Neretva, which met the most essential needs of Sarajevo. The overhead transmission lines over Mount Igman were erected and the cable running through the tunnel installed under extremely difficult conditions in the last three months of war-torn 1994, as part of the project code-named S-35.

To the south-west, the tunnel emerged in a narrow strip of territory that was defended and successfully held throughout the war by the 4th Motorised Brigade commanded by General Fikret Prevljak. The zone was then further extended in the Mount Igman and Konjic direction, and later towards Herzegovina and the outside world.

The Igman–Bjelašnica area was then being defended by the 81st and 82nd Alpine Regiments and parts of the 8th Motorised Brigade. The defence was a real motley crew, since it also included the Zulfikar and Silver Fox Units. There were problems with the leadership and command, since some units did not recognise the authority of the Igman Operative Group, which was supposed to bring under a single command all military activity in that broad region, which was of major strategic importance for the defence of Sarajevo. To make matters worse, during the three months leading up to the attack three commanders of the Igman OG were replaced.

The enemy found our weak spot and launched its attack. Trnovo fell on 13/14 July, and enemy troops broke through to the Igman plateau on 1 August. Our troops retreated in disarray. From Trnovo, Dejčić, Rogoj and other places 4,000-5,000 refugees poured down the mountain, sleeping scattered throughout the forests. There was a real danger that

Sarajevo would be completely cut off. It was in these circumstances that I had to travel to Geneva for talks, being led for the European Union by Lord Owen. As he saw me off, Kemal Muftić, for BH Press, asked me: 'You are travelling abroad to seek justice for Bosnia. What are your expectations?' I replied that I felt like a thirsty man setting off through the desert in search of water.

'My army is finally in control of Allah's road,' boasted Ratko Mladić to Juan Goytisolo during the Igman offensive. In the Serb propaganda we were Islamic militants wanting, with Turkey's help, to establish a 'Balkan caliphate,' and the Chetniks were warriors protecting Europe from the Islamic threat. This was notorious nonsense, of course, but Mladić was also wrong in yet another matter: 'Allah's road' remained in our hands.

As I crossed Igman, I did something that by military logic was highly unusual: I used the radio to call on the 7th Muslim and the 17th Krajina Brigades to come to the assistance of the troops on Igman that found themselves in an almost total impasse on this important mountain saddle. The military commanders were shocked by this open appeal, but they issued the necessary orders. Parts of the 7th Muslim and 17th Krajina Brigades made all speed to Igman and helped the troops already there to halt the Serb incursion. We succeeded in defending the strategically important forest road over Igman and held it throughout the war, although in certain places the Chetnik trenches were no more than 200-300 metres away. The road itself, and any vehicle travelling along it, were constant targets of attack. Holbrooke describes the Igman road, where 'the wreckage of vehicles that had slid off the road or been hit by Serb gunners littered the steep slopes and ravines.' Apart from the airport, which we used with the assistance of UNPROFOR, and which was often closed on account of hostilities, all our communications from Sarajevo went on this road.

There was another circumstance that played a role in our holding on to Igman, as the following passages tell. We succeeded in outwitting Karadžić with a carefully thought out diplomatic and military trick. The idea was simple and, as time would show, very successful. In the presence of Lord Owen we acted as though we were ready to continue the talks and perhaps even accept his peace plan. We said, however, that we could not and would not do so as long as the Chetnik offensive on Igman continued. We did not say anything that was not true, we simply allowed Lord Owen to believe what he wanted to. In fact, his plan – the one he had drawn up jointly with Stoltenberg – was not acceptable to us at all.

Lord Owen, a very competent and stubborn British diplomat who had been Foreign Secretary in the Labour Government in 1976-1977 and 1977-1979, put it to us that the offensive would cease as soon as the accord was signed. This was not at all what we wanted. We called for an end to the offensive and for the withdrawal of enemy troops to their positions before the start of talks. Every day we came to the UN building where these mind-numbing and pointless talks were being held, to announce that the offensive was still continuing and that we would not negotiate under these conditions. We would then return to our hotel, to repeat the performance the following day. This went on for several days. In despair Lord Owen, believing that he held the key to peace, and perhaps a Nobel prize as well, began to persuade Karadžić that he should call off the offensive. I imagine that he said something like this: 'You really don't need this offensive. You have peace and the map of Bosnia the way you wanted it. The Muslims are ready to sign if you call off the attack and withdraw your troops to their original positions.'

Owen's plan was as much to Karadžić's liking as it was contrary to ours. The plan, known as the Owen-Stoltenberg Plan due to the involvement of the former Norwegian Foreign Minister Thorvald Stoltenberg, provided for a Bosnia and Herzegovina as a union of three republics – one Serb, one Croat, one Bosniac – with the right to secession.

Owen's persuasion finally succeeded, with the backing of announcements of air strikes on Serb troops on Igman. Karadžić in turn succeeded in convincing General Mladić to call off the attack and, what is more, to withdraw his troops to the positions they had held at the time the talks began. Mladić did not give in easily: he agreed to withdraw only on condition that the area vacated by his troops be occupied not by us but by UN troops. This was how the famous Igman Demilitarized Zone (DZ) arose, which was to be maintained until the end of the war. Mladić also gave the order that every hotel and tourist facility on this Olympic mountain be destroyed during withdrawal.

The agreement on the withdrawal of Mladić's troops from the territory they had seized, reached with the unwilling mediation of UNPROFOR, was rather obscure, but one thing was absolutely clear: Mladić had to relinquish the territory he had occupied on Igman. This can be clearly seen from an interview that I gave at that time to *Večernje Novine*.

> *Večernje Novine*: The agreement on demilitarisation and withdrawal to original positions signed in mid August 1993 is very short and rather imprecise. At this very moment some of our own troops are withdrawing from their positions around Sara-

jevo, and in Pale General Rose recently promised Karadžić that he would 'fill in' all our trenches dug since the agreement was signed. To what extent is the agreement an impediment to any action by our army that might lead to lifting the siege of Sarajevo?

Izetbegović: Yes, the agreement is very brief and not exactly a model of precision. Given the conditions in which it was drawn up, what remains unsaid was obviously deliberately or unavoidably omitted. Nevertheless, the obligations it lays down are fairly clear: it requires Mladić's army to withdraw from Igman to the line where it was positioned on 30 July 1993. As for our army, all that is said is that it will remain in its current positions and that it will not move to occupy the territory abandoned by Mladić's troops. These provisions are clear. This means that General Rose cannot fill in any of our trenches outside the explicitly designated territory. A map is appended to the agreement, showing the lines of confrontation on 30 July and 14 August 1993.

This was characteristic of the conduct of General Rose and certain other British and French officers, in attempting to prevent the withdrawal of Mladić's troops, claiming that it was not necessary and that their presence on Igman was of no great military significance. But our stubbornness in refusing to negotiate won the day.

When the withdrawal of Mladić's troops was complete, Lord Owen expected the talks to be drawn to a conclusion and his plan to be accepted, but to his horror we announced that we must return to Sarajevo for consultations and that we must obtain the consent of the Parliamentary Assembly of Bosnia and Herzegovina to the peace plan.

Just before the parliamentary session, the Second Bosniac Assembly was held, in which representatives of the Bosniac people from all over the world took part. Under UNPROFOR escort, delegates even came from occupied parts of the country, Bosanska Krajina and the Podrinje enclaves of Srebrenica, Žepa and Goražde. Both the Bosniac Assembly and then the Parliament voted on the Owen-Stoltenberg Plan with 'We agree, but...' This 'but' meant, in effect, the rejection of the plan, since we made our acceptance of it conditional on the inclusion in the Bosniac republic of all the municipalities that had had a majority Muslim population according to the 1991 Census. The military situation, and morale, at the time can be clearly judged from the fact that this wholly reasonable and justifiable condition of ours was totally unacceptable to the Serbs, as we well knew.

Much later I learned of the clash between Mladić and Karadžić over the latter's agreeing to withdraw from Igman. Mladić never forgave Karadžić, and even accused him of being guilty of giving up certain military victory that would have led to the total suffocation of Sarajevo and our ultimate defeat. In this case, Mladić was largely right. Fortunately for us, Karadžić got it wrong.

During the Igman campaign of July-August 1993, the Serbs stepped up the pressure on the enclaves, shelling them daily and impeding the entry of food convoys. All this was going on as the peace talks were being conducted in Geneva. On 9 August I sent a letter to the US President calling for air strikes against Karadžić's forces. I based my request on Article 51 of the UN Charter, on the right to self-defence, and Article 1 of the 1948 Convention on the Prevention and Punishment of the Crime of Genocide, to which the USA is a signatory.

The President's reply, dated 13 August, was vague. True, President Clinton did express his determination to put a stop to the siege of Sarajevo (which was finally to happen two years later), and said that he was encouraged by the decision of the NATO allies to use air strikes if the parties on the ground did not fulfil the conditions set during the peace talks, which were still going on (this, too, was only to happen two years later). His letter ended with the words:

> The Secretary-General and members of NATO, including the United States, are monitoring the situation closely, so as to determine when and whether air strikes will begin. We agree with you that convincing threats of air strikes or – if need be – actual strikes will contribute significantly to the Geneva process. A negotiated settlement remains the final goal of our activities, for we are convinced that such an agreement is the only solution to the Bosnian tragedy. The United States will continue to work with you to that end.

Elsewhere, the HVO attacks had not ceased, but had become even more vicious, and every attempt to secure the release of the civilians languishing in various camps had proved fruitless. I decided to inform the UN Security Council of this.

Letter To The UN Security Council
(19 August 1993)

Dear Sirs,

I write to inform you that the violations of human and national rights of the Bosnian Muslims by troops of the Croat Defence Council (HVO) in Herzegovina are reaching the proportions of a true human catastrophe.

Tens of thousands of people have been forcibly expelled from their homes and their country for the purpose of creating ethnically pure Croat territories.

Men between the ages of 15 and 70 are being arrested, subjected to ill treatment and selectively liquidated. The Chairman of the SDA in Herzegovina, Zijad Demirović, was arrested with his entire family in Mostar at the beginning of June and since then there has been no trace of him. The Chairman of the SDA in Čapljina, engineer Boškailo, was murdered in cold blood outside his own house in the presence of his family and neighbours. Men are being held prisoner in improvised concentration camps, as follows:

City	Location of prison
Mostar	Heliodrom, University building
Čapljina	Dretelj, the Grabovina Barracks, the Military Depot in Gabela, the former cattle farm in Čeljevo
Stolac	The Military Barracks, the Tobacco Depot, the school in Crnići, the Steelworks
Vitina	The former state farm
Ljubuški	Otoca Prison
Prozor	The nuclear shelter, UNIS, the High School Centre, the Fire Station

Every Muslim house in the villages of Gubavica, Bivolje Brdo, Hasića Glavica, Stanojevići, Pijesci, Ševaš-Polje, Škaljevina, Lokve and the Mostar suburbs has burned down. The mosques in west Mostar, the villages of Višići and Dubrave have been blown up. The HVO has driven UNPROFOR, UNHCR, the Red Cross and journalists – witnesses of torture and forced expulsions – out of Mostar. Muslims are permitted to leave Herzegovina on condition that they sign a statement declaring that they are voluntarily giving away their entire property. In Mostar alone more than 8,000 such permits have been issued.

Stolac, Tasovčići, Čapljina, Ljubuški, Višići, Čeljevo and the Mostar residential areas of Balinovac and Đikovina, together with the areas around Mostar Cathedral and the Police and Interior Ministry buildings have been ethnically cleansed of their Muslim population. Some of the people who were forced to leave, mainly women and children, have been herded into east Mostar, Blagaj and Počiteljsko Polje, where they have been left without food, water, medicine or electricity.

We call upon the Security Council:

1. To send UNHCR and UNPROFOR representatives immediately to Mostar and other places at risk, in order that they may determine the facts on the ground and report to the Council and to the world public;

2. To enable via UNHCR the urgent delivery of humanitarian aid for the displaced population in east Mostar and in the concentration camps throughout Herzegovina;

3. To order the HVO to release all civilians and to treat military prisoners of war in accordance with international conventions;

We also reiterate our demand that the city of Mostar be proclaimed a protected zone.

Unfortunately, I must emphasise the fact that in addition to the two nationalist armies, responsibility for the tragedy of the Muslims in Bosnia also lies with those in the international community who have imposed an arms embargo on this people, which has effectively tied its hands and deprived it of the right to self defence guaranteed by the UN Charter.

Gentlemen,

This time I call upon you to grant to the people who are not permitted to defend themselves at least the right to survive.

There was no real reaction other than verbal condemnations. Every objective observer had the impression that Bosnia had been abandoned to its fate. Noel Malcolm, who was just then completing his book *Bosnia: A Short History*, wrote:

> The years 1992 and 1993 will be remembered as the years in which a European country was destroyed. It was a land with a political and cultural history unlike that of any other country

in Europe. The great religions and great powers of European history had overlapped and combined there: the Empires of Rome, Charlemagne, the Ottomans and the Austro-Hungarians, and the faiths of Western Christianity, Eastern Christianity, Judaism and Islam.

In the early hours of 16 April 1993, HVO soldiers invaded the village of Ahmići, near Vitez, and committed atrocities that shook the world. More than 100 civilians were killed and massacred, among them many women and children. The perpetrators of this atrocity are on trial before the Hague International Tribunal.

There is no such thing as a clean war or a blameless army, however. All wars are dirty, to a greater or lesser extent. Although we took every opportunity to remind our soldiers of their duty to uphold the laws of war, and to control their behaviour as much as we could, from time to time news reached us that things were not as they should be on our side either.

In early August I received a letter from the Co-Chairs of the Geneva Conference, Owen and Stoltenberg, on alleged atrocities by the Bosnian Army in the village of Doljani. The accusations came from the Croat side. I called General Delić on the telephone and asked for information on what had happened, and on 8 August sent him a letter reading as follows:

> A few days ago I requested by telephone that the accusations of the HVO that one of our army units massacred a number of civilians of Croat nationality in the village of Doljani near Jablanica be looked into.
>
> I have not yet received any report on this, and I must ask you to inform me of the results of the investigations and to make these known to the general public.
>
> Please take every opportunity to remind our troops of their duty to uphold the laws of war. Do not hesitate to punish offenders severely nor to inform the general public of this. We have nothing to lose thereby.

A few days later, Delić informed me that there were no indications whatsoever that the Bosnian Army had committed any atrocities in Doljani. I sent a copy of Delić's response to Owen and Stoltenberg, proposing an international inquiry:

> Dear Sirs, in reference to the accusations by the HVO that a number of civilians of Croat nationality have been massacred in the village of Doljani near Jablanica, I requested the Chief of General Staff of the Army of Bosnia and Herzegovina to investigate these charges and to inform me of the results as a matter of urgency. I enclose a copy of my letter and the response from General Rasim Delić (in both Bosnian and English).
>
> Since the information he supplies conflicts with the charges of the HVO, I request your assistance in establishing the truth in relation to these events. I have full confidence in the findings in this regard of the International Red Cross and UNPRO-FOR. I am convinced that we shall meet with your understanding and cooperation in this regard.

Owen and Stoltenberg said nothing further on the matter.

However, if the accusations of an alleged atrocity in Doljani was the product of Croat propaganda, the atrocity in Grabovica against Croat civilians was the brutal truth. On 8 September 1993, during the course of the operation 'Neretva 93', a group of our soldiers massacred 27 Croat civilians in this village on the River Neretva. On learning of the atrocity, General Delić called on Sefer Halilović, who was commanding the 'Neretva 93' action, to submit a report, but it appears he never received it. However, many of the circumstances of the tragedy would become known two months later in the context of the military and police action 'Trebević 1', conducted in Sarajevo on 26 October. During the investigation into the insurrection and crimes in Sarajevo, the Military Prosecutor's Office, which was part of the Ministry of Justice, acquired a great deal of information on the atrocity in Grabovica, but the charges and trial were set up solely for the Sarajevo case. In autumn 1997, the Department of Military Security submitted criminal charges on the Grabovica atrocity to the Cantonal Prosecutor's Office in Sarajevo. The prosecution took up the case and, in accordance with the Rome 'Rules of the Road', requested the agreement of the Hague International Tribunal to initiate court proceedings against the suspects, upon which the Hague Tribunal took over the entire case and all the documentation relating to it.

The proclamation of the Autonomous Region of Western Bosnia issued by Fikret Abdić on 27 September 1993 further exacerbated the already extremely difficult position of the Army of Bosnia and Herzegovina, in particular the 5th Corps. The opening up of a third front, and Fikret

Abdić's collaboration with the Serb and Croat aggressors, made the overall military and political situation in Bosnia and Herzegovina as difficult as it could be.

On 4 October I travelled to New York to address the UN General Assembly.

Extracts From Speech At The United Nations General Assembly

(New York, 7 October 1993)

The international community has neither a defined policy nor a clear plan of political action to alleviate the transition from the communist structures that were in power for 50 years to the concepts founded on freedom and democracy...

The negative aspects of this problem are portrayed to the fullest extent in my country. It is clear to see that we are under pressure from surviving forces of communist aggression, and that the eradication of every chance for democratic development has taken place before the very eyes of Europe, America and the world as a whole. This was effected by the use of force, involving mass murders of civilians, the elimination of every trace of civilisation and culture, and the barbaric tactics of burning and ravaging our country.

At the same time, this unprecedented violence is being used as an experiment for the political vivisection of our country. It is being carried out by the international community, which is evidently using Bosnia and Herzegovina as the testing-ground for various models of a post-communist state...

The first experiment was that of the London Conference. This concept, which sought to halt the aggression, was abandoned without even a single attempt to implement it. All that happened was that the war being fought over our land increased in intensity. There then followed an attempt to find in constitutional, legal and political reform a solution to an ever-deepening crisis. No one even tried to apply this solution, known as the Vance-Owen Plan. It was abandoned in order to be replaced by another, based on the flawed thesis that what was happening in Bosnia and Herzegovina was a civil war between three peoples, and that for this reason the only solution was territorial partition... As a result of this, the uncontrolled course of events continued, with renewed sufferings for the people.

Mr. President, the people of Bosnia and Herzegovina face a choice today: either a just war of defence or an unjust peace. If the war continues, there is a heightened risk of the people suffering still further, and even of our nation's destruction. It could mean the deaths of thousands of people. An unjust peace is unacceptable, since it is based on a concept of ethnic partition and apartheid that is proven by history to be a failure...

And yet these unacceptable elements in the so-called peace plan being imposed on us are not merely of a philosophical nature. Firstly, any plan that legitimises genocide and promotes ethnic partition is far more likely to sow the seeds of further aggression and to light the fires of revenge. Secondly, any peace that pays no attention to the causes of the war will, at best, offer only temporary surcease, but not a true solution, which is now fundamental...

In conformity with its authority and responsibility, the UN Security Council should evaluate the Plan drawn up by Lord Owen and Mr. Stoltenberg, to determine how far it is consistent with the United Nations Charter and the numerous Resolutions earlier adopted by the Security Council.

The Council cannot evade its responsibility by taking cover behind the often-repeated excuse: 'We shall accept everything that the three sides agree upon...' when one side, that of the victim, is under pressure from the real threat of mass starvation and genocide...

After a year of siege, the signs of anarchy began to make themselves seen in Sarajevo. Some of the units defending the city were increasingly disregarding military discipline and the authority of the Supreme Command HQ, of which the then Chief was Sefer Halilović, a competent officer, but a man of insufficient personal courage. In December 1992 open armed conflict flared up between the army and the so-called Special Purpose Unit commanded by Juka Prazina. Jealousies arose between individual commanders, threatening to undermine the defence of the city – from the very start there had been a latent conflict smouldering between police units and the army. News came in of ill-treatment of Serbs and of illegal raids in which civilians were conscripted for the dangerous task of digging trenches at the front. Everything indicated that Sefer Halilović had insufficient authority among the troops to be able to handle the situation. On 30 May 1993 we suffered a catastrophe on Trebević. In a heroic but ill-conceived action 29 combatants of the 1st Alpine Brigade were killed. It was the straw that broke the camel's back. I resolved to propose that Halilović be dismissed from the topmost post in the army. At a session of the Presidency of the Republic of Bosnia and Herzegovina held on 8 June 1993, the office of Commandant of the Army was introduced and Rasim Delić was appointed, a serious man and a very highly trained officer. Prior to this the post was offered to Džemail Šarac, a prominent general of the former Yugoslav Army, but he refused on the grounds that the post required someone younger and in better health. All operational authority in the army was transferred to the Commandant. Halilović retained the position of Chief of General Staff of the Supreme Command, but was subordinate in all respects to the new Army Commandant.

There was another circumstance that influenced this decision. A few days earlier (to be precise, on 27 May 1993), I received a four-page letter from General Divjak, then Deputy Chief of Staff of the Supreme Command. In his letter Divjak complained of the attitude towards him and of the behaviour of armed people towards the citizens of Sarajevo, citing as instances:

– that when visiting the Konjic-Jablanica front, troops from the local brigade had arrested him and held him in custody for 27 days;
– that individual commanders of military units on the ground were behaving very heavy-handedly towards civilians;
– that there were private prisons in Hrasnica and Dobrinja;
– that sick people were being conscripted to dig trenches and made to work for 12 hours a day;
– that in all these cases the violent conduct of the Commander of the 10th Alpine Brigade, Mušana-Cace Topalsvic particularly stood out.

Divjak did not say so explicitly, but it could be deduced from his letter that the attitude towards him was caused by his being a Serb and that the victims of ill-treatment were for the most part Serbs, though not exclusively (a tailor by the name of Hajro was mentioned, and one Mehmedović Meho, both Muslims, etc.).[8] I sought an explanation from HQ of Divjak's complaints. It was clear from the report that Divjak was surrounded by distrust and suspicion, and that many of his accusations were well-founded. Unproven but persistent stories of the ill-treatment of Serbs in the city were in any case becoming ever more frequent. The accusations also related, though to a lesser extent, to the soldiers of the

[8] The full text of Divjak's letter is to be found in the Appendices.

9th Brigade, of which the *de facto* Commander was Ramiz Delalić Ćelo (who was formally Deputy Commander).

The 9th and 10th Brigades held a large part of the northern and southern lines of defence of besieged Sarajevo (the 9th Alpine Brigade held the line Slatina-Grdonj-Pašino *brdo* (hills), and the 10th the line from the Assembly building on the River Miljacka to Debelo *brdo* and Ćolina *kapa* (huts)). The troops of these brigades had bought their firearms at the beginning of the war, and were intensely loyal to their commanders. To tame these mutinous people and impose military discipline on them was like trying to saddle wild mustangs. Any showdown with their commanders could lead to a clash with the entire brigade, and to their abandoning the lines. It was essential to proceed with extreme caution.

On 2 July 1993 some of the men from the 9th and 10th Brigades blocked all the bridges over the Miljacka from the Vijećnica (Town Hall) to Skenderija, and the police stations throughout the eastern part of the city. Through the good offices of the Commander of the Delta Unit, Dino Aljić, I negotiated all night and succeeded in having the rebel soldiers withdraw to barracks and their lines. I decided, however, to do everything necessary to ensure that the situation did not repeat itself and finally to introduce proper order among the units defending the city. The following day I summoned the Army Commander Delić and the Minister of the Interior Alispahić, who was in charge of police units, to my office. I told them to draw up a plan to put an end to the arbitrary behaviour of the two renegade brigades.

The preparations for this highly delicate and risky operation took much longer than we had expected. It was necessary to take armed action against our own units in a city that was surrounded by a far stronger enemy. The action, originally planned for September, was postponed until October, and then again postponed day after day almost until the end of the month. Meanwhile, as an integral part of the plan, one by one members of the Crni Labudovi or Black Swans from Kakanj were transferred into the city through the tunnel under the airport runway in order to take part in the action.

The Executive Board of the SDA issued a statement on lawlessness in the army during its session of 23 October 1993. The statement read:

> Based on the duty and responsibility of the Party for Democratic Action to strengthen the defence capacity of the peoples of Bosnia and Herzegovina, and in the light of the current military and security situation in Sarajevo, the Executive Board of the SDA finds that in certain units of the 1st Corps of the

Army of Bosnia and Herzegovina the leadership and command system has been under serious threat for some time now. This directly calls into question the effectiveness of carrying out combat missions and undermines the efforts of the Army of Bosnia and Herzegovina and the people in their difficult struggle against the aggressor. Occurrences of crime and arbitrary conduct among members of the Armed Forces are also becoming more marked. By their unlawful behaviour, individuals in certain units in Sarajevo are damaging the good name acquired by these units in the heroic defence of the city. The Executive Board of the SDA therefore calls upon the authorities, above all the Presidency of Bosnia and Herzegovina and the Supreme Command Headquarters of the Army of Bosnia and Herzegovina, to review the situation and to take steps to introduce law and order and thereby restore the wavering confidence of the people in their army and their state. Only an organised and synchronised battle can be successful; war, and the state of war, cannot be an excuse for self-will and lawlessness.

In order to maintain the secrecy of the operation, the session of the Presidency at which the decision would be taken on the operation was convened on 25 October just before midnight. The action was planned for the early hours of 26 October.

The decision was also taken at this session to order the dismissal of Mušana-Cace Topalsvic and Ramiz Delalić from their command positions in the 9th and 10th Brigades and to take them into custody. 'The use of force in order to implement this decision, should it prove necessary, is permitted,' the Presidency's decree states.

Sarajevo awoke to complete silence on 26 October. By chance, there was not even any shelling. Part of the 9th Brigade, stationed in buildings opposite the Catholic graveyard on Koševo, soon surrendered, at seven in the morning. The rest, in Romanijska Street, continued to resist until late in the afternoon. Dr. Haris Silajdžić and Bakir Alispahić went into the base, which was surrounded on all sides, and persuaded Ramiz Delalić that further resistance was pointless. Mušana-Cace Topalsvic had barricaded himself into his night base in Bistrik, along with a large group of civilians as hostages. He was lying in wait for incautious policemen, and killing them one by one – nine of them in all. We did not know what to do. If we stormed the building, it would mean the death of the hostages, of whom there were between 40 and 50, mainly women and children, hastily collected up from the surrounding houses.

In the early evening I sent Jusuf Pušina, an Adviser to the Presidency, to see if he could convince Cace to surrender. Cace refused, and Pušina brought us the news of the policemen he had killed, whose bodies were lined up in the courtyard.

The hostages' agony continued. I called Cace on the telephone and told him that at 11.30 Jusuf Pušina and my escorts Haris Lukav and Osman Mehmedagić, whom he knew well, would come for him. I also told him not to open fire, that he would be taken to Command HQ and that he would be treated according to the law.

Around midnight Cace and a number of the men in his command surrendered without a struggle. He was taken to the Command HQ of the 1st Corps in Đure Đakovića Street (now Ali-pašina street). There he was physically attacked by friends of the policemen he had killed. There was a real danger of his being lynched. To avoid the worst, he was bundled into a car with the intention of transferring him to the District Prison. On the way, as the car was making its way along Koševo Street, Cace suddenly wrenched himself free, opened the car door and tried to escape. The guards opened fire. This was the official report. In the first news broadcast of the morning, the TVBiH announcer reported that Caco had been taken prisoner the previous night and had been killed while attempting to escape.

150 men from the 9th and 10th Brigades were held in custody while an investigation was conducted. Most of them were soon released, and sent to the front lines on Trebević and Grdonj. Eighteen of them were charged and tried for murder and armed insurrection. Law and order prevailed in the city. Danger now threatened only from the hills.

Immediately before these events, in October, Foreign Minister Dr. Haris Silajdžić had finally returned from abroad after a period of dealing very successfully with affairs relating to the recognition and affirmation of Bosnia and Herzegovina as an independent and sovereign state. We needed to form a new government. It was assumed that the new prime minister would be Haris Silajdžić. At the end of October, Silajdžić formed a Government without great difficulty, and presented it to the Presidency (Edib Bukvić, Hamdija Hadžihasanović, Bakir Alispahić, Irfan Ljubijankić, Sead Kreso, Kasim Trnka, Rusmir Mahmutćehaić, Faruk Smailbegović, Munever Imamović, Dragoljub Stojanov, Arif Smajkić, Mustafa Beganović, Enes Duraković and Ivo Knežević). There was some discussion about who should have the Refugee portfolio. The SDA candidate was Amila Omersoftić but Haris preferred Dr. Arif Smajkić and his choice was accepted; the real drama, however, arose around Rusmir Mahmutćehaić. Silajdžić proposed that Mahmutćehaić's portfolio be split, with Energy moving across to the jurisdiction of the Ministry of the Economy. It had been noticed that Mahmutćehaić was using his control over energy supplies (at that time chiefly petroleum) to gain control over the army and even other portfolios. One day, when I was looking for General Delić, I found him waiting in line outside the office of the Minister of Energy and Military Industry (as Mahmutćehaić's Ministry was called) to obtain the Minister's personal warrant for some fuel for the army. Mahmutćehaić opposed the separation of Energy from his Ministry, and gave an ultimatum that if it was separated he would resign. The problem remained unresolved for a few days. One evening, during a visit to the Zenica Steelworks, Mahmutćehaić came up to me and asked for my support in retaining Energy Affairs within his Ministry. When I refused, Mahmutćehaić resigned. Thereafter, he changed from being a minister into a 'critic of everything in existence' in Bosnia.

During the second half of November 1993, immediately after the liberation of Vareš, I spent 12 days in free territory (from 6 to 17 November). I visited 17 towns, and spoke with the war leadership of 32 municipalities. On my return, I gave a long interview to RTVBiH which was conducted by the General Manager of RTVBiH, Mufid Memija. I have selected three questions and answers for inclusion here.

Interview for RTVBiH
– Abridged Version –
(18 November 1993)

Memija: The problem of food has become the prime question, and I fear that this misfortune may become even more dangerous than the Chetniks and the Ustasha.

Izetbegović: This is an issue that weighed on me the whole time during my tour of free territory. The people are not demoralised, however, although they are faced by this problem and know very well what the situation is. But then, even as we speak, a conference is going on in Geneva with our delegation present, headed by Silajdžić; it's up to him to do everything to lift this blockade, in other words to find a way for food to get through. Our view is that it's not important whether it comes in via Serbia or via Croatia; we even agree with the Bar-Sarajevo corridor. Of course, there is also the food that might come from Macedonia. It left Skopje yesterday, in a commercial convoy, and we are anxiously waiting to see if it will get through or not. In short, food remains an issue that we have to face, and that we shall continue to try to resolve with all the determination that such an important matter merits.

Memija: Certain stages in your tour of free territories should be particularly highlighted. Vareš, above all. You were in Vareš immediately after it was liberated by units of the 2nd and 3rd Corps. You then issued an appeal that was exceptionally well received both among the international and, of course, our own general public, calling on the Croats who had not moved out to remain, and on those who had already left to return.

Izetbegović: Yes, and that appeal still holds good, although it is difficult to make contact with those people. We arranged for a delegation to leave here, but it was stopped up on Kobiljača. The delegation included Monsignor Vinko Puljić and Fra Petar Anđelović. The people who had left their homes were in a sense torn between the HVO militants, who were seeking to convince them not to return to Vareš, and ourselves, who were appealing to them to return home. This emigration of the Croat population was clearly an integral part of a plan, the so-called Boban Plan, to create a kind of Croat statelet down there in which all the Croats of Bosnia and Herzegovina would be brought together. Boban said – and I have read the material – that there are 700,000 Croats scattered throughout the region, from Neum in the south to the River Sava in the north, and that they should be brought together to form a compact unit in a single territory. The diversity of Bosnia does not bother us, on the contrary, for us it is an enrichment. I must be honest and say that our people asked me why we want the Croats back when Boban is forcing us to leave Herzegovina. My answer was that Boban's methods are not ours, for we are a state while they are a parastate; we are an army while they are paramilitaries, or in fact just gangs. One can certainly say that it was gangs of people that carried out the ethnic cleansing of Mostar and Stolac, and that recently destroyed the Old Bridge in Mostar. But there is another, more practical side to the issue. One of these people was from Herzegovina, and I asked him, 'Do you want us to return to Stolac?' He naturally said that he did. So I told him that the only way for us to return to Stolac was for the Croats to stay in Vareš. Boban's ugly plan had two stages, you see. The first was to cleanse the area, to clear Mostar,

Stolac, Čapljina, Ljubuški, Livno and so on of Muslims, and then to herd his own people into that Bobanistan, as we call it, from the north, from Bosnia, from the south, like cattle. But if we don't want the plan to be carried out, we have to convince our Croat fellow citizens to stay in their own homes, we mustn't help Boban by driving the Croats out of Vareš. So that is the practical side of the problem, if we set aside for a second the purely moral, principled side of the issue. Bosnia and Herzegovina must be a true state governed by the rule of law. People should know that just before leaving Vareš, HVO militants were using megaphones to call on the people to go, telling them they had an hour to leave the town, because the Bosnian Army was coming and, the militants claimed, was burning and killing everything that came in its path. The people didn't know what was really happening and couldn't take the risk. In any case, we shall never be the ones who expel people. You see how strangely history repeats itself. Here and now in Bosnia we are seeing images like those of the Second World War. I remember that war very well. I was 16 when it began, and 20 when it ended. Then, too, there were Chetniks and Ustasha; and here they are again. The difference is that these Chetniks are worse than the Chetniks of that time, these Ustasha worse than those Ustasha. I can say this with complete confidence, because the Ustasha of that time didn't destroy the Old Bridge, nor the mosques of Mostar, and these have done so…

Memija: Would you care to comment on Tuđman's latest statement on Bosnia and Herzegovina?

Izetbegović: Yes, it is a very regrettable and a very unpleasant statement. If I understand it correctly, it announces some kind of invasion of Bosnia. Unfortunately, we are already seeing an invasion, though not perhaps on a mass scale, since we know that there are already Croatian Army troops fighting around Gornji Vakuf. I gave orders yesterday for the precise details to be determined. We shall then request a session of the UN Security Council and call for protection. It seems that Mr. Tuđman tried to use the HVO to conquer part of Bosnia, and that when this failed, since the HVO has been defeated here – that is the rebel part of the HVO, he decided to become directly involved in order to conquer where the HVO had failed. But Tuđman has given other statements, too. He has called for a kind of crusader war against what he calls the creation of an Islamic republic here. Our people know whether an Islamic republic is being created here or not. Naturally, we want Islam to be present here and we want the Muslims to be free, but we have absolutely no intention of creating an Islamic republic. Tuđman is taking the Milošević line, except that he is doing so a few years later.

On 9 December I was invited to give a lecture to graduates at a seminar held by the Department of Morals of the General Staff of the Army of Bosnia and Herzegovina, which was being held in the Army Club in Sarajevo. I used the occasion to speak about the conduct of soldiers:

> When you leave here, it will be to tell the soldiers certain things. Tell them that they must not persecute the weak. Ensure that the people have no fear of this army. I do not know to what extent this is the case at present. To some extent it is so. Passions are running high, terrible things have been committed on all sides, and people often cannot distinguish one thing from another. Recently two priests were killed in Fojnica. The case is still being investigated. But assuming that the murderer was one of us, whether a civilian or a soldier, his attitude would have been – they destroyed our Old Bridge, let's get back at them… But who is this 'them'? The Franciscans and the Ustasha are not the same. This way of thinking gets us nowhere. I repeat, we must be an army that the people regard as their own, and we shall then be unconquerable. Even if all the satanic forces of this world were to be assembled, they will be powerless against us if we have the people with us. This is my first message. Convey it to the people, and do so in simple language, so that the man in the street can understand you.
>
> You see, God has presented us with a painful challenge. We have been slaughtered, our women and children murdered, our mosques destroyed, but we shall not kill women and children, we shall not destroy churches. We shall not do so, because this is not our way, although it has happened in isolated cases. There are combatants here too, and I take this opportunity to tell them – and this is a message that should be passed on to everyone here and elsewhere – that we shall be victorious because we respect others' religions, and others' nations, and other political convictions, and because we strive to be decent people even in our difficult situation. In any case, the destruction of others' places of worship is explicitly forbidden to us. It is thanks to this prohibition that in Serbia, where the Turks

ruled for 400 years and who were not exactly the mildest of people, to this day the Dečani, Gračanica and Sopoćani monasteries are still in existence. They remained untouched because it is so written in the Book that we respect. It is written that such acts must not be committed, and people have observed this. When we do so and when we say that we wish to respect churches and the faith of others, we are not only upholding the finest traditions of European democracy, which the world has slowly groped its way to through the ages, but also directly and literally respecting the precepts of our Holy Book.[9]

Here is how the conversation on the same subject went for the German newspaper *Stern* (5 November 1994):

> *Stern*: Mr. President, you are known as a Muslim of the European tradition and tolerance, open to the world as a whole, but reports are appearing in the Western press now of the so-called Islamisation of Bosnia and Herzegovina. Are these merely rumours?
>
> Izetbegović: I shall be very frank: these are not merely rumours. A return to faith is an almost universal phenomenon wherever communism brutally suppressed religion for 50 or 70 years. There is Islamisation, as you call it, in Bosnia, but only to the same extent as Christianisation, in the form of a renewed interest in religion among Bosnian Catholics and Orthodox Christians. But Christianisation does not register with Christian Europe, which is not sensitive to the phenomenon, something I understand and do not hold against it. I must just correct you on one point, however: my tolerance is not of European but of Muslim origin. If I am tolerant, it is first and foremost as a Muslim, and only then as a European. Europe has some delusions from which it is completely unable to free itself, despite the glaring facts. During this war in Bosnia, for example, hundreds of churches and mosques have been destroyed. All of them were destroyed by 'Europeans', not one by Bosniacs. The Turkish authorities were not the mildest of rulers, but every Christian people and all of their most important mediaeval monuments survived the 500 years of Turkish rule. That is a fact. The famous monasteries of the Fruška Gora hills, not far from Belgrade, survived 300 years of Turkish rule but did not outlast three years of 'European' rule. They were burned down during the Second

---

[9] Izetbegović, *Čudo Bosanskog Otpora* (The Miracle of the Bosnian Resistance), 1994, pp. 27-28.

World War. Fascism and communism are not Asian products but European. And even now, Europe has not shown much sensitivity towards the emergence of fascism in the Balkans. I value and appreciate Europe, but I think it has too high an opinion of itself.

During the winter of 1993-1994 the situation on the lines of confrontation with the HVO was exceptionally difficult, particularly near Mostar and Gornji Vakuf. The pointlessness of the conflict was obvious, but it continued all the same. Food was running short in the besieged towns. Religious leaders in Sarajevo and Zagreb were behind initiatives to send food convoys to the areas most at risk. The first two convoys were sent to Bila, which was under HVO control, and Maglaj, under the control of the army. The Bila convoy reached its destination, but came under crossfire near Gornji Vakuf. The Maglaj convoy was halted in Zenica, since the HVO refused to allow it to go through Žepče. Very soon after this, on 23 December 1993, I received a letter from Tuđman in which he blamed the army for the attack near Gornji Vakuf. I checked out his allegations and replied by letter on 13 January 1993. I informed him that we had approached the Security Council, and indirectly proposed talks, with the warning that we could not be expected to negotiate with the executioners of the Bosniac people. I was thinking, of course, of Boban.

> I write in reply to your letter of 23 December 1993. I agree that the humanitarian situation in Bosnia and Herzegovina is extremely grave, but this, it seems, is the only matter on which the two of us can wholly agree at this time. It is obvious that we see certain facts relating to this situation in a totally different way. First, the convoy for Nova Bila reached its destination, that for Maglaj did not. The Maglaj convoy is still parked and waiting in Zenica... We are sorry for the victims, but we did not start this war, nor did we start the incident near Gornji Vakuf. The Army of Bosnia and Herzegovina is legally defending this town against the HVO paramilitary units that are attempting to seize it and are responsible for ravaging the town and for the death of hundreds of its inhabitants. The alleged message from the Deputy Commander of the 3rd Corps, D•emo Merdan, is a complete fabrication from start to finish. Our army is not killing women and children. What evidence do you have, Mr. President, for this grave libel against the Army of Bosnia and Herzegovina? I regard it as wholly inappropriate to introduce an unverified, and in my view fabricated, statement

into our correspondence. As for the Army of Bosnia and Herzegovina, I should like to make myself perfectly clear; the presence of the Army of Bosnia and Herzegovina on every part of the territory of Bosnia and Herzegovina is legal and legitimate to the same extent that the presence of other military units that do not recognise the supreme command of the Presidency of Bosnia and Herzegovina is illegal and unacceptable. The Army of Bosnia and Herzegovina cannot be the aggressor in its own country. Only an army sent in from other centres without the consent of the Presidency of Bosnia and Herzegovina can be so… The authorities under HVO control have set up camps and incarcerated tens of thousands of innocent civilians in them. You have persistently rejected this assertion as defamatory. A few days ago your Foreign Minister boasted, in a letter to the UN Security Council, of the fact that the Croatian Government had, I quote, 'released 5,600 Muslim prisoners.' How is it possible to release prisoners from camps that do not exist? I deliberately do not introduce here the background to the conflict in Herzegovina, accompanied by the ethnic cleansing of the Muslim population from Mostar, Stolac, Čapljina, Livno and other places, of which the crowning act of barbarism was the destruction of the Old Bridge. I do not quote the disturbing facts on the presence of the Croatian armed forces on the territory of Bosnia and Herzegovina, which points to the open interference of Croatia in the internal affairs of Bosnia and Herzegovina, since this is the subject of our letter to the UN Security Council. But despite all this, I want to convey to you our sincere interest in improving relations between our two countries, and the development of all forms of cooperation, but, for all this, genuine changes in your policy towards Bosnia and Herzegovina are needed. What is more, as I have already told you several times, you cannot expect us to negotiate on improving relations with those who are known to be the executioners of the Bosniac people.

Not long after I sent this icy response, Tuđman used the good offices of Dr. Mate Granić, his Foreign Minister at the time and one of the more reasonable people in the Croatian Government, to offer talks on an end to the conflict. The message was conveyed to me by Dr. Haris Silajdžić, and I accepted at once. There followed talks in Washington and the establishment of the Federation of Bosnia and Herzegovina. According to certain information, the brains behind the idea of creating the Federation was Ivo Komšić, a highly-regarded independent Croat politician who was at the time a member of the Presidency of Bosnia and Herzegovina.

Nevertheless, I believe that the combination of our military and political pressure had an impact on Tuđman's rapid decision to sit with us around the negotiating table. The military pressure was that of our forces on Vitez, which began on 15 January 1995 and reached a peak in early February. The political pressure was more important, and related to our threat to notify the Security Council of the blatant interference of Croatia in the war in Bosnia and Herzegovina. This second matter was particularly awkward for Tuđman, particularly after the atrocities in Ahmići and Stupni Do.

The Federation that was established by the Washington Agreements – which was the result of force, not conviction and political will – vegetated for a long time. It needed a great deal of time, with steps forward and back again, to establish freedom of movement and a partly mixed police and administration, but what was most important was that the fighting stopped almost at once. Many of the institutions of the supposedly abolished parastate of Herzeg-Bosnia have continued functioning to this day. They are gradually dwindling away, however, not gaining in strength.

Immediately after the New Year 1994, I received a greetings card from a soldier. He enclosed a letter with the card, complaining that his commanding officer had taken the name of God in vain. He asked why he had to endure this now, as he had had to in the former JNA, where such curses were to be heard every day. I addressed this issue in a speech I made at a formal session of the SDA Main Board, held on 12 January in Sarajevo:

> Four or five days ago I held a consultation with the military leadership near Konjic. I concluded the meeting with a recommendation to our officers. The recommendation was very short, and read thus: 'Resemble the nation you originate from. It is a courageous, intelligent and proud nation, there is no need to shy away from resembling it, and even sharing some of its shortcomings.' When I addressed this message to the soldiers, I was thinking of something quite specific. Our nation is a nation of believers, even if it does not cross the threshold of the mosque so often, as we well know. But don't touch any of the things it holds sacred. There are occurrences of some officers cursing God. This must not happen. We shall not ask

our officers whether they observe the fast or go to the mosque. We ask of them that they fight honestly, and let them believe what they will. But they shall not curse God. This is my message today, and I think that it is the message of all of you. Unfortunately, these things happen, and many of our soldiers complain about it to me.

Perhaps I was a little unjust to our officers in this speech, since respect for religion was the rule in the Army of Bosnia and Herzegovina. The instances I referred to were the exception.

On 3 February 1994 there was a rather stormy session of the Presidency of the Republic of Bosnia and Herzegovina. Nijaz Duraković complained that sessions of the Presidency were not being held often enough, that certain decisions were being taken individually, independently of the institutional system, and that responsibilities and duties should be equally distributed among the Presidency members. Both Kljuić and Pejanović shared his criticisms, albeit in somewhat milder form. For the most part the objection was justified, and I said so during the session. It was important to maintain the unity of the Presidency in these exceptionally difficult times. A statement issued after the session noted, among other things:

> In the light of certain quandaries and controversial views that are being brought into the public domain, relating primarily to the situation of and relationships within the Presidency itself, the Presidency of the Republic of Bosnia and Herzegovina has resolved as follows:
>
> First, there are no personal clashes nor is there a power struggle being conducted. On the contrary, full political unity is expressed in regard to the basic issues of the internationally recognised State of Bosnia and Herzegovina, the struggle to safeguard its territorial integrity and sovereignty and its democratic, civil character. Full support for the liberation struggle and the Army of Bosnia and Herzegovina is also expressed, together with the commitment to establish a just peace, so that the Presidency rejects as unfounded and malicious all speculation in this regard.
>
> The members of the Presidency are of one mind in their view that there is no place for political dissension at these decisive historical moments, and such criticisms as exist are primarily directed at strengthening the position and role of the Presidency itself and of the other legal institutions of state.

The Chetnik 'speciality' was attacks on hospitals, libraries, marketplaces and the queues for bread and water. The last type were particularly tragic: a single well-aimed shell could kill dozens of people, sometimes entire families. On 15 January 1993 a shell was launched at a water queue in Sarajevo. It was two in the afternoon, when about 300 people, including women and children, were waiting on that icy January day to fill their canisters. Eight people were killed, including a married couple, Azra and Asim Lačević, their daughter Dalila and another 40 people were seriously injured (Dalila is now living in Chicago, where she has married). On 5 February 1994 a shell fired from Serb positions on Mrkovići killed 68 civilians and injured 142 when it landed on the packed Markale Marketplace. Only the day before, nine Sarajevans were killed by shelling in the suburb of Dobrinja. Among the dead were a brother and sister, Mirza and Selma Spahić.

On 5 February, and again on 7 February, I sent a letter to Manfred Werner, the then NATO Secretary-General. The second letter ended with these words: 'Gentlemen, the hell in Sarajevo has already lasted for more than 700 days. It is high time that the Serb killing machine, which kills people and destroys places of worship, schools and hospitals, is brought to a halt and eliminated.'

These two tragedies involving the citizens of Sarajevo, following hard one upon the other, for a moment awoke the conscience of the West. On 9 February NATO sent an ultimatum to the Serbs to withdraw their heavy weapons from around Sarajevo to a radius of 20 kilometres from the city centre (the 'exclusion zone'), with a deadline of ten days. After procrastinating for a while, the Serbs accepted the ultimatum but – believe it or not – celebrated it as a victory. They barbecued oxen and celebrated by firing into the air on Trebević. On 20 February the UN Secretary-General's Representative in Bosnia and Herzegovina, the Japanese Yasushi Akashi, announced that there was no reason to call for air strikes against Karadžić's Serbs since, in his judgement, they had met the demands.

It will never be known for sure whether the Serbs had really withdrawn their heavy weapons from around Sarajevo or whether Akashi simply wanted to see it that way; whether he had had the wool pulled over his eyes and, if so, whether willingly. But in spring news began to reach us that the Serb artillery was all around the city. By July this was confirmed beyond doubt. On 31 July, I sent a letter to the NATO Secretary-General and to the UNPROFOR Headquarters in Zagreb requesting effective action to protect all the 'safe areas', and particularly the exclusion zones around Sarajevo and Goražde. Nothing was done. Both the UN and NATO passed over the violation of their 9 February ultimatum in silence. In August the shells began to land on the city once again, at first here and there, but by September it was the same hell as the year before. This was to last another full year, practically until the mass air strikes by NATO that began on 30 August 1995. At one point during this period, on 7 May 1995 to be precise, Dr. Haris Silajdžić appeared before the TV cameras in the presence of a number of ambassadors accredited to Sarajevo and, on the occasion of the shelling of Butmir where nine were killed and more than 40 injured, quoted the numbers of victims of the continued shelling of Sarajevo. These figures showed that in the previous eight months, in other words since the introduction of the exclusion zone, shells and sniper bullets had killed 240 civilians in Sarajevo, of whom 26 were killed in April alone. On 1 May, there were 14 civilian casualties in a single day. His statement made a certain impression on those present, but the shelling continued.

There was a particular cynicism around the constant suspicions that we were shelling ourselves. Almost invariably, when an opinion was called for on the position from which a particularly murderous shell had been fired, UNPROFOR experts (never named, always remaining anonymous) would give an unspecific response: the shell could have been fired from either Serb or Muslim positions. NATO Commander General Joulwan, in an interview he gave many years later for the Sarajevo daily *Avaz*, on 8 July 2000, was to complain that UNPROFOR officers 'would never give a clear name to things. I asked them to interpret the events as they were, but it didn't happen,' said Joulwan. The intentionally vague responses paralysed all action in advance, even had there been the political will for action in the first place. The indifferent world could go on living without any pangs of conscience, and the killing of civilians continued. At the SDA Convention on 25 March 1994, speaking of the situation in Sarajevo, I said:

> Sarajevo will be remembered worldwide as a symbol of suffering, but also as a symbol of resistance. It is said that 700,000 shells have been fired at us. So it was a kind of test of human resistance. Thanks be to God, we have withstood that test. It has been shown that it is not important how strong someone is to deliver a blow, but how strong he is to resist the blow.

In an action code-named 'Spring 94', on 12 April 1994, our troops stormed and seized the stronghold of Vijenac near Tuzla. In this attack 1,200 troops of the 2nd Corps forced back about 400 enemy troops from their position. 53 enemy soldiers were killed and 56 taken prisoner. Our losses were three killed and 25 wounded.

Also in spring 1994 (from 27 March to 25 April), Serb forces prepared and carried out an offensive operation on Goražde, which had been declared a UN safe area, with the objective of occupying it and liquidating or expelling the town's defence forces and civilian population. The crisis reached a peak in early April. On Sunday 10 April, NATO carried out limited air strikes on Serb positions around the town. At this time demonstrations in support of the defenders of Goražde were being held in Istanbul and certain other Turkish towns, and on 12 April a large number of students demonstrated outside the French Assemblée Nationale in Paris, as a sign of protest against Serb attacks on this 'safe area'. Though heavily outnumbered, the defenders of Goražde – some 6,000 of them – supported by the entire population of the town, managed to hold out against the attacking forces for almost a month. Both our and enemy casualties were very high.

On 10 October 1994, troops of OG-7 South carried out an attack on the Husar Compound and liberated it in a 20-minute attack. This was important for operations towards Teslić. From 1 to 3 October and from 28 to 31 October, troops of the 1st Corps carried out two offensive operations in the Treskavica area and liberated 60 km^2, which to a large extent drove the Serb forces back from the 'gateway' to Sarajevo.

Bosnia was changing under the terrible impact of the war. I wondered what was left of it after all this; was it still alive after enduring so many blows? At the SDA Convention on 25 March 1994 I tried to answer the question:

> I often wonder what Bosnia is, after all that has happened. What is Bosnia today? I can say for sure what it is not. Bosnia has changed. 200,000 people have been killed, the most modest estimates indicate that 600,000 have been forced to leave their homes, 800 mosques have been destroyed, hundreds of villages and towns ravaged… and the inescapable results of all this are changes in the way people feel. Bosnia will be better or worse, but certainly different. Naturally, we hope and believe that it will be better. We are fighting to preserve Bosnia within its

present borders... We have the right to do so... but in all our calculations and analyses we must bear in mind that terrible changes have taken place. We must bear this in mind as serious people... Since they have not killed Bosnia, they have strengthened her...

I said that our Bosnia and Herzegovina has become in a sense a moral test of humanity and, while on this subject, you know that many have failed that test. It is a great comfort to us, however, that the better part of humanity has been with us. When I was in America recently, they suggested that I go to see an exhibition of contemporary American artists. I did so, and I saw that the entire exhibition was dedicated to Sarajevo. I almost made the unforgiveable mistake of not going to the exhibition. But the people who had put it together, more than 50 artists, had done so to show us how they felt about our city and to try in their own way to help us. So Bosnia is a moral issue, and issues of a moral order are always universal, and are the concern of every man and woman.

On the initiative of the Presidency of the Republic of Bosnia and Herzegovina, on 5 August 1994 I addressed our fellow citizens in the areas under occupation by Karadžić's army:

I address you, citizens of the Republic of Bosnia and Herzegovina in the temporarily occupied territories, in the name of the Presidency of Bosnia and Herzegovina.

Whatever the reasons for your remaining where you are, I appeal to you to make a commitment to peace.

The 'Greater Serbia' project has irrevocably failed.

It failed because it was founded on the destruction of Bosnia and Herzegovina as an internationally recognised state and, worse still, because it was based on genocide and ethnic cleansing. Can any viable state, whatever it may be, be founded on the murder and expulsion of a civilian population, on the destruction of places of worship, libraries and hospitals?

Do you know, have they informed you, that so far 83 states, among them every major country of the world without exception, have recognised Bosnia and Herzegovina?

All of you whose hands are not soiled with the blood of the innocent are welcome. We accept you as citizens with full rights in our common state, provided only that you are committed to peace and against war.

Our army, in which both Serbs and Croats are serving, is not an avenging army. It is not an anti-Serb army. It is the golden fleur-de-lis that flutters on its flag, not the death's head.

Our common homeland of Bosnia and Herzegovina meets all the conditions to become, finally, a state in which the rights of all will be respected and protected.

Meanwhile, do everything that you are bound to do as human beings: come to the defence of the small number remaining of Bosniacs, Croats and other neighbours of yours in Banja Luka, Prijedor, Sanski Most, Bosanski Brod, Brčko, Bijeljina, Trebinje and other temporarily occupied towns in our country, people who are at risk of expulsion. Cease to obey those who are calling upon you to continue the war and the suffering. There can be no success for something the whole civilised world is opposed to.

After the liberation of Velika Kladuša in August 1994, most of the population of the town retreated with Abdić's paramilitaries. We appealed in vain to them to return. Not even the offer of an amnesty was of any use. Abdić's poisonous propaganda had done its worst. It was a textbook example of the satanic power of the media over the human mind. In addition, the Knin Serbs were preventing the return of refugees. For why would they let go of a potential 5,000 strong force of the Army of the Republic of Bosnia and Herzegovina whom Abdić had so elegantly handed over to them? When asked, in an interview with *Slobodna Dalmacija* (2 September 1994), about Fikret Abdić's fate, I replied:

> I think Fikret Abdić is politically dead. He has caused enormous damage to the cause of Bosnia and Herzegovina, and to the just struggle of our people. There are some unfortunate symbols of what happened. At the end of the story, Abdić finds himself together with those who killed the people of the Krajina in Prijedor and Kozarac, and who destroyed everything we hold sacred in Banja Luka and throughout Bosnia. This is the logical end for people like him. It is only to be regretted that in this misfortune, Abdić took with him a number of innocent people. We are doing, and will continue to do, everything to rescue them from their predicament.

The great powers continued to equivocate. An *Oslobođnje* journalist (30 August 1994) asked me: 'What sort of future awaits us all?' I replied:

> As last winter approached I tried to put on paper all the factors that were then influencing the immediate future of our country. I listed them one by one, and soon had a list of almost 30. And then I tried to define the specific significance or impact of each of these factors. I found that the behaviour of most of the factors was completely unpredictable. Of course, it is not surprising that among these unpredictable factors was, for example, the winter – would it be long, would it be mild or harsh – but the strange thing is that the same question marks appeared against the way a certain number of the world's influential countries would behave. Their policies appeared to me to be just as changeable and unpredictable as the coming winter. Remember one thing: before this war, while the so-called New Europe was being created with such pomp and ceremony, who could have believed that this same Europe would behave in so cowardly a fashion, and tolerate a war of aggression against a country it had just recognised, that it would close its eyes to genocide, concentration camps and so on? But that is what happened, and is still happening, and we all feel surprised by it.

On 27 September 1994 I was once again in New York, at the 49th Session of the UN General Assembly. The situation at home was extremely serious. I tried, for the umpteenth time, to draw the attention of the world to the situation.

> I come from Bosnia and Herzegovina, a distant country much talked about these days.
>
> Unfortunately, I must begin my address by repeating some facts that are, or should be, already known to most of you.
>
> When Yugoslavia was inexorably breaking up, a little more than three years ago, we did everything we could to ensure that the dissolution would take place in a peaceful fashion, without violence.
>
> When Slovenia and Croatia left and the dissolution of Yugoslavia became an inevitability, we organised a referendum to decide the future of Bosnia and Herzegovina democratically. The citizens of Bosnia and Herzegovina went to the polls on 1 March 1992 and voted by an almost two-thirds majority of

the entire registered electorate for the independence of the country. There followed not only the international recognition of Bosnia and Herzegovina, but also the aggression. The decision on recognition was taken on 5 April, and published the following day, 6 April 1992. The aggression against Bosnia by Serbia and Montenegro began on 5 April, the very day that the decision to recognise the state was taken.

This aggression has been going on, with greater or lesser intensity, ever since then, without any prospect of soon coming to an end.

The war forced upon Bosnia and Herzegovina and its people, which has entered its 31st month, is one of the bloodiest in the history of mankind.

The results of this unequal struggle are: 70% of the country's territory was occupied in the very first months of the war, more than 200,000 civilians have been killed, more than 1,000,000 of the country's inhabitants (that is, one quarter of the population) have been forced to leave their homes, and hundreds of towns and villages are in ruins.

So this has not been a classic war between two armies. It has been a war of an army against civilians, accompanied by genocide and the unprecedented destruction of cultural and religious buildings.

The world has not responded appropriately to this barbarism. Terrified by the brutality of the attack, or morally and psychologically unprepared, or even embroiled in their own conflicting interests, the world has merely appeared confused and indecisive. Even when the images and news of new concentration camps in the heart of Europe appeared, the general public was shocked, but people in positions of responsibility for the most part remained silent. Tens of thousands of people have been killed in those concentration camps, and there is no trace of thousands of others.

The crueller the attacks, the more the world vacillated.

The free world did not defend and safeguard freedom.

Our people, faced with the threat of annihilation, resolved to defend themselves. But they then came up against another absurdity. They found their hands tied. For before the war began, the United Nations adopted the famous Resolution that banned the import of arms into the entire territory of former Yugoslavia. Then everything changed. The war began. Attackers and victims appeared on the scene, but the arms embargo remained exactly the same, as if nothing had changed in the meantime. Justice turned into blatant injustice. The attacking forces had arms – they had been stockpiling them for 40 years – and the victims were unarmed, left with their hands tied behind their backs.

The Resolution on the arms embargo turned into the very reverse. By maintaining the arms imbalance, it prolonged the war, and turned peace negotiations into the dictate of the better-armed side.

We sent a message to the world: you don't have to come to our defence. But come and untie our hands, and at least allow us to defend ourselves. While our children are being killed, our women raped, all that we hold sacred reduced to ruins, recognise our right to defend ourselves.

However, the arms embargo is still in place today. Practically speaking, our troops are fighting against artillery and tanks with only the rifles they carry. We have lost many soldiers. Reliable statistics show that 90% of them have been killed by tank and artillery shells. Our cities, towns and villages are left at the mercy of this mercilessly powerful machinery in the hands of murderers.

In the city of Sarajevo alone, more than 10,000 people have been killed and more than 50,000 wounded. There is hardly a family without casualties, killed or wounded.

And the only message we have received from the world on all this is: negotiate!

Believing that the only justified path was to continue to defend our country and that the freedom-loving world would come to our assistance in that just struggle, we refused for a long time to negotiate.

Finally, faced with the unendurable sufferings of the people and the indifference of the world, we had no choice but to agree to negotiate.

It was soon clear that the attackers were using negotiations merely as a way to buy time and as a cover for continuing the aggression.

In March 1993, after long and difficult negotiations, and many concessions on our part, we signed the Vance-Owen Plan. The attackers refused to sign.

There followed another bloody round of war, and then yet another round of talks.

The result was the peace plan of the Contact Group of five countries (the USA, Great Britain, France, Germany and Russia) of July this year.

This time, too, we opted for peace. And this time, too, the attackers opted for the war to continue. We accepted a blatantly unjust peace offer in order to bring the war to an end. We did so because we believed that an unjust peace plan could be rectified during the years of peace. Knowing the soul of Bosnia, we believed, and still believe, that peace will save but war will destroy what we call Bosnia.

And what we call Bosnia is not merely a slip of land in the Balkans. For many of us, Bosnia is an idea. It is the belief that people of different religions, nations and cultural traditions can live together. If it were to happen that that idea were buried for ever, and if that dream of tolerance between people in this region were to vanish never to return, the blame will lie with those who have been killing Bosnia with their artillery for 30 months, but no less with the many world powers that could have helped, but refused to do so.

I left Sarajevo two days ago. I did not leave by air, because the airport is closed. I left by mountain and forest roads, which are under constant fire and where people are killed daily. For days now the city has had no electricity, water or gas… The city is completely cut off, and is literally dying.

Nothing has been done.

Yesterday, when I came to this building, I received a letter from Srebrenica, a town on the Drina that has been surrounded since the beginning of the war. It should have been a report, but it is, rather, a cry from a true living hell. I could not find the strength to read the letter again.

A new wave of ethnic cleansing has been going on for three months now. Thousands of civilians whose only crime is that they are not Serbs have been forced to leave their homes in Banja Luka, Bijeljina, Janja and other towns under the control of Karadžić's army.

And again, nothing has been done. It is as if the world were gradually becoming accustomed to allowing the most fundamental norms of international law to be violated. This is a sick condition, and one that is the concern of every man and woman in the world, no matter how near to or far from Bosnia they may be.

I refused for a long time, and I still refuse, to believe in conspiracy theories, that is, in the explanation that all this is happening in Bosnia because it has a majority Muslim population and that some dark forces are deliberately inciting the Serbs to annihilate the Bosnian Muslims.

Those who make this claim have their own arguments. I believe you have heard them. For it is obvious that Bosnia is in the grip of overt aggression accompanied by genocide, concentration camps and other forms of the most sinister fascism. The world would have to be blind not to see this. Either it is blind, or it is consciously accepting this evil. Since it is not blind, there remains only the second possibility. This is how they argue, and more and more people are coming to believe it every day. It would not be well if the billion Muslims of the world were all to accept this argument.

The latest events relating to the Contact Group Peace Plan have added to the armoury of arguments of the adherents of the 'conspiracy theory'.

For five great powers are behind the proffered peace plan for Bosnia and Herzegovina, which means the majority of the international community. It was explicitly stated that any party rejecting the plan would be punished and the party accepting it would be protected. What happened, however, was the reverse: the Serbs rejected the plan and were rewarded with a suspension of sanctions. We accepted the plan and were punished by Sarajevo's being totally cut off from the outside world. These processes unfolded simultaneously and in parallel.

The message we are receiving from the most senior positions in the United Nations is: if you call for and obtain a lifting of the arms embargo, United Nations troops will withdraw from Bosnia and Herzegovina.

I have not, of course, made this long and exhausting journey from Bosnia to America solely to inform you of facts that are already known to the majority of you. We in Bosnia believe that good and justice cannot be defeated, whatever the obstacles and difficulties. We have not yet lost our belief that the world can be better and that we must always strive anew for this. It is with this conviction that I have come to address you and to present our proposals, despite all the disappointments and frustrations we have experienced.

We call upon this Assembly and upon the Security Council:

1. To implement all the Resolutions adopted by the UN Security Council on Bosnia and Herzegovina;

2. To introduce effective measures to control the borders between Serbia and Montenegro on the one hand and Bosnia and Herzegovina on the other and to prevent or to discover in time the cross-border transport of troops, arms and military equipment;

3. In the event that such transport is discovered, to annul forthwith the decision on the suspension of certain sanctions against Serbia (Security Council Resolution No. 943) and to introduce the stricter sanctions set out in the Contact Group Plan of July 1994;

4. Under no circumstances, to further ease the sanctions against Serbia and Montenegro until these countries recognise Bosnia and Herzegovina and Croatia;

5. Forthwith to adopt a Resolution to reinforce the protection of and to extend the Safe Areas of Security Council Resolution Nos. 824 and 836, in accordance with the commitments set out in Point 6 of the Contact Group Plan;

6. To adopt a decision to prevent the throttling of Sarajevo. These measures should include provision for the city to be opened along the northern lines of road communications by the creation of a 2.5 kilometre demilitarised zone on either side of these roads. Only United Nations troops and police should remain in the demilitarised zone. The possibility of using force to prevent the throttling of Sarajevo is envisaged in Paragraph 4 of the NATO Decision of 9 February 1994.

On these conditions, and on condition that UNPROFOR continues to fulfil its mission, the Government of Bosnia and Herzegovina would be willing to accept a new and modified formula for the arms embargo issue.

We would in this case limit our demand for the arms embargo to be lifted only to the adoption of a formal decision, with the implementation of the decision postponed for six months.

In this case, United Nations troops could remain in Bosnia and Herzegovina, the Contact Group would have fulfilled its promise, and Karadžić's Serbs would be sent a clear message.

I should like finally to set out our two fundamental commitments:

1. Our non-negotiable objective is a democratic Bosnia and Herzegovina within its internationally recognised borders and with national, religious and political rights for all its citizens. In such a Bosnia and Herzegovina, the Serbs could have the right to the highest degree of autonomy, but could not have their own state within a state.

2. We believe that, like every other nation, we have the inalienable right to self-defence. For this reason, if our compromise proposal on the arms embargo is not accepted for any reason whatsoever, we shall call upon our friends to lift the embargo immediately, even if they must do so unilaterally.

Finally, I take this opportunity to thank all the friends of Bosnia and Herzegovina who support her struggle for survival and freedom.

Having no choice, then, I set aside our demand for the arms embargo to be lifted. My feelings can be judged from a statement I gave to *The Times* of London at that time (18 November 1994):

The Times: What would you like to happen now, militarily and politically?

Izetbegović: My aim is to preserve Bosnia and to ensure that the Muslim people have their own place there. You are wrong if you think that I should like you to come with your army and bring our people their state and their freedom. Our people must secure its own place under the sun. We are not asking anyone to give us freedom on a plate. We are not, therefore, seeking your direct help, we are asking you not to impede us in our struggle for survival, but you often do impede us, making our already difficult struggle even harder. A recent example is the UNPROFOR blackmail: if you want arms and freedom, you will be left without bread and medicines. It reminds me of Jesus' temptation by the devil in the desert. We are forced to play tactics, but I am sure that we shall not sell our soul to the devil.

Tactics, however, were combined with military action. A little before this interview with *The Times*, we carried out the Kupres Operation. For the first time since 1992, the HVO was explicitly on our side and against the Karadžić troops. The operation was planned and conducted from 19 October to 3 November 1994, with the involvement of about 5,500 troops of the Army of Bosnia and Herzegovina. In this operation Kupreška Vrata, or The Gates to Bosnia, the town of Kupres and a wide surrounding area were liberated.

But the war continued, zig-zagging to and fro. News of military successes alternated with news of crises. Barely had the euphoria over our forces' liberation of Kupres subsided when bad news began to come in from the Krajina. In the first ten days of November 1994 a widespread attack by Karadžić's army, together with Fikret Abdić's troops, began in the Bihać region. After a few days these troops were joined by paramilitary Knin Serbs under Martić. The enemy was advancing on all sides, even threatening to take Bihać itself. On 22 November I received a letter from NATO Secretary-General Willy Cleas informing me that the previous day, 21 November, NATO air forces had bombed the Udbina airport in the Knin border region. The purpose of the attack, the letter informed me, was to halt the attacks against Bihać, which had been proclaimed a 'safe zone' by UN Security Council Resolution. Since the airport that came under attack was in the Republic of Croatia (although it had for four years been under the control of Martić's rebel Serbs), prior to the bombing NATO sought and obtained the consent of the Croatian President, Tuđman. The attack on Udbina did not help much, however. We had to abandon Velika Kladuša after 45 days of heavy fighting. It seemed that defeat was inevitable, which led the US Defence Secretary, William Perry, to issue a hasty and irresponsible statement saying that 'the war in Bosnia has ended with victory by the Serbs, and the world must accept this.' I was shocked by this statement. I replied to him at the OSCE Summit in Budapest, and in so doing incidentally replied to many others.

SPEECH AT THE OSCE SUMMIT
(Budapest, 5 December 1994)

The latest events in our country have filled me with bitterness, so I shall be brief and direct.

Inescapable Questions

There is really something ironical in the fact that I am present at this important forum of an organisation created 20 years ago for the purposes of security and cooperation, and that bears those two fine words in its very title, but have to speak of something completely contrary to this: of insecurity and lack of cooperation. For what is happening in Bosnia is, to put it mildly, a failing of the West. Unfortunately, it is also something much more serious.

A month ago the aggression against Bosnia and Herzegovina took a new turn. Rebel Serbs in Croatia, in the so-called UNPA Zone, attacked our 5th Corps from the rear, leading to the so-called Bihać crisis. An offensive was organised that was conducted from the protected zone in one state against a safe area of another. Nothing was done, or rather it was claimed that nothing could be done. The entire global community, embodied in the United Nations and the powerful NATO alliance, could not save one town that was at risk. Was it, could it be true? Here are some facts:

During the six months prior to the offensive, the Bihać region had been starving, for humanitarian convoys were simply not getting through (of 143 convoys, only 12 were allowed to enter and 131 were turned back), and immediately before the attack was launched the French Battalion quit the Bihać region. It was replaced by troops from Bangladesh, few in number and poorly armed. A total media blackout was imposed, for there was not a single foreign correspondent in the entire region, and in its reports UNPROFOR minimised the significance and extent of the offensive. Can all this be a coincidence?

With cynical indifference, one senior office-holder announced to the world at large and to the people threatened with slaughter and annihilation that the Serbs had won – as though this was a football match, and he was blowing the whistle to announce that time was up. But because this was a case of 'to be or not to be,' it wasn't the end, and the fighting continued, with the result that Bihać and Kladuša, and Cazin and Krupa, are still holding out after a month-long offensive. I could cite, for the gentleman I have just referred to, a handful of examples of utterly incorrect forecasts by his eminent colleagues. Exactly the opposite of what they foresaw and predicted has happened.

Paris and London have from the very start spoken out as patrons and defenders of the Serbs, blocked the Security Council and NATO, and thereby prevented every step that could have been taken to halt the Serb offensives and the war as a whole. This is not my assertion – it appears in a recent statement by the Society for Endangered Peoples from Goettingen.

And what can I say about Russia's role? It exercises its veto against Security Council Resolutions and votes for the Croatian Serbs to be supplied with fuel oil at the very time that these same Serbs are preventing food and medical supplies from getting through to the starving population of the Bihać region. And there is of course an inescapable question: Karadžić's Serbs have deployed missile systems throughout Bosnia, more than 150 in all. Where did they get them from?

What will be the outcome of the war in Bosnia that is dragging on like this because of this blend of incompetence, vacillation, and sometimes outright ill-will on the part of the West? The result will be: the United Nations discredited, NATO weakened, Europeans demoralised by the sense of their inability to respond to their first post Cold War challenge. It will be another and worse world, in which relations between Europe and America, the West and Russia, the West and the Muslim world, will never be the same again. I would agree with those who predict that (and I quote) 'shame and humiliation because of the shameful withdrawal from Bosnia will characterise the Western world at the end of this century.'

Many have clearly underestimated what is happening in Bosnia. To begin with it was a regional crisis, then it became European, and now, beyond any doubt, it is a world crisis. The defence or fall of Bihać therefore has global implications, and is an issue that concerns all of us in this hall today.

The West reacted to brutal aggression, to a genocide of unprecedented extent, to concentration camps, with a so-called humanitarian response. It used tranquillizers to treat a serious illness, and the illness, as expected or even planned, is worsening. And then that 'humanitarian response' turned into blackmail, and of late into the double blackmail, of our people.

We have deserved assistance, for we did not simply sit back and wait with arms folded. We put up an unexpected, and for many inexplicable, resistance. At the beginning of the war, with a mere hundred or so groups of from 20 to 150 people armed only with light weapons, we have created an army of 150,000 men, who have put out of action several tens of thousands of hostile troops and destroyed more than 1,000 of their tanks and armoured vehicles.

The stronger our defence became, the less was your readiness to help us. Why? Is there an answer?

Mr. Chairman, what is happening in Bosnia was and is, in truth, a clash between democracy and the vilest forms of nationalism and racism. Our opponents recognise only one nation, their own, only one religion, their own, and only one political party, also their own. Everything that is not theirs is condemned to extinction. Even graveyards have been ploughed up. Read the latest report of the United Nations Special Rapporteur, Mr. Mazowiecki, on what is going on in the areas under the control of the enemy forces.

I should like to ask some of the gentlemen who are working dedicatedly to create a state from the monstrosity that styles itself 'Republika Srpska', the Serb Republic – and some of those gentlemen are sitting in this very hall – will they soon be seeking to have that 'republic' recognised and its creators sit here with us next time? I would ask those gentlemen whether they are making preparations for that creation, founded on violence and genocide, to be invited to join the family of civilised countries.

Tomorrow I am going to Geneva to a meeting of the ministers of Islamic countries. As I have to you here today, I shall tell them the truth about what is really happening in Bosnia and why. I shall tell it to the leaders and send a message to the peoples of Muslim countries.

In wars of liberation there are some intangible quantities that elude analysis. This is why some military and political analysts in the West continually get their predictions wrong. Our people are fighting for their freedom, and for more than that, for their very survival. Such struggles are usually hard-fought, but seldom lost. Not a single war of liberation in the past 50 years has been lost. I don't know why ours should be any different. No one can force our 150,000 soldiers, by any means whatsoever, to lay down their arms. I would recommend that each of you takes this factor into account, both for our sake and for your own.

I hope that the friends of Bosnia will not reproach me for these words, and as for the others, after all, it's no concern of mine. Thank you.

On returning home I answered a few questions put to me by BH Press (7 December 1994). The conversation went like this:

BH Press: Mr. President, after your return from Budapest and Geneva, have you anything more to tell our general public about war and peace in Bosnia and Herzegovina?

Izetbegović: I think that I have spoken about this a good deal of late. Perhaps I could add that the fact that when we occasionally speak out more harshly it does not mean that we are less interested in a peaceful solution to the war that has been imposed on us. On the contrary, we shall continue, as we have up to now, to strive to achieve an honourable and early peace, for peace is what our people need. But it is essential that from time to time we tell the world what is being done here, and what that world is itself doing. It is clearly anxious to bring the war to an end at any price, and the easiest way for it to do so is to favour the stronger side. But it has to be told that this is in fact prolonging the war. In this search for peace, we shall use both military and political means. Military wherever we have to, and political wherever we can.

BH Press: But they reproach us for having rejected a cease-fire yesterday at the OSCE.

Izetbegović: This is not correct. We rejected the attempt by the Russians to equate us and the aggressors. They call upon 'both sides' not to prevent the passage of food convoys. They also call upon 'both sides' to cease hostilities, and so on. This implies that we too have blocked the passage of convoys, which is absolutely untrue. We have never halted a convoy. They cannot get away with this any longer. We say: call on the Serb side to let the convoys through, put a name, finally, to those who are using food, gas, water and medicines as a means of war. Does not this whole miserable affair, which has already lasted three years and which is constantly being prolonged, prove that nothing can be achieved with lies and half-truths, that it merely prolongs the agony? Say, finally, who is committing this evil in Bosnia, and you will help us. And as for that cease-fire, without restrictions and conditions it means in effect perpetuating for ever the occupation. The Serbs, who are 31.7% of the population of Bosnia and Herzegovina, have occupied 70% of the country, and would now stay put. It seems that the Russians sympathise with and support them in this demand. We have offered a cessation of military activities for a period of three months, and that proposal is still on the table.

BH Press: Does our situation have anything to do with the crisis in NATO, assuming of course that you agree that there is such a crisis?

Izetbegović: The crisis you refer to is glaring. NATO arose as the response of the West to the Soviet threat. If I may so put it, it is the offspring of this confrontation between two worlds, which lasted for more than 40 years. The Europeans are now reasoning like this: the confrontation is no longer there, the threat is no longer there, we don't need America and its NATO any more. I think that these conclusions are premature, but we shall see. The unfortunate thing is that this reflects negatively on the situation in our country. Our drama is being played out in a world that is changing, in which everything is fluid and undefined. New alliances are being formed. This sometimes creates unexpected and unpredictable difficulties.

BH Press: What kind of outcome can we expect, then?

Izetbegović: There is absolutely no one in the world who could give you a reliable answer to that question right now. The only thing that is certain is that we shall continue to defend ourselves.

The military situation in the Krajina was becoming worse by the day. The attacks by Martić's troops from Croatian territory were particularly worrying. Although the Croatian Government was not responsible for these attacks – since they were the work of Martić's rebel troops – I wrote to the Croatian President, Tuđman:

As you know, for the past ten days a powerful military offensive is being conducted against the safe zone of Bihać. Most of these attacks are coming from Croatia, particularly from the UNPA Zone in your country. There is also reliable information that new forces are currently gathering in the UNPA

Zones, in readiness for a direct assault from several different directions on Bihać and Velika Kladuša.

Three days ago the region also came under air attack. The aircraft flew in from Udbina airport, again therefore from Croatian territory.

Although the specific circumstances under which Croatian territory is being used for the preparation and launch of attacks on the territory of Bosnia and Herzegovina are known to us, we call upon you, in the spirit of the provisions of international law, to undertake without delay all necessary measures to prevent attacks upon Bosnia and Herzegovina from the territory of your country.

We also expect you to undertake these measures in the spirit of Article 8, on military cooperation in the border areas between our two countries, of the Agreement on Friendship and Cooperation of 21 July 1992 and the Annexe to this Agreement of 13 September 1992.

Whenever we were under pressure militarily, the situation was exploited to exercise additional political pressure on us: this time it took the form of a confederation of the Bosnian Serbs and Yugoslavia (Serbia). This is indicated by a question from an interview I gave to the weekly *Ljiljan* of 10 December 1994. This was the question:

Ljiljan: The latest plan of the international Contact Group for Bosnia and Herzegovina is said to be the lowest threshold of national politics, the bottom line. Isn't the political objective of the Serb offensive on Bihać to shift this bottom line so that once again, from the position of blackmailer, they can insist on new approaches, in practice on the legalisation of aggression? What were the intentions of the Serb aggressor in launching this offensive, and what lies behind the veiled assent of the international community, so-called, to such aggression?

Izetbegović: To put it at its simplest, this was an attempt to soften us up. It is no coincidence that at the very height of the offensive on the Cazin border region we also have a political offensive, an invasion of visits of which the message has nothing to do, as one might expect, with checking the attacks on Bihać, but with a political solution. Many estimate that the time has now come. As you know, we are successfully resisting the military offensive against the 5th Corps, and also the political offensive on the peace plan.

And on 28 November I sent a message to the people of the Krajina region:

> Dear courageous people of the Krajina,
>
> For the past 25 days our people have been breathlessly following your heroic struggle for life and freedom. The enemies from the east and the west have joined forces with the traitors. We want you to know that you are not alone in that unequal struggle. We are doing all we can to assist you. The enemy will be defeated, and we shall bring the criminals and traitors to justice.
>
> Our army, of which you are an integral part, is active on all fronts with the aim of alleviating your situation and assisting you. It is trying to tie down considerable enemy forces along a long front line, and thereby to support your resistance. It has to a large extent succeeded in that endeavour.
>
> The enemy is spreading pernicious propaganda. When it loses a battle, it speaks of victories, and when it suffers a defeat, it calls upon us to negotiate.
>
> Do not listen to the enemy, and do not fall for their stories, which are aimed at sowing confusion among our ranks and undermining our will to resist.
>
> Similarly, do not expect much from the outside world. Our best personnel are charged with these contacts, and they are tirelessly doing their job to a high standard, but our fate is being resolved in Bosnia and depends upon all of us.
>
> Let us therefore turn to ourselves and close ranks. Let us support the brave troops and the command of the 5th Corps everywhere! Let us preserve our dignity both when we are giving and when we are receiving blows. Let every individual carry out his task to perfection, play his part, and – with God's help – victory will be ours!
>
> I repeat: we want you to know that you are not alone. The army is fighting alongside you, and our people are watching your struggle with admiration and prayers.

The idea of a confederation of the Bosnian Serbs and Serbia continued to be put about. It was heard more and more often in statements issued by certain Western diplomats. I had the impression that these statements were not just coincidental. On 30 November, therefore, I sent a letter to US President Clinton, letting it be known that we would never accept such an idea. The letter read:

> I am due to receive representatives of the five-country Contact Group for Bosnia and Herzegovina here in Sarajevo today. We are informed that the Contact Group will propose a constitutional arrangement that would give the Serbs the right to form a confederation with Serbia.
>
> It is very clear that the end result of such a solution would be the end of Bosnia, and would directly call into question the survival of our people.
>
> For this reason we cannot accept such a solution.
>
> We remind you that we have already accepted the Contact Group's Peace Plan, that two days ago we offered a three-month cease-fire throughout Bosnia and Herzegovina, and that we have accepted the UNPROFOR Plan for an immediate cease-fire in Bihać.
>
> Every previous proposal for a peaceful resolution to the conflict in Bosnia has been rejected by the Serbs.
>
> It is with regret that we note that from the start of the aggression against Bosnia, unprincipled concessions have been made to the attacking side, which recognises only one people (its own), only one faith (its own), only one political party, and has condemned everything that is not its own to extinction.
>
> Since it is a matter of the survival of our people, I am bound to inform you that we shall not capitulate, and that we have no choice but to continue the struggle, whatever may be the outcome.
>
> With respectful regards.

The response was rapid and unequivocal. In a letter bearing the date 4 December 1994, President Clinton wrote, among other things:

> I want to make myself clear: the USA continues to stand for the preservation of Bosnia and Herzegovina as a unitary country within its existing borders. As for the issue of a 'confederation' which you mention in your letter, our position has not altered. We do not support a confederation of the Bosnian Serbs with Serbia.

I described the state of the army and the balance of power in the second half of 1994 in my response to a question from a journalist from the Sarajevo daily *Oslobođenje* (30 August):

> We knew that any denouement favourable to us would have to be preceded by the creation of an army of 200,000 men, and that takes time. We are now at that stage. A certain balance of power has been achieved. It is not symmetrical. We have the advantage in the human factor (in numbers and morale), they in the technical. We are endeavouring to at least reduce the gap between the two armies as regards military hardware, and to some extent we are succeeding. But it is still not sufficient. By ensuring that we have up to date anti-tank weapons we are succeeding in neutralising their superiority in armoured force. We still do not have an adequate response to their artillery. As for mortars, I think that we shall soon be able to parry them.

Muslim countries played an important part in Bosnia and Herzegovina's struggle against aggression. They provided significant political, material and military aid. Never, in the last hundred years, had the Muslim world been so united as in the case of Bosnia, claimed Samuel L. Huntington, noting that 'the Bosnian cause was universally popular in Muslim countries... Sunni and Shi'ite..., Arab and non-Arab Muslim societies from Morocco to Malaysia all joined in.' Finding here further evidence for his theory of the 'clash of civilizations', Huntington describes this as 'the broadest and most effective civilization rallying... on behalf of the Bosnian Muslims.' Although Huntington's 'clash of civilizations' theory is repugnant to me, in this case his assertion of the unity of the Islamic world in the case of Bosnia was accurate.

Adopting a proposal by Iran, the Organisation of the Islamic Conference (OIC) founded a group to lobby for the Bosnian struggle in the United Nations and, following this, as a member of the group and in the name of the OIC, Turkey proposed a resolution calling for military intervention in conformity with Chapter 7 of the UN Charter.

In May 1993 the Organisation of the Islamic Conference fiercely criticised the plan put forward by Western countries and Russia for the so-called 'safe areas', accusing them of the ghettoisation of the Muslims in Bosnia. A month later, at the UN Human Rights Conference, the OIC succeeded in pushing through a resolution condemning the Serbian and Croatian aggression and calling for a lifting of the arms embargo against the Bosnian Army. In July 1993 the OIC offered 18,000 troops for the UN peace keeping forces. The West agreed to take 7,000 troops, from Turkey, Pakistan, Malaysia, Indonesia and Bangladesh. These joined the UN forces in 1994-1995.

In December 1994 I was invited to the OIC Summit to be held in Casablanca, Morocco. I addressed the assembled heads of state and governments of more than 50 Islamic countries:

Speech At The Summit Of The Organisation Of The Islamic Conference
– extracts –
(Casablanca, 13 December 1994)

I greet you and thank the King, the Government and the people of Morocco for the hospitality they have extended to us.

I presume that you know much of what has been happening in Bosnia and Herzegovina over the past two and a half years. A Turkish historian said recently that the only event that surpasses in horror the Greater Serbian genocide of the Muslim people of my country was the Mongol invasion of Baghdad in the 13th century (…)

Here and there in the Islamic world one can hear expressed the view that we should not have left Yugoslavia, and that if we had remained with Serbia in Yugoslavia we might have avoided the war.

Gentlemen, this is a superficial, and perhaps even a malicious interpretation!

We invited the political leadership of Serbia and Croatia to form with us a confederal Yugoslavia, in which the Muslim people would be on an equal footing with the other peoples of the country, and Bosnia and Herzegovina on an equal footing with Serbia and Croatia. Those who launched the aggression against Bosnia and Herzegovina on the very day that my country gained international recognition did so in order to bring us under the yoke of their own state construct, 'Greater Serbia', in which both the Republic of Bosnia and Herzegovina and the Bosniac (Muslim) people would have ceased to exist as a political factor. Furthermore, in such a state the Muslims would have been cannon fodder in the Greater Serbian war against everyone else, including the Muslim peoples, in the Balkans.

In a referendum we rejected this subordinate and inferior position, which had already been devised for us many years previously. We had no choice but to fight in defence of our very lives, our faith and our dignity. And as soon as we began to fight for the first time against the genocidal tradition in the Balkans, we provoked unprecedented ferocity on the part of our enemies, overt and covert, known and unknown.

In this war that was forced upon us, we have shocked the world twice. The first shock was our resistance. Both our enemies and the world at large expected us to suffer rapid defeat. What happened was that our resistance became daily ever stronger, and more and more soldiers sprang up as if from the soil. Despite the massive technical superiority of the attacking forces, we succeeded in saving 30% of our territory and forcing the enemy out of almost every major town. Wherever we were fighting man to man, our troops proved superior and emerged victorious. Our problem remains the enemy's heavy weapons.

The second shock was the political side of our struggle. Because of the horror of the atrocities, and also because of their own ingrained prejudices, the world expected reprisals from us. This did not happen. On the contrary, we proclaimed a democratic society, founded on religious and national tolerance. It became clear that we were not at all extremist or fanatic, as our people are frequently labelled by European orientalists and certain Western media. We preserve our Islamic identity, remaining open to all that is of value in both the East and West.

We like to say that our aim is a state in which no one will be persecuted because of his faith, nationality or political convictions. We are committed to this principle and shall continue to uphold it.

Thanks to these two facts, of which the first relates to the military aspect and the second to the political aspect of our struggle, with God's help we shall finally put an end to the series of genocides against the Muslim people, which began three centuries ago.

For this time, for the first time, an organised armed resistance has been offered to the perpetrators not at the local level, but by the people as a whole. No such resistance has been offered before, so the tragedy kept repeating itself. Furthermore, this time the resistance is developing in a different historical context. We are no longer alone, we have the entire Muslim world with us, growing into a powerful political factor that can no longer be ignored, and we have all the peoples of the world with us, if not all the world's governments.

Finally, we have succeeded in bringing Bosnia into the focus of the general public worldwide. Two important summits, one held recently in Budapest and this one being held today in Casablanca, have dealt with Bosnia.

The enemy's attempt to carry out its murderous task rapidly in silence has failed. Everything that is happening in Bosnia is under the spotlight, and no one will be able to say that he did not know. This circumstance assists the defenders and makes the attackers' task more difficult...

You need to convince the countries of the West that it is in their interests to cooperate with the Islamic world and that they must change their policies towards Bosnia. You also need to convince the Orthodox world that it has nothing to gain from its nationalism and force, and that it would be better for it to avoid a potential confrontation lasting many years with the Islamic world.

Both the West and the Orthodox world must be shown that a confrontation with the Islamic world will not pay, and that Bosnia is the test of a different politics. Do this, use your influence, it is high time.

On returning to Bosnia I found an invitation to the parliamentary session of the Republic of Bosnia and Herzegovina, informing me that the Parliament looked to me for a report on the current military and political situation in the country. At the parliamentary session that took place on 17 December 1994, I said:

> I have just come from faraway Morocco, where I witnessed a manifestation of solidarity with Bosnia and her struggle for freedom. We are not and will not remain alone in that struggle. And yet what will decide the fate of our country will be what we do here in the country, that is, what we alone know how to, want to and are able to do.
>
> As regards the general situation, it can be described as difficult but not bad. The situation is difficult despite the fact that we are stronger than ever before, for of recent days there has been

a concatenation of circumstances that are negative for us. The difficult military situation in the Bihać region has been exploited to bring political pressure to bear on our country. Together with the offensive on our 5th Corps, there followed a political offensive against our positions, which is less visible but no less intense. In accepting the five-country Contact Group's Peace Plan of July this year, we defined the lowest threshold of our policy, below which we will not go. The Serb military offensive, clearly synchronised with the international political offensive, had the objective of shifting that threshold. We are coping successfully with both these pressures. I think that it is now clear to both the Chetniks in Bihać and various power centres in the world at large, which have organised an invasion of visits and various initiatives, largely to our detriment, that we have withstood and survived this pressure.

That was a concise assessment of the general military and political situation in the country at this time.

Since the political situation depends more on the military than vice versa, I shall first turn in the briefest of outlines to the situation on our fronts.

The general characteristic of the military situation in Bosnia and Herzegovina from the start of the war is the very long front line. The length of the front alters and varies between 1,200 and 1,300 kilometres, and is only marginally less than the Eastern Front in the Second World War and the front in the recent Iran-Iraq war.

This very long front has imposed enormous problems. Our only comfort is that it has imposed the same problems on the other side. Our other military problems are, as a rule, different from those of our opponents: we have better people, they are better equipped; our morale is better, the logistics are better on their side. These circumstances have a decisive effect on our combat tactics, which consists in delivering hundreds of small blows to the enemy along the entire length of the front. Since we do not have sufficient heavy weapons, in particular artillery, no strategic reversal is yet possible in the theatre of war. Our aim at this point is to force our opponents into peace. Since the obvious political and war aim of the enemy was the destruction of Bosnia as a state and the annihilation of the Bosniac people as the backbone of that state, our aim is to force them to give up that genocidal plan. When they give this up, it inevitably means their political and military defeat.

I said that our objective is peace. It is our objective both for our own and for Bosnia's sake. For our sake, because our people need peace. For Bosnia, because the war is destroying what Bosnia is and what we want her to be. Peace can save her. And to the same extent that we aspire to peace, the enemy, given the nature of its objectives, wants war and is doing everything it can to prolong it. The aggressor is pulling the wool over the eyes of its own people and the general public abroad when it says that the proposed maps are the reason for not accepting the peace plan. The truth is that it cannot accept peace, for peace means the end of its genocidal plan and the start of accountability for the atrocities committed. It is realistic, therefore, to expect the enemy to keep thinking up new reasons for undermining every peace initiative and prolonging the war indefinitely. Of course, nothing alters the fact that the notorious factors that set the aggression and genocide in motion will adopt the mantle of peacemakers and speak of peace so as to fool the naïve and those who want to be fooled. As you know, a farce of this very kind is being prepared right now.

The battle for Bihać is raging right now. This is no ordinary battle. The soldiers know this, and the rest of us ordinary people, and the world at large, sense it. Much is being tried out and resolved right there, in that relatively small area in and around Bihać. Hence the desperate struggle, which has entered its seventh week. Thanks be to God, we have held on to our vital positions. Of course, it will remain unclear why Croatia did not become actively involved in something that was also its concern…

And now some observations and views on fundamental political issues. The Serbian side has still not accepted the Contact Group Peace Plan. When and if it does accept it, talks on everything are possible. Until that time, there is nothing to be talked about. I mean here talks on a political solution. We can, of course, talk about and even agree on humanitarian issues or a cease-fire if the other side is interested in doing so, and under reasonable conditions.

The lifting of sanctions against Serbia was premature. The border between Serbia and Bosnia and Herzegovina has quite obviously not been sealed. Every objective observer agrees on this, and it is confirmed by the Chetnik offensive in the Bihać region, which would have been impossible without logistical support from Serbia. We are therefore opposed to any further lifting of sanctions until Karadžić's Serbs accept the peace plan and Serbia recognises both Bosnia and Herzegovina and Croatia. We note with regret that Russia is almost overtly on the side of those who are attacking Bosnia and Herzegovina, and we ask the British Government whether it is sure that the British public agrees with the legalisation in the Balkans of a creation that does not in the least recognise the notion of human rights, that is founded on genocide and ethnic cleansing and for which arrogance and violence are the only rule of conduct. We note and welcome the stance taken by France towards Bosnia and Herzegovina, and ask America and Germany finally to define their policy towards Bosnia and to stick to it. As for the Islamic world, we expect it to fulfil its promises made in the Declaration on Bosnia, adopted yesterday.

We still need UNPROFOR. We shall be happy when the day comes for us to thank it and request it to leave. Until then, we expect its senior representatives to uphold the Security Council Resolutions, not the political directives of their governments, and we call upon our people to show a friendly attitude towards the United Nations troops, the great majority of which are carrying out their duties properly.

A federation of Bosniacs and Croats is our objective and our path. Our objective, since we see in it partly achieved our dream of the integration of Bosnia and Herzegovina; our path, for in it we see a way of continuing and completing that integration. Difficulties in implementing the federal constitution are clearly to do with different views on the fundamental question of the survival of the state as the supreme interest of our people. Our common friends abroad, who have sincerely and loyally backed this project, ask us where the difficulties lie. Our response is that the implementation of the federation is ultimately a problem of democracy. The mono-national, mono-religious, one-party character of the authorities in the regions under the control of the Croat Defence Council is contrary to the very concept of the federation and its constitution. Only democracy can resolve this knotty problem. Until then we shall go round in circles looking for problems where none exist. This democratic evolution in the regions I refer to is in the interests of the Croat people and of the

Republic of Croatia, and they should be encouraging and supporting it. But despite all the difficulties, the Washington Agreement has played an historic role. Even if it had merely put an end to the wretched war between Bosniacs and Croats, it would have been worth all the effort. But it opened up many other possibilities, which it is true to say have not been taken advantage of, but which are still not lost.

Our attitude on the arms embargo remains unchanged. If the Serbs do not accept the Contact Group Peace Plan, the arms embargo must be lifted, with a deferral period of six months, but by 30 July 1995 at the latest.

It is now time for us to use this occasion to turn, even if in the briefest of detail, to our successes and failures, to enquire if in this general chaos and confusion we have made some serious mistakes and whether we could have done much better. The only reliable answer to this question is one that is made after the lapse of some time. Of course, you have the right to make your judgements here and now, and you will be heard with due attention. I think that we have succeeded in at least two important matters. We have succeeded in organising our defence by creating in wartime an army of 200,000 men, and in establishing and preserving the democratic character of governance. We have also succeeded in maintaining the focus of world attention on Bosnia throughout, thereby making the task of the attackers and criminals more difficult...

On the other hand, we have failed to provide more or less stable financing for such important social needs as health, education, the judiciary, pensions... Nor have we succeeded in making any essential move on the refugee question.

Someone quite rightly said that what we are seeing in Bosnia is a world war, obviously meaning that every relevant world power is involved on these visible and invisible battlefronts of ours. A maximum of history is taking place here in a minimal space. In such a situation, while passing through an extremely turbulent period of world history, in which thus-far powerful empires are vanishing and thus-far stable international institutions are being eaten away, we are trying to bring our country to some peaceful haven, in the hope that a miracle will happen and the storm will die down.

And finally, on freedom.

Our non-negotiable aim is for Bosnia, regardless of what it will be, to be a country in which no one will be persecuted because of his faith, nation or political conviction. I often repeat this phrase almost word for word, but given what has happened around us, to right and left, I have to do so. This formula is the practical expression of our commitment to a principle of the highest order: the principle of freedom. Freedom is what gives our lives meaning. It makes those lives bearable and sheds a gentle glow over this difficult and painful struggle of ours.

A few hours before the year 1994 came to an end, with the mediation of former US President Jimmy Carter, we signed a four-month cease-fire. On 28 December, during a critical period in the talks, I received a letter from Secretary of State Christopher in which he encouraged us to reach agreement on the cessation of hostilities. We had just a little earlier signed the Cease-fire Agreement. It proved to be beneficial. With the exception of Bihać, during the week that followed the signing we had no casualties, either dead or wounded, along the other fronts.

Our immediate motive in accepting the cease-fire was to halt the offensive on Bihać, followed by the desire – if possible – to avoid loss of life among our people, without at the same time calling into question our fundamental aim: Bosnia and Herzegovina as a state within its internationally recognised borders, and its future development as a free and democratic country.

To avoid Karadžić's taking advantage of the agreement to extend indefinitely the occupation of our country, the Cease-fire Agreement was for a fixed period. Meanwhile, talks were supposed to begin on a political solution to the conflict. In order for those talks to begin, we called upon the Serb side to accept the five-country Contact Group's Peace Plan. Without their explicit confirmation of this, there would be no political talks.

A day earlier, the Government of the Republic of Bosnia and Herzegovina had adopted two programmes for the coming year: strengthening our defence capacity, and ensuring an existential minimum for every citizen. They were complex programmes that included a large number of quite specific tasks. In accordance with their respective constitutional authority and obligations, the Presidency would deal primarily with the first and the Government with the second, although the two programmes were interlinked and interdependent. In a hungry country, the defence cannot function properly and for there to be production, the country must be defended. The defence is linked by a hundred threads with the economy. Both the troops and the business community must understand and respect that.

My new-year message to the people of Bosnia and Herzegovina included these words:

> The war must not last a day longer than it has to, but nor can peace be accepted at any cost.
>
> For this reason we talk where we can, and fight where we must.
>
> If, during the next four months, the enemy does not show its willingness for a reasonable political solution, the cease-fire will not be extended, and we shall call for the arms embargo to be lifted with effect from 1 May next year...
>
> At this time we remember, with respect and feelings of a debt owed, those who have fallen in the struggle for freedom or as victims of the war. We also remember our refugees, and wish that they may soon be able to return to their homes. We also lend our thoughts to our soldiers who are on the front line on this cold December night. May the souls of the dead rest in peace, and to the living all congratulations for having endured the past year righteously and properly. And naturally, best wishes to all of you for the coming year.
>
> God will help a people that works and strives for freedom.

The third winter of the war dragged on, day by day, painful, hungry and cold. We fixed our eyes on spring with a certain undefined hope. Just let January and February go by. The weapons had for the most part fallen silent, except in the Krajina region.

A modest celebration was held in the Army Hall to mark 1 March, Bosnia and Herzegovina's Independence Day. I addressed those present; the following is an abridged version of my speech:

> Today reminds us of the dilemmas and anxieties we then faced, but also of our sufferings, of our struggle, of heroism, of the victims ... Since that March, three long years have elapsed. True, three years is not a long time in the life of a people. But during those three years, more events have taken place in this

small country, both good and ill; more battles, more atrocities, more treachery and more heroism, more life and death than in any three centuries of our history...

The enormous scale of the suffering and death raises one inescapable question: was this suffering, this struggle for freedom the only possible choice; was there any way this tragic clash of ours with history could have been avoided?

The answer to that question takes us back to the turbulent year 1991: to the war in Slovenia and Croatia, to their referendums, to the dissolution of Yugoslavia, to Vukovar and Dubrovnik and everything that accompanied this. We found ourselves at a historic cross-roads: the choices were to either bow our heads and remain in a rump Yugoslavia, or more precisely in Greater Serbia, or to hold our heads high and take the right path, with all the risks that this choice carried with it.

We opted for the second. I say 'opted', although I am not sure this is the right word. For in fact we had no choice. ... It all unfolded as relentlessly as in some ancient Greek drama. We could not use our freedom in any other way. Free people are in fact slaves to freedom.

So the 1st March was our destiny, and it is inappropriate, and indeed meaningless to ask if it could have been otherwise. For we would not have been what we are if we had chosen subjugation for the sake of a dubious security.

It is, of course, appropriate to ask what kind of security that was. This can be clearly seen in the position of Montenegro, in the position of the people in Kosovo and the Sandžak.

True, we are suffering and being killed, but for the freedom of Bosnia. Had it been any other way, we would have been killed on someone else's account, on fronts against Croatia, the Sandžak, Kosovo, for the glory of a Greater Serbia.

So there was only one way ahead for us, and our people took that path, three years ago. That is the meaning of 1st March, our national holiday today. ... Our aim is a Bosnia of free people, a Bosnia in which the human being and human rights will be respected. We oppose the concept of mono-national, mono-religious, one-party parastates – in the plural – with our concept of a free and democratic Bosnia. We oppose hatred and intolerance with freedom and democracy. When we inscribe this motto on all our flags, then we must continually strive for it, correcting our path daily and tirelessly rectifying everyday injustices.

We are not doing this for them, for we owe them nothing. We are doing it for ourselves.

Every people has its promised land. Our promised land is Bosnia. We call upon you to fight for it and win it.

Our response to the Serb offensive in the Krajina region was the Vlašić Operation (carried out between 19 and 30 March 1995) with the codename 'Domet-1'. About 21,000 troops of the Army of Bosnia and Herzegovina took part in the operation. This daring and hard-hitting operation was planned and conducted by the command of the Army's 7th Corps, headed by its then Commanding Officer General Mehmed Alagić and reinforced by troops from the 3rd Corps, in particular from the 7th Muslim Brigade, elements of the 4th Muslim Brigade and the Guards Brigade of GHQ, all in exceptionally difficult weather conditions of blizzards and very low temperatures. About 51 km^2 of territory was liberated, with the facilities of Crni vrh, Šantić, Paljenik and Galica, and the very powerful RTVBiH transmitter on Vlašić mountain, of particular importance for the Army of Bosnia and Herzegovina's communications system. The enemy casualties amounted to around 200 killed, 180 wounded and 12 officers and men taken prisoner, together with a large quantity of arms and equipment. Our losses, too, were high: 61 combatants killed, 75 wounded and five taken prisoner.

At the end of March 1995 a session of the SDA Main Board was held. I spoke of the problems in the federation and the blockades being maintained by the HVO. The Croatian media reacted sharply. On 30 March I gave an interview to *Oslobođenje*. Asked about this reaction and how I had responded, I said:

> I have read some of these articles. They try to suggest to the Croatian readership that I have spoken about Croats in the same terms as about the HVO, or to put it better, about some elements of the HVO. They are not the same to me, and it is a good thing for the Croats that they are not. I have a high opinion of Croats and know that most of the Croat people, whether here or in Croatia itself, have feelings of friendship towards the people to which I belong. I appreciate this very much. I cannot say the same of the HVO. I would remind you of my inter-

view in which a foreign journalist remarked that the Croats had destroyed the Old Bridge in Mostar. My response was, and I quote exactly, 'It was not the Croats who did so, it was done by some people from the HVO'.

Asked by *Oslobođenje* whether I had called them fascists, I replied:

> I repeated certain facts that, unfortunately, are not in dispute. And that is that in the areas under HVO control, national, religious and political exclusivity rule; only one nation is recognised, the Croatian, only one faith, Catholicism, and only one party, the HDZ. Everyone knows what the world calls such mono-national, one-party concepts. Well, fine, let them give another name to that concept if they want. One thing is sure, it is not democracy, but the negation of democracy. I do not speak of this regrettable phenomenon as an enemy. I would like the situation to be rectified. I shall be happy when I hear that Bosniacs and others are living in freedom in Stolac, Prozor and Čapljina, that the *azan* can be heard there and that critical words and parties other than the HDZ can be heard there too. Until this happens, things are what they are regardless of what we call them.

There were two occasions in April in which I addressed non-Bosniacs: Serbs at the second assembly of the SGV, the Serb Civic Council, and Jews on the occasion of Pesach. This was my address to those attending the Assembly of citizens of Serb nationality, on 9 April:

> I should like to greet you and to wish you success in your activities.
>
> I also want to express my respect for you in representing the conscience and the other, spotless face of the Serbian people.
>
> I congratulate you on your courage in coming to Sarajevo and in speaking the truth. Witnessing to the truth has always called for a large measure of courage, and above all today.
>
> You do not represent the armed element of the Serbian people, you are its unarmed, empty-handed element. They have arms, but you have words, and words of truth have so many times been shown to be a powerful weapon.
>
> The aim of the legal government of Bosnia and Herzegovina, in the name of which I am speaking to you, is a democratic Bosnia and Herzegovina or, as we like to say, a state in which

no one will be persecuted because of his faith, nation or political convictions. We believe that in this lies the essence of civilisation.

We also believe that people of different faiths and nations can live together in tolerance and peace. Some say that this is utopia in this region. Our response is that this is the only human way out of this present extremity, which has affected so many innocent people of all faiths and nations, and we continue to believe this. And a utopia in which people believe ceases to be utopia.

And to the Jews:

Permit me to congratulate you on today's holiday and to hope that you may spend it in peace and joy, as far as this is possible of course in these circumstances.

This gives me particular satisfaction for three reasons. First, as your fellow citizen, you are my neighbours and your joy is my joy; second, as a Muslim, the Qur'an has some moving words on the event you are celebrating today, for the Qur'an speaks in vivid imagery of the slavery of the Jewish people in Egypt and their journey to freedom. Third, I do so as a human being. Pesach is a traditional festival of freedom, and freedom is an exalted word and a universal value which is the concern of everyone and of every nation.

I say this with some emotion, for this is a time when the freedom of my people is threatened and a dramatic struggle is going on to save and preserve it.

I said that I wish you a joyful day, but for reasons we know very well it is not that joyful. And yet, we shall agree that it is more joyful than the last, and even more than the year before. I mean that things are going the right way, and that we are entitled to hope that you will celebrate next year's Pesach in better circumstances, and even, if it be God's will, in peace.

Finally, I appeal to you not to leave Bosnia, but to remain in this country, which is your country too. Our aim is for it to be a tolerant community of faiths and nations, as it has been for centuries. It is a difficult task. With you among us it will be easier for us to reach that important and worthy goal.

On 11 April 1995 good news came from Paris, where the Committee of the Parliamentary Assembly of the Council of Europe was in session: I was one of three candidates for the European Human Rights award. The session of the Committee was attended on behalf of Bosnia and Herzegovina by Miro Lazović, Chair of the Parliamentary Assembly of Bosnia and Herzegovina; and Prof. Abdulah Konjicija, Chair of our Human Rights Commission. I did not win the award, but they say that what's important is entering the race, not winning it.

All of us living in Sarajevo were in constant danger during the siege – this was true of everyone living there. The Presidency building was hit several hundred times (the exact number is not known) and was less than 500 metres from the front line on its southern side. I moved into an office in the inner part of the building, which I jokingly called the coward's office. In every other regard I was in the same position as the majority of Sarajevans – neither better nor worse. And yet there were exceptional situations.

In April 1995 I was visiting some of our troops in northern Bosnia. I concluded my tour with a visit to the HQ of the 3rd Corps and troops of the 7th Muslim Brigade. The tour, and those indispensable meetings, were running over time – everything was running three to four hours late. That evening, instead of taking off from the Zenica Stadium at five o'clock, it was late at night when we left. Our intended destination was Tarčin. The most critical point was the flight over Vranica mountain. Everyone in the helicopter fell silent, willing the journey to come to an end as quickly as possible.

We were above Vranica mountain when one of the pilots came to tell me that a red light had come on, which meant that there was something wrong with the helicopter. I do not understand these things, but he explained that some controls were not functioning. He said, 'We aren't far from Fojnica, if it's lit up we'll try to land there in the stadium.' Our helicopters had not been receiving regular technical inspections, nor were they equipped for night-flying. It couldn't have been worse: a faulty helicopter in total darkness. I doubted if we would make it.

At the bottom of the helicopter, Arijana Saračević, an RTVBiH journalist, and Hakija Topić, a cameraman, were sitting in the dark. Bakir Sadović was beside them. I later learned, when talking to them, that they had gathered something was wrong.

By good fortune, there was electricity in Fojnica. The pilot told us to hold on tight to our seats (there were no seat belts) and began to manoeuvre the helicopter down. The minutes dragged by, but finally we touched down, albeit with a bit of a bump. A number of figures, probably astonished by their unannounced visitors from the skies, could be discerned in the semi-darkness of the Stadium. The pilot opened the helicopter door and called one of them over. 'Which brigade is this, and who is the commanding officer?' I asked. 'Tursumović,[10] Mr. President, 145th Brigade,' replied the man, recognising me. I already knew Colonel Husein Tursumović from the 'Black Swans'. He was known as a serious man and combatant. I asked for him to be called at once.

Tursumović put us in three cars. I sat in the front seat of his big Toyota, and we set off on the long night journey over the hills. Although it was April, there was still snow on the heights below Lopata. First one of the cars and then, after a few kilometres, another ground to a halt, not being equipped for winter conditions. We all crammed into Tursumović's Toyota, which got through to Tarčin, helped along by being pushed from time to time, shortly after midnight.

Coming down into Bradina, on the way in towards the lights, I saw two or three soldiers standing on the road watching us as we drew near, their rifles cocked. The only thing I could think of was, are they ours or theirs? Not whether they were good or bad people, but simply: whose side were they on. The tragedy of war is that one loses one's ethical standards.

On 30 April 1995 the four-month cease-fire expired. During this time the fighting had died down, but not entirely stopped. Karadžić had attacked the Bihać region, and we had responded with an attack on Vlašić. But apart from these actions, there was a lull on all the other fronts. Should we extend this illusory truce when two-thirds of Bosnia and Herzegovina was under occupation by Karadžić's troops? On 10 April I convened a session of the Presidency of Bosnia and Herzegovina, at which it was resolved:

> 1. Our delegation would receive representatives of the Contact Group, hear what they had to say, and confirm that we still stood by the proposed Contact Group Plan (the maps).
>
> 2. We would not enter into any kind of political negotiations with Karadžić until he accepted the Contact Group Plan. In this regard, even the mediation of former President Carter was not acceptable at this time. We welcomed any peace initiative, but Carter's visit,

---

[10] Husein Tursumović is now Commanding Officer of the 7th Mechanised Brigade (formerly the 7th Muslim Brigade).

objectively speaking, would not contribute to peace, because it could be interpreted as an alternative to the en-deavours of the Contract Group, and would prolong the uncertainty. For if Carter made the same offer as the Contact Group, then his visit would be superfluous, since we had already accepted their Plan. And if he offered something different, his visit would even be damaging.

3. If Karadžić accepted the Contact Group Plan, this would open the way to direct negotiations in which certain modifications to the maps could be considered, provided the ratio of 51:49 was maintained by mutual consent.

4. In the event of talks, the Serbian Civic Council (SGV) must also be included, following the proposal of the assembly of citizens of Serb nationality of Bosnia and Herzegovina, as representatives of a significant sector of the Serb people and a group that had not taken part in the aggression against Bosnia and Herzegovina.

5. A confederation between the self-styled Serb entity in Bosnia and Herzegovina and Serbia would be unacceptable in the future constitutional order of Bosnia and Herzegovina. Special relations would be possible, on condition that the same kind of relations were to be provided for between Bosnia and Herzegovina and the Bosniacs in Serbia.

6. In relation to demands that the cease-fire be extended, the Presidency adopted the following position:

a) If Karadžić did not accept the Contact Group Plan by 30 April, we could not extend the cease-fire, since it carried with it the risk of a gradual legalisation of the status quo, which was extremely unfavourable to us (Karadžić's troops were holding 65% of the country's territory at the time).

b) This did not mean that we would take any offensive actions.

c) If Milošević recognised Bosnia and Herzegovina, we were ready to extend the cease-fire for two or three months, to investigate the possibility of reaching a political solution to the conflict.

d) If Karadžić accepted the Contact Group Plan after 30 April, a cease-fire would automatically enter into force formally on the date of acceptance.

e) In any case of extending the cease-fire, we would require every clause in the Agreement on Cessation of Hostilities dated 31 December 1994 to be implemented during the first seven days (an end to the fighting in the Bihać zone, opening all the 'blue routes', free access throughout for convoys, in particular to Bihać and the Drina enclaves, and so on). If this was not done, the cease-fire agreement would no longer apply.

7. No easing of sanctions against Serbia until it recognised Bosnia and Herzegovina, which meant recognition of the territorial integrity of Bosnia and Herzegovina as a state within its internationally recognised borders.

8. In the event of any suspension of sanctions against Serbia, we would call for UN troops to be posted along the borders with Serbia and Montenegro in sufficient numbers to ensure the effective closure (control) of the borders.

9. We would accept only a suspension of sanctions. A lifting of sanctions would be possible only when a peace agreement on Bosnia was implemented in cooperation with Serbia.

10. The Presidency protested against the renewed attacks on civilians in Sarajevo and the continued blockade of the city. We called upon the international community to protect the city in accordance with the commitments it had undertaken. In this regard, we let it be known that if Karadžić's forces continued to shell the city, and the international community did not prevent them from doing so, our army and the citizens of Sarajevo would be called upon to liberate the city.

11. As a peaceful solution to this situation, we offered the demilitarisation of Sarajevo with a radius of 20 kilometres, including the withdrawal of all troops. A proportionately composed force of UN troops and the police would take over the control of law and order and security. We linked this proposal with the earlier idea of a two-year UN administration of the Sarajevo area.

12. We sought no alteration to the mandate of the UN troops, but would call for a strict implementation of the existing mandate, since it was clear that it had become totally distorted during the process of implementation. A study was being drawn up listing the main areas of this distortion. An abridged version of the material would be sent in letter form to the UN Secretary General, heads of state and foreign ministers of the

> Contact Group countries, potential co-chairs for issues relating to former Yugoslavia, and other relevant actors.
>
> 13. The Presidency expressed its particular dissatisfaction and protest at the withdrawal of UN troops after the threats from Karadžić's troops at the illegal check-point in Kasindolska Street. This check-point was contrary to the agreement on Sarajevo airport, dated 3 July 1992, and was a direct threat to the safety of people and goods at the airport, as well as to the airport itself. We demanded that the check-point be abolished.
>
> 14. A unified delegation would negotiate for our side with representatives of the Contact Group, composed of Izetbegović, Zubak, Ganić, Silajdžić, Pejanović, Komšić and Ljubijankić, together with Begić and Sabrihafizović as advisers to the delegation.

Just before the expiry of the four-month cease-fire, I responded to some questions from BH Press. In one question it was alleged that both sides had violated the agreement. I replied:

> By its very nature, a cease-fire is indivisible. Karadžić thought he could have peace where he wanted and attack where it suited him. Specifically, that he could have peace in Tuzla and central Bosnia, but attack Bihać and continue the strangulation of Sarajevo. We warned both him and international actors several times that this would not do. When our services discovered that, under cover of the cease-fire, Karadžić was transferring significant forces to Bihać with the aim of breaking the 5th Corps, we carried out the Vlašić action, to show him that he had calculated wrongly. We do not hide this, but it is obvious that our action on Vlašić cannot be seen in isolation from the attacks on Bihać, which have been going on without interruption since November last year, right through the cease-fire period, which is a direct and continual violation of the signed cease-fire Agreement.

The phoney cease-fire was still in place when I was invited to address the German Association for Foreign Policy on the situation in Bosnia and Herzegovina. On 17 March, in the Association's packed hall in Bonn, I spoke of the aggression against Bosnia and the attitude of the world, of life under siege in Sarajevo, on religious renaissance, on the encounter of

East and West in Bosnia, and so on. The lecture is included as one of the appendices at the end of this book.

In Sarajevo, as in most of the rest of the world, Victory Day was celebrated on 9 May. I noticed that former Communists were trying to take advantage of this day to draw attention to themselves – as though the struggle against fascism had been a struggle for communism. My message read as follows:

> Dear citizens, I address you on the occasion of tomorrow's Victory Day.
>
> Many responsible people worldwide do not claim that this was a victory over fascism, since it is obvious it was not. A major and significant battle against fascism was won, but the war against fascism, unfortunately, was not. Bosnia today is the living and tragic witness to that fact.
>
> History does not begin with us. For this reason we should remember all that was good, but we should not forget any of what was bad. The world that emerged from the victory of 50 years ago was not much better than the old. In large areas of the world, societies without freedom continued to exist or were newly established, responsible for the suffering and deaths of millions of people, and the so-called free world continued as before with its own interests, hypocrisy and indifference. In the Soviet Union we had Stalinism and the gulags, and in Yugoslavia a one-party system with Goli Otok, a large Communist prison for political detainees on a deserted island in the Adriatic, and many other *otoks*.
>
> The army that ravaged Vukovar and Dubrovnik, and that is now ravaging Bosnian towns and killing civilians, is both materially and psychologically the product of the system that ruled over the past 40 years. Had there been freedom, and the freedom to criticise, that army would not have been what it is, and would not have committed the evils that it has committed.
>
> So we have no reason to idealise the past and to disseminate illusions.
>
> Our current protest against fascism, therefore, does not mean that we wish to return to a society without freedom. Some of those being feted forget this. After everything they have endured, our people have the right to both – peace and freedom. Unfortunately, evil will never be wholly defeated. Mankind is

faced with a continual struggle against evil. We believe that this is where the meaning of our lives and of human history lies.

In sending you my message of good wishes for Victory Day, the victory over fascism 50 long years ago, I wish you also another victory, over the evil of these days, whatever that evil may be called.

The evil of those days, whatever it was called, achieved yet another bloody victory. On 25 May 1995 it mowed down our youth at the Tuzla Kapija. A shell fired from Ozren, almost 20 kilometres away, killed about 70 people on the spot, most of them young men and girls (the final count was 71). A team of experts (three of ours and five European observers) established that the shell had been fired from an M-48 cannon of Russian manufacture. Our entire struggle was a clash between evil and good, but the contrast between these two principles was complete in this case: between the bearded killers on the Ozren hills and the serene faces of the boys and girls on the Tuzla promenade.

Tuzla was in shock, but the funeral had to be arranged. The mortal remains of 47 of the victims now lie together in the central city park in Tuzla. The funeral was at first fixed for 28 May, but in fact it took place at dawn on 29 May. It was postponed because of the danger of renewed shelling from those monsters in human form, who liked to target funerals, where large numbers of people are gathered together.

I don't like early telephone calls. Ever since the war broke out they had never brought me good news. That morning, 28 May 1995, I was called at around six in the morning by General Delić who said, in a voice that boded the worst, 'I have some very sad news for you.' He paused briefly (how long brief pauses of this kind seem) before continuing. 'Last night our helicopter was brought down over the Knin Krajina, with Minister Ljubijankić in it.' I suppose I said nothing, for once again the General's voice could be heard: 'Did you hear me, Mr. President?' I had heard, of course, but I was speechless, appalled by this terrible news. Who would tell Irfan's wife and children, and how?

Dr. Irfan Ljubijankić was the Foreign Minister in the Bosnian Government of that time, a founder of the SDA in the Krajina in 1990, and a good, courageous man.

Around noon I learned that our entire delegation, returning from a visit to the Cazin Krajina, had been killed. Besides Minister Ljubijankić, the four-member delegation included Dr. Izet Muhamedagić, Deputy

Minister of Justice, Dr. Mensur Šabolić, an official in our Zagreb Embassy, and Major Fadil Pekić, Dr. Ljubijankić's escort. The three Russian crew members, paid high 'wages of fear' to pilot the helicopter on this highly dangerous route, were also killed. The flight was exceptionally risky, since it crossed the Knin Krajina, territory under the control of Martić's rebel Serbs. A few days earlier, the helicopter had flown by night from Zagreb to a heliodrome not far from Bihać without any problems; it had been on its return flight.

The brave passengers boarded the craft in Ćoralići on 28 May some time after two in the morning. At around four the alert was given when the helicopter failed to appear at Zagreb airport. The Croatian Army's security services recorded the following conversation of a Serb crew who had obviously been informed about the flight and were waiting, ready to open fire:

Freq:	235800 – Vardar.
	245800 – Drina.
Drina:	Lala here.
Vardar:	Have you seen it?
Drina:	I've seen it 25,00 away due north.
Vardar:	(silent)
Drina:	I can't see, I have to go from this cabin to another.
Vardar:	(silent)
Drina:	I still can't see it, I'll call you as soon as I see it. Have you begun the job?
Vardar:	Yes, we have, is there anything?
Drina:	Just be ready, I'll call you.
Time:	02.44
Drina:	Hullo, here it is 110,25 in your direction.
Time:	02.49
Drina:	Have you hit it?
Vardar:	Of course, here goes the main one.
Drina:	We saw it being fired.
Drina:	Give us the position.
Vardar:	KPDJA.
Drina:	OK, congratulations, come down, cheers!

Our military service comments that the conclusion to be drawn is that the helicopter was hit ten minutes into its flight, at a distance of some 30 kilometres from the take-off point. The helicopter came down near Kremen, five kilometres from Slunj, in territory that had been under the military control of Croatian Serbs since 1990. The area was liberated in operation 'Storm' in early August 1995. Five years later, a modest memorial to the Bosnian delegation was erected on the site of their death.

Irfan Ljubijankić, a medical doctor by profession, was an artistic soul. He wrote poems, and played the piano well. He was in love with his Krajina region, which had been surrounded for more than three years. He paid for his desire to see the Krajina with his life. He left behind him a wife and two young children and was buried in his native Bihać.

Yet another desperate attempt to lift the siege of Sarajevo was made in the second half of June 1995. Perhaps it is inappropriate to compare this operation with similar attempts in the second half of 1992, but from the military perspective the causes of failure were the same: insufficient firepower and insufficient knowledge of the situation on the other side of the line. One thing was clear: the only method that stood a chance was a high-speed breach, a kind of blitzkrieg. Time was not on our side for an action of this kind. As the days went by, the technical superiority of the enemy became ever more marked. After almost a month, with heavy losses on both sides, the operation was halted.

On 19 June 1995, the Army of the Croatian (Knin) Serbs attacked from the western side of the Bihać pocket. The 5th Corps retreated, while putting up a fierce resistance and slowing the enemy advance. I had several telephone conversations with General Dudaković. For the first time, Dudaković was not optimistic. He was worried. I thought: this time the situation is serious, or more precisely, it was critical. A miracle happened, however. When the crisis was at its height, Tuđman called me unexpectedly and suggested that I come to Split for what he called 'important talks'. We were welcomed there by a high-level Croatian military and political delegation. They proposed a joint military action in western Slavonia and the Bihać enclave, with the code-name 'Storm'. Silajdžić and General Delić were with me. We immediately accepted the offer. The action began early in the morning of Friday 4 August, and was brought to a successful conclusion in less than three days. The Croats liberated the Knin Krajina, and we broke through the three-year blockade of the Bihać region. Salvation had come from where it was least expected. I saw in this a sign from God; He had fulfilled His promise to help a people that strives on its own behalf.

Finally, on 30 August 1995, more than three years too late, there followed mass air strikes on the positions of Karadžić's troops throughout Bosnia. These days, characterised by crime and punishment, merit more detailed description.

I had an invitation from the French President, Chirac, to visit France officially on 29 August 1995. We left Sarajevo on 27 August in the late afternoon, and spent the night in Mostar, where we were to be joined by Safet Oručević, Mayor of Mostar. The following day, 28 August, we woke to a beautiful, clear, late summer's day, with no presentiment of evil.

We were supposed to leave the base in Mostar at 11 o'clock and head for the helicopter waiting for us in Jablanica. My son Bakir was supposed to leave at the same time by car for a military airport near Pula in Croatia, where he would take off for Iran in a transport aircraft which had delivered arms for Bosnia. Since we were running late, I was hurriedly getting ready when I was told that Sarajevo was looking for me urgently. The voice on the other end of the line told me that about ten minutes earlier a shell had landed on Markale Market and that there were many casualties, both dead and injured. Along with the Tuzla shelling of 25 May 1995, this was the worst tragedy caused by shelling since the 5 February 1994 massacre when, only about 100 metres from where this one had fallen, the same kind of shell had killed 67 men and women and injured 142.

Chaos prevailed everywhere, so to speak – in the skies and on the ground. Within a short time the skies clouded over, and a storm broke out. I decided to cancel my trip to France. It was better, I thought, to go to Sarajevo and be present at the *janaza* of those who had been killed than to waste my time doing the rounds of European governments that had remained indifferent to atrocities at the heart of Europe. Safet Oručević thought the very opposite: this was the very moment for Europe and America to declare themselves. They should be asked explicitly whether they were ready finally to punish crime and actively support the peace talks that had already been going on for two weeks. And the question should be put to them the following day, in Paris. The arguments were clear. This was indeed the moment.

We set off for Jablanica, where a helicopter was waiting to transfer us to Split. But the further we travelled inland from Mostar, the worse the weather became. There were times when the cloud was so low and the downpour so heavy that visibility was reduced to zero. The heavens and the earth were awash. We reached Jablanica, but there could be no question of the helicopter taking off. We arranged, via Sarajevo, for another helicopter to be prepared at Polog Airfield south of Mostar. Before take-off, via the journalist accompanying us I sent a message to the citizens of Sarajevo:

> The news of this morning's Chetnik atrocity in the Sarajevo marketplace came to me when I was in Mostar on my way to France. I hesitated for a moment on whether or not to continue my journey. We have enemies, but we have also plenty of friends in the world. Unfortunately, the majority of people are indifferent. From the very start this fact has been at the basis of the unprincipled policy towards Bosnia and Herzegovina, and towards the entire crisis that has arisen here. Today's tragedy, the scene of mangled human bodies that we see on our television screens, is the result of the unprincipled policy of a world that abandoned us to our fate and even tied our hands behind our backs.
>
> I am going to Europe to ask people in positions of power there how much longer this is going to continue, and to tell them that we shall no longer put up with this violence. We shall use all means at our disposal to find the way out from this terrible predicament. I emphasis: all means.
>
> As for today's murderers, my message to them is that they will not go unpunished. And that their punishment will come very soon. The day is nigh.

We were welcomed at Orly airport in Paris at 4 pm. We had arrived three hours late. A guard of honour was there to welcome us, and a large group of journalists. The news of the Sarajevo marketplace tragedy had already gone round the world. In the transit area I said that we expected an urgent armed response by the West to the killing machine on the heights above Sarajevo, and that without such action the peace talks were dead. I was to repeat this statement, in various forms, on every possible occasion that evening and the next day.

It is true that it was not easy to make the decision to launch air strikes. When NATO had carried out limited air strikes on 25 and 26 May 1995, the Serbs had captured 375 UN personnel (mainly military observers) and tied them to the pillars and balustrade of the bridges in Pale and other surrounding objects. The memory of this humiliation was still fresh.

The following day I was received at 10 am. by the French President, Chirac. He said: 'We are ready, the Americans are hesitant.' Leaving the

Palais de l'Elysée, I repeated for the umpteenth time that there could be no peace talks if Karadžić's criminals went unpunished.

Throughout those days Richard Holbrooke, the brilliant American diplomat who had launched an American peace initiative in mid August, had been following me like a shadow. I was not surprised to learn that he was now in Paris. Twice during the day he tried to arrange a meeting with me, but I refused. My message to him was that only resolute NATO action could save the peace talks.

To avoid pressure, I accepted the invitation of a group of French intellectuals to a discussion and dinner at the French Institute of International Relations. Krešimir Zubak, Miro Lazović and our Ambassador to France, Prof. Dr. Nikola Kovač, accompanied me.

Our host was Jean Barrio, the prominent French intellectual and member of the Institute Jean Barrio. In a discussion lasting more than two hours, I replied to questions that Jean Barrio described as 'iconoclastic', relating to the possibility of peace, the attitude of the great powers and in particular of France, on Mitterrand and Chirac, my attitude towards the Serbs, so-called Islamic fundamentalism, the future of Bosnia, and so on; in all more than 20 interesting questions and, in my view, open replies.[11]

When we left the meeting, it was past 9 pm. Night had fallen over Paris, and it was raining. I suggested we change into casual clothes, put some kind of caps on our heads and walk along the Champs-Elysées. We were about half way along when a group of people we did not know came up to us. They introduced themselves as people from the American Embassy, and told us that Ambassadress Harriman was inviting us to dinner. I sensed what this was about, and tried to get out of it. I said that I was not properly dressed, and that I had to return home early next morning. Then one of the Americans came up with a powerful argument: 'Madam Ambassador has a very important message for you.' I at once forgot my drab clothes (I was wearing a windjacket and my trousers were soaked with rain), and we set off.

The American Embassy in Paris is in a fine building with a large garden not far from the Champs-Elysées, on the right facing towards the Arc de Triomphe. As we entered the courtyard, I noticed an elderly lady smiling at us from the porch. This was Pamela Harriman, the US Ambassador to Paris, widow of the famous 'roving' diplomat Averell Harriman.

---

[11] The full text of this discussion appears as an Appendix to this book.

Mrs. Harriman welcomed us warmly and led us into a large antechamber. I immediately noticed (guess who!) Richard Holbrooke in the corner, on the telephone. I nodded at him in greeting, whereupon, to my surprise, he beckoned me over, pointing to the telephone receiver. It was obvious that everything had been carefully synchronised, and without doubt the only person who was surprised was me, and none of the Americans. The telephone was answered by Strobe Talbott, Deputy to US Secretary of State Warren Christopher. He spoke to me in approximately these terms: 'Please continue cooperating with Ambassador Holbrooke in seeking conditions for peace in Bosnia. I am aware of your dilemmas and understand them. I assure you that yesterday's atrocity against the citizens of Sarajevo will not go unpunished. We shall carry out air strikes against Karadžić's positions.' He sounded very resolute and convincing, and took his leave of me, evidently wishing to end the conversation as quickly as possible. Nevertheless, I managed to say to him: 'This is good news, Mr. Talbott, but you have not told me when this will happen.' He replied: 'I cannot tell you that, because I myself do not know exactly. The only thing I do know is that it will be soon, very soon.' I replaced the receiver, still trying to understand the real meaning of this dramatic message. We then went in to dinner, and to discussions that lasted until past midnight.

Early the following morning, 30 August, I was awoken by a loud knock on my hotel room door. My escort, Osman, excitedly told me that the Chetnik positions had been attacked and that the skies above the city were red from the strikes on the surrounding hills. I learned later that other targets throughout Bosnia had also been hit. And thus began a new phase of the war in Bosnia, that would end on 21 November with the initialling of the peace accord in Dayton.

The air strikes sent shock waves through the defence system of the Serb Army, and made it considerably easier to carry out the final operations in western Bosnia and Vozuća. The latter was carried out on 10 September 1995 in a joint action by troops from the 2nd and 3rd Corps of the Army of Bosnia and Herzegovina, commanded by Sead Delić and Sakib Mahmuljin, now Generals in the Army of Bosnia and Herzegovina. The main strike in this well planned and conducted operation was carried out by a unit of *mujahidins* composed of volunteers from Muslim countries.

Sarajevo airport was opened on 15 September, after having been closed for five months. The road into Sarajevo via Hadžići, which had been closed throughout the war, would also soon be re-opened. Thus the iron grip around Sarajevo was finally broken, after 43 months. Research conducted by the long-time Commanding Officer of the 1st Corps of the Army of Bosnia and Herzegovina, General Nedžad Ajnadžić, indi-cated that 6,581 soldiers were killed during the defence of the capital city, of which 6,104 were Bosniacs (92.7%), 240 Croats, 223 Serbs and 18 from other ethnic groups. During that same period, more than 10,000 Sarajevans were killed by sniper bullets or shells (the exact number is still not known).

The last major operation by the Bosnian army took place in western Bosnia between 13 September and 12 October 1995, involving about 16,000 troops. Kulen-Vakuf, Bosanska Krupa, Otoka, Bosanski Petrovac, Ključ, Nanica and Sanski Most were liberated. Estimates of enemy casualties are more than 900 soldiers killed and more than 1,000 wounded. Our casualties were 178 men killed, 588 wounded and 41 taken prisoner. However, prior to these significant successes by our army, the tragedy of Srebrenica took place.

Chapter 5

※

SREBRENICA

Security Council Resolution No. 819 – Srebrenica a safe area. Famine in Srebrenica. May 1995 – helicopter downed. Two meetings with Naser Orić. Start of massive attack. Letter to President Clinton. General Rupert Smith announces air-strikes – General Janvier cancels them. Disorganisation in the town and the army. Fall of the town. Exodus and massacre of civilians. Mladić moves against Žepa. Evacuation of civilians from Žepa. Letter to John Major. Letter to the UN Security Council. Report by UN General Secretary – international community acknowledges responsibility for tragedy in Srebrenica. Replies to David Harland's questions.

In the spring of 1992 the situation of our defence against aggression was extremely serious throughout Bosnia and Herzegovina, and in particular in the Podrinje region. Besides the JNA troops regularly stationed in Bosnia and Herzegovina at that time, there were also the corps that had withdrawn from Croatia. Bosnia and Herzegovina was the largest barracks in the world in those days. The aggression against Bosnia that began with the attack on Bijeljina continued with the invasion of Zvornik, Višegrad and Foča – in other words throughout the Podrinje. It is a small miracle that we were able to hold out in Foča for five days, and that we retained Srebrenica and Žepa right up to 1995. The initial resistance was possible thanks to the courage of our people and some defence preparations that the SDA had organised through the Patriotic League. Later the defence was taken over by the Army of Bosnia and Herzegovina.

There was a plan to form a special 8th Corps to defend the Podrinje. The plan provided for the units then defending Goražde, Žepa and Srebrenica to form this corps. In the meantime, however, the agreement on the demilitarisation of Srebrenica and Žepa was signed. This agreement, signed on behalf of our side by the then Chief of General Staff of the Supreme Command, Sefer Halilović, was reached at an exceptionally difficult time for Srebrenica, and enabled the town to survive for more than another two years. Instead of the planned corps, the 81st Division was formed, with its headquarters in Goražde. Srebrenica thus remained within the zone of responsibility of the 2nd Corps, headquartered in Tuzla.

During the winter of 1992-1993 I insisted, in vain, that the 2nd Corps should send reinforcements to Cerska and Konjević-Polje, which were directly at risk. It was said that the Commanding Officer of the 2nd Corps at that time, Željko Knez, favoured the northern sector at the expense of the Drina, but I could not confirm this. I would prefer to say that we had insufficient troops to enter into offensive action towards the Drina. For the Chetniks, any breakthrough by our troops to the Drina would mean their north-south communications line would be cut, so they defended that sector with all available resources, rather like the Posavina corridor.

I must admit that there was a firm conviction that the UN would protect Srebrenica and Žepa, both proclaimed safe areas by UN Security Council Resolutions Nos. 819 and 824 in April 1993. As far as I know, the people of Srebrenica believed it too. Nevertheless, just in case, we delivered the essential military supplies to Srebrenica – as far as we were able, of course, since we could do so only by helicopter. There were sufficient quantities to provide a defence against tanks.

Whenever we raised the issue of lifting the arms embargo, we were threatened with the withdrawal of UNPROFOR troops. This was a serious threat. If UNPROFOR did leave, all three Podrinje enclaves – Goražde, Žepa and Srebrenica – would have been in a particularly difficult, even hopeless, position. It was for this reason that when attending the general assembly session at the end of September 1994 I postponed for six months our demand that the embargo be lifted. I had no choice. The UN troops were the hope of these enclaves, but that hope was betrayed in the summer of 1995.

Plans were made to breach the siege of Srebrenica, but they came up against the fact that this was a formally demilitarised and protected UN zone. Any action of this kind by us would be exploited by the UN as a pretext for withdrawal. The decision was exceptionally risky. What if the action failed. In that case the Chetniks would occupy the town and carry out reprisals, and we would be directly responsible for the tragedy. The only possibility was to maintain the status quo, with the help of the

UN troops, until the entire situation in Bosnia and Herzegovina was resolved by means of peace negotiations. When that happened, it was already too late for Srebrenica and Žepa.

UNPROFOR, which was composed at that time of troops from 13 countries, was only ostensibly under a single command. In reality, each of the major units was under parallel command from the headquarters in its own country. For example, the French, who held the sector around Sarajevo, including Sarajevo airport, and eastern Bosnia, were in fact under the command of the French General Janvier and received their orders direct from Paris. This was an open secret. My talks with President Chirac on 29 August 1995 confirmed this; Chirac did not even attempt to hide the fact. I think that he even wanted me to come to this conclusion.

Some of the people in Srebrenica needed to be replaced, but because the town was officially demilitarised, we could not send new officers. We could only train the ones we had, which we did. Because of a helicopter crash in May, a group of military officers were unable to return to Srebrenica, among them the then Commanding Officer of our troops in Srebrenica, Naser Orić. Orić's Deputy, Ramiz Bećirović, had been in the helicopter, with four doctors. Three of the doctors were killed, and Bećirović was seriously injured. The fact that we were despatching the Deputy Commanding Officer of the Division and four military doctors proves our determination to defend the town. We had also considered sending a state delegation, but UNPROFOR refused to provide transport and escorts, and without these it was impossible.

In the town itself, the situation was extremely serious in every regard. Food ran out from time to time, and there was a constant shortage of salt. A report by an international group describes the sorry state of affairs in Srebrenica in 1993:

> There is no food, and people are stealing and begging from each other. Pneumonia plus malnutrition was killing 20 to 30 people every day, and there were 100-200 extremely ill patients as well as some 300 less seriously ill but who required evacuation. The population had swollen far beyond the capacity of the town's water supply and its sewage capacity. There were some 60 cases of tuberculosis (quoted in Owen, *Balkan Odyssey*, p.131).

The situation was so serious that the idea of exchanging Srebrenica and moving the population elsewhere often came up, only to be rejected. This was the result of consultations with the political and military leadership of Srebrenica. They believed that the town could be defended. It seemed to me that in the event of mass enemy attack the situation was untenable, and I was for evacuation, but I did not insist. As far as I recall, the troops were not in favour of evacuation either.

As a result of being under constant threat and of the specific syndrome of a town cut off from the outside world, there were tensions in Srebrenica, with quarrels, mutual accusations, fights and even murders. We summoned Naser Orić so we could find out just what was going on, for then, as now, there were conflicting accounts. We were surrounded here, as they were there. It was hard for us to get at the truth. We would have had to question dozens of people, and confront them. All this was impossible in such conditions.

I met Srebrenica's Commanding Officer, Naser Orić, on two occasions, the first before the assault and the second during the assault on the town in July 1995. On both occasions the meeting took place in Kakanj, in the 'Black Swans' Barracks. I asked him to return to Srebrenica. It was impossible on foot, and after the May 1995 helicopter crash he refused to go by ordinary helicopter. It's true that it was extremely risky. The attack on Srebrenica was actually going on when I met him for the second time. I asked him to gather a group of volunteers in Tuzla and to meet the mass of civilian refugees making for Tuzla. Thanks to this action, in which troops from the 2nd Corps also took part, a large number of civilians and combatants were saved.

Everything that later became known showed clearly that the Serbs had planned in advance the liquidation of all three Podrinje enclaves – that is, besides Srebrenica and Žepa, of Goražde as well. The genocide, too, was pre-planned. 'The massacres of civilians took place on 14, 15 and 16 July, and on 17 July all the graves were filled in,' stated Jean-René Ruez, a French political commentator, when testifying before the French Parliamentary Mission to investigate the 'Srebrenica case'. Attacks by Serb forces in the safe area of Srebrenica were a daily occurrence, which had led UNPROFOR to abandon five checkpoints and withdraw deep into the safe area.

The final assault on Srebrenica began on 6 July, but at first it resembled all those earlier attacks of limited extent. It was only on 8 and 9 July that one could reach the conclusion that this was a mass assault on the town. We called for action by NATO air forces. We believed that the international community would not allow UNPROFOR troops and a safe area to be overrun. On the other hand, we also expected more from the Srebrenica defence itself, since it had at its disposal significant anti-tank weapons, including almost 300 RPG missiles and dozens of 'Red Arrows', which would have been quite sufficient to halt a tank assault. As far as I know, in the general panic these weapons were not used, or not to the extent they should have been.

The general assessment is that the Serb decision to attack Srebrenica and Žepa was hastened by the news that a Rapid Reaction Force was to be deployed to reinforce UNPROFOR and restore its shaky credibility after the hostage-taking and the humiliation of seeing UNPROFOR troops handcuffed to posts. There was Allied artillery deployed on Igman, the famous 155mm howitzers, light British assault guns, and heavy French mortars. The Serbs decided to pre-empt this action.

On 7 July the Bosnian Serbs attacked an observer post of the Dutch contingent in Srebrenica and took 55 Dutch troops hostage. In order to save the hostages, the international community refused to carry out air strikes and, in effect, sacrificed Srebrenica. On 9 July I sent an urgent message to US President Clinton, and also spoke on the telephone with the Turkish President Demirel and the Iranian President Rafsanjani about the situation in Srebrenica. In my letter to President Clinton I wrote:

> The crisis over Srebrenica, which has been under siege since the start of the aggression, has lasted for a long time.
>
> Security Council Resolution No. 824 proclaimed Srebrenica a UN safe area. It was also demilitarised in 1993 on the basis of an agreement with UNPROFOR. Despite these facts, Srebrenica has been exposed to shelling. Yesterday, however, the Serb aggressor launched a mass mechanised and infantry assault. The UNPROFOR troops, who are few in number in this enclave, had neither the will nor the capacity to protect the town from this assault. The lives of more than 60,000 civilians, mainly women, children and elderly people, are in mortal danger.
>
> Please use your influence on the international community to meet its commitments to this UN safe area and prevent further acts of terrorism and genocide against the civilian population of Srebrenica. I beg you to take urgent action.

Late in the evening of 9 July I had set off to leave Sarajevo through the tunnel under the airport in order to go to Zenica when General Rupert Smith, UNPROFOR Commanding Officer, called me from Split. Sounding agitated, he told me that NATO air strikes on the Serb positions had finally been ordered and would follow without delay. I know that General Smith had been in favour of such action from the very first and that he had sincerely advocated it. Someone senior to him had blocked it, General Janvier or Akashi, and perhaps even UN Secretary-General Boutros Ghali.

In January 1994 the French General Jean Cot, who had at one time been UNPROFOR Commanding Officer in Bosnia, stated in *Le Monde* that he had asked Boutros Ghali on several occasions to give the clearance for air strikes, but that the Secretary-General had refused. Many years later, General Joulwan, NATO Commanding Officer for Europe, stated: 'We in NATO were concerned at that time at the UN's indecisiveness in calling for the use of our military force, although this was a clear violation of a safe area' (in an interview for the Sarajevo daily *Avaz*, 8 July 2000, on the eighth anniversary of the tragedy). It is now known that during the Srebrenica crisis aircraft were taking off from bases in Italy but being turned back in mid-flight.

Hearing the news of the action from General Smith, I continued on my way to Zenica with relief. We were on the alert all night and the whole of the following day, 10 July, expecting a report on the strikes. But no report came. In the late afternoon of 11 July the news began to get through that Mladić's troops had entered the town but no NATO action had followed. Not for the first time, unfortunately, I felt betrayed. It was with these feelings that I issued a public statement on 12 July, reading:

> We call for:
>
> 1. The UN and NATO to use force to establish the safe zone of Srebrenica within its pre-attack area, that is, as it was in May 1993. If they are unable or unwilling to do so, let them say so explicitly.
>
> 2. All available means to be used, including air drops, in association with UNHCR, to provide tents, food and medical supplies around the safe area for the retreating population, including the evacuation of sick and injured civilians. If they are unable or unwilling to do so, let them say so explicitly. The very least that they owe this country, a member of the UN, is a clear and unambiguous response to the above demands. The current confusion in the statements being issued is merely exacerbating an already extremely difficult situation.
>
> 3. Finally, a negative response from them will mean that they openly assent to the legalisation of force in international re-

lations and accept the genocide as a *fait accompli*, as well as accepting war criminals as equal partners. This is the reason for their avoidance of a clear response and the reason this clear response is necessary for us.

The only reaction came from French President Jacques Chirac. He called for the possibility of Srebrenica's being restored to UN military control to be considered. I saw from everyone else's silence that there would be no action, but I sent the French President a letter of thanks:

> I write to you on the occasion of your latest statement on the role of UN troops in Bosnia and the need, following the Srebrenica tragedy, to bring to an end the negative development of the situation in Bosnia which threatens to lead to a conflagration of war in this part of the world.
>
> Your statement was received here with acclaim and the hope that the international community would finally begin to fulfil the commitments it had made towards Bosnia.
>
> We ask only that the Security Council Resolutions, on which international consensus was reached, be implemented consistently and without vacillation.
>
> As a major power and a permanent member of the Security Council, France has particular rights and obligations in this regard.
>
> Mr. President, it is really high time that Serbia and the Serbs ceased to dictate European policy.
>
> Please continue your endeavours to put a stop to the violence in the Balkans.

Our chief handicap was the lack of reliable intelligence on the strength and intentions of the enemy. UNPROFOR certainly had information on the concentration of Mladić's troops, but even they could only guess at his intentions. It was not difficult to conclude from their conduct that they had been caught unawares. This was also evident from their indecisiveness in giving the order for air strikes. The air force would receive two different orders within an hour. The Chetniks took full advantage of this circumstance.

In his *Avaz* interview of July 2000 referred to above, General Joulwan said: 'If we had been more resolute, the Srebrenica tragedy could have been avoided.'

As for the situation in the town under assault, it was characterised by panic and disorganisation. This was the impression I gained from a large number of telephone conversations I held between 7 and 11 July. Later I learned that many smaller units and individuals had fought courageously to the death, but I think that from 9 July onwards there was no longer a unified command. I heard the first news of the fall of the town in Zenica. I think that it was General Delić who told me; he was in continual direct contact. About 20,000 women and children were evacuated from Srebrenica in buses. A long column of men accompanied by troops spent days forcing their way through towards Tuzla and Kladanj. The truth is that the Srebrenica combatants making their way to Tuzla did so with more élan than the troops sent from Tuzla towards Srebrenica. I do not want to shy away from the purely human explanation: the more powerful motivation of troops making their way to safety than that of troops advancing towards danger. A second reason could have been Chetnik cowardice. The Chetniks avoided encounters with the armed and highly motivated combatants who were forcing their way out. They preferred to confront unarmed civilians, of which there were many. The objective, to occupy the town, had already been achieved.

Thanks to satellite images, the headquarters of the great powers knew that a massacre of prisoners and civilians was going on. We could only guess, and hear the news with disbelief as it became worse and worse. I recall that two or three days after the fall of Srebrenica we intercepted a telephone conversation between two Chetniks. One said: 'We sorted them out yesterday.' 'How many, were there 30 of them?' asked the second. 'Add two zeros,' the first answered. I believe that the recording is in the Presidency archives. What really happened, however, exceeded even our darkest forebodings. The International Committee of the Red Cross counted 7,079 civilians and soldiers killed in the first four days of the massacre alone. This is not the final figure. Who is to blame? When a tragedy of this magnitude occurs, no one is innocent. Each of us is to blame for there being a world in which Srebrenica was possible. Each of us must believe that he could have done more. I am not wholly satisfied with the activities of the army at the critical moments, it appears to me that it 'sneaked' around the Chetnik positions. The troops believe that they did everything within their power in those circumstances. In Srebrenica itself a clash between the civilian and the military authorities was constantly simmering. In any event, unanimity was not at the level called for by circumstances. This was in part the result of the psychological situation in a town that was cut off and where living conditions were as difficult as they could be.

On the second anniversary of the Srebrenica tragedy, on 11 July 1997, I sent a message to the women of Srebrenica:

> Whether a tragedy of this extent could have been prevented is a question that will be presented to the conscience of each of us and of every responsible person in the world until a just and honest answer is given. Those were indeed very painful and terrible days for Bosnia. The unsuccessful attempt to lift the siege of Sarajevo 20 days prior to the Chetnik offensive on Srebrenica, the enormous advantage in power of the enemy, which was receiving direct assistance from Serbia, the indifference of the world, the cowardly conduct of UNPROFOR troops at that time, your long isolation and the internal problems that it gave rise to in the besieged town – all this was against us in those terrible days of July.
>
> I want you to believe that we are doing and will continue to do all we can to help you. I know that it is never enough, but after this four-year war of destruction Bosnia is full of wounds that need healing. Srebrenica is just the largest and deepest of them.

As a sign of protest at the cowardly conduct of the international community in the case of Srebrenica and Žepa, on 27 July 1995 Tadeusz Mazowiecki resigned from his position as UN Special Rapporteur for Human Rights. 'One cannot credibly speak of human rights while the international community and its leaders have not the courage and resolve to protect those rights,' wrote this honourable man in his letter of resignation.

In December 1999 the UN Secretary-General Kofi Annan published his report on the Srebrenica tragedy. The report was penitent. International factors acknowledge their responsibility for the tragedy. However, the names of the officials bearing the greatest responsibility were merely timidly hinted at, although the guilt of General Janvier and of Akashi is beyond doubt.

I am not sure whether we shall ever know all the circumstances of the tragedy. Perhaps in 30 years, when all the documents come into the public domain. In this context, there is an interesting detail from my conversation with President Chirac on 29 or 30 August 1995 – a little more than a month after the Srebrenica disaster. I told him that I regarded General Janvier as one of those responsible. He was genuinely surprised, and rejected the very possibility. 'No, he is a very correct officer,' he said. I replied that I had reliable information that it was Janvier himself who had blocked the air strikes, and that he had met Mladić during the crisis. He repeated that he did not believe it, but that he would investigate the matter. A month later, Janvier was recalled.

Encouraged by the world's passivity in the case of Srebrenica, Mladić moved on to Žepa. His plans also included Goražde, but he was stopped. On 17 July 1995 I spoke twice with the UNPROFOR Commanding Officer for Bosnia and Herzegovina, General Rupert Smith, to look into the possibility of evacuating civilians from Žepa with UNPROFOR's assistance. I offered direct talks at the military level with the enemy side on this issue. At the same time I gave instructions to our Foreign Minister, Muhamed Šaćirbegović, to raise the issue of safe evacuation in the UN Security Council and other international institutions. I requested him to lay particular emphasis on the responsibility of the international community for the fate of the population in zones that the UN Security Council had proclaimed as safe areas.

On 20 July I sent a letter to the British Prime Minister, John Major, with a request that he submit it to the foreign and defence ministers of the Contact Group countries at the meeting being held at that very time in London. I wrote:

> While your meeting is being held in London, the drama of the people in the so-called safe area of Žepa continues.
>
> 5,000 women, children and exhausted men are in deadly danger.
>
> After Srebrenica, and the murder of several thousand people in that demilitarised enclave, no one has the right to remain passive and thereby enable the Serb terrorists to commit another mass atrocity.
>
> I therefore call upon you to use all available means to prevent the slaughter of the innocent people of Žepa.
>
> Please, Mr. Prime Minister, inform the participants of the contents of this letter before the start of the meeting.

Five days later, with the attacks still continuing, I sent a letter to the UN Security Council:

> The safe area of Žepa is still the subject of brutal attacks. As a result of uninterrupted shelling, the population has abandoned

> the town and has taken refuge *en masse* in the surrounding forests. I call upon the Security Council to order the safe evacuation of women, children, the sick and the injured from Žepa. I request that the evacuation be conducted under the full protection of UN troops and that General Smith be permitted to use all means, including the use of force, if convoys with civilians come under attack.
>
> After what happened in the safe area of Srebrenica, and after your refusal to defend Žepa, which you also proclaimed a UN safe area by Resolution, saving women and children is the very minimum that you are bound to ensure. Do so without delay and without any hesitation or reservations.
>
> I request that this letter be read at the start of today's session and that it be forwarded to all members of the Security Council.

Generally speaking, both the troops and civilians of Žepa displayed more discipline in this difficult situation than those of Srebrenica. The major credit for this goes to two courageous people: the Commanding Officer in Žepa, Colonel Avdo Palić, and the Mayor of the town, Mehmed Hajrić. Since those tragic days, nothing further has been learned of the fate of these two true heroes. In an attempt to save the civilian population of Žepa, they went to negotiate with Mladić, and never returned. Žepa fell on 25 July 1995.

The misfortunes of Srebrenica and Žepa had a major impact on the events that followed. Our appeals and criticisms, apparently unsuccessful, nonetheless reached critical mass. On 30 August 1995, less than two months after Srebrenica, there came air intervention by NATO on Serb positions throughout Bosnia. The immediate occasion was the shell fired on 28 August at Sarajevo's marketplace, Markale, but I think that the true reason was Srebrenica. Srebrenica also had a direct influence on the Hague indictment of Karadžić and Mladić. For all of us the tragedy of Srebrenica remains the greatest misfortune that could happen in our lives; too great a misfortune for little Bosnia.

As time passes, the world's interest in the Srebrenica tragedy is growing, not diminishing. On 16 July 1999 I received David Harland, Head of Civil Affairs of the UN Mission in Bosnia and Herzegovina, and replied to some of his questions.

Replies To David Harland

(16 July 1999)

Harland: Mr. President, you are no doubt aware that the UN General Assembly has passed a resolution to investigate the circumstances of the fall of Srebrenica in the summer of 1995. The UN Secretary-General has passed a verbal note to the UN Mission in Bosnia and Herzegovina authorising me to assist with the preparations of this report, in accordance with Paragraph 18 of the Resolution. To enable me to do so, I should like to ask you to answer a number of questions on some of the events surrounding the fall of Srebrenica, which are perhaps known to you.

My first question is: did the authorities of the Republic of Bosnia and Herzegovina support the evacuation of civilians from Srebrenica in March–April 1993?

Izetbegović: Yes, although not from the town itself, but of a certain number of civilians who had retreated after the Chetnik offensive on Cerska and Konjević-Polje to Srebrenica. Srebrenica was already seriously overcrowded. There was a serious humanitarian crisis in the town. It was mainly the sick, elderly people, invalids, women and children who left the town then, from areas that Serb forces had occupied in the offensive of March–April 1993. The decision to evacuate these civilians was made by General Morillon. We did not oppose it.

Harland: Did the authorities of the Republic of Bosnia and Herzegovina believe that the Serbs could enter Srebrenica in their offensive of March–April 1993?

Izetbegović: The authorities considered every possible way of preventing Serb forces from entering Srebrenica. A long-term solution was sought for the protection of the inhabitants of the town. If they were unable to enter in March 1993, the Serbs could have attempted to do so later. Srebrenica was completely cut off from the remainder of our free territory. It was impossible to deliver equipment, arms and ammunition for a longer-term defence. The greatest concern was how to feed the inhabitants. These were the reasons for our accepting the idea of safe areas. The Army of Bosnia and Herzegovina troops in Srebrenica were disarmed. All heavy weaponry was excluded. Positions facing the Serb forces were filled in. There were UNPROFOR commitments and guarantees in regard to the UN Resolutions on the safe areas. The people believed that these commitments would be honoured. It is true that the population continued to leave Srebrenica, but this was less out of fear of Chetnik attack and more because of the serious humanitarian situation and in order to join their families.

Harland: Did the authorities of the Republic of Bosnia and Herzegovina consider that the NATO ultimatum of 9 February 1994 contributed to the decision of the Serbs to withdraw their heavy weaponry from around Sarajevo or to place it in weapons collection points to be controlled by UNPROFOR?

Izetbegović: The NATO ultimatum was only partly effective. A high proportion of the arms were not placed under control, nor was UNPROFOR willing to implement the decision fully. The Serbs took weapons away whenever they wanted. There is the well-known case of the removal of heavy weapons from the collection centre in Lukavica. This was in March or April 1994. Obviously their assessment was that at this time it was merely a verbal threat from NATO.

Harland: Did the authorities of the Republic of Bosnia and Herzegovina consider that the Serbs could enter Goražde in their offensive of April 1994?

Izetbegović: There was a real danger, but we believed that Goražde would hold out, and hold out it did, with the utmost effort.

Harland: Did the authorities of the Republic of Bosnia and Herzegovina consider that the NATO ultimatum of 22 April 1994 played a certain part in the decision of the Serbs not to continue their offensive against Goražde?

Izetbegović: It did, without any doubt. However, it was the defence of Goražde by the Army of the Republic of Bosnia and Herzegovina that was crucial. The offensive had lasted almost a month prior to the ultimatum. If troops of the Army of the Republic of Bosnia and Herzegovina had not had the capacity to defend Goražde for that month, the ultimatum would have come too late.

Harland: From the perspective of the authorities of the Republic of Bosnia and Herzegovina, why didn't the Serbs enter Srebrenica prior to July 1995?

Izetbegović: The course of events during 1992, 1993 and 1994 gave the Serbs the impression that the international community was irresolute and indecisive. There were differing assessments among the Serb leadership on the readiness of the world to intervene. Mladić decided to take the risk in Srebrenica. As it turned out, his judgement that the international community would not decide to act was right. I presume that he came to that conclusion, among other things, from the discussions the Serb leadership had with Akashi and General Janvier.

Harland: To what extent did the authorities of the Republic of Bosnia and Herzegovina consider an exchange of Srebrenica and Žepa with the Bosnian Serbs as part of a peaceful solution? What talks were held on this subject internally, and what with the Serbs?

Izetbegović: No talks were held with the Serb side on this issue, but in Dayton, along with everything else, the Americans asked us to accept the final version of the map of the entities in Bosnia and Herzegovina. The map altered during the negotiations. Finally we succeeded in getting Sarajevo and a corridor to Goražde, but not Srebrenica and Žepa. When I did not want to agree to Brčko being in Republika Srpska (this was on 20 November) the talks were on the point of collapse. All we could have done was to return to Bosnia and continue the war under extremely unfavourable circumstances, in total isolation from the international community. It appeared to us then that we would be able to some extent to compensate for the loss of Bosniac majority areas in the Podrinje by the return of refugees and displaced persons to those areas, which was guaranteed by Annexe 7 of the Dayton Accord. I still believe in this and act accordingly.

Harland: Is it possible that the thought that Srebrenica would be ceded to the Bosnian Serbs in the peace accord influenced the willingness of the defenders of Srebrenica to put up a fiercer defence?

Izetbegović: I have said that prior to Dayton it was never even imagined, let alone spoken of, that Srebrenica could be ceded to the Serbs. The evidence is the defence weaponry that we sent to the garrison in Srebrenica. We had also supplied them with TF-8 anti-tank weapons, and in the last helicopter flight for Srebrenica, which was brought down in May 1995, there were four military medical officers as well. Three of them were killed when the helicopter was downed, and the Deputy Commanding Officer, Major Bećirović, was seriously injured. One does not send military medical officers and sophisticated arms to a town that one intends to abandon.

Harland: Was the Army of the Republic of Bosnia and Herzegovina ordered to supply military equipment to the defenders of Srebrenica even after 13 April 1993? If so, why? If not, why not?

Izetbegović: Yes, the army was tasked with supporting the defenders of Srebrenica as best it could, but I stress, not with offensive but with defensive weapons.

Harland: Did the authorities of the Republic of Bosnia and Herzegovina know of any kind of attacks outside the safe area of Srebrenica after April 1993?

Izetbegović: Not as far as I am aware.

Harland: In the opinion of the authorities of the Republic of Bosnia and Herzegovina, why did UNPROFOR fail to apply its mandate to deter the attacks on the safe areas of Srebrenica and Žepa? Were the authorities surprised by this failure? Did their plans assume such lack of success?

Izetbegović: UNPROFOR always justified itself by saying it had no mandate to use force. However, when Srebrenica and Žepa were declared UN safe areas, we believed that UNPROFOR would use its authority to call for NATO air support. It could and should have done so, since the Security Council Resolutions on the safe areas in Bosnia and Herzegovina were adopted on the basis of Chapter VII of the UN Charter, which means that they could be implemented with the use of force if necessary. We had every reason to believe in an airborne response from NATO in the event of more robust attacks by Serb forces on Srebrenica and Žepa. You know that the decision to do so was taken, then withdrawn, then taken again, and then finally again withdrawn. Why and how is a question that only Akashi and General Janvier can answer. They know about the game that was played out behind the scenes on 8, 9, 10 and 11 July 1995. General Smith called me late in the evening of the 9th to tell me that NATO air action had been ordered and would follow early in the morning. I think that General Smith was a very correct officer and that he was ashamed of the irresolution of UN political leaders, who consented to suffer violence against and even the humiliation of

UN troops by Serb generals. Unfortunately, neither his nor my expectations were met. The powers-that-be higher up in the UN, or some other powers, decreed otherwise.

Harland: Did the authorities of the Republic of Bosnia and Herzegovina expect the Serb attacks in July 1995? Did they expect that Srebrenica could fall? Did they foresee that the Serbs might massacre the majority of boys and men they took prisoner?

Izetbegović: Naturally, nothing could be wholly excluded. There were certain indications, and intelligence reports, but not wholly dependable ones. We in Sarajevo were under siege, cut off. There were always suspicions of possible military stratagems and deliberate disinformation on the part of the Serb headquarters. I can only tell you my own personal view: I did not expect an attack on Srebrenica with the aim of occupying the town. Nor did I expect the Serbs, even after everything that had happened, to opt for a massacre. I believed that this time the international community would not tolerate something of this kind. But what one expects seldom happens, especially if one hopes for the best.

Harland: Did the conquest of Srebrenica and Žepa make the final peace accord easier?

Izetbegović: I do not think that is so, except in another specific sense: our fear that yet another Srebrenica would occur, and another, and another. The attitude of the world did not encourage us. Quite the contrary.

Harland: Did the Dayton Peace Accord have more advantages for the Bosniacs than earlier proposals for a peaceful solution that provided for Srebrenica and Žepa to remain within the areas under Bosniac control (for example, the Vance-Owen plan, the Contact Group Plan, the HMS *Invincible* Plan, and so on)?

Izetbegović: I think that for us the Vance-Owen Plan was more favourable than Dayton, precisely because of the Bosniac majority areas in the Podrinje. But the Serbs rejected the Vance-Owen Plan, and the war continued. However, the Dayton Accord has another, very important advantage over the Vance-Owen Plan. An international military implementation force was an integral part of Dayton. The Vance-Owen Plan, even if the Serbs had formally accepted it, would in my view have remained a dead letter in every aspect that did not suit the Serbs.

Harland: Were the authorities of the Republic of Bosnia and Herzegovina aware of any involvement, direct or indirect, of the Federal Republic of Yugoslavia in the attacks on Srebrenica and Žepa?

Izetbegović: I have already responded to that question. So, to a certain extent, yes.

Harland: When did the authorities of the Republic of Bosnia and Herzegovina begin to believe that the majority of men and boys taken prisoner by the Bosnian Serbs had been massacred? What were the sources of information?

Izetbegović: We learned of individual killings as soon as the first refugees reached Tuzla and Kladanj. But what in fact happened exceeded even our worst imaginings. I don't think anyone could ever have supposed that something so terrible would occur.

Harland: Why, in the opinion of the authorities of the Republic of Bosnia and Herzegovina, did UNPROFOR call for major NATO air strikes on 29 August 1995 when it had not done so earlier? In the opinion of the authorities of the Republic of Bosnia and Herzegovina, would such air strikes have been of greater military or political benefit if they had been used in August 1993 (Igman), in February 1994 (Sarajevo), in April 1994 (Goražde) or in July 1995 (Srebrenica and Žepa)?

Izetbegović: Everyone agrees, both we in Bosnia and Herzegovina and responsible people abroad, that the strikes at the end of August 1995 were at least three years too late. And why did it finally come to air strikes? Well, it seems that the last straw had finally come. The world, whatever it may be, could no longer look on indifferently. This is one reason. Another could be the assessment that it was still possible to reach peace on the basis of compromise. A peace without either victors or losers suited the international community. A peace of this kind was still possible in the autumn of 1995. The following year we might have decided to go all the way. This did not suit the world, so it opted for military and political action.

Chapter 6

War and Jaw

Carrington's mediation. Vance-Owen Plan. Karadžić rejects the plan. Persuasion in Athens – Karadžić signs, the Serb Assembly rejects it. So-called Joint Action Plan – the West yields to Karadžić. Proclamation to the citizens of Bosnia and Herzegovina. Vance withdraws, Stoltenberg replaces him. Owen-Stoltenberg Plan. UNPROFOR's double-dealing. Pressures. Meeting on the British aircraft carrier, HMS Invincible. First Bosniac Assembly and Parliamentary Assembly of the Republic of Bosnia and Herzegovina in session. Richard Holbrooke and the American peace initiative. Tragedy on Igman. Air-strikes halted. Letters to Presidents Clinton and Chirac. Meeting with Holbrooke in Ankara and Republika Srpska. Geneva Conference and Basic Principles. Answers for Sky News. Tuđman's interview with Le Figaro. Meeting in New York. American ultimatum and cease-fire.

I loathed the war, and still clearly remembered the one that took place 50 years ago. When it swept over Yugoslavia, I was 16. I remember the hunger, the bombing, the refugees, the lawlessness of war. In that experience I differed from many of my younger associates and friends, who knew something of the Second World War only from books.

Negotiate wherever we can and fight wherever we have to – that was the principle I stuck to, or to put it better, which I had to stick to in the given circumstances.

But I was negotiating on behalf of a militarily much weaker side. The weak must appeal to principles, for they have no power. It's hard on a negotiator whose only trump card is principles.

When I received Lord Carrington, the European Community Representative for Yugoslav Affairs, on 3 July 1992, there were three months of destructive and bloody war behind us. We were both disappointed with the meeting. I with his unwillingness, or in fact the unwillingness of Europe, to protect a small European country that was the victim of aggression; he with my demand – to me, a wholly reasonable one – that as a condition of talks a seven-day cease-fire be ordered and the JNA heavy weapons be placed under UN control.

I was not that surprised. An EEC report dating from 1988 foreshadowed this vacillating attitude of Europe towards the emerging crisis in Yugoslavia: 'The agreement signed in Belgrade in 1988 [between Yugoslavia and the EEC] is defined as an agreement *sui generis*, in the sense that political motives overruled economic ones, primarily because of the worsening situation in the country, and also because of the growing role of the SEV Zone in Yugoslav foreign trade and the sensitive political moment that followed the death of President Tito. Almost all the sweeping deficiencies in the commitments of Yugoslavia to reciprocal concessions are based on motives of a political nature.' Thus the second paragraph of Clause 17 of the report by Giorgio Rosetti, Deputy to the European Parliament, submitted on behalf of the Foreign Relations Committee. The report was adopted at the European Parliamentary session in January 1988 and was a typical example of the pragmatic rather than the principled approach. Europe had long since ceased to strive for ideas. Everything had been turned into calculated interests.

I must admit that in one matter Lord Carrington was very fair with me: not for one moment did he allow me to remain with the illusion that the world, and in particular Europe, would help Bosnia under attack. On the contrary, he was very clear and explicit: 'Don't count on it, because it won't happen. Try to negotiate with the Serbs, it's the only way out.' We were both silent for a few minutes before he stood up. I accompanied him to the exit from the building. On the landing between two flights of stairs he suddenly paused and asked me: 'Well, what do you intend to do?' 'We'll fight,' I replied. 'What do you mean, do you know who you're dealing with?' 'I know,' I answered, 'but do we have any choice?' He made no comment, but I am sure he thought I was mad.

Luckily we were all a little mad at that time. Much later, at a gathering of officers and men from the Bosnian Army, I told them to go out among the people and get to know them:

> Why would it be a good thing for you to do the rounds of Bosnia? You need to know your people. I have been rediscovering the people for myself these days through direct contacts. They are good people, and in particular, brave people. Strange things are happening. They tell me: 'Mr. President, we have no

bullets, we have no food.' And then I expect them to say to me: Come on, try to find a way out. But then there follows an unexpected sentence: 'But please, don't let them get away with anything. We have the strength, and we shall fight to the end.' I have sometimes been somewhat taken aback, not knowing what to say to them, but it happens almost every time. ... Some might say, where's the logic in this. There is no logic! And it's a good thing there is none. I would not wish now to digress into the philosophy of the relationship between life and logic, but we shall agree that it was a good thing we were not wholly logical. For if we had been, we would have surrendered at the end of April or the beginning of May 1992. The entire logic of the world was against us at that time. And now we have these illogical people: we have no food, we have no bullets, but we'll fight and win. What is one to do with them? They are good, courageous people.

(From an address to graduates at a seminar on morals convened at the General Staff of the Army of Bosnia and Herzegovina, Sarajevo, Army Hall, 9 December 1993.)

On 4 July 1992 the self-styled Croat Community of Herceg-Bosna was proclaimed in Grude, and the very next day it took its first action against the Bosnian State: it confiscated 38 trucks loaded with arms and equipment that we had secretly procured for the defence of Sarajevo (this robbery was reported in the *New York Times* on 6 July).

As a condition for the continuation of talks on the Cutileiro-Carrington Plan, I called for the withdrawal of heavy weapons around Sarajevo to be ensured in accordance with Security Council Resolution No. 752. In a letter dated 26 July 1992 I informed Lord Carrington that after the London talks further mass atrocities had taken place and that concentration camps were sprouting up all over Bosnia and Herzegovina. I ended the letter with the words: 'I assure you that unless the heavy weapons are eliminated, as agreed in London on 17 July, the aggression against Bosnia and Herzegovina will continue, and that in such circumstances talks would merely be a cover for the continuation of aggression and the legalisation of the occupation of territory by the use of force and ethnic cleansing.'

There was no response. Instead, the London Conference on former Yugoslavia was convened for 26 August, with more than 40 participants. After two days in session, and numerous meetings, several documents were adopted including the Declaration on Bosnia and Herzegovina. Among other things, the declaration confirmed the integrity of Bosnia and Herzegovina's borders. Cutileiro and Carrington resigned, and future talks were entrusted to Cyrus Vance (for the UN) and Lord Owen (for the European Community).

In October Vance and Owen submitted a preliminary document entitled 'Possible Constitutional Structure of Bosnia and Herzegovina', which envisaged a decentralised state with between seven and ten provinces, chiefly based on the ethnic principle. Of course, there were also the principles of parity and consensus, which it seems Bosnia cannot escape. The Vance-Owen Plan envisaged a nine-member Government (3+3+3) which would adopt decisions by consensus.

Problems arose when it came to working out the maps of the provinces. The Bosnian delegation, which the Croat representatives Ljubić and Brkić had left in the interim, proposed a map with 13 provinces. The Croat and Serb representatives continued to insist on their 'Croat' and 'Serb' provinces, with the Serbs including in theirs large areas with a majority Bosniac population.

At a meeting in Zagreb in mid December 1992, Owen demanded, in the form of an ultimatum, that I agree to direct talks with the president of the SDS, Radovan Karadžić. If I did not, he threatened that the international community would withdraw not only from the talks but from all forms of involvement in Bosnia and Herzegovina. There was no way I could allow this. Without some kind of involvement of the outside world, in particular without deliveries of food and medical supplies, Bosnia could not have survived, under attack as it was. I agreed to talks with Karadžić.

The long and exhausting Geneva talks began, resulting in a draft peace plan for Bosnia and Herzegovina. The proposal comprised four documents: an Agreement on Bosnia and Herzegovina, an Agreement on Peace in Bosnia and Herzegovina, the Maps of the Provinces and an Agreement on Transitional Measures.

Once again it was a decentralised state, this time with ten provinces. The jurisdiction of the state itself covered foreign affairs, foreign trade, citizenship, taxes for the state budget, a central bank with a single currency, international and inter-provincial communications (railways, roads, post office and so on) and the energy supply system. In addition: a multi-ethnic government on the basis of the 1991 population Census, freedom of movement throughout the country, human rights to European standards and with international control, democratically elected state and local governments with a mechanism for resolving disputes between them.

The maps of the provinces were to a large extent based on the ethnic principle, and clearly honoured the results of aggression and ethnic cleansing. Thus, for example, Bosniacs, who formed 43.74% of the population according to the 1991 Census, were allocated a mere 26.36% of the territory (without counting Sarajevo). It was an attempt to buy peace with this unprincipled compromise at the expense of the weaker.

The essence of our position as the world saw it was defined by Carl Bildt with these words stated in the Bosnian edition of his publication: 'To put it simply, [the Muslims] could choose between having 30 per cent authority over 100 per cent of Bosnia or 100 per cent influence over 30 per cent of Bosnia… The alternative of 100 per cent control over 100 per cent of the territory of Bosnia did not and could not exist' (Carl Bildt, *Peace Journey: The Struggle for Peace in Bosnia*). This leaves open, of course, the question why 30%? Why should the almost 50% Bosniac population (Muslims, as they say) have the right to only 30% of Bosnia? This was European justice for the Bosnian Muslims.

To highlight the American involvement in the peace process, the talks moved to New York.

We were unhappy with the proposal, but in the meantime disturbing news began to come in from the field of potential open conflict between the HVO and the Army of Bosnia and Herzegovina. From far-away America, it seemed that this conflict could mean the end of Bosnia, since it would open yet another front for the Army of Bosnia and Herzegovina, and the single supply-line via Croatia and Herzegovina would be cut off. The war had to be brought to an end, since it threatened not only the destruction of Bosnia but the end of the Bosnian idea itself. In these circumstances, I signed the Vance-Owen Plan in New York on 25 March. My signature was accompanied by a restricting clause which read:

> First, our signature on this document will become invalid and will be considered legally null and void if the following conditions are not met:
>
> – all interested parties, in particular the aggressor party, sign the document without any alternatives or reservations;
>
> – the international community undertakes effective measures for the implementation of the signed agreement within an appropriate time frame;

– the aggression does not continue.

Second, no provision of the signed document may be interpreted or understood in such a way as to diminish the integrity and sovereignty of Bosnia and Herzegovina as an independent and indivisible state entity.

Prior to this, at its session of 15 March 1993, the Parliament of the Republic of Bosnia and Herzegovina adopted decisions supporting the peace process 'in order to end the aggression' – as minuted, and welcomed the work of our delegation at the talks in New York. The vote on these decisions was unanimous.

The Croat side also accepted the Vance-Owen Plan, which was to be expected, since it met all their conditions. Karadžić rejected the Plan. There followed a process of persuasion combined with threats to bomb Serb positions and to tighten the sanctions against Serbia. Finally, on 2 May 1993, in Athens, after a 'work-over' lasting all night, Karadžić put his signature to the document, but this time too with a condition that made it effectively worthless: that the self-styled Serb Assembly approve the document. Those who were well informed of the state of affairs knew what that condition meant.

Both the Greek Prime Minister, Mitsotakis, and the Serbian President, Milošević, were involved in persuading the members of the Serb Assembly, which met in Pale late on 6 May 1993. Despite some rumours to the contrary, I think that the endeavours of these two to convince the Serb Assembly to accept the agreement were sincere and, to begin with, successful. Milošević believed that the Serbs had attained their true goal, and economic sanctions were becoming too heavy a burden for Serbia to bear. It seems that the affair was thrown off the planned course by Krajišnik's craftiness. After a long debate, and just before the vote was to be taken, Krajišnik proposed that the session be adjourned for a shared dinner. This was done, but lobbying followed, and when the assembly reconvened after dinner, the mood had changed completely. The vote to accept the peace plan was lost, and the war continued with heightened intensity.

There was not long to wait before the great powers retreated. As early as 22 May 1993 the USA, Great Britain, France, Russia and Spain launched the so-called Joint Action Programme, which meant in effect abandoning the Vance-Owen Plan. In essence it was a concession to Karadžić's Serbs, which Noel Malcolm calls 'the final death warrant for Bosnia.'[1]

[1] Noel Malcolm, *Bosnia: A Short History*, p. 250.

The Serbs would not be required to hand back occupied territory. Only the so-called UN safe areas for the Muslim population would be guaranteed in future. I reacted bitterly. On 23 May I addressed the people of Bosnia and Herzegovina:

> Citizens of Bosnia and Herzegovina,
>
> I am sure that you, like me, listened anxiously last night to what the Big Four would say in far-away America. I am sure that you, like me, are shattered by what the bleak announcements hinted at.
>
> We heard, if we heard right, that the aggressor will not withdraw from occupied territory, which means that our people who have been forced to leave their homes will not be able to return, that a part of our people will be provided with so-called safe areas, which means reservations, etc.
>
> If that is so, we can only say that this new plan is wholly unacceptable to us.
>
> If the international community is really not ready to defend the principles which it itself has proclaimed as its foundations, if it is ready to recognise the law of force in international relations, to close its eyes to unprecedented violations of human rights and international law, and what is more to reward aggression and genocide, let it say so openly both to our people and to the people of the world. Let it proclaim a new code of conduct in which force will be the first and last argument, and let it proclaim that the UN Charter and the painstakingly and patiently constructed laws of the international order are no longer valid.
>
> Citizens of Bosnia and Herzegovina, God and men are our witnesses that we did everything to avoid war, and when it came to war, to find the way to peace.
>
> But this can only be a just peace. And a just peace includes, as a minimum, the return of occupied territory and the return of our long-suffering population to their homes. Without this, there can be no peace.
>
> When we signed the Vance-Owen Plan, we said our last word, the bottom line below which we will not and cannot go. We shall no longer waste time on fruitless talks. Instead, we shall turn to our people, to all our citizens who love this country and who cherish Bosnia and Herzegovina in their hearts, and

> call upon them to unite and to use all means, all admissible means, to defend an independent and sovereign Bosnia and Herzegovina and its integrity and freedom.
>
> Dear citizens, the world has not left us much choice. I believe that I share your thoughts and feelings when I say that we shall not bow our heads, and that we shall accept the risks of the struggle for freedom and dignity.
>
> Do not be afraid, and do not doubt, for a people that fights for survival and freedom, if it truly fights, cannot lose.

It was typical that Germany took no part in this conspiracy against Bosnia. The German Defence Minister, Folker Ruhe, called the Joint Action Programme a 'moral catastrophe', and the German newspaper *Westdeutsche Zeitung* wrote at that time: 'Those who are killing, expelling and raping, have won.'

Lord Owen did not give up. After Cyrus Vance resigned, a new pair continued working, this time Lord David Owen and Thorvald Stoltenberg. After the Serbs rejected the Vance-Owen Plan, it was taken for granted that the only way to find a solution was in concessions to the Serb side, and this is what happened.

Instead of a decentralised state with ten provinces, the new plan proposed a confederation of three republics: Serb, Croat and Bosniac. In effect, a solution was sought in the partition of Bosnia, which was what the Serb side, and to a lesser extent the Croats, had insisted on from the very beginning.

New talks began in July 1993, in circumstances that could hardly have been more unfavourable for us both politically and militarily. We were fighting on two fronts, and barely holding on to our positions. During the talks, the Serb General Mladić launched an offensive on Bjelašnica and Igman, while representatives of the international community issued shocking and confusing statements about this Serb action and about the war in Bosnia and Herzegovina as a whole. From this distance it appears that military action by the Serb and Croat forces was tolerated, and perhaps even encouraged, so as to compel our side to make concessions. For example, on 16 August 1993 UNPROFOR Lt.Col. Barry Frewer announced that Sarajevo was not under siege but was militarily surrounded (!?), and the British Brigadier Hays, a few days earlier, said that the problem was not the Serb offensive on Bjelašnica and Igman, but the offensive of the Bosnian Army in Gornji Vakuf and Prozor.

On 9 July the *New York Times* published an article by its Washington correspondent, according to which Mrs. Ogata had announced the possibility that UN forces would be withdrawn if the Presidency of the Republic of Bosnia and Herzegovina refused to negotiate. The seriousness of this threat can be judged from the fact that, thanks to the presence of UN troops, who protected Sarajevo airport and convoys, UNHCR was bringing in up to 8,000 tonnes of food and medical supplies a week (UNHCR data). Thanks to this, there were still no cases of large-scale deaths from starvation. Now that danger too loomed over wide areas of Bosnia, in particular the towns.

The Serb actions on Bjelašnica and Igman, which were intended to finally close the stranglehold around Sarajevo, were the subject of a tough diplomatic battle at the Geneva talks, in which we succeeded in outwitting the Chetniks. I have already covered this interesting detail in Chapter 4 of this book.

Meanwhile the Security Council twice debated the call to lift the arms embargo. On the second occasion this was on the basis of a proposal from Islamic and a certain number of non-aligned countries. The voting result is interesting: six *for* (the USA and five non-aligned countries), and nine abstentions (including France, Britain and Russia). Bosnia and Herzegovina was deprived of the right to self-defence. The message from the three great powers, particularly Great Britain, was that there was no way out for Bosnia except to negotiate and to accept whatever was offered. This message was equivalent to blackmail.

During the negotiations for the earlier Vance-Owen Plan, I could not say that Lord Owen was biased or that he favoured only one side. But I cannot say the same of Lord Owen in the case of the talks aimed at achieving the Owen-Stoltenberg Plan. His conduct that time was a case study in *real-politik* and, clearly, *real-politik* and morality do not go together. He began to exert strong and systematic pressure on our government to accept the partition of the country, even the possible partition of Sarajevo, and then opposed the bombing of Serb positions because of their continued aggression, stated that the Serbs owned 65% of the land in Bosnia and Herzegovina (Karadžić's data), and finally tried to break up the existing Presidency of the Republic of Bosnia and Herzegovina, proposing that instead of the legal Presidency a nine-member coordinating body be formed on the principle of parity, with three members each from the Serb, Croat and Bosniac peoples. Given this behaviour, on one occasion I said that Lord Owen was the Chamberlain of our time, which *The Washington Post* – not without a certain malice, I believe – reported on 10 August.

At the height of this crisis, demonstrations by refugees from Bosnia and Herzegovina were held. An enraged crowd of several thousand people rocked and threatened to break down the fence around the UN Headquarters in Geneva. I came up to them from the other side of the fence, shook hands with many of them, and asked them to disperse.

In everything he proposed and did this time, Lord Owen had the support of Milošević and Tuđman. What is more, at a session of the Presidency of the Republic of Bosnia and Herzegovina held in Zagreb on 9 July 1993, he put forward a joint Serb-Croat – in fact Milošević-Tuđman – plan, composed of constitutional principles for a peace accord and transitional arrangements. This plan meant in effect the abolition of the state of Bosnia and Herzegovina and a break in its legal continuity as a state, which had been confirmed in every previous document from the London Conference onwards. This plan envisaged Bosnia and Herzegovina as a kind of confederation of three statelets on the basis of agreement.

We rejected this proposal. Instead, at a session held on 17 and 18 July 1993 the Presidency of the Republic of Bosnia and Herzegovina and political parties drew up their own plan, in which Bosnia and Herzegovina was a federation with international personality and exclusive jurisdiction over human rights issues, the defence of its territorial integrity, foreign affairs, statehood and the basis of the economic system. Armed with this proposal, the Bosnian delegation went to Geneva for talks convened for 26 July. Without much discussion the Serb and Croat representatives rejected the proposal. The only thing on the table was the Owen-Stoltenberg Plan and its alternative – a continuation of the war. I requested that a session of the Assembly of the Republic of Bosnia and Herzegovina be held in order to reach a decision. The Assembly met on 27 and 28 August. In my introductory speech I said:

> Our position is characterised by two impassioned nationalisms in our immediate neighbourhood and the strange and incomprehensible indifference or passivity of the rest of the world. In such a situation, constantly confronted with the alternative of the war continuing, we could no longer defend the concept of a unified Bosnia and Herzegovina. We decided to defend its integrity for future, and I hope more reasonable, generations. In the meantime, it appears that we have to partition. We can do so at the negotiating table or on the battle-

field, in a war in which, unfortunately, almost every law is gradually ceasing to be observed. I think it is better that we do so at the negotiating table. And yet, history must remember: we did not want partition, it was imposed upon us.

In this situation, a question from a journalist from *The Times* of London sounded cynical:

The Times: What would you answer to critics who say that you want to establish an Islamic state?

Izetbegović: I would say that they are either ill-informed or ill-intentioned. I advocate the integrity of Bosnia and Herzegovina, and an integral Bosnia and Herzegovina, since it is multi-national, cannot by definition be an Islamic state. Only a partitioned Bosnia can be that, and it is in fact certain European governments who are working ardently for the partition of Bosnia. Thus we have the paradox of Europe creating an Islamic state in Bosnia.

The debate in the assembly took place in the atmosphere of an extremely serious military situation and with the feeling that Bosnia and Herzegovina had no choice. Among the decisions adopted by the assembly on the second day of the session was the following: 'The peace talks in Geneva should continue with the aim of finding a solution that ensures a durable and just peace, the continuity of the statehood and international personality of Bosnia and Herzegovina ... The constitutional agreement on a federation of republics must undergo significant changes in two respects: it must specify that this does not involve the abolition of Bosnia and Herzegovina as a state, but rather the transformation of its internal organisation as a state into three republics, and it must clearly define the joint functions at the state level of Bosnia and Herzegovina, with a minimum that, in addition to international personality and foreign trade, includes citizenship, border control and the basis of the economic and legal systems.'

In regard to the maps of the 'republics', the Assembly of the Republic of Bosnia and Herzegovina concluded that the territory of the 'Bosnian Republic' must include all the territories with an absolute or relative Bosniac majority, taking the 1991 population Census as the baseline. Given the known stance of the aggressor side, this demand meant in effect the rejection of the plan. The talks as a whole took place in two stages, the first in July and August, the second in September and October.

In early September there came the news that trucks carrying fuel oil for Sarajevo were being held in Metković. It was a time when the mood in Bosnia and Herzegovina was nearing rock bottom. Recalling those days, Noel Malcolm writes in the Introduction to the Bosnian/Croatian edition of his *Bosnia: A Short History*:

> I wrote this book in August and September 1993, gripped by almost overwhelming despair at the future of Bosnia. It seemed that the outside world had given up every serious attempt to save Bosnia from collapse; it also appeared that the Serb politicians and military commanders who had planned the occupation of territory and the mass expulsion of the population had almost wholly achieved their aims. (p. ix)

On 9 September I received a letter from the French and German Foreign Ministers, Juppé and Kinkel, informing me that the peace talks must continue, and that these two countries would insist on the Bosnian Republic being guaranteed access to the sea. Somewhat prior to this Tuđman had refused to agree to that access being in Neum.

We began the second round of talks with the demand that political freedom and party pluralism be ensured throughout Bosnia and Herzegovina. By decision of the assembly, the Bosnian Government Delegation was composed of Izetbegović, Silajdžić, Lazović, Komšić, Ljubijankić, Filipović, Abdić, and experts Trnka and Čukle.

On 20 September there followed a meeting of the delegations on the British aircraft carrier HMS *Invincible*, which was sailing the Adriatic sea. Tuđman and Milošević attended the meeting. In inviting us to meet on the carrier, Lord Owen clearly wanted to impress us. We, all accustomed to powerful feelings and witnesses to extremely dramatic events, however, remained indifferent. What can make an impression on you when you know that at that very moment thousands of people are starving in Croatian concentration camps?

I took advantage of Owen's wish to obtain a decision on a peace accord to bring together, with UNPROFOR's assistance, participants in the Bosniac Assembly, followed by deputies to the Assembly of Bosnia and Herzegovina from all the areas that had so far been inaccessible.

I gave the introductory speech at the assembly: an analysis of the reasons for and against the proposed plan. My proposal for a resolution of this 'dilemma between a just war and an unjust peace,' as I defined it, did not appear. Although I listed nine reasons for accepting and four against the plan proposed by Owen and Stoltenberg, it was clear that the smaller number carried the greater weight. The plan was effectively refused, in diplomatic terms, since its acceptance was subject to a wholly reasonable, but to the Serbs unacceptable condition: the return of all territories on which the Bosniacs were an absolute or relative majority according to the 1991 Census. The situation is best illustrated by this fact: a wholly reasonable condition was unacceptable, and both we and they knew it.

The European Union continued to exert pressure on the Bosnian government, through its foreign ministers, to accept the peace package. The British Foreign Secretary, Douglas Hurd, demonstrated particular heartlessness when he announced that Britain would not take part in the operation to deliver humanitarian aid the following year. No more serious threat could have been expressed, for the population of a whole series of Bosnian enclaves, among them Sarajevo, Maglaj, Srebrenica and Goražde, were already near starvation.

At a meeting held on 22 December, in order to cajole us into accepting the Owen-Stoltenberg Plan, the European Union foreign ministers offered a rectification to the map of the 'Bosnian Republics' with the original 28.3% increased to 33.3% of the territory of Bosnia and Herzegovina, but we rejected it. Although we had objected to the plan on territorial grounds, our true reason was the unacceptable constitutional structure proposed. After the continuation of talks on 18 January and 12 February 1994, it was clear that the Owen-Stoltenberg Plan was dead. There followed the direct involvement of America in the problem of Bosnia.

The Croats and the Bosniacs resolved to end their conflict. On 9 February 1995 a cease-fire was signed, following which, on 19 February, there followed talks in Frankfurt on a peaceful solution to the crisis, with more talks in Washington between 26 February and 1 March. The result was the Framework Agreement on establishing the Federation on the areas of Bosnia and Herzegovina with a majority Bosniac and Croat population. The talks were led on our behalf by Dr. Haris Silajdžić, at the time Minister of Foreign Affairs of Bosnia and Herzegovina.

The Croat-Bosniac conflict was staged for the purpose of creating Greater Croatia at the expense of Bosnia, and lasted almost a year. When we put up an unexpected resistance, particularly in Mostar and central Bosnia, the attempt came to an end, or rather was postponed, or to put it still more precisely, was continued by political instead of military means. One thing was certain: we neither wanted nor began the conflict. In our situation, with the Serb aggression at its height, only a madman would have dreamed of opening yet another front. The Croatian leadership could – and obviously did – reason quite the other way around: while the Bosniacs are busy dealing with the Serb aggression, let's exploit the situation and take a piece of Bosnia for ourselves. As it turned out, they had miscalculated. At the beginning of 1995 we clearly held the military initiative in central Bosnia. Vitez was on the point of falling, but despite this, we accepted the peace offer and talks in Washington. Our generals were not too pleased that the action had been halted, but we decision-makers thought otherwise: we could regain Vitez, but given what might then happen there, the idea of Bosnia could suffer an irreparable blow.

On 5 July 1995, Mostar was handed over to an interim (two-year) administration by the European Union. At the formal inauguration of European Union Administration in Mostar, attended by the Croatian President Franjo Tuđman and the Foreign Ministers of Germany, France and Greece, Kinkel, Juppé and Papoulias, I said:

> This agreement between the Bosniac and Croat communities of Mostar to hand over the administration of the town temporarily to the European Union is a huge and courageous step for all involved.
>
> Mostar has gone through a veritable hell of war.
>
> I am sure that the notion of urbicide, the murder of a town, has never been more vividly encountered than in Mostar, unfortunately.
>
> In our Bosnian and Croatian languages, Mostar means the town with a bridge. The bridges that gave the town its name, and its beauty and its soul too, have been destroyed, one and all. Even the famous Old Bridge, part of the world's cultural heritage, did not escape that fate.
>
> Historians will probably long seek the answer to the question how and why the tragic Croat-Bosniac conflict broke out after 500 years of something that was more than ordinary tolerance…
>
> But I think we have no choice and that, despite everything, we must look to the future.
>
> In signing this agreement today, we are making a new start for Mostar, for Bosnia and Herzegovina, and for Europe.
>
> If we are once again to build bridges over our rivers, we must first build them in the souls of our people.

War and Jaw

The war between the Bosniacs and the Croats, in which troops from the Army of the Republic of Croatia also took part, was no more, but there remained distrust and a cold peace. Nor is it much better today, as I write these lines.

On the other side, efforts were being made to bring the war throughout Bosnia and Herzegovina to an end and find a comprehensive solution. Thus on 25 April 1994 it was announced in London that a four-member Contact Group had been formed for the purpose of coordinated action in the efforts to bring the war in Bosnia and Herzegovina to an end. The group, originally composed of the USA, Great Britain, France and Germany, was soon joined by Russia.

America gave way under European pressure, tilted towards European *real-politik*, and in effect accepted the partition of the country into the Federation and a Serb entity on the basis of a 51:49 ratio. This was the well-known and controversial Contact Group Plan, which was in fact the dictate of the world. The war would last more than a year longer, but the political fate of Bosnia and Herzegovina was sealed with this plan. Everything that subsequently happened was to be determined by this compromise, which had every relevant world power behind it from America to Russia. Faced with this world ultimatum, I decided to propose that the Parliament of the Republic of Bosnia and Herzegovina and the Bosniac Assembly be convened simultaneously.

At the Parliament of Bosnia and Herzegovina, held on 18 November 1994, Silajdžić informed the deputies that the international community had, for the first time, expressed a willingness to implement the Contact Group Plan with the aid of troops, including a NATO contingent, and that this was a very important development. The Assembly accepted the plan by majority vote, with 17 against and two abstentions.

The session of the Assembly of Bosnia and Herzegovina preceded the Second Bosniac Assembly, attended by 355 delegates from all the free territories of Bosnia and Herzegovina. Everyone pointed out the injustice of the plan. I said that there was no need to prove the obvious, and that we should focus on a way out. In my short address to the assembly, I said:

> The plan offered to us, and on which we must take a position, is unjust. I say this in order to save both you and myself time and effort. For these days some people are wearing themselves out trying to prove this self-evident fact. But there is no need to prove the obvious. Some are doing so out of conviction,

> naïvely believing that they will be helping, and some, in fact the majority, are doing so to avoid answering the real and much more difficult question: what must we do in such a situation... The proffered plan, despite all its deficiencies, is one we cannot reject. It is unjust and unsatisfactory, but every option that would arise if we reject it, and which we are in a position at this time to assess, would be even worse for our people. ... Our struggle for the integration of Bosnia will depend to a large extent on us, on what and who we are and what we can do. Whether we can and will make of the parts of Bosnia we control a modern, democratic and free country... Will its light shine brightly enough to illuminate the far corners of the country and dispel the darkness of chauvinism, or shall we imprison ourselves in the anxieties of chauvinism and hatred. Bosnia cannot endure exclusivity. Such as she is, multi-national and multi-religious, she seeks those who are not perturbed by diversity. And we are they. We are not troubled by churches or cathedrals, we have learned to live with people who think and feel differently from us, and we regard this as our advantage...

When the vote on the plan was taken, 330 delegates voted in favour, 46 against, and there were six invalid ballots. With this the choice between a just but hopeless war or an unjust peace was made. Things continued to proceed in a zigzag line, but the direction was ordained. Bosnia was not saved by this. What was saved was the idea of an integral Bosnia, for which it would be necessary to fight patiently in the long years to come.

I was in Zenica in early August 1995 when I was informed that the French Foreign Minister, Hervé de Charrette, was coming to Bosnia. De Charrette delivered a personal message to me from President Chirac. The message included an invitation to visit France in my official capacity, and proposed that a resolution to the conflict be sought in direct contact with Belgrade. I replied by letter on 7 August:

> Our people welcomed your personal endeavours to save Srebrenica, and then Žepa, with sympathy and gratitude. Unfortunately, the indifference of the international community once again made yet another mass genocide of innocent people possible.

Despite this, we try to recognise every signal leading to an end to the fighting. Monsieur de Charrette, I am sure, will be a faithful interpreter of our willingness to open the door to peace, wherever it may be announced.

In this regard, we are open-minded even to proposals from Belgrade. Unfortunately, I must inform you that even as he is sending letters and calls for the war to be brought to an end, Milošević is also sending his army and military hardware to Bosnia. 6,000 troops from Serbia and Montenegro took part in the latest offensive against Bihać alone.

We are in constant contact with Mr. Carl Bildt, whose mission we sincerely welcome. We believe that the mutual recognition of Bosnia and Serbia, in other words the mutual recognition of all the states that arose from the dissolution of Yugoslavia, would direct the entire crisis towards a just and lasting solution.

France, as a great power, can contribute much to such an outcome, by direct involvement and by influencing its partners in the European Union and the UN Security Council.

France was soon to play a significant part in the decision to approve NATO air action (30 August), which would mean the beginning of the end of the war in Bosnia and Herzegovina.

The following day, 8 August, via Zagreb I reached the Bosnian Krajina, which had been surrounded and cut off for more than three years. It was liberated in a joint action ('Storm') by the Bosnian and Croatian armies in western Slavonia and our Krajina between 4 and 7 August 1995. I was on the move the whole day. I toured Bihać, Cazin, Bužim and Velika Kladuša, which had been liberated the day before. I visited the fresh grave of the Bosnian Army's youngest general, the late Izet Nanić, killed two days earlier in the battle to break out of the Krajina stranglehold. On returning from the Krajina, I responded to some questions by RTVBiH Editor Belmin Karamehmedović (13 August 1995).

The first question related to the continuation of military cooperation between the Army of Bosnia and Herzegovina, HVO and the Croatian Army. I did not let myself get carried away by illusions:

> Izetbegović: I think we should not nurture too much optimism in that regard. Croatia will go to the limits in its own interests. The most that we can expect is technical assistance, assistance

with equipment. Perhaps there will be a little more cooperation with the HVO, but even that is limited. I do not think we can expect anything spectacular.

Karamehmedović: Antony Lake is currently touring European capitals. He has visited London, Bonn, Paris and Madrid, and it is said that America is ready to back off from the Contact Group Peace Plan. There is much speculation, which we are aware of principally from the media, since there is as yet no official plan; there is mention of such possibilities as the exchange of territory, Goražde for parts of Sarajevo, the possible extension of the Brčko corridor, a confederal or even federal linkage between Pale and Belgrade, and so on. This is an opportunity for us to learn from you at first hand how things stand with the American initiative.

Izetbegović: I think there is no such plan, only an initiative. I too am left with only speculation, in a way. I read the reports by certain news agencies, but I do not know how reliable these reports are. Today I had a telephone conversation with the US Vice-President, Al Gore, and tried to find out a little more from that conversation. He said that an American delegation is coming to Sarajevo the day after tomorrow, headed by the Deputy Secretary of State for Europe, Richard Holbrooke. They will explain the essence of the initiative to us. One could say that there is an incomplete American plan currently being drawn up. For now, it is more of an investigatory mission. They are looking into the possibilities. Knowing this to be so, I told the US Vice-President today that I had heard of the speculations about Goražde, and that we would not surrender Goražde even if we had to fight for another 15 years. During the conversation he confirmed something very important for us, which is that the initiative is based on an affirmation of the sovereignty and territorial integrity of Bosnia and Herzegovina within its internationally recognised borders. He added that we need fear no compromise of any kind in that regard. There might have to be compromises over territorial issues. In my view, this gives notice of a certain receding from the Contact Group Plan. We shall know more when they come to Sarajevo. We are told of American involvement in the implementation of such a plan, and threats to the Serb side that if they reject such a peace they risk the use of force against them. It has been confirmed to me that it is absolutely certain the arms embargo against Bosnia and Herzegovina would then be lifted and that there would probably be air strikes against Serb positions. Al Gore finally said that it would be a fair and equitable plan.

Karamehmedović: All the variations mention the existence of a Serb entity in Bosnia and Herzegovina. Without prejudice to the future relations of such an entity with the rest of Bosnia and Herzegovina, over the long term, would such an offer, in your view, lead to the integration or the disintegration of Bosnia and Herzegovina?

Izetbegović: You are right, there will be some kind of Serb entity, but how it will be organised, I don't know. We offered a federal structure, though this too has certain disadvantages. They would then have the right to delegate certain people to the central governmental bodies. If they were to be pro-Chetnik, what would the state look like, and so on. But this is in a way the price of retaining Bosnia and Herzegovina. Whether it leads to integration or disintegration depends to some extent on us. It is a game that is neither won nor lost. It depends on what we are here, whether we shall create a progressive element of Bosnia and Herzegovina on the territory under the control of the legal authorities, a competitive element of which the model, in the economic, political and social sense, will be clearly superior to the other. Will civil society be established there, with human rights, respect for property, democracy, and shall we make the best use of everything that the world is ready to do for Bosnia, thereby contribute to the integration of Bosnia and Herzegovina? I think that this will be the case.

Karamehmedović: A moment ago you mentioned the new European mediator for talks on the former Yugoslavia, the Swedish diplomat Carl Bildt. This is not much talked about in our general public. Let us recall that Croatia proclaimed Bildt *persona non grata* after his statement that President Tuđman should be indicted for war crimes. It seems to me, although we have not said much about it, that there are nevertheless certain reservations on the part of the legal authorities of Bosnia and Herzegovina towards Mr. Bildt's mission. Can you confirm that?

Izetbegović: We have a somewhat less critical stance towards Mr. Bildt than the Croats, but it is critical for all that. Bildt's appr-oach gives rise to certain reservations. I have just spoken about one element of his plan, which is the Serbian recognition of a Bosnia and Herzegovina that does not exist, or that exists in Milošević's visions. Bildt is urging us to accept this, which has given rise to justified doubts among us. Second, we called for that recognition to be invariably combined with the effective closure of the borders along the Drina, which is something Bildt did not show much sympathy for. We pointed out that a truncated recognition of Bosnia and Herzegovina of this kind, for which Milošević would be rewarded with the lifting of san-ctions, would enable him to play a double game. He would simultaneously get a lifting of sanctions and continue to build Greater Serbia through this porous border. We had to warn Bildt of this, which should have been clear to him, as an ex-perienced diplomat, from the very start, but it wasn't. There's the Igman road, too. At one point he said to us that he would ensure that the city was supplied via Kiseljak, which means through territory controlled by Karadžić. We replied that this was no kind of solution. One doesn't need to be all that smart to know that the Chetniks could close the road at any time. He said that he understood this, but that he was nevertheless ready to give up the Igman road, because Karadžić had prom-ised him to open the road via Kobiljača. He is a bit too ready to believe in Karadžić's promises, after all.

Karamehmedović: The way Karadžić and his followers have been behaving these past few days in fact gives the lie to his promises, because he is again obstructing entry to the city by that agreed route.

Izetbegović: It was strange to us that we had to point out to an experienced diplomat the trap he was falling into. But Bildt committed these oversights.

The American peace initiative, led by Ambassador Richard Holbrooke, began in mid August 1995. It was made possible by the recent military successes of the Croatian and Bosnian armies in western Bosnia, and the tragedy of Srebrenica was a further warning that something must be done.

We were preparing to meet the American peace-makers when the news came that three members of the American negotiating team, Robert Frasure, Joe Kruzel and Nelson Drew, had been killed on the Igman road on the way to Sarajevo. While passing a French armoured vehicle on the narrow road, their vehicle had plunged 100 metres down the steep slope. The mission was thus characterised by misfortune from the start.

I went to the US Embassy with Silajdžić and Šaćirbegović to express my condolences. Richard Holbrooke, visibly shaken by the tragedy, tried to do his job and take the lead in the talks. He said that as a starting point we must say explicitly what kind of a Bosnia we wanted. 'You can have an integrated but decentralised state or exclusive governance over part of the country. Which of these two do you want?' he asked me, pointing to the map on the wall. 'The first,' I replied without hesitation. Given the circumstances, the conversation was brief, but as time would show it was also decisive. Much was resolved by this short conversation.

A few days earlier, on 18 August, in order to inform Holbrooke and everyone else interested in the matter and to influence their potential demands, I published a document entitled Twelve Point Plan for Peace in Bosnia and Herzegovina, in which I set out our aims in peace talks for Bosnia and Herzegovina. The following is an abridged version:

> 1. Any peace solution must be based upon the sovereignty and territorial integrity of the Republic of Bosnia and Herzegovina, and Serbia must agree to the mutual recognition of all the states that arose from the dissolution of the former Yugoslavia;
>
> 2. The five-country Contact Group Plan of July 1994 remains in force for us. We think that this should also be the case for its authors...
>
> 3. The issue of Sarajevo must be resolved as part of a comprehensive peace plan. After Srebrenica and Žepa, we are not willing to hand Sarajevo over to UN administration;
>
> 4. The issue of Bosnia is an issue of democracy. We recognise the equal rights of Serbs in Bosnia, but we recognise no rights whatsoever of the Pale regime. That regime, since it is founded on genocide, must either be militarily defeated or wholly isolated. We are ready to negotiate with a leadership of the Serb nation that will respect the fundamental rights of the non-Serb population in Bosnia and Herzegovina and conduct itself in accordance with the norms of the civilised world...
>
> 5. Since a peace agreement at this time would make it impossible to integrate Bosnia and Herzegovina by military

means, the constitutional order of Bosnia and Herzegovina may not include anything that would impede the country's peaceful reintegration in the future, and must include everything that would make that reintegration possible...

6. War criminals must continue to be prosecuted vigorously and the process should be stepped up...

7. The implementation of the peace plan should be guaranteed by the presence of troops from the five member countries of the Contact Group. Since the USA is the initiator of a new peace initiative, significant American troops should also be included...

8. The signatory countries shall establish a special reconstruction fund for Bosnia and Herzegovina...

9. The signatory countries shall support the strengthening of the Federation both politically and financially...

10. Talks with the Serb side should be led by the President of Serbia, Slobodan Milošević...

11. The signatories to the peace accord will assist Bosnia and Herzegovina in assuring her future defence. They will also support Bosnia and Herzegovina's membership of the IMF, the World Bank and other international organisations of global and regional importance...

12. The peace accord will be signed not only by the countries with a direct interest, but also by the members of the Contact Group and a representative of the Organisation of the Islamic Conference.

Certain important elements of the future peace accord concluded in Dayton in November 1995 can be recognised in this plan.

On 27 August the International Congress on Genocide was held in Bonn. I was unable to attend, but sent the following message:

> Bosnia and Herzegovina has been the subject for four years of brutal aggression on the part of Serbia and Montenegro, in which thousands of innocent people, most of them Bosniacs, have died cruel deaths, more than a million people have been forced to leave their homes, and hundreds of towns and villages have been ravaged. An indigenous spiritual and cultural substance, which has accumulated over an entire millennium,

encountering and being permeated by diverse civilisations, cultures and faiths – a substance that we call the Bosnian spirit – is under violent attack.

Bosnia was already what the civilised world wants to become. But instead of the international community defending its own formally proclaimed principles here, it betrayed them. The sufferings of Bosnia, with rare exceptions, were accompanied by a strange indifference and even shameful silence on the part of the world.

It is for you, gentlemen, to shed objective light on this anti-civilisational decline. Do so with brutal honesty, so that another Bosnia may never happen to anyone else.

The following day, 28 August, a shell landed on the Sarajevo marketplace. The images of massacred civilians were seen all around the world, and stung the conscience of people in positions of responsibility. In the morning of 30 August there followed air intervention by NATO against Serb positions, which altered the entire course of the war, as we have already seen.

It is interesting that the same evening Milošević and Bulatović met representatives of the Bosnian Serbs in Belgrade. It was agreed that Milošević would lead the Serb team and that he would have the decisive word in the peace talks set in motion by America. Patriarch Pavle was a witness to this agreement.

The bombing of Serb positions lasted for two days and nights, and was then stopped, although not a single military or political goal had been achieved. I sent the same letter to Presidents Clinton and Chirac, protesting against this lack of resolve:

> There are signs that the action begun by the UN and NATO against the Serb killing machine being used against civilians in Sarajevo has been called off. The old game is continuing. The same people are still in place who have from the very start paralysed every action on the part of the international community, prolonging the war and the agony of Bosnia and undermining the credibility of international institutions.
>
> The Serb artillery surrounding Sarajevo has not been destroyed, the Igman route is once again under fire, and the same regime as has prevailed until now is proposed for the Kiseljak-Sarajevo route, which means that the route will be open one

day and closed for ten, depending on the will of those who have been terrorising the city for 40 months.

In his letter of 1 September, the Serb Commanding Officer Mladić dictates terms. It appears that General Janvier is ready to accept those terms. The game with the fate of Bosnia and its people continues, therefore.

I assure you, Mr. President, that this is not the way to advance the peace process that has been begun – quite the contrary.

I therefore ask you to use your influence wholly to fulfil all the commitments that have been made, and to send a message to those who have committed these unprecedented atrocities that they are not the ones who should be dictating terms.

On 3 September US Vice President Al Gore called me and confirmed that the strikes would continue.

A few days later the strikes began again, lasting until 14 September, when they were finally and definitively called off.

On 4 September I was on an official visit to Turkey when I was told that Richard Holbrooke was in Ankara and wanted to see me. I was not greatly surprised, but because of the protocol that had already been arranged, our talks began only at 11 pm. The meeting was held in the residence of the American Ambassador to Ankara.

Holbrooke had been preparing a meeting of the foreign ministers of Serbia, Croatia and Bosnia and Herzegovina, which was to be held on 8 September in Geneva. The purpose was to determine the basic principles of a peace accord for Bosnia.

The basis of Holbrooke's thinking was compromise: we would recognise Republika Srpska and, in return, the Serbs would recognise the state of Bosnia, or to quote the precise wording, 'Bosnia and Herzegovina will continue its legal existence with its present borders and continuing international recognition.'

At first I resolutely opposed the idea, because of 'Republika Srpska'. There followed persuasion alternately from Holbrooke and Robert Owen, with the most diverse arguments raised. Carl Bildt called me to insist, on behalf of Europe, on compromise. Robert Owen, a specialist in international law in Holbrooke's team, indicated that this word 'republic' in the title of Republika Srpska meant little. What was important was how the entity would be defined in the future constitution of Bosnia and Herzegovina. 'Look here, Texas is called a republic, but it's just one of the federal states forming the USA,' he claimed. I recalled that in our case, too, the federal states forming the former Socialist Federal Republic of Yugoslavia were called republics. But this 'republic' had been created by Karadžić on the basis of genocide.

You could like or dislike Holbrooke, but you couldn't help respecting him. His argumentation displayed a trenchant intelligence, exceptional talent and an extensive knowledge of the problems. They say that diplomacy and power are two ends of the scale. The more power you have, the less diplomacy you need. In the extreme case – if you are a superpower – you don't need diplomacy of any kind. Holbrooke gave the lie to this theory. Although he represented the greatest superpower – in fact, the only true superpower in the world – he was to the fullest extent a diplomat, and used his persuasive skills like the most powerful of weapons. The power of America is taken for granted here.

If you used a logical and incontestable argument against the standpoint he represented and on which he did not wish to (or could not) yield, he would use neither threats nor blackmail. When you had finished, he would say: 'Mr. President, you are absolutely right, but...' I don't know how many times since our first meeting in Sarajevo in August 1995, and all our subsequent meetings, I heard that famous phrase: 'You are absolutely right, but...' What else did you have to demonstrate if you were 'absolutely right'?

This time, too, in Ankara, when I had told him for the umpteenth time that we could not accept a Serb republic because ... and set out all the arguments of which he was perfectly well aware, Holbrooke again used his famous phrase: 'You are absolutely right, and I wholly understand you, but...' The discussion, lasting almost three hours, finished at around 2 am, with the words: 'We cannot leave Republika Srpska out of the draft. I'm sorry, but there's nothing more I can do.' I decided that I would convene a session of the Presidency immediately upon my return to Sarajevo, to inform the members of what was awaiting us in Geneva.

It was not easy for me, then, with Holbrooke, but it seems it was not easy for him with me either. In his book *To End a War*, p. 274, recalling the difficult talks in Dayton, Holbrooke wrote:

> The most difficult meetings were with Izetbegović. In the last of our three meetings that day, we tried to talk in personal terms to the Bosnian leader. We reminded him of all the benefits peace would bring, and listed the substantial achieve-

> ments the process had already brought Bosnia: a cessation of hostilities, the lifting of the siege of Sarajevo, the partial opening of roads, the damage NATO bombing had done to the Bosnian Serbs, the $50 billion World Bank package that awaited the country after a peace agreement, the equip-and-train program for the Bosnian Army. Christopher concluded with a drama unusual for him: 'President Clinton has put an enormous amount on the line to save Bosnia,' he said. 'But he will no longer assist your government if you turn out to be the obstacle to an agreement in Dayton.' Izetbegović said nothing in response, and outwardly seemed unmoved by Christopher's statement.

Perhaps Holbrooke found it difficult to deal with me because he did not know me. I think he had certain prejudices about me. This is how Holbrooke saw me (ibid., p. 97).

> At the centre of this tangle was the remarkable figure of Alija Izetbegović. He had kept the 'idea' of Bosnia alive under the most difficult circumstance… At the age of seventy, after surviving eight years in Tito's jails and four years of Serb attacks, he saw politics as a perpetual struggle … His eyes had a cold and distant gaze; after so much suffering, they seemed dead to anyone else's pain. … He reminded me a little of Mao Zedong and other radical Chinese communist leaders – good at revolution, poor at governance.

This impression of Holbrooke's of me and my personality amused me a little. I wondered whether my eyes really looked 'dead to anyone else's pain'. I have a wholly different conception of myself. Although our own view of ourselves is the least reliable, that does not mean that Holbrooke was right.

During the morning of 8 September, when the Geneva meeting was due to begin, I was telephoned by Secretary of State Christopher, insisting that we accept the draft Geneva document without any alterations. He said that it meant a 'powerful recognition of the status of Bosnia,' and that America would be resolutely behind its implementation.

The Presidency was in session at that very time, and the Geneva document was the only item on the agenda. I conveyed Christopher's message to the members without comment. The document was accepted with an evident sense of unease. And thus began a new era in the history of Bosnia and Herzegovina, full of quandaries and ambiguities.

The first part of this important document reads:

> 1. Bosnia and Herzegovina will continue its legal existence with its present borders and continuing international recognition.
>
> 2. Bosnia and Herzegovina will consist of two entities, The Federation of Bosnia and Herzegovina as established by the Washington Agreements, and the Republika Srpska (RS).
>
> 2.1. The 51:49 parameter of the territorial proposal of the Contact Group is the basis for a settlement. This territorial proposal is open for adjustment by mutual agreement.
>
> 2.2. Each entity will continue to exist under its present constitution (amended to accommodate these basic principles).
>
> 2.3. Both entities will have the right to establish parallel special relationships with neighbouring countries, consistent with the sovereignty and territorial integrity of Bosnia and Herzegovina.
>
> 2.4. The two entities will enter into reciprocal commitments (a) to hold complete elections under international auspices; (b) to adopt and adhere to normal international human rights standards and obligations, including the obligation to allow freedom of movement and enable displaced persons to repossess their homes or receive just compensation; (c) to engage in binding arbitration to resolve disputes between them.

'This is not an outcome of which the West can be proud,' was the comment made by Antony Lewis in the next day's *New York Times*, on the recognition of Republika Srpska.

On the day the Geneva Conference was held, I replied to some questions from a *Sky News* journalist:

> *Sky News*: What are your expectations from the Geneva Conference?
>
> Izetbegović: Peace, the survival of Bosnia as a state and a constitutional solution that will make possible its full reintegration by peaceful means in the future.
>
> *Sky News*: Political and military pressure on the Serbs has been increased. Is this pressure sufficient?

Izetbegović: No, it isn't. The air strikes of a week ago and this new round have caused serious damage only to the infrastructure of Karadžić's Army. According to our information, damage to mobile targets – tanks and artillery – is relatively small. The killing machine surrounding Sarajevo has not been destroyed. Sarajevo is still at risk.

Sky News: Are you ready to withdraw from certain territories currently held by your army?

Izetbegović: As regards the drawing of internal borders, the five-country Contact Group Plan is still valid as far as we are concerned. We have accepted the possibility of certain minor modifications, but I must emphasise that our army will not withdraw anywhere. We can only gain territory – less or more – but withdrawal from even a foot of land is out of the question.

Two days later, on 10 September, I gave a general assessment of the results of the Geneva Conference in a special article for the Sarajevo daily *Oslobođenje*:

Last Friday in Geneva the foreign ministers of Bosnia and Herzegovina, Croatia and Serbia agreed certain basic principles for a future peace in Bosnia and Herzegovina.

Nothing has been signed, but something has been agreed, and this will be the basis for further talks. I shall try to set out my personal view of this. Essentially, it was a classic compromise, and every compromise has a bitter taste.

What was agreed in Geneva? The most important issues can be reduced to two points:

1. Bosnia and Herzegovina continues to exist as an integral and sovereign State, a member of the United Nations, within its internationally recognised borders.

2. Bosnia and Herzegovina will in the future consist of the Federation of Bosnia and Herzegovina and the Republika Srpska, with the internal division of territory in the ratio 51:49 in favour of the Federation.

So the Serbs have had to recognise and accept the State of Bosnia and Herzegovina against which they fought the war, while we have had to accept their Republic which arose out of aggression. In addition, they have had to accept the internal ratio of 51:49, which from the very start they categorically rejected, and there is no confederation with Serbia.

These important circumstances, and in particular the fact that the Serb Republic is part of Bosnia and Herzegovina and that there will be no confederation, have been kept from the Serb people by Karadžić's media, but nothing is altered by delusion and self-delusion.

Why did we accept this compromise? The answer is simple: to end the war. The misery and suffering of the people are already far too great, every day of war brings new victims and invalids, our refugees and displaced people living in others' homes or countries are losing patience and hope, and the number of refugees is not diminishing but increasing, just as the number of destroyed homes and factories is increasing. If the war were to continue, the outlook is uncertain, since the world has sent us a clear message that we have their support for peace, but not for war. If we reject the peace, a peace that the world regards as reasonable, the arms embargo almost certainly will not be lifted, and it is possible that there will be pressure on our surrounding countries to impede our obtaining supplies and continuing the war. Since war is by its very nature a process that is hard to control, it is possible that it could escalate at any moment, with the involvement in the war of Serbia, Russia and so on. If things were to take this turn, it would be all or nothing, and we could lose everything.

The attitude of the West is not illogical, as is often claimed. It is defined, and will continue to be defined, by the interests of individual countries, but still more by one fact that is less visible and little spoken of: fear of Russian atomic bombs. That fear is greater now than it was in the time of the Soviet Union. At that time they were under full control, but now all kinds of unpleasant surprises are possible there. This fact, about which Westerners think all the time but are reluctant to speak of, is one that our analysts, too, continually overlook. However, it lies behind this 'incomprehensible' behaviour on the part of the West. And it will continue to be the case, so when we speak of war and peace in Bosnia, we must not lose sight of this important circumstance.

The world is as it is, and we cannot change it. What we can do is to familiarise ourselves with it and not close our eyes to the facts.

What is this bitter peace bringing us? I shall try to make a list:

1. The Federation is getting about another 15% of the territory of Bosnia and Herzegovina, including, among others, the towns of Bosanska Krupa, Sanski Most, Donji Vakuf, Jajce, Trnovo, Brčko, Odžak, Derventa, Doboj, Bosanski Brod, Šamac and others. It also gets a ground link with Goražde, which will mean Goražde is no longer cut off. It most likely gets Sarajevo, which will remain an undivided city. I say most likely, because this is still not absolutely certain, but it is certain enough – this is a condition that we cannot give up.

2. All our refugees may return and settle in this extended Federation, and begin to live normal lives again.

3. Instead of humanitarian aid, we shall receive aid for the reconstruction of the country. By reopening our factories, schools and universities, and thereby the prospect of a normal life for our citizens, we shall be in a position to give jobs back to people who are capable of work, schools to our young people, and pensions to our pensioners. Systematic care of invalids and *shahids'* (fallen soldiers) families would also finally begin.

4. Finally, with these as a basis, the process of the peaceful reintegration of the parts of Bosnia currently under Chetnik control could begin. This will be a painstaking task for the next two generations, but two basic prerequisites for this would already be created:

First, the very principle of an integral Bosnia, accepted by all relevant countries of the world and formally confirmed yesterday in Geneva, and

Second, a part of Bosnia successfully defended, now constituted as a Federation, in which a high degree and tempo of political and economic development can and must be achieved.

The first is the formal and the second the material basis for the future reintegration of Bosnia. Whether we shall take full advantage of this opportunity depends to a large extent on us, on what we are and whether we are in a position in this part of Bosnia to create a model of a democratic and progressive state of a kind that will be victorious over the darkness that lies over the scattered pieces of the so-called Serb Republic.

There is only one alternative to this route: that is a continuation of the war so that Bosnia could be reunited by military means, by military victory. Could we achieve this, and how much would it cost, above all in human lives? How many more casualties, people killed, mutilated, how many more refugees, voluntary or enforced? We are a small people. Where is the limit of endurance of this people? And did we not agree that war continues to ravage the very essence of Bosnia, while peace can save it? Did we not agree that a continuation of the war suits the war criminals from Pale, that it feeds and nurtures them, and that one way or another peace will be their ruin? Ethnic cleansing is what is obliterating Bosnia. Just see how far things have turned for the worse in this respect in the past few months, after the atrocities in Srebrenica, Žepa and Banja Luka. Despite the army's successes, Bosnia is now further away from being a multi-ethnic community than it was a year ago. Will not a continuation of the war merely exacerbate this further?

For all that, if we have to, we shall continue to fight, but we would then have to be sure that there was no other choice.

On 10 September 1995 I spoke on the telephone with the President of France, Jacques Chirac, and the US Ambassador to Sarajevo, John Menzies. The conversation was on the same subject. Both informed me that Karadžić's Serbs were not withdrawing their heavy weapons from around Sarajevo, on the pretext that the Army of Bosnia and Herzegovina would take advantage of the altered situation to occupy parts of the city that were at the time under their control, and that on this basis Serb lawyers abroad were calling for the NATO and UN action to be called off. In order to eliminate this trumped-up excuse, I offered both the French and the American sides guarantees that the Army of Bosnia and Herzegovina would not undertake any offensive actions in the Sarajevo area, nor would it try to gain the military advantage on the basis of the withdrawal of the Serb artillery. The Army of Bosnia and Herzegovina would uphold this commitment for the duration of political talks on the status of Sarajevo, with the proviso that such talks began at once and were concluded within a reasonable period of time. I stressed that this carried the implication that the commitment would no longer hold good if at any time the Serbs attacked the city. I drew particular attention to the need to avoid a repetition of what happened in February 1994, when Mladić's troops ostensibly withdrew their heavy weapons, but in fact merely concealed them and began attacking once again.

At the session of the Assembly of the Republic of Bosnia and Herzegovina held on 18 September, there was a stormy debate about whether or not Republika Srpska should be recognised. There was almost universal revulsion among the deputies at the idea. A professor of constitutional law spoke at length on what a modern, normal state should look like, naturally advocating that this was the kind of state we should be declaring ourselves in favour of. I had to take the floor to bring everyone back to reality:

> I would immediately vote for the proposal just set out for us by the esteemed university professor, whom I greatly respect, but professors generally know a great deal about theory and are unaware of certain matters in practice. An ill of this kind cannot be eliminated by declaration. If it could, we should not hesitate for a second, we should immediately pronounce such a constitution and resolve the issue today. Unfortunately, even if we did so, the Chetniks would still be on Trebević, and would go on killing our children and cutting off our gas and electricity supplies. It would give me great pleasure if we here today were to vote for the future state as a federation of cantons, not national but mixed, based on communications, economic and whatever other criteria. But if we do so, the Chetniks still will not withdraw. They will still be in occupation of Zvornik and Bijeljina, will continue forcing our people to leave Banja Luka, and a million of our people will have to continue living as refugees or displaced persons. True, we would have a constitution that we could uphold with the greatest of pride, but nothing would have happened, nothing would have been changed. Everything would be as before.
>
> They say that in politics one should make a list of what is fine and desirable, and then immediately cross off the list everything that is unrealistic, things that for this reason or that cannot be achieved. There is nothing more futile in politics than to talk about wonderful but unattainable ideas. There is no benefit to be gained from this. Such talk may be interesting for poets and for literature, but different rules prevail in politics. A realistic compromise is better than a handful of ideal prescriptions that remain only on paper.

Our military successes in August and September 1995, in particular the NATO air strikes, marked a turning-point in the war. The military situation altered to our advantage, but there were forebodings of problems of another kind that arise from peace and military success. These new dilemmas and fears can be clearly seen in my address to the session of the Assembly of Bosnia and Herzegovina on 18 September 1995:

> Some people have at times reproached me when I have said that no one is providing guarantees for the integral Bosnia that we plead for. These days, no one guarantees anyone anything. They all say: make the attempt, fight, win it for yourselves. This is why I say here that whether Republika Srpska begins to fade away and whether its decline will continue or not depends on whether we are in a position to continue militarily. Do we have sufficient strength and courage to do so and, in particular, will we be in a position to create in the parts of Bosnia that we control a model state, an example of a democratic and economically developed society, will the funds the world will give us be turned into factories or into cars and weekend cottages, will we misuse it or will we use it for the people, for the general good – will we be able to do all this? Will we stamp out corruption, so that the best people can work, will we uphold the promises made to our soldiers, our invalids, our *shahids'* families, or will we betray those promises, and so on? I am thinking of these and many other crucial issues when I say that the future depends in very large measure on us, on who and what we are.
>
> In this regard, I recall a war novel in which it is said that the first people to go to war are ordinary soldiers, then come the squad leaders, the officers, the admirals, then the generals, then the ministers, and finally the war profiteers. That is how things go in war, and when peace comes someone says 'About turn – left,' and the first in line are the war profiteers, then the admirals, the generals, the ministers and so on, and at the tail-end are the other ranks, with behind them again, of course, those most unfortunate of combatants who have lost arms and legs. Will this same story of the dismal truth of war and peace repeat itself here with us, or not?
>
> Another question is whether, under the influence of our military successes, we will forget ourselves and begin to make some wrong moves, and turn the world against us, or will we continue to be serious and responsible people. Victory is a burden and, to tell you the truth, I no longer fear defeat. Defeat is something behind us, but victory brings its own problems. Remember, even now it is already bringing them. I wonder

whether now, when we are victorious, we could be and remain decent human beings, as we were when we suffered blows. You see, we succeeded in gaining and retaining the sympathy of the world. When I say the sympathy of the world, I do not mean the sympathy of governments, but of ordinary people... I have travelled a great deal these years, and have seen what ordinary people think of Bosnia, what the policeman standing guard at the entrance in Geneva, the customs official in New York, the man in the street thinks, I have seen how ordinary people welcome us. The other day I was in France, and I felt this. I mean that the world, the best part of the people of the world, and the best part is usually the poets, artists, crazy idealists, the slightly 'zany' or freakish – these are usually the finest people, and it is these very people who are on our side.

I say to our troops above all, do not forget yourselves. Victories are a severe temptation, some victories hold within them the germ of the defeat of the victorious peoples. We now, therefore, if we are victorious, must strive to remain the same people that we were when things were at their worst for us. Let us respect the laws of war, protect the civilian population that we come upon in the territories we liberate, and ensure that prisoners are treated according to the law.

At the end of September Croatia's President Franjo Tuđman was in Paris, and gave an interview to *Le Figaro* which caused a great commotion among the people. The newspapers were full of articles about it. RTV-BiH invited me to comment, on 29 September. The question from the Editor was:

> Karamehmedović: How would you comment on the statement by Croatia's President Tuđman that Croatia has been given the task of Europeanising the Bosniacs and that the Federation was created, for example, because Europe and the world could not allow a Muslim state to be created in Europe?
>
> Izetbegović: First of all, President Tuđman knows very well that it was in fact Europe that was forcing us into creating a Muslim state. Wasn't that precisely what the Owen-Stoltenberg Plan was, and didn't we reject it? The Bosniac people has hitched its waggon to an integral and civil Bosnia, and is resolutely following that route.

As for the Europeanisation of the Muslims here, look, we are a European country and a European nation. I do not state this as some kind of advantage, but simply as a fact. If I were to go to Africa and claim to be an African, no one would believe me the moment they saw me. I think that it is wrong to divide the world into Europeans and the rest, it is insulting to the rest. I know that many nations and people in the world are insulted by this categorisation. Finally, Karadžić and Mladić, too, are European, and so is the general who destroyed the Old Bridge in Mostar. He too is a European, but it didn't help matters. I think that people should be divided into civilised and barbaric, and that is the only true division. Everything else is insulting nonsense.

Karamehmedović: If I may, another question relating to the Croatian President's interview. Among other things, he said that there are a number of pragmatic people among the Bosnian leadership. What does it mean, in this statement, to be pragmatic?

Izetbegović: Well, I don't know exactly, but I presume that it means what it means generally. Pragmatists are people who see but pretend not to see, who hear but pretend not to hear, who remember but pretend to forget, and so on. Sometimes, in the interests of our people and of Bosnia and Herzegovina, we pretend not to see certain things that we do see, not to hear certain things that we do hear, to have forgotten certain things that we can never forget. We strive to look to the future. In the interests of certain higher goals, in this case in the interests of our people and this country, we are sometimes ready to pass over certain things in silence. Except when it is essential, as it is tonight.

As for Tuđman's boast that some Europeans had entrusted him with the 'Europeanisation' of the Bosnian Muslims and preventing the creation of a Muslim state in Europe, I think that there was some truth in what Tuđman said. Many people in both Europe and America, with honourable exceptions, looked at what was happening in Bosnia with suspicion. Everything that they regarded as an Islamic renaissance in the country was to be stamped out. Many ugly things were done to achieve this end. One of them was the criminalisation of the Bosniac authorities in Bosnia and Herzegovina, which would intensify after the war and reach its apogee with a *New York Times* article in August 1999.

I knew that there were serious differences among the allies on the continuation of bombing Serb positions. It was no secret that France, Spain, Canada and Greece were opposed to it. The Russians went a step further and threatened to offer direct assistance to the Serbs if the strikes continued. At the height of this debate there came the news that Holbrooke was meeting Karadžić and Mladić in Belgrade. The two of them had already been proclaimed war criminals, but they say that in politics the end justifies the means. I was shattered by this news, but one good thing came of it: Karadžić agreed to withdraw his heavy weapons and to end the siege of Sarajevo. In return, the bombing would be suspended. It was 14 September 1995.

Also in mid September, Holbrooke announced a meeting in New York which would go a step further than Geneva: to specify the central institutions, allocate the responsibilities of the state and the entities, and define the competencies of the Council of Ministers and the way in which the Presidency and Assembly of Bosnia and Herzegovina would be elected. Holbrooke's team was working with our representative, Šaćirbegović, who was in constant touch with us. Things were going well, and we were for the most part satisfied with the draft, which was completed on 22 September. Now Milošević had to be convinced.

The American team, composed of Owen, Hill and Pardew, travelled to Belgrade on 23 September for talks. Milošević first left them to wrestle with Karadžić and his companions, who would not hear of state institutions of any kind. When the negotiators were already pretty tired, and were at their wits' end, Milošević got rid of the Bosnian Serbs and played the 'peacemaker' and 'man of good will', accepting much of what Karadžić and Co. had rejected. But not everything. If you compared the paper after Milošević's intervention with what Karadžić had been demanding, it was good. But if you compared it with what the Americans had brought with them to Belgrade, it was absolutely unacceptable.

We were kept informed about what was happening in Belgrade, but the Americans now committed yet another blunder. Instead of coming to Sarajevo to agree the text with us once again, they simply went back to America. Thinking that this was not fair, we announced that we would not come to New York. The Americans were already half way home by that time, had already overflown Ireland, but Secretary of State

Christopher ordered the team to return to Bosnia. It seems it did not go smoothly. After a long persuasion, they finally altered course, landed in Ireland, rested and returned to Bosnia. There then began the toughest round of talks, lasting, with brief interruptions, almost an entire day and night. Finally, only one provision remained to be agreed, but it was a very important one. We insisted on direct elections for the Parliament and Presidency, the other two sides on indirect elections. It was clear that different political philosophies lay behind these attitudes. Serbia and Croatia wanted a weaker head of state, we wanted a stronger one. On 25 September, Holbrooke called me after midnight. I told him briefly that we must have direct elections. 26 September dawned, the day when the conference was to be held, and there was still no agreement on this point. All the delegations, and hundreds of journalists, were already assembled in New York. Fifteen minutes before the start of the conference, Secretary of State Christopher called me and asked me to rescue the conference at any price. We then told Šaćirbegović to accept the document with the proviso that the Contact Group stated that it understood elections to mean direct elections, and the American side explicitly stated that it upheld the integrity of Bosnia and Herzegovina and would oppose any kind of partition. The Contact Group issued the statement we asked for, and for the Americans, President Clinton confirmed our proviso personally while the meeting was still going on, with the words: 'Bosnia will remain a unified internationally recognised state. America will strongly oppose the partition of Bosnia.' Thus this dramatic episode came to an end.

From mid September onwards the Americans had been insisting at first on a deceleration, and then on a complete halt to the Croatian-Bosnian offensive in western Bosnia. It is true that Holbrooke encouraged us to take Prijedor and Bosanski Novi, but he was resolutely opposed to any continuation of the operation towards Banja Luka.

It was not hard to convince Tuđman, especially when his idea of exchanging Tuzla for Banja Luka with the Serbs faced opposition. It appears that this nebulous idea was put forward by a number of Western officials. Tuđman no longer had any interest in pursuing the action eastwards. The news that several Croatian soldiers had been killed attempting to cross the Una in flood on 18 to 19 September also contributed to this. So from 20 September onwards we were in effect alone in the battle against Karadžić's troops, who had begun to consolidate their positions following their defeat.

Things were beginning to move towards a cease-fire. Holbrooke launched an initiative to this effect on 2 October. Karadžić and Mladić accepted the proposal without much persuasion. With the exception of one set-back near Ključ, we had the military advantage. The Croatian Army, however, was conclusively brought to a halt. The Americans had begun to oppose a continuation of the fighting and announced a complete halt to the Iranian logistical support that was coming in via Croatia.

Prior to this, we had received yet another eloquent warning. Suddenly the air force of Karadžić's Serbs became active. Its fighter planes were taking off from Banja Luka airport and strafing our troop convoys on the move, and those of the Croats. NATO did not react. The message was clear: there must be no victor in the Bosnian war. Or: the Serbs must not be wholly defeated, which came to the same thing. At the Mostar meeting Holbrooke had already informed me that the bombing would be halted to give political talks a chance. Three thousand, four hundred flights had already been executed. The attitude was that the Serb position had already been sufficiently softened up and that there was no need to go too far.

According to fairly reliable data, the daily toll in human lives of the war in Bosnia was 150, military and civilian. Taking all these facts into consideration, I reached the conclusion that there was no choice.

On 5 October I signed the agreement on a cease-fire, but made an end to the conflict conditional on Sarajevo's receiving gas and electricity and on the road to Goražde being opened for food supplies. I reckoned that in this way we would get another few days, enabling us to take Prijedor and Bosanski Novi. Holbrooke accepted the terms and incorporated them into the document.

When the cease-fire was signed, with the exception of the Krajina the fighting died down almost the same day. Everyone was obviously tired of war. One can see what this meant from the fact that during the war there had been an average of 2,000 armed incidents recorded daily. General Rupert Smith, for example, stated that on 24 May 1995 alone about 2,700 smaller or larger actions had been recorded along the front line and in the rear. Another thing that indicates how fierce the fighting was in the Bosnian war is the fact that up to 16 May 1995, 162 members of UNPROFOR had been killed and 1,420 wounded (data from the report by the UN Secretary-General, Boutros Ghali, to the Security Council). By the end of the war, according to certain sources, UNPROFOR had lost 204 soldiers, the European Union six monitors, and the USA three peace negotiators.

The military, in particular Dudaković and Alagić in the Krajina, were not delighted by the signing of the truce. It seemed to me that they had greatly overestimated our potential, and in particular that they did not see the political context: the American attitude, and the opposition by Croatia to a continuation of the war. Tuđman openly threatened that not a single bullet would enter Bosnia via his territory.

Yet another event gave us pause for thought: our set-backs and losses in the Serb counter-offensive near Ključ at the end of September. The town of Ključ, which we liberated on 15 September, was practically abandoned for several hours.

This crisis, relating to Ključ, will also be remembered for the largest manoeuvre carried out by our Army in the war. Since the 5th and 7th Corps were engaged further to the north, the only way to stabilise the wavering front along the Otoka-Sanica-Ključ line was to bring in troops from other lines, mainly from central and northern Bosnia. Within six days, from 2 to 7 October, using helicopters, buses and lorries, parts of the Guards Brigade, specials from the Ministry of Interior, the 'Black Swans' and parts of the 146th, 309th, 210th and 225th Brigades from Visoko, Kakanj, Tuzla and Banovići were transferred to the Ključ front, a strength of some 8,000 men.

During the cease-fire talks the Serbs continued their ethnic cleansing. On 5 October I sent a letter to Richard Holbrooke:

> Despite our earnest endeavours to reach a cease-fire, we have of late encountered the problem of ever more extensive expulsions of Bosniacs and Croats from the parts of Bosnia and Herzegovina under occupation by Karadžić's Serbs. This scandalous process of forcing people to leave their ancient homes, instead of being halted after the Geneva Agreements, has still further intensified. According to data from the Office for Refugees and Displaced Persons of our Ministry for Refugees, in the last ten days alone more than 5,000 people have been forced to leave Bosanski Novi, Prijedor, Banja Luka, Doboj and other places.
>
> Given that this conduct by Karadžić's Serbs is contrary to both the letter and the spirit of the Geneva Agreements, please demand that President Milošević halt the expulsions of the non-Serb population immediately. Please also require him to withdraw the infamous troops of Željko Ražnjatović Arkan from the territory of Bosnia and Herzegovina.

On 11 October gas and electricity supplies reached Sarajevo, and humanitarian convoys set off for Goražde, which meant that the conditions for the cease-fire had been met. Russia's President Boris Yeltsin personally used his influence to restore the supply of gas to Sarajevo. I received a letter from him, via the Russian Embassy in Sarajevo, in which he appealed for a truce in Bosnia to be reached and confirmed Russia's commitment to preserving the integrity and sovereignty of Bosnia and Herzegovina.

Emotionally, Russia was strongly on the side of the Serbs, but it remained principled on the question of the integrity of Bosnia and Herzegovina. 'We have our own domestic reasons for that,' said the Russian Foreign Minister, Andrei Koziriev, hinting at the situation in Russia itself. I took advantage of my reply to Yeltsin to highlight this fact:

> Thank you for your letter of 4 October.
>
> I agree with you that a turning point is approaching in the resolution of the Bosnian crisis.
>
> I hope that a first important move in this regard will be made in the next few hours with a cease-fire throughout Bosnia and Herzegovina.
>
> We have always considered, and still consider, that Russia has an indispensable part to play in resolving the problems in the Balkans and between the states that arose from the dissolution of Yugoslavia. In this regard, we fully understand your interest.
>
> We greatly appreciate the support of the state bodies of the Russian Federation in all the peace initiatives thus far for Bosnia and Herzegovina. Your personal support for the principle of preserving the integrity of the Republic of Bosnia and Herzegovina, and the clear and principled stance of your Government on this issue, is received here with appreciation and satisfaction.

The fighting in the Krajina continued, however.

On 12 October I was visited by the new American Ambassador, John Menzies, who had submitted his credentials only a few days earlier. He conveyed to me a warning from America that the cease-fire agreement must be honoured. General Delić had already issued the appropriate orders, but the fighting in the Krajina had not stopped. News was getting about – largely unfounded – that Banja Luka was on the point of falling. Columns of Serb refugees were jamming the roads across the Posavina corridor, heading for Serbia. Faced with this wave of refugees, and under pressure of the criticisms from Karadžić and Mladić, Milošević, for whom these angry and disillusioned refugees were a new threat to the stability of his regime, threatened to become directly involved in the conflict. Two or three Serbian divisions were mentioned for involvement on the side of Karadžić's troops. I did not believe this, but the Americans did. Ambassador Menzies came to see me again, and in a very serious tone of voice conveyed to me the message that NATO air forces would take action against our troops if the fighting was not halted. He said that this was a serious threat and that it would be carried out. Since orders by telegram or telephone did not hold water, I asked General Delić to go at once to the Krajina and implement the cease-fire decision. The fighting was finally called off on 13 October. The day before we had succeeded in liberating Sanski Most, the last town to be liberated in this war.

And thus a war that had lasted for 1,280 days, and of which the human and material balance-sheet was horrific, was finally brought to an end. Ahead lay the painful peace talks.

Chapter 7

Dayton Diary

Sixteen-point peace plan. Speech at the 50th Session of the UN General Assembly. Meeting with President Clinton. Meeting with Mohammad Ali. Statement on peace. Aviation Museum at the Wright-Petterson Airbase. Talks with Milošević and Bulatović. Talks with Granić and Šušak. First part of the General Framework Agreement for Peace. Arms balance in the region. Central Bank and currency. IFOR – Multinational Implementation Force. The issue of elections. Institutions. The question of Sarajevo. Corridor to Goražde. Signing of the Agreement on Implementing the Federation. About Tuđman. Talks with US Secretary of State Christopher. Maps, maps, maps. Talks with Bildt and three European political foreign affairs directors. Zubak rebels. Talks with Shattuck. Supervision of elections. Voting of refugees and displaced persons. Talks with Antony Lake. Reservations about Project 'Delta'. Talks with Secretary William Perry. Milošević retreats – IFOR to police the entire territory of Bosnia and Herzegovina. Brčko corridor. Milošević hands over Sarajevo, but not Brčko. One-night collapse of negotiations. Milošević agrees to arbitration on Brčko. President Clinton announces peace. Initialled in Dayton, signed in Paris. Speeches. Repeal of state of war. Statement for El-Mundo. 'Civil war' – a fraud.

In my long life I have done the most varied of jobs: as a convict, I delved ground, carried mortar, cut woods, and later, as a free man, ran a construction site, represented in court, wrote articles. Still, my hardest occupation was negotiating. To negotiate means to decide, and deciding is the most difficult job for the unfortunate human being.

My problem was that I could neither win a satisfactory peace nor lead a satisfactory war. Negotiations were held in conditions of blackmail and with a Damocles sword held over Bosnia's head. People, attacked, outnumbered and out armed, were subject to terrible sufferings, and the offered peace was opposed not only to my principles, but to elementary justice as well. I could hardly accept such a peace, and it was even harder to go back home carrying a message of the war's continuation. My dilemmas were difficult. I felt crucified.

Ten days prior to the beginning of the Dayton negotiations, in the meeting of the SDA Executive Board (20 October 1995), I defined our goals. This was my August programme of 12 points, this time worked out in greater detail:

> 1. Our goal is to maintain Bosnia and Herzegovina as sovereign and integral. This aim can be accomplished through military and political means. I think that we have reached the point when the war can stop and we can continue our way towards a sovereign and integral Bosnia and Herzegovina by political means. The forthcoming peace negotiations will test how correct this expectation is.
>
> 2. Common institutions and functions of the state guarantee the integrity of Bosnia. Among others, these institutions are the Parliament, the Presidency, Government, the Constituent Court and a central emission bank; the functions are: foreign affairs, defense, human rights protection, outer borders protection, communications, currency, customs and foreign trade, budget and financing at the state level. The Serbian side will do anything to reduce the number of common functions. Our interest is, of course, vice versa.
>
> 3. In the situation as it is, regarding the probable parity constitution of common organs, the main problem is the possibility of blocking common institutions' functions by veto. We need a state which can function, and we cannot allow a repetition of the 1991-1992 situation when, because of consensus (veto) practice, not one decision of essential importance could be reached. We need (a) an integral Bosnia and (b) a state that can function. It seems that these two requests are contradictory and that before us lies the task of undoing this knot. Some suggest deciding by majority, but then there is a real danger of two reaching an agreement to the harm of the third, and the third one could be the Bosniac side. The way out may be implantation of an unblocking mechanism. It would probably be the Constituent Court, which would in this case include a few foreign judges. In any case the way of deciding and the block-

age possibility remains the most serious question facing Bosnia as a constituent state.

4. An important step in the reintegration of Bosnia is the Bosnian-Croatian Federation. It is not functioning, though. Canton forming is not happening, or is happening very slowly. The Federation Government is, actually, the government of only a part of Federation territory, and this is the one under the control of the Republic of Bosnia and Herzegovina Army. In the part of Bosnia under HVO control the so-called Herceg-Bosnia Government is still functioning, and shows no signs of its intent to self-dissolute. In this respect, the formation of a federal police and the return of refugees is somewhat stagnant and freedom of movement is restricted in many areas. Therefore, a new effort should be made in order to finish the Federation installation, for it is in our vital interest. In today's meeting, within the second point of our daily schedule, Prof. Ganić is to outline a programme of action that could lead to our goal. It is intended that these actions take place at the same time or in close proximity with each other, and that the plan is partially coordinated with the Croatian side.

5. The Contact Group map is to be valid, if we do not agree on changes. We will not back down from Goražde and Brčko as we have made clear to American mediators on several occasions.

6. When it comes to Sarajevo, we have a few options, but all the solutions are based on the concept of a unique, undivided city. This is, along with the problem of common functions, definitely the most difficult point in negotiations. In relation to this, it is recommended that we immediately step up the reorganisation of the city of Sarajevo by forming the Sarajevo District, conforming to directions, which, according to the Federation Constitution, are valid for canton formation. We should exercise extreme caution and stay within the limits in level and dynamics during the transfer of authority from municipalities to the District. The Federation Constitution neither demands imperative nor automatic deauthorisation of municipalities and allows flexible solutions in this case. The transfer of authority from municipalities to cantons should be eventual and gradual.

7. The peace agreement, if anything is to be signed, can be implemented only with the help of strong international forces. It

cannot be UNPROFOR. It can only be NATO forces, perhaps supplemented by soldiers of other friendly countries. If Russia is to offer its soldiers, the number of them must be balanced with the number of soldiers from Muslim countries.

8. The peace implementation troops should be deployed in the form of garrisons throughout the whole of Bosnia and Herzegovina. It is unacceptable for us that they only be deployed at borderlines.

9. The financing of soldiers from Muslim countries is to be done by the United Nations.

10. International military forces for peace implementation may not interfere with the defensive efforts of the Bosnia and Herzegovina Army.

11. Peace implementation forces may stay on Bosnia and Herzegovina territory for a year, which is to be prolonged only at request from the Presidency.

12. Republic of Croatia military troops may stay on the Republic of Bosnia and Herzegovina's territory for a period of 30 days maximum after the signing of the peace agreement, which is to be prolonged only at the request of the Republic of Bosnia and Herzegovina Presidency.

13. We welcome the readiness of the international community to supply economic support for the reconstruction of countries affected by war in the former Yugoslavia, and especially for the reconstruction of Bosnia and Herzegovina. However, we explicitly demand that this help is to be according to the following terms: a) respect for the territorial integrity of Bosnia and Herzegovina by neighbour countries, b) respect for human rights and the rights of national minorities, c) respect for refugees and displaced persons rights to return to their homes. In this way, Western countries will not be able to continue to make mistakes by agreeing to new unprincipled compromises. Economic help – for all sides need it – is a strong device to induce leaderships and the public to start walking the path of respect for the law.

14. Democratic elections throughout Bosnia and Herzegovina are a great chance for criminal regimes and nationalist fanatics to be dethroned. This is an opportunity that must not be passed by, which will happen if conditions for truly democratic elections are not ensured. To do this, it is necessary: a) to ensure the

essential minimum of freedom (freedom of activity for political parties, freedom of the media, personal and proprietary safety for citizens, etc., b) to return the larger part of expelled citizens to their homes, c) to facilitate efficient international election control, d) to enable the elections to be held during the presence of international military forces for peace implementation. Elections for the Parliament and Presidency must be direct.

15. Persons who are suspected by the Hague Tribunal to have committed war crimes are not to take part in the elections.

16. It would be useful to establish mixed commissions and bureaus for acceptance and help to refugees in all the larger parts of the Republic of Bosnia and Herzegovina.

After an interval of ten days I travelled to America twice. The first occasion enabled me to talk in front of the General Assembly of the UN; there, I delivered my opinions on peace and my vision for Bosnia in the future. This is the speech I gave on 24 October.

Speech At The General UN Assembly
New York, 24 October 1995.

The UN organisation, whose jubilee we celebrate today, was a constant source of our hope, but also the constant reason behind our disappointment. Some say that at the same time it is the greatest and the least efficient organism in human history. The number of unrealised resolutions confirms this. Such as it is, our organisation probably reflects the imperfection of our world. If to constantly repair the world is not in vain, then further perfecting of the UN is not only needed, but possible as well.

Our highest goal is to maintain peace. The UN has contributed to the prevention of a global war, but has proven itself less efficient in halting regional conflicts. However, the sum of disastrous consequences in local wars since the founding of the UN up to this day is tragic.

The UN efficiently worked to stop the Gulf crisis. Unfortunately, this efficiency was not repeated in the case of aggression against my own country. The price of hesitation was terrifying. My people paid this high price.

I wish to repeat the words of Georgia's Minister of Foreign Affairs who, two days ago, standing at this very booth said: 'we must have the courage and the will to call aggression by its name and to call genocide by its name.'

As you know, there was very often a lack of either courage or will, and sometimes both.

In a couple of days the negotiations for peace in Bosnia are to begin. We approach this initiative started by America and its President in the best of faith and with much hope. Our people need and want peace. We did not start the war, and although we are winning, we never dreamed of winning a war. We have always worked for peace and we want to be winners in peace.

We wish to create a society based on political and ethnic pluralism, respect for human rights and private contractor companies. Since everything is the opposite on the other side, our ideas, we are certain, will triumph in a peaceful game in the next five to ten years. Thanks to the exceptional superiority of our society and country model, we will, with the help of God, win.

The Bosnian Government and Army will not accept the splitting and disintegration of the land, no matter what the package it might be served in. Dividing Bosnia would lead to the continuation of war, whether immediately or later.

True democratic elections in Bosnia are a huge – if not the only – real chance for the removal of war criminals and national fanatics who initiated the war and who will continue to poison relations between people and nations from the commanding political and military functions. Terms must be established, so that this last chance for democracy in the Balkans does not get lost. These terms are liberty and the efficient international supervision of elections.

If the peace negotiations come to a successful end, the reconstruction of a war-devastated region must follow, especially in Bosnia. The international community has promised significant support to the reconstruction plan. Related to this I would like to make a, probably unexpected, proposal: make conditions for this support. Send a clear message that the side that will not respect human rights and freedoms will not get the help. And make a decision for the strict respect of these rules. Do not make mistakes again in the hope to buy or better criminals and tyrants by new concessions. Go a step further. Isolate criminals and tyrants. This is the only way.

Men who have led people along the path of crime must be removed. Without this there will be no peace or safety, not in Bosnia nor in the region.

We wish and have the right to integrate Bosnia, which has not been broken by the will of its people, but rather by the power of weapons. The Bosniac-Croatian Federation is an important step in this direction and all friends of Bosnia should support and help this project.

To accomplish peace – and for it to survive – there must be a balance in arming. This balance can be established at higher or lower level. We give advantage to the second option and ask for a reduction of Serbian heavy artillery. If the Serbs do not accept this, the only choice is to equip the Bosnian Army, which would, strengthened, become a factor of peace and stability in the region.

Now, almost all our cities are in the range of Serbian artillery. This artillery has to be removed or destroyed. We cannot and will not accept to continue living under constant threat. And finally: in the last two days, many speeches have been given. We have heard many nice and high words on democracy and freedom and everything that goes along with it. On freedom and justice many have spoken who themselves have stepped over elementary human rights and who continue to do so. One old Holy Scripture says: 'Judge them by their deeds.' So, let us listen to what they say, but ask them what they do. The moment they get back home they will keep on doing things their way. Of course, this is so only if we let them.

After my speech to the General Assembly of the UN, I was received by President Clinton in the *Waldorf Astoria* Hotel in New York. I received important news during this meeting: the Russians had agreed to place their troops in Bosnia under the command of NATO, which practically meant under American control. This was the first time this had happened in NATO's existence.

On this occasion in America, another of my wishes came true: I met Mohammad Ali, the boxing legend. He had come to New York that day (I do not remember from which city), accompanied by his manager. The first thing I said to him was that I am Ali as well. He said he knew, nodding his head. Ali still looked good, but had difficulties moving and speaking. I felt an almost brotherly closeness with this man. For years I had watched every one of his fights, when possible, and cheered for him. Of course, I will never forget the unfortunate Ali vs. Frazer bout that had taken place 30 years previously. Sarajevo was awake through the night and reached the dawn sadly. With a witty smile on his face, Ali offered me a boxing match and, raising his hands to his face, took his stance. I accepted the game. Mohammad Ali was a big boy, to him went the credit that a harsh sport like boxing could be called a 'noble skill'. Upon my return to Bosnia, more people asked me about my encounter with Ali than with President Clinton.

The masses in Yugoslavia were indoctrinated by nationalist propaganda, and the leaders were prisoners to a monster they had often created themselves. Many who knew Milošević, wondered if he was a nationalist himself, or if he only used nationalism as an instrument of power. To be supported and chosen, he had to convince the Serbs that he was a great nationalist. In this respect, the saying that people have the leaders they deserve holds true.

I felt an aversion for official lunches and informal political meetings in general. It seemed unnatural to eat and attempt to chat with people who were not my close friends. I have to admit that it took me a long time to realise that smiles and sincere diplomat greetings mean nothing. For at the same time, they could be signing your death warrant. In general, there are no geniuses or men to especially admire in politics. The true geniuses are in science and the arts. When it comes to politicians, everyone is more or less average, the 'big' ones and the 'little' ones. Only ambitions and vanity are huge. Of course, there are rare exceptions. Official lunches in the end are nothing but forced smiles, vanity, affectation and acting, all that spiced up by a food you do not like.

1 November. Such lunches and dinners were a part of the Dayton Agreement's protocol and I avoided them as much as I could. One official lunch in the *Hope Hotel* in the American airbase *Wright-Petterson* in Dayton, Ohio, started the peace agreements. This was on 1 November 1995. Besides me, in our delegation were Haris Silajdžić, Krešimir Zubak, Jadranko Prlić, Miro Lazović, Ivo Komšić and Muhamed Šaćirbegović, as well as legal experts Kasim Trnka, Kasim Begić and Džemil Sabrihafizović.

Before lunch, State Secretary Warren Christopher and Ambassador Richard Holbrooke held separate conversations with each of the three delegations: the Serbians, Croats, and ourselves. In the plenary session that followed, Warren Cristopher, Carl Bildt, Tuđman, Milošević and I gave introductory expositions.

Christopher pointed out the readiness of the USA to help maintain the unique state of Bosnia and Herzegovina, founding the Federation and maintaining the multiethnic character of the Republic of Bosnia and Herzegovina. He made comparisons with the Camp David negotiations to stress the necessity of not communicating with the press. The State Department loudspeaker, post consultations with delegation representatives, would give statements to the press. Christopher also pointed out President Clinton's involvement in everything that happened in negotiations and, of especial importance for us, he talked about the USA's preference for maintaining a unique Sarajevo as the Republic's capital.

In turn, I said:

> We are here to negotiate in good faith and determined to do everything in our power to achieve a righteous and permanent peace. Whoever comes with the same intent will find complaisant collocutors in us.
>
> We have expressed our terms for peace very clearly in many recent instances. Still, I consider it necessary to repeat our basic points of view here today. First of all:
>
> 1. A sovereign and integral Bosnia and Herzegovina is essential. This should be based on democracy, pluralism and respect for human and minority rights, so that there will be conditions for the return of banished persons to their homes.
>
> 2. Such a Bosnia would consist of two parts: the Federation and the Serbian entity. The Federation was formed by the will and decision of the Bosnian and Croatian people as two equal constitutional nations of Bosnia and Herzegovina.
>
> 3. Bosnia and Herzegovina will maintain common institutions which are crucial for its functioning as an independent, sovereign and internationally recognised country. A decision on these institutions must be made in a manner that enables possible blockades to be quickly and efficiently removed.
>
> 4. The inner borderline map, on the issue of the Federation, cannot, in a quantitative and qualitative way, be below the map of the Contact Group.
>
> 5. International military forces should ensure implementation of the agreement. These forces should be deployed throughout

the entire territory of Bosnia and Herzegovina and on international borders.

6. The prosecution of war crimes must be continued. We ask Serbia and Montenegro to cooperate with the International Tribunal in the Hague.

7. Efficient international election control must be ensured; elections must be free and direct for entity parliaments, the national Parliament and the Presidency. Participation of our refugee voting body in these elections must be ensured.

8. Economic help for the reconstruction of Bosnia and the regions must in all parts be conditioned by respect for human and minority rights.

Before I finish this short speech, I consider it necessary to point the attention of this assembly towards a matter that strikes me as the most important of all at this moment. That is to say, while we negotiate here and make festal statements and promises, in the territory under the control of Mladić's army, especially in Banja Luka and western Bosnia, intense terror against the non-Serbian civil population is in progress.

The war on the fronts has ended, but the war against civilians is continuing and even intensifying. Women and children are being thrown into the streets while the male population is taken away into the unknown. Dark news on mass murders reach us daily – read any of today's issues of American newspapers.

Our people need peace, and we have come to achieve it, but I ask you: how can we negotiate while genocide against our population continues?

So, I ask President Milošević to immediately give out the order to stop this banishing. I call upon the international community with the United Nations Security Council at its head to take steps to deal with the situation. I ask Presidents Clinton, Chirac, Yeltsin, Chancellor Kohl and Prime Minister Major to use their influence in order to finally put an end to the sufferings of civilians in Bosnia.

At the end of the meeting we were handed a part of a general initial agreement on peace in Bosnia and Herzegovina, which contained provisions on ending hostilities, separating forces and elections. The demand not to give statements to the press was repeated in the interest of the normal flow of negotiations – a thing we only partially honoured.

2 November. The following day, our negotiation team met with President Tuđman and members of the Croatian delegation. The mediator was Holbrooke. There were arguments on the founding of the Federation and the problems which followed this. However, the return of 200 families from the Croatian and Bosnian sides to Travnik, Bugojno, Jajce and Stolac was agreed upon.

3 November. I held meetings with the ministries of foreign affairs representatives from France, Great Britain, Germany and Russia. All four delegations pointed out the importance of negotiations and offered help from their governments in the peace process.

During the day, we were handed Annexes on human rights, the return of refugees, and cultural monuments. And before noon I had a meeting with the President of Serbia Slobodan Milošević, the first one during these agreements. I had met him on several previous occasions, most often in meetings of the Yugoslavian Presidency in Belgrade.

I am not certain if I know Milošević well, but it often strikes me as though he and his politics are two different things. I can hardly combine what he does with my impression of him as a person. He is not a repugnant person. The truth is, he is always a bit drunk – or at least he seems to be – and in a mood to talk. It appears as if he believes what he says. He must be brave, but I would not say that he is a hypocrite. He may well be a split personality, but that is another thing. However, it does seem that the other, the evil side of his personality, is prevalent, so Milošević inevitably produces evil.

A detail during the Dayton negotiations might illustrate Milosević's contradictory judgement. After long negotiations, he suddenly changed his attitude towards the matter of Sarajevo and generally accepted our request. Leaving the room, he addressed Silajdžić and myself with the words: 'It's easy for you, you got Sarajevo, I have to put a helmet on and go among those fools.' He meant Krajišnik and Koljević who were anxiously awaiting the result in the other building. I do not think that he was putting on an act at that time. On the contrary, I am certain that it was his sincere opinion of Karadžić's companions.

That night, we were invited to visit the *Wright-Petterson* air force base where the negotiations were taking place. Here, there was an aviation museum, the largest in the world. It was true aviation history from the first flying device by the Wright brothers to the latest tomahawk missiles. The B-52 airplane from which the first atomic bomb was released (on Hiroshima) on 6 August, 1945, and a model of the bomb were exhibited. In a wide space between or underneath these impressive exhibits was an improvised restaurant with dinner tables set out for the occasion. We could hear music. I was not in the mood for dinner, so I looked around. I do not know if by accident or not, but the table for Nikola Koljević, a close assistant of Radovan Karadžić, was placed immediately under a huge tomahawk, a weapon which was used on the night of 11-12 September 1995 on Banja Luka from submarines in the Adriatic Sea (Koljević was from Banja Luka).[1]

4 November. The day began with a meeting between our team and that of Richard Holbrooke and his advisors. We discussed the structure of the Presidency, the way it would be selected, our demand that Karadžić and other war criminals be forbidden to stand as election candidates, the dilemma about whether the national government be directly elected or appointed, general elections, as well as matters of so-called vital national interest.

Thereafter, I studied the material on the solution to the Federation problem, prepared by Michael Steiner, the German Representative of the Contact Group. And late at night we had dinner with representatives from the Croatian team, Mate Granić and Gojko Šušak.

5 November. On the fifth day of negotiations I received a visit from Mrs. Elizabeth Rehn, the UN Special Reporter for Human Rights and Mrs. Christine Wallich from the World Bank, whose task it was to handle cooperation with the Republic of Bosnia and Herzegovina. Our delegation then met with the Croatian one headed by Minister Mate Granić. We discussed our views on the Federation material put forward by Steiner. This was followed by Silajdžić's and my almost three-hour meeting with Milošević and Bulatović.

6 November. A meeting was held with the American General Suel about the organisation of common command over the Federation military forces and American help regarding this.

Ambassador Steiner presented a new proposal on the Federation, after partially accepting written remarks from our delegation. Then came the issue of cooperation with IMF, relations between the Republic of Bosnia and Herzegovina Government and the Federation in matters of defense and how to gather customs and distribute them. Then a further two-hour meeting with Milošević and Bulatović took place. The day concluded with a dinner with Richard Holbrooke and leaders of the negotiating teams at which Holbrooke confirmed the readiness of America and its allies to send military troops to Bosnia for implementation of the peace agreement.

[1] Koljević committed suicide in 1997 (official version).

At all previous peace agreements, I had been concerned by one thought only: how to implement what had been agreed upon, regardless of the contents of the signed documents. Previous international negotiators had no military force at their disposal. How would this peace agreement look if Karadžić were willing to implement it voluntarily? It could only mean our capitulation. In this regard, the Dayton situation was different. It was made clear, and this time commitments were made in public on the subject, that the agreement would be implemented even if the use of force proved necessary. Among all of its defects, the Dayton Agreement had this advantage above all previous agreements.

But this advantage also had another face, its other side of the coin. If there was something I wanted and hated at the same time, it was having foreign troops in Bosnia. But a reasonable man between the devil and the deep sea will choose the lesser evil. Is having foreigners bad? Because they are an authority without control, and every authority without control inevitably turns into self-will; it would happen in Bosnia too. We were facing a dramatic choice: either foreigners (Americans, British, French) or local extremists. Either the foreign arrogance or the open violence of Serbian and Croatian hardliners and separatists. Neither was good, but there was no third option. I figured it was better to have foreigners who do not love you, than locals who hate you.

7 November. The day began with a 'face to face' meeting with Richard Holbrooke. The future balance of armaments in the region was considered. Holbrooke remarked that thus far in the negotiations certain progress on the matter of the Federation had been made, but that there was no progress concerning Sarajevo. He claimed it necessary for me to speak to Milošević every day in order to arrive at a solution. After seven days of negotiations, the American team was clearly not satisfied with the results.

Afterwards, I met with Milošević and Holbrooke in the presence of Montenegro President Bulatović and Serbian Foreign Affairs Minister Milutinović. In an argument over Sarajevo, the Serbs asked for it to be divided. I looked at Holbrooke. He categorically refused, stating that city partition was not negotiable. Instead, the American side proposed a 'federal district' solution for Sarajevo; meaning for it to remain within the Federation but under ethnically balanced administrations and unique police forces. I had earlier been especially keen that the Americans take a determined stance so that what happened in Mostar did not repeat itself. Our demand was also that the role of IFOR (International Forces for Agreement Implementation) be agreed during the Dayton negotiations.

The Americans further agreed with our proposal that the elections for the National Assembly and the Presidency be direct, but they also suggested a so-called mixed model: general elections for the National Parliament, and appointments for the Presidency with three, six, or nine members. I suggested that there be more than three persons in the Presidency. Otherwise they would only represent the nations that chose them. Holbrooke also supported the Croatian demand that the Croats have the ministerial office of foreign affairs and accepted the need to establish exactly who answers to whom (the premier to the national assembly, government to the premier, etc.). In Europe there are different solutions: the government answers to the head of the country (in our case, the Presidency) or to a national assembly. During the afternoon, I met with the President of the Federation Zubak, and in the evening with the French delegation and again with Milošević.

8 November. The meeting began early in the morning. This is when the most difficult questions were raised. Present were Holbrooke with his negotiating team, Premier Silajdžić, Federation President Zubak and Presidents Milošević and Bulatović. I proposed the Contact Group Plan as the basis for conversation, which in effect meant that we got Žepa and Srebrenica back. For his part, Milošević insisted that the formula for a peace solution required two entities and a clear definition of which territory belongs to each. 'The moment each side realises what is its territory everything will be clear (…) Let's not be frozen by existing positions,' he said. With this statement Milošević defined exactly his strategy during the war and after it.

There were several breaks for rest and consultation. During one of the breaks, Krajišnik joined the conversation. Holbrooke pointed out the need to discuss the constitution, maps, and above all Sarajevo. He repeated the three election models for the Presidency and the necessity that one of the members be in a superior position. I asked for the conditions for fair elections to be secured throughout the entire Bosnia and Herzegovina territory (freedom of speech, press and movement, etc.). If this were not the case then any elections would remain a pure formality. I also suggested that we talk about how these elections be conducted. In particular, I expressed my idea of how national institutions should be: parliament is a political body that reflects the political configuration of the country. The government answers to the parliament, and the presidency has the right of veto. Both the parliament and the presidency should be voted for in direct elections.

Milošević proposed a delegation system for the Presidency. According to him we should keep in mind the specificity of Bosnia and Herzegovina and the need to establish as simple a model as possible, which would disable any obstructions. I must admit that I did not quite understand how such a delegation system would prevent obstruction, but this was his explanation. Milošević was also for entity elections taking place as quickly as possible. He repeated that there should be direct elections in both the Federation and Republika Srpska for the 'continuation of the life of both entities with existing constitutions, which will be accorded to the Bosnia and Herzegovina Constitution.' He considered that 24 representatives from the Federation and 12 from Republika Srpska be delegated to the national parliament. He also suggested that the Federation have two positions in the Presidency, Republika Srpska one; the two Presidency members from the Federation to be the President and Vice-President of the Federation. Ambassador Holbrooke intervened at this proposal, pointing out that the Presidency, as head of the country, represents the country as a whole. Premier Silajdžić implied that direct elections were acceptable to everyone and that what we needed was a country with a certain consistency, which would itself maintain integrity. In his opinion what Milošević was suggesting was actually a union. The Bosnian Serbs needed to understand and accept the fact that Bosnia and Herzegovina would be their country as well. Zubak was in favour of a combination of direct elections and appointments and stressed the need for the government to reflect the national structure.

Holbrooke thought that control points throughout the entire territory of Bosnia and Herzegovina should be removed before elections. He again emphasised that Sarajevo be an undivided city. Myself, I once again returned to questions about Srebrenica, Žepa, Goražde and Sarajevo, arguing that Goražde must have a territorial connection to the rest of the Federation, through Rogatica or some other way.

Holbrooke repeatedly stated that there was no chance of some sort of a walled structure or similar in Sarajevo or anything else that would remind us of what Berlin used to be. In spite of this, Krajišnik asked for Novo Sarajevo to belong to Republika Srpska. Komšić implied that the city could be split neither in war nor in Geneva. 'Sarajevo will continue its existence as an integral capital city,' he said, and supported the special district proposal. I asked for the question of security within the city to be solved and proposed the formation of unique police forces in municipalities. I stood against the removal of military forces from the city. Since the snipers were still active, and since Karadžić's army was still positioned around the city, we could not afford the risk.

Krajišnik suggested that communication with Tuzla remained under our control, and that we build a bypass for Zenica in Ilijaš. Yet again, then, we faced reminders of Karadžić's bypasses, tunnels, overpasses and bridges. Ambassador Holbrooke repeated his affirmation that the USA and the Contact Group's goal was to resolve the conflict and offer a solution for Sarajevo as a special district.

A third meeting on the subject of the Federation was also held. Present were Steiner, Daniel Server, the State Department's Special Coordinator for Federation matters, Croatian ministers Granić and Šušak and the Federation President Zubak. A new proposal on the 'Agreement on the Realisation of the Federation in Bosnia and Herzegovina' was made. Zubak insisted on separating the competences of the two governments, federal and state. Lesser changes in the offered text were also proposed.

9 November. Six meetings in total that day. First, Minister Šaćirbegović and I met the American advisory team, headed by General Clark, to discuss their future mission in Bosnia and Herzegovina (help in coaching personnel and the proposal of an army and armaments organisation).

Afterwards, our entire delegation met Ambassador Holbrooke, General Clark and the American mapping team for further arguments. I pointed out our priorities: the Brčko corridor, Sarajevo and Goražde. An argument followed on borderlines in relation to the Contact Group Plan. Conversations continued with a talk about the constitution, elections, and the role of the OSCE. For example, was the OSCE to organise or only supervise the elections? I was in favour of the OSCE doing both. After lunch came a meeting with Tuđman and Minister Granić. Šaćirbegović was also present. A part of our daily schedule was the revision of accomplished agreements with projections for the future.

During the late afternoon, Premier Silajdžić and I met Robert Owen for a discussion on constitutional solutions. Owen told us that Milošević did not like the idea of having a bicameral parliament. Milošević was also opposed to the OSCE organising the elections (his proposal being that the OSCE only supervise them). He also requested that people living outside of Bosnia and Herzegovina go to Bosnia and Herzegovina and vote. We pointed out that the Constitution of Republika Srpska was not in conformity with democratic principles and the Constitution of the Republic of Bosnia and Herzegovina and asked for a deadline for accordance. The OSCE must solve the question of the rights of the non-Serbian population in the territory of Republika Srpska. Owen asked, on behalf of the Serbian side, when they would begin to participate in the organs of the state authority.

Our negotiating team met General Clark and representatives of the Pentagon, once again, to discuss the Serbian map proposal. We found the proposal unacceptable and suggested that, from now on, corrections and proposals be sketched on the Contact Group map, for purposes of comparison.

Late that night there was a further meeting with Owen and Ambassador Menzies about constitutional questions and the proposed American text on elections and OSCE supervision. There was also a discussion on how to interpret the words 'supervise the elections'. We asked for national assembly elections to cover the entire territory. We also asked for it to be made possible for the non-Serbian population living in Republika Srpska to have equal access to voting, as well as to enable Serbians who did not live in Republika Srpska to enter the list for the Presidency. By the end of the day, I received the final text of the Agreement on the Realisation of Federation in Bosnia and Herzegovina.

10 November. Early in the morning, Premier Silajdžić and I received first Ambassador Steiner and talked about the Federation; then we received the Secretary of State Christopher and Ambassador Holbrooke. The State Secretary emphasised the importance of the accomplished agreement on the Federation and asked for a rational division of main positions in authority during the transition period. I suggested that the Croats get the vice-presidency of the government and foreign affairs ministerial positions, and that Silajdžić remained Premier. I explained that we had already given concessions to the Croats by virtue of parting the Federation Government from the Bosnia and Herzegovina Government, and also emphasised the condition that these two governments part in parallel with the end of Herzeg-Bosnia's existence. State Secretary Christopher pointed out the importance of clear and precise peace regulations, because only on that condition would President Clinton, after signing the peace agreement, speak to Congress and ask for US troops to be a part of IFOR.

American public opinion objected to military involvement in Bosnia. The Pentagon, too, attempted to reduce this engagement as much as possible, proposing that IFOR deploy troops only in the Federation. I said that this was absolutely unacceptable: IFOR was to take positions throughout the country, including Bosnia and Herzegovina's borders.

American sensitivity to military engagement was roused by their bad experience in Vietnam and more recently in Somalia. They had to count on losses and this made them cautious. I assured all American functionaries that such trouble was not to be expected in Bosnia. My statement proved to be true. It was in part a result of IFOR soldiers' correct behaviour, but also our politics, our messages to the people and a feeling among the people themselves that foreign soldiers were necessary at this point. Still, not even the greatest optimist would have believed that after five years not one assault on SFOR soldiers would be recorded. (Note: IFOR, the international military force, was renamed SFOR, a Stabilisation Force, in 1997 and also given a new mandate.)

Holbrooke repeated that Milošević agreed for elections to be direct, the first mandate for both the Presidency and Assembly being two years. He insisted that we should talk more with representatives of the European Union and Carl Bildt, so that they would be obliged to commit their forces to an international force for implementation of the agreement. He again pointed out that the USA could not commit itself to anything unless it had the concordance of Congress, which depended exclusively on the clarity of the peace regulations. Premier Silajdžić asked for obligations to help the country's reconstruction to be included in the annexes to the agreement.

After this meeting, which lasted for almost two hours, there was the signing of the Federation Agreement ceremony. Introductory speeches were given by State Secretary Christopher, Ambassador Ishinger on behalf of the European Union and Holbrooke, followed by the three Presidents Zubak, Tuđman, and myself. I was in a dilemma about the carrying out of the agreement and about the signatories themselves. My experiences with Tuđman had thus far been very bad, and this could be noticed from the very first sentence of my speech:

> I shall not name this day historical. I will leave it to historians to mark its importance in a distant future. They will judge not by what is said today, but by what will be done. I will rather call this day the day of our determinacy or the day of hope, as State Secretary Christopher has put it.
>
> We have once again confirmed our determinacy to continue with the efforts to establish the Bosnia and Herzegovina Federation that we agreed on more than 18 months ago in Washington. With this goal, we have agreed on certain changes described in the documents that we have just signed. As reasonable people, we have decided to correct what did not

function, keeping unchanged the basis on which we built our Federation.

The source of our hope was the fact that all factors of a permanent character were on the side of the Federation. The others were temporary and the coming time will leave them behind. This judgement, in spite of everything else, was the source of our patience, though this was sometimes incomprehensible to others.

Together with today's agreement we have also settled on the return of a certain number of families to Jajce, Bugojno, Stolac and Travnik. It is a small, but very significant step. For both sides, it is a test of good will and a readiness for the execution of everything that has been agreed. The condition is clear: safety in those towns. On our side, I wish to state here that we are determined to guarantee safety.

Of no lesser importance is our agreement on Mostar. We have settled on terms that will help to overcome the separation of the town as it is today.

I am happy that America and Europe strongly support this concept and thankful to Mr. Christopher for the statement he made today regarding this.

In his speech, Tuđman treated the Federation as a state and spoke of its relations with Croatia. I did not like Tuđman. There was something upstartish in his behaviour, and his protocol was on the verge of kitsch. He constantly wanted to have a piece of Bosnia – whether larger or smaller. I have not read his doctoral dissertation, but I'm familiar with the fact that it was on the subject of *Banovina* Hrvatska, established in 1939, by the Cvetković-Maček Agreement. The *Banovina* was according to his taste and measure, because it included large parts of Bosnia. I assume that he read Huntington with delight. Actually, Huntington's 'conflict of civilisations' made a good theoretical excuse for his appetite towards Bosnia.

Divisions according to Huntington's line were his fixed idea. When the Kosovo crisis in 1999, during NATO's air attacks, was at its peak, Tuđman came up with his proposal to divide Kosovo into two parts, Albanian and Serbian. He loved the word secession. When asked for a comment, I said that the only thing missing in his proposal was that it wasn't proclaimed in Karađorđevo.

Still, Tuđman was one thing for Croatia and another for Bosnia and the rest of the world. His merits for Croatia are priceless. He put forward the basis for the Croatian State that will one day – when he has gone – become a democratic and progressive state. His merits for Croatia are permanent, his mistakes temporary and repairable. Regarding his influence on happenings in Bosnia, things are mostly the other way round.

I was sceptical about the Croats' ability to fulfil the obligations they had taken on because the idea of a Federation had been in place for almost two years. But we had to try over and over again, for there was no choice. This time we went a step further: we accepted to leave the foreign affairs function to the Croats. Šaćirbegović resigned so that Prlić could take this position. State Secretary Christopher had sought to persuade us that this was the condition for common institutions to start functioning: 'Common political and economic institutions that will unite two communities will be formed,' said Christopher. Christopher's optimism has not as yet proven justified. The Federation is still just a formality without substance. There are still two armies, two payment funds, double pension funds, double teaching plans, post offices, railways and a divided Mostar. Still, things are moving towards the Federation, not against it.

Closing the ceremony, Christopher emphasised that the central government of Bosnia and Herzegovina would keep its authorisations, which included the matter of the state's sovereignty, foreign politics and trade and monetary politics, while the work of the police, courts, tax inspectorate, health and education departments would be transferred to the Federation. He also said that this agreement obliged the Federation to respect the human rights of all citizens, making it possible for them to move freely over the entire territory of the Federation, and also removing all inner customs control points.

At the end of the day Silajdžić, Šaćirbegović and I met once again with State Secretary Christopher and Ambassador Holbrooke. Christopher pointed out the importance of the day and urged us to speed up the realisation of the agreement, expressing hope that progress would be made regarding the maps. He said that he and the American negotiating team regularly reported to Congress on the course of negotiations. I assured them that we would do everything to achieve peace and pointed out the need for establishing the way of Bosnia and Herzegovina's defense after the departure of IFOR forces. We handed the American side our *aide-memoir* on the subject. Premier Silajdžić repeated the necessity of bringing in a clause on the obligation of the international community to help in the reconstruction of Bosnia and Herzegovina, and Christopher once again stressed the importance of the higher involvement of the European Union in the peace agreement.

When I left Sarajevo, I considered that negotiations could last up to ten days. However, ten days had passed and nothing essential had been achieved. I lost the little optimism I had brought to Dayton. I ate and slept poorly; my thumping heart woke me in the night. It seems that Holbrooke noticed my condition, because he came to me after the day's meetings and unexpectedly suggested that one of my children join me in Dayton. I turned it down, but from this offer I drew the conclusion that Holbrooke was not pessimistic like myself and that he had no intention of giving up easily. It seemed to me that every day I was getting closer to a heart attack. It happened, but three months later. Still, I am sure that I 'earned' it in Dayton.

11 November. The second round of negotiations began with the continuation of arguments about geography. Holbrooke came out with the completely unacceptable proposal made by the Serbian side. A discussion followed about the lines, which according to the Serbian proposal they and we should pull out from. In the argument on the Brčko corridor, we refused the demand that it be broadened. Holbrooke then suggested that the Brčko lines remain unchanged, because the Serbs would never voluntarily retreat from this territory, and NATO forces, according to Holbrooke, were not prepared to force them out. He proposed that we call this line a 'temporary line of parting'. We, however, expressed our fear that a new war might erupt because of Brčko. Silajdžić reminded everyone that Milošević had ensured that sanctions were loosened because he accepted the Contact Group Plan, and that plan did not provide for corridor broadening. In the afternoon hours we held separate meetings with Robert Owen. The subject: the involvement of Serbs from Republika Srpska in common Bosnia and Herzegovina organs and the supervising of elections.

Late at night I was called from the RTVBiH. I told the journalist on the other end of the line that there was no essential progress yet and added: 'One thing is for sure: we will have to share something, either territory or authority. We would rather share authority.'

12 November. Komšić, Lazović and I met Schwarz Schilling, the European Union mediator for Federation matters. Schilling stressed his view that the signed agreement on the Federation was very important for the strengthening of the peace process and expressed his belief that the following three days of negotiations would be a deciding time. According to him, a strong Federation, attractive to international capital, would

be a factor in the reintegration of Republika Srpska in Bosnia and Herzegovina. He gave the example of the Federal Republic of Germany and the former DDR, which united after almost 50 years, thanks to the economic power of the Federal Republic of Germany. He emphasised the need to enable legal proprietary owners to return to their properties, and proposed that a commission for these matters be formed immediately in cooperation with the countries that had accepted our refugees. This would help avoid any new humanitarian catastrophe should a peace agreement be signed and domicile countries decide to immediately return our refugees home.

That day members of our delegation met with the families of the American negotiating team's members who had perished in Igman in the August of 1995 (namely, Frasure, Kruzel and Drew). I expressed my condolences to their wives and children and highlighted the contribution these men had made to the peace process. The conversation continued more informally with the children involved. Finally, I invited members of these families to visit Bosnia and Herzegovina and see the place where their closest ones had been killed.

Thereafter came a meeting with Holbrooke and his team, and also with Šaćirbegović and Zubak. Ambassador Holbrooke put forward a geographic proposal presented by Milošević, but appended by a note to the effect that he was only a messenger, and that he did not stand behind it. The map thereof was in any case utterly unacceptable. Holbrooke also handed us a proposal in document format entitled 'Elements of Agreed Principles for Sarajevo' containing 11 points, worked out by Robert Owen.

Late at night a working meeting of our entire delegation and legal experts concerning constitutional matters was held.

13 November. Silajdžić and I met Ambassador Holbrooke and the American team. The Serbs repeated their unchanged mapping proposal. I marked this as unallowable and threatened that I would speak to the media and let them know about the pressure that was being inflicted upon us. I also handed Holbrooke our comments on the 'Elements of Agreed Principles for Sarajevo' material.

The meeting that followed was with Paulina Neville-Jones and Alan Charlton from the British Foreign Affairs Ministry. Mrs. Neville-Jones, who never tried to conceal her dislike for us, came to express her concerns regarding the lack of progress in negotiations and threatened to withdraw UN forces from Bosnia. 'You have to be aware that the international community is prepared to stay in Bosnia only if an agreement is reached. A negative signal from here would lead to the withdrawal of UN forces, which have reduced the suffering of your people. The consequences are much higher if you do not reach an agreement now, because we will not return to status quo, said, or rather threatened, Mrs. Neville-Jones. She also added that she came to 'warn us on time'. Taking this as open and unjustified pressure, I replied: 'Defend your map – the Contact Group map, and do not let the Serbian side be rewarded for the genocide they have committed.'

In the continuation of the conversation, the British delegation defended the Serbian demand for a broader Brčko corridor, without hiding the Serbs' wish to separate. I protested: 'You are here to help us maintain the integrity of the state. The world does not know that we are under pressure here. You should not be supporting killers. Milošević needs a lifting of sanctions, he desperately needs that, pressure him, not us,' I said without any attempt to conceal my angst.

Neville-Jones continued in the same tone, stating that our positions would be much weaker than the Serbs should negotiations stop and that the consequences would be more difficult for us than for them. I tried to explain that Milošević only wanted to broaden the corridor so that he could cut off Republika Srpska and that Great Britain should not support separatism. The polemic continued. Silajdžić's comment was as follows: 'The Serbs have committed genocide and created this situation and you have no right to defend their stands,' to which I added that we had agreed to these negotiations only after Milošević had accepted the Contact Group Plan, and that there was no corridor facility in that plan. 'You have to remind him of this and threaten him,' I said. The British representatives left dissatisfied with the meeting.

News arrived of the Bosnian Croats' disobedience of Tuđman, the first after Kljuić's in 1992. Zubak had refused to surrender Posavina to the Serbs, to which Tuđman had previously agreed, and maybe even dealt in a replacement for a 'clean Baranja'. 'It will be with you or without you,' Tuđman allegedly said to Zubak. 'Then without me,' Zubak had replied.

We continued with the previous day's dialogue with Schwarz Christian Schilling. Schilling repeated his belief about the need to strengthen the Federation as a factor in Bosnia and Herzegovina uniting. We argued about questions of a financial nature, about what dilemma the Federation might face before the international community when it came to credit and about the kind of financial relationship it would have with the international community in comparison with the state. Šaćirbegović emphasised that the state must have the means to repay debt. Silajdžić expressed the opinion that the Federation could not appear as an international subject because it required the authorisation of the central government. It was decided that Mrs. Wallich from the World Bank be invited to bring needed explanations. I repeated my critical assessment of the mapping proposal, reiterating that we were under pressure from the USA and Great Britain to accept the same, and informed the delegation that our response was clear: 'This is a map of your governments, not ours. Defend your map. If the pressure continues, we will talk to the press.'

In the afternoon we met Ambassador Steiner and Christian Clages from the German Foreign Affairs Ministry. Clages suggested that we correct our comments to the proposed 'Elements of Agreed Principles for Sarajevo'. We had arguments on the ruling regarding the transitory period and the way of supplementing personnel as well as the scheme that would function until elections were held. Steiner's proposal was that for the first two years the President of the Presidency would be a Bosniac. I proposed instead that the President be the candidate with the highest number of votes. We continued the conversation speaking about the military structure and the manner of military commanding. When it came to the government, I suggested it be a government of experts.

Our delegation then met Carl Bildt and political directors of the foreign affairs ministries of Great Britain, Germany and France. We talked about the problem of safety in Sarajevo after the departure of IFOR forces. We suggested an international police force. I again informed those present that the maps which were still on the table were unacceptable to us, especially as regards the Brčko and eastern Bosnia corridors.

Afterwards, Šaćirbegović and I met John Shattuck, the Assistant to the USA State Secretary for Human Rights. Since this coincided with Shattuck's return from Bosnia, my first question related to conditions in Banja Luka. Shattuck said that there was a large number of missing persons and pointed out the problem of forced work in the territories under Serbian control. Šaćirbegović said that Milošević knew these as concentration camps but justified their existence with the excuse that 'everyone has to work'. Šaćirbegović argued as follows: 'We have a resolution from the UN Security Council, which says that work camps must be dismissed and that everyone must obey the Resolution.' John Shattuck mentioned the situation of 17 prisoners, 'Merhamet' employees, who were visited by representatives of the International Red Cross and who the Serbian side claimed they were willing to exchange. In this respect, we asked for his help to ensure the exchange took place, which he promised.

Holbrooke came three times during the day, each time bringing a new geographic proposal.

14 November. A conversation with Secretary of State Christopher, Ambassador Holbrooke, Silajdžić, Šaćirbegović, Zubak and myself was held. Christopher expressed contentment that he had the opportunity, on his way to Japan, to stay in Dayton for a day and speak to each of the delegation heads. I stated that we were still being pressured into accepting a geographic solution that was totally at odds with the Contact Group map. I repeated that there was a line below which we would not go. I handed a letter to the State Secretary (addressed also to all representatives of the Contact Group in Dayton) in which our delegation detailed its complaints. Essentially, that the Serbian President Milošević had received a suspension of sanctions on the basis that he accepted the plan of the Contact Group which was being ignored. We had come to the negotiating table on the condition that the Contact Group Plan be honoured. We were prepared to discuss changes to the Contact Group map but only if qualitative and quantitative balance was maintained. In discussing the corridor near Brčko, Zubak pointed out that Milošević insisted on a wide corridor, purely because he was counting on division. Not only was this obvious, it was unacceptable.

During the day, Christopher came three times after conversations with Milošević and Tuđman, on the last occasion at sometime after midnight. At each one of these meetings, the map was discussed as well as the possibility of receiving Foča and part of the Drina River for building the hydroelectric power station for our needs, retaking Srebrenica and Žepa, etc. Christopher informed us that the Serbs definitely refused to return Doboj and that negotiations henceforth were at stake.

At the third meeting, Sarajevo was the subject matter. The American team presented the Serbian, revised proposal for 'The Elements of the Agreed Principles for Sarajevo'. The paper was completely unacceptable because it implied a division of the city, for the proposal stated that every municipality was to maintain a local police force. It was agreed that our experts should propose the necessary alterations. The Secretary of State emphasised that the Americans were absolutely on our side in this matter and that President Clinton had spent three hours with Congress, talking about Bosnia so as to secure the necessary means in the budget. Then, Christopher turned directly to me: 'We really want to help. In this moment we have a great chance to establish a united state, to end the war, to get funds for the reconstruction and I am appealing to you not to forego this unique opportunity. You Mr. President, at this moment, are the only person that can point out the necessity of a positive approach to these proposals. Do not let these details prevail, which are not very important in comparison with the entirety of the solution. We are pressuring Milošević to give up Karadžić and Mladić, so we can actually implement things we agree in Dayton. If we achieve a stable agreement here, Congress will support sending our troops along with IFOR forces. But if this does not happen, some people in the USA will be happy and say: "let us wash our hands of everything, we tried sincerely and now there is nothing more we can do".' At the end of the meeting, Secretary of State Christopher said that he would return to Dayton on Saturday, 18 November, and help with last minute questions.

Thereafter I received representatives of the European Union, Carl Bildt and three political directors of the foreign affairs ministries from Great Britain, France and Germany. I introduced the meeting with discussions from the previous day and with the problems surrounding inner borders.

Late at night, Silajdžić and I received Milošević and Bulatović. We talked about Sarajevo and the release of captives.

15 November. Things were still not progressing forward. There was still no safe territorial connection with Goražde, Sarajevo was partially solved, but they would not yield Srebrenica, Foča and Višegrad. A number of constitutional questions also remained unsolved. At the same time, there was pressure from all sides. President Chirac, Prime Minister Major and President Demirel all called saying the same thing: this is the best chance there is to achieve a satisfying peace, later it would only become more difficult. Carl Bildt also came with a message from the European Union ministers that the negotiations, which were at a standstill, must be continued and a solution found. Soon there would be no new negotiations. This was the last chance to catch the 'train of peace'. The messages were almost identical and America's handwriting was instantly recognisable.

Next, a meeting with John Shattuck, Ambassador Menzies and Jak Zekulić from the State Department took place. The conversation centred around captives in the region of Banja Luka. It was agreed that Shattuck submit a proposal about the release of all captive civilians, recalling Security Council Resolution No. 1019, 9 November 1995, whereby the Bosnian Serbs were asked to allow undisturbed access to captives from Srebrenica and Žepa, and also to ones from the regions of Banja Luka and Sanski Most. According to this Resolution, the Red Cross was to be allowed to register all captives and to have access to all places of their captivity. Jak Zekulić informed us of the Serbian request that refugees and evacuated persons vote in the place and for the municipality they were in at the time of the elections. This I firmly rejected.

Croatian representatives were also in favour of letting those people vote in the place where they lived now, which meant in those places where they had taken others' properties and homes. It was the future well-known procedure of P-2. Our opinion was different and was such that refugees and displaced persons vote in the municipalities and for the committees where they had lived in 1991. The meaning of this different access was clear. The Serbian and Croatian side – at least through the people who represented them then – wanted to maintain and fortify the demographic picture of the Bosnia and Herzegovina created by the war, that is by the expulsions and ethnic cleansing. Such a demographic situation implied or at least potentially held the possibility of a three parts division of Bosnia. There is no other place where the different politics towards the existence and future of Bosnia are stated more clearly than in the use of the P-2 form.

I also identified the problem surrounding the interpretation of the term 'supervising' the elections by the OSCE. The Serbs understood this as presence at the elections only, while for us it meant organising as well as supervising those elections. After our proposal for voting in accordance with the 1991 Census, the attitude of the American Government was that the OSCE should register all refugees and that a deal should be made with those countries that had accepted our refugees. This so that they could vote without fear of being returned by their host countries (Germany, Austria, Switzerland) directly to Bosnia.

Later, our delegation met Carl Bildt and the three representatives of the European Union. Mrs. Neville-Jones protested at the so-called mistreatment of humanitarian workers and UN observers in central Bosnia. In turn, I assured all present that I would order the accusations to be examined. Carl Bildt asked how far the peace negotiations had matured. I replied that, unfortunately, we did not have any good news, despite the former day's work on the maps, from 9.00 am till 12.00 pm. The problem was that Milošević's solutions differed completely from the maps of the Contact Group. Work on the Annexes continued, but there were still differences over many questions. Nonetheless, I expressed the view that we should be able to solve such issues. Minister Saćirbegović expressed his less than optimistic view and highlighted those indications which seemed intent on dividing the country.

Ambassadors Ishinger and Neville-Jones suggested I go to Washington and ask Congress for its full support in the agreement's implementation. Knowing the American attitude, I said that I could do that only with a worthy document, because Congress required a clear and strong agreement. The European Union ambassadors assured us that NATO was determined to lead the soldiers immediately after the signing of the document and that difficulties on this matter did not stem from Europe but rather from the USA.

Then the ceremony of signing the Agreement on establishing the Council for Collaboration between the Republic of Croatia, the Republic of Bosnia and Herzegovina and the Federation proceeded. I led our delegation and Tuđman the Croatian one. Upon its completion, we held two shorter meetings with Holbrooke. This was basically an extension of our discussions about geographic allocations.

16 November. A meeting between our delegation and Bildt together with the three political directors from Germany, France, and Great Britain proceeded early in the morning. We discussed the timing of the three conferences: in Paris where the peace accord would be signed, in London about the economic reconstruction of Bosnia and Herzegovina and finally in Brussels about the implementation of the civic aspects of the peace accord. President Zubak, who had by then resigned asked, 'What is the importance of the accords if we lose the people as they are not coming back to Posavina because it remained under Serbian control?' I said that I could be partially optimistic if we secured a solution for Goražde. I informed the collocutors that I had just spoken with Prof. Ganić, who was in Sarajevo, on the telephone. Ganić had warned me that Serbian propaganda, headed by Karadžić, had sent a message to the Bosnian Serbs not to accept the plan.

Thereafter, Silajdžić, Saćirbegović and I received Antony Lake, President Clinton's Advisor for National Security. Ambassador Holbrooke joined the meeting. Lake informed us that he had just spoken with President Clinton and he brought us a strong message from the American Administration, to the effect that this was the right time to bring about a solution. He listed the advantages achieved so far in the negotiations: a united Bosnia and Herzegovina within internationally recognised borders and, in his opinion, a righteous solution. He emphasised the fact that the USA would not force anyone to sign the agreement who did not believe that it could be accepted. The USA's role in all this was not only to achieve the accord, but also to find the best achievable agreement. If the negotiations were not completely workable in Dayton, then unresolved questions could be decided in Paris. He pointed out that Congress was divided about sending American troops to Bosnia, as well as about equipment and our army training. To secure the accord we would have to be ready to make concessions. This despite the fact that people always emphasise things that have not been achieved as opposed to those that have.

I explained that we were doing everything we could and informed Lake about the Serbian propaganda that encouraged Bosnian Serbs not to accept any accord. Holbrooke advised us that Milošević accepted the Goražde corridor, but not wider than three kilometres, and that he was ready to return Grbavica if the Serbs gained parts on the northeast side of Sarajevo. Premier Silajdžić explained that the Serbs wanted such a narrow corridor for Goražde, so that people would be scared and, hence, leave the city. For his part, Saćirbegović identified that there were insufficient established mechanisms for the implementation of the agreement, as well as police forces for the security of returning refugees and also for supervising elections.

Lake expressed concern about the refusal of some Congress members to accept the 'Delta' Project (the programme for the equipment and training of our army by American experts). Šaćirbegović asked whether it were possible to discuss special relations between Bosnia and Herzegovina and NATO or rather the possibility for a statement from NATO that Bosnia is important for the overall stability of Europe as well as for NATO. Silajdžić referred to the problem with Sandzak, especially the fact that there was no observing OSCE mission there. He requested the beginning of discussions about the matter with the Europeans.

A break for lunch was made and thereafter we again spoke with Anthony Lake and Ambassador Holbrooke. In the discussion about geographic allocations, I made it clear that we could not ease up any further and that it was necessary to examine whether Milošević was serious about these negotiations. Holbrooke said that General Joulwan would speak with Milošević the following day and explain to him that the Goražde corridor, only three kilometres wide, was unacceptable from a military point of view and that Grbavica could not, by any means, become Serbian. He also informed us that Milošević had agreed with NATO's presence under NATO's conditions, which in effect meant without a double key.

17 November. A meeting with William Perry, the US Defense Minister. Holbrooke too was present. Perry stated that in his view this was a historic moment, and that everyone in Washington was watching it

closely and that huge progress had been made as compared with the situation two weeks ago. He explained that the USA was ready to engage its forces for the implementation of the agreement, but that Russian support would be needed so that the plan could be applied with the minimum of risk. The Europeans, he advised us, do not have the same obligations towards Bosnia. Furthermore that everything was being done for the establishment of a strong Federation. I explained that Christopher, Secretary of State, had put forward a geographic proposal, which we accepted, but which the Serbs had refused, and that in this way, we had made huge concessions. Holbrooke advised that subsequent to his long talk with Milosević the previous night, the latter had agreed that the Goražde corridor be eight kilometres wide. Perry again referred to NATO's engagement, and how important this was not only for Bosnia, but for Europe also. Thereafter, a tour of the USA mapping agency took place, where the video of the corridor and avionic slides of the Goražde region were demonstrated.

Once the meeting resumed, General Joulwan joined the discussion. He confirmed that the Russians, at a meeting with President Clinton, had agreed to put their forces within IFOR under American command within 20 days. I already knew about this unusual detail, which, in itself, revealed the complexity of the relations between these two countries.

Holbrooke informed us that Milošević accepted our request for IFOR forces to be spread over the whole Bosnian territory, and that this was definitely a step forward. I pointed out that the Serbs had to withdraw not only from Grbavica and the Jewish cemetery (parts of Sarajevo) but also from the hills above the city. General Joulwan stated: 'I explained to Milošević that our forces could be vulnerable if the Serbian troops stay on the hills above the city, and also that we will sharply reply in the case of an attack.' Šaćirbegović asked what would happen if civilians were attacked, whether IFOR would act then as well. General Joulwan did not give a direct answer. I asked for the demilitarised zone around the Goražde corridor to be shortened from two to one kilometre from each side and suggested that people would stay in the city if they felt safe, if not they would leave. Joulwan said that he would insist that a military annex be signed by representatives from the Serbian Republic as well. I did not agree with this because Milošević was authorised to sign in the name of the Bosnian Serbs only. Holbrooke explained that Congress would not send troops without the signature of the Republika Srpska military representatives to Annexe One (the military annex). 'We are not dividing your country, it is only a signature that their army agrees with our arrival,' said Holbrooke. The explanation did not sound particularly persuasive. A long discussion about the people who would sign the Military Annexe and about the legacy of their signature followed.

Later that evening, I received Bildt and the three European political directors. I explained the mapping situation, as well as critical points and the discussion about the Goražde corridor's width. Zubak spoke about the need for a solution to remaining questions, especially about a central bank and mutual monetary system. Afterwards, the discussion about elections followed, including how refugees would vote. Was it in the place where they were registered in 1991 or where they were currently living now? Bildt pointed to difficulties and asked that the international community conduct only the supervision of elections. This we had earlier refused. I replied with a request for OSCE observers and other international institutions to come earlier, during the election campaigns, and not only at election time.

During the night, I held a meeting with Secretary of State Christopher and Ambassador Holbrooke. Silajdžić and Šaćirbegović were also present. Christopher said that he had been informed about our intensive activities, about meetings with Minister Perry and Advisor Lake and expressed satisfaction on the proposed widening of the Goražde corridor. I explained that there was no solution so far for the building of the hydroelectric power station on the Drina River and that the Brčko problem remained unsolved. Holbrooke proposed that America offer a written guarantee for the hydroelectric power station and some other items. I then advised them that the following day we would seek to conclude the map equation and the day after that any remaining unsolved questions.

18 November. Ambassador Menzies and General Kerrick informed us about the necessity of achieving an agreement today, before midnight in order to enable documents to be completed and the initialing ceremony to take place on the Monday. I repeated that if there was no agreement about Brčko, there would be no solution, and no ceremony. Secretary of State Christopher joined the discussions. He advised that we had reached the moment where it was necessary to decide whether negotiations be continued or suspended. He repeated the timing for the agreement and ceremony which had been put to us earlier that day.

Ambassador Holbrooke presented the benefits for Bosnia that would ensue from the peace agreement. He listed them as follows:

1) One national government with a democratic constitution and central institutions, continuity and recognition of the country, freedom of travel through the whole country, a Bosniac as the president for the first mandate, direct elections for the Presidency and Parliament, the firm protection of human rights, exclusion of war criminals from governmental authority, democratic elections in both entities that would be supervised by the international community, a central bank with one currency and an internationally sponsored programme for police training and supervision.

2) A package for economic reconstruction (international donations, IMF and IBRD programmes with the intent of fast reconstruction, the writing off of a large part of Bosnia's debt, credits and guarantees for the reconstruction of the infrastructure, membership and concessive credits of the IMF and World Bank and a starting support from the USA of $500 million).

3) IFOR forces led by NATO under American command; 60,000 soldiers, of which 20,000 would be Americans, a separation of forces but with IFOR in both entities, regional control of armaments, lifting of the arms embargo, and military parity with the Bosnian Serb forces.

4) A significantly strengthened Federation (the new agreement on the Federation would secure a clear definition of governmental powers and the dismantling of the Herzeg-Bosnian government)

5) The territory of the Federation would be augmented from 50% to over 55% during the negotiations,[2] and that this was compact, maintainable territory. Goražde was secured and accessible, IFOR (or others) would build a new road through the Goražde corridor, and until it was complete, IFOR would control fully the Rogatica and Foča roads. There was also a committee for the implementation of the agreement, and this would be led by a steering group from Brussels, whilst the work of different international agencies would be coordinated by the high representative from offices in Sarajevo and, in accordance with the need to ensure and create necessary measures of confidence and protection of human rights, elections would be supervised by the OSCE and other international organisations.

---

[2] This percentage would decline to somewhere a bit above 51% again.

6) Stronger protection of human rights, the guaranteed right of refugee return or compensation for loss of property, support for the War Crimes Court, release of all civilians, the exchange of war captives, and establishing a commission for war crime investigations.

7) Belgrade's agreement to normalise relations with Bosnia and Herzegovina including the addition of confidence measures (President Izetbegović's, Premier Silajdžić's and other authorities' visits to Belgrade, a direct air transport link between Belgrade and Sarajevo, Belgrade's recognition of Bosnian sovereignty and territorial integrity, opening of the embassies in Belgrade and Sarajevo, collaboration in matters of transport and the use of electricity, water and gas, trade and economy collaboration, establishing a 'hot line', direct telephone communications system, mutual economic chamber, cultural, sports and scientific collaboration, an exchange of armed force delegation visits, and the creation of a customs union, etc.).

Silajdžić noticed that the European Union representatives were against the idea of the OSCE organising elections. They agreed only with OSCE supervision of elections, but Silajdžić demonstrated that it would then be impossible to talk about 'internationally led' elections. As regards the possibility of lifting the sanctions against Serbia, Ambassador Holbrooke emphasised that this could only happen after free and fair elections.

Afterwards, a discussion on geography and maps again took place. Holbrooke informed us that Milošević had asked for the corridor near Brčko to be 15 kilometres wide but that he, Holbrooke, had stated that this was impossible for us. Silajdžić pointed out that this question could not remain unsolved. In turn, I asked for the Brčko solution as per the Contact Group Plan. Holbrooke answered that we could not secure Brčko, and that our unyielding position meant a return to the battlefield. Secretary of State Christopher reminded us that the price for peace was high and that it was impossible for us to achieve more.

Later, David Lipton from the World Bank joined us. We were talking about establishing a unique currency and unique fiscal institution. After a long discussion, Zubak agreed with the proposals.

An ordinary daily briefing followed with Carl Bildt and the three European political directors. This was part of our daily schedule and in this instance unsolved problems with the maps and constitutional provisions were discussed. Premier Silajdžić referred to the Sandžak problem in particular. He insisted on the necessity of sending European human rights observers into Sandžak.

Thereafter came a meeting with Secretary of State Christopher, and the fiscal expert again. I requested a statement, a letter about future financial support. I also asked for a clearing up of the question about how refugees would vote – where they were registered or where they currently lived. During a new discussion about geographic allocations and dissatisfied with the proposal for Goražde, I stated that I was not ready to discuss the matter further and concluded the meeting.

Then, a turnabout occurred. Milošević decided to give up on Sarajevo. This dramatic moment Holbrooke describes in the following way, pp.291-292:

> Finally, early Saturday afternoon, I asked Milošević to take a short walk around the inner compound. I complained bitterly that his behavior was going to cause a breakdown of the talks, and concentrated on Sarajevo. 'Some issues can be set aside or fudged,' I said, 'but Sarajevo must be settled in Dayton.' 'Okay,' he said with a laugh, 'I won't eat today until we solve Sarajevo.'
>
> A short while later, while I was chatting with Hill and Clark, the door to my suite opened without a warning, and Milošević walked in. 'I was in your neighborhood and did not want to pass your door without knocking,' he said, smiling broadly. Clearly, he had something important to tell us.
>
> 'Okay, okay,' he said as he sat down. 'The hell with your D.C. model; it's too complicated, it won't work. I'll solve Sarajevo. But you must not discuss my proposal with anyone in the Serb delegation yet. I must work the "technology" later, after everything else is settled.'
>
> 'I tell you,' he continued, 'Izetbegović has earned Sarajevo by not abandoning it. He's one tough guy. It's his.'
>
> These words were probably the most astonishing and unexpected of the conference. As he talked, Milošević traced on a map with a pen the part of Sarajevo he was ready to give to the Muslims. Immediately Chris Hill objected: it was a huge concession, but it was not all of the city. Milošević had retained for the Serbs Grbavica, a key area across the river from the center of town. Although a dramatic step forward, Milošević's proposal didn't quite unify Sarajevo.

When Hill pointed this out, Milošević exploded. 'I'm giving you Sarajevo,' he almost shouted at Chris, 'and you talk such bullshit!' We told Milošević that while his proposal was 'a big step in the right direction,' it was likely Izetbegović would reject it.

Hill and I went immediately to see the Bosnian President. Izetbegović did not acknowledge the importance of the offer, but focused solely on its defects.

'Sarajevo without Grbavica cannot exist,' he said with passion. The area that Milošević wanted to retain for the Serbs jutted directly into the center of the city and was known to Western journalists as 'Sniper Alley'. Still, we all recognized that the negotiations over Sarajevo had entered a new phase.

Taking a detailed street map of Sarajevo, Hill, Clark, and I went back to Milošević's suite. We began examining every road and every terrain feature. Milošević seemed flexible; Hill predicted after the meeting that if we stuck to our position we would get all of Sarajevo the next day. Feeling suddenly encouraged, we adjourned with our hopes soaring.

This is how Holbrooke describes the moment and he wonders why Milošević did so. Holbrooke believed that with the Sarajevo surrender, Milošević wanted to weaken the Serbs from Pale. I, however, do not think this explanation is correct. Instead, I believe that Milošević, after 18 days of negotiations, figured out that there were no compromises to be made on the matter of a united Sarajevo, especially given that the attitude of the international community was firm and unanimous on this occasion.

The poet Abdulah Sidran in one of his later discussions put forward his own explanation: Milošević needed 150,000 Sarajevo Serbs to fill out the towns next to the Drina River. This is what Sidran thinks, but then the question still remains as to why Milosević refused any discussion about such an idea for 18 days. Perhaps we will never find out Milošević's real motive, but our major goal in Dayton was achieved.

19 November. This critical day began very early (or very late). At two o'clock after midnight Silajdžić, Zubak, Šaćirbegović, Trnka, and I met with Robert Owen and his team of legal experts. The discussion centred around a controversial constitutional matter. At Zubak's repeated request, two Houses of Parliament and the appointment procedure for ministers (nominate) and their approval by Parliament were agreed upon.

In the early afternoon, with Zubak and Šaćirbegović I visited a group of our scholars and students, who were studying in Ohio and other neighbouring states (all in all around 40 students). Secretary of State Christopher and Ambassador Holbrooke later attended this meeting too. In friendly and informal conversation, I tried to explain the present Bosnian situation and our goals.

Secretary of State Christopher then arranged a lunch for Silajdžić, Zubak, and myself. Ambassadors Holbrooke and Menzies were present. The discussion continued about our various positions and those controversial matters that remained outstanding. This continued until the early evening. I again explained that the maps were the stumbling block and Secretary of State Christopher summarised the results achieved so far. He recalled the obligations that Secretary of Defense Perry had taken on due to the enlarged Goražde corridor, and whereby Perry believed the deployment of IFOR troops and their efficiency significantly alleviated any problem. I repeated the problem with regard to Brčko. Christopher emphasised that he was aware of the importance of Brčko, and referred once again to the positive solution achieved regarding Goražde and Sarajevo, as also President Clinton's letter obligating the USA to begin the procedure to lift the UN Security Council Resolution regarding the embargo on weapons to Bosnia and Croatia immediately after the peace document was signed. The Americans insisted on our yielding and achieving the agreement. I tried to explain my determination. To save the negotiations, I suggested a postponement of the Brčko matter and that this be confined to a commission presided over by Americans and consisting of two Bosnians, two Serbs and one Croatian, with the aim that it be solved in the following two months.

At Christopher's request, everyone left the meeting except our two selves. Christopher emphasised that it was of the greatest importance to stop the war, and that I should appease my position on Brčko. This because Milošević could easily lose control over his delegation and if we continued to be unyielding then everything could fail. I repeated the idea about leaving Brčko as unsolved and explained that our people would not accept a bad solution. My arguments, however, did not appear to leave any impression on Christopher.

At a meeting for all members of our delegation, Holbrooke gave a long list of the successes we had reached and the exact same list of consequences if the negotiations were to fail.

Thereafter, I do not know when the next thing happened: whether it was on Sunday night or Monday morning. Night and day had become inseparable. Indeed, we stayed awake almost the whole time from Saturday night until Monday. Silajdžić was busy in negotiations with Milošević and the American delegation from early evening onwards. I was sitting in my little apartment and from time to time was informed about the negotiations' happenings. I had left Silajdžić to struggle with Milošević that evening. He was younger and in better shape than I. He came to me during the evening and again around two o'clock after midnight. 'It is good,' he said. At four o'clock in the morning I had put on my pyjamas and was preparing for bed when I was asked to go and celebrate the agreement. I slipped on a winter coat over my nightclothes and went to the neighbouring building, where the whole group had gathered: Christopher, Holbrooke, Hill, Clark, Milošević, Silajdžić, and the others. I felt some kind of uneasiness. I was thinking about Brčko. When they spread the map before me, the only thing I looked at was this spot on the Sava River: I noticed that it had been left to the Serbs. I was silent for a while. Holbrooke read my mind. Hesitating, he finally asked me if I was satisfied. I said that I was not, and that without Brčko I could not accept the agreement. I noticed consternation among all those present. Later, I found out why: they had already celebrated the agreement and the successful ending of the peace negotiations in Dayton. I spoiled the party. We dispersed without a goodbye.

20 November. This was the last day of the negotiations. Visits, invitations, pressures, promises, and appeals kept us busy all day long. I met with Christopher, Milošević, Tuđman, General Clark, the expert mapping and constitutional teams several times, and of course Ambassador Holbrooke.

Before the end of the day, we again stated that the issue of Brčko and the 1.5% of the territory that we should, according to the maps and the 49:51 relation, return to the Serbs, be left unsolved. Late at night, around 11 o'clock, Secretary of State Christopher visited me asking for an hour of my time and the answer to two questions. Namely, were we ready to give Brčko to the Serbs and were we ready to return an excess of 1.5% of the territory. If we were not able to do this, then the negotiations he advised me would end and be considered unsuccessful. I immediately consulted our team, and answered through Šaćirbegović. We will return 1% of the territory, but not yield on Brčko. Shortly thereafter, John Kornblum came to my room and brought a paper which said that, despite the efforts made thus far, peace negotiations were unsuccessful and hence closed. The sides in the war were further urged to restrain from adding fuel to the conflict. The messenger asked me to sign for receipt of this letter. I signed it and went to sleep peacefully for the first time in five days.

During the night, however, there was a further twist to events. Milošević accepted the Brčko arbitrage. Holbrooke describes this event as follows, p. 308:

> Suddenly Kati burst into the room. 'Milošević is standing out in the snow in the parking lot waiting to talk to you,' she said. For the first time I noticed that it was snowing. She ran back out and pulled him into my room, where Christopher and I met him. He looked as if he had not slept all night.
>
> 'Something has to be done to prevent failure,' he said wearily. 'I suggest that Tuđman and I sign the agreement, and we leave it open for Izetbegović to sign later.'
>
> 'That's quite impossible,' Christopher said firmly. 'We cannot have an agreement that is not signed by everyone. It is not a viable contract.'
>
> 'Okay, okay,' Milošević said. 'Then I will walk the final mile for peace. I will agree to arbitration for Brčko one year from now, and you can make the decision yourself, Mr. Christopher.'

I did not know what was happening, I was preparing for my return to Bosnia. Around eight o'clock in the morning, I received a note that Christopher wanted to see me urgently. He arrived accompanied by Holbrooke, refused to sit down and asked me almost from the doorway: 'Do you accept the Brčko arbitration?' I was confused for a moment, then I answered, 'Yes, I do.' 'Then it is all right,' he said. Holbrooke said something to him in a semitone, they said goodbye and almost ran out of the room.

21 November. At 11:40 am, on Tuesday, November 21, President Clinton went out onto the White House lawn and in front of countless reporters declared that the agreement for peace in Bosnia and Herzegovina had been reached:

> After almost four years, two hundred and fifty thousand killed, two million in refuge and terrors which horrified people around the world, people in Bosnia finally have a chance to exit dread of war and enter promise of peace.

At that moment it was 5:40 pm in Bosnia. My daughter Sabina later told me: 'On my return from work that evening, I entered the hallway and, taking my coat off, through a half opened door, saw President Clinton on the television screen, telling the gathered journalists that peace had been reached. I barely understood what this was about because during the entire day we had received news that the situation was totally the opposite: about the collapse of the Dayton negotiations and the return home of our delegation. For the entire morning, I had thought about another difficult and uncertain winter ahead of us and how I would have to go on walking my children to school, wondering if they would be back safe and sound. We would go on, not knowing for how long, living in fear, day and night. Now, suddenly peace! When I realised what had happened I burst into tears unable to stop.' I think that a large number of men and women in Bosnia that night thought and felt like my Sabina.

The ceremony for initialising the agreement was scheduled for 3 pm American time. Christopher, Bildt, Ivanov, Holbrooke, and the three of us, Presidents Milošević, Tuđman and myself each gave speeches. For my part I said:

> This is a historical day for both Bosnia and the world. For Bosnia, because the war – we hope – will be replaced by peace. For the world, because the Bosnian tragedy and everything that went along with it was a moral question of the first degree, and a moral question concerns every man and woman in the world.
>
> The documents we have just signed guarantee the maintaining of a sovereign and integral Bosnia and Herzegovina and the further building of an open society based on tolerance and freedom.
>
> We consider this the main and largest result of the negotiations that have just finished.
>
> We are determined to fulfill the obligations we undertook.
>
> We ask the world for support and help in this.
>
> We expect this support and help especially from the United States of America, its President, its Congress, and its people.
>
> Do not hesitate to do this, because it will put an end to the sufferings of many people and help stamp out a dangerous war pivot, which represented a threat to peace both in the region as well as the world.
>
> And to my people, I say, this might not be a just peace, but it is more just than a continuation of the war. In the situation as

> it is, and in the world as it is, a better peace could not have been achieved.
>
> God is our witness, that we have done everything in our power so that the extent of injustice for our people and our country will be decreased.

Upon my return from Dayton, a journalist from *Ljiljan* asked me for my meaning of the words: 'In the world as it is…' I answered: 'It is a world in which it is possible to lead an unjust war and impose an unjust peace.'

So that France, actually Europe, would be happy, it was decided that the ceremonial signing of the peace agreement would take place in Paris (in Dayton it was only initialised).

Everyone who in any way had taken part in the Dayton negotiations, several hundreds of them, gathered on 14 December in the French capital in the Elysée Palace. The atmosphere was ceremonial, but I wished I were alone. After the signing, speeches were given. Mine was as follows:

> We came here to sign the Peace Agreement, which we initialised in Dayton 20 days ago.
>
> Our people and our Parliament have accepted this Accord. They did this without enthusiasm, like a man taking a bitter but useful medicine. Still, I wish to assure you of our determination to consistently and honourably put the signed Contract and all of its components into action.
>
> Our goal was and is an integral and democratic Bosnia. Provisions of the Agreement guarantee this, but whether these provisions become live or remain a dead letter on paper for this moment greatly depends on us, on what we want and what we can do. The battle for these goals is not lost, nor is it won. It goes on through other peaceful means, not with weapons of power, which we were deprived of, but with the power of ideas and spirit. We believed and claimed that our model of a multinational community and open society was superior and that it could not lose. Now is the time to prove this to ourselves as well as to others.
>
> With these thoughts we are sending a message to the Serbs that the war is over and that evil is to stop. We again declare that there is no revenge or payback, but that there is and should be

justice. Human rights must be established everywhere. Banished persons have rights to their homes and the culpable have the right to their punishment. This because punishment is the human right of a criminal.

The Serbs around Sarajevo should be given a choice: to leave or to stay. We invite them to stay and go on living in safety. The only condition is that they respect the laws of Bosnia and Herzegovina, which order freedom and forbid violence. Let them help their neighbours return to their homes and let them cooperate with the legal authorities of Bosnia and Herzegovina in establishing law and order. We will ask IFOR and international organisations to mediate in making contact on all levels during the transition period so that the rules of the agreement signed today be implemented in whole.

We call upon the world to help Bosnia in this historic moment. Send your troops to implement the peace contract and fulfill your promises regarding economic help for the country's reconstruction; Bosnia will return this favour to you in the best way it can, by becoming a factor of peace and stability in this part of the world.

On 22 December 1995, I put my signature on the Bosnia and Herzegovina Presidency's decision on the abolition of the state of war in Bosnia and Herzegovina. The decision stated:

1. In the territory of the Republic of Bosnia and Herzegovina the state of war, introduced by the Decision of the Presidency of the Republic of Bosnia and Herzegovina from 20 June 1992 ('Official record RB&H', Number 7/92) is abolished.

2. The decision on the proclamation of immediate war danger from 8 April 1992 ('Official record RB&H', Numbers 1/92 and 13/94) remains valid.

3. All state organs will without delay make preparations and step up the implementation of the general broad peace agreement on peace in Bosnia and Herzegovina.

4. The Ministry of Defense will take necessary measures in order to implement this decision, in cooperation with the Bosnia and Herzegovina Army's General Headquarters and other state organs.

5. The Presidency of the Republic of Bosnia and Herzegovina will inform the UN Security Council on this decision.

The last interview I gave in that year of war was for the Spanish *El Mundo* (28 December 1995). It concerned the concluded peace in Bosnia and Herzegovina:

El Mundo: In your speech in Paris, you defined this peace as 'bitter' for the people of Bosnia and Herzegovina. Could you explain to us what you meant by that?

Izetbegović: That peace was bitter for many reasons. The main reason, of course, was the fact that the peace, as it is, practically admits the results of the war of aggression at Bosnia's door: especially the divisions and ethnic cleansing. What would Europe look like if some heavenly force had stopped the war in the summer of 1944? Wouldn't that peace have been bitter for many nations? A war of aggression has to end with the defeat of the assailant. Any other outcome is unjust and leaves a bitter taste.

El Mundo: Which was your most difficult personal moment in these three war years, in the 'days without a future' for your country?

Izetbegović: There were many very difficult days: not least the Srebrenica tragedy, where people close to my heart, many of them, were massacred. Still, 9 November 1993 stands out. On that day the Old Bridge in Mostar, that little architectural miracle of unseen beauty, was purposely demolished in tank fire. For a moment there I hated human kind. Those were the hardest days of this war, 'days without hope', as you name them. My people were literally under siege on every side. Complete darkness surrounded us. There was no hope and it seemed that the resistance lost any meaning whatsoever and that it continued only by inertia.

El Mundo: How does the man who led the Bosnian people feel after signing the surrender of Žepa, Srebrenica, Zvornik, Brčko, Bijeljina and other parts of Bosnian territory?

Izetbegović: I feel bitter but I do not despair, because there was no choice. The limit of our people's endurance had been crossed a long time ago. However, I do not believe that those cities are lost forever. Brčko, definitely, isn't. Someone counted that in the last 300 years we lost Srebrenica nine times and took it back nine times. Why can't we do it a tenth time?

El Mundo: Who are the winners in this war from your point of view?

Izetbegović: We are the moral winners. There are no military victors. Everyone both won and lost.

This is how a bloody and demolishing war ended. When the public began to forget both the causes and beginning of the war, a dilemma on the character of this war was craftily released on air: was it aggression or a civil war? This matter became an infallible test for differentiating Bosnia's friends from its enemies. To friends, it was a classic case of aggression; to enemies it was a civil war.

Political accountants in the Bosnian opposition found the silence on this inevitable question useful in so far as they could maintain a platitude of equal responsibility on all three sides for the war in Bosnia and Herzegovina. The most efficient way for them to harm the Democratic Action Party (SDA), which headed the defense, was to put it in the same basket as the HDZ and SDS, and the easiest way to do this was to announce the conflict as civil. Other forces in the world also preferred to name it a civil war. If aggression and genocide took place, the world was obliged to do something in order to protect those who were attacked and there were explicit obligations, according to the UN Convention, on punishing genocide crimes dating from December 1948.

However, the truth gradually surfaced because the facts were obvious and inexorable. Furthermore, our diplomatic duo, Silajdžić and Šaćirbegović, did a huge job in ensuring the same. To back track a little and look at the evidence it is necessary to recall the 15 May 1992 UN Security Council Resolution No. 752, which demanded the 'immediate ending of all forms of interfering outside Bosnia and Herzegovina, including JNA's troops and elements of the Croatian army...' (operative paragraph 3 of the Resolution). Since the Belgrade regime disobeyed the demands of Resolution 752 on 30 May 1992, the Security Council repeated the demand for the immediate ending of interference by neighbours in the internal affairs of Bosnia and Herzegovina, and asked them to respect the territorial integrity of Bosnia and Herzegovina. It further introduced sanctions against Serbia and Montenegro.

In Resolution Number 787 from 16 December 1992, in operative paragraph 5, the UN Security Council demanded that surrounding countries stop the infiltration of irregular military groups into Bosnia and Herzegovina, this time apostrophising elements of the Croatian Army as well.

The word aggression was for the first time explicitly mentioned in Resolution Number 47/121 under the heading 'The Situation in Bosnia and Herzegovina' dated 8 December 1992. Expressing grievance that the sanctions introduced by the Security Council had had no effect, the UN General Assembly accused the ex-Yugoslavia Army of 'direct and indirect support to aggressive actions against Bosnia and Herzegovina'. Furthermore, operative paragraph 2 of the Resolution 'strictly condemns Serbia, Montenegro, and Serbian forces in the Republic of Bosnia and Herzegovina for the disturbance of sovereignty, territorial integrity and political independence of Bosnia and Herzegovina and for their behaviour contrary to relevant resolutions of the Security Council, UN General Assembly and London Peace Agreement of 25 August 1995'. In paragraph 3, the UN General Assembly demanded that Serbia and Montenegro immediately halt 'their aggressive actions and hostility and to wholly and unconditionally cooperate their behaviour with the relevant resolutions of the Security Council...' (The specification of UN Security Council and General Assembly Resolutions thus far reached followed). In paragraph 7, the General Assembly called upon the Security Council to 'use all needed means in order to establish and maintain the sovereignty, territorial integrity and wholeness of the Republic of Bosnia and Herzegovina'. The Resolution for the first time referred to Chapter VII of the Charter, which allows for the use of force for implementing a decision. These demands were repeated in the Resolutions of the UN Security Council No. 819, 16 April 1993, No. 838, 10 June 1993 as well as in Presidential Statements from 24 April 1992 and 17 March 1993. In Resolution No. 48, dated 20 December 1993, it states that the aggression against Bosnia and Herzegovina continues and it demands that the Security Council immediately implement the orders of Resolution No. 838 from 10 June 1993.

Due to the hesitation of the great powers, the UN Resolutions were not conveyed, and military intervention for stopping the genocide did not follow. This despite the fact that unequivocally and in several instances it was stated that this was an act of aggression against Bosnia and Herzegovina. The Islamic countries, without exception, however, supported the Resolutions on Bosnia, and initiated them in some cases.

Speeches made by representatives of most Western countries were in no doubt about the nature of the conflict in Bosnia and Herzegovina. On the occasion of the adoption of the VS 757 Resolution, 30 May 1992, statements such as the following were heard:

Hungary: 'Provisions of the 752 Resolution are not being conveyed at all. Aggression against Bosnia and Herzegovina is continuing with full intensity.'

Venezuela: 'This Resolution condemns the behaviour of one country, which misused its military power and jeopardised the sovereignty of another country – a member of our organisation – Bosnia and Herzegovina.'

Austria: 'The decision made today by the Security Council to impose sanctions against Serbia and Montenegro is bitter but necessary. It has become necessary because of stubborn and irresponsible behaviour by Belgrade authorities, military as well as civilian. Their policy and practice have caused sufferings and demolition on such a huge scale that it overcomes imagination in our age. They will be judged not only by history but by their own people as well.'

United States: 'The aggression of the Serbian regime and its military forces against Bosnia and Herzegovina represents a threat to international peace and safety and a serious challenge to values and principles on which are based the Final Act from Helsinki, the Parisian Charter, and the United Nations' Charter.'

The Russian Federation: 'Belgrade ignored good advice and warnings and did not cooperate with the international community's demands. Doing so, it has caused the United Nations' sanctions by itself. Voting for sanctions, Russia is performing its duty as a permanent member of the Security Council in order to maintain international law and order.'

France: 'The European Union and its countries' members have already adopted a course of measures against the Federal Republic of Yugoslavia and called upon the Security Council to convey a similar action.'

Great Britain: '…Truly there is no doubt of where the main responsibility lies now: on the authorities, civilian and military, in Belgrade. This cannot be hidden; they cannot prove that they have nothing to do with what has been going on in Bosnia and Herzegovina. Multiple-barrel rocket-launchers cannot be found in a peasant's barn. They come from the Yugoslavian National Army (JNA) warehouse. They supply themselves with ammunition from their storage. If the Belgrade authorities truly wanted to assure us of their innocence, I doubt that they would be shelling Dubrovnik today. They would have to believe that we are really stupid people.'

Our services possess numerous original documents – orders, records, military maps and such – confiscated in JNA and Republika Srpska army barracks, on the occasions of the liberation of parts of Bosnia and Herzegovina (Sarajevo, Vozuča, Bihać region) – from which conclusions can be made about the preparations of the Yugoslovenian Headquarters for war in Bosnia and Herzegovina, about the explicit arming of the Serbian people during 1991-1992, the forming of paramilitary units for entering Bosnia (Arkan's, Šešelj's, and the like), about the transformation of the second military region in Sarajevo into the Republika Srpska Headquarters with Mladić at its head, about paying and solving status matters of the officers in Mladić's army by JNA Headquarters and about logistical support to the Republika Srpska Army as a part of the JNA.

In his memoirs, Borislav Jović provides a broad description of his meeting with Milošević on 15 December 1991, in which they discussed the question of the 'future conflict in Bosnia and Herzegovina'. It was concluded that it would be necessary for the SDS management in Bosnia and Herzegovina to take command over what they called 'the Serbian part of JNA'.

In his *Balkan Odyssey*, Lord Owen describes how in a conversation with Milošević and Ćosić, at the end of April 1993, he pointed to the direct involvement of the JNA in the Bosnian War: 'Ćosić was pretty shaken, so it is possible that he was not in the whole familiar with the complete range of its involvement. Milošević, however, didn't twitch because I gave him facts that he was, I am sure, very well aware of, since he probably approved of every aspect in military relations' (p.165).

The Hague Tribunal, judging according to accusations for war crimes, has so far in two cases judged that the war in Bosnia and Herzegovina was an international conflict. In the valid verdict in the Tadić case the Tribunal jury decided: '...that the forming of this Republika Srpska Army was a legal fiction, and that even after 19 May 1992 the command structure of JNA remained unchanged, renamed itself the Yugoslavian Army and went on continuously controlling the Bosnia and Herzegovina Bosnian Serb Army (VRS). The same weapons, same equipment, same officers, same commanders, mostly the same troops, the same logistic centres, the same goals and tasks and the same actions remained. FR Yugoslavia was involved in the conflict while its Government essentially remained the same force that ruled over the Bosnian Serbs'. The court jury concluded: 'the Bosnian Serb forces acted as *de facto* organs of another state, the Federal Republic of Yugoslavia'. In the valid verdict in the Aleksovski case the court jury concluded: 'Military forces of Bosnian Croats acted under command of Croatia and HV's control in executing armed attacks on Bosnia and Herzegovina. Accordingly, this conflict was of an international nature'.

Finally, in the comment for *The New York Times* issued on 23 May 1999, regarding the air campaign by NATO in the case of Kosovo, the US President Bill Clinton characterised the Bosnian War explicitly as one of aggression. The goal was ethnic cleansing for the forming of Greater Serbia, in which entire nations were condemned to extermination for their ethnical or religious belonging. 'This was first seen in Croatia and Bosnia, but then the international community reacted with a neutrality which makes the victim and the aggressor equal,' concluded President Clinton.

Chapter 8

AFTER DAYTON

Serbs attempt to postpone the handover of Sarajevo. Letter to Admiral Smith. The storm over Father Christmas. Rome meeting. Pogorelica. Letter to Mme Agnelli. Heart attack. Message to the people of Mostar. 'Rules of the road.' Integration of Sarajevo. Serbs leave, burning Sarajevo, IFOR looks on. Message to the Serbs. Law on amnesty. Games over Brčko. Letter to Carl Bildt. Speech in Zenica. Speech in Žuca. First signs of corruption. Speech in Gelsenkirchen. Speech in Grebak and what The New York Times' journalist heard. End of the War. Presidency of the Republic of Bosnia and Herzegovina. Speech in the 51st Session of the UN General Assembly. Arms reduction. Responses for Avaz – the balance sheet for 1996. More games over Brčko. Considering resignation. Award from the American Center for Democracy. Meeting with President Clinton. The Pope's visit to Sarajevo. Bonn Conference. The battle for a single currency. Speech at the OIC Summit in Tehran. The mistake in French protocol. Letter to President Chirac. Mitterrand and Chirac. Bernard Henry Levý. Croatia continues its dual policy. General elections, and victory. Treaty on the use of Ploce Port and Agreement on Special Relationship with Croatia. Last meeting with King Hasan. Madrid Conference. So-called 'Secret Report.' Final decision on Brčko. My testimony. Refugee returns proceeds at snail's pace. Unsuccessful presidential initiative on returns. Opposition campaign steps up. Kosovo crisis and NATO air-strikes against Yugoslavia. Speech in the Council of Europe. Silajdžić's initiative to revise the Dayton Accord. Summit of the Stability Pact for South-Eastern Europe. Klein's statement on corruption in Bosnia and Herzegovina. The NewYork Times' article on corruption in Bosnia and Herzegovina. Open letter to the High Representative. Report of the International Commission. New York session on the Presidency of Bosnia and Herzegovina – decision on border services. My 'rabble-rousing' speech. General Elections, April 2000, and electoral setback for the SDA. Deteriorating health. Resignation from the Presidency. Rule by foreigners.

And with God's will, peace awaits us. Not immediately, but soon. Be well prepared for this peace. Our Prophet, upon his return from a hard battle, said that he was going from a small battle to a large one, meaning the battle of peace. And really, what awaits us when the peace comes will not be easy at all. I am afraid that we will often think of the days when there was only war. When a man is ill, he has only one wish – to gain health, and when he does – then come a hundred wishes and he turns even unhappier than when he was lying sick in bed. It is similar with people in war and in our situation. It seems: when the shelling stops and peace comes, everything will be easy, it's a straight road ahead. Most of you here are young people. Be aware, huge problems are ahead of you: destroyed industry, unemployment, hunger... The world is feeding us now. Everyone, more or less, receives the same amount. However, what is to come, are absolute inequalities – there will be wealthy people, war profiteers who will exploit the common people that are unemployed. So, you who will have to lead this battle in peace, be well prepared! Do not live in illusion or spread the illusion that it will be easy! It will be very difficult. We are a country that will get out of war with tens of thousands of injured people – invalids. A large number of them will be completely unable to do any job. They will need our help. We will have a huge number of families without breadwinners, numerous orphans. I forget the number, but I remember being horrified when a woman from 'Sumejja' or 'Fatma' told me how many orphans they look after now. And then, of course, there are inevitable matters of justice and injustice. So, may God be with us.[1]

I spoke these words 20 months before Dayton, at an SDA conference (25 March 1994). I was, obviously, not carried away by illusions. I predicted a lot of things, and would have been happier if I had not.

After the signing of the peace agreement in Paris, the Serbs initiated a desperate diplomatic effort to prevent the uniting of Sarajevo. They achieved a certain success in this respect. They managed to make the Commander of IFOR Admiral Smith, who was in charge of implementing the peace agreement, indecisive. Admiral Smith entered the negotiations about Sarajevo without caution. I warned him pretty

---

[1] A. Izetbegović, *The Wonder of Bosnian Resistance*, pp. 47-48.

harshly that he was not authorised to do this. The day after I heard about his conversations on Pale, I wrote to him saying:

> Your conversations about Pale on 26 December 1995 and your susequent statements have caused deep distress among our citizens.
>
> With their attempts to bury the peace agreement, the Pale regime will do anything to force a discussion about the Dayton Agreement on Serbian Sarajevo. I do not consider it necessary to prove that there is no special agreement on Sarajevo or a special Serbian Sarajevo. There is a huge package in the peace agreement and this package is a whole. Sarajevo can in no way be observed separately which is exactly what the Pale regime wants. We have made great sacrifices to have a unique town and that is why any separating observation of Sarajevo is absolutely unacceptable.
>
> Your promise to consider the possibility of delaying the implementation of the agreement in the part concerning Sarajevo could have the consequence of questioning the agreement implementation in many places that are part of the package with Sarajevo. It will also strengthen the Pale regime, delay refugee returns and lead to the postponing of elections. In short, it will create a political climate that could harm the peace.
>
> If you, as well as we, wish to make it easier for Serbian civilians in Ilidža and elsewhere, to stay in their homes, then speed up the departure of Karadžić's soldiers instead of delaying it. Shorten the deadlines instead of prolonging them. That is the only way you can help. Any delay will only cause new difficulties.
>
> Mr. Admiral,
>
> We know that you have the authority to change deadlines in the agreement's implementation, but this right is about military and technical problems (weather and terrain conditions), and not ones of a political nature. Political negotiations were finished in Dayton and this book is now closed. You were assigned the implementation mission, not the mission to change the accomplished political agreement.
>
> For all these reasons, we expect you to wholly and consistently implement the agreement and to inform the Pale regime about this. Any other answer to the request by the

> Pale regime would cause diffidence to the correctness of your actions and would lead to failure.
>
> Mr. Admiral, I ask you, in the interest of peace, not to repeat UNPROFOR's mistakes.

The letter was effective. Sarajevo was united according to the plan.

Rarely did a statement by me cause such a bitter reaction as the one I gave after New Year's Eve 1996. It is known as the 'Grandpa Snow Statement'. Actually, I was protesting against the inappropriate manner in which some people celebrated the conclusion to 1996. All of this can be seen in my open letter to the editors of radio and television facilities in Bosnia and Herzegovina on 2 January 1996:

> Gentlemen,
>
> I felt a certain unpleasantness watching last night's news and some scenes which you claim depict the New Year celebrations in Bosnia. I think that a large majority of our people, especially warriors, felt the same dejection after this show. They were wondering about where they live, really.
>
> Because what you show as a national celebration on New Year's Eve is actually a celebration given by a minority, definitely not more than one percent of the people in our country. What about the other 99 percent of our citizens? If they celebrated at all, if they had the opportunity and the will, they did it humbly and in a way that would not hurt the feelings of the people who lost their homes and their loved ones. Only a small number of cheeky and heartless individuals dared to get drunk and make faces in front of the cameras, while graves and wounds are still fresh, as if nothing had happened.
>
> And you, editors of radio and television, have your share of responsibility. You showed and followed this without a comment, and it seems, even approvingly.
>
> We are a European country, but that does not mean we should open the door widely for all European vices: alcohol, pornography, drugs and recklessness of every sort. We will look up to European accuracy, diligence, a sense of organisation, but we will not follow America and Europe in all their ways without measure and criteria.
>
> I would also like to ask you not to impose some 'grandpa snows' or other symbols foreign to our people. Everyone can

keep them to themselves, in their homes, if they want to. Television is a public institution, and our people are not gullible enough to have their noses pulled.

We will not of course reach for censure or prohibitions, but we will make sure that the people reject and despise various implausible values which some are trying to impose in the name of culture and freedom, actually a false culture and a false freedom.

A year and a half later, when I considered the Grandpa Snow episode forgotten, I received a letter from the Editor of *The New York Times*, O'Connor, in which he expressed the wish to discuss a number of questions with me. One question, especially emphasised, was he said, about St. Nicholas. He was referring to my statement about Grandpa Snow. I replied to him via a letter on 28 December 1996:

Dear Mr. O'Connor,

I have noticed a difficult and rather funny misunderstanding. There are two characters that are vaguely similar but are completely different, to be precise similar on the outside but different on the inside: Santa Claus and Grandpa Snow. They wear the same suits and appear almost at the same time, so the people mistake one for another, both the people here and especially you in America. Saint Nicholas comes from the Christian tradition and appears on Christmas Eve, Grandpa Snow comes from the ex-USSR and appears on New Year's Eve. Here, on ex-Yugoslavia territory, as was the case in the entire former eastern block of countries, there was no Saint Nicholas or Santa Claus in public, only the New Year's Grandpa Snow. He has nothing to do with religion and was made up in the USSR after the revolution in order to put an end to religious tradition.

In the open letter I wrote at the beginning of 1996, I reacted in anger to the inappropriate behaviour of some individuals on the occasion of that year's New Year's Eve celebrations, reminding them that our wounds were still fresh and that not even six months had passed since the Srebrenica tragedy. In this letter, I also mentioned Grandpa Snow and said that he was not a part of our tradition, because he is not. There was not a word in that letter about Saint Nicholas.

Here in Bosnia Christmas is celebrated in a dignified way. Muslims respect other's symbols, but are not prepared to accept them as their own, identify with them, nor can it be asked of them.

Hoping that my explanation will reach your readers, I ask you to give them my best wishes for a merry Christmas and a happy New Year.

On 17 February 1996, we were invited to Rome for the first meeting of Croatian, Yugoslavian and Bosnia-Herzegovinian Presidents after the signing of the Dayton Peace Agreement. Mrs. Susanne Agnelli, who was then the Minister of Foreign Affairs in Italy, and also the President of the European Union, scheduled the meeting. The importance of this meeting could be seen by virtue of the fact that, besides others, it would be attended by the US State Secretary Warren Christopher and NATO commander for Europe, the American General Joulwan. Richard Holbrooke's presence went without saying.

There were a large number of matters on our daily schedule, one harder than the others: checkpoints, lawful (unlawful) arresting on the road, cantonal borderlines, Sarajevo (district-canton), international police forces, customs' control of the Federation, the uniting of pension funds, etc. Emotionally, I was concerned with the matter of Mostar.

There was a crisis in Mostar at the beginning of February when the then Representative of the European Union for the town, Hans Koschnik, produced a plan for organising Mostar with a large central district. The Croats did not accept this, and instead organised demonstrations; attacked Koschnik and the man barely got out with his head on his shoulders.

Mostar is the town that, along with Sarajevo, was the most destroyed. We called it our Hiroshima. It is located on the right and left banks of the River Neretva, connected by a number of bridges. One of them, a crescent-shaped arch of stone, over 500 years old, was torn down in 1993 by target fire from armed Croatian units that had proclaimed their own republic.

We did everything to unite a town separated in two parts by the war line. Koschnik tried with his large central district, which would be under common management, to reduce this separation and also make a step forward towards uniting it. Our side hailed the plan but the Croatian side rejected it bitterly.

Instead of supporting the plan of its Representative, the European Union, faced with the threat of Croatian extremists, backed down. As had happened so many times before, the European Union asked us to negotiate the solved matter again.

On 9 February I sent a letter to Mrs. Agnelli. It stated:

> The matter of Mostar, that we discussed late last night by phone, is basically a question of democracy and human rights.
>
> In the western part of Mostar four elementary human rights have been suspended: freedom of movement, freedom of faith, freedom of political activity and the right to property.
>
> Mostar is the only place in Europe (and maybe in the world) where public expression of religious feelings is forbidden, except for those who belong to one religion.
>
> Two nights ago, demonstrators banished Bosniacs and Serbians, took their properties and refused to return them.
>
> They want a divided city so they can maintain this unnatural and unjust state and that is the essence of resistance to propositions made by European Manager Hans Koschnik.
>
> We were prepared for certain concessions – and made them – to avoid conflict, but now there is a much more important question: will the violence be legalised and continued or will there be an open path for freedom and respect for human rights? And a question of that sort does not only concern one city, but Europe and the whole world in general.
>
> Any further compromise would be unprincipled bargaining at the expense of the standards and values that the contemporary world chose.

On the same day as I travelled to Rome, it was 16 February, IFOR performed an action in Pogorelica, the base of our Ministry of Internal Affairs, located in the hills, 16 kilometres west of Sarajevo. All the world's press published headlines such as: 'IFOR discovers illegal Iranian military base in Bosnia,' 'Weapons and means for terrorist action found,' 'Izetbegović broke the Dayton Agreement,' etc. Never before had I heard of this base but, if we forget press exaggerations and drama, there was some truth to all this. Weapons and means of suspicious purpose were found in Pogorelica. The Minister for Internal Affairs, Bakir Alispahić, explained that these means were used for training only, which sounded not quite credible even for us, his friends. Thereafter, he was forced to resign and had to leave.

The press speculated that IFOR knew about this base before, but that they planned their action in time for the Rome meeting so as to make my situation more difficult. I do not know the truth, but my position in Rome was certainly extremely difficult. This was compounded by the European Union's pressure for a revision of Koschnik's Plan. A significant reduction of the central district in Mostar was proposed, and at first we turned it down. This was followed by the European Union's threat to withdraw from Mostar altogether, which came through Minister Agnelli.

The whole of Saturday right through to Sunday evening was spent in meetings. Papers were written, changed, rejected, and rewritten. I felt my strength leaving me. If I accepted the reduction of the central Mostar zone, my citizens of Mostar would feel defeated and Croatian extremists would celebrate. If I did not accept it, the European Union would abandon Mostar, and this would mean a farewell to unity. I knew that both sides in Mostar anxiously followed every word spoken in Rome. I told the journalist who wrote the report from this meeting to start with the words: 'This here is a madhouse.'

I asked Oručević what we should do. His answer, that he would accept whatever I decided, did not help. Faced with the possibility of the European Union leaving, which was the goal of Croatian hardcorers, I decided to accept the corrections to the plan. Feeling betrayed by the European Union, Hans Koschnik resigned. It was easy for him; he could resign, I could not. At least I thought I couldn't.

The acceptance of the European Union's dictate and the district revision sent a shock wave through eastern Mostar. I sensed that the citizens of Mostar were cursing my name, but then they did not know the whole truth. I returned to Sarajevo. Ramadan was to end the next day and the holiday (*Bairam*) would begin.

Troubles don't come alone, they like to arrive in groups. I was sitting in my office, finishing God knows which phone call when the secretary brought me a letter marked 'personal'. It was Safet Oručević's resignation from the position of Mostar Mayor. I could only imagine that the situation in the city had made Safet take this step. I replied that I did not accept his resignation. There could be no resignations until some important things in Bosnia were achieved.

Earlier, I had promised to visit paraplegics in the State Hospital on the first day of the holiday. Before this, I went to the mosque for the *Bairam* prayer and shook hands with at least a thousand people. Talking to paraplegics is talking to people without hope. I stayed for more than two hours and listened to their stories, one by one. I felt that I lacked ideas and words. What could I say to a people who feel deprived for the rest of their lives? The following morning, on the second day of *Bairam*, the day of *Shahids* (heroes/fallen soldiers) in the Shahid Cemetery at Kovači, the situation repeated itself. The mothers, wives and sisters of the dead could not cope with their loss. They seemed to be pleading with me with their eyes, and I could say nothing to help them. Can I even understand them at all? What does it feel like to lose a son, a husband or a father? Can the rest of us, who did not experience this, truly understand?

This was a working day and in the afternoon I went to perform regular *Bairam* visits: to my brother and three sisters. I almost ran from one house to another and felt no joy at all. I also had to make my appearance at the *Bairam* reception organised by *Reis-ul-ulema*, the Islamic religious leader, that evening. Could I find an excuse not to go? But then I had to go. I just wished *Bairam* would end as soon as possible. Early the following morning, I felt a strong pain in my chest and I was transferred to the hospital. The doctors diagnosed a heart attack.

A month after that unfortunate Rome meeting, I sent a message to the citizens of Mostar:

> Dear women and men of Mostar,
>
> I am familiar with the way you feel about the news that came from Rome almost a month ago. I had intended to visit you immediately after that meeting, to talk to you and face your anger. I was disturbed in this intention by illness, therefore I am contacting you this way, with delay and still from my sick bed. What happened in Rome was inevitable. It might not have been a good solution, but any other, according to my judgement, was even worse.
>
> When we arrived in Rome, the Europeans were already opening Koschnik's 'package'. They were seeking a so-called mutually acceptable solution. This they made clear to us.
>
> For those who know less, I will make one explanation: Europe is an economic giant and mostly powerless politically. It can hardly reach any radical conclusion due to its decision making processes. If 15 countries, for example, are in favour and one is not, the decision cannot be made. This is, among the rest, one reason why it was possible to prepare, start and lead a genocidal war in the heart of Europe and all Europe did was watch it powerlessly.

We, of course, could have held onto Koschnik's arbitration and left Rome demonstratively, but what would we have gained from this? The truth is that the other side would not celebrate it, and perhaps some more principal European governments would have stuck to our side, but nothing would have been done. The state in Mostar would have been frozen for a long period of time, which would objectively help Croatian extremists. Because, if nothing is done, time is not on the side of an integral Mostar and Federation, but against it. After a few wasted months, we would once again have had to sit at the negotiating table, and look for a so-called mutually acceptable solution. I was thinking: if I have to compromise in a few months, I will do so now and maintain at least a slow tempo towards our goal. It is important that things do not stand still, that they move, and if they are moving, they can only go in one direction: towards an integral town. Finally, what do we have to lose, do we have anything on our hands anyway? Those were my thoughts.

We must not be too impatient. In these years, the destiny of our people for the next century is being made, and this requires less emotion and more thinking, determination and patience.

Our strategic goal is clear: an integral Mostar and strengthened Federation on that basis, a maintained freedom and a democratic state. We should go towards this goal overcoming obstacles daily and trying again and again. This goal is located on the general path of humanity and civilisation and we cannot lose.

From the above you can conclude there is something that I eagerly wait to tell you: that is that the decision on Mostar, whether it is wrong or right, is mine and nobody is responsible for it but me. I believed and I still believe that it will prove right in the long run. If that is not the case, you must know the truth: I made that decision and I am responsible for it, to history and to you. Nobody else.

And in the end: do not be too sad for some individuals and groups celebrating on the other side of the Neretva River. Those besieging Sarajevo acted rudely and violently and look how they were finished. Law and justice are finally stronger than anarchy and force, but we have to endure.

One good thing happened in Rome: a decision under a strange name was made: namely the 'Rules of the Road'. The essence of those Rules was that nobody could be imprisoned or charged for war crimes without the approval of the Hague Tribunal. The goal was to broaden freedom of movement that was decreasing by the day because of people being randomly taken into custody under the charge of war crimes. The decision was accepted loosely but proved to be very useful. For with it came unique vehicle plates, and freedom of movement was almost completely re-established.

The uniting of Sarajevo was executed according to the plan. It began with Vogošća on 22 February, and finished with Grbavica on 18 March 1996. This is when the huge exodus of Sarajevan Serbs occurred. Since they had not succeeded in disturbing the uniting of the town, they decided instead to tacticly 'torch the land'. They left the town with nothing but devastation behind them. I cannot find a better and more competent witness of what happened than Richard Holbrooke himself. In the 20th Chapter of his famous book *To End a War* he describes this apocalypse as follows, pp.335-357:

> Sarajevo was unified precisely on schedule. On March 18, 1996, a group of ragged Bosnian Serb policemen, their voices barely audible over a scratchy recording of the anthem of precommunist Yugoslavia, lowered their flag from the police station in Grbavica and left for Pale. 'We saved this area militarily,' said Milenko Karisik, a Bosnian Serb Deputy Interior Minister, 'but we lost it at Dayton.' The next day, the Bosnian Serbs handed over to the Federation the Serb-controlled portions of Sarajevo. There was no fighting, no attempt to prevent the event.
>
> But at the moment that was one of Dayton's greatest achievements, the Bosnian Serbs exploited the passivity of IFOR and the weakness of the enforcing powers to salvage something for their separatist cause. In the two weeks before Sarajevo's unification, Pale ordered all Serbs in Sarajevo to burn down their own apartments and leave the city. They even broadcast detailed instructions on how to set the fires. (Pile all the furniture in the middle of the room, douse it with kerosene, turn the gas on, and throw a match into the room as you leave.) Young arsonists, mostly thugs from Pale, roamed the streets warning Sarajevo Serbs that if they did not destroy their

homes as they leave, they would be punished severely, perhaps even killed.

For those Bosnian Serbs who had moved into Sarajevo from the countryside during the war, destroying apartments they would have to leave anyway was easy. But tens of thousands of Sarajevo Serb families had lived in peace for generations in a once-cosmopolitan city. Most were ready to stay had they not been forced to leave. Kris Janowski, the spokesman for the United Nations High Commissioner for Refugees, estimated that before the exodus there were seventy thousand Serbs in Sarajevo, of whom at least thirty thousand wanted to stay. After the intimidation tactics of Pale, fewer than ten thousand remained, many of whom would leave soon thereafter. In the week before March 19, a steady stream of Serbs clogged the roads out of Sarajevo, most carrying furniture, plumbing fixtures, and even doors. Behind them rose the smoking remains of Grbavica and Ilidža. 'We must not allow a single Serb to remain in the territories which fall under Moslem-Croat control,' said Gojko Kličković, head of the Bosnian Serb Resettlement Office (and later Prime Minister of Republika Srpska).

Journalists reported nearly incomprehensible scenes: a Serb woman beaten and raped by a young Serb thug before he set fire to her apartment; an elderly Serb couple who survived the entire war in Sarajevo appealing futilely to Italian troops as a Serb thug blew up their apartment. Robert Gelbard, Assistant Secretary of State for International Narcotics and Law Enforcement, was visiting Sarajevo at the time at my suggestion; he watched in disgust as IFOR and the International Police Task Force refused to apprehend the marauding arsonists and IFOR kept its own fire-fighting equipment inside the IFOR compound. Desperate, the Moslems sent their antiquated fire-fighting equipment into the Serb portion of the city, where they were attacked by rock-throwing Serb arsonists. But their requests for IFOR protection were refused. Gelbard watched buildings burn as IFOR troops stood by less than 150 metres away, and observed British General Michael Walker, IFOR's second-ranking officer, coolly reject the pleas of the Deputy High Representative, Michael Steiner, for IFOR intervention. 'I was ashamed to be associated with it,' Gelbard told me later, 'to be unable to get IFOR to do anything.' A year later, appointed by President Clinton and Secretary Albright to coordinate the faltering implementation effort, Gelbard would make a difference.

The tragedy could have been easily prevented if IFOR had taken action. But although unchallenged and feared, NATO/IFOR did almost nothing. An IFOR spokesman said that while the burnings were 'unfortunate', the Serbs 'have the right to burn their own houses.' IFOR, said another spokesman, 'is not a police force and will not undertake police duties.' Shocked by IFOR's sudden passivity, UN officials, in an ironic role reversal, now criticized NATO for its inactivity. 'If (NATO) had been tougher, things would be different,' said Kris Janowski. 'We're seeing a multiethnic Bosnia being flushed down the toilet.'

I was criticised for not doing enough to keep the Serbs in that part of Sarajevo that was transferred into the Federation's jurisdiction. Bildt wrote: 'Moslem leadership, especially Izetbegović, betrayed multiethnic Sarajevo. To tell the truth, Izetbegović reacted to the worst violence from time to time..., but he did not show a bit of that daring statesman skill that was needed to offer a hand of peace so that the little number of Serbs that still lived in Sarajevo would stay there' (Bildt, *Misija Mir*, (Mission Peace), page 227, Zid Sarajevo, 1998).

Readers can judge the truth of Bildt's words through the already quoted Holbrooke description of the situation in the integrated part of Sarajevo in February and March of 1996, and also from the following facts. In the assembly on 22 December 1995, the Presidency called upon the Serbs to remain in their homes. The statement said:

> The Presidency of the Republic of Bosnia and Herzegovina calls upon citizens from areas of Grbavica, Ilidža, Vogošća, Ilijaš and Hadžići to accept the peace solution for Sarajevo and remain in their homes and on their land.
>
> The Presidency states that it is prepared to ensure the full human and citizen rights and safety of all citizens of Sarajevo in cooperation with the international community.
>
> The Presidency will at the same time make efforts to punish war criminals accordingly.

In its session on 21 February 1996, before the beginning of integration, the Presidency stated that a Law of Amnesty was declared primarily because of citizens of Serbian nationality in the future integrated Sarajevo. In the announcement on this occasion, the Presidency stated:

> The Presidency is once again asking Serbian people not to be lured in by the propaganda of the Pale regime that wants to classify Serbs into national ghettos, to move them out of their homes. Do not believe false promises. Know that according to the Dayton Agreement everybody will have to return to their homes. Do not let them evict you later from other people's lands and homes that they so gallantly offer you now. Stay on your own property.
>
> All those who remain in Sarajevo are safe and the organs of the State and Federation of Bosnia and Herzegovina guarantee their integrity, freedom, personal and proprietary safety.
>
> Serbs of Sarajevo,
>
> The Amnesty Law is accepted. All honest people are safe and equal according to it. Do not leave your homes. Those who want to hide and justify their crimes are the ones making you leave. You also have the guarantee of the international community. Stay in integral Sarajevo and let us all together build our future. The Bosnia and Herzegovina Presidency is asking the international community to prevent the eviction of people by force, the robbing of property and the stirring of fear among those who want to stay in their homes.

These appeals from the Presidency and the amnesty were honest, but it was after all just theory. The practice was something else altogether. Bad things were happening in the field, and the Serbs were truly disturbed. The tension of many years was taking its toll. Asked about this in an interview for RTV BiH, I said (10 July 1996):

> I believe that many complaints regarding this were founded. I have to be honest and say so. It is no good to deny some things that are happening. If you deny them they will never stop. In my opinion, the Serbs do have troubles in these parts. On the other hand, it is in no way as widespread as to justify Steiner's recent statement ('I am ashamed of Sarajevo'). This is about different, so to say double criteria. When one Serb experiences something unpleasant near Sarajevo, then everyone talks about it, the world press writes about it. At the same time in Kotor Varoš, Banja Luka, the evictions of Bosniac families followed by beatings continues. No big fuss is made over this,

the world is used to it and does not react to it. But, anyway, if we want to be a democratic and lawful state, we have to suppress any kind of violence. In my opinion, that is how we get the right to follow this principle throughout Bosnia and Herzegovina as well as the moral right to spread the model of a democratic and lawful state further. But we have to implement this model here, before all. A man who refuses Karadžić's call to leave his house and stays here trusting this authority and its promise that he will be protected, must be protected. Anything bad that might happen to that man cannot be justified. That is what is truly unacceptable.

The Pale authority directed a large part of Serb refugees from Sarajevo towards Brčko. The logic was: we have lost Sarajevo, let's at least ensure a refund for Brčko. Carl Bildt, who was then the High Representative of the International Community and Admiral Smith, watched this happening with unexplainable passivity. They claimed that they had no way of stopping this. On 9 March I sent them a letter:

> By evicting Serbs from the outskirts of Sarajevo, the Pale leadership is continuing the genocidal politics of ethnic cleansing that it implemented during the entire war.
>
> You claim that you have no way to influence these politics that are obviously controversial to the spirit and word of the Dayton Peace Agreement.
>
> You also claim that you have no way of influencing the movement of these columns and their destination.
>
> Still, I think that the freedom to choose the place to live in, that the Serbian leadership repeatedly states, has one absolute exception – Brčko.
>
> The Serbs do not have any right to take their misfortunate people, whom they for no reason move from their homes to Brčko because, according to the Dayton Peace Agreement, international arbitration is the way to decide the destiny of this city.
>
> This means that Brčko is under a special regime in the meantime and that all actions that stand for prejudicing arbitrated decisions cannot be allowed. If Serb occupation of Bosniac houses in Zvornik and Foča is unlawful, doing the same thing in Brčko represents a double violation of the Dayton Agree-

ment, because the goal of this is obviously to create a finished fact and hardened legal solution of this maximally delicate matter.

I consider you responsible for seeking a way to stop this harsh unlawfulness and action against the Dayton Agreement.

I wish to assure you of our intentions to protect our rights concerning the city of Brčko.

The letter had no effect.

After leaving the hospital, I answered a few questions for a journalist from the Sarajevan magazine *Ljiljan* (24 March 1996):

> *Ljiljan*: It seems that the trip to Rome was truly an event with a bad omen. It seems that it was of more importance than is now realised. Finally, it was sudden, wasn't it? Our public, you will allow, was shocked, especially a part of the Herzegovinian Bosniacs. What did, actually, happen in Rome? What solution were you facing? What were the dilemmas? How did the participants in Rome act? Can you broadly explain Rome to our public?
>
> Izetbegović: I cannot agree with you completely when it comes to the importance of the meeting in Rome. We neither gained nor lost anything of special importance. The Croats turned down Koschnik's Plan, and Europe, as usual, backed off. Does this surprise you and is it something new? Didn't they say to us in the most difficult days of genocide: negotiate, you have no other choice. Who were we to make a deal with? Killers! This is why I don't understand why someone should be shocked or disappointed now. This had all been seen before. Koschnik's plan and his larger central district was just a project, not something we had and then lost in Rome. The main thing the public needs to know in order to understand Rome is that the European Union had abandoned Koschnik's Plan before we got to Rome. They were already holding meetings and looking for a so-called mutually acceptable solution. The German Representative to the European Union told our expert Dr. Kasim Begić very explicitly: 'If you do not agree today the Union will withdraw from Mostar in three days.' I had just one goal in this situation: to oblige the Croatian side to accept freedom of movement and a mixed police force throughout the city. I knew that this would not be done

completely but the important thing was for the world's pressure in that direction to continue and not diminish. I think that the recent meeting in Geneva allowed me to do this. As concerns the atmosphere at the Rome meeting, it truly was hell, because there were three meetings taking place simultaneously in three rooms over the entire previous night and following day. New papers were constantly produced, rejected, changed, then rejected again. On Sunday night I saw our journalist writing a report from Geneva, and I told her to begin the report with the words: 'This here is a madhouse.' Fortunately, she did not do so, but she wrote something similar.

Ljiljan: Your illness has brought the unthinkable temptation to Bosnia and Herzegovina and the Bosniac people. First, did the countries that signed Dayton abandon the Republic of Bosnia and Herzegovina? We have the impression that in the period following Dayton entities were pushed forward instead of the multinational state of Bosnia and Herzegovina, then the Europeans agreed on the concept of national states in Bosnia and Herzegovina... Yesterday Mr. Zubak stated in *Slobodna Dalmacija* that Bosnia and Herzegovina is only possible as a federally-confederative formation. It seems that new clouds are moving in over the Bosniac people in case the world community heads into any one of these adventures. In a recent interview you said that you weren't sure if our public was aware of the seriousness of the situation. Did you have the same thing in mind?

Izetbegović: I think that this is the right question, unlike issues from Rome. Forces of disintegration in Bosnia, both internal and external are at work. The thing that worries me the most is the fact that even after Dayton, ethnic cleansing has continued. And the absolutely most important provision of the Dayton Agreement for Bosnia and Herzegovina was eventual ethnic reintegration. The return of displaced persons is not going ahead and so far we cannot see a way to get this thing moving in a positive direction. This is the greatest problem and largest threat hanging over Bosnia's head. There are attempts to convince the world that we are all equally guilty, that not even the legal Bosnian authority is immune to narrow minded thinking and nationalism and that Bosnia as a state is not possible. Some of our mistakes – and there are some – are used in this poisonous propaganda. However, the situation is such that there must not be mistakes because the world places an equality sign between our mistakes and their crimes. This is sad, but the world is that way and we cannot change it. What we can know are the facts, never mind if we like them or not, then put them into an equation and try to get the result as correct as possible. Our propaganda is largely wrong as well. The media are competing in publishing the crimes that Serbs and Croatians have inflicted upon Bosniacs. Of course, crimes should not be kept silent about and covered up, but is there anything good and human between those three nations? Does ever one gesture of care happen between people of different confessions and nations in this country of ours? I do not think that it does not exist, but nobody mentions it, I don't know why. And that is exactly what should be pointed out in a situation like this. Because, constantly showing nothing but trouble between the three nations is showing nothing but that Bosnia is not possible, and I think that Krajišnik and Boban are doing this job pretty well themselves. Our job is to prove it wrong. It is our task to find positive examples and point them out. Of course, we should not make them up. You are asking me if the world has agreed on the concept of national states in Bosnia and Herzegovina. The problem is not if the world has agreed. The problem is that it seems as though we have agreed to this or at least we act like it. For example, look at some articles in our press, even in your own magazine. Reading them will not strengthen the belief that Bosnia is possible as a multinational state at all. Quite the contrary.

At the beginning of 1996, the opposition began a political offensive. Aspects of the atmosphere then can be decoded from my speech in Zenica (Bilino Polje Stadium, 14 April):

> Our interior situation is at boiling point. New parties are being formed and the opposition is radicalising its mostly unfounded critics. A sort of bad will, discouraging energy is being artificially created. The opposition thinks that the presence of a foreign army and foreigners in general is giving it a chance. I think they are wrong, because at the bottom line, it will be our population, not the foreigners who will make decisions in the elections.
>
> The opposition's tactic is to constantly point out what has not been achieved, and to overlook, let's say ignore, all that has

been achieved, often in the most difficult circumstances. They say: Podrinje has not been freed, the land is destroyed, Chetniks have stayed in almost half of the territory, demobilised soldiers are unemployed, IFOR is limiting the country's sovereignty, the Federation won't budge, refugees are not returning, etc. All of this is mainly true, but they keep silent on some things, they don't say: there is peace, people are not being killed and are not suffering any more, the dying and crippling has stopped, half of Bosnia has been defended, there is a strong army made from almost nothing, Bosnia is recognised by over a hundred states, the Bosniac people have been saved from the extermination announced for us. They keep silent about these important facts. They also keep silent about the fact that in the autumn of 1991 Bosnia was facing a choice to either become a part of Greater Serbia or be destroyed; they do not say that Bosnia neither became part of the Greater Serbia nor was it destroyed. Rather it defended itself, that it is slowly rising from the ashes, that life is better compared to a half a year ago, that Sarajevo, which knew only of grenades, hunger and darkness, is now free, lighted and full of merchandise, that a large number of our fighters are now employed, that people in Bosnia are free to say, write, found political parties, even free to lie – nobody is prosecuting them for their words.

The troubles that unprovoked genocidal war has left behind, and all this good and positive development, is constantly overlooked and kept silent about.

Why is this done? In order to confuse the people and take over power. Lies and partial truths are being used as means in this struggle.

Without the SDA Bosnia would either be a province of Greater Serbia today, or it would have been destroyed. The SDP could not have saved it and some minor parties even less. If there wasn't the SDA, the SDP would not exist either, there would be an alliance of Bosnia and Herzegovina communists or Milošević's Socialist Party (SP) as a part of some docked Yugoslavia SP. We have made the transformation of SK to SDP possible, we have opened the democratisation process in this part of the world and, from a historical perspective, we have paid a huge price for this from 1945 to 1995.

Yesterday, a new party was founded in Sarajevo. Its founders claim to fight for a Bosnian Bosnia. I suppose they want to say that we are fighting for a Muslim Bosnia. Well, let them say it, but it is more likely they are fighting for power in Bosnia, not Bosnia itself and these are two different things. Because in the parts of Bosnia freed by the Bosnian Army, the struggle for a Bosnian Bosnia is won, this struggle should be led and won also in the part of Bosnia which is under Serbian and Croatian control currently. Will they ground this plan – Bosnian Bosnia in Banja Luka, Bijeljina, Čapljina, Livno? If yes, their efforts are worth every compliment, and all of us would vote for this party. But there is no hope for this. They do not plan to do this. They want to once again free the already freed Bosnia, and leave its unhappier, unfreed part to others.

This is why I say it is a struggle for power. True, a struggle for power in a democratic Bosnia, the way we created it. It is a legal thing, so good luck to them. But a struggle for power should not be mistaken for patriotism. Patriotism and looking after democracy are different things.

If it is not a struggle for power then it is an attempt for the Bosniac people to come to reason, because they have come to their senses too much and ask for too much. These people should be calmed down a bit.

There are some who claim that fundamentalism, Muslim of course, is at work here. The proof of this theory is that the President of the State goes to a mosque for prayer on Friday. Honourable President Clinton and Chancellor Kohl go to church as well, and nobody considers this suspicious.

I used to ask my critics from the opposition to tell me what they would suggest. It is true, I say, that the Federation is not working – what do you suggest? There are three armies in Bosnia, which is very bad; what should be done to make one army, a Bosnian army? In Mostar the HVO (or HDZ) is stalling, what do you think should be done to put an end to obstruction? Croatia is leading the politics of hypocrisy, do you suggest we shut down our relations with them? As you know there are plenty of such and similar questions. My collocutors were usually men with academic titles, but never, never did I get an answer or did I feel my erudite collocutors knew it. These critics are like a doctor who tells you that you have a fever – which you already know yourself – but they neither

> prescribe you a therapy nor know of one. Anyway, you know them, ask them the questions I have mentioned and you will be sure of what I am telling you. So, I reach the conclusion that I should not care about what they say and that I should go my own way. There is no magical solution, there is only patience and hard work.
>
> The opposition as opposition, has no everyday problems on their back, so they have time for propaganda and media. They are catching our mistakes, and are right, if we give them material to do this, and it happens.
>
> So, for instance, a municipality mayor, a member of our party, does not find time for a month to meet with a soldier who was banished from his apartment with his family. Can a mayor have anything more important to do than to receive a visit from a soldier who finds himself in the street along with his wife and two children? Since he has more important things to do, he sends the man to an authorised service, which pulls out some rules, and these rules say that the apartment belongs to a woman who spent the war years in Belgrade etc. This is a story about people and regulations, bad people and bad regulations, it is not a coincidence that I am telling it, because this story about indifference and injustice in different variants, repeats itself, if not every day then very often. It is a story about power, every power as well as ours, how power spoils people and how services inevitably become bureaucratised and move away from people and how care should be taken from day to day so that this power serves the people and not itself.[2]

In the large gathering of people for the anniversary of the battle in Žuč, on 8 June 1996, we paid our respects to the Serbs and Croats who fell defending Sarajevo and Bosnia and Herzegovina. Speaking to the rally of over 20,000 people, I said:

> Dear soldiers of the Army of Bosnia and Herzegovina, dear citizens of Sarajevo, dear citizens of Bosnia, wherever you come from.
>
> I greet you and thank you for leaving your business for a moment and coming here so we can together bring back the memory of those difficult and glorious days of the battle for the salvation of Sarajevo and Bosnia and Herzegovina. The

---

[2] Izetbegović, *Year of War and Peace*, pp. 73-80.

survivors of the crucial battle in Žuč have gathered today, and we have come to pay our respects. I asked the organisers not to forget anyone of the battle participants who survived the battle and I believe they have tried hard to ensure this.

You are here in a large number on this hot day, which means that there is no oblivion and that there will not be.

You see, today has begun in the appropriate manner, with the anthem and respect for those killed in the defense of Sarajevo. Although most of them, a majority, were Bosniacs, not only *Fatiha*, the Islamic prayer for the dead, was made, but we also rose for a minute's silence and paid our respects to dead Croats, Serbs and others. But if only one Croat or one Serb was killed defending Sarajevo, and it wasn't one but many, we should get up and pay our respects to him appropriately. We should because this is Bosnia. I wish to say a few words about this Bosnia, about this dream of Bosnia.

We have always imagined it as a land of good, proper and straight people. And we believed that in this lies the power of Bosnia as well as the helplessness of attackers who again and again tried to conquer it. When analyses are made one day, when this wonder of Bosnian resistance is solved, it will be found – I am sure of this – that this secret was somewhere in the souls or characters of the people.

Remember spring and summer of 1992. We were almost barehanded, they were armed to their teeth. And then, we banished them together with their monsters of steel, gradually from the city up to the woods where they belong. It was a true conflict of good and evil, between man and brute. The spirit won. According to no military logic or count did they have to leave Sarajevo at that time. All military trumps were on their side, not one on ours. Still, they lowered their heads and left, both in 1992 and now in 1996. Why?

We should think about this for the sake of our dilemmas, doubts and possible errors. Even today some wonder if we will manage to struggle with the threatening number of legal and political catches which are made against an integral Bosnia. The answer is as it was four years ago: we will be stronger and win if we are better than our opponents, if along with the military force that we must have, we at the same time carry proven human values, against one-track minds, barbarism, extremism and violence of any kind. And vice-versa:

we will lose this battle if we go by logic: all they did unto us we will do unto them. This is where we lose our moral and political advantage, and their greater material as well as power in numbers will prevail. We must not make this mistake.

One of these strange battles of this sort, of which the outer history is known to a certain extent – some of it you have just heard in General Delić's speech – but its internal history is yet to be written, took place four years ago in the areas where we stand now. This battle did not last for a few days, I would rather say that it continued for the next two years, and maybe to the end of the war. Almost exactly a year later, in June and July of 1993 not far from here, were killed, in short time spans, almost one after another, two famous commanders, Šeha and Safet. I had the honour to personally know these two humble men and great fighters as well. In those difficult days, it was the time of the Igman crisis, Chetniks threw literally thousands of grenades onto this little piece of land in which today's calmness seems almost unreal. Then they continued their attempts to take over Žuč, and this went on almost till the end of the war. The surviving warriors that I see here today in large numbers, remember this hell and can say more about those days than I. Ibro was just telling us something about this, and it is just a small part of the exciting story about the incomparable courage of a generation that lived and died for Bosnia.

From time to time, news was received about a misuse of power. Some people used their positions to grab things that did not belong to them. Power spoils people. This inexorable law had obviously started to work in Bosnia and Herzegovina. On 6 July 1996, I sent an open letter to all SDA municipality organisations in Bosnia and Herzegovina. The letter said:

> I have received the bad news of the unjust giving of business premises in some municipalities. Usually, the plaintiffs are invalids and demobilised soldiers who claim that they have been completely avoided in those allocations and that the majority of business offices have been received by war profiteers and cousins or friends of important people.
>
> If there is even some truth in those complaints – and it seems that, unfortunately, a large part of it is true – then it is a sure sign that our human and political sense has failed. Human,

> because the fighters deserve to be taken care of and we have promised them this. Political, because we will face their dissatisfaction and justified anger.
>
> I invite you to pay your attention to this question and to prevent misuse in the assignation of those business rooms. Do not cite rules and regulations for poor decisions. If rules are not just and right, change them or suggest their change. In any case, without delay, do something to eliminate the injustice.
>
> Soon, I will ask for a debate in public (the press and television) on this question and culprits will be called to account for themselves.

Later happenings showed that my letter did not produce any important effect. Misuses continued, only with more skill and secrecy.

Together with such bad news came other information from the elective campaign that was taking place at that time. Croatian representatives Stjepan Kljuić and Ivo Komšić, my good comrades in war, had been harshly offended at a political meeting in Gradačac and Kalesija. According to the circumstances, it was possible to conclude that the attackers were SDA members. In my statement, on the 15 August 1996, I condemned the incidents:

> I express my deep disagreement and sorrow because of this, and send a word to everyone, no matter who they are, not to mention my name when they go into similar incidents. I was fighting for the Bosnia where people would be able to think and speak freely. I am unhappy when I see that individuals, instead of arguments, yell and draw hoes at each other and in this way help the enemies of Bosnia.
>
> I know Kljuić and Komšić very well, I know their behaviour in the war and now in peace. For me they are, regardless of their different political attitudes, honourable people, worthy of respect.

At the end of August, it was a rainy day, at the Gelsenkirchen Stadium in the Federal Republic of Germany. Here, a large number of Bosnians had gathered, and I was invited to speak. With me, there were also General Dudaković, Safet Oručević and a number of famous fighters from the war: Mutevelija, Prevljak, Lovac, Humo, Muderis and others. I made a long speech from which the following represents a shortened version:

After Dayton

We made a peace in Dayton. Now, we are facing more or less an absence of war rather than real peace. Dayton was a compromise, and compromises are not justice. However, there is no more dying in Bosnia. Death had been present every day. It had to stop and we should not regret this. If sometimes, we do regret the signing of the agreement, we should remember those who stayed alive, thanks to that peace. It is a matter of thousands of boys who would have become invalids in a continued war. For them, that peace was good, because there was too much dying. The number of our people is small and we could not continue to count the number of dead and disabled every day.

Germany gave you its hospitality, accepted and gave you the protection when it was hardest for you and us. I express my gratitude to the German Government and the great German people. Honour should be given to the people of this country, who did not ask for names while the trouble was on. You should be thankful to this land. And the best gratitude is to respect its laws. I want to believe that you have been doing this till now, and that you did not stain the honourable name of our people. I am very happy when I hear that our children learn well and behave nicely. They should be the best in everything, should learn their host language so that there can be connections between two peoples and two friendly countries.

We want peace. Do not hesitate if you are voting or working for peace because Bosnia needs it. The war was destroying not only our lives and our homes, but the Bosnian idea as well, which cannot survive without peace. The war had split our people, sent them all over the world, and now we are sauntering along to gather them. Therefore, our permanent slogan was: we will negotiate whenever we can, fight whenever we have to.

That is why we will do anything to keep the peace. The Dayton Agreement is a balanced entirety of different elements, made by long and hard negotiations. It cannot be implemented in parts. It is not possible to choose: this order suits me, so I will implement it, this one I do not like, so I will not take it. That is exactly what the Serbian side is doing, and the world is still shutting one eye in the face of this fact. This will not be so. The most important decision of the Dayton Agreement, for the sake of which we swallowed many bitter pills, is the one about returning everyone to their homes. The Serbs accepted this in Dayton and they will have to implement it, or there will be no Serbian Republic. We paid a high price for our people to be able to return to their homes and there is no, nor can there be, a bargain about this. The struggle for your return to villages and cities that you have been banished from, was always an important goal. From this day, it is the most important assignment, and all others will be subordinated to that. We will constantly ask this from all those who signed the Dayton Agreement, and our cooporation in every field and matter we will condition with the fulfillment of this, the most important decree of the peace agreement. They have done their ethnic cleansing; we will do the opposite process, return people to their homes. These two processes are as opposite as two mathematical operations: multiplying and subdividing or addition and subtraction. These two processes stand with different moral signs and relate to each other like evil and good or crime and punishment.

Part of this process is our message or recommendation to you, to vote for the institutions of the places where you had lived before the war: Trebinjans for Trebinje, Banja Lučans for Banja Luka, Stočans for Stolac, Zvorničans for Zvornik, etc. Oppressors, ethnical cleansers and destroyers of Bosnia, as you know, did absolutely the opposite. They persecuted their own compatriots from villages and towns where they had lived, and now they are forcing them to vote there. This means: to keep them definitely in other people's homes and properties – that is houses and properties of persecuted Bosnians. The international community created the famous form P-2, which gave them the ability to legalise that status. Some say that this was done on purpose, some claim that it was done out of ignorance, as if it is important. The only important things are the consequences, and they are catastrophic in this case. We have declared war on P-2 and have proclaimed it a means of the continuation of ethnic cleansing, as some sort of 'final solution' to the ethnic question in Bosnia.

In my speech at the pre-election meeting of the SDA in Jablanica (4 September, 1996) I recalled our two fates: an April war and the Dayton peace:

I mentioned the things that were unavoidable, I can state two of them: an April war and the Dayton Agreement. Those two things were our destiny.

The war was planned. For those who do not understand this, I would recommend the Hague Tribunal testimonies of those so-called political witnesses. For those who do not find it persuasive enough, go ten years back, to 1991 and 1992. The SDA did everything it could to prevent the war. Just remember all those futile negotiations in the summer of 1991 and our initiatives. In June, the attacks of the JNA on Slovenia happened, in July the aggression against Croatia. Those two countries declared their independence from the ex-Yugoslavia and at the end of 1991, the international community accepted them. Bosnia stood in front of the dramatic choice: to stay or not in the defective Yugoslavia. That was, indeed, a dramatic dilemma: to either stay in a defective Yugoslavia with Serbia and Montenegro or to declare our independence, and risk war. As you know, we addressed the people for this important decision. A referendum was held, the result is known, and aggression followed.

The second unavoidable decision was the Dayton peace. Dayton was as unavoidable as the April war. Those two destinies were bound to happen, whether they were good for us or not.

There are those who are big generals after the fight. Some of them claim that we could have avoided the war. Maybe we could, if we had bowed our heads, but because we could not do so, we carried that destiny in ourselves. The whole historical context of the world as it was and our proud people, all meant NO for an ex-Yugoslavia. Just as well then those historic circumstances occurred in 1995. An American peace initiative, possible military intervention, thousands of dead and wounded, hundreds of thousands of refugees, our people who melt abroad like a snow, a coming winter, a possible last chance and promises, even pressure from the big world power, all of this was not possible to ignore. Dayton peace, whether it was good for us or not, was our destiny and everyone accepted it then, as you know.

Nevertheless, we should get back to this: everything that was done, good or bad, was the success or a mistake of the party. The opposition is ready to admit everything that was bad or was omitted, but not everything that was good.

Of the good things, at first there was the organisation of our defense. Because they know they did not do a lot in this respect, except maybe give verbal support, they want to deny it for us too. They created a whole theory about how our defence was made and developed in Sarajevo and through Bosnia spontaneously. Everything happened by itself. Because they were not there, the SDA was not there either. With a little bit of irony, I call it 'a doctrine of spontaneity'. If this 'doctrine' is correct, then the mobilisation and organisation of 200,000 fighters, their equipment, training and armament occurred spontaneously. We had on our back two embargoes on weapons and we fought both of them. They say spontaneous. And the tunnel under the airport was dug by itself, somehow, here and there. Acquisition of the helicopter that assured our defense in besieged places around Goražde and especially Krajina – these too were spontaneous. And that no one died of hunger in Bosnia – that too happened somehow, by itself. Strangers came and fed us. The dinar is stable, that is by chance. And hard political outwitting, starting from the first days of 1993, until now, according to them, all happened by itself. When they say spontaneously, they mean without SDA merit.

In my speech in Jablanica, I answered an interesting question about the activity of the opposition in Sarajevo. I said that it would be useful if they spread their influence, as they had promised, to the other entity. It would be detrimental, in other words, if they stayed only in the territories controlled by the legitimate authority. As is now known, the opposite happened, and the position of the Bosnian people was weakened.

A few days later (31 August), I was speaking about Grebak, a place of unseen suffering for our people during 1992 and 1993. I could hardly resist my emotions. People were exclaiming the *tekbirs*, shouting Allah is the Greatest. Because, where there is death, faith is close by. Although it was a political meeting, it was religiously coloured, and I did not mind. However, one Western newspaper did mind.

The New York Times Sarajevo correspondent heard some messages that I did not send, and then heard some that I did send. He wrote, for example, that I had called on people to take up arms, though I did not even mention this. He exaggerated incidents in the pre-election campaign, and saw them only under the control of the Bosnian government. He did not see the things that were happening under Serbian control.

Essentially, he complained about two things. First, that I said the Serbs would have to implement Annexe 7 of the Dayton peace agreement or there would be no Republika Srpska. I did say this and I still think the same way and do not see what is wrong with such a view. Second, that I said elected Serbs, no matter which ones, will have to pledge themselves to the Bosnia and Herzegovina Constitution if they want to enter common institutions. It is sure that they will. I did not say that they will have to put their hand on the Qur'an, but on the Constitution of Bosnia and Herzegovina, and that is Dayton's constitution, but this gentleman still doesn't like what I said. Why? At the end of my speech on Grebak, I also said something that the American ear may like, but that this gentleman certainly did not. I said: 'We want for Bosnia to be a democratic country, a country where everyone can pray to God like his mother taught him and where no one will be persecuted because of their religion, nation and political belief.' Although I said this, the gentleman in question did not hear this and instead concluded: 'President Izetbegović wants a Moslem Bosnia.' I do not want a Muslim, but a complete democratic Bosnia. A Bosnia in which our people can be free, on their own, and where genocide cannot happen again.

The elections loomed closer, and with them the end of the mandate of the Republic of Bosnia and Herzegovina war Presidency. At the session of the Republic of Bosnia and Herzegovina Parliament on 11 September 1996, I submitted a report on the Presidency's work for the period from 20 December 1990 to 10 September 1996. The introduction of that report was as follows:

> Hundreds of investigators would have been necessary to complete a detailed and truthful report on the Presidency's work, which led Bosnia and Herzegovina during the most tumultuous and most critical period of its history.
>
> This that is in front of you is not a survey. It is a collection of summary notes that will give you a certain picture about the work of this most important institution of the Republic at a time that is now behind us.
>
> This work of the Presidency illustrates the fact that it held 325 sessions during the time of its mandate and that it observed over 2,000 points from the daily schedule, while materials, decisions and correspondence include over a few thousand pages of different texts.

> We expect that this is going to be a subject for research and objective analysis one day, and, I hope, as well, impartial and just judgement of our work.

I concluded the report with the words:

> We, the members of this body have our own critical attitude towards the result that has been reached. Nevertheless, we believe that the defensive war, which was the major occupation of this institution, considering the extremely hard circumstances in which it was led, was successfully finished. The results created the basics so that, with political means, in peace the fight for the complete and democratic Bosnia and Herzegovina would be continued.
>
> That is going to be our goal even when we will be ordinary citizens of this country.

Membership of the Seven-Seat Presidency had changed during the war. From the end of 1993, that structure became stable and looked as follows: Alija Izetbegović, Ejup Ganić, Nijaz Duraković, Stjepan Kljuić, Tatjana Ljujić-Mijatović, Ivo Komšić and Mirko Pejanović (three Bosniacs, two Croats and two Serbs).

At the 51st Session of the General Assembly of the UN, I made a speech that was graded as shocking. It seems that the unwritten rule is to repeat some generally accepted phrases. It is a question of 'nice behaviour' in this UN institution. I do not care much for such rules. In the plane, on my way to New York, I got hold of a copy of *The Washington Post*, where it reported, in a negative context, the arming of our army during the war, and whereby they published some insinuations. The next day, in front of the Assembly, I was very direct:

SPEECH AT THE GENERAL ASSEMBLY OF THE UN
New York, 25 September, 1996

> While travelling to New York yesterday on the plane I read an article published in an honourable American newspaper where it said something about the armament of the Bosnian Army during the war. The writer does not say it openly, but it is obvious that everything that is Muslim reminds him of terrorism. For him, it is enough for someone to have a Muslim name and to have a beard to be suspicious. The writer also mentions some names as well. Their only guilt was that they

helped the Bosnian Army secure some weapons during the war. Today, there are over a billion Muslims in the world. I do not know whose interest it is to push them, with this and like minded articles, into the embrace of extremists.

Our land and our people went through hell. The world assumed that it had a right on the embargo of weapons, we thought we had a right to self-defense. In competition with two rights, we think that our right was stronger. That is why I do not have any intention of apologising because we did everything we could to obtain weapons during the war to defend ourselves. Quite the opposite, I give recognition to brave people and thank friendly countries that helped us during a war. That page of our history is over, we turned the other one: peace.

I thank the United States of America for starting the initiative for peace and for trying, together with other countries, to consolidate that fragile and complicated peace.

We are a small country, and that is why we have to lead an open and just politics. Secret diplomacy and double games are the privilege of large countries. For this reason, and many others, one of them being the above mentioned article, I will repeat some facts and our goals.

Bosnia is possible only as a democratic country of three autonomous peoples and free citizens. This basic provision of the Dayton Peace Agreement we accept with all its consequences. That is the famous formula: one country, two entities and three peoples.

Usually it is claimed that the Dayton Agreement is not good. It is good because it stopped the dying in Bosnia and because a better agreement does not exist. The major shortage is not in itself, *per se*, but rather in its implementation. All of the deficits of the Agreement would be reclaimed if it were justly and completely implemented. Unfortunately, this is not the case.

It was ordered in the Agreement that 'Herceg-Bosna' would cease to exist, formed as it was as a parallel country during the war. Nevertheless, it still exists and disturbs the implementation of the Federation of Bosnia and Herzegovina.

It was also ordered that the second Bosnian entity, Republika Srpska, should allow the return of all expelled Bosnians and

Croats to their homes. Not only has that not happened, but the banishing has continued.

Generally, the problem of the Dayton Agreement is in its selective, that is, partial implementation. The Serbs, for example, like Paragraph 2 from Annexe 4 that mentions Republika Srpska; they do not like Annexe 7 that requires the return of refugees. They accept the first order but refuse the second. The world and especially the members of the Contact Group have said clearly: the Dayton Agreement is an entirety. If there is no return of those who have been persecuted, there can be no Republika Srpska. If this is not the case, the Dayton Agreement will grow from little and tolerable, into large and intolerable injustices, and unbearable injustice leads to new conflicts.

According to the Dayton Agreement, human rights should be respected across the whole territory, but they have been violated, more or less, across that whole territory.

The September Elections and the pre-election campaign were a chance to check the situation in the field in a very effective way. An especially bad position in this regard is on the territory of the Serbian entity. For people from the Federation, there was no freedom to travel even before, or it was very limited, and only Serbian political parties could act. In addition, elective organisations that registered the voters and counted the votes were, in this entity, uni-national in all cases, and often uni-party.

Concerning the freedom of the press, important progress was made only on territory under legal Bosnian Government control, where a vast number of independent newspapers and magazines, 40 radio stations and 12 TV stations perform. In the pre-election campaign (the last 50 days) on state television (TVB&H), at prime time (8 pm-12 pm) the leading party had 1/10 of the time and the opposition 9/10 of the time. The Government also gave provisional permission for work for an OBN (Open Broadcasting Network). It is ready to give permanent permission for this on condition that the OBN cover the whole territory of Bosnia and Herzegovina and be open to all political tendencies – left or right.

The problem of Brčko will, practically, be solved by an arbiter, an American, Robert Owen, because the Serbian side does not attend the meetings of the Arbitration Commission. Both sides have stated their arguments. I want to emphasise that the major arbiter does not have complete freedom in deciding. He is limited because we must respect the principles of justice and equity, as is said in Annexe 2, Part 5 of the Dayton Agreement.

In this short analysis of the implementation of the Dayton Agreement I will finish by stating that the major war criminals, Karadžić and Mladić, are still free in spite of Dayton, despite the requests of the Hague Tribunal and despite elementary claims to justice.

We would like to proclaim the principle for the reconciliation of all the people and nations. Bosnia needs it. Nobody advocates the collective guilt of the people. Guilt is always individual, no matter how many culprits exist. However, for the people to reconcile themselves, the criminals ought to be punished. That is why the Hague Tribunal was established, but, as we all know, neither the main Prosecutor, nor the President of the International Court in the Hague are satisfied with the international community's behaviour. They are calling for the culprits and issuing wanted circulars, but all in vain. The world is asking for some painless, middle solution in this matter. When we talk about crimes like those that happened in Bosnia, every compromise is a shameful betrayal of justice. Unpunished crimes will continue to poison the world and to destroy its institutions.

Some people in Europe and America are asking the question is Bosnia possible, after all? Those people either do not know the facts or they are morally dull. It seems as if they do not know that half a million people were killed or persecuted in the Serbian entity, that is about 40% of its original (pre-war) population. They are indifferent to this fact. My answer is: if unpunished genocide is possible, Bosnia is not possible. I agree that punishing the criminals is an expensive thing, but the price of not punishing them is much larger for the whole world.

So, the first question is not whether different nations can live together, it is more concrete and simple that says: does a bigger nation have a right to chase away a smaller one, and then, under the transparent 'we cannot live together' take its property and ask for all the violence to be forgotten and legalised? That is, actually the question of Bosnia, and for people of principles and morals the answer is clear.

In the end, what is the future government of Bosnia and Herzegovina supposed to do in this very critical and historic moment for Bosnia and Herzegovina? It should, in my opinion, constitute a maximally representative Government, made up of all relevant political forces in accordance with the election results, including the opposition in both entities as well.

Then it should proclaim a programme to consist of at least three points. Firstly, it should ask everyone who signed the Dayton Agreement for its full and just implementation. Now, all inner international factors, at least verbally, express a support for this Agreement. The Government should take them at their word. International pressure in this direction will be necessary for a long time.

Secondly, the Government should proclaim a reconciliation of the people and nations involved in the harsh persecution of war criminals.

Thirdly, the Government should secure freedom of the press, as a way of healing the country. The press began the war, a few years before, with its unbelievable spreading of hate. The press could stabilise peace with the spread of tolerance and understanding between people as well. State RTV offered an example of this during the pre-election campaign. OBN could, as well, help this if it could be open for all political parties, and if it is under the observation of the Assembly.

This programme, the Government cannot implement alone. Bosnia is still a patient, and she needs a world's support. The presence of international military forces and economic help will be necessary for a long time.

Before I finish, I want to say a few words about the United Nations. We support the reform of the United Nations' system. Changes are necessary not only in organisation, but in psychology as well, if I can put it like that. Changes are necessary in the organisation of the Security Council, along with changes in the world, but also, a new attitude towards obligations is needed. The United Nations cannot take over obligations that they cannot perform. They cannot declare a protected zone and then leave it to its destiny. It is inadmissible! My people have paid an endlessly high price for this negligence. The protected zone of Srebrenica and its 8,000 innocent lives is not the only example, but they are the hardest example of this unclear relationship. We do not know who is responsible, but we are asking for changes that will make sure that this practice will not happen again.

Yesterday, in this building, I signed an Agreement on the universal prohibition of nuclear testing. We are a small country and my signature does not carry much importance. However, we want, at least symbolically, to participate in everything constructive. One day, Bosnia will, through her representatives, sign an agreement for terrorism prevention, and in support of the struggle against drugs, organised crime, etc. Bosnia will, I hope, join every action whose goal is to prevent evil, and the constant movement of this border towards the direction of a good, better and safer world. Thank you.

Weaponry was important for the Bosnian defense, but the proper solution was in limitation of armaments in the neighbourhood. We had already acceded to the 1994 Vienna Protocol on Regional Arms Control. In Dayton the balance of armaments on a lower level was agreed, through the relation Yugoslavia – Bosnia and Herzegovina – Croatia (5:2:2) and inside of Bosnia and Herzegovina on a relation to the Federation-Republika Srpska of 2:1. Concrete quotas and phases of weaponry reduction were strengthened with the Agreement on sub-regional armament control (Florence, July 1996).

The first phase of this reduction ended in December 1996, and from that time, almost 1,700 pieces of heavy artillery have been destroyed. A goal of the first phase was a reduction of 40% in arms of mass destruction in the category of military planes, helicopters and artillery tools, and 20% of tanks and warlike transportation. The SRJ destroyed, in the first phase around 400 pieces of such armaments. The Federation of Bosnia and Herzegovina destroyed around 700 pieces, mostly mortars of smaller calibre, and by doing so fulfilled the obligations of the first phase. Republika Srpska destroyed, at first, less than 50 pieces, which is below the requested quantity. After international pressure, Republika Srpska destroyed about 1,100 pieces of armament.

In the second phase of reduction, Republika Srpska registered the annihilation of 2,000 pieces of weaponry, including a vast number of heavy ones. The Serbian side began this second phase of destruction in

May 1997. Around 550 pieces of weaponry were so destroyed by September. The Federation of Bosnia and Herzegovina registered, for the second phase around 1,300 pieces of weaponry and by September 1997 had destroyed around 500 pieces. With this tempo, our side fulfilled the requested number for 1997. In this phase, Croatia destroyed around 600 pieces of weaponry, mostly artillery, which was higher than had been requested. The SRJ announced around one hundred pieces for the second phase, including a vast quantity of heavy weaponry. They started with this implementation in July, but with a condition to finish it by the end of September 1997. An international observers' survey identifies that the SRJ will destroy the requested quantity of weaponry by the appointed time. Altogether, for the second phase, the assessment was for the annihilation of 4,600 pieces of weaponry, and 2,000 have already been destroyed. By the end of this phase, 6,200 pieces will be destroyed in total. For the security of this part of the world, it is important that this job be successfully done.

While answering one question put by Banja Luka's *Nezavisne Novine* (29 October 1996), I assessed the democratic developments in neighbouring Croatia and its influence on relations with Bosnia and Herzegovina:

> Considering the geopolitical position of Bosnia and Herzegovina, cooperation with Croatia is necessary and all Bosnian Governments, regardless of their philosophy, will have to respect this fact. This cooperation existed even during the harsh clashes with the HVO during the war. Generally, those relations will depend on the development of democracy in Croatia. With its growth, relations will grow. Personally, I believe that Croatia, with influence from the inside and the outside, has to follow the democratic course. That is why I believe in good relations with Croatia in the future.

On 2-3 December 1996, a conference about Bosnia was held in Lisbon. In my report, called 'A Short report from Bosnia', I spoke about the slow and imperfect implementation of the Dayton Agreement, and the difficulties this had created. I finished my speech with the words:

> Let me finish this little survey with one final comment, which is very actual in the present Bosnia. It is about the moral principle of equality and justice.
>
> In Bosnia today, that word, that great word, equality can often be heard, but it is abused to the same extent.

I want to express my personal attitude: it is the equality of all people. YES, the equality of all Bosnian citizens. YES, the equality of all nations. YES, the equality of Serbs and Bosniacs, Bosniacs and Croats, etc. YES. But the equality of killers and their victims, then NO, no matter who the killers or the victims are.

The end of a dramatic year, 1996 was coming to an end. In an interview with Sarajevo's *Avaz* I answered a few of the editor's questions about how I saw the passing year. A blood-coloured Bosnia beginning to reveal some shades of grey.

Avaz: How do you see this past year as regards a Bosnian situation? What pleases you and what does not?

Izetbegović: I would like, just as everyone else, to say that I am happy with peace, the end of the fires and the dying... however, when a country finds itself at peace overnight, the criteria change quickly. You find yourself in an everyday situation, where a job, salary, electricity, heat, pensions, prices, etc. become important. If I turn to those standards, I cannot be satisfied because unemployment is high, salaries low, the gas supply is on and off every minute, the same thing with the water, and injustice is everywhere. Perhaps I could be satisfied if I recall how everything could be even worse. There could be hunger and beggars, but there are not, huge inflation may have happened, but it did not, there could have been no electricity whatsoever, but there is, thank God, etc. But if we measure it by world standards, it is all very weak. There is a heroic scale where Bosnia held first place in the world, but there is also another scale, a living standard scale, where Bosnia is at the bottom, and this is uncommon for our Bosnia and for us.

Avaz: Still there are strategic interests and goals for our country, and I believe that they are on both scales. May I ask you about your personal obligations as regards your being the 'father of the nation' although you may disagree with this interpretation?

Izetbegović: I have an aversion towards so-called 'fathers of nations' and I do not like that title, but I will answer the first part of your question. In short: it is the entirety of the land and its democratic character. It seems to me that these go together in Bosnia. The concept of the division was always followed with a practice of genocide or at least violence. Without that, division did not work. And the opposite: if you are for the democratic principle, then that also means a united Bosnia. So you could express our goal in one word, and that is freedom, freedom to be Bosniac, Croat or Serb, or simply a citizen, to write or speak freely, to travel through Bosnia freely, in short to be limited only by the law.

Avaz: Although emotions should not dominate, how did you personally feel while you lead the negotiations with Krajišnik?

Izetbegović: That is part of my job, and in that job there are very few pleasant things. For the most part, they are unpleasant, so I just got used to it.

Avaz: A major trial and a great test for the international community was arbitration for Brčko. How can this decision affect the possible return of war or strengthen peace in Bosnia and Herzegovina, considering the ever stronger war-like vocabulary which we hear every day from Pale while we are waiting for a decision on this city?

Izetbegović: Brčko is, indeed, a great trial, the greatest trial for peace since the signing in Dayton. I cannot see how our people can bear an unjust decision on Brčko. I think that the glass is full. Nor are all injustices the same. There are those that cannot be swallowed. Brčko is, considering its origin, population, and ownership – our city. The genocide committed against the Bosniacs in 1992 is one argument more, exactly the one that brings this present situation to the absurd. This is because the Serbian request means searching for the reward for their crime. They do not even try to prove that the city should be theirs, only that it is theirs, because they are the ones holding it. They are quiet about the rest, but it is obvious: we killed and persecuted the real owners and we hold the city, so it is ours. If you do not concede it to us, we will use force again. However, this is not 1992 anymore, and they are not a power anymore. They know it and I think that the world knows it too. That is why I do not believe that injustice is going to happen again.

Avaz: The Serbs are not permitting the return of non-Serb refugees. In places under the control of the Bosnia and Herzegovina Army, Serb refugees are constantly returning. Though this latter development is positive, could all this bring about the hermetic closure of Republika Srpska and HVO controlled territories for Bosniacs, on the one hand, and an increased percentage of Croats and Serbs in the territories controlled by the legitimate government on the other? How can the government ensure two-way returns without having to resort to the methods applied by the Pale regime and those of west Mostar?

Izetbegović: You have just described our huge dilemma. Sometimes it seems unsolvable. If we stay firmly with reciprocity, the process of refugees' return could be definitely blocked, and plans for ethnic cleansing practically supported. If we neglect that principle and consistently, it means a one-sided application of the law, and we could produce a situation which even Roman law defined as *summum ius, summa iniuria*, that is, the situation in which the law causes injustice. For example, a Serb, who keeps a Muslim house in Zvornik could regain his former one here, so he could end up with two houses and the Bosniac none. That is why we have to maintain reciprocity. What we can do is not to be too stiff, and be ready to make the first step in order to open up the process and hold it open for good. What I refer to here about reciprocity relates to material goods, houses, apartments, etc. However, if we are talking about human rights, reciprocity is not valid. You cannot say: you do not permit religious rights to us, so we will not permit them to you either. This does not work. It does not work for two reasons: first, human rights are above the principles of usefulness, and second, even if they were not above that principle, human rights are in the interest of the community or society who implements them. It is proven that democracy and freedom are useful for a society and a country that applies them. Totalitarian communities always decline. It follows that you should respect the freedom of another man because of yourself, not because of him. In my own opinion, we should respect human rights because of moral principles.

On 14 January 1997, Reuters spread the news that Brčko had been decided in favour of Republika Srpska, with some guarantees for the Federation. Supposedly, the Americans made this proposal. This called for an immediate state of high alert. I invited the ambassadors of the Contact Group (USA, Germany, Great Britain, France, Russia) and told them that if the news were true, I would resign my membership of the Presidency that very day and ensure that the whole world knew the truth about the injustice that had occurred. I despatched a letter to them conveying that.

> Rumours have been circulating that arbitration, under the oppression of one part of the international community, should give Brčko to the Serbs.
>
> If that happens, I will immediately resign and leave my function in the Presidency of Bosnia and Herzegovina.
>
> That would be my protest against open violations of the principles of justice to which the Arbiter was specifically obliged according to Article 5, Annexe 2 of the Dayton Agreement, and because of this last in a row of injustices that the world has done to democratic Bosnia and its people. Even though we were attacked, the world tied our hands with an arms embargo which enabled the killing of the Bosnian people, starting with those in Zvornik in 1992, up to the massacre in Srebrenica in 1995. In those tragedies, the part played by the international community was not always very clear. Brčko is a different case, because the decision to punish a victim, and award a criminal for genocide was this time made consciously.
>
> With a world that is ready for something like this I would not be able to cooperate, but because of my function I would have to, so the only way for me is to resign, so someone else can do so. Nevertheless, for now, I cannot see that person among the Bosnian people. Because, as far as I know, Silajdžić would act alike, and I believe Bičakčić, Ganić and Muratović too, just like many others. In that case, I see chaos in Bosnia.
>
> I do not think that there is anyone who would be able to explain to the Bosnian people that they should calmly accept this last injustice. The glass is finally full.
>
> If I resign, because of the reasons listed above, I will do everything to explain to ordinary people in the world – those in the East and the West – what happened in Bosnia during the past five years and why it has happened, in the hope that the space for cynicism and vanity in world diplomacy will be shortened.

I do not know exactly how, or to what extent my letter influenced things, but it looks like the Arbiter's decision, at American request, was modified, such that the final decision was double sided. The Serbs did not get Brčko, but they would have it, if in one year they fulfilled certain conditions concerning human rights, a mixed police force and administration and especially the return of persecuted Bosniacs and Croats to their homes. I knew that the Serbs neither could nor would ever fulfill those requirements.

Tension and political manouevrings about Brčko continued for two further years, until finally Arbiter Robert Owen found a Solomonic solution: on 5 May 1999 he declared Brčko a District, a sort of third entity in Bosnia and Herzegovina. This District would have a multi-ethnic government with its own court and police force. Fighting for implementation of the decision still continues and an end to the situation is impossible to foresee.

At the end of March 1997, I was invited to New York to receive an award from the American Center for Democracy. The President of the Center, Professor Weinstein, the American Ambassador to the UN at the time, Bill Richardson and I all delivered speeches, with myself using the occasion to express my gratitude for the award. In essence, I spoke about the situation in Bosnia and Herzegovina, especially about the slow implementation of the Dayton Agreement. From my speech it is possible to see all the difficulties and troubles we dealt with at that time:

> The defence of democracy in Bosnia is a merit of many people who belong to the various nations and different political parties in the country. Today's act I consider recognition for them all. For all who kept their compass in those hard days of war and public confusion, and stayed firm in the direction of tolerance and democracy. That is why I asked Mr. Miro Lazović, President of the wartime Parliament and Prof. Dr. Ivo Komsić, a member of the wartime Presidency of the Republic of Bosnia and Herzegovina, to be present at today's celebration. I thank them for answering my calls.
>
> My vision of Bosnia is clear: it is of a whole and democratic land. I believe that you perceive her in the same way. That is a vision, for life and reality are far different.
>
> War always leaves hard trials for democrats and democracy. That is what happened in Bosnia. You know very well how much we succeeded in resisting those challenges, as well as how much we did not. Personally, I think that our moral

victories were greater than our defeats and that is how I understand this award of yours today.

One of my American friends asked me if I believe, after all, that a multinational Bosnia is still possible. The same question has been asked of me by many good-intentioned people throughout Europe. This question, I usually answer with another question: what is the alternative? If you think this concerns only a divided Bosnia, you are simplifying the problem unpardonably. The thing is much more complex. Considering what has happened, beginning with the aggression in the spring of 1992, through the genocide, till the current playing with everything that was secured in Dayton, division would not only be a political defeat for Bosnia, but a moral debacle of the world with its countless consequences. That would be a definitive recognition of the force and fraud in international relations, the legalising of genocide and violence, a defeat for democracy and the triumph of two small, but poisonous, fascisms one on one side and one on the other. Could this huge defeat for democracy and the law be a matter only to concern Bosnia, or would it not rather relate to the lives of every woman and every man in this world? In Bosnia, the moral strength and courage of the modern world are tested. Until now, unfortunately there are far more evidences of its moral weakness.

The other day, one important American politician stated that American soldiers would withdraw from Bosnia in the predicted time, even if it meant a return to the clashes. He literally said: 'If Bosnians, Serbs and Croats want to fight, it is their choice.' I was shocked: is it really a matter of belligerent sides that want to continue the fight, aren't there other reasons that may lead to the restoration of the war? It is about the fact that the world is tolerating the hard violations of the Dayton Agreement, helpless to stop this obvious erosion. There is no freedom of movement, no return of refugees, and the Pale regime publicly states that it won't deliver war criminals nor accept a central bank and common currency: which it was obligated to do by the agreement. There is no right reaction to this. I know good, common people in Bosnia do not want to fight, they want peace, they desperately need peace. Small and large leaders may want to continue the war, but that is another thing and should be discussed separately.

Since the Dayton Agreement is balanced by an entirety of different elements, made by long and hard negotiation, it is only worthy as a whole. The nature of similar accords does not bear partial implementation. Hence, Republika Srpska cannot take from the negotiations only what it likes, and refuse the parts that it does not. But that is just what the Serbian Republic is doing. Annexe 7, which guarantees the refugees' right to return to their homes, is not being implemented at all, and it damages the multinational character of the Bosnian state as a whole, which was our major goal in Dayton. For the Pale regime is, not by use but by misuse of the agreement, accomplishing its goals. However, our goals – I will mention only the return of refugees and the integral entirety of the land – we are not achieving. If this negative trend doesn't stop, the Dayton Agreement will no longer exist, and the situation will get out of control.

That is how things are with the civilian aspects of the Dayton Agreement. Some in the West thinking that peace has been reached answer with this: that the military part has been successfully realised, and the separation of military forces on the field. I am free to declare that this does not represent a lot. If the civilian part of the Dayton Agreement is not implemented, the military results will soon be denied, like they never existed, and we can start the war again. Only the implementation of the peace accord as a whole can secure peace in this region which is still in a state of crisis and turbulence. I think that the world does not really observe this fact.

What can we do in a situation like this? Even though we have lost a lot of time, I want to emphasise that it is still not too late, and to our friends in America and elsewhere I recommend: secure the righteous and consistent implementation of the Dayton Agreement. The time of and for negotiations is over. This is the time for implementation. High ranking representatives should not call for new agreements, but finally ask for the fulfillment of what was agreed.

Stop the politics of giving way to evil, because it only encourages extremists, and do not say that everyone is guilty in the same way, because it is a historical lie. A lie does not help. It only enables confusion to grow.

Force all sides to accord their constitutions with the Dayton Agreement and destroy the surplus of weaponry according to the Vienna protocol.

Reconciliation of the people is possible under two conditions: punishment of war criminals and freedom of the media. First, one should switch collective guilt with that of the individual, and second one should sober people from chauvinistic and racist delusions.

We know that the largest part of the job we have to do ourselves, for it is the matter of our land. However, in the situation as it is we need your help.

For that reason, do not leave Bosnia. Positive or negative developments will influence the whole region that is currently in a state of crisis. Bosnia is a land – a bridge. Two worlds, three cultures and four religions meet here. For that reason, the Bosnian problem here and now, is a major question of democracy.

During this visit to America, I was invited to meet President Clinton at the White House. It was an informal meeting, and I used the opportunity to learn more about the personality of this man for whom strange circumstances, since the beginning, had connected him with Bosnia's destiny.

A long time ago, back in March of 1992, I received a picturesque document, actually a charter about the fraternisation of the federal state of Arkansas and Bosnia and Herzegovina. At the end of the Proclamation, which states that citizens of Arkansas establish tight cultural, educative, economic and scientific links with Bosnia and Herzegovina, it was stated: 'As a testimony to this, I hereby lay with my hand the seal of the State of Arkansas, affixed in the capital on the Big Rock, on the eighth day of February, in the year of our Lord, nineteen ninety two.' Signed: Governor Bill Clinton and the Secretary of the State (signatures illegible). This bringing together of Arkansas and Bosnians at the beginning of the 1990s was the result of one Bosnian group's efforts, headed by Dr. Edib Korkut, who lived and worked for a long period in America.

In July of 1992, Bill Clinton, at the time Governor of Arkansas, gave permission for his electoral headquarters in Little Rock to proclaim, concerning the war in Bosnia, that the USA should request the UN Security Council to issue an agreement for air raids against those who were preventing humanitarian aid from arriving at its destination, and that the USA had to be ready to offer corresponding military support for this operation. At the end of the statement, it was said: 'We have to say clearly that the economic blockade against Serbia will be tightened, not only for armaments, but for gas and other goods, necessary for the survival of Slobodan Milošević's apostatic regime. The UN should give permission for European and American marine forces on the Adriatic Sea to stop and search ships that may be smuggling goods into Serbia and its ally Montenegro.'

When he was elected president and took office (in January 1993), Clinton became noticeably restrained. I think that Secretary of State Warren Christopher, the 'electronic brain' of the American Administration at the time, advised him to do so. Christopher would appear to have asked him not to bring too many emotions and ethics into politics. When Christopher returned from his tour of Europe, in the spring of 1993, where he went to investigate possible military intervention in Bosnia and Herzegovina, Senator Biden complained how the Secretary of State faced 'a mosaic of apathy and cowardice' in Europe. I remember my anxiety while I observed this tour. I knew the result beforehand. Christopher went to Europe to find apathy, and he found it. However, Clinton won over Christopher when he, at the end of the August of 1995, after Srebrenica and the shelling on Sarajevo marketplace, confirmed the air raids against the Karadžić army in Bosnia.

When we were separating, President Clinton shook my hand in a friendly manner and smiled at me widely. There was something boyish in the man, whom Senator Biden described as the most intelligent man he had ever worked with. I will never forget that he refused Holbrooke's request to pressure us when negotiations in Dayton stumbled. 'I do not want to pressure the Muslims,' he answered to Holbrooke's request.

While I was leaving the White House, a group of journalists waited for me in the courtyard. They asked about the possible arrest of Karadžić, whether President Clinton promised American action in that respect, and also about the possibility of IFOR's withdrawal from Bosnia, given that they only had a temporary mandate there. I answered the first question vaguely, and they were clearly not very pleased. As for the second, I said that there were four conditions. I counted them: implementation of the Agreement on Subregional Control of Armaments signed in Firenca in July 1996, for Bosnia to become a member of the Partnership for Peace, the complete realisation of the American programme for Federation Army armaments, and finally, complete integration of the Croatian military component into the Federal Army.

On 12 April 1997, after a number of postponements, Pope Jean Paul II came to visit Sarajevo. I harboured a sincere and deep respect for this man. I admired him while he was still a bishop of the Polish Church, and as Cardinal Karol Vojtila announcing a freedom for his land from communist dictatorship. His tireless work for peace and understanding between nations is one of the bright pages of 20th century history.

I was still in prison when Cardinal Vojtila visited Morocco (1965) and in front of the 80,000 Muslims spoke about 'our common ancestor Abraham' (Ibrahim), and after that, in April 1986, visited a Roman synagogue. It was the first time in history that the head of the Catholic Church stepped over a Jewish threshold, an act which meant offering a hand to the people who had been accused, over the previous 20 centuries, of Jesus Christ's killing.

In Bosnia and Herzegovina, the Pope was especially popular because he used every chance to draw the world's attention to the situation in our country. In one of his famous speeches he said:

> A century which has been marked with maybe the most cruel crimes in human history is coming to its end. A century which opened with a dramatic war that started in Sarajevo, that century, at its very end, is facing again the tragedy which has its painful level of misunderstanding and hate. Sarajevo, a martyr town, is a symbol for many places in the world who are still afraid of war.

At Sarajevo airport, a cool north wind was blowing. It did not prevent a warm welcome for the Pope. While greeting him, I said:

> It is a great honour for me to greet you today in this long-suffering town. I am sure that your visit is equally welcomed by all those with good will, no matter what their religion, nation, or belief, here in Sarajevo as well as throughout Bosnia and Herzegovina.
>
> This undivided respect you deserve with your persistent devotion to peace and freedom everywhere in the world. Your convictions about the violence in Bosnia, said not only once, but on many occasions, were a balm for our wounds and meant encouragement and hope for all of us.
>
> Your Holiness, you are coming into the city of not one religion but four confessions: Islam, Catholicism, Orthodoxy, and Hebrew.

> It is possible to conclude from a panorama of this town that over the centuries, one next to another, in close proximity mosques, cathedrals, orthodox churches and synagogues all stand together.
>
> This view is not accidental. It originated from the wisdom of our ancestors, who believed that in faith there is no force and that every sort of celebration is for the one and only God and is worthy of respect.
>
> For centuries the capital of tolerance, Sarajevo was a victim of an unseen violence and the place of human suffering. From incidental pictures, from the airport to the town, you will be able to see only a small part of the hell which this city has gone through...

The Pope led a prayer gathering, which completely filled Koševo Stadium. During those two hours of prayer, two annual seasonal changes were witnessed; we went from a January snow storm to an April spring sun.

At the end of July, I gave an interview to Belgrade's *NIN*. Here, I document the answers given to two interesting questions posed by journalist Gordana Igrić:

> *NIN*: Do you believe in the possibility of a united Bosnia and Herzegovina's survival? Why didn't you accept the entrance of Bosnia and Herzegovina into a 'shortened' Yugoslavia?
>
> Izetbegović: Not only do I believe in but I also work for the survival of an united Bosnia. I have the full support of my people and the result cannot be escaped from. Considering the second part of your question, the answer is simple: because we could not accept being second rate citizens, and that is what could have happened to us at least. That subordinate status we carried for over 100 years. But then we decided to risk going it alone because we are a proud people.
>
> *NIN*: Last winter and spring, a rumour was heard about a possible offensive by the Bosnia and Herzegovina Army against Republika Srpska. Later, the media close to your party launched new maps for the ethnic division of Bosnia. Do you think that a Bosnia with only Bosnians in it, a Serbia and Croatia with only Serbs and Croats, could be a perspective for these countries in the longer-term?

Izetbegović: Here we have Croats from Neum to Brčko, Bosnians from Višegrad to Bihać. The same is true with the Serbs. So how can you establish national states there? You can, of course, do some bloody demographic engineering, and force the people into national sheepfolds. That is what the Ustashas and Chetniks in the Second World War and in this one, 1992-1995, tried to do. But your question can also be understood in the following way: do you agree with ethnic cleansing? Of course, I do not. It follows that national states in Bosnia are impossible from a moral and legal point of view. It is possible if moral and legal norms are brutally broken. As you know, that is exactly what was done, but I think that the time has come when you can not base a state on bare violence. Well, perhaps you can, but it will not survive.

The Pale authority[3] continued to obstruct Bosnia and Herzegovina however it could. It maintained its delusion of people that Republika Srpska was a separate state, and not an entity within Bosnia and Herzegovina. It sabotaged the functioning of state institutions, avoided everything that was common between the entities, and in every possible way tried to avoid mention of the name Bosnia and Herzegovina. By way of answer to this, aversion for Republika Srpska grew amongst our public.

I decided to identify this problem at the Conference on Bosnia and Herzegovina, which was held in Bonn, 9 December 1997:

> Part of our public was shocked at the time we accepted the Republika Srpska and we did it unwillingly. However, we had two good reasons for this: we stopped the war that threatened us with a new spiral of death and destruction and – what we want to specially emphasise here – we assured the survival of Bosnia and Herzegovina as a united and internationally recognised country.
>
> That was our mutual compromise and it was done on the basis of Dayton.
>
> Considering this basic fact and present Serbian behaviour, and also the hesitation of the international community, I have to say this: if the Serbian power does not recognise Bosnia and Herzegovina as it is defined in Article 1 of the Consti-

---

[3] The Bosnian Serbs' power, under the control of Karadžić, was called according to its residency in Pale, a place not far from Sarajevo.

tution of Bosnia and Herzegovina, then we do not recognise Republika Srpska and ask for the world, who guaranteed this agreement on peace, to follow this logic and status through with all its consequences.

Ignoring this basic fact of the Dayton Agreement is the reason for our failure today. All other failures in the future implementation of the agreement will eventually cause its complete collapse. All the efforts, connected with so many victims and at such expense, could be lost.

I finished my presentation with a request for the implementation of the accord between the Constitution of the entity and the Constitution of Bosnia and Herzegovina, and I especially emphasised establishing the constitutionality of all three nations in both entities, Serbian in the Federation and Bosnian and Croatian in Republika Srpska. Soon thereafter, I submitted a formal request in this regard to the Constitutional Court of Bosnia and Herzegovina. The Court accepted this request on 1 July 2000, with a vote of five to four, after a long procedure that lasted for almost two and a half years and which was dramatic, sometimes involving Serbian and sometimes partial Croatian obstructions. The decision was formally made, but before us is the vast work for the implementation of the Constitutional Court decision, maybe the most important one after Dayton. All circumstances point to the fact that it will be a hard and painful job.

The behaviour of the Pale Government can be vividly illustrated in the harsh debates surrounding the new currency of Bosnia and Herzegovina. We wanted a unique Bosnia and Herzegovina currency; the SDS wanted two different ones: one for the Federation and the other for Republika Srpska. According to them, Republika Srpska was a state, and everything should be different. This debate about the new Bosnian money which had begun in 1997 then lasted for almost another year.

In April of 1997, in the Land Museum in Sarajevo, the Presidency met Kornblum, Gelbard and David Lipton, an expert from the World Bank, for a debate on this question, which was very important for the future of Bosnia and Herzegovina. Krajišnik was ready for the discussion: he immediately proposed that Bosnia and Herzegovina should not have a unique currency. Let the Federation have the mark and Republika Srpska the dinar. After this was rejected, he said that he would present his own design, and that the Federation should propose its own. It was obvious that the fight for a unique Bosnia and Herzegovina currency was going to be hard and unpredictable.

At the beginning of July 1997, there was a meeting between the Presidency and Gelbard and Holbrooke in Lukavica. I asked for the Bosnian currency to bear a neutral design, while Krajišnik continued to make proposals which emphasised national symbols. He brought sketches of crosses, churches, Kraljević Marko, Njegoš, the Saint Sava Church in Belgrade, etc. High Representative Carl Bildt was ready to compromise in order to solve the problem. The Governor of the Central Bank at the time, Robert Serge, a Frenchman, did not show any interest in influencing a solution, and by doing so practically helped Krajišnik.

The meeting lasted for hours but Krajišnik did not give up. On one occasion, he took from his pocket shabby notes and coins bearing English and Scottish pound symbols, claiming that Great Britain, although one country had different currencies for the national entities therein. He recalled similar examples from Argentina and Panama.

In his letter to High Representative Westendorp (a copy was given to me), Krajišnik, on 10 July 1997, wrote:

> Considering the request of Mr. Izetbegović, for a design with symbols exclusively related to Bosnia and Herzegovina, I want to inform you that this proposal is unacceptable.
>
> The agreement about the design is connected to the symbols of the Serbian people, but because Serbian national space is also spread outside Republika Srpska, it is logical that the eponyms of the money should have symbols that are related to places outside of Bosnia and Herzegovina.

In accordance with this letter, Krajišnik submitted proposals for the bank note for 100 convertible marks, with pictures of Petar Kočić and the Gračanica Monastery. Other bill proposals (50, 20, 10, 5, 1 and 0.5) bore the same elements, including characters like Branko Ćopić, Ivo Andrić, Meša Selimović, Njegoš, Nikola Tesla, Jovan Dučić and the Gračanica Church, the Ostrog Monastery, the Žitomislić Monastery, the Mostanica Monastery, the Saint Sava Church, the Ozren Monastery and the Monastery of Krka.

Krajišnik had taken great care to ensure that the colours, sizes and shapes of letters and motifs, were always different from those on the Federal proposals for the currency. If we had red, the Serbian would be blue, if we had a flower, they would have a building. It did not matter what it was, as long as it was different.

On 13 January 1998, a session of the Bosnia and Herzegovina Presidency took place and Gelbard, Westendorp, Klein and the new Governor of the Central Bank Nicol, were present. Krajišnik came up with the proposal that four S[4] letters should appear on the bills, justifying this by the equality of the various entities, and with the Serbian right to 'pay with their own money, so the international community cannot order which money they carry in their pockets'. The proposal, of course, was rejected. Realising that the fight was purposeless, Krajišnik made a last, desperate attempt: he proposed that Bosnia give up its currency and that the money be the German Mark. This he considered would be accepted by people unanimously. Before this, he had proposed the use of the dollar so that 'Muslims, Serbs and Croats could be Americans for at least six months'. According to Krajišnik, we could save 30 million DM which would be the cost of printing our own currency. Westendorp was completely at a loss. He was afraid that any money chosen by his own decision would not be accepted. Gelbard, for his part, stated at the press conference that 'unfortunately, the three sides did not reach an agreement', so avoiding any public declaration that Krajišnik was guilty of failure.

I decided to play the trickster. Before the Bosnia and Herzegovina Presidency meeting, which was scheduled for 19 January 1998, I asked for the deposition of all the designs in the Central Bank of Bosnia and Herzegovina. After this was done, to everybody's surprise, especially Krajišnik's, I said that I completely accepted the Serbian design, but without national and religious symbols. I listed the names and symbols that were then currently displayed on the money. Krajišnik could not believe it, and his expression was as if he had found himself above the chasm. The situation was tragicomic. He said that if the Federation accepted his design, then he did not. A dispute began between Krajišnik and Gelbard. Gelbard called him aside in his room, from which Krajišnik angrily left. Gelbard returned, noticeably upset, saying that everything was all right. Two days later, Westendorp and Nicol revealed the appearance of the new bank notes. The characters on them were from different nationalities, but all from Bosnian literature. Kemal Muftić, my Press Advisor was the first one to suggest this so simple but cunning idea to accept the Serbian design. 'Is it really important if we have money with vines and trees on it instead of flowers, as long as we make sure that the size and the colour of the money is the same?' he explained.

[4] A great Serbian slogan: 'Only concord can save the Serbs' – four words which, in Serbian, start with the capital letter S.

However, to be honest, I have to say that I did not feel hatred towards Krajišnik, nor did he belong to the worst kind of people I had met. The worst kind are betrayers (Dante places them in the ninth circle of hell), and Krajišnik was not a betrayer. He served the Serbian people, in a way that he perceived them and their interests.

The Bosnian currency, having a strong deposit back, won. It suppressed the intruders, the Croatian kuna and the Serbian dinar, that had been sovereign in many parts of Bosnia and Herzegovina before.

At the height of these currency debates, within an interval of only five days, three major international conferences were scheduled. I was invited to attend the Session of the Islamic Organisation for Education, Science, and Culture (ISESCO), planned for 7-8 December 1997. A very important conference for the implementation of the peace in Bosnia and Herzegovina was planned for 9-10 December, in Bonn, and, finally, the Summit of the Organisation of Islamic Conference (OIC) was scheduled for 10-11 December in Tehran.

On 6 December, I took off for Riyadh on a special Saudi plane. Saudi Arabia made me happy not only with its holy places, but with its obvious prosperity as well. At the universities of Saudi Arabia, there were over 150,000 students, and it was planned that in the year 2000, their own professors would lead the education programme. Only half a century earlier, Riyadh had been surrounded with fences and muddy roads, and the Kingdom contained a large number of illiterate people.

On the morning of 7 December, in the large hall of the University of Riyadh, I was handed the diploma of Honourable Doctor of Legal Sciences. In the afternoon, I visited King Fahd in his residency, which reminded me of the ones in fairy tales. This was our fifth meeting.

The King received us in his solemn saloon. He was ill and sitting in a wide armchair, swirled in a black thin robe, the traditional Arabic outfit. He could hardly speak. 'You had heart problems, how are you now?' he asked me. 'Whenever I come to Saudi Arabia, I recover,' I answered. I outlined to him briefly the situation in Bosnia and told him about the Conference in Bonn. I added that I was in Saudi Arabia at the invitation of the University of Riyadh and that I would be travelling to Tehran to the OIC Conference. 'I learnt today that Saudi Arabia has 150,000 students, and that in the near future you will not depend on foreign teachers,' I commented. '*Sahih*,' (that is true), he replied, proud of this success for his land. It was, actually his own success, because he was the one who, as minister of education, 40 years previously started this process of intense education. Parting, the King shook my hand and smiled, wishing me a good journey and success in both conferences. 'Next time you come, we will play soccer,' he joked, obviously directing his amusement at both our bad healths.

Crown Prince Abdullah, a tall and corpulent man, waited for us in the neighbouring saloon. He greeted us heartily. He spoke briefly, but quickly. When I told him that I would be attending the OIC Conference in Tehran, he asked me whether I intended to speak there. 'Yes, I will speak, and moreover, I will speak about the problem of Muslim nations lagging behind. Here, yesterday, I received information from those responsible in ISESCO. Can you imagine that even today there are Muslim countries in which the illiteracy rate is over 60%?' 'Yes,' he answered, 'that is one problem, the other one is discord, Mr. President. Can you see how many fools there are among us? I will improve our relations with Iran. There is no reason for squabble,' he said resolutely.

I had already prepared a speech for the OIC Conference in Tehran. However, after my acknowledgments in Riyadh, I threw it away, and wrote a completely new one the night before the Conference. At around five o'clock in the morning I gave it to Hajrić for translation, and went to sleep for a few hours. The speech was a little bit heretical, and it collected vivid comments.

The Iranians, the hosts for the OIC that year, presiding over this meeting of Muslim countries' leaders, had erected a special building in a huge park, in the north of Tehran. The Conference Hall was equipped with the most modern of technologies. However, a huge amount of snow fell the night before. There was damage to the roof installation and suddenly the elite of the Muslim world found themselves in the dark. My speech was postponed for a few hours. This accident made me deliver my speech during the midnight hours, when all of the large television stations of the Muslim world were following the Conference live.

Speech At The OIC Conference
Tehran, 11 December 1997

> It is a great privilege for me to have the chance to speak in this important gathering of Muslim countries. I have just returned from the Conference in Bonn. That was a specific conference devoted to Bosnia, where the situation in my land was observed, and some important decisions were made. Unfortunately, the time for this Summit and the Bonn Con-

ference overlapped, so I am addressing you now. Thank you for this exceptional occasion.

Respecting your time and today's Conference programme I will focus on only one subject tonight: the East and West and my Bosnia in between. I got the idea for this subject during my current and continuing journey. For during this week I have flown from Bosnia to Saudi Arabia for the Conference on Education, then to Europe for the Conference about Bosnia and finally here, today, in Tehran for the Islamic Conference. That is: East-West-East.

I think that I know these two parts of the world rather well. On this journey of mine, I established some new facts, some of them good, some of them bad.

I discovered the encouraging fact of about 5,000,000 pupils and students in Saudi Arabia, but a bad one as well: there are around 68.5% illiterate people in another Muslim country. The second piece of good news, which I have just heard, is that 20,000,000 people attend school in Iran, but the bad news is that illiteracy among women in almost all Muslim countries is inadmissibly high. Women represent half of the human race. Uneducated women cannot bring up the generation that will lead our nations into the 21st century.

Forgive me, for I will now be very open. Nice lies do not help, but sour truths could be a cure. The West is not corrupted or degenerated. The 'Rotten West' of a self-deceiving communism paid a high price for this. The West is not rotten. It is strong, educated and organised. Their schools are better than ours and their cities are cleaner than ours. The level of human rights in the West is higher and social care for the poor and less able, better organised. Westerners are, most often, responsible and accurate people. Those are my experiences with them. I know, as well, the dark sides of their progress, and I am not letting them out of my sight.

Islam is the best – this is the truth – but we are not the best. Those two are different things and we always switch them. Instead of hating the West, we should compete with it. Did not the Qur'an order us to do just that: 'Strive to achieve the virtue of deeds...' With the help of religion and science, we can create the power that we need. It is a long and hard road, it is an exhausting climb up the hill, the hill that the Qur'an talks about, but there is no other way.

So, let us establish funds for education everywhere. Do not let any child of ours remain uneducated. Rich Muslim countries should help the poor ones in this regard. Let's do this today or convene a conference on the same.

Some people think that advantage can be reached by terror. That delusion spreads quickly. Terrorism is a consequence of our present and of our future weakness. It is not only immoral, but it is unproductive as well. Immoral because innocent people are hurting and unproductive because it has never and nowhere solved anything. All serious political movements in history rejected terrorism. I think that the Qur'an forebade it with a specific sentence: 'It is the same to kill one innocent human being as it is to kill the whole of humanity…' Unfortunately, there are those who forget that.

Now a few words about the Bosnia that I have come from. I mentioned the East and the West. Bosnia is positioned between these two, on the Big Border, as we like to put it. Every tenth Bosnian died in the past war. We paid a high price for our right for survival and freedom. That is why you should not let new injustice happen in Bosnia. Tell everyone that Bosnia is a holy country to you, because it has been drenched with the blood of innocent people, your brothers in faith.

When I finished, there was tense silence in the hall, a sure sign that my words had left a certain impression. I felt some sort of relief in my soul. While I was walking away from the hall, I noticed one young man pushing his way through the crowd and he gave me a small piece of scribbled paper. The message was in English, and consisted of two sentences; actually one question, and one assertion. It read: 'Did you forget that the West, that you are praising, left your people to extermination? Remember, only Muslims are truly your friends.'

In April 1998, two important Frenchmen came to visit Bosnia: President Jacques Chirac and the writer and philosopher Bernard Henry Levý. Over the previous six years I had held a few meetings with President Chirac, the first one in 1992, when he was mayor of Paris, and planning to proclaim his candidateship for President. I was surprised by how little he knew about Bosnia and its problems. When I saw him again in 1995, the situation was quite different, he even knew about the Kiseljak-Sarajevo road, about Igman, and French calibre 155 cannons on that mountain.

Chirac was quite the opposite of his predecessor Francois Mitterrand. Not only ideological differences, but their characters divided them as well. Mitterrand was introverted, thoughtful, reserved, while Chirac was always on the move. When talking to you he would look you right in the eye and try to convince you of what he was saying. During one lunch, I told him that he was not a diplomat. At this remark, he was silent for a moment, in doubt. I explained that I was paying him a compliment. He smiled at me widely and expressed his thanks.

Mitterrand and Chirac — two different men holding two different policies towards Bosnia. Rather, I think that it was a matter of two different approaches to Serbia and the Serbs. For Mitterrand, this relation was determined by memories of the First and Second World Wars when the French and the Serbs shared the same side. Some called it 'fraternity through weaponry'. Nothing could change this penchant from the past. Maybe Chirac held similar feelings, but they were suppressed by one new memory: a picture of French soldiers whom the Serbs had tied up against pillars in Pale, in the April of 1995. It represented a brutal humiliation for France and its army, and Chirac could not forgive it.

During the infernal days of June 1992, Mitterrand paid an unexpected visit to Sarajevo under siege. This on June 28. He was accepted as a saviour: he visited the place of the massacre near the Sarajevo market place, the hospital and — what was important — there was no bombing that day. However, up to this day there is doubt. What was his motive: to help Sarajevo or to prevent the military intervention of the international community against the aggressor? The number of those who believe in the second is still increasing.

While I have been writing these columns, a book was published in Paris about Mitterrand's ambiguous visit to Sarajevo. The author, Mathieu Braunstein, published, for the first time, the fact that Mitterrand held a short meeting with Karadžić and Mladić at Sarajevo airport, which was, in his opinion, organised by UNPROFOR Commander, Canadian General McKenzie. Braunstein writes:

> Although Mitterrand had literally a one minute meeting with Karadžić and Mladić, he told us that he did not come to officially visit the country which had just gained independence, and this is why he bears part of the responsibility for everything that has happened in the succeeding three years (...) Moreover, President Izetbegović informed Mitterrand about the existence of concentration camps, and said exactly where they were. The French President did not react, and kept silent

about this in Paris. Instead of requesting an international investigation, one month later the Keraterm and Omarska camps were discovered by the Anglo-Saxon press.

When Srebrenica happened, President Chirac proposed military action to re-establish the destroyed UN protected zone. The Americans and British found this plan unrealistic, and any action was declined. However, French hesitation under Chirac was also to become apparent. The main attorney of the Hague Tribunal, Louise Arbour, at the beginning of 1999, vehemently criticised the French Government because of its poor cooperation with the Tribunal, and in February President Chirac received Biljana Plavšić, President of Republika Srpska, with every honour that a head of state deserves. Our public was shocked.

I sent a letter of protest to the French President. The answer that followed stated that the French only wished to express support to a person who represented a new, moderate course in the politics of the Bosnian Serbs and that it sent a message to the Pale regime to the effect that it does not have legitimacy and international support. We, of course, did not consider this was the best way of sending such a message. For *Le Monde*, Paris, (4 April 1998), I stated:

> When it comes to welcoming Mrs. Plavšić in front of the Elysée Palace, intentions could have been one thing, but the political effect was something completely different. France's intent, as it was explained to us later on, was to send a message to the Pale regime that the other kind of Serbs, those headed by Mrs. Plavšić, enjoy French support. Nevertheless, we saw the other side of the medal, and that is state protocol. Both the Serbs and Bosnians accepted it as recognition of the statehood of Republika Srpska, the Serbs with one feeling, the Bosnians with another. According to the Dayton Agreement, only Bosnia and Herzegovina is a State, and Republika Srpska is an entity in that State. Again, it has been shown that intentions in politics do not mean a lot, that only the consequences are important, and they are as I have already stated above. Some of this bad effect has, however, been removed by President Chirac's letter.

The other great Frenchman never hesitated. The famous French intellectual Bernard Henry Levý was visiting Bosnia for the twelfth time. His first visit was back in June 1992. The war was still raging and Sarajevo was under siege. About his first visit to Sarajevo, Levý wrote:

> The first time we came to Sarajevo, in June 1992, the city was under siege, people lived under bombing, children lived and played in the basements, and before the picture of that hell, there was no more political thinking, no more historic memory, traditional friendship with this and that land of the region. The fact was that we were forced to take an attitude towards the situation. Antifascism before it even became an idea, was a reflex (interview with Sarajevo's *Oslobođenje*, 15 July 2000).

Levý later wrote a book, made two movies about the Bosnian tragedy and, with Gilles Herzog, a film about the Bosnian Army. These two Frenchmen – Levý and Herzog – who had an almost religious devotion to Bosnia, proposed that I ask Chirac to enable the Bosnian Army to have the ability to step into the city first during the redemption of Sarajevo, just like the French soldiers had stepped into Paris in 1944. This did not happen, for known reasons, but I cannot forget the romanticism of these two true Bosnian friends.

On 8 April 1998, I handed Levý a 'Silver Decoration of the Bosnian Arms', presented to him by the war Presidency of Bosnia and Herzegovina. I made a little speech in accordance with this:

> Six years have passed since the beginning of the aggression on Bosnia and Herzegovina; those were tragic happenings, tragic not only for Bosnia but for the whole of Europe and the world. Force tried, like many times before, to triumph over freedom. Force did not win but it did not lose either. As throughout man's entire history, the end does not exist, and the struggle for freedom continues.
>
> You were the first one who came and encouraged us in those hard days. As far as I remember, it was in June 1992, when the aggression was in full swing. You were one of the first to realise that it was not an ordinary war, that there was something deeper and more important concerning every free man and woman in the world.
>
> After you, other dear and close people came, and so it continued until today. However, you were the first one who opened the door and gave an example for our colleagues, independent intellectuals, writers and artists. During the hard times of the war, your visits and the visits of those brave people were like a balm for our wounds, a light that kept on shining upon a dark age.

The modest and belated recognition that I am handing you today, is a sign of our gratitude for your brave step in that horrible June of 1992, for your brave words, for the book with its symbolic title *The Lily and the Ashes*, for the movie *One Day in the Death of Sarajevo*, for the movie *Bosnia*, for your cooperation in the movie *Army* and all the other things that you have done for Bosnia that are impossible to number in this short congratulation.

I want to assure you, Mr. Levý, that Bosnia will regardless of the hesitation and unavoidable dilemmas, continue to develop in accordance with your and our ideals of freedom and tolerance, and that you will never regret remaining on the Bosnian side in those hard days.

Thank you Mr. Levý, and through you, thanks to all the anti-fascists of France and the world.

On 30 June 1998, I was invited to a ceremony at Istanbul's University of Marmara where I was to be honoured with the title of Honourable Doctor of Law. Air conditioning does not help much on a hot summer's day in a brimming university hall where a few hundred professors and students had gathered, together with a great many guests including the President of the Republic of Turkey, Suleman Demirel. At the top of the hall was a choir with a vast number of girls and boys, singing some Turkish songs similar to marches.

After they had dressed me in a solemn toga identifying me as a doctor of sciences, I made a little speech, coloured with personal overtones:

> I am sorry that my short report, instead of being a long speech about the law and legal science, of which you know more than I do, will have a personal note to it.
>
> Law was my ambition from my youth. As a young man, maybe as a child, I dreamt of being a lawyer so I could defend what I consider to be justice. However, when the communists came to power, I was sent to prison, and after three years of punishment, listening to my father's advice, I enrolled in the study of Agronomy. At the time, the common belief was that un-likeminded lawyers did not stand a chance in a communist system. After the three-year course on Agronomy, I did however return to my first love – the Law.
>
> The Law was not only a profession for me. It was my determination, my faith, some sort of life philosophy. I always

believed that the so-called right of the stronger is not the true right, but a mere fact, that lawyers are made to protect the weaker elements of society and that freedom of thought is primarily the freedom to think differently.

This was what I believed in as a young man and this I have continued to believe in as an adult. I paid for this belief with my freedom twice, being in prison for almost nine years.

But my major temptations were not those years in prison. Quite the opposite. The real temptations were the years of power. By taking, for over eight years, a part of the responsibility for the destiny of one small country, attacked from the outside and torn from the inside, I continued to check the beliefs from my youth. On one, not huge but nonetheless brutal occasion, I had the chance, accidentally, to examine myself and others, to closely watch the relationship between the law and force, between principles and interests, morals and politics. The survival of the people, to whom I belong, came into question, as never before in its long history. The imperatives of that fight, and the imperatives of justice and law, were constantly tested.

It is not my job to judge whether I passed this endlessly hard and important test. In the end, the least relevant is what we think of ourselves. I just want to assure you that I did everything I could to accord with those two imperatives as much as it was possible. If this honour is about how much I strove – and I am not talking about results – I believe that I deserve your recognition.

Croatian politics towards Bosnia and Herzegovina under Tuđman did not change. It was littered with nice statements, but the practice was consistently focused some other way. On 8 September 1998, a correspondent of *Free Europe* visited me and asked a few questions. Two of them related to the politics of our neighbours:

> *Free Europe*: How do you perceive the fact that President Tuđman calls for the agreement in Zagreb of all presidential candidates – Croats – and that there are, for example, in the Croatian Parliament delegates who represent Croats from Bosnia and Herzegovina? Do you consider this disrespects Bosnian sovereignty?

Izetbegović: Tuđman's influence on the Bosnian Croats is weakening. At a meeting the other day, of the nine invited, only two showed up. Obviously, Tuđman's intercourse with the inner matters of Bosnia and Herzegovina is not 'in' any more. A different time is on the horizon. As far as the second part of your question is concerned, this practice is obviously illegal and unique in the world. Croatia wants to enter European integration. With this kind of practice, it will not be able to. They will have to sign an agreement with Bosnia and Herzegovina for double citizenship. That is how it was ordered by the Dayton Accords. In the Agreement, the active and passive right to vote, army service, payment of taxes, etc. are particularly explained. As everywhere else, the criteria is permanent residency. Things are inevitably moving towards normalisation, I think this is so of the future. The present situation is a relic of an abnormal situation that events are putting aside.

Free Europe: How important are Serbia and Croatia politically for Bosnia and Herzegovina? Could there be basic democracy in Bosnia and Herzegovina without democratisation of political life in Serbia and Croatia?

Izetbegović: The influence of our neighbours on processes in Bosnia and Herzegovina is very important, but not crucial. Not so long ago we experienced some sort of racism and fascism in parts of Bosnia and Herzegovina, but still there was a certain level of democracy in the places where the Sarajevo authority had control. Affirmation of the Bosnian State will be relieved by two facts: democratisation of Croatia and the further weakening of Serbia. We expect developments of this kind in the future. Democratic resolution in Serbia I cannot see in the near future. Of course, miracles can happen. The whole episode is a story about unpredictable and unexpected happenings.

Three days later, I was asked similar questions by a correspondent from Istanbul's *Cumhuriyet*:

Cumhuriyet: What do you think of the Croatian and Serbian sides and how can their decisions shape the future of Bosnia?

Izetbegović: Among the Croats and Serbs, there are two main streams: pro-Bosnian and separatist. They call them soft and hard, or moderate and radical streams. The development of things and Bosnia's status depend upon the common relationship of these two streams in the Croatian and Serbian corpus. I think that moderate powers will win. Nevertheless, the attitude of the Bosniacs is crucial for Bosnia's destiny, and our attitude is clear: we will not give up Bosnia.

Three more days passed, general elections were polled in Bosnia, and a correspondent of *Voice of America* wanted an interview. The questions and answers to the same were distinctive:

> *Voice of America*: Mr. Izetbegović, almost three years have passed since Dayton's signature and the end of the war. Many things have been done, but Bosnia and Herzegovina, according to the international community, especially the USA, is not in a phase of stable and permanent peace yet. How do you judge the actual situation in Bosnia and Herzegovina?
>
> Izetbegović: More than two and a half years of peace have gone by. I recently read an analysis that says that a country needs three times more than the time it spent at war; so for every year of war three years of peace. It is the truth that the peace cannot be stable and self-preserving, but a long path has been walked. Maybe yesterday's elections can illustrate that progress in the best way. They were implemented without any serious incident and people crossed entity borders freely, and this was not even imaginable last year.
>
> *Voice of America*: International economic help for Bosnia and Herzegovina is greater than for Germany after the Second World War, but the Bosnian economy is still not able to manage on its own. Politically, hardly one agreement can be reached without international arbitration. Is Bosnia and Herzegovina an independent and sovereign state? In other words, to what extent is it a country, when there are two entities, and three realities, and when all important decisions are made by High Representative Carlos Westendorp?
>
> Izetbegović: Bosnia looks like a man who has been crushed in a car accident, the fault of which is not his own. Because he is hardly mobile, he needs help from a third person, in this case the international community. But the patient is getting better, and this is evident in the last period. You mention the rehabilitation of West Germany after World War Two. I do not think that our rehabilitation can go faster. I am speaking according to memory, but there are at least three major differences between Bosnia and Germany, that is three comparative

advantages which Germany had. First, Germany did not have a national problem. She is a nationally united land. Second, Germany was a more developed country, with good engineers, economists, and a vast number of good repair persons and executives. Third, Germany had, in spite of its fascistic political organisation, a kind of capitalistic economy or that sort of consciousness. Here, socialism was in power for over 40 years. Now when we want to implement privatisation, we have not only to change the relations in the economy, but change the state of peoples' minds as well. Finally, the Bosnians are not Germans. We have some virtues that they do not have, and they have some that we do not possess: a high degree of discipline and diligence. We are more easy-going, I have to admit. I respect the Germans very much, but I am happy that I am Bosnian.

Voice of America: In Bosnia and Herzegovina, people usually live in closed ethnic communities. Can Bosnia and Herzegovina really become multi-ethnic and what have you and your party done in this regard?

Izetbegović: We are doing everything we can. We are recommending tolerance and the possibility of life together, we are educating people. In practical terms, we are supporting the return of refugees and persecuted people to their homes. The return of refugees, that is implementation of Annexe 7 of the Dayton Agreement, is the most powerful factor for correcting the damaged demographic picture of Bosnia and Herzegovina, but every return, to be permanent, has to be double sided. It is not like that right now. In the Federation, there are around 200,000 returned refugees, in Republika Srpska very few. The elections were held yesterday and I hope that after them, returns of refugees will reach a new impetus. But Bosnia will unfortunately never be multi-ethnic and mixed like it was for centuries, for genocide did its job too well.

Voice of America: Are religion and nationhood overly present in the SDA and other national parties?

Izetbegović: Religion and nationhood are present in the SDA, but in a moderate and positive sense. Our slogan is: love your own, respect others. The presence of faith is a reaction to 45 years of communism. You know that the goal of the aggression was annihilation of the Bosnian people. Biological endangerment always results with a gathering of the people.

Voice of America: Many claim that the international community, by helping opposition parties wants to tear down the SDS before all, then the HDZ, but the SDA as well. What is your comment?

Izetbegović: These three parties can in no way be put in the same basket. Whoever does that is making a huge mistake. In the war that happened in Bosnia, we were on different sides, different sides of the barricades, as they say. The SDS, and later the HDZ attacked Bosnia and we defended it. We maintained a level of democracy and freedom, I mean freedom of the press and political activity, as much as possible in a cruel war. Besides, the SDS and the HDZ are accused of war crimes, the SDA is not. Today, as well as before, we represent the idea of an integral and democratic Bosnia – the coalition of four parties that we initiated is entitled this – while there is a spirit of totalitarianism and separatism present among the SDS and HDZ. All of this is very obvious. If somebody doesn't want to see this, it is a mistake, and mistakes are most often paid for by those who make them.

Voice of America: We have discussed the present and future of Bosnia and Herzegovina. The immediate past can not be avoided. For the end, looking from this distance, tell us: if it was possible would you have changed anything in your own as well as the politics of the SDA during the war in Bosnia and Herzegovina?

Izetbegović: Maybe some details, but not in general. No strategic mistakes were made. Let me remind you: we tried to maintain Yugoslavia while it was possible. When Yugoslavia collapsed after Slovenia and Croatia left, we organised a Referendum of Independency and fought for our country to be recognised. When we were attacked, we organised the defense of Bosnia. We defended Bosnia and negotiated at the same time, seeking peace. As soon as a more-or-less fair peace was possible, we concluded peace etc. So, not even from this distance do I see that things could have been different, at least on our side. It seems that the parting was inevitable, but it did not have to be so bloody. The others are directly responsible for the second element.

Then came questions from the other side of the world. A significant Japanese daily paper based in Tokyo, *Asahi Shimbun*, applied for an interview (23 September 1998).

Asahi Shimbun: For how long will Bosnia need an international presence, especially military, like SFOR? Would you agree with the idea of reducing the number of SFOR soldiers beginning from next year? Also, talking about the role of the international community, especially after the Bonn Conference, the more active participation of Mr. Westendorp is noticed in solving some problems by his imposing decisions through the High Representative Authority. It is also known that Mr. Westendorp did not conceal his will and hope for 'alternative parties' to win in the elections. Can you give us your opinions about such international community points of view? Do you consider Mr. Westendorp's behaviour fair?

Izetbegović: First in Sintra, then in Bonn, I supported the extraordinary authorisations of Mr. Westendorp and I cannot be angry when he uses them. His cheering, I will use this sporty expression, for so-called alternative parties was not completely fair, but it also had no impact on the elections. Our people like foreigners, we are both nationally and religiously a very mixed society, but people do not like foreigners to tailor their justice. I think that the High Representative should be ideologically neutral and that implementing, or not implementing, the Dayton Peace Agreement should be the only criteria for him. It is the only productive thing for Bosnia.

On 22 November, in Zagreb, on the behalf of Bosnia and Herzegovina I signed the Contract on the use of Ploče Port with Croatia. Before this Prof. Ganić signed the Agreement on Special Relations between the Republic of Croatia and the Federation of Bosnia and Herzegovina.

I have to admit that the signing of each of these two agreements was not followed by the same emotions in my mind. It is not a secret that in Bosnia, and especially among the Bosniac public there existed a certain aloofness when it came to the Agreement on Special Relations with Croatia. Subsequently, some changes were brought into the initialised text of the agreement, so that it was acceptable in its corrected version. In a short speech after the agreement signing, I said:

> To those who would stay reserved towards this agreement, I would recommend they look to the future, that is, to include a factor called time into their judgement. Things do not stand in one place, they do not stay still, they move forward and in my perspective I see a democratic Bosnia and Herzegovina, a democratic Croatia and the two neighbouring countries

entering European integration. In this new situation, in this new historical context, this agreement also seems a lot different. Because, the same things in different circumstances are not the same anymore.

Tuđman, who signed both agreements on behalf of Croatia was obviously not thrilled by my speech. He invited us for lunch but was silent all the time and extremely cold though polite. I pretended not to notice.

The implementation of peace in Bosnia and Herzegovina continued to run late, in spite of the Conferences in Sintra (30 May 1997), Bonn (9-10 December 1997) and Luxembourg (9 June 1998). On 15 December 1998, a new conference about Bosnia and Herzegovina was scheduled in Madrid, this in an atmosphere of unhappiness and nervousness. I did not think that I should try to soothe the dissatisfaction expressed by the international community. On the contrary, I created a balance of duty fulfillment from previous conferences and found that 15 conclusions from Sintra, 32 conclusions from Bonn and even 35 from Luxembourg were only partially or not at all implemented, especially the ones that would have a positive impact on the internal integration of Bosnia and Herzegovina.

In my addresss in Madrid I stated the following:
1) that the obligation of exposing state symbols in some parts of the country was not respected at all,
2) that Yugoslavia still made conditions for establishing diplomatic relations with Bosnia and Herzegovina, in spite of the clear rulings of the Dayton Peace Agreement and those from Sintra, Bonn and Luxembourg,
3) that most of those accused of war crimes were still free and that local Republika Srpska authorities had done nothing to hand them over to the Hague Tribunal,
4) that police reconstruction in Republika Srpska was running late,
5) that negotiations on ex-Yugoslavian property succession were being obstructed,
6) that the Republika Srpska Constitution was still not in harmony with the Bosnia and Herzegovina Constitution on some points,
7) that the return of the minority population was inadequate everywhere, and its rate in Banja Luka small and meaningless,
8) that the results of municipality elections had not been completely

implemented (Srebrenica was not the only, but the most obvious example),

9) that payment circulation, judiciary and police force were not integrated in some Federation cantons,

10) that the Republic of Croatia keeps on directly financing the HVO, which disturbs the efforts to integrate a Federation Army etc.

In conclusion I said that although it was not the most important example of resistance to Bosnia and Herzegovina integration, it was still the most striking. Namely, the stubborn maintaining of special telephone codes in Republika Srpska and in some parts of the Bosnia and Herzegovina Federation and resistance to the unique 387 code for the entirety of Bosnia and Herzegovina. This despite the fact that this decision was repeated in the Bonn and Luxembourg Conferences.

I asked for six more points to be added to the prepared draft of the Declaration for the Madrid Conference. One of them (Point 2) demanded that the conference support the principle of the constituency of all peoples in Bosnia and Herzegovina, and the proposition in Point 4 said: 'We call upon the Arbiter for Brčko to hold on to legality and equity principles while making his decision, as explicitly stated in the Dayton Agreement; he should also define a solution for Brčko, which will be satisfactory not only for one but for all three nations and all citizens of Bosnia and Herzegovina.' This proposition openly suggested a solution for Brčko in the form of a district, out of both entities, within the Bosnia and Herzegovina State. One more declaration was passed, the Madrid Declaration, which led us into the year 1999.

Half-and-half results from conferences held thus far on the subject of Bosnia, the incomplete implementation of the Dayton Peace Agreement, the slow inner integration of Bosnia and Herzegovina and the dilemmas and speeches heard at the Madrid Conference caused justifiable anxiety in the Bosniac people's faith in Bosnia and Herzegovina. Extremists on both sides had obviously not been defeated and were patiently waiting for their moment.

It was the time to finally decide which way to go. How to keep foreigners in Bosnia and Herzegovina who were crucial, and yet not become a protectorate? In my opinion, two things were to be done: join Europe and maintain our national identity. Is it possible to do both, doesn't one exclude another? Still, this formula, pretty complicated though it is, seemed to be the only one.

Immediately upon my return from Madrid, I called for a session of the Main Board of the SDA, announcing a discussion about the condition and future of the Bosniac people at the threshold of this new century. I handed out a previously prepared paper, which I had drafted on the plane, on my way back to Sarajevo. The paper stated (18 December 1998):

> Dear brothers and sisters,
>
> Respected members of the Main Board,
>
> Today, in this gathering, I wish to open a debate of extreme importance for the future of Bosnia and the Bosniac people. My address will be short and its extent is not in equal proportion to the importance of the subject.
>
> I will begin with the just finished Conference in Madrid. It lasted two days, 15-16 December 1998 and ended with a Declaration and Annexe of 160 points in the whole. The most important ones are of course those about strengthening and maintaining the integrity of the Bosnian State and the return of refugees. The High Representative has kept his authorisations, which is not bad, a border police will be established, the convertible mark penetration will continue, the Ministerial Council will broaden, the role of a Permanent Military Committee will be a nucleus of the future integral and defensive structure of Bosnia and Herzegovina, there is an initiation for the establishment of a judicial institution at state level (at this moment we only have the Constitutional Court), a general election law will be made for the entire country; in short, the Bosnian State will strengthen. None of this has been an issue for us so far. The only question is how to implement it.
>
> However, although not explicitly stated, one message can be clearly seen in the 'spirit' of the Madrid Agreement and speeches made by numerous representatives of the international community. Such a Bosnia, considering all the circumstances, geographical and political first of all, should be included in European integration and turn into a citizen state, weakening any nationalist charge and with a domination of what we usually call Western civilisation.
>
> When it comes to this second matter, there obviously are some dilemmas within the Bosniac public and our party members. The time has come for us to decide what we want.

Do we want such development and such a country? Should we resist this or accept the flow? What should the party do and which way should we lead people?

This is the question I want to discuss with you today. We cannot avoid it, we are facing it every day in different forms. We should make a choice with all its consequences.

I propose that we hold a discussion on this tomorrow, and think about it in the meantime.

I will tell you my point of view: we should bravely move towards Europe, to ensure this umbrella over Bosnia's head, because all other alternatives carry a great amount of risk.

Our people are still endangered, biologically, which means spiritually as well. In order for one to be anything, one must exist. Peace in Bosnia is maintained, thanks to the presence of foreign troops. It is very uncertain what would happen (or will happen) should they leave. Will we be at war again? Will our children (or our grandchildren) live to experience suffering, rape, banishing? Our people have found themselves pressed between Serbia and Croatia. They did not choose this place nor do nations choose their neighbours. We found ourselves where we are, the only thing we can do is survive physically and spiritually.

We are not responsible for this uncertain unenviable situation. Our general geopolitical position is the way it is and, besides, in a Balkans that constantly rumbles. So far, we have not made one strategic mistake. Whenever we got to a historic crossroad, and we got there several times in the last ten years, we always managed to pick out the option with less evil in it. While Yugoslavia existed, we supported it. We tried to reconstruct it, which was absolutely legitimate. When it broke apart with Croatia and Slovenia stepping out, we announced independency because it was a better solution than an incomplete Yugoslavia (actually a Greater Serbia with Milošević and Karadžić at its head). When we were attacked, we chose resistance and managed to resist. When, 43 months later, we were offered a realistic peace, we accepted it as less bad than a continuation of war. In a dilemma between an integral Bosnia and Herzegovina (the way it is now) and a little Muslim country in a part of Bosnia, we chose the first. I do not think that we have made a mistake, no matter what the problems that follow this decision. A little Muslim country, considering its possible geopolitical position, would turn into a ghetto, and a ghetto is a worse choice than the state we are in now.

We are at a crossroads again and we have to decide where and how to proceed.

The difficulties we are currently facing have nothing to do with our ability to build a state. Our people would no worse than others know how to make a national country. But the circumstances have placed a different task ahead of us: to create a multinational state, which is incomparably more difficult. Such countries are very rare in the world. Almost all the difficulties we are facing today relate to the nature of this project, a multinational state. It is the most difficult, but also the most valuable part of the Dayton Peace Agreement for our people. It is an experiment to test the possibility of a common state for three nations, three religions and three cultures. The success of this experiment will have historical significance not only for us but for the whole world.

Some circumstances are on our side. I am talking about inevitable changes in our surroundings. Democratic forces will come to power in Croatia, and they will bring new politics towards Bosnia and Herzegovina. Serbia will get weaker for a long time, and it will turn to democracy in Europe after many mistakes and a long wandering. So, in the first decade of the next century, we have a weak Serbia in the east and a democratic Croatia in the west.

We will also have to question our priorities, constantly bearing in mind that our main opponent is not a Bosnia-oriented opposition but Serbian and Croatian extremists, or literally – Chetniks and Ustashas. We have to promote a clear Bosnian criteria in everything.

As we have emphasised many times before, our goal is not the party but the people. The party is just the means. It is good that the party is in power, and we will fight for it to stay that way, but the elementary security of the Bosniac people must not depend on the election results of the party in the future. It would be too risky, because political parties win but lose as well. The security of the country must be based on other, more constant factors.

This security I can only see in a Bosnia that has become a truly democratic country and also a member of European integration. In a civilised country there are no Bolsheviks, Chetniks or Ustashas, and therefore there is no risk for the physical survival of the Bosniac population. A safety of sorts would be established, as far as possible, because there is no absolute security in history.

Of course, such a choice carries its risks. They concern the preserving of national identity, in the full meaning of the word. We will save the body, but will we save the soul?

We will keep our identity if we deserve it. Freedom is a debt, a responsibility and a constant struggle which the weaker lose. We are not spiritually weaker and we should not lose this battle. Anyway, we daily face the challenges – good or bad – of a Euro-American civilisation and this is as useful as inevitable. Of course, we will have to learn hard and work hard. If we are to be defeated for neglect and laziness, it will be because we broke one of God's unchangeable laws: the law of work and struggle, and we will have no one to complain to.

Since this paper was marked 'confidential', some newspapers, whose possession it got into, instantly named it 'The Secret Paper of Alija Izetbegović' and some called it my political testament. I did not deny this.

As 1998 passed, the final arbitral decision for Brčko moved closer. Annexe 2 of the Dayton Peace Agreement obliged the international arbiter to hold onto the principle of legality and equity in making the decision. Would the arbiter go by these principles or would he succumb to political pressures and pragmatic views? Our reasons for worrying were plenty.

To be righteous and lawful, the arbitrage decision would have to give the city to the State of Bosnia and Herzegovina or its Federation. But then the entity called Republika Srpska would be territorially cut off, which would create unsolvable problems for the great-Serbian project. The Serbs could use their common weapons – issue threats of force and the destabilisation of this and the broader area. The Americans, who sent 20,000 of their soldiers to Bosnia, definitely would not allow a situation that would endanger the life of one single soldier. And yet the Serbs started intimidating both SFOR and us. The head of their state was a certain Poplašen, an extreme politician, who delivered disturbing statements about mobilising Serbs for actions SFOR would not wish to see. Besides, in a part of the municipality of Brčko, just next to the city, with the help of the High Saudi Committee for support to Bosnia, we repaired the damage and built over 1,000 new homes, hospitals, schools, mosques and returned some of our population. Serbian extremists found our thousand red roofs a provocation. In one word, this was an ideal opportunity for a Western politician to propose a status quo for the sake of 'peace at home'.

I decided to address one of our influential friends who could neutralise negative political pressures. I chose the King of Morocco, Hasan II. The King was as equally influential in the West as he was in the Muslim world, and a huge friend of Bosnia as well. I decided to visit the King immediately before the Madrid Conference for Peace Implementation that was scheduled for 15 December 1998.

Several of us were seated in a small Cesna with eight seats: Dr. Silajdžić, Dr. Trnka, Džemal Latić, an interpreter, bodyguard and myself. Professor Ganić did not come with us as he promised. As a joke, we said that he was afraid of airplanes, knowing that there was a grain of truth in this. When we found ourselves flying over the Alps, and when the Cesna started falling through vigorous wind whirls, we admitted to ourselves that Ganić had been cleverer than the rest of us. We felt relieved when we landed in Malaga for a short rest on a mild and blushing evening. It was not yet dark when we flew over Gibraltar. This was a unique chance for us to see this rock. Of course, we immediately started talking about the legendary Tarik and his crossing of Gibraltar, which was not only tight but – as it seemed to us from the plane – shallow, like a puddle spread between the deserts of Morocco and the rocky coast of Spain. After everything that had recently happened in Bosnia, one does not have to be a Muslim to remember the tragic fate of Spanish Muslims on this occasion. 'God, God, where did You sow us!' the poet Latić quoted a sentence from Skender's *Ponornica*.

King Hasan was in Marrakech, where the climate was better for his already ailing health. We were welcomed by Dr. Abdellatif Filali, who was once the Moroccan premier and then minister of foreign affairs, and as we later found out, a relative of the king.

The hotel we were staying at was agreeable, built in Berberian style, and located in a lush park. As soon as I walked in, I noticed large photographs of Winston Churchill hanging on the walls of my suite. Yes, this was the suite that Winston Churchill secretly stayed in for the first years of the Second World War and from where he planned military preparations against Hitler's armies in North Africa, which he describes in his memoirs. I had the honour of staying in the same suite as that great statesman had more than half a century earlier.

King Hasan waited for us in front of his residency, in a yard full of green, sun, water, pillows and pillars. He was short, like a Bosnian boy, but cheerful and classy. He almost whispered when he spoke. There were photographs of him hanging behind where he sat, in Moroccan traditional clothing, a long red fez and a white dress.

King Hasan was known as a very educated Arab sovereign. He knew Islamic law and the Qur'an, spoke several languages, spent time with teachers of religion and organised special sessions with them. He welcomed us in French, stating that he kept a careful track of what happened in Bosnia. 'What is the current situation and what can we do for you?' he asked me at the outset. I got straight to the point and told him the reason for our visit: justice for Brčko. He listened to me carefully, nodding his head. 'Mr. President,' he said after a short pause, '… just go on your way. I think that you are leading correct politics. Regarding your problem, in my opinion, Muslim countries should express an interest in the matter of Brčko and demand that the decision be legal, not political, which is in your interest.' I answered that this was all we asked for. That was our last meeting. King Hasan died in the summer of the following year.

So, we entered 1999 with the burden of worry about Brčko. It was announced that Arbiter Robert Owen would make the final decision that year and that this was to be expected by the end of February or the beginning of March.

On 21 January I was visited by the General Director of the Sarajevan daily newspaper *Avaz*, who had asked for an interview about Brčko. The following are some of the questions and answers that ensued:

> *Avaz*: Mr. President, the most actual and important question in Bosnia and Herzegovina is currently the Brčko problem. Is there a possibility that the arbiter, or more precisely the international community, or even America, will hand the town over to Republika Srpska?
>
> Izetbegović: I cannot say that such a possibility does not exist in theory, but it would be a tragic mistake.
>
> *Avaz*: I agree with you, but could you explain your answer a little better for our readers?

Izetbegović: Well, I think chaos would emerge. Nothing would be the same after such a decision? The Bosniac people would not only feel this as a betrayal of their vital interests, but also as a mocking of international law and justice. You know that such a solution was unacceptable in Dayton as well. There is a line, actually a level of injustice that can not be swallowed.

Avaz: What are our main arguments for the forthcoming arbitration?

Izetbegović: All, absolutely all, arguments are on our side and have been numbered in more instances already. The burden of proving is on the other side, because our right is obvious.

Avaz: But, their argument is the territorial whole of Republika Srpska?

Izetbegović: What do they need territorial integrity in a common state for? The Federation is not whole, either. Their argument reveals an intent for secession, because they would need territorial connection only in that case. This is another reason why Brčko should be conferred to the Federation. In that way, one injustice of Dayton would be corrected and at the same time this would deliver a strong message that nothing will become of the secession idea. Those who ask for Brčko for Republika Srpska, and those who support them, are practically going towards secession, and the breaking of Bosnia and Herzegovina and we are clear about that.

At the end of the conversation, Radončić asked me if I still intended to resign my position in the Presidency should Republika Srpska get Brčko. My answer was positive. 'And Mr. Silajdžić?' he asked. 'There is no doubt in my mind that he would do the same,' I replied.

The job of coordinating our efforts for Brčko was given to the State Commission for Brčko Arbitration with Dr. Ejup Ganić at its head. He was then a member of the Bosnia and Herzegovina Presidency, later Federation President. The Commission had the task of collecting documentation and preparing our arguments for arbitration and did this job very professionally and successfully.

The Tribunal for Brčko was put to work on 15 July 1996 when the President of the International Court of Justice named the Presiding Arbiter, American lawyer Robert Owen.

The first arbitration meeting was held in Rome from 11-16 January 1997. A so-called Temporary Arbitral Decision was made. It introduced an international bureau and supervision in the part of the municipality with the actual 'Serbian majority', but the matters of territory and city status remained unsolved. The decision was a reflection of *real politik* not justice and legal regulations. The Contact Group members' worry and fear of the possible need for military engagement in implementation of a just decision in Brčko had influenced Arbiter Owen. In spite of clear arguments for giving Brčko to the Federation of Bosnia and Herzegovina, he postponed the final decision to the last moment, which prolonged the factual situation of Republika Srpska running the city. Since the arbiter brought international supervision, relevant international circles (members of the Contact Group: namely, the USA, Germany, Great Britain, France, Russia and Italy) considered the decision fair. The supervisor was given significant authority in the area of local laws and regulations, policing, the return of refugees, elections, economic reconstruction, port revitalisation, establishing border crossings and custom services, etc.

Implementation of this Temporary Arbitral Decision began with the opening of the Supervisor's Office in Brčko in March 1997. American Robert Farrand was assigned as Supervisor. The State Commission for Brčko was transformed into the Federal Commission for Implementation of the Arbitral Decision for Brčko. It had the task of representing the Federation of Bosnia and Herzegovina in contacts with the Supervisor, to make concrete proposals and undertake activities for him, as also to implement the obligations placed on the Federation of Bosnia and Herzegovina that arose from his decisions. During 1997, the Supervisor gave out eleven orders and four supplements to orders for the establishing and functioning of a multiethnic assembly, police force, head offices and judicial institutions.

When a year later the second session of the Arbitrage Tribunal for Brčko was held (5-12 February 1998), our public tensely followed the session and every word that was spoken. Our legal representative, American lawyer Edward DeLaney, stated that the Serbian side had done nothing for the implementation of the Arbitral Decision made in Rome (January 1997) and that it was unable to do anything. He proposed that Brčko be given to the Federation or to conclude a compromise solution, which would mean putting Brčko under the authority of the central government of Bosnia and Herzegovina.

Arbiter Owen made a so-called Supplementary Arbitral Decision on 15 March 1998, which postponed the final decision for Brčko for another year. Although he used legal terms and repeated the words justice and equity a lot, Owen's explanation made it clear that the decision for Brčko had passed from the legal sphere into the sphere of political decision making and this in no way suited us.

After the Supplementary Decision was published, I answered a few questions for *Dnevni Avaz* (15 March 1998):

> *Avaz*: My first question is: are you surprised by the Arbitral Decision for Brčko?
>
> Izetbegović: Frankly, I am not surprised. When it comes to the world, or the international community, as you please, they stopped surprising me a long time ago.
>
> *Avaz*: Did our team, with Prof. Ganić as its head, do their job well?
>
> Izetbegović: Not well, but very well in my opinion. I saw the material and documentation they handed over to the court. It was all done very systematically and well. They brought almost all relevant witnesses, from the TKP Governor Dr. Jamakosmanović, to Bešlagić, Komšić, Orošolić, Dr. Hudolin, people from the Government and Brčko Municipality, almost all political parties, SGV, even the mayor of Osijek Cr. Kramarić. Officials from international organisations: SFOR, IPTF, UNHCR, etc. were heard on our proposal. Besides our experts, American lawyers were engaged, and at the end Prof. Ganić visited the United States, France and Germany. We made a whole line of political steps on our own. But, as they say, winking to the blind is in vain. This was clearly a political decision made by the great powers.
>
> *Avaz*: Our journalists, who were present in Vienna, are not praising our team in that manner. They say that they were pale compared to Dodik who drew incomparably more attention from the media and the like?
>
> Izetbegović: The last thing you said is true, but all of this does not have much to do with the Arbitral Decision. Neither did Dodik offer some serious arguments in the colloquium, nor did his arguments play a role. He threatened that Brčko must be a part of Republika Srpska, or he would resign, a threat he did not fulfill, nor did anyone expect him to. It is true that Dodik was noticed by the media, but the reason for this was completely different: finally, a normal Serbian politician had appeared on the political scene after seven years. People went to see this miracle as they would a rare occurrence in nature. Of course, there are many normal Serbs among the common

people, but they are very rare when it comes to politics. And when it comes to the press praising or criticising, it is something of a trend now, it's popular, and maybe profitable to attack the authority in Sarajevo and praise its opponents.

Avaz: You say that the decision is of a political nature. Could you be a little more precise?

Izetbegović: Well, the pre-election campaign has already begun. America and Europe want to strengthen Dodik. The decision for Brčko, the way it is, is a clear message for the Serbs to vote for Dodik, not the Pale regime. And for now we are paying the price of this.

Avaz: What do you mean by 'for now'?

Izetbegović: If you read the decision carefully, you will also find other interesting messages in it: Dodik must return Bosniacs and Croats to the town, establish a multinational police force and authority, clean Brčko of war criminals, establish a free economic zone together with the supervisor, and make it possible for state organs to open, the port, etc.

I said that he was unable to do this 'homework' for that would have to wait until the following year. Predicting this did not require much lucidity.

The third, and last arbitration for Brčko took place in Vienna 8-17 February 1999. Six international community witnesses were heard, 17 witnesses were proposed by Republika Srpska and 16 by the Federation. On 16 February I took the stand as the twelfth Federation witness. I expressed the following:

> Expressing respect for Arbiter Owen and his colleagues, I want to state the following: Brčko should belong to the Federation of Bosnia and Herzegovina. The reasons being:
>
> 1. In Dayton we definitely refused the solution according to which Brčko entered Republika Srpska. On 20 November 1995 I signed a document about leaving the peace negotiations and the return of our delegation to Bosnia just because of Brčko. That is when this arbitration was offered, followed by the signing of the general peace agreement. This fact is not contestable, and I think that you as well Mr. Owen are familiar with it since you participated in the Dayton Agreements.
>
> 2. The Annexe for Brčko (Annexe 2, Point V) explicitly says that the Arbiter will go by the principle of legality and equity

when making the decision. So, the Arbiter does not have a free hand to make the decision. He cannot go by pragmatic political reasoning, and overlook legal reasons. He is bound by two principles. His decision must be legal and righteous, or it will not be in harmony with the Dayton Agreement.

3. Brčko was a Bosniac-Croatian majority town before the war. The official Census of 1991 shows that Serbs and others were in a relation of 21% to 79% with non-Serbs in the advantage. The property proportion is alike. At the outset of the aggression (May-June 1992) ex-JNA and Serbian paramilitary formations performed genocide against the Bosniac and Croatian population of Brčko. One part was killed and most of them were banished. The situation now was made and maintained by force, not by law.

4. Due to stated facts, not one peace plan for Bosnia and Herzegovina, and there were many of them (the Cutileiro, Vance-Owen, Owen-Stoltenberg, the Contact Group of five great powers, etc.) said that Brčko should be given to the part of Bosnia under Serbian domination. On the contrary, all peace projects so far said that Brčko is to be returned to its true owners – the people of Brčko.

5. The behaviour of Serbian authorities both during the war and after it, in Brčko and generally in Republika Srpska, show that this authority cannot ensure a minimum of rights and justice for the non-Serbian population, actually the great majority of its pre-war population. There is much more justice, freedom and tolerance for minorities in the Federation. This is the current state of affairs and, according to general evaluation, this situation will be even worse in the future.

6. In case the Arbiter decides to ignore the above stated facts and makes an unjust decision, it will definitely trigger dissatisfaction among most of the Bosnia and Herzegovina population and stop the implementation of the Dayton Peace Agreement.

It is because of all that is stated here, as well as for other reasons, which our delegation has made clear during this and the two earlier sessions of this arbitration, I consider that your decision should be: 'Brčko belongs to the Federation.'

On 5 March, the Arbiter declared his final decision: Brčko would belong neither to the Federation of Bosnia and Herzegovina nor to

Republika Srpska. It would be a Special District within Bosnia and Herzegovina. The District would be run by a multi-ethnic government and would, until called off (no deadline was made), act under supervision of the international supervisor.

Our predictions that Dodik could not (or would not) fulfill the demands of the Supplementary Decision of 15 March 1998, proved to be true. In Points 6 and 7 of his final decision Arbiter Owen stated:

> 6. In the course of hearings in Vienna 1999 it was concluded that RS has not fulfilled the demands of the Supplementary Decision from March 15th 1998 regarding the demanded evidence. The presented evidence should demonstrate an active and trustworthy program of change and respect for the Dayton Agreement and previous arbitral decisions during 1998. In spite of RS Premier Milorad Dodik's good intentions, the Serbian political leadership that had direct local control over Brčko, and especially individuals connected to anti-Dayton oriented parties like the SDS and SRS, locally as well as at the entity level, tolerated and even supported a significant level of obstruction of the Dayton Agreement and Tribunal goals, especially about the aspirations to (a) encourage and make it possible for banished persons and refugees to return to their homes, (b) help the development of democratic multi-ethnic establishments and (c) cooperate with the international supervision regime.
>
> 7. The Tribunal has also found that the level of local obstructionism will not efficiently reduce as long as the anti-Dayton political elements, especially parties like the SDS and SRS led by the newly elected president of RS Nikola Poplašen, are allowed to keep the dominant role in the part of Brčko located within RS. Actually, if the pro-Dayton oriented structures could have implemented their programs in Brčko during the past year, the Tribunal's decision now to ask for a change of administration would probably not have been necessary, but the implacability of the SDS and SRS left no other choice for the Tribunal.

A few days after the proclamation of the final decision I answered a couple of questions for BH Press. One question related to Brčko:

> BH Press: The struggle of two sides for Brčko has finished, speaking sportingly, with a tie, which is not that bad for the

Bosnians. Some people say that you are the one with most credit for this.

Izetbegović: My reply might surprise you, but I frankly think that the merit belongs to Poplašen.[5] It is no secret that the international factors considered the possibility of leaving Brčko to the Serbs for a long time, not because this would be fair, but because it would be easier for them. With his reputation as a Šešelj's man and especially thanks to his behaviour in the past six months, Poplašen definitely convinced them that this was not possible. All our arguments about injustice from hell if Brčko was to remain under Serbian control gained weight exactly because of Poplašen and this finally took its toll. The other man with credit for this decision is Arbiter Owen, who had the courage to admit this fact. Poplašen was a strong argument for him as well. Owen wrote so in his decision. So, thanks to the two of them. We will talk about the credits of the rest of us on some other occasion.

Implementation of the final decision is moving slowly and with great difficulty. However, its most delicate part – district demilitarisation – was finished successfully and without incident. The last units of the Federation Army left the district area on 31 December 1999 and those of Republika Srpska on 6 March 2000. The Rubicon was crossed.

The most important ruling of the Dayton Agreement, the return of refugees, was implemented slowly. The returns were not only slow but unequal, especially to towns under Serbian and Croatian control. Since Ante Jelavić, the Croatian member in the Bosnia and Herzegovina Presidency verbally supported the returns, I decided to test practically the sincerity of these words.

During the middle of February 1999, I started the initiative for the return of 1,000 families of Bosniac and Croatian refugees to Mostar and Sarajevo. As usual, Jelavić said 'no problem'. In the session of the Bosnia and Herzegovina Presidency held on Tuesday, 23 February, the initiative was accepted, but also supplemented, so it would include Serbs and returns primarily to the towns of Banja Luka, Mostar and Sarajevo.

Two days later, the Bosnia and Herzegovina Presidency organised a dinner in honour of the General Secretary of NATO Javijer Solana and Commander of the NATO forces for Europe, General Wesley Clark, who were visiting Bosnia and Herzegovina at the time. High Represen-

[5] The removed president of Republika Srpska.

tative Westendorp and SFOR Commander for Bosnia and Herzegovina General Meigs were also present. These were the most important people if you wanted to do something for the return of refugees.

Over dinner, General Clark raised the issue of returns and the presidential initiative. He said that they (he meant the foreigners present) were ready for political, military and financial support of the action. The word 'military' in this sense referred to the safety of those to return. Returns to Sarajevo, Mostar and Banja Luka were the major destinations of those returning and the toughest as well as most important places. Activity in the three cities should be exemplary and present a step forward. The specificity was also that detailed plans for returning would be made (I named them 'phone books') containing the names of those to return, their current address, the address they wanted to go back to, the state of the object they should return to, where the current resident should be moved (if the property were temporarily occupied), etc. Lists would be coordinated and exchanged. Coordinators would be appointed and they would solve the problems that would inevitably emerge, together with local authorities and representatives of the international community.

After all that had happened, I was not at all optimistic. I was worried because demagogic slogans immediately appeared: we want no numbers, we want 'everyone on their own property'. Or: we want a general plan of returns to Bosnia and Herzegovina made. Such a plan, of course, would never be made and that sort of proposal usually comes from people known to do everything so that everyone can stay where they are, most often on somebody else's property. 'Everyone on their own property' is a nice slogan, but in some cases it becomes an alibi for nothing to be done.

Returning people to their homes, for those who work on it, is a difficult job. Usually, with right or not, someone is living in the house or flat of those to return, a refugee, soldier or a person in authority occupies it. The first two, refugee and soldier, have moral rights that no one can ignore, you have to find them another adequate home, and officials usually have strong connections and struggle with all their power. They all usually have wives and children.

During the entire 1999 the talks about returning 'everyone to their own property' continued, especially to the three large cities. A lot was said, little was done. The returns to west Mostar and Banja Luka were so little as to be negligible. According to data by UNHCR, the UN Agency for Refugees, 2,683 minority families returned to Sarajevo canton, 98 to the west part of Mostar municipality, and 133 to the area of Banja Luka municipality. The process of ethnic cleansing in the period 1992-95 was fast, and the process opposite to this – returning people to their homes – very slow.

On Saturday, 28 February 1999 the statement about the union of the two parties who had the social-democratic attribute in their titles was published: the SDP in Sarajevo and the Party of Social-Democrats in Tuzla. The uniting of the social-democrats was supported by foreigners with all their might both publicly and secretly. In my regular weekly address to *Avaz* from Sarajevo, I answered a question by one reader about how unification could affect Bosnia and Herzegovina (4 March 1999):

> My reply is: there can be good effect, no effect at all, or bad effect, and this explicitly depends on their will and how much they will do in Republika Srpska and the part of the Federation that we usually say is under the control of the HDZ. What I will say to you is my sincere opinion: if they become a relevant political power there, if they get a significant number of voters from the Serbian corpus in Republika Srpska and the Croatian part where the HDZ is dominant now, then it will create a whole new quantity in the political life of Bosnia and Herzegovina. This is about them 'crossing the Rubicon'… If they do not do this, if they remain on this side of the 'river', then it is all 'boil the water, cool the water', or worse: a transparent attempt to take away authority from the Bosniac people under the veil of social-democracy. Because in that case everything comes down to the question: will the Bosniac people (I emphasise – the Bosniac people, because that is what this is all about) be lead by Alija, Heris, Edhem, Safa tomorrow, or will it be Zlatko, Tokić, Ljubiša and Karlo, or actually some other Alija and Zlatko and his comrades in the far future. The price of this course will definitely be some sort of oblivion for the national emancipation of the Bosniac people. Nevertheless, if they succeed in the Serbian and Croatian corpus, which I sincerely wish for them, because of Bosnia, we should support them, and when it comes to oblivion, we will make sure that there isn't any.

In the Municipality Elections in April of 2000, the united Social-Democrats enjoyed significant success among the Bosniac people and complete failure among the Croats and Serbs. The SDA lost many municipalities that had been under its control for the previous ten years, and the Serbian and Croatian national parties, the SDS and HDZ, strengthened their positions.

Since nothing of importance could be accomplished among the Serbs and Croats, the opposition and its media directed their attention and attacks towards the Bosniac corpus and the SDA. In their propaganda, the SDA was co-guilty for the war and everything that the war had brought. Nobody mentioned anymore the Eighth Assembly of the Serbian Communist Union (September 1987) in which the decomposition of Yugoslavia really began, and the word aggression was carefully avoided. Some of the most important historical facts were forgotten or unsaid because they did not fit into the scheme of the struggle for authority. Therefore, I decided to use the following Independence Day as a means to go against this attempt to confuse and bring about oblivion.

ADDRESS AT THE RECEPTION FOR INDEPENDENCE DAY

Sarajevo, Presidential building of Bosnia and Herzegovina,
1 March 1999.

Honourable ladies and gentlemen, dear friends,

I asked you to join us to celebrate our great holiday – the Independence Day of Bosnia and Herzegovina. Before I say a couple of words about the magnificence of this day for the citizens of Bosnia and Herzegovina, let me greet the present. Special regards to the high representatives of religious communities, I see present Reis Dr. Ceric, Bishop Mr. Sudar, Vladika Nikolaj, Mr. Finci from the Jewish community, our honourable Franciscans with Fray Petar as their head, etc. I also want to welcome our friends from the world, representatives of friendly countries' embassies, representatives of OHR, SFOR, UNHCR, OSCE, as well as governmental and non-governmental organisations which are here on missions of peace, members of the Council of Ministers and the Government of the Federation, high cantonal officials, representatives of political parties and all of you that share the joy of this day.

This humble ceremony is in memory of a referendum that took place on this day seven years ago, when almost two-thirds of the citizens of the then Socialistic Republic of Bosnia and Herzegovina voted for the independence of the country.

The motto of the referendum was: 'For an integral, independent and sovereign Bosnia and Herzegovina'. That motto remained the guiding principle of forces that defended the independence of the country and it remained as a motto through an extremely hard period, until today.

The government of the then already incomplete Yugoslavia, the then existing Army and paramilitary units of the SDS, decided to ignore the will of the people and rejected this decision.

On 6 April 1993, countries of the European Union recognised the independence of Bosnia and Herzegovina, and on 23 May, the United Nations accepted the Republic of Bosnia and Herzegovina into membership of the United Nations. The government of the incomplete Yugoslavia, its Army and paramilitary units of the SDS again ignored this unanimous decision of the world and chose not to accept it.

Instead, they began an aggressive war against the youngest member of the United Nations.

The war, which took place, was long and merciless and resulted in a huge number of human victims and the unseen destruction of villages and towns, factories and historical and cultural monuments.

We call this war, with every right, aggression because it was led against an internationally recognised state and because it aimed to obstruct by force the will of the majority of Bosnia and Herzegovina's citizens.

We righteously considered ourselves legal and legitimate defenders of Bosnia and Herzegovina, because, in those critical days, we acted in accordance to the will of this citizen majority and in harmony with the rules of international law.

So much about the past, which we go back to on these occasions just as much as we have to.

As the first step towards the future many talk about 'truth and reconciliation'. Truth and reconciliation YES, but justice also. Some people are forgetting this justice intentionally or unintentionally. This is why we are going to strongly support the work of the Hague Tribunal, no matter who is in question, and why we are not going to accept the oblivion of war crimes.

A war in which such a high price was paid ended a little over three years ago with the peace agreement in Dayton. A new inner organisation of the Bosnian State was established. According to many, it is not functioning because Dayton's solutions were not good. There is some truth in this, but this is not the whole truth. The Dayton Agreement would have been good if it was consistently implemented. The war was stopped, but it has continued by other means. This new kind of war is called obstruction, and it is, unfortunately, at work in lots of sensible places in the Federation and the State.

The only solution for this is our determination and the world's determination to consistently and completely implement what has been agreed and signed in Dayton. This determination is missing, or there is not enough of it. I admit that in everyone there is more of it in words, than in deeds. Accomplishing the decisions of the Madrid Conference is a good test. However, there are signs of hesitation and tiredness. I wish that in future this situation would change. In my name and in the names of all those I represent, today and here, I wish to confirm our readiness to invest new efforts in strengthening the peace and security of the country, bringing back the refugees, building up a free market economy, fighting corruption and organised crime and transforming the judiciary, in short building an integral, democratic, prosperous Bosnia and Herzegovina, a country which will act in the interests of all citizens, regardless of their religion, nation or political beliefs. This effort of ours will be more successful if a just solution for Brčko can be found, if the constitutionality of all three nations on the territory of Bosnia and Herzegovina is recognised and if political and material support to Bosnia and Herzegovina, as a multinational country consisting of two entities, three nations and, I hope equal citizens, continues.

With these thoughts and wishes I thank you for being present at this humble celebration and, of course, once again I congratulate you on this historic day of ours. Thank you!

Never peace in the Balkans! This time the Belgrade regime decided to make a 'final solution' to the Kosovo issue. Day after day, the ethnic cleansing of Albanians in Kosovo escalated. It swept away everything in front of it with an iron broomstick. Over a million men, women and children left their homes and headed for Macedonia, Albania and Montenegro. About 20,000 came to Bosnia, and several thousands went to Western countries. As a response, on 23 March NATO began an air campaign against targets in Yugoslavia. News about the mass murder of Albanian civilians poured in, but also about the hesitation of Western allies about the continuation of the air campaign. On 7 April, I sent the following message to the Organisation of Islamic Conference that was holding a meeting in Geneva at that time:

> Expressing my sincere respect and gratitude for the today present representatives of member countries of the Organisation of Islamic Conference (OIC), especially members of the Contact Group, I wish to ask members of the OIC for emergency help to the people of Kosovo, who are going through a very difficult time.
>
> First, I suggest that the OIC supports the ongoing action of NATO forces without hesitation. Almost a million Albanians have been banished from their homes. Misfortune is turning into one of the largest human catastrophes after the Second World War. This unseen banishing of a civilian population can be punished or not, and more important, it can be with a hope for their return, or without it. If NATO action is stopped, the crime will remain unpunished, and banished people will never return to their villages and cities.
>
> Second, I ask members of the OIC to offer, without hesitation, any kind of help to refugees from Kosovo, especially with tents, clothing and medication, and, to establish a committee for coordinating help for this purpose. I thank Saudi Arabia and Turkey who have already delivered the right example.
>
> Third, I also ask you to send words of courage and solidarity with the Bosniac national minority in Sandžak through a document which is to be made by this high committee.
>
> Expressing wishes for the successful work of today's meeting of the OIC, I send you brotherly *salaam* and express my deepest respect.

Unanimity obviously didn't exist in the Presidency of Bosnia and Herzegovina regarding the issue of NATO action. On two occasions, the Serbian member of the Presidency of Bosnia and Herzegovina wanted to put forward the question of using Bosnia and Herzegovina's air space for air attacks on Yugoslavia on the daily schedule. I asked him if he had evidence about Bosnia and Herzegovina's air space being used for these purposes. He answered that he didn't have evidence and that he had asked the IFOR commander, General Meigs the same question. I then said that I wasn't ready to discuss presumptions, and that NATO had the right to patrol the Bosnia and Herzegovinian sky according to the Resolution of the UN about the so-called no-flight zone (forbidden flight zone), which had been effective since 1993. Proof for the necessity of this was the recent taking down of two Yugoslavian MIGs that had penetrated Bosnian air space near Tuzla.

The bombing of Serbia was halted on 10 June, after Milošević accepted the withdrawal of the Yugoslavian Army from Kosovo.

Considering the chaotic conditions in the Balkans, it was pretty clear that only the admission of Bosnia and Herzegovina into European integration circles could ensure its long-term security. On 27 April 1999, our delegation travelled to Strasbourg for a meeting of the Council of Europe. Bosnia and Herzegovina had for the three years prior to this tried to become a member country of this body which was some kind of a lobby for entering the Partnership for Peace and later the European Union. A European policy for Bosnia was my definite choice in spite of all temptations otherwise, which I explained in my address that journalists called 'Secret' (December 1998). We went to Strasbourg to convince them to speed up this process. My speech was given in front of a full hall of Council members.

I have to admit that my speech was too optimistic. It looked like a picture without shadows. It matched the occasion. I could not go to Europe and ask them to accept us, in front of 600 delegates from 19 countries, not counting journalists and a public audience in the large gallery, and then tell them that conditions were bad. Others would take care of that. There are a lot of enemies and a lot of completely indifferent people (the latter I find more repulsive), who talk about problems in Bosnia and Herzegovina. My job was to improve the picture a little and to show some hope and a way out in which I could truly believe. It seems as though I partly achieved that. At the Committee of Ministers meeting (over a 100 officials were present), three members of the Presidency gave introductory addresses and then answered questions. The representatives from Slovenia, Italy and Cyprus addressed me. Their questions concerned the return of refugees (conditions and chances), human rights in Bosnia and Herzegovina (considering the unsatisfactory report about this) and the influence of NATO air strikes on conditions in Bosnia and Herzegovina. I answered that there were several prerequisites for the successful return of refugees (security, accommodation, jobs, school teaching programmes), but there were two main ones: the regulation of a multi-ethnic police force, a job which was only half done, and the equality of all citizens in all parts of Bosnia and Herzegovina. As regards the second, I said that we had started a procedure in front of the Constitutional Court of Bosnia and Herzegovina (our request for the constituency of all three nations in all parts of Bosnia and Herzegovina). I explained that nobody would come back (nor were they likely to do so) if they would be second-class citizens. This situation reflected on the issues of accommodation, jobs and education. On the issue of human rights, angry about the report, I requested that the Council of Europe reporters make specified reports and check the information and data they put in them. I said that the condition of human rights in Bosnia and Herzegovina was very different, and that it varied from town to town, being in one like in Austria and in another like in Enver Hodža's Albania, and that any general judgements could not be given. General reports, that are made now, help only the hiding of brutal violators of human rights within that 'average rate'. It is impossible to 'mix' data about human rights in Sarajevo and in Foča and to derive some average from it. But that's what was going on. Specific situations in Sarajevo, Tuzla, Zenica, Banja Luka, Bihać, Bijeljina, Višegrad, etc. must be described. I think that members of the Committee understand me well. My answer to the third question was that there were obvious differences in judgement about the necessity of NATO's action, but there was an absolute consensus between all three members of the Presidency and for sure among the majority of Bosnia and Herzegovina citizens, to leave our country out of war. All of us, of course, had different reasons for our stands, but the conclusion was the same and that was good.

We held separate talks with the General Secretary of the Council of Europe, Daniel Tarschys, and the President of the Parliamentary Assembly of the Council of Europe, Lord Johnston, a great friend of Bosnia. The bitterest discussion, however, took place during the meeting with reporters of the Council of Europe about human rights in Bosnia and Herzegovina. I found a number of mistakes in their reports, especially concerning Sarajevo. Where they got this information (disinformation) from I do not know, but the reporters stated that the population was leaving the city, due to the bad state of human rights, ('more people have left the city, than entered it' – they said). I said this was just a lie and asked them if they knew the following: in Sarajevo, which has been a majority Muslim city since its foundation, there was a large Catholic centre with a secondary school, a gymnasia and a medical school, there were two Catholic universities and the largest Croatian cultural association 'Napredak' was active; that the Croatian political parties there were freely functioning; that over 60,000 Serbs and Croats were then living in Sarajevo; that BH television was not an SDA media (I suggested they ask for information about editors and journalists of TV B&H); that our delegation in the Council of Europe was not an SDA delegation because only one of its five members was from the SDA (Bičakčić), of the remaining four there were two Serbs and one Croat, etc. I think they heard this for the first time. And, yet they consider themselves reporters on conditions in Bosnia and Herzegovina. I finished with this statement: if things everywhere were like in Sarajevo, Bosnia and Herzegovina would have been accepted by the Council of Europe immediately after the Dayton Agreement, but the way things are, who knows how long we will have to wait for that. I suggested that they try to answer this precisely.

At the end of the day in a Committee of Ministers meeting, Živko Radišić, the Serbian member of the Presidency made a speech and talked of nothing but Bosnia and Herzegovina. I was left just to say 'amen'. In a previous meeting of the Military Committee, after a similar speech, I said this out loud. The General Secretary of NATO, Javijer Solana and NATO Commander for Europe General Clark, who were present in the meeting, laughed heartily to my 'amen'. This time, I did not say 'amen' (I just thought it to myself), but I had a short briefing afterwards in which I said that I agreed with Mr. Radišić completely and that I would sign every word he had just said.

After the meeting, the Italian representative came up to me and said: 'I think that you are very close to your aim, do something important and positive as soon as possible, help us so we can help you.' That was how this very dynamic and exhausting day ended.

In May, Dr. Haris Silajdžić initiated the idea of changing the Dayton Agreement. This idea provoked great interest amongst the public. In an instance, the camps *pro et contra* were created. Those against often alleged that the initiative was illegal, that it meant the destruction of the Dayton Agreement and other such nonsense. The truth is opposite. The idea contained a legal basis in the contract. In its most important part – Annexe 4, that is the Constitution of Bosnia and Herzegovina – a mechanism for changes and corrections was implanted. The Constitution of Bosnia and Herzegovina can be changed by decisions of the

Bosnia and Herzegovina Parliament and I believe that this is going to happen in the future.

The request is legal, but is it realistic? A two-thirds majority in the House of Representatives and consensus in the House of Peoples are necessary in order to change the Constitution. With existing relations between the various political forces, I think that this is completely unrealistic. That is why, at this moment, the only productive use of energy is the realisation of some very important practical questions for Bosnia and Herzegovina, such as the implementation of the Madrid Conference decisions, especially those concerning the return of refugees, a border police and transformation of the Council of Ministers. Next, we have to see to concluding the contract about dual citizenship, property questions and a market regime with Croatia, for the realisation of promised donations from the Third and Fourth Donation Conferences, for our citizens outside Bosnia and Herzegovina to have their passports on time, in a word for some more temporal and more realistic things. In this moment the best way to 'revise' the Dayton Peace Agreement is to implement its better sides as much as possible. Opening other, for now completely hopeless questions, is good for those who change the hard work of realising possible things for useless arguing about the impossible. A good example of this is the meeting between the Prime Minister of Republika Srpska, Milorad Dodik and Gelbard on the 9 June. Instead of talking about the 70,000 Bosniac and Croatian refugees that he had promised to return to Republika Srpska, Dodik craftily turned the discussion into a polemic about the Silajdžić idea. Dodik scored two points: he presented himself as a defender of the Dayton Agreement and Serbian interests and avoided the question of the refugees' return. Why wouldn't he do this, when he had the opportunity?

Summer in Bosnia started stormily. First, the High Representative Deputy Jacques Klein published an article on corruption in Bosnia and Herzegovina, saying that it was rooted in the culture of this country and giving some, in my opinion impossible, numbers about corruption in Tuzla canton. Then, the Minister of Internal Affairs in Sarajevo canton complained about the inefficiency of public prosecutors and judges regarding the issue of persecuting criminals. By the end of it all, Dr. Silajdžić was left to question the legitimacy of Republika Srpska because it did not work on implementing the Dayton Peace Agreement.

Aspects of the atmosphere can be seen from the interview I gave during these days (24 June 1999) to Sarajevo *Avaz*:

Avaz: There were some polemics in our magazine between Mr. Klein and yourself about the corruption in Bosnia and Herzegovina. Then the American Ambassador Kauzlarich, and before him Mr. Sklar talked about the same matter. Your reactions were, if I can say, unexpected, because you were always talking about the Americans as our biggest allies.

Izetbegović: I didn't say Americans, I said the United States of America. America is an ally and friend of ours and I strongly believe in this. I don't know about the Americans. There are people who like us and those who don't, but the majority does neither, they do their jobs and don't care about what is going on in the world far away from them.

Avaz: However, the stinginess in your responses was a bit unexpected. Especially those to Mr. Sklar: 'Get off our necks.' And now there is your response to Mr. Klein. Some people think that you lost your temper and that this could be a disadvantage for relations between Bosnia and Herzegovina and the USA?

Izetbegović: Speaking of Mr. Sklar, the whole sentence was: 'Tell us what you know, or get off our necks,' and that is very different. I did not lose my temper. Actually the opposite, my words were conceived and, if I may say, I said them on purpose.

Avaz: Why?

Izetbegović: There are lots of reasons for that. The first one is to make them more specific, and the second because 'I don't have any nuts in my pocket,' so I can afford this luxury. I live in a two-room apartment, which is the property of the Presidency of Bosnia and Herzegovina, without servants or any luxury. I don't possess anything but elementary things. My children also have no property. They have apartments, humble furniture and cars, but this is what half the citizens in Sarajevo have. In the Izetbegović family, including my children, there are lots of educated and competent people. However, none of them are ministers, or mayors, or ambassadors. All this gives me the right to call everyone and everything their true name.

Avaz: However, there is a rumour that your son, Bakir, is a very powerful man in Sarajevo.

Izetbegović: It is not a rumour, it is what one local magazine writes, all the time, from issue to issue. It's their favourite subject. The Sarajevan people know that this is not true. Bakir is not a powerful man but Bakir is his own man, and everybody who is on their own, is powerful in a way. He says and does what he wants and some people don't like that.

Avaz: Yes, but this is not without consequences. There are some implications that foreigners take these stories for the truth.

Izetbegović: Yes, some foreigners, I know that, but what can you do? It would be better for them to check things. To believe in lies also damages those who believe in them.

Avaz: This subject of corruption is dangerously shaking the SDA, some say also destroying it. Have you ever heard of such statements and what is your reaction to them?

Izetbegović: Let me remind you: we (the SDA) started this subject. This argument can only make the party stronger. Silence and swamping is the worst thing out. Only frogs hatch in the swamp. Everything that is happening implies that the party is alive, and it is a strong organism fighting against a dangerous attack of illness. We are going to walk out of all this cleaner and stronger.

Avaz: Do the foreigners, I mean those from the European Community, help with this or not?

Izetbegović: If they only talk about corruption in general, they don't help. If they show us concrete cases and give us information, they do help, but this happens rarely. The story according to which corruption is rooted in the culture of our people and that hundreds of millions of marks are disappearing from public funds, is a lie and helps to fight the authority, not the corruption.

Avaz: Our next subject is very close to the last one. It is about criminals, the police and the law, which started with the public speaking out of Minister Ismet Dahić. Dahić complained about the inefficiencies of public prosecutors and the courts. What do you think about this?

Izetbegović: I share Dahić's opinion. In the last two years I have spoken about this twice. At the beginning of last year I said that prosecuting offices and courts are the most inefficient institutions of the system and, if you remember, got a very repulsive response from the court associations. I told Prof.

Ganić that we are not going to win the battle against crime with these people in prosecuting offices and I suggested to him some radical changes. Decisions are within his jurisdiction as President of the Federation. I don't know why, but he didn't listen to me. Two or three nights ago I listened to the statements of prosecutors and judges on TV B&H as a response to Dahić's remarks and I didn't hear any real answers. As people used to say: he talks of one thing and they of another. The man has filed about 70 entries against 14 people and he wants to know what happened. They comment on 10 or 15 cases, and then talk about other things. I don't question the size of somebody's guilt but this obviously isn't the way to do it. I will suggest that the Canton Parliament asks the public prosecutors and judges to come to the Parliament and answer Parliament representatives' questions. Let us hope that they won't say this is an attack against their independence.

Avaz: NATO's action led to an epochal change in the Balkans. Is your strategic formula: a weak Serbia in the east and a democratic Croatia in the west, still valid?

Izetbegović: The first part of the formula will probably change. This means that a democratic, and even stronger, Serbia on the east is desirable. The only question is when? If there is, and as long as there is dictatorship there, a weak Serbia is better. Bosnia and Herzegovina will be happy and safe if it starts living in a democratic, and this means powerful and politically stable region. I believe that time is coming.

The campaign about corruption reached its climax on 17 August when the American journalist Chris Hedges published an article about corruption in Bosnia and Herzegovina in *The New York Times*. He alleged, among other things, that a billion dollars from public funds and help sent by Western countries had been embezzled in the last two years in Bosnia and Herzegovina. Three days after the first article, *The New York Times* published a correction: about 20 million dollars of foreign aid had disappeared, and the rest was domestic money. This was not true either, but it was the rectification of American papers.

The article caused a shockwave in Bosnia and the world, especially America. Before this Hedges had been in Bosnia for ten days, contacting opposition journalists and he picked up 'friendly' information from them. He accepted all they said to him. Later, it was discovered that some foreigners were a part of all this. Allegedly, they did not give out any specific information, but followed Hedges' doubts with acclaim. Somebody said: 'they nodded'. Hedges called upon a 4,000 page OHR report about corruption.

Considering that Hedges called upon the High Representative Office as a source of his article, the same day this article was published I sent an open letter to the High Representative headed 'I ask for truth and publicity, Mr. High Representative'. The letter read:

> Citizens of Bosnia and Herzegovina, and especially my people, must know:
>
> An article has been published by the journalist Chris Hedges entitled 'Leaders in Bosnia stole a billion dollars' in today's issue of *The New York Times*. Among the rest, this article states the following:
>
> – that a billion American dollars was missing or stolen from public funds,
>
> – that the anti-corruption group of the High Representative's Office is investigating 220 cases of abuse and corruption and that it made a 4,000 page report on this, which is hidden from the public,
>
> – that Bosnia reached the end of the war with two million refugees and that two million of them are wandering all over the world,
>
> – that in Tuzla, a Muslim city, as the author of the article had tagged it, 200 million dollars disappeared from this year's budget, and 300 million dollars over the last two years,
>
> – that Tuzla's schools were painted four times from Government resources, although they were already reconstructed and painted from international help,
>
> – that there is a story saying that Bakir Izetbegović, son of President Izetbegović, was controlling the City Development Institute which has 80,000 apartments in city property and that many of these apartments that were the property of Serbs and Croats, were given to members of the ruling SDA, but others can also have an apartment if they pay Izetbegović 2,000 dollars. Bakir Izetbegović is – the article states – the owner of 15% of Air Bosnia, a state air company and he gets a share of money that city gangsters take from shop owners, etc.
>
> I claim that all of these are lies and I claim that they were devised to backbite the Bosnian government and to prevent

friendly countries from fulfilling military and financial engagements in Bosnia and Herzegovina.

Fortunately, some lies are obvious. The entire budget of Tuzla Canton for the years 1997 and 1998 as well as the first half-year of 1999 was, in total, 612 million KM. According to the article's author, there were 500 million dollars missing, in other words 900 million KM, which is, almost 50% more than all the Canton budget put together.

As for the 80,000 public apartments in Sarajevo that the article writer mentions (the number is incorrect, there are 69,000), these are not under the administration of the City Development Institute, and have never been, but are rather the property of hundreds of state companies and institutions and this fact is known to everyone. The City Development Institute has nothing to do with these apartments, it is an organisation for the revival and reconstruction of the city and it is occupied with the revitalisation of destroyed and damaged buildings.

These two facts illustrate just how familiar with the facts the writer of this article is as well as his sources.

I want to say that it is impossible to continue working in this way. Secret reports cannot be made, which are secret just to make it possible to bring out lies and nonsense without responsibility. This is why I ask OHR to clearly answer:

– are the allegations of the article based on reports of OHR officials,

– are these reports true and correct, and if they are, to publish them completely,

– will the officials of OHR answer how, if this data turns out to be incorrect and untrue.

The purpose of this article was to backbite what Chris Hedges calls the Bosnian Government. We were not killers, we did not pilot genocide, they cannot, unfortunately for them, impute this to us, but they can present us as thieves through fake and secret reports. And they do this, with all the instruments at their disposal.

And the moment for publishing the article was well chosen. The former High Representative, Mr. Westendorp, has just left and he cannot react. The new High Representative, Mr. Petritsch has just come and he cannot react either. In the meantime the lie can freely spread and do damage to Bosnia throughout the world just like the war which it went through.

Introducing our public with this, I expect it to ask the High Representative for the whole truth.

Somebody made a big mistake at Bosnia's expense here. Whoever it is – must answer for it.

I sent a letter to the American State Secretary, Mrs. Albright, as well, appealing to her to use her influence for the so-called 'Secret Report', if something like that existed, to be published completely. Almost immediately after this, the High Representative's Office reacted by stating that such a report did not exist.

Some of the media recognised in *The New York Times* a political attempt against me. One *Avaz* reader asked me directly (*Dnevni Avaz*, September 1999):

Avaz reader: Mr. President, some people think that the article in *The New York Times* is a political attempt against you personally and that the American Government is behind this.

Izetbegović: As you know, there was a correction of this article, published by *The New York Times* itself, which is a very rare case with this paper. Denials by OHR and some of our institutions followed, and I asked for the publishing of the so-called 'Secret Report', the existence of which everybody is now denying. I also requested an international inquiry about the allegations of *The New York Times*. There is no answer. They are silent. This silence tells more than a denial. I believe that this case will stimulate everybody and everyone, even the representatives of the international community, to take stories from our 'yellow pages' and various gossips with reserve in the future, that is to check them before turning them into 'discoveries' and reports.

You are mentioning a political attempt against me. I could agree with this, that is how I feel about the article, but I do not agree that the American Government is behind it. The American political leadership has no interest in calling the Bosnian project, in which America invested so much, a failure, a mistake, and that is exactly what this article has called it. Maybe some American circles were behind it. After all, Chris Hedges himself mentioned some Americans from OHR. And, as you know, OHR denied any connection with any of this. Who knows? Anyway, the political effort happened, I was hurt by it, if it was a difficult wound, I do not know, but I have survived. That's all for now.

The New York Times article inflicted huge moral and material damage on Bosnia and Herzegovina. I asked for an international inquiry in the letters I sent to a number of heads of states. Around the middle of September, the American Administration named Robert Frowick, a good expert in Bosnian issues, as Chief of the Anti-corruption Team, and the Federal Government engaged an American law company, McDermott, Will and Emery (MWE), to inspect the reliability of accusations published in *The New York Times* in the name of Bosnia and Herzegovina.

The international team of legal experts led by Paul Williams gave the first 'preliminary finding' at the end of October. Paul Williams stated for the media: 'We did not find anything true in *The New York Times* text. Those who gave the information to journalist Hedges regretted it.'

In the meantime, the High Representative Office spokesman, Alexandra Stiegelmayer, stated that the Office did not give out any information to Chris Hedges, and much later, when the storm had somewhat calmed itself, in an interview for *Oslobođenje* (8 May 2000), she said: 'For sure, the most unsuccessful cooperation was with Chris Hedges and *The New York Times* when they made the story about corruption. That journalist worked sloppily, made mistakes in hundreds of things, and the story had enormous repercussions. This was the biggest scandal.'

The Final Report of 53 pages (with more than 200 pages of Annexes) was submitted by the international legal team of experts on 10 February 2000. At the beginning of this report, there is a statement that American, Canadian and British Governments, the UN and High Representative Office publicly denied that aid funds were stolen and that the report of High Representative Office mentioned in Chris Hedges' story does not exist.

The main findings were compressed into the first two points of the Report. The first point stated: 'Text in *The New York Times* has oversights in the basics because it concentrated on the exaggeration of corruption concerning international aid. The Commission found little evidence for his most important allegations even in the "corrected" form.' The second point was more important, it proved that the problem exists: 'Corruption is a serious problem in the Federation. As it was noted, it consists of the

Federation's, cantons' and municipality districts' incorrect use of funds and breaking of federal laws, especially the ones related to taxes, customs, public bills and supplies.'

The story about corruption will be greatly exploited in the pre-election campaign that is to take place in April 2000. The painful thing was that the story about corruption – although not by a long shot close to what *The New York Times* wrote – was true. The bitter taste of knowledge that it is present in Bosnia, remained.

The second half of 1999 started with the signing of the Stability Pact for Southeastern Europe, which was initiated by the new chief of German diplomacy, Joschka Fischer. A Pact Summit was held in Sarajevo on 29 July and, at the time, it brought back a feeling of confidence and hope. All leaders that had some importance in the world were present, starting with the American and French presidents, Clinton and Chirac; British Prime Minister Blair and German Chancellor Schroeder, to the Turkish President Demirel. In my closing words just before the end of the Summit I mentioned one great European man whom I always admired and whose spirit was, I felt, present in the hall: the late president of France, Charles de Gaulle. I said:

> A duty referred to me is to be the last speaker in this important meeting, before the presiding Ahtisari makes the balance of today's meeting in which over 30 and maybe even 40 speakers participated.
>
> My duty is, in the name of Bosnia and Herzegovina, the host of today's Summit, to thank you for being here, to wish you a pleasant return to your countries and, of course, to express hope for the fastest possible realisation of this important meeting's decisions. We all know that this is a process, which will take some time, but I think we must act without delay.
>
> Expressing those wishes, I must notice that today we have the realisation of the vision of the great French president Charles de Gaulle about a 'Europe from the Atlantic to the Urals' in front of us. Unfortunately, south-east Europe stayed out of this historical process for a long time. The Stability Pact Summit, which is just ending in Sarajevo, is correcting this mistake. Hence, what late president de Gaulle predicted is happening. But things he maybe didn't predict are happening as well. I can think of one important fact in this respect, that the United States will participate heartily in this great project as well.

After Dayton

By November of that year, nearly four years had passed since the signing of the Dayton Peace Agreement. The Sarajevo daily newspaper *Dnevni Avaz* asked me to give my opinion on this, as they put it, historic event. I answered:

> Lots of events are not historic even though people call them that. Dayton is. It didn't just bring the peace, which is very important itself. Dayton ended the dying and further crippling of our people and Bosnia. There was an unbearable amount of dying and wounding, especially of civilians, for such a little nation as ours. Besides, the peace at least saved even the idea of a whole and democratic Bosnia. Prolonging the war daily sent this perspective further and further away. And considering the results of a four-year-old peace, they are as follows: all bridges and roads are repaired, and almost all schools and hospitals. The PTT network has been reconstructed, as well as the electricity supply, and power stations. Today, we have more pupils and students than before the war, hospitals and post offices have better equipment, we have electricity for export. We have a unique currency, which is stable too. More than a million refugees and displaced persons have been brought back. Sarajevo was a dying city in November four years ago. You can see how it is now. It's true that we have difficulties with the functioning of state institutions, but that wasn't at all unexpected. Essentially, it is about the technology of making laws and decisions. The opposition is pointing at discord in parliament. Well, all real parliaments in the world have discord and they are supposed to be in discord. In communist time we had unanimous parliaments, but they were not parliaments at all. Besides, Bosnia isn't a country like Austria, Hungary, Holland or Italy. These countries are mostly mono-national with some national minorities. All the decisions there are made by majority votes. Bosnia is a country of three nations, three religions, and even three cultures. To make any important decision, consensus is necessary, which is a rare case in the world. Difficulties mostly come from the nature of the project which is very specific and called Bosnia. For instance, we were supposed to make a draft of a law about the border service yesterday in the Presidency – you will read about it in today's papers – and we didn't. When it comes to something like this, all our differences, which aren't primarily party or ideological differences but are just in the foundations of Bosnia itself, come out. The ar-

rangement of relations is an issue of long evolution, but things are going forward and will come in to place. We need less destructive attacks and more friendly critics, time and passionate work.

At the end of November 1999, Richard Holbrooke suggested that the Presidency of Bosnia and Herzegovina visit New York for the UN Security Council Conference. The real reason for the trip to New York was the Presidency Session, in order to accept the New York Declaration with Holbrooke's mediation, and the real objective of this declaration was to found the State border service in Bosnia and Herzegovina. Holbrooke masterfully played this part. What seemed impossible just a month earlier, was solved: after four hours of argument the decision on the border service was reached.

Almost at the same time, High Representative Petritsch changed 22 officials in Bosnia and Herzegovina and in neighbouring Croatia fever grew before the upcoming general elections. I answered the question about changing officials at a meeting in New York and about the Croatian elections in the regular weekly column in *Avaz* (2 December 1999). The questions and answers went like this:

> *Avaz*: Mr. President, Petritsch and Barry's decision to change 22 officials caused different reactions among the public. Can you give your comment on this move by the international community representatives, especially when it comes to Bosnian representatives in government?
>
> Izetbegović: The decision has good and bad sides. There are, however, more good ones. The hard liners, who obstruct the returns to Republika Srpska and west Mostar were removed. The change of Bosnian staff I see as a price for that. Bosnia obviously could not do without its famous 'key'. You know what happened in communist times: they arrested a Chetnik or an Ustasha, and then they added a Muslim priest, not for his guilt but for 'peace at home'. So everyone is equally happy and unhappy. Can we, for example, compare the mayors of Goražde and the so-called Serb Goražde, Hrelja and Topalović? The first one wants to bring Bosniacs to Kopači and to receive Serbs in Goražde, and the second one doesn't want to do anything. And then the 'internationals' put them in the same basket with a sign 'they obstructed return'. Or they take down a man in Sarajevo, impute he's dishonest, provide no

proof of that, and then talk about human rights. They want us to trust their word. They place a sign of equality between the mayor of Banja Luka, who publicly forbids the building of the destroyed Mosque Ferhadija and the governor of USK where all sacral objects were open even during the war. The international community obviously doesn't have the courage to act according to the truth, rather they do things the easy way for them. And it's easier to give everybody equal blame. But this is not a long term solution for problems. Only truth and courage move things forward. However, the decision is one thing, we can't split it, it must be accepted as a whole or rejected. I don't think we have a choice.

Avaz: The New York Declaration once again affirmed the territorial integrity and sovereignty of Bosnia and Herzegovina through its most important decisions. However, some government representatives in Republika Srpska denied the whole essence of the declaration just upon the returns. What essential moves for the implementation of the Dayton Agreement will, in your opinion, the decisions signed in New York make?

Izetbegović: The New York Declaration is a very important act. I know these post-return hesitations. But thanks to these 'internationals', that we are sometimes angry with, the declaration will be implemented, point by point. The first point, the most important one, is partly finished. The Presidency, shortly after its return from New York, ratified the project of the Border Services Law. The Law is to be confirmed by the Bosnia and Herzegovina Parliament. It is the most important law after Dayton, the most important from the aspect of the integrity and stabilisation of Bosnia and Herzegovina State. I expect some difficulties in the Parliament, but still I think that the Law will be accepted. Unique passports are going to be introduced too, I have no doubt of that. True, the introduction will go step by step. So, existing passports will be in use until their term expires or they will exist in parallel with the new ones. It is important to have the possibility of having a unique passport.

Avaz: Neighbouring Croatia is for parliamentary elections. Already there is a rumour about the post-Tuđman era in this country. You were often accenting a democratic Croatia as a predisposition for a better future in Bosnia and Herzegovina. Will something change if the HDZ loses its power in elections in Croatia?

Izetbegović: Yes, for sure something will change, but we don't know by how much. Personally, I think that there will be a significant change. We expect the government in Zagreb to send Bosnian Croats to solve their problems in Sarajevo instead of in Zagreb. That is the most important change. If we take into consideration the changes in Serbia too, the complete situation in our region is changing to Bosnian benefit. Finally, behind us remains an extremely difficult decade and before us the new incoming one, which with God's help, will be a better one.

Events were running their course. The opposition, as elections were approaching, exploited the issue of corruption maximally, in an abstract way, and with expected exaggeration; production had grown from a modest 10% (modest considering its low base), the unemployment rate had reduced a little, the Brčko District was being established slowly, things with Croatia were falling into place and waiting for better days, there still as yet was not a ratification of the Ploče Contract, nor a contract about commercial relations. Dodik played his game: be good with foreigners, be eloquent, make promises but do not let Bosniac and Croat refugees return (since the end of 1999 only 2% of them have returned, and it will take 50 years for them to return at this rate), etc.

In such an atmosphere we approached the municipality elections. They took place in April 2000. Behind us there were the ten most difficult years in the history of Bosnia and Herzegovina, a time when the country boiled and looked like a volcano. But, a lot had been done. Bosnia had been defended in the war and an army created, all schools were reconstructed in peace time, as well as all hospitals, electrical and power stations, destroyed PTT traffic had been revived and most of the bridges and roads were repaired. That was one side of the medal. The other one was much darker: the economy was recovering very slowly, and many people were unemployed. A strong fall in the SDA's rating was predicted and proved to be true. In the April Elections, the SDA lost many municipalities where it ruled. I was sad but not surprised. I recalled one interview from more than three years earlier. After my second victory in the elections of September 1996, Sarajevo *Večernje Novine* Editor, Jasmina Šabić, asked me whether I was happy about my victory (interview, 3 January 1997). I said:

Let me tell you right away, I am not. Now I recall one smart, or better to say, cynical tale about love. It is said that every love story has a tragic end: they either get married or break up. Political struggle is like this: you lose or you win, it's not a happy end in any case. A mother whose son disappeared in the Srebrenica tragedy asks you to find him, a refugee in Germany asks you to return him to his home in Bijeljina or Dubica, an unemployed soldier asks you to find him a job, a factory director to find him money for the start of production, etc. And in Bosnia there are thousands of missing persons, unemployed people, hundreds of villages and cities were demolished. Who can fulfill all these expectations, all completely reasonable from certain points of view? Disappointments are inevitable.

And disappointments came. An unseen media campaign started against the SDA. This campaign called the SDA nationalistic and, what was political impudence and historical falsification, put it in the same basket as the two nationalistic parties, the Serbian SDS and Croatian HDZ, whose assault the SDA had to defend Bosnia from and succeed in that defence. Foreigners openly joined this campaign as well.

Equalising the SDA with those two nationalistic parties made some people angry and the naïve sad. In any case, it was negative for our rating with the people. Ex-communists, who had changed their name to social democrats, were speaking about Yugoslavia with nostalgia. Not without reason; they had omnipotent power and privileges then. To younger generations they started to show Tito through idyllic glasses: peace, construction and concord in contrast with a condition of war, conflict and stagnation in today's democracy. They left out the dark sides of the Yugoslavian system and the causes of its end. When confronted with real evidence, they admitted there was no freedom, but it was safe. Opinion was created that the communists offered security without freedom, and we offered freedom without security, again this aboriginal dilemma wherein the devil tempts Jesus in the desert.

I have already said that there was one thing I both hated and wanted at the same time: foreign troops in Bosnia. Foreigners help you at the outset but, as the days pass by, they become bosses. Strange things indeed happened in this respect. On Friday, 3 March 2000, I delivered a speech at a pre-election SDA meeting in a Sarajevo municipality. The meeting was held in the Great Hall of Skenderija Complex in Sarajevo before

7,000 supporters of the SDA mostly from Centar municipality. Three days later on local television and in the newspapers, the High Representative for Bosnia and Herzegovina, the Austrian Wolfgang Petritsch and the Head of the OSCE, American Robert Barry, both qualified that my speech had been 'extraordinarily provocative'. They claimed that the speech 'harms the perspectives of living together and reconciliation in Bosnia and Herzegovina', because of its mentioning Chetniks and Ustashas, etc. Here, then is that 'provocative' speech so that readers can judge for themselves:

> Dear brothers and sisters,
>
> First of all, I'll ask you to sit down. My old mates from jail criticise me; it's like making a cult of Alija Izetbegović, though it's not my fault. So I want to ask you not to rise for me.
>
> These days I receive many letters from different sides. There are questions about pensions, privatisation, certificates, the opposition, foreigners, etc. But two questions are exceptional for their importance. The first is about the past, the second about the future of Bosnia. I choose, therefore, to answer these two questions at today's meeting.
>
> The first question read (I will quote as I remember): was it possible to avoid the war and killings during 1992-1995? At least, it went something like that. Here is my answer: before Slovenia and Croatia left Yugoslavia war could have been avoided. Thereafter, nothing could be done.
>
> After Slovenia and Croatia left Yugoslavia, Bosnia and we, the Bosniac people together with our country, found ourselves at a crossroads: one way led to an incomplete Yugoslavia, which meant a state federation with Serbia and Montenegro, ruled by the Milošević-Karadžić duo; the other led to independence. There was no third option. War and dying, could not be avoided because we were weaker and the aggressor would not negotiate. We could choose to be slaves, and could have become the Kurds of Europe. This did not happen, thanks to the resistance that the SDA organised. It is true that our party was not the only one which resisted, and its members were not the only ones who fought, but it was the organiser of the resistance and the leading power that permanently led the fight for the political and spiritual survival of Bosnia and the Bosniac people over the last ten years. Do not let them steal that truth from you. Thanks to this, we can gather here today

and talk freely. Thanks to this, our political opponents can also gather freely and talk. Milošević's and Tuđman's projects were defeated. We came out as the moral and historical winners of the fight against these projects.

The second question I want to answer at this meeting concerns the future of Bosnia. What do we want to achieve in Bosnia and what are we hoping for?

Our objective is a whole and democratic Bosnia and Herzegovina. If this is our aim – and it is – our main enemies are not the opposition parties, they are just our political opponents, and that is something else. Our main enemies are the Chetniks and Ustashas. They are the ones who rose their hand against innocent people, they are against the State of Bosnia and Herzegovina and everything that it stands for, so they are against the border service, the functioning of state institutions, a unique passport, etc. They want to freeze the situation with three armies in Bosnia, they are against including Bosnia and Herzegovina in Europe and the world, they are against the returning of everyone to their own property, hoping to forever maintain the condition created by war and by ethnic cleansing, etc.

And as far as the opposition is concerned, I'm talking about those parties that do not throw away the Bosnian State, they only see things a little bit different, and we compete with them. It is like an important football game for us, in which we cheer heartily because we believe we are better and we deserve victory. We ask you to look at things and today's meeting this way. We can talk like this because we are strong. Because we look at things in such a way we will win.

We need peace in Bosnia for our children and our grandchildren, of course, peace and freedom for each and every person who wants the good of this country, no matter what their nation, religious or political beliefs.

That is why I ask you in the end to confirm our destination with an applause: for every man who wishes the good of this country, for living together, for freedom, forgiving and reconciliation wherever it is possible, and finally, for a strong Bosniac people in a strong Bosnia. Thank you and cheers!

That was the speech that foreigners called 'provocative'. I replied to their criticisms on the same day, saying that the reaction of foreigners was a request for oblivion. 'We can talk about forgiving and reconciliation, but not oblivion,' I said:

> Of course, there is still the question of why Petritsch and Barry reacted in this way. I believe the following explains it: when genocide occurred between 1992-1993 and the death camps emerged in Bosnia and Herzegovina, most European politicians closed their eyes in face of the facts. Instead of using force, or even words, they shamefully remained in silence. Today, they do not like to recall this infamous episode. They experience problems even when mentioning it and those who took part in it. They would like it to be forgotten. Perhaps they can forget, but we must not and we cannot, because a forgotten genocide repeats itself.
>
> A foreign power in a country is a great evil. The only comfort we have is the fact that Bosnia did not have a choice and that there were bigger evils than these facing it – not least the Chetniks and Ustashas.

However, here I should stop and make one remark: High Representative Wolfgang Petritsch pushed the Bosnian state project forward with true devotion, in the way he understood Bosnia and that project. His good will is beyond doubt. Are his moves also? I certainly respected his intentions, but not all of his decisions.

My first public misunderstandings with the High Representative occurred soon thereafter, in the matter of the eviction of Bosniac refugees. When the Bosniacs were banished from their homes in Podrinje during the war, most of them came to Sarajevo, Tuzla and other local places, settling in houses and apartments that the Serbs had left. The Dayton Agreement ordered the returning of 'all to their own', but that process was slow and partial. To the parts of Bosnia which had been under our control, the Serbs were returning ten times faster (or they had their homes and apartments returned) than the Bosniacs were returning to the part called Republika Srpska.

Some of our people, under foreign influence, eagerly practiced the laws for returning property, sometimes even ignoring elementary justice. At the beginning of September 1999, a refugee Dugalija Sulejman was evicted from a Serbian house together with his wife and two children. I protested against this practice which overstepped the mark. My statement (7 December 1999) read as follows:

> Today I discovered that a refugee Dugalija Sulejman together with his wife and two children were evicted from the apartment he temporarily occupied. He was evicted by court order, which was signed by Judge Karahodžić Indira. Dugalija Sulejman was banished from Pale in 1992. On 7 December, nine months ago, he filed an application to enable his return to the house, which is his own property. That was not made possible for him.
>
> Concerning this matter I state the following: the eviction of a refugee who is expelled from his own home and who can not return there, is absolutely unacceptable. Nobody can order something like this because it is the opposite, not only to elementary rules of justice, but also to the words and spirit of the Dayton Agreement. The Dayton Agreement did not order the eviction of refugees but rather their return to their homes. To make the situation worse, the earlier tenant Prelić Vlastimir did not ask for the apartment so he could come back, but in order to sell it. The emptied apartment is now used by Odabašić Jasmin from Sarajevo. The court was familiar with this fact.
>
> As a member of the Presidency of Bosnia and Herzegovina, chosen by the people in free elections, I ask everyone to refuse bringing and carrying out orders for the eviction of refugees who are not enabled to return to their own homes, because these orders are immoral and illegal. Those who do not have enough civic courage to do their job in accordance with their conscience should resign their functions.

A part of the media was on my side. The oppposition press, however, accused me of advocating 'abstract justice' against the law. Some wrote that unjust law had to be respected as well, others embroiled themselves in academic arguments about the relations of justice and law. An OHR official went one step further and said that I had urged people to break the law, etc.

All foreigners led by the High Representative Wolfgang Petritsch condemned my stand, saying that laws about property are 'complete and without reservation'. 'One person's right to return to their property does not depend on the other person doing the same. These two matters cannot be connected,' the High Representative's statement said. In effect, however, this 'unconditionalising' led to the above mentioned disproportionate returns of people to some parts of Bosnia and practically meant the continuation of ethnic cleansing.

My health varied from day to day; although, in general, I enjoyed pretty good luck when it came to health matters. I was ill on only three occasions in my life. The last time it had been a heart attack in 1996. But the years have passed since then, and I was still only half-way through my four year mandate. Could I endure another 30 months?

Before the elections in September 1998, I seriously thought about not running. I was in doubt. On 18 May 1998, I wrote a letter that I addressed 'To my friends' and sent it to about 30 addresses. In it, I announced my withdrawal from the position of Presidency member. My reasons being age, health, and tiredness. It would not be fair of me to occupy a function if I were unable to fulfill all the demands thereof.

Most of my closest associates decisively rejected any idea of my withdrawal before the elections. I myself was in a dilemma as well. I decided to ask the SDA member base about this. During May and early June 1998 consultations were held in all local organisations of the SDA in which the members were to answer a number of questions concerning the forthcoming elections. One of the questions was: 'Do you think that President Izetbegović should (should not) run for member of the Bosnia and Herzegovina Presidency in the upcoming elections?' This was a three-answer multiple choice question: 'He should not be a candidate', 'It would be good if he was a candidate' and 'It would be necessary for him to be a candidate'. Ten municipality organisations checked the answer to number one, six to number two, and thirty-five to number three.

The issue was also revised in the assembly of the Main Committee of the SDA, held on 11 June 1998. I asked for secret voting and said that I would accept the decision of the Main Committee. When the voting tickets were counted, it turned out that out of 76 members, 58 thought that I should run for election. 18 members thought the opposite. Thereafter, I ran for the elections and won 80% of the Bosniac votes.

I continued my work in the new mandate and thought about retiring over and over again. In August of 2000, I turned 75 and it was my tenth year of office in the highest organ of the state. I had experienced two huge wars, one in my youth, the other as an old man, and two long periods of imprisonment in between. Wasn't this enough for one lifetime?

Although in less than five years of peace huge successes had been made in the consolidation and reconstruction of the country, the consequences of a bloody and destructive war were still present, especially in the economy. The opposition press kept silent about our successes, and emphasised only our mistakes and shortcomings. It embroiled itself in an unseen campaign that stopped at nothing. In politics, wolfish laws rule: there is no mercy, no truth, only a goal.

Finally, on Friday, 2 June 2000, while returning from *Džuma* prayer, I made my decision. I invited Senad Hadžifejzović to my office, the then main Editor of Radio Television B&H and asked him to schedule an appointment on air for me such that I could make an important statement. He set up the interview on Tuesday, 6 June. That day I showed up at the main news offices at 7:30 pm and read the following statement:

> Dear citizens of Bosnia and Herzegovina,
>
> I wish to inform you about my decision to retire from the Presidency at the expiration of my mandate as the President of the Presidency of Bosnia and Herzegovina, on 12 October this year.
>
> In the meantime, legal rules can be made about replacement of a Presidency member whose function is running out. Such regulations currently do not exist.
>
> There are several reasons for my retiring but the main ones are my age (I am to turn 75 in August) and my health. The function of Presidency member in these conditions demands a physical and nerve condition that I no longer have.
>
> I thank all of those who supported me during the past ten difficult years of our history.
>
> I wish for the Bosnian patriots' dream of an integral, democratic, prosperous Bosnia and Herzegovina to come true.

After this statement, Hadžifejzović asked me two questions. To his question about what I considered my greatest success, I replied that it was the independence of Bosnia and Herzegovina. 'During 1991-1992 there was a real danger of Bosnia becoming a province of a Greater Serbia. I prevented this and I consider it my biggest merit.' The second question followed naturally by itself: 'And what about your greatest failure?' 'The slow process of establishing an integral, democratic and prosperous Bosnia and Herzegovina in peace,' I replied.

Foreigners received the news of my resignation with pleasure and disbelief. They considered it to be a pre-election bluff and asked about my true intentions. In the middle of July during one conversation that took place in my office, Robert Barry, Head of OSCE for Bosnia and Herzegovina, directly asked me whether I was really retiring or not, and if yes, then why. I told him that I was afraid I would die a president and I do not like lifetime presidents. He laughed. Knowing Barry, I bet that he would not have believed my explanation at all.

But my decision to retire was sincere and final. On 24 July, I sent a letter to the Bosnia and Herzegovina Presidency in which I formally confirmed my intent to withdraw from my function. This is when the arguments about the law on the filling of the empty position in the Presidency of Bosnia and Herzegovina started. Foreigners wanted 'their' man in the Presidency, the Parliament wanted theirs. The Parliament voted in a law, but the foreigners changed it.

There was also an assumption that I wanted my son Bakir to be my successor, which was a plain lie. That story had been alive for almost four years. In August 1999, a journalist from TV OBN directly asked me who would succeed me and how much truth there was in the rumour about Bakir. I answered:

> Who will succeed me? It is not mine to decide. And regarding my son Bakir, he is, like any very capable man, also an independent man. What he will do with his own head is always his decision. You have to believe me that this is so. He is my best unofficial advisor, but I can say that we are talking more about philosophy than about politics. When I was arrested in 1983 and sentenced to 14 years for something I wrote, Bakir was 26. Back then, like all young people, he lived carelessly, played the guitar very well and had a wide circle of friends. Then, he suddenly had to become earnest. For six years he fought for my life and freedom. He had one foot in prison himself because of this. By the end of 1986 one man from the UDBA visited me in prison and told me to restrain Bakir, or they would arrest him. Bakir would not be intimidated. He travelled, met with the Serbian and Croatian opposition, got people abroad interested in my case, Helsinki Watch, Amnesty International, Pen-clubs. When I came out and formed the party, he became actively involved. He worked in a number of important programmes in war time. If you think that he listens to me, you are wrong. Like me, he usually does what he wants. He is not an active participant in politics, although he is a member of the SDA Sarajevo Canton Committee. I do not get the impression that he will change something while I

am alive, and after that he will decide for himself what he wants to do and where he will go (OBN, 12 August 1999).

Nevertheless, the process in Bosnia, albeit slowly, moved in the right direction. There were less and less of those who still hoped for Bosnia's secession. From a geopolitical and historical context, the realistic perspective of Bosnia's inclusion in European integration discouraged Serbian and Croatian separatists and radicals. In their statements you would more frequently hear the formerly prohibited words – Bosnia and Herzegovina. Freedom of movement was for the most part established, the Constitutional Court made a decision about the equality of all nations in the Bosnia and Herzegovina territory, the newly established border service gradually took control over border crossings, a unique monetary currency and unique passports were created and talks about a unique army began. In the summer of 2000, Bosnia and Herzegovina had 50 diplomatic representations open in the world (embassies, missions, consulates) and it was gradually becoming a real state. There were times when, in spite of everything, I felt happy because my vision of Bosnia was going ahead.

To tell the truth, a lot of this would not have been achieved without the help of foreigners and that was the reason for our schizophrenic situation. 'God forbid there are none of them, woe is us that there are them,' a prominent Sarajevan intellectual described this situation wittily. We felt as though we were crucified between their goals, which we supported in general, and their methods, that were unacceptable. A large amount of foreign aid assigned to Bosnia was spent on their high salaries and expenses during their stay in Bosnia. And, more importantly, they started to act as if they were Bosnia's protectors. Gradually, they established their own authority that was not responsible to anyone. This increasingly reminded me of the communists. They interfered directly in the work of parliament, the judiciary, the administration, and the media as well. Because we felt weak, instead of our pride a certain serving mentality developed, and there were more and more journalists who wrote on order and less and less who wrote according to their own conscience. No government can resist the temptation of dictatorship, if it is not controlled with efficient instruments. And the foreigners' authority was under no one's control in Bosnia. Anonymous, sometimes completely incompetent people in different services of the Office of the High Representative, the OSCE and certain UN organisations, made inadequately studied, unexplained, sometimes totally wrong, but always irrevocable decisions. They came here to stay for a certain period, usually for two years, often with no elementary knowledge of the country they were coming to, or, even worse, with prejudice towards the Bosnian culture and its people. Most of them got their idea of Bosnia from Andrić's novels that are popular in Europe and with his picture of Bosnia, where, I quote: 'Those belonging to three religions hate each other, from birth to death, irrationally and deeply, passing this hate on to life after death… They are born, die and grow up in this hate…etc.'[6] along with Andrić's well-known aversion towards Muslims. It was difficult to break this wall of prejudice.

What we needed was not tutorship, but a partnership of the world with Bosnia. Foreign authority was necessary as long as there was no confidence between the three nations in Bosnia and Herzegovina. This authority should be in proportion with the degree of distrust. It would or should end when confidence was rebuilt. So, it is clear what should be done for the foreign protectorate over Bosnia to end: we should work on the reconciliation of the three nations in Bosnia. This is the highest task for all responsible and wise people in this country.

On 15 October I left the presidency building in which I had spent almost ten years of my life, the normal ones, the tough ones and the terrible ones. I do not like farewells, but I felt no sorrow.

Before this, in short intervals, I received warm letters from President Clinton, President Demirel, Prime Minister Blair and many others, important or less important men and women who were in one or another way involved in the Bosnian drama over the last decade of the 20th century. Farewell parties were organised with my colleagues of many years standing. At one of them there were almost all the members of the then opposition. I made a short speech and shook hands with hundreds of people, who, more or less sincerely, wished me the best in life.

Everything proceeded as if it were a mere duty, as if it did not concern me. Even now, I do not know if I felt anything. Still, there was one exception. On 11 October, a meeting with pupils and students was organised. The Great Hall of Army House and the hallways were full of young boys and girls. I had not prepared a speech for the occasion. Instead, I told them that I had come to bid them farewell and my voice shivered.

I do not know if everything is a coincidence or whether happenings have an invisible connection that cannot be reached. Close by, only the

[6] Ivo Andrić, *Gospodica*.

street separated us, stood, just like half a century earlier, the building of the First Male High School in which I had spent eight years of my childhood and early youth. There were then two more high schools in the street, Normal and Commercial Schools, and down the street, just across the small wooden bridge was the Ladies' School. As I spoke at that day's meeting, pictures of a world from more than 50 years ago followed one another in the mists of my memories: young and cheerful faces like those today in the Hall of Army House. Strict professors and a lunch break at half past ten. Running through dusky corridors, in the light of the street crowded by boys and girls, and ice-cream salesmen shouting and praising their products. A little shop selling buns with sour cream. First sights and first loves, fierce discussions about justice and injustice, and talk of building a new, better world, as exciting as vain. For a moment there I returned to my youth, the early youth, when all nice illusions were gathered together. Then life came and, like a strong wind, blew them away, one by one.

What we call happiness is sometimes the accordance between our life and circumstances, our biography and history, our personal aspirations and historical currents. If I look at things that way, I can say: I was born too early to be happy. But birth is one of the many things we do not get to choose. It is a part of our destiny.

If I were offered life again, I would refuse it. But, if I had to be born again, I would choose my life.

Contents

Appendices

Appendix 1
General Divjak's letter

Appendix 2
From a conversation with Sidran

Appendix 3
Lecture to the German Association for Foreign Affairs,
Bonn, 17 March 1995

Appendix 4
Talks at the French Institute for International Relations,
Paris, 30 August 1995

Appendix 5
Two interviews for the Sarajevo weekly *Dani*
11 December 1994
March 1998

Appendix 6
Lecture at the ISESCO meeting,
Riyadh, 6 December 1997

Appendix 7
Some more important opinions and statements

Appendix 1

General Divjak's Letter

Divjak Jovan Deputy for NŠVK OS RB&H
02/688-1
Sarajevo, May 27th 1993

Resignation to the Deputy function in
NŠ VK SO   VK OS RB&H
                                             Alija Izetbegović

I am forwarding you the written resignation to the Deputy function in NŠ VK OS RB&H
  Reasons:
  1. In May I handed you my resignation because there were numerous violent criminal acts against the citizens of Sarajevo. On this occasion, Topalsvic Mušana-Cace's gang severely wounded my son Želimir. Upon your request to think this over and consider what it would mean to the interests of Bosnia and Herzegovina, I thought that you seriously meant that you needed me as the third member of the constitutive nation in the Territorial Defence of Bosnia and Herzegovina Headquarters. Only for this reason, the reason of my confidence in your sincere intentions, did I withdraw my resignation.
  2. The course of events in the following period showed that I often represented only 'decoration', as certain members of the VK OS Headquarters would say. In 13 months of war I was never treated as the Deputy, but rather as 'the third one'. Proof is the fact that I was never included in operations, battle and fight planning and the organisation of the Bosnia and Herzegovina Army. For instance, I know nothing about Operations 'Jug-92' or 'Envelope-92', because I was treated as an 'untrustworthy' person. There were certain statements to the effect that I was in direct contact with Chetniks.
  3. None of my suggestions for forming and organising units and cadre problems were either considered or accepted. I did not want to agree to brigade commanders who were men with insufficient military-profes-

sional knowledge (you are familiar with the case of brigade commanders in the Old Town municipality) and those who could not command the OG Igman (Haznadar Medo, Čaušević Mirsad, Mehić Ređo), but this was overlooked. Upon my return from the free territory I made a report about the conditions in the Igman, Konjić and Jablanica territories. However, nobody wanted to consider the report seriously and take action to prevent what led to the HVO attacking the Bosnia and Herzegovina Army.

4. I did not agree with the behaviour of ŠVK OS about the 'case' in Konjić and me being imprisoned in Parsovići for 27 days. According to NŠVK OS orders, we were supposed to meet in Igman upon my return from New York. Since the ŠVK did not come out to Igman, I was made a 'human ball' for 100 days. I did not even have the minimal conditions in which to work. I strolled from quarter to quarter without any protection, and was put in a situation between life and death. For Bosnia and Herzegovina, yes, but I do not know for who else as well! I do not know the reasons why the ŠVK OS did not declare publicly that I was not a criminal as the Mostar HVO reported. This should be explained by the responsible organ. I ask you, High Commander of OS RB&H, was it not my place to visit the free territory by your side in October, November and December of 1992 like Jasmin Jaganjac and Armin Pohara?

5. I do not agree with the behaviour of Army Headquarters and the High Command in the current, so far the toughest period in the war. No one is taking adequate action against the criminal behaviour of some military personel towards Bosnia and Herzegovina citizens. (I do not accept the statement that they are meritories of Bosnia and Herzegovina Army commanders.)

For several months now, roughly speaking, some individuals have been found in the highest positions in the Army in strange circumstances, and these are inflicting great damage on the Bosnia and Herzegovina Army. I do not know who gave permission for the existence of private jails in Hrasnica and Dobrinja. The International Red Cross report on the visit to Hrasnica Prison on May 2nd 1993 should be read. What is going on in the city of Sarajevo is unsuitable even for tribal armed units in Africa! You should receive information about Adnan Solaković's unit from honourable Sarajevo citizens – wives, parents and friends. Just one example – about 30 days ago on his way to work NN (I have correct data) was stopped in the street by Solaković's men, he showed them his working duty certificate, they tore it up and took him down to the unit by force. NN is one of the men who are important for the functioning of the waterworks and sewage system and who does not serve in the Army because he has had a kidney disease from birth. Although he tried to explain his health situation he was not heard, but instead included in very difficult and complex battle training. In the meantime, he had a kidney attack, but he was not granted any excuse, so he passed out. He was urgently transferred to a hospital, where he received medical help. However, Solaković sent two of his policemen to the hospital who returned him to the unit from his bed. I am unfamiliar with his further destiny.

Still, the most difficult situation in all this relates to the Republic of Bosnia and Herzegovina Army. The dealings of the 10th Brigade commander are inadequate regarding citizens' sacrifices and those of soldiers. Although information on criminal behaviour is available to VK OS, no measures are being taken against him. I know that VK OS are familiar with the conditions, but I will nevertheless bring out concrete data dealing with the 10th Brigade command. I do not claim the data is fully correct, but it can be indicative.

In the Ablakovina (Nadlipa) area there is a group of citizens and soldiers of the Bosnia and Herzegovina Army operating on a different basis. In most cases all their personal documents have been taken away. They are divided into five groups: the first group consists of prisoners. There are about ten of them. Their names are Dragan, Siniša, Ivo... (I do not know the others). They have been in this group for 40-50 days, without personal hygiene facilities, bathing... (trust me – they stink!). I am told that Tiho, Director of GP 'Bosna' is also among them. They dig trenches every day from 8:00 am to 8:00 pm. The second group consists of punished brigade members. They are here for larger, smaller or minimal reasons. For example, the brigade's tailor Hajro is among the 'trench-diggers' just because he made a joke about not having summer cloth for uniforms. The third group presents those taken into custody. Some of them are there for a month, a fortnight or a week. They work for 12 hours a day. You can ask the following people about their conditions: Slobodan Lučić, Deputy Health Minister; Safet Hadžihasanović, Haris Alatović's mother, whose son works on a computer in ŠVK OS, who is 18 years old, and does not possess a day of military training; Željko Vujković's mother, whose son has acute internal bleeding, he has been released from duty by the brigade doctor but was ordered by the commander to go digging; the wife of Mehmedović Meho, the man who was taken away in the street when going to work, wearing a summer suit, tie and shoes and about a hundred others whose dignity is destroyed.

I ask you: how do their families feel? A fourth category has also been formed. They are brigade soldiers. They will tell or history will. The fifth category consists of people brought to work for the brigade through CZ. Their Commander is a certain Mirsad. Let him say what he knows. I am familiar with the fact that this group works from 8 am to 4 pm. I wonder who will carry the burden of responsibility for these people being sent to the front line to dig trenches, five of them being killed and about 20 wounded in 20 days.

6. As a member of the Bosnia and Herzegovina Army I have reservations about the assertion that there is no need for cooperation between the Government, Army Headquarters, MIA, MO, MFA and other subjects in a liberation war, as the situation is now. My requests that the issue of combat activities should be resolved at that level was not taken seriously. I cannot accept this and I do not wish to take the responsibility for the un-cooperativeness of subjects in armed battle.

I would like the conditions in Dobrinja Prison to be checked.

I ask for a transfer from VK OS Headquarters to the duty of Bosnia and Herzegovina Army soldier.

And when you receive a report in 10–15 days saying I was killed for trying to desert to the other side, please do not believe them. My heart and soul is with your Republic of Bosnia and Herzegovina.

Applicant,
Jovan Divjak

Appendix 2

From a Conversation With Sidran[1]

Short version.

Sidran: I am a writer and I like to start from the beginning of a human life. People know that the cities you mentioned as important in your biography are Belgrade, Šamac and Sarajevo, but there is nothing more detailed known about this. We are truly curious about what Belgrade means to you, which family descendants lived there, how they came to Bosnia and what the historical circumstances are behind this?

Izetbegović: My family lived in Belgrade up until 1868. This is the year when the Muslims left Belgrade. One group went to Užice, another to Turkey, and the third group were given land near Šamac. At that time, the town of Šamac did not exist. The other day I read a book about the town's 100th birthday, which was published in 1968. At the outset, Šamac was named Azizija after Sultan Aziz who gave the Muslims from Belgrade a piece of land on the mouth of the Rivers Bosna and Sava, on the right side of Bosna. That is when a number of Muslim families from Belgrade started living literally off the land; I do not know how they passed those first days of building shelters, then houses. That is how the town of Šamac was created.

Sidran: Is it true that there was an Upper and a Lower Azizija, so that there were two towns on the River Sava?

Izetbegović: Very possibly, but I do not know much about this. I know that my grandfather, who was also named Alija, I was named after him, was the Mayor of Šamac before the First World War and that he went to court with Austria, or the then authority of Belgrade, because of Ada Ciganlija, where we still had a large piece of land. Since I mention this grandfather, it might be interesting to say something important about

[1] Conversations with Abdulah Sidran, screenplay writer and famous Bosniac poet, were published in a magazine from Sarajevo *Slobodna Bosna* on 11 and 25 August and 8 September 1996.

my personal life. After the attempt on Ferdinand in 1914, the Austrian army took Serb hostages in almost all the larger parts of Bosnia and Herzegovina. They did not manage to do this in Šamac, because my grandfather stood up against it. This is an important moment in my personal life. In 1944 the Chetniks arrested me near Gradačac, where some of my cousins were refugees after the Ustashas took over Šamac. I went there from Sarajevo. When the Chetniks arrested me, my life was in danger. However, a group of Serbs came to intervene with the then commander, Colonel Keserović, head of the Chetniks. They told him the story of how my grandfather saved 40 Serbs in 1914 and that it was his duty to return the favour. Thanks to this circumstance, I left with my head on my shoulders.

Sidran: What did your father do for a living?

Izetbegović: My father was a merchant in Šamac, but he lost out because he was not talented in sales. He had a partnership with a man who tricked him and my father failed. Then we went to Sarajevo. I was only two years old back then. That is why I feel more like a man from Sarajevo than from Šamac. I visited Šamac from time to time during the summer holidays to see uncles who still lived there. But I have lived in Sarajevo since 1927.

Sidran: How was life upon your arrival in Sarajevo?

Izetbegović: Difficult. My father was a clerk in a small company. There were five of us children, three girls, my brother and myself. I am proud to say that I attended the First Male High School, which was famous. I attended that building, the First Male High School, the one next to Army House, for eight years. People complain that life is short, for me it seems very long. I finished six grades there in the time of the old Yugoslavia, and graduated in the time of the NDH in 1943. I should have presented myself to the army then, but I did not, and instead decided to run away. Gradačac, where I went, was ruled by Chetniks and Hadži-efendić's Muslim militia. Both sides were armed but there was a sort of truce between them. In this area there were no criminal acts or banishing of Serbs or Muslims during the entire Second World War. There was a strange phenomenon there. The most horrible criminal acts took place in the north of Bosnia this time. In the last war, no Muslim was killed by a Serb in Brčko, Šamac, Gradačac or Modriča, as least as far as I know.

Sidran: So, you continued your education, high school, in Sarajevo? For how long were you away?

Izetbegović: I was a deserter from 1943 and hid in Gradačac and Modriča for the entirety of 1944. I would secretly visit Sarajevo on certain occasions. In 1945, the Partisans came. When they entered Sarajevo on 6 April, I was very ill from typhus. They knocked on my door on the night of 5-6 April. Later, when my health recovered, I joined the army. At the end of this, when I had served the required time in the army, I was arrested. This was on 1 March 1946. I was court martialled by the 6th Army and sentenced to three years in prison. I acted like I opposed both the Ustashas and Partisans, because I ran away from the Ustashas, and in the conversation about whether I would join the Partisans, I openly said that I would not. They knew it.

Sidran: I see this as some sort of catharsis, a final scene in a film that ends in an unjust act: an innocent defendant is sentenced to 14 years in prison, his facial expression is overwhelmed with a sad silence and a magnificent tranquillity. You can see this on the side as well, in a sharply shadowed profile of a head slightly leaned backwards. This is how Socrates' face must have looked, or so I think, when the judges of Athens confirmed the death sentence and that he must execute himself.

Yes, the year was 1983, a trumped-up process against Muslim intellectuals, the accused Alija Izetbegović, lawyer, horrifying sentences, although, a day or two earlier, we had left the courtroom as on wings, after hearing convincing and flawless pleas by the defense team. Who can – I thought – say guilty after such a defense? Nobody, nowhere in the world.

This Bosnian historical shame, this trial, was never proclaimed closed to the public, but the 'viewers' could be counted on the fingers of one hand: the state chose a small courtroom, and when the defendants, security, relatives and accredited press were seated – there was no room for anyone else. After a lot of trouble, I finally got some sort of a pass from Nidžo (Slobodan Nikolić, a friend from sittings in 'Seljo'), court secretary, and I went there for days, to see Melika and so she could see me. I filed documentation at home, for a future film... from all the things I saw and heard then in the courtroom, the image that remained sharply and unforgettably carved in my memory was only the face of Alija Izetbegović, in the moment of the passing of sentence upon him.

I saw that look on his face once again, ten years later, he brought it with him from his presidential chambers, to the microphone, after a conversation with one of the international murderers of Bosnia. It did not rest in spoken sentences, I later found out why it was there. This international, authority figure tried to convince him that 'the Muslims are the defeated side in this war, and one must go from that fact when trying to find a peace solution' (the statement that the Dayton Peace

Agreement saved the Chetniks from a total military defeat was closer to the truth).

I am though interested in your spiritual interests at that time: literature, philosophy? How were your ideas formed, indeed how were they formulated at that age?

Izetbegović: I had the fortune or misfortune that I read a lot, and in my opinion sometimes unnecessary books on philosophy. Today, I sometimes think I read so many useless things and it would have been better for me if I had learnt English language well. Practically, for the work I do now, or so it seems to me, I would have had much more use of two languages, let's say French and English, than of Indian philosophy, for I do not know if the latter was good for me or not.

Sidran: How perceptible was it for a young man?

Izetbegović: You swallow these texts and something sticks.

Sidran: I'm now tackling such works and am struggling with them.

Izetbegović: I read the *Bhagavad Gita* then, it is a part of the *Mahabharata*. I had reading attacks like toothache; I wouldn't read anything for three to four months, then I would frantically read for the next three months. Then, the process would repeat itself. I read nearly all that was written by Dostoevsky, Tolstoy, and almost everything by Kant. When I was 19, I read his *Critique of Pure Reason*. I still remember well some parts that had a special impact on me, in particular his famous antinomias in the central part of a *Critique of Pure Reason*. Among the books I remember is Spengler's *The Decline of the West*. I could not rid myself of his schemes for a long time, they are some sort of steel scheme that a man falls into and cannot think differently from.

Sidran: In those years that book went around intellectual circles and had a place in my father's library. I opened it as a child, someone had underlined parts with a red pen. I did not understand anything, but still I read it. I was maybe 15 or so.

Izetbegović: I was impressed by Spengler's huge knowledge of facts. There are actually two volumes. I think that the work has altogether a thousand pages. The publisher is, I think, Kosmos from Belgrade. This library published many capital works in world philosophy. Bergson is also important. He was an extraordinary stylist. Bergson was actually a scientist, a biologist. It is, so to say, an extraordinary and dangerous combination that of a scientist and philosopher. His best work is definitely *Creative Evolution*. People considered him the greatest stylist among philosophers. This as opposed to Kant who never was a stylist. Some say that his 'Critiques' could have been written in one third of the space that he took. With Bergson it was a thick, concise text, with excellent sentences, extraordinary metaphors. What he wrote in *Creative Evolution*, in my opinion could not have been explained without metaphor.

Sidran: Since we skipped a part of your time in jail, and we will address that subject in the future, it might be convenient if you tell me about the way of life in prison in both the first and second case, beyond political, beyond legal, beyond state elements. Were you spared physical work, what is the difference between the time when you served your first imprisonment and the second, was it physically too difficult to stand, what was the status of a young man, a political prisoner, among the others who were in jail for criminal and other bad deeds?

Izetbegović: You see, it could be said that immediately after the Second World War, there were political prisons. Statistically, in those prisons, there were 90% political prisoners and 10% criminals. When I went to jail again in 1983, the situation was vice versa: 90% criminals and 10% political convicts. That is why the first prison was easier for me than the second where I was among criminals. Still, I do not have any particularly unpleasant memories from those prisons. The first time, in my youth, my colleagues were people who thought differently so we could broadly talk (whisper) about anything. The second time, rather weirdly, I was a lawyer, and lawyers are very much appreciated in jail. Convicts need a lawyer to write complaints, requests and the like for them. So, this circumstance made me very respected and loved by these people. Sometimes they would tell me things that they had not even confessed to during trial. So, I knew their stories, their destinies. Convicts also have the misfortune of being left by their wives, so there are divorce proceedings taking place. So, when writing these requests and papers, one gets to know the drama of divorcing people who have children. It is a horrible human experience. On the other side, criminals in jail are not the way we imagine them. There are very good people among them. When I was in jail for the second time I was in Room 90. That was the killer room. There were between 90 and 100 people in this room that we called a suite. This was a large space with a lounge, four dormitories and a bathroom. This is how I got to know the story of each murderer, because I was serving my sentence for almost six years. In many cases I would have done what they had done. So, when we look at these people from the outside, we see things in black and white. For us, they are criminals and nothing more. When it comes to thieves, I do not know what kind of people they are. But, when it comes to killers, they are a special breed of people. Criminals in one way, and yet in another men with character and honour who could not live with an insult or unfairness, or outrage. Your Junuz Kečo Kuduz[2] was with me in Foča, for two or three years. I know him well, we were in the same room.

Sidran: Did he work in the joiner's workshop?

Izetbegović: Yes, we were both assigned to the joiner's. I worked there for a while, I think for the first half of the time I served. The second half, I did not work there anymore because I caught a bronchitis that I still have to this day. Working on wood is not a bad job, but there is a lot of dust involved. Upholstering makes a sort of dust that makes me ill, because I had had bronchitis before, I've had problems with it ever since and I will probably even die of it.

Sidran: Let's get back to Kečo.

Izetbegović: I know his story about that little girl. However, Kečo does not look like that man from your film.

Sidran: Yes, Ademir hired a face that was too pretty.

Izetbegović: Kečo was very silent, solitary and unhappy. That is just the way to say it, an unhappy but good man. So, he is one of those good men I told you about. I would not kill for my wife's unfaithfulness, but he did. If I cannot justify it, I can at least understand the situation. There were many people who could not put up with some sort of injustice, violence, and they reacted in that way. There were murders in effect. I had a friend in jail who committed murder defending his father. He was building a house that day and was supposed to do the roof when some people came and said that his father was being attacked in a coffee shop. He went to the affray and saw his father lying under the table, and men kicking him. He grabbed the first thing he could get his hands on and killed a man. Experiences with those sorts of people are very strange.

Sidran: What was the first job you got thereafter, and was it difficult to find employment with the political tag you had been labelled with?

Izetbegović: No, it wasn't. There were plenty of things to do, but salaries were very low. The Partisans tried to do and build something. The administration was just multiplying. Whoever was literate could find a job. I found employment immediately, because I had finished high school. I got a job 12 days after I got out of prison. I went out looking on 4 March and started work on 16 March as an employee.

Sidran: You were employed in a building company called 'Put'?

Izetbegović: Yes, I was employed in 'Put' and worked there until 1964, when I switched to IPSA, an engineering company. I was in court for a year in the meantime, I think 1962 to 1963. I was taking legal exams. I

[2] The main character in the film *Kuduz* (scenario by Abdulah Sidran).

had to be in court for a year as a trainee to ensure the conditions were met for passing that exam.

Sidran: I have the impression that we did not do enough to maintain the Bosnia and Herzegovina Army's multiethnic structure. In Sarajevo, as well as in some other towns in 1993 the structure of our military defense forces was analogous to the population's structure. If we agree on the statement that the survival of Bosniacs is conditional upon the survival of the multiethnic country of Bosnia and Herzegovina in its historical borders, what should be done for the Army to be truly reflective of all its nations?

Izetbegović: First, you are not correctly informed: nowhere, not even in 1992, and not later, was the structure of the Republic of Bosnia and Herzegovina Army analogous to the national population structure. This was unfortunate, but the facts are as such. The situation was a bit better in Sarajevo and Tuzla regarding this, but not even in these cities was the proportion established, not by a long shot. In other parts, the relation was 9:1 or worse, and getting even worse. Why? One, for sure we did not chase them away. Two, Bosnia was defended by Bosniacs, more precisely Bosniac units. We can try to hide this fact, but historical facts are not to be ignored, for they will come out into the open sooner or later. It is better to take them for what they are and see what to do for a start in some better direction. Whether this is possible, depends on the general development in Bosnia and Herzegovina now and in the future. This is the question of the success or failure of integration in Bosnia and Herzegovina and so on, but that is another, much broader subject.

Sidran: In one meeting it seemed to me that you easily accepted the idea of forming a Bosniac television. It seemed sad to me, because it brings about the question: does this contribute to the destruction or salvation of Bosnia? If someone proves a totally impossible thing that a separate Bosniac national television contributes to the salvation of Bosnia, then the question is which institution should back this television up? The editing office of a publishing house? Why shouldn't the decision of running such a television station be made by the Bosniac Assembly or, for instance, the Council of Bosniac Intellectuals Congress?

Izetbegović: This is not about trading a Bosniac for a public TV, the current RTV B&H, it is about establishing another television house, besides RTV B&H. If this was a trade, I would be the first one against it. But when it comes to Bosniac TV, the real question is: is the strengthening of the Bosniac people in the interests of an integral and democratic Bosnia or does it pull in the other direction? Or to make it simple, which of the following premises is correct: a stronger Bosniac people, a stronger Bosnia, or vice versa: a weaker Bosniac people, and a stronger Bosnia? There are people who consider the second variant true and believe that an integral and democratic Bosnia would need, or even require, a certain 'oblivion' of the Bosniac people. According to them, it would be good if the Bosniacs forget their faith, their name, their past – all of this would strengthen Bosnia. I do not know your opinion, but I must say that I do not feel that way. On the contrary, I believe that a strong and conscious Bosniac nation is the spine of Bosnia and Herzegovina and, if not the only, then the main guarantee for Bosnia and Herzegovina's survival, especially in the forthcoming situation of aggressive 'great state' projects both from the eastern and western sides of Bosnia. In such conditions, only a strong Bosniac nation can save and gradually integrate Bosnia. It is the only real guarantee that a curtain will not fall over the Bosnian State.

If this dilemma is solved, the rest should follow by itself. The gaining of consciousness among the Bosniac people – and it is always a certain knowledge about the past and future – cannot be expected from RTV B&H because by its definition it is not or should not be national, it should be Bosnian not Bosniac. It cannot specifically promote Bosniac values, among which is religion, without going against its beyond-national character. People in public TV constantly face this dilemma and do not know how to solve it.

Of course, the presumption for all this is that Bosniac TV would not let down the traditions of the Bosniac spirit, that is, that it would not teach hate, but tolerance and everything that comes from that. Anyway, not everything national is bad. National feeling is not divine like cosmopolitism, but it is a natural and healthy state and has been a strong driving force in history. It is just a matter of measure. Destruction in the name of this principle is more an exception than a rule. Finally, if an idea of pluralism can be Soros' or Bildt's TV, why could it not be Bosniac?

Sidran: When a political party is choosing its slogan for elections, a parole, a collective attitude, then it must do that in a serious way. The SDA election slogan 'In our faith, on our land', in my opinion, quite reduces the platform on which we gather in the battle for an integral and multiethnic Bosnia. I would like to have your comments on how we inject the Bosnian medicine to the entity if we are speaking of our religion and our land?

Izetbegović: I'm sorry, but it seems to me that you are starting from a wrong presumption. You go from the premise that the SDA is Bosnian, and it is actually a Bosniac party. The SDA is Bosnian as far as it goes but its structure is Bosniac, and we do not hide it. Furthermore, the SDA believe that this must be so. Bosnian feeling will emerge from Bosniac or it will be an amalgam of the two, after many years of mutual interaction, sparks and the inevitable toing-and-froing that history is full of. It is difficult to predict how things will flow, since nations in Bosnia are already formed. European nations are creating a strong union, but they remain French, German, Swedish, etc. They call Europe, or Europeism their mutual interest and a sum of certain mutual values. For the nations of Bosnia and Herzegovina, Bosnia is the name of the mutual interest and a sum of values we have in common.

Sidran: Looking at this closely, I find a stunning likeness between the SDA that you are at the head of with what used to be the late Communist Union. Lenin wrote somewhere that there are three phases in the history of mankind: matriarchate, patriarchate and secretariate. However, the Communists spent much longer on this journey then the pets of the 'secretariate'.

Izetbegović: Obviously, we look at the world through different eyes. I, for example, see no likeness between the SDA and the ex-Communist Union when it comes to management methods. There is stunning likeness only in the equal opposition to Chetniks and Ustashas, but when it comes to internal functioning the only stunning things are the differences. Democracy is always the basic question for internal organisation, and this is where there is absolutely no likeness between the SDA and the Communist Union. A few days ago in *Oslobođenje* I read an analysis of media conditions in Bosnia and Herzegovina, from which it can be seen that there are more than 200 media active in the area under the control of the legal authority, around 150 magazines and newspapers, 40 radio stations, 12 TV houses, and 4 press agencies. I am stating these numbers from memory, but I think that they are more or less correct. The great majority of these media are either in opposition or independent. Political parties act freely, there is no censorship, and not one editor of a public, I mean state, RTV is an active member of the SDA. Could the same situation be imagined under Communist domination, and could you have spoken with some important 'comrade from the committee' like this? Would you dare to tell him that his authority stunningly reminds you of everything that was bad in the 'old' regime? I do not know if you will believe me, but while we talk I feel a certain satisfaction, because, in spite of the stinginess of your questions, I find proof in them that in your soul you believe in freedom and law in this country. Otherwise, you would not ask them or you would not dare to ask.

Sidran: Mr. President, I would like to ask you for your comment on the difficult question of the future historical definition of the character and deeds of Alija Izetbegović, that we spoke about before the microphone was turned on. It seems very important, almost inevitable in a conversation like this one. Do you remember my statement that Alija Izetbegović will be one thing if Bosnia and the Bosniacs survive, and quite another should they disappear from the face of this earth?

Izetbegović: I do not like to talk about the character and deeds of Alija Izetbegović, but I would like to talk about Bosnia and its future. I believe that the idea of Bosnia will win, and that Bosnia will survive. I believe in this for at least three reasons. First, the proved strength of our people; second, a weak Serbia for a long time, a Serbia that will not be able to get into a 1992 adventure again; and third, the inevitable democratic developments in Croatia. In other words, 'great state' projects that represent the main danger for Bosnia and Herzegovina will not function. Serbia will not be able to and Croatia will not want to destroy Bosnia. So, our growing power in Bosnia, and a weak Serbia and democratic Croatia outside, is a vision or historical picture I see slowly being created in this territory. In such a historical situation, Bosnia will survive and gradually affirm itself as a democratic and integral country.

Sidran: The last time we spoke, we mentioned your family. People know that you have three children and five grandchildren.

Izetbegović: More precisely, five granddaughters. I will tell you the external side of the story, the inner one I will keep for myself. Back in 1943, when I was 18, I met my wife Halida. We were seeing each other until I went to jail in 1946. I was very much in love with this girl, it is not shameful to say this to you, you can understand it. It was a love to die for, as you poets say.

Anyway, I went to jail and this girl waited for me for the three years. When I was released, we were married. I have three children from this marriage: Lejla, Sabina and Bakir. I had all three of them by the time I was 31.

As for our grandchildren, two of them were born before I went to jail for the second time, and three of them while I was in jail. The first of them, Bakir's daughter Jasmina was born when I was on trial, a few days before the verdict. Later, when I was in Foča the last two girls were born. There is a little joke about this. We all expected that the fifth baby would be a boy. However, Bakir let me know: 'Dear father, you got one more granddaughter,' and then commented on this: 'Who will get them all married?' What else could I say: my oldest daughter Lejla graduated in mathematics, Sabina in linguistics, and Bakir is an architect. Selma, my oldest granddaughter is studying journalism. All my granddaughters speak English very well, better than me anyway.

Sidran: You did not tell me how life was?

Izetbegović: Very difficult in the beginning, I did not have a flat for a long time. I finally got it in 1958, after nine years of work in the company. I had to do fieldwork in Montenegro to deserve it.

Sidran: What, Montenegro in all this as well?

Izetbegović: Yes, I worked in Montenegro for seven years, from 1953 to 1960, within the Niskogradnja–Put company, that worked on the Perućica hydropower plant. I was head of the construction site. Those are the anomalies of that time. The locksmith was a marshal, and the head of the construction site a lawyer, etc. It was a huge site, employing a thousand people and hundreds of construction machines and trucks. It was a big experience for me, maybe even important for the job I do today. A construction site is like a little state: managing people and things. In 1960, when Perućica started running, Tito came and that was the first time I saw him closely. I thought he was taller, but he was my height, but much more corpulent.

Sidran: Those were terrain barracks you lived and slept in?

Izetbegović: Yes, but it was like that only for the first year, and then we built a more solid house in Nikšić. In the first year I was in a barrack because the first site entailed digging a big tunnel about 4,000 metres in length. The way out of that tunnel was at the place from which you can see the Ostrog Monastery in the mountains. What I remember from those days, I was 28, is that there were snakes everywhere and one received rather weird welcomes from the Montenegro people, peasants, who still carried a memory of the Turkish age and saw in me a Turk. True, we got along well but they always saw me as a Turk and called my wife a *bula* although her hair was not covered. They just felt that way about us.

Sidran: The fieldworkers are usually alone, without their families.

Izetbegović: My wife and children were with me during the season, usually from April to October, and returned to Sarajevo to spend the winter. You could say that this was a nice time in a way, something was built, made, and – what was very important – we were young.

Sidran: This, maybe, has nothing to do with our journalist business. However, one year, when I was a graduate, I went to earn some money digging a road, it was also GP Put, the Donji Vakuf–Bugojno road. I was shovelling for 15 days, and it was too difficult for me, but I remember the site manager. His name was Nikola, nicknamed Hitler by the workers. He was strict, so we could not lose time and I could not endure this so I went back with around 20,000 dinars earned through the Student Service. I mean, I have tasted field life and seen how loneliness often takes a fieldworker down the path of sin, so they start gambling and drinking.

Izetbegović: Yes, it is almost a rule. The largest number of them, men from construction sites, technicians, engineers, and workers go to beer-houses to break the monotony of a lonely life. But they also work hard. In the finishing season, year 1960, when the hydropower plant was to be opened, I used to get up at 4 am and work till 10 pm.

Sidran: All hours are working hours: if it starts raining, workers must get up at any time of the day or night to prevent the concrete from hardening.

Izetbegović: In the site we are talking about there was always the risk of flooding. So, you had to be there all the time, and deadlines were very short. There was not enough mechanical equipment either. We worked day and night, 24 hours on the tunnel. That is how a construction site is. However, a dead season comes, works are stopped and men stay alone, feeling lonely. And, of course, they deal with the monotony somehow.

Sidran: You were released from prison in 1988. So, how did the radical shortening of your sentence occur? Was it after filing a complaint, a request, some procedure, lawful or constitutional?

Izetbegović: In August of 1983 I was condemned to 14 years in jail. After half a year, it was during the Olympics, there was a second-degree process for our complaint to the Supreme Court of Bosnia and Herzegovina. It seemed we would get a significant shortening of the punishment. However, we were disappointed. The sentences were only symbolically shortened. I received two years off, so 12 years was my so-called final verdict. We had the right, since this was a political trial, to a re-questioning of the verdict at the Supreme Court of Yugoslavia, and of course, I filed the request. This process lasted for almost two years. The punishment was reduced to nine years and the deed was re-qualified. First, I was accused for so-called contra-revolutionary action, and now it was qualified as the notorious Article 133, the verbal delict.

Sidran: So, a radical change of qualification, and a symbolic change in punishment?

Izetbegović: Exactly. According to the law you could get ten years maximum for word or verbal delict. I got nine. With that verdict, I finally started to do my time. In February of 1987, I was made a strange offer, I do not know how or why, but I think it was through Nikola Stojanović, who was then a CK Presidency member. My two daughters were invited to the Presidency, right in this building where we are talking now, by Zdravko Đuričić, who was the Secretary for the Pardon Commission. He handed them a proposition, which contained my plea for pardon. He said: 'Take this to your father to sign it and he will be released'. It was the classic plea in which I realise that my ideas are wrong, that I do not intend to deal with politics any more and that I will withdraw and lead a peaceful life, etc. You know what I mean. Anyway, I refused to sign it. Stojanović was not happy. He angrily shoved the paper into his briefcase and we never spoke of it again. I remained in jail for almost two more years. In November of 1988, I was informed that the Presidency of Yugoslavia had decided to grant me a pardon.

Sidran: So, this was, after all, the result of what we wanted to talk about. Did you, imprisoned, feel the radical changes taking place in the outside world?

Izetbegović: Yes, I definitely felt changes in the world situation, and especially in Yugoslavia. There was the process of the decomposition of the Soviet Union, a huge, so to say, global happening. We saw in the scene Gorbačov, *Perestroika*, the Berlin Wall crisis, the fleeing of East Germans, etc. In Bosnia and Herzegovina, there was the crisis of Neum villas, Agrokomerc, Pozderac's fall and his drama, conflicts in the Central Committee. In my opinion, the reason for this was, most probably, doubt in the social concept arising all around as a result of the global failure of the socialistic concept, socially and economically. Besides, there was external pressure on Yugoslavia for its non-honouring of human rights, the arrival of a number of commissions addressing that question, and because a large number of people were in jail for verbal delict.

Sidran: How did you feel in prison, to be inside, did you watch TV, receive newspapers?

Izetbegović: Yes, I did. I was well informed. We had a TV in the living room, where we spent time after work. We also received newspapers. They were censured during the investigation. Still, you could clearly see what was going on in the world if you followed happenings from day to day. Globally, the USSR crisis, Milošević's climb up in Yugoslavia, the so-called Eighth session, the growth of nationalism, the dissolution of the united Communist League of Yugoslavia. All of this was clear and whoever was interested could have known where things were going.

Sidran: Whoever had problems politically probably experienced watching people running to the other side of the street to avoid greeting them. I know this from hundreds of examples, and I had some experience of this myself. I want to know, what were your encounters with people immediately after you were released from prison in 1988. Did they mostly act so cowardly?

Izetbegović: When I left prison, there was no more of that, but my closest ones experienced that during my trial and for a year or two afterwards. Later, something began to change in people as a consequence of the crisis, and maybe because of the more and more frequent news that the process was fabricated, so the public started to look at these things a bit differently. So, when I came back, I felt none of what you are talking about. It seems to me that I was warmly received. I think that the regime was already quite weakened, so the fear that was present in 1983 for instance had disappeared.

Sidran: What led to the ripening of ideas for the need to politically organise the Bosniac people: it was, I assume, a process?

Izetbegović: I left jail in November of 1988, and began forming the party exactly a year later, in November of 1989. The next year, 1990, also in November (with me, all those Novembers were somehow important), I entered this Presidency building. I thought of forming a party while I was still in jail, because then it was obvious that things were inevitably going towards democracy, that is that a one party system would not survive, that more parties would be formed like everywhere else in the world. But my party was initially imagined as Yugoslavian.

Sidran: That is what the first documents say.

Izetbegović: This can be seen in our Programme Declaration. Actually, the group of people gathered around me wanted to reconstruct Yugoslavia through the party. We thought the Muslims were alright with Yugoslavia, but not the way it was, a one party country, and not with Serbian hegemony implied. We cared for a Yugoslavia in which republics would have more self-reliance and more equality for all nations. Those were the two main requests when it came to a new political course and there were many people who shared my opinion, but dared not say it. In November of 1989, I travelled to Zagreb to talk to a group of people about this idea and we agreed to form the party. It was exactly one year after I had left prison.

Sidran: Was the party's name a matter of necessity because the law forbade identifying any national category in the title. Actually, was the name willingly chosen or given because nationality could not have been mentioned in it? I do not remember which.

Izetbegović: I do not remember exactly either, but I know that the proposal for it was made by Safet Isović, our famous artist. First I considered remaking Spaho's Yugoslavian Muslim Organisation (JMO). However, in my conversation with Adil Zulfikarpašić, this idea was dropped. As you know, he too was one of the party's founders. He thought that this was not the solution to go for. Frankly, I did not quite like Safet's idea for the name, but the abbreviation (SDA) was good, it sounded fine. The proposal was accepted.

Sidran: So, your Yugoslavian orientation was beyond doubt?

Izetbegović: We wanted a democratic, reconstructed Yugoslavia. Some parties avoided saying it, but we did not. We thought that it clearly depicted the fact that we wanted to untangle the situation peacefully. We did not opt for tearing Yugoslavia apart, we wanted it reconstructed so it would become a democratic country where all nations were secure, among them the Bosniacs too. On the other side of the equation, the Muslims did not live only in Bosnia and Herzegovina, there were many of them in Sandžak, Macedonia, Kosovo and Croatia.

Sidran: It seems that in one phase of the negotiations between all presidents of all former Yugoslavian republics, we reached a point where we would accept anything Belgrade and Zagreb agreed upon just to prevent war. This seems to have been forgotten little by little.

Izetbegović: We could say that the decision for an independent Bosnia and Herzegovina was in a way extorted. It was forced upon us because we wanted more self-reliance for Bosnia and Herzegovina within Yugoslavia, but the independence of our state, the way it was demanded later, was a result of Croatia's and Slovenia's independence. We said that any Yugoslavia with Croatia and Serbia in it was acceptable, and that any Yugoslavia without either of those countries was not. When Croatia left Yugoslavia, we faced the choice of staying in a partial Yugoslavia with Serbia and Montenegro or opting for independence. We chose the second option. I still believe that the other choice was not possible.

Sidran: I agreed with this decision to struggle for independence, with efforts for Bosnia as a federal unit to be entitled to everything other republics in Yugoslavia were entitled to. This is why I did not consider this act as a secession, as a bad act. I wrote once that one cannot exit a house that does not exist. And Yugoslavia did not exist anymore in 1992.

Izetbegović: This is important because that is usually the breaking point for placing the blame for the conflict that took place, blame for war. The Serbs accused us of tearing down Yugoslavia, preventing them from living in Yugoslavia. From the documents made in the first days of the SDA it is clear that this is not so, and that the Serbs were actually not prepared to control their national selfishness. As for those 'presidential meetings' in the first half of 1991, that you have just mentioned, it was obvious in advance that there could be no agreement, because two key men – Milošević and Tuđman – were against it. Do you remember that President Gligorov and I brought out a proposal for a confederate Yugoslavia. This proposal was close to being accepted but the problem of the control over the army remained unsolved. Serbia wanted a united army. Croatia did not accept this, so the project failed. Anyway, I still think that if this plan had succeeded, it would have saved the former Yugoslavia from dissolution and of course from war. However, Croatia gained independence, an absolute misbalance was created and Bosnia was supposed to remain in an incomplete Yugoslavia. We could not agree to this.

Sidran: I do not know if I am right, but there is a certain public belief that for the first time during those conversations you found out about Milošević and Tuđman's agreement in Karađorđevo to split Bosnia. It seems that you were informed about this for the first time in Split, by the two of them. It is important that you describe those moments, psychologically, humanly, politically.

Izetbegović: No, it was not in Split. I was told this first by the Macedonian President, Gligorov, on his arrival at Sarajevo for the meeting of the six presidents. Gligorov came for this meeting a day earlier to let me know about Milošević and Tuđman's conversation in Karađorđevo that had taken place a few days earlier and of which he had completely trustworthy information. It was not known if they had agreed to divide Bosnia into two or three parts. As far as I know, no document from Karađorđevo has ever been published, and it was even denied that the agreement was ever made.

Sidran: Your journey to Split happened very quickly after President Gligorov's warning.

Izetbegović: Yes, soon after I received an invitation to go to Split for a meeting with Milošević and Tuđman. Since I had been informed by Gligorov, I sensed what the topic of conversation would be. It is interesting that they did not directly mention division, but the entire conversation, led in a coded, hardly understandable language, was oriented towards convincing me that the survival of Bosnia was impossible and that we should seek some other, as they said, realistic solution. I was pitting my wits against them all day, and when I returned to Bosnia that evening, the press asked me if we had spoken of dividing Bosnia. I said only one sentence: 'It is impossible to discuss with me dividing Bosnia!' However, today it is clear that what happened in Karađorđevo marks the entire history of our relations and explains the happenings that followed in all the four to five years thereafter.

Sidran: I see a question here in my notes about your vision of Bosnia in the year 2030?

Izetbegović: How am I to know what will happen in 30-40 years time? This is not just a change of century, but in millennium as well. Some claim that it will definitely be a new page in the book of history. Futurologists predict that there will be huge changes, that Europe will become a province and the Far East the centre of the world. That America will lose its influence because of its moral stumbles. That is the context in which the future of Bosnia is to take place. I believe that in 2030 Bosnia and Herzegovina will be alive and well! Without this, without such a belief I could not do my job. In my opinion, it is more our immediate surroundings that affect Bosnia than the rest of the world. Happenings in Croatia and Serbia are more important for us than those in the USA, Europe, or Russia, because those two countries directly affect the State of Bosnia, and I would say, Croatia rather more than Serbia. I am sure that in the next five to ten years Croatia will transform itself into a modern democratic country. Serbia will remain weak for a long time. Such a situation opens up a perspective for Bosnia and Herzegovina. So, Bosnia has a chance with a democratic Croatia and a weak Serbia!

Sidran: Or maybe, a Serbia that has come to its senses!

Izetbegović: Well, you could say that, but in any case, Serbia will be too weak for a long time to enter an arena like it did in 1992. The third and the most important factor is, of course, our population that has learned a lot in this war, a people that proved themselves to be very strong and very tough.

Sidran: Do you think that we, you as political leadership and us as common citizens, will have the strength to resist the desire, or naïve need, to manage the area that we control in the way the destroyers of Bosnia manage theirs? I mean, one party, one nationality, a monolith domination. I sometimes have the belief that we could return Bosnia and Herzegovina to its constitutionally-legal system without one bullet being fired, just by living in the territory we live in now in the way of an integral Bosnia. That is, with much more respect for 'multi'. To be brief, I believe that we could have the entirety of Bosnia without one bullet being fired if we organised our part as if it were the entirety of Bosnia.

Izetbegović: When I said — and I have said this many times — that we could defeat the darkness that surrounds us with the strength of our political model, I was referring to the same thing you are speaking about now. The basis of this is democracy in the best meaning of the word. It implies liberty of people to think and believe differently. It is also the strength that can defeat this single-minded behaviour that surrounds us. But, we cannot do this alone. The Bosniac people are, obviously, in favour of this concept, or they are, in great majority, in favour of it. Over the past months the Bosniac population has been going through a certain crisis relating to this, which is depicted in the course of events.

Sidran: Excesses?

Izetbegović: I think that the people have been struck by certain disappointments, regarding the behaviour of one part of the Serbs and Croats. It is hard to maintain control over people in such a boiling situation. But, in my opinion, the thinking part of the Bosniac people will never lose their bearings because it is clear that Bosnia and Herzegovina has a bad geo-political location anyway, even with internationally recognised borders, and especially in…

Sidran: And especially with reduced…

Izetbegović: Especially with reduced. Let's leave ideals and principles out for a while, and let's just talk about the interests of the Bosniac people, that has tied their destiny to the survival of the State of Bosnia and Herzegovina. As I said, the part of the Bosniac who people think, understand this. All of them, unfortunately, do not, because they are under the influence…

Sidran: Of inertia…

Izetbegović: Yes, inertia from two sides. Still, we have not trampled down the principles of tolerance in war, even at the very outset we said that we did not want revenge. We have prevented two revenges here, two hard revenges. First, the possible revenge against the Communists when we took over power in 1990. Second, any revenge here against Serbs in the time of the worst Chetnik crimes. There were groups who wanted revenge and retaliation. That means that our authority has passed a very difficult test. Furthermore, we did not censor the press, even though there were requests from the army to do so, because they often leak military secrets. Remember when a man stepped in front of the cameras in the middle of war on our television and said: 'In Sarajevo, there is bread for only two more days.' I was wondering whom he was telling this to. Because the Chetniks who see and hear this, will conclude: if this is so, let's go for it, because they are almost finished.

Sidran: There is no doubt this is a great political capital for our government and it should, from my point of view, be supplied with some efficiency in sanctioning excess cases on our side. There is sorrow in my heart because we never established who killed the young reporter in Zavidovići. We have four or five examples of such individual sad destinies. For instance, the handball player, who was once the goalkeeper for the national team, a Serb, orthodox, who is a dentist, and has spent the entire war serving the army, and cannot find work after he has been demobilised. I think that this government lacks the determination needed to sanction what happens to us in such excesses but not as a rule.

Izetbegović: I am also hurt by injustice. But, don't forget, Avdo [Sidran's forename], that we have passed through hell, and remained sane people in spite of everything. This is our victory.

Appendix 3

Lecture to the German Association for Foreign Affairs

Bonn, 17 March 1995.

'Ladies and gentlemen, dear friends,

I am told that these days mark 40 years of fruitful activity by your association. I would like to use this opportunity to congratulate you on your jubilee and wish you much success in the years to come.

The work of an association like yours can be of great help to people who make decisions. When it comes to the Bosnia that I come from, I can immediately state at least two matters on which we could use and need your help: first, there is a lack of ideas for solving problems in the territory of the former Yugoslavia and especially Bosnia and Herzegovina. Second, there is a need to re-examine the functioning of some important international institutions: the UN, the Security Council, NATO and others, because all mechanisms of collective security have obviously failed in the case of the Balkans conflict. International factors have made erroneous moves. You can help to reduce the number of these mistakes in the future.

In a few days, it will be three years since the aggression against Bosnia and Herzegovina began. It is the same number of years that the world has passively watched the unequal wrestling of a well-armed attacker and its victim.

There is one delusion that I immediately want to correct. It was said: the international community did not want to (or could not) interfere in the war in Bosnia and Herzegovina. This statement is not true. The international community did interfere in this war, but in the wrong way, and this should be remembered. This was through an embargo on weapons that practically affected only the victim. Instead of helping us, by military intervention, to arm us, the world did exactly the opposite: it forbade the arming of the attacked country and deprived us of our legitimate right to self-defense.

The explanation, as it was repeatedly said, was: an embargo is necessary because without it the war will be long and bloody. Now, after three years, we Bosnians have the right to ask: wasn't the war long enough and bloody enough? Could it have been longer and bloodier?

We have every reason to claim that if there were no embargo, the war would have been over by now, and Bosnia as well as the principles of international law would have been defended. This way, we have both a bloody war and an unprecedented breaking of all laws and moral norms.

When it comes to this terrible war, three things stand out as lacking any logical and rational explanation:

1. The quantity of evil poured over Bosnia,
2. The world's indifference to this eruption of evil, and
3. The wonder of our resistance.

You have to admit that none of the above was expected and that you were startled.

Did you really expect that in the middle of Europe, after Auschwitz and the Gulags, someone would be impudent enough to form death camps in which thousands of people disappeared, and cold-bloodedly and in a planned way tear down mosques, churches, libraries and hospitals?

If you could have seen this happening in your darkest premonitions, could you have believed that the civilised world would watch this happening passively, that it would shut its eyes in the face of genocide, aggressive war, death camps, ethnic cleansing and absolute violence?

And, finally, the third miracle, this time positive, our resistance. Could you have foreseen in 1991 or 1992 that the barehanded Bosnian people would manage to stop the well-armed Yugoslavian (Serbian) Army?

In May of 1992, Lord Carrington visited me in Sarajevo with one and only one message: negotiate, and when I told him that they requested our capitulation and that this was the only thing they would negotiate, he asked me: 'Well, what will you do?' I said: 'We will fight.' Carrington replied in resignation: 'You obviously don't know what you're dealing with. I am sorry, but you don't have any chance.'

As you know, we decided to resist. With only a few thousand lightly armed fighters we succeeded in keeping the strategic part of Bosnia and, to create an army, in war, that nobody can now ignore.

Those were the three miracles that await explanations. History is unpredictable and stories about unexpected things do occur. Libraries of books will be written in an attempt to explain the three phenomena mentioned above, but no true explanation will be found.

Evil in Bosnia was already named metaphysical, which obviously meant that it was unexplainable and outside of known categories. One writer said that in the languages of civilised nations there is not a word ugly enough to name some aspects of this evil.

And when it comes to the world's behaviour, this strange line of contradictions, a bizarre thought comes to mind that an unexplainable break happened in peoples' souls over the last two or three generations. Our fathers wrote those exalted creeds, declarations and conventions that forbade the use of force, about peaceful coexistence, about human rights. We have treated these documents as if they were papers of no value. Were our fathers different men? What happened to us in the meantime?

A crucially serious question imposes itself and it concerns every nation and every country in the world from now on: will breaking international laws on such a high level as in the Balkans tear down the standards that have been formed through the ages? Will the international community accept new rules of behaviour that will legalise force as right? Is it prepared for this?

When it comes to our resistance, one day all the facts will be known, but this will not reveal the phenomenon. This is because the resistance had a strong moral component, a fact of spiritual order, and facts of this sort defy scientific analysis. Sarajevo is not the only, but may be the most persuasive and the most illustrative example.

We in Sarajevo have been living and working practically on the first front line for three years now. In some locations this line comes as close as 500 metres to the Presidency building. The building was directly shelled over 120 times in three years, 57 people were killed both inside and around it. It experienced 1,000 days of siege. In that time, at least half a million grenades hit the city. Over 10,000 citizens were killed, including about 1,300 children, etc.

This is the tragic side of the coin. The other side is the following: the university did not stop working for one single day. More than 1,500 students were awarded their degrees during the war and over 55 doctoral dissertations were accepted. In the same time over 250 concerts and 1,000 theatrical plays were held. Sometimes it happened that the TV news programme informed viewers of the number of victims that fell that day and of a concert or play performed that evening. Intensive dying was followed by intensive living. It is true that those concerts were more than just mere musical happenings, but they represented our answer to evil and violence from the hills, our human reply to an unseen inhumanity.

Still, they want to divide such a town and build a wall through it. You, Germans, know best what walls through a city mean, you know better than others what a state of spirit can stand behind this dark idea. All those who build walls between people are the same. When they built the Berlin Wall, the Stalinists said that they were defending freedom. Today, we know that their real reason was panic, a fear of freedom. Those who are dividing Sarajevo, and those who are tearing the city down, are telling us the same thing, and they are obsessed by the same fear. They want to kill the symbol, which is witness against them, to kill the town that is all that they are not.

Sarajevo is a witness that people of different religions, nations and cultures can live together. There is only one condition for this: that they are normal human beings. Inhumane ones cannot do this.

In Bosnia today, in the part under the control of the legal Bosnian government, 12 parliamentary and out-of-parliament political parties are active. Some of them do not have many members, because they are stronger on rhetoric than deeds, and the people can see this, but nobody forbids them from continuing their activities and winning new voters. I read the report by the Special Reporter for Human Rights, Mr. Tadeusz Mazowiecki the other day, with pride and satisfaction. He reports that three TV stations are active in Sarajevo, along with eight radio stations, as well as some others in other parts of Bosnia. RTV B&H is the only State station, all others are either independent or under the opposition's influence. In recent days, in Zagreb, there was an exhibition of 175 papers and magazines published in Bosnia and Herzegovina during the war. Most by an independent press. There is no censorship of the media in Bosnia and Herzegovina, never was one publication forbidden, nor was a journalist persecuted for his or her writings.

On the other hand, on our left and right there are little fascisms that are proud of their one-national, one-religion and one-party concept. Winds blow from there, trying to put out this little flame of light shining through the free territories of Bosnia and Herzegovina. They opt for one argument in so doing: Islamic fundamentalism. They claim that THEY are the ones defending Europe from the Islamic danger. Maybe this is a good chance, the right time and place, to make it clear about this so-called Islamic fundamentalism in Bosnia. First of all, do not let them defend you, even if it is from Islamic fundamentalism. Has Europe stooped so low that it needs those who destroyed sacral objects and cultural monuments to defend it from anything? There is Islam in Bosnia, but there isn't fundamentalism, and if someone cannot tell the difference between those two, then it is their problem. After 50 years of Communist repression, religion is awakening and this is a natural process. This process is a part of the national awakening of the Bosniac people and it will continue.

Religious renaissance in Bosnia will not be followed by radicalism and extremism, because it is natural and free. It has already played a positive role in the humanisation of our struggle for freedom. Religion emphasised the difference between good and evil, and, in spite of everything, we did not allow the differences between the allowed and the forbidden to be erased. Everything urged us to uncontrolled revenge. We have overcome those temptations, thank God.

This delusion, mistaking faith for fundamentalism, is still there thanks to the silent consent of aggressors and the West. The interest is the same, the reasons are different. The interest of Serbian aggressors is to avert the West from helping Bosnia, using the ruse of Islamic fundamentalism. The interest of the West is to have a good excuse for its passivity, for doing nothing. The West accepts being persuaded into something that relieves it from any duty.

Here are two examples: when a few months ago there was an incident in the city market of Sarajevo, concerning pork (the citizens asked for shops to be separate), the Western press wrote about this as a dangerous thing for days. There were more articles published in the Western media about pork in Sarajevo than about all the Serbian death camps where thousands of innocent people disappeared. As for the second example, when talking about war in Bosnia, a high ranking Western politician said: they are all equally guilty, and, to be quite clear, states: Bosnians as well as Serbs as well as Croats. His colleagues talked about so-called warring sides and a civil war in Bosnia. The reason is as transparent as simple: if this was not aggression and genocide, the West was not obliged to react, and an arms embargo was not only legal, but also crucial. How can we, Bosniacs, think of this, if not as of ultimate partiality and bias?

But, then it happens that one respected and very informed American institution – you know which one – states that 90% of all crimes in Bosnia were committed by Serbs. So, we are not equally guilty, and thank God this is so. This way, at least hope is saved. And if we have committed one crime, we would not hold ourselves innocent, because we believe that principles and numbers cannot be added and subtracted. There is no place for arithmetic in this. When a few days ago, two children were killed in crossfire in the Serbian part of Sarajevo, our army was brave enough to take the responsibility for its soldier and persecute the crime. The same was done in a few other situations, because three years of a horrible war like the one in Bosnia, brings unpredictable, hard to control situations. Still, we were sometimes the ones to blame because we were the weaker side. It seems that the weak ones do not have the right to make a mistake. They have to be perfect, the strong ones do not. Not accepting this stance invented by the powerful, we will continue to believe in the undefeatable and unexplainable power of law and humanity over force.

To end, allow me to finish this speech with some personally coloured observations:

I come here in my official function, but also – why not say it – as a Muslim from Bosnia. I personally feel both a Muslim and a European, and I do not think that one excludes the other. I do not accept that there are differences between people and civilisations that cannot be overcome. If each civilisation is first of all a group of values – which are in the final analysis moral values that are believed in – then we can talk about a possible unity of civilisations.

A long time ago, as a young man, I wrote an article on Kant's categorical imperative. The article's thesis was that the moral principle formulated by Kant and known under the title above, can be found in very old teachings almost in literal form, beginning from ancient Jewish wise men and Confucius in ancient China, to Tolstoy and Martin Buber in our century, so this basic moral principle is practically out of space and time out of history. For me, this meant that there are no differences between civilisations that cannot be overcome and that all cultures are similar or even equal if one goes down to their roots. To me, this question was a matter of human equality.

There is an exciting sentence in the Qur'an that begins with the words: 'Come and gather around the word that is common to us…' The invitation is meant for Christians and Jews. So, I invite you to turn down the invitations for building artificial partitions between Islam and Christianity, between East and West. Rather look into this to see if some intolerance is caused by the selfishness and injustices of the West. Furthermore, many differences that you can see and feel are not essential, they come from differences in the level of cultural and social development.

I would like to finish my speech with the wish for Germany to take the place in the world that belongs to it as a cultural, moral and economic force of the first degree. Germany has no reason to hesitate. Germany and the world will only gain from this. Thank you.

Appendix 4

TALKS AT THE FRENCH INSTITUTE FOR INTERNATIONAL RELATIONS

Paris, 30 August 1995.

Jean Barrio: Mr. President, I would like to thank you for accepting our invitation for this evening. Everyone knows about the pressure that has burdened you for years. Among your qualities that we know, I would like to mention one, that deserves special praise, and that is your bravery. Your personal bravery, your physical bravery, your political bravery.

Allow me to ask you the first question to get this conversation going. Is it true that we are approaching a true peace process today, or are we, on the contrary, moving towards a new round of war?

Izetbegović: Before I answer your question, I would like to thank you for your cordial invitation. It is an honour for me to have the opportunity to talk to such a large number of eminent French intellectuals. There are four members of our delegation with me, who can also answer your questions, and I can rest a bit while they reply. You have asked me the question at the right moment. I sent a letter only this morning to the UN Security Council and Contact Group members, the Western one and the one of Islamic countries that will meet in Geneva tomorrow. In this letter, I ask for the destruction of Serbian artillery surrounding Sarajevo. Since this is a killing machine, that has annihilated more than 10,000 Sarajevo citizens of which 1,300 of whom were children as well as 41 other citizens yesterday, I asked for an efficient action to destroy this machine. I said that we would suspend our participation in peace talks until this is solved.

If the hesitation of the international community continues, peace will certainly not be reached for a long time. Since we have to find the means to neutralise this artillery surrounding Sarajevo by ourselves, this obviously means the prolongation of war.

I do not know if you are content with my answer, but I think that I was at least clear.

Jean Barrio: A game rule in these dinners is to ask questions a bit 'iconoclastically' and I would like to ask you such questions as well. Sometimes there is the impression that Bosnia actually wants the continuation of war because it is sure that the evolution of forced relations is convenient for it. What do you think of this interpretation?

Izetbegović: Our delegation came to France on a peace mission. At the time of yesterday's massacre, we were in Mostar, on our way to your country. As you know, we arrived late, and I will explain why. We hesitated for a few hours. We were considering returning to Sarajevo. After hours of rethinking, we decided to come here after all. The Serbs might have shelled Sarajevo to disturb the peace process. We should not fall into this trap and go for provocation. We came to Paris expecting the fast reaction of the international community, either yesterday or today. We have waited for this reply all day today, but it has still not arrived. The world thinks it can tie our hands behind our backs and do nothing. I do not know if you remember: I was here two years ago on your TV. I put my hands in a tied position and showed them, because you really did so tie our hands with the arms embargo. We thought the world would do something to help us, since we were faced with this embargo. And, as you know, nothing was done. We can say that just the opposite happened, that the international community betrayed Bosnia and Herzegovina in a shameful way. On 9 February 1994, NATO reached the decision to remove the artillery surrounding Sarajevo. This was respected for only about half a year. In August, grenades started hitting Sarajevo again. To begin with, one grenade every few days, and then more and more frequently. The Serbs tested the international community to see if it was prepared to hold onto its decision and fulfill its duties. They realised that it was weak and not prepared to do anything. Then the attacks followed, like yesterday.

To answer your question, if we are for peace or the continuation of war, I will say that we have accepted two peace plans so far. The Vance-Owen Plan at the beginning of 1993 and the Contact Group Plan last year, exactly a year ago. Both these plans were unjust for Bosnia and Herzegovina. We accepted them because they led to peace. The Serbs refused both plans, so you can draw your own conclusions.

Jean Barrio: I will ask you one more question but I want others to ask questions as well so that this does not become just a dialogue, so, ladies and gentleman, please prepare your questions.

Mr. President, my next question is: can you tell me what you think of the solidity of the Croat-Muslim Federation, is it existing thanks to pressure from the USA? What does the solidity of this pact consist of and how can the maintaining of Bosnian State integrity be imagined while a part of the country is in a confederate relationship with another country, Croatia, and yet another with Serbia? How can such an order have meaning in the context of international law?

Izetbegović: First, this is a rather lengthy question.

Jean Barrio: Yes, you are right.

Izetbegović: You have Mr. Zubak, Federation President sitting on your right, and he can say something about this. The establishment of the Federation is moving pretty slow. I still believe that the Federation is not an artificial thing imposed by external influence. The Federation was founded more than a year ago and it immediately led to peace. Not a bullet has been fired since.

According to our opinion, this is a great test for the value of this plan, although its implementation is difficult. On the day we signed the Federation Agreement, the war literally immediately stopped. I think this is how our Federation passed the test. I believe that Mr. Zubak and I will manage to establish it completely. It is not an unnatural alliance. On the contrary, we can say that the conflict that preceded the Federation was unnatural. Since there is deep sympathy between the Bosniac and Croatian people, the conflict was obviously caused artificially. Only some groups were against the Federation. In favour of the Federation were Bosnian and Croatian intellectuals, all the opposition parties in Croatia, and the party that holds power in Croatia signed the agreement. The Catholic Church, that is very powerful in Croatia and Bosnia was also for the Federation. So, all influential factors were in favour of it. This is why I believe that the Federation has a future.

Jean Barrio: Mr. President, you saw Mr. Chirac today. Are you disappointed by the French support to the project of Sarajevo demilitarisation?

Izetbegović: Frankly, I am not familiar with the full content of this proposal. President Chirac did not mention the subject in our conversation. On the contrary, we spoke of Sarajevo opening with the help of French forces. President Chirac promised to use French forces to secure the route over Igman and the airport that will open Sarajevo. The conversation was very open and useful. I have a feeling that Bosnia has a friend in President Chirac, judging by the way we see Bosnia and the way he sees it. And we see Bosnia and Herzegovina as a democratic country in which human rights will be respected and tolerance will be present. President Chirac stated that he supports Bosnia and Herzegovina because it is the attacked country. He said: 'If you become the aggressor one day, we will be against you. As long as you are attacked, we are on your side. Because it is the moral obligation of France.' This is the main thing that he said.

Jean Barrio: Mr. President, is there a difference between President Chirac and the ex-president Francois Mitterrand concerning the Bosnian question?

Izetbegović: I think there is. I cannot claim that President Mitterrand held anti-Bosnian positions or anti-Bosnian feeling. But, President Chirac's position about Bosnia is clearer. Of course, this is my impression, but I think that a difference obviously exists.

Jean Barrio: Is the American plan, according to your knowledge, a simple opening that does not oblige the Americans to anything? Do they want the administrative division of Bosnia according to the percentage: 49% for Serbs and 51% for Croats and Muslims, since Radovan Karadžić demanded 64% of the territory last week, plus an outlet to the sea, plus a part of Sarajevo? What do you think about Karadžić's statement from this morning in which he said that he accepts the American plan?

Izetbegović: I did not hear that statement. I have been very busy today and I did not hear the news. But, I know that Karadžić gives ambiguous statements to postpone the reaching of a decision or to facilitate confusion. Karadžić needs to accept the Contact Group Plan and to say it clearly as well as to accept the integrity and sovereignty of Bosnia and Herzegovina. Not indirectly, but explicitly.

Jean Barrio: Mr. President, during a dinner a bit like this one, that took place in London, Tuđman sketched his division of Bosnia. What was your personal reaction when you saw this drawing and did you ask President Tuđman for a personal explanation.

Izetbegović: Before I spoke to him, he denied this story. Since we do not like pinching the devil if possible, we decided not to investigate this matter. Tuđman denied it and we accepted his denial. You know, there is never absolute trust in politics. But, there should not be a permanent distrust that paralyses any action. Nations do not get to choose their neighbours. Croatia is our closest neighbour and most important partner. We have to live with Croatia. We like for things there to go well, not badly. This is why we accepted President Tuđman's denial.

Jean Barrio: So, you are not negating the existence of the sketch, you are just accepting the denial?

Izetbegović: You could put it that way.

Jean Barrio: Mr. President, we suppose that the arms embargo will finally be lifted. Do you think that the conflict will be limited or that it will spread over into other regions of the ex-Yugoslavia or maybe even broader than that?

Izetbegović: Both possibilities are realistic: that the conflict will spread, or that it will remain on Bosnia and Herzegovina territory. The second is more likely, out of fear of the conflict spreading. As you can see, sometimes fear plays a positive role. Spreading this conflict over Croatia and Serbia could lead to Albania, Greece and even Russia. Fear of such development can hold the war within Bosnia and Herzegovinan borders. Therefore, I consider this more likely.

Jean Barrio: Mr. President, after almost four years of war, what do you think about Europe's role? Do you think that there should be an European capability to help solve conflicts, would it do any good, did you feel the lack of it?

Izetbegović: I think that Europe failed the test, which reflects the bad state of spirit in Europe and the world in general. I just mentioned an obligation that NATO and the United Nations undertook, I meant the ultimatum protecting the city of Sarajevo. This obligation was betrayed completely. Srebrenica happened recently. The United Nations proclaimed Srebrenica a protected zone. And not only this. They convinced us to accept the demilitarisation of Srebrenica, on the basis of which our army handed over its weapons to the UN. Following this, they left Srebrenica to its fate, and the worst crime after the Second World War happened. I think that this was a shameful betrayal. As a young man I read *The Decline of the West* – the famous work by Osvald Spengler. I was under the influence of this strong work for a long time, and then I started to relieve myself from the idea of the West's decline, and started thinking of it as a utopia. Under the influence of this war, I started to believe this idea again. How could Srebrenica be handed over to its assassins after clearly made and stated obligations? Do you know that 4,000 people were killed in just four days? All this is happening and the civilised world is watching it without any obvious protest! A world that can betray its obligations in that way and leave thousands of people to their cruel destiny must stop and think about itself. Let me repeat: I again believe in the decline of the West. It seems that the Einsteinian spirit of relativity is hanging over everything. Nothing is sure and stable any more, everything is falling to pieces.

Jean Barrio: Mr. President, listening to some Bosnians, and some of your friends, like Bernard Henry Levý in France, one gets the impression that we, countries of the West, are guilty because Serbians, Bosnians and Croats have been killing each other for four years already. But, are there reasons, strictly local, for those massacres? Still, this should be considered from time to time. How is it possible that people who have lived together for 70 years and more, are now killing each other?

Izetbegović: It is a question of nationalism in this part of the world. Remember European happenings during this century when normal people under monstrous ideologies suddenly started to commit evil. Fascism is Europe's child, stems from a civilised part of Europe, not the Balkans. Bolshevism is the same story. You see, evil springs from somewhere. It is hard to find its source, but you get the impression that its quantity is permanent and that it just changes place and form. And I am saying that good did not stand up against evil. Evil emerged in the Balkans, this is true. But there were no forces of good in Europe to stop it. It still remains unexplained why an independent country, that was in spite of everything an oasis of democracy or a light in absolute darkness, was deprived of the right to defend itself. Only in that part of the world under the control of the Bosnian Army and authority, was there democracy, freedom of the press, political opposition, and churches, both Catholic and Orthodox. All are in one piece. In spite of all this, our hands were tied. We had no chance to defend ourselves. Again and again new reasons were construed not to allow us to defend ourselves. Why?

Jean Barrio: Let's go back to a very real question. Is the idea of Slobodan Milošević formally recognising Bosnia and Herzegovina realistic or not?

Izetbegović: I do not know if you have noticed a certain hidden note in the recognition we were offered. Milošević is offering unilateral instead of bilateral recognition and is asking a very high price for this. He is recognising some of Bosnia, which does not exist. He is recognising a Bosnia and Herzegovina according to his taste. The price he asks is lifting the sanctions. We said that we were not interested in something like this. It is obvious that Milošević wants to secure two things: the lifting of sanctions by formally recognising a country that does not exist and at the same time continue with the realisation of the Great Serbia plan. Since Milošević is presenting himself here as peacemaker, it reminds me of Klauzevic's witty thought: 'When the aggressor reaches his goals, he turns into a peacemaker.'

Jean Barrio: You said that the West has betrayed Bosnia, which means that Bosnia is closer to the Islamic world. What do you think, what can Bosnia expect from the Muslim world?

Izetbegović: Bosnia is an European country. I am a Muslim, but a European at the same time. I feel good about being able to be both. A very similar thing is going on with Bosnia. It belongs both to the East and West. It is an interesting country, a land on the so-called Big Border. The line of interaction between the East and West moved over Bosnia for hundreds of years and it has created what we call a Bosnian spirit. The main characteristic of this spirit is tolerance, the ability to live with someone who is different from you. Recently massacres in Srebrenica and Žepa took place. There was no attempt by the Bosnian people to get back at the Serbian people for these. So, this is my reply. We belong to two different worlds at the same time and we are happy that this is so.

Jean Barrio: Allow me to ask you one more question Mr. President. The Western press insists on inner division among the Serbs, it is said that Mr. Milošević knows about the diplomatic card, and that Mr. Karadžić is an extremist. General Mladić would be the one closer to Milošević, the man you can negotiate with.

Izetbegović: There is not much difference between Karadžić and Mladić. On the other hand, the two of them are different from Milošević. Milošević is less a nationalist, more a striver for power.

Jean Barrio: The main problem between Croatia and Serbia is East Slavonia. Will Serbia withdraw from this Croatian province or will there be war? What is your estimation?

Izetbegović: I think they will withdraw from Slavonia. But this cannot be done immediately. The doctors say that you can't have two injections on the same day. One has to be left for the next day. But Serbia will withdraw, I am almost sure of this. In a few months maybe.

Jean Barrio: I would like to ask you a somewhat personal question. First, did you have friends among the Serbs before the war? Do you still have those friends and what do you talk to them about? And the third question is: do you think that some day you will make peace with the Serbs?

Izetbegović: Two of my friends are present here, both Serbs: Prof. Kovač, our Ambassador in Paris and Mr. Miro Lazović, President of the Bosnian Assembly. I was not raised in hate. If we are talking about mentality it could be said that the Bosnian mentality is closer to the Serbian than the Croatian, because we used to live together for a long time under Turkish authority. It is said Bosnians and Serbs have something in common: they like beautiful women and good horses. I do not think that evil nations exist. There are nations with bad leadership. The Germans are a good example. I always believed that the Germans were a good people. Goethe, Beethoven, Einstein were Germans. But, at one time an evil team led the German population and they committed horrible crimes.

Jean Barrio: Now one question concerning the cause of war. What do you think of the moment when Croatia and Slovenia were recognised as independent states? I think I heard that you said this was done at the right time. What do you think of that decision, did it contribute to the development of happenings?

Izetbegović: That was a good decision for Slovenia and Croatia, but bad for Bosnia and Herzegovina. Maybe, and I say maybe, it made the peaceful solution initiated by Lord Carrington impossible. The question is: could things have gone another way? But this takes us into the philosophy of history: why did something happen in history? If Hegel is right, Yugoslavia had to fall apart. Do you remember his statement that all that failed in history failed for a reason? And Tolstoy wrote that big book, his famous novel, to show that people do not rule history. Nobody knows why history flows the way it does. I do not feel capable of finding and understanding the reasons for the course of history. God is the One with His plan. This is what I believe.

Jean Barrio: Allow me to contradict you with your own words. You just said that people were not bad themselves, but that they are led by some group. Isn't there a contradiction between the two?

Izetbegović: Yes, it apparently may be a contradiction. Every important judgement on life is usually contradictory.

Jean Barrio: Mr. President, I was about to thank you for this conversation, bearing in mind your obligations. But, let me ask you, do you consider possible the establishing of some new, old Yugoslavia? Also, minding the fact that Yugoslavia means South Slovenians, would establishing a new political whole in some 20 to 30 years be possible?

Izetbegović: I don't think so, because those key factors that could form such a Yugoslavia – Slovenia and Croatia – decided to go their own way, while Bosnia and Herzegovina was in between. I think that Croatia and Slovenia would never again accept Yugoslavia because of their bad experience with it. Since we have a few more minutes, I can tell you that in the beginning Yugoslavia was not a bad idea, but Serbian national egoism ruined it. For the entire time, the Serbs tried to maintain their hegemony in Yugoslavia. I apologise to my Serbian friends, but this is unfortunately true. Yugoslavia could have been a country of equal nations and survived like that. In 1990 and 1991, I still believed in Yugoslavia. But it turned out to be a machine that could not be repaired. If I was to give some sort of diagnosis, I would say that Serbian hegemony was in the basis of Yugoslavia, so the Yugoslavian idea became unacceptable for Croatia and Slovenia.

Jean Barrio: Do you think that Yugoslavia was a bad idea?

Izetbegović: I don't think that it was a bad idea, but the implementation of it was bad.

Jean Barrio: Why did the Serbs for such a long time accept having a Croat running them?

Izetbegović: This question regards the character of the Communist system. In the eyes of many, Josip Broz was not a Croat, but the leader of the Communist Party. But, of course, this is more complicated. Bolshevism is a system that was based on the idea of communism, and this idea, at least in principle, rejected the idea of nation and nationalism. However, that situation is always temporary because nations are a reality.

Jean Barrio: What is the role of religion in this conflict, and what do you think about it?

Izetbegović: After many years of communist repression came a return to religion and it is an almost general phenomenon. Religion is a great idea that is very often misused. This is what happened in the Balkans these last few years. Personally, I am a religious man, but I can give you a whole bunch of examples of religion being misused in history. But this will not run down religion, nor has many sad previous episodes. Christ's idea outlived the Crusades and bad popes, and many tragic and bad things, because faith is indestructible, like life. But this is another subject.

Jean Barrio: Mr. President, thank you, we have run out of time. I wish to express our admiration for your personality, you have managed to draw great sympathies with the sublimity of your ideas and the goals you fight for and your endurance on that path. Thank you.

Appendix 5

Two Interviews for the Sarajevo Weekly *Dani*

Among numerous interviews from that ten-year period, I have picked out two for these Appendices, both published in the Sarajevan magazine *Dani*. These interviews were made three years after each other. The first one in December 1994, at the height of the war, the second in March 1998 when we were at peace. I will quote them without comment. In essence, I consider that the questions depict the situation and changes better than the answers do. Both interviews were made by Senad Pećanin, the leading editor of *Dani*.

First interview – 11 December 1994
Dani: In the long history of Bosnia and Herzegovina, its fate has been decided either by foreign conquerors or big powers. But, in either instance, the people living in the country decided its fate the least. Will history repeat itself now and more drastically than ever?
Izetbegović: I would not on the whole agree with you. We are actively taking part in creating what is called our destiny. The matter of results is a different question. It is not a question of our greater or lesser involvement, but the relation of forces. Very powerful factors have become involved in our destiny, either by inertia or by action. The West mostly by inertia, but inertia is a force as well. Still, if I should estimate the final outcome of all this push and pull, I think that our people will finally have their state and their say.
Dani: The role of Russia, Great Britain and France in aggression against Bosnia and Herzegovina is, although neither logical nor understandable, pretty clear. But, it seems to me that the greatest unknown quantity in our politics is the intent of the USA concerning Bosnia and Herzegovina. Do you believe that the current American Aministration will

overcome its 'politic-strategic provincialism' of the thesis according to which 'America, actually, does not have security interests in Bosnia'?

Izetbegović: Recently, I read of a study by a group of competent American authors. According to this study, Bosnia falls into the third category of American interest, which is pretty low. This tendency has been present from the beginning of the crisis in ex-Yugoslavia. We have always, mostly without success, tried to convince America of the need to actively, not as a watcher, involve itself in the solving of the Bosnian crisis. The answer was always, directly or not, that Bosnia is primarily a European problem and European responsibility.

Frankly, I do not understand this underestimation of the problem, but we cannot do anything in this regard. When I met President Clinton, a few days ago in Budapest, I made the last attempt, telling him that the Russians had reached the Mediterranean. My allusion was clear, that this had happened during the time of Bill Clinton's presidency. That was nothing new. I would like to remind you that the USA took the same reserved stance at the time of crisis between Yugoslavia and the USSR when Brežnev directly threatened Tito. Asked the question of whether the USA would take Yugoslavia into its protection, American President Jimmy Carter simply said that that would be a very serious matter, but that the USA would not intervene militarily. Some people said that Carter then offered Yugoslavia to the Russians on a plate. As you can see, things have not changed. My strongest personal opinion is that America does not have defined politics when it comes to Bosnia. That is why we should keep on working so that these politics are in Bosnia's interest.

Dani: Would you accept the announced military help in man-power terms from the group of Islamic countries (Malaysia, Iran, Pakistan, Turkey), should the UN Security Council withdraw peace-keeping forces from Bosnia and Herzegovina? What would be the consequences if you decided to accept this offer?

Izetbegović: Yes, I would accept it. I am aware of the risks of such a decision, but in the situation as it is and as it could become, it would be irresponsible to make the opposite decision. People would not understand nor would they approve it.

Dani: Mr. President, it seems that both Bosnia and Herzegovina and you personally differ from all little and new European states and officials, because neither Bosnia nor you are under the control or protection of any large state in the world. There is no state official who can call you and determine Bosnia's attitude on any question. Could Bosnia and Herzegovina have been an interest-politic dominion of the USA,

Germany, Iran or Turkey for instance, and to which extent was your independence in decision-making an obstacle for the inner bonding of Bosnia and Herzegovina and some 'protector state'?

Izetbegović: We acted independently, but we refused no one's shield, which does not mean that we would have accepted anyone's protection. There are 'death embraces'.

Dani: Could such a bonding at the outset of the aggression against Bosnia have reduced its consequences and could such a bonding eventually save Bosnia in the future?

Izetbegović: The Americans have a saying that every success comes from the inside. We have to keep our defense on some level high enough, by ourselves, we must endure and then we will find allies in the world. I see no other way. Anyway, if it is about our influence, the possibility for our influence succeeding is very high on the inside and very reduced on the outside.

Dani: Mr. President, your charisma for the Bosniac people is not in question. You are no longer just the President of a party or the highest state organ, but you have also become a symbol of the Bosniac people and the first great leader of these people in their history. Although I will risk feeling like one of the many Yugoslavian journalists who interviewed President Tito (I have no bad intent with this parallel, not to flatter you nor to offend you) I want to ask you: what after you? Do you see people around you who could replace you in the historically most delicate moment for the Bosniac people? I know many different people, from those who adore you to those who negate you, but all agree that you represent one of the crucial defense factors for the survival of the Bosniac people?

Izetbegović: I have to gather myself a bit after hearing your question. First of all, I think you are exaggerating. I am just a president chosen in free elections and I know what that means. I am flattered by what you have said, but if I think it over better, I also have reason to be sad, worried and maybe even angry. Allow me not to agree with the idea that I am so important for the defense and survival of the Bosniac people. It would not be good if this was so, but, thank God, it isn't. Thousands of people are fighting, I make it easier for them as they do for me, but they would fight without me and they will continue fighting when I'm gone. I was sure of this in October of 1992. This was the first time that I went all over Bosnia at the height of war. I repeated this tour two months later, in December. I went to Gradačac, that was defended and would definitely be freed after a battle on November 1992, when we destroyed their tanks in the plains surrounding Gradačac. What did I and the people around me in Sarajevo do to help them? Not much! We helped them by organising the people before the war and preparing some guns, unfortunately not many, and by delivering them some anti-armour weapons before this crucial battle in November. They did everything else by themselves, on their personal initiative, organising help from our people in Europe. They showed a great deal of independency, skill and imagination in this. Remember the armoured train that soldiers from Gradačac lured in and destroyed. That was not our idea, they both planned and executed it. I could give you a bunch of such examples. Reviving our military industry is a special story when it comes to local wit and local initiative. These people, fortunately, do not depend on individuals. The blockage of Sarajevo had one good side: it contributed to the growth and independency of people. They developed faster going through these sufferings and facing immediate danger. This is why I consider the statement – when Alija is gone Bosnia will shake – dangerous and false. Already, in the party, government and presidency, there are completely formed people. The party has for a long time been run by Bičakčić, the government by Silajd•ić and the presidency by Ganić. I will urge these men to continue making agreements and cooperation. People will some day say who will be at the head, as soon as they have the opportunity in free elections. Until then, they should be patient and work together with the people.

Dani: In Bosniac people, and even in the SDA and authority itself, the gap between two lines is becoming deeper and deeper: the radical line, that we could call religious, and the moderate, civic line. Is this division slowly becoming a serious threat and is the 'religious fanatism' of the first line or the 'cosmopolitanism and lack of patriotism' of the second line responsible for it?

Izetbegović: The SDA is a large party and it is no wonder that it has more streams. It reflects our people the way they are, maybe along with some of its contradictions and inconsistencies. Our people like religion, but without exaggeration. It is a typical nation on a Big Border, the borderline of two worlds. Our faith is Eastern our education is European. Our hearts belong to one world, our minds to another. There is some far Bogumil component of forgiveness and goodness in all of that. Any of us who are honest must admit that they often ask themselves: who are they, what world do they belong to? My answer is that I am a European Muslim and I feel comfortable with this definition.

I have strayed away a little from your question. So, it would be bad if the streams in the party went on hardening so that the religious line sharply separates from the common. I would like the party to continue to look like our people, and for it to be so. These two tendencies must not grow farther apart. They should grow closer. This way we will have the most efficient combination for the future.

Dani: You are viewed as a tolerant man and a democratic politician, in spite of or maybe thanks to the fact that you have experienced the repression of the former totalitarian system yourself. But, the party of which you are the founder and representative is beginning to act exactly the same as the last one. It is much easier for Bosniacs to live, fight, work and claim their rights if they are members of the SDA. In plebian language: where is this leading?

Izetbegović: Lately we have seen a strong influx of people that belonged to the former system into the SDA. Of course, there is the question: are they coming in for their convictions, ambitions or as a result of pressure. One thing is sure: there is no direct pressure, maybe indirect. Talking about people from the former system we respect those who stayed with the people and continued to honestly work and fight in the places they were in. On the other side, those people respect the SDA that persistently kept on fighting for Bosnia and these people. So, recognition and respect is mutual. Of course, there are ambitions and indirect pressures here and there, especially in the provinces, but this is not the main trend and it cannot explain the situation. Anyway, all parties have full freedom to act, some have their own media and skilled staff. The state of war might be contributing to homogenisation, but this is not urged by the SDA. People faced with danger instinctively feel the need to come together, or at least not to scatter around. And about that 'easier life' – as far as I know, everyone has a difficult life.

Dani: Mr. President, with the strength of your authority and power you are able to influence the course of all social movements – from the economy, to education, the position of religious communities, to cadre, foreign or internal politics and defence. How do you privately cope with that fact, how do you carry such a burden?

Izetbegović: I think that you are overestimating my authority and my influence. The only thing I know is that I have a lot of work, that I am always in a hurry, that I hardly manage to get things done on time and that I am endlessly thankful to anyone who does not ask me much and does their job well.

Dani: Are you afraid of the possibility that the forced lines of international politics and dishonourable interests might overlap at a point when it will be clear that there will be no Bosnia and Herzegovina and that further struggle could be counterproductive?

Izetbegović: Somebody said that a world war is taking place in Bosnia but that this is not seen. They obviously aimed at the strong involvement of almost all relevant world forces in this conflict. If I was to rank the forces which influence the events in Bosnia, I would still put on top our military and political influence, because it is, unlike others, direct and because we know the situation better than others, generally and in detail. Nobody has the right to say that there will be no Bosnia any more and that fighting for it might be counterproductive. There is no right of opinion on that matter.

Dani: Will Bosnia and Herzegovina exist in 100 years and when will the war end?

Izetbegović: I think that I have just answered the first part of your question, and when the war will end I do not know and am not ashamed to say so. I am certain that at this moment no one in the world knows this. There are so many changing and unpredictable factors. Our job is to work and fight and to do the best we can, and God runs history. This is what I believe.

Second interview – March 1998
Dani: Mr. President, if we were to agree that the last arbitrated decision on the status of Brčko is actually a decision made by the American Administration, is there room for drawing further conclusions about the USA's relations to Bosnia and Herzegovina or maybe the Bosniacs?

Izetbegović: Yes, some changes in the behaviour of the American side are noticeable, but it can still not be judged if they are of a tactical or strategic nature. If they turn out to be strategic, our media contributed to it hugely, by keeping silent about everything good in Bosnia and exaggerating whatever bad there was. In any case there are still not enough elements for reaching conclusions on what this is about. We will see.

Dani: I believe that you too are familiar with the fact that officials of the American Administration at various levels, as well as High Representative Westendorp, together with today's opposition leaders openly and without circling, are pointing out the importance of tearing you down politically. Are you aware that there is no place for you, as well as for the actual leaders of the Croatian people, in the Western perspective of prosperity and stability in Bosnia and Herzegovina and in the region?

Izetbegović: I do not believe and I am not aware of such speculations, but it seems that you are openly cheering for foreigners. I do not know why, after everything that has happened, you believe that foreigners are better friends to these people than me. But that is your choice. As far as I am concerned, I always cheer for the home team, even if they are worse, and these people are not bad, they are good. Anyway, the people do not even exist in your question at all. You have Americans and Westendorp and the Western perspective, but there are no people whose head this is about in your vision. You have forgotten them completely. I think they have some say about this, or at least they should have. And whether I will be present in all this, I will decide. My comfort is, if I need comfort at all, that your predictions are usually wrong. I do not read your magazine regularly, but I could give you a bunch of your predictions and diagnoses that were a complete miss. I will only mention the last one, that you personally signed, that the Arbiter would hand Brčko over to Republika Srpska and that it was a closed deal. It did not happen nor will it happen. And all this putting me in the same line with those that you call Croatian leaders and your stubborn equalling of aggressors and those who defended Bosnia, I leave it to the reader's judgement. One thing is sure: this equalling, no matter who does it, does not help Bosnia, on the contrary.

Dani: Many were surprised when recently, among oppositionists, at the call of British Minister Cook, Edhem Bičakčić, Jadranko Prlić and Neven Tomić appeared at the meeting. Do you believe that the West will use the same scenario to tear down the SDA and HDZ, the scenario they used to tear down the SDS, and will Western officials among Cook's collocutors from authority look for a 'Biljana Plavšić'?

Izetbegović: They can look if they have nothing smarter to do, with the regard that we did not have Karadžićs, Mladićs, Bobans, and we will probably not have a Biljana Plavšić either.

Dani: Academic Muhamed Filipović told me that your current situation reminds him of the situation Hamdija Pozderac found himself in before his resignation from the Central Committee. But, according to Filipović, there are two differences: Pozderac was taken down by great-Serbian hegemonists, and you by the international community with America at its head; and second, Pozderac did not withdraw for the well-being of Bosnia and the Bosniacs, and you should have done just that. How do you see this observation?

Izetbegović: I don't know what Mr. Filipović told you, or what you told him, but you both have the right to your opinion. You mention two differences between Pozderac and me, but you have forgotten the third, most important one: Pozderac's fate was decided by the Central Committee, and mine will be decided by my people and myself.

Dani: A great part of the public was surprised by your recent negative stance concerning the role of Branko Mikulić and Hamdija Pozderac in later Bosnian history. Understanding your personal ruin, a feeling of suffering that they are responsible for, I want to ask you: don't you think that your judgement was too harsh and that a great part of the public, Bosniacs if you will, does not see them in that light, especially not after the war?

Izetbegović: How do you know what 'a great part of the public' is thinking? And my opinion about Mikulić and Pozderac does not have much to do with my feelings, although their Central Committee once sentenced me to 14, yes, 14 years of imprisonment for nothing more than the written word. How many years of prison would you get for your writing, if this notorious law was not abolished on the initiative of the SDA that you hate so much? Let me remind you: in the show that you are mentioning, I said that those two politicians were good Bosnians but that they were not democrats. And I suppose that most of the public agrees with me on this. Or, do you think that the two of them were democrats? If so, try to explain that in your papers.

Dani: No matter how much, partially still on no basis, international officials 'rubbed your nose' with Milorad Dodik, it seems to me that you have not managed to find an adequate answer to the radical turnabout in the politics of Republika Srpska's Government. I think that such an answer cannot be found by the nature of your authority, but it is far more important what you think of this.

Izetbegović: I still do not see any true turnabout in the politics of Republika Srpska. I have to admit that I was startled, especially by the 'famous' idea about a uni-national pluralism, that was supposed to be taken as a lesson by us. For a moment then I thought that I did not know what pluralism was, but I soon gathered my wits. It seems that you have not as yet. You take Mr. Dodik's statements for granted. Serious people do not do that, and neither does America, I think. I do not see any realistic, and even less radical, turnaround in Dodik, so I have no reason to reply. If you see something more than words in Dodik's dealing, you can try to explain that in your paper as well.

Dani: It seems to me that lately you often have the need to reconsider the two most important political decisions you have made in your life –

the one about war (the independence of Bosnia and Herzegovina) and the one about peace (accepting the Dayton Agreement). Do I have the right impression?

Izetbegović: Yes, you are right. I think about these things very often, I must admit. The price of both was very high and only an irresponsible man could put those matters *ad hoc*. I have asked many wise men that question, could it have been done differently or in another way. No competent person from among the Bosniac people said that different decisions were possible. One exception though is Mr. Halid Čaušević, but the man turned 80 a long time ago.

Dani: Is the reason for your more and more frequent unmeasured qualifications and insults that you throw onto your critics the feeling of a gradual loss of power? When your colleague Tuđman does that, it is not a surprise. But I am shocked by the manner in which you disqualified Halid Čaušević, for example, because of his opinions published in his interview in *Dani*.

Izetbegović: A great number of people, I mean those who do not know Čaušević, were shocked by his statement that the Bosniacs should have remained in a rump Yugoslavia, that they are the one to blame for the war, etc. And I am shocked too by your writings, especially by the fact that everything Bosniac is strange and ugly to you, and everything non-Bosniac close and beautiful. You have an unjustified complex. I assure you that love and respect for your own people, especially if it is worth the respect, as the Bosniacs are, is not nationalism of any sort. It is a normal human feeling.

Dani: When you recently came down on 'magazines' from Sarajevo, you called upon your right to reply to the journalists who attack you. It is true that presidents in democratic societies can choose the way to reply to the media, but you do not have that democratic right because of the nature of your authority. This is why your speech in the Congress of Bosniac Intellectuals Council marked the beginning of prosecution against 'magazines': first *Reis-ul-ulema* spat on us, then the regime's media, followed by problems in print and distribution, then RTV B&H forbade our paid marketing, then came a court trial for which I could envy you the treatment you had during your own. I do not believe that you wanted or ordered these consequences, but you must have been aware of them. Would you repeat your speech and opinions on 'magazines' today?

Izetbegović: Of course I would, because I condemn lies. I did not condemn the media, but the lies in them. I do not know why I should change my opinion on lies and why I should not call a lie its proper name. And I also do not know why I should not answer you harshly? Why do you think that journalists are untouchable? You can put out lies and people remain silent or else you will immediately shriek out that you are endangered. You are not. The endangered ones are those who are slandered with your words and who can hardly get satisfaction for that. You have offended thousands of brave men who defended this country, and aroused justified anger in the public that you call persecution and pressure on a so-called free media. It is well known that the media are not innocent in creating hatred and causing this war. When some reasonable people pointed this out at that time, it was also said that the freedom of the media is jeopardised. You went to court because you offended your journalist colleague and he sued you. Why do you involve other people in this? And then you say that you had a court trial that was more brutal than mine. That is the real measure for your objectiveness. You really are a man who thinks that you just need to launch new and new untruths until something sticks. I do not see why you think that you are entitled to lie just because you are a journalist? So, I would again today repeat what I said, but I doubt that you will once again write so scandalously about Bosnia and its army. Not because authorities would hold it against you, but because your readers would. Mr. Pećanin, you are underestimating these people. You think they are stupid and uninformed, and they are not. You cannot maintain your edition level on sensations only.

Dani: To the oft-repeated calls about the honesty of people from your close surroundings (Čengić, Šahinpašić) you have only replied with your personal opinion that Hasan Čengić was an honest man. Your answer seems incomplete to me. When will you finally show the bills for donations for the defense of Bosnia, the money routes, spending practices, about who helped Bosnia and how much in the war…? How many people are familiar with those secrets but you and your son? If it is still not the time to publish this information, is there one state organ that you feel obligated to report this to?

Izetbegović: I cannot file a report because I did not protocol this, nor was it my obligation. This was done by the National Bank of Bosnia and Herzegovina and it has all donation documentation that went through me. There are a few hundred, maybe even over a thousand points. One part of the donations went to the *Šehid*-invalid fund that has its own service. Talking to Mr. Slišković, President of the Federal Parliament Commission, I brought out these facts. I do not know if he asked for and got data from the National Bank. I personally think that no one has complete evidence of all the donations for Bosnia and Herzegovina because they were not centralised and most of them did not go through the government, but directly to some cities, humanitarian organisations and army units, etc. The report of use of a donation is regularly given to the donor, and as far as I know, this is what Čengić did. I still think that Čengić is an honest man. He is not a person who would take something for himself, I am sure of that. And look at your question. It is an example of an imputation. You mention my son, as if by the way, but what you are really doing is making him suspect. What does my son have to do with donations? If you know something, bring it into the open like a man, not like this as if you said something but then you didn't. Let me remind you: two or three years ago you published a story that I was preparing my son as successor and other such stupidities. So, what do you say now, am I preparing my son to take my position? You never apologised for this disinformation, not to me, not to the public, you just keep on and on with it.

Dani: I would like to continue, if you don't mind. What is it that has changed since November last year when you stated: 'With this mind, I will not run for the next elections'?

Izetbegović: Well, a lot of things changed, which can be seen by virtue of your questions and my answers. A strange campaign has begun. It started, among other things, to seek to convince us that Dodik's uni-national authority, a 100% uni-national, and uni-national Serbian media, a 100% uni-national, and ethnically totally cleansed territory of Republika Srpska, incidentally it is not 100%, but 97%, that all of this is an example of pluralism and democracy that we should follow up. I have to admit that this twisted logic confused us for a moment. I do not know if there is a connection, but it was coincidental with my statement that I would probably retire. Then I started thinking should I help them in this way. This does not mean that I have decided to run for election, I am just stating some of my thoughts.

Dani: How do you explain the fact that your former closest associates now present you in a very bad light? The last case of this is Sefer Halilović's book, and I hear that Rusmir Mahmutčehaić is also finishing a book that you will not like at all.

Izetbegović: You mention only two men who are not fond of me, and I think that there are a thousand like them. I never thought that all people should like me, why would they? Much better men than I had bitter enemies, why shouldn't I? Jesus was handed over to the Romans by his fellow citizens, Gandhi was not killed by Englishmen, but by his own people, he was not a good enough Indian for them, Rabin was not killed by an Arab, but by his own man, he was not a good enough Jew for them, etc. What can we do? Soon, green grass will grow over all of us, but people do not think about that.

Dani: You have explained the reasons why you gave up the idea of SDA civic profiling. But, did you not overestimate the strength of the rightists in the Bosnian national corpus? And more importantly, who else can remove the danger of the political radicalisation of the party on a religious basis, if not you?

Izetbegović: As long as Islam is free in Bosnia, there will be no political radicalisation of the SDA. Radicalism will occur here and there, but those will be individual cases. There is radicalism in every nation and every state. That is nothing unusual.

Dani: How do you see the more important presence of Wahabi believers and those who agree with the Taliban movement in public. Should the Islamic community have an opinion on this?

Izetbegović: My understanding of Islam is obviously different from theirs. I do not think that a woman should cover her face. Not only do I not think so, but I am against it. In the Harem of Makkah, I did not see a woman with a covered face, or they were very rare. Why should they be in Sarajevo? But those are some religious questions under the jurisdiction of the Islamic community. I do not know how many Wahabis there are in Bosnia, and as long as they use allowed means, that is words, their activity is legal. This is a free country. If you, Mr. Pećanin can say and write whatever you please, why shouldn't they? Such views are interesting to the authorities only if the people expressing them want to impose their opinions by force or urge violence.

Dani: You call upon us to 'all be a little less Bosniac, Croat and Serb and a little more Bosnian'; I understood as your confession that Bosnia cannot exist as a happy country on the basis of national parties' projections, not even those before the war. To be so, is it necessary to give up a part of Bosniac-ness, Croatian-ness and Serbian-ness for the maintaining of Bosnia?

Izetbegović: The sentence you quoted frankly expresses my opinion. And it is: to be Bosnians, it is not necessary that we stop being Bosniacs, Croats and Serbs, let's be Bosnians along with that. Of course, Bosnian-ness is not an ethnical pointer here.

Dani: Do you believe that the final destiny of Bosnia will be determined by a 'Huntington' clash or just by classical interests of outer and inner political actors?

Izetbegović: Finally a good question. History is not exact in the way that mathematics and physics are. Here it is important what you believe and that you know in which direction you are going. I can just say that I do not believe that a conflict of civilisations is inevitable. I do not believe that it is one of the inexorable laws of history and I do not believe at all in the existence of something called history laws, some sort of determinism in history. History is, at least in some measure, a domain of human freedom. That is why its course is unpredictable. Therefore, in one part of the world something very close to a conflict of civilisations may be taking place and yet in another at the same time, something contradictory: dialogue and cooperation. This depends on people, or great people, who are significantly influencing happenings at the moment. When it comes to Bosnia, we wish for dialogue and cooperation. But this is just my wish and my striving that collides with many other factors that might pull to the other side. What the result of all those factors will be is hard to say. Ours is to work. The outcome is not in our hands. I am pleased for I believe the outcome is in God's hands.

Dani: And finally, what did you think when you stood over the grave of General Hajrulahović and said in your speech: '…With all protocol exaggerations…' Do you know that many people did not like these words?

Izetbegović: I do not think so. On the contrary, I think that the late Mustafa would have agreed with me. On that occasion I also said many beautiful words about the General. The others noticed this. You, as usual, did not.

Appendix 6

Lecture at the ISESCO Meeting

Riyadh, 6 December 1997.

It is a great honour to speak to this magnificent gathering of cultural representatives from all sides of the Islamic world.

Before I get on with my speech, I have to thank God for helping us to hold this significant meeting.

I also want to express three gratitudes to the Keeper of the two Sacred Temples, King Fahd bin Abdul Aziz, the Government and people of Saudi Arabia: first, for hosting this assembly, second, for the efforts put into building Islamic cultural centres worldwide and third, for the support and help they provided for my country in the hardest days of its history. God will reward them for this great effort.

Although I have been separated from writing for many years, I will try to bring out and explain some thoughts on the exceptionally important issue of education and of our common Islamic culture and civilisation. These are the subjects that many significant Islamic writers and reformers have written about in the past two centuries.

As you know, they were all dissatisfied with the conditions that pertained to these matters. They all wondered why the followers of Islam of the day did not hold on to the oft-repeated and very clear commandment of their faith concerning learning. To remind you, the commandment is: 'Watch…', and varies throughout the Qur'an continually (Qur'an, verses 3/164, 6/95-99, 21/33, 22/45-46, etc.) and reaches its literal form in some verses of the Holy Book: 'Will not they watch a camel the way it was created, and the sky the way it was risen, and mountains how they were placed, and the land how it was spread (88/17-20)… Did you watch the seed that you plant…and the water that you drink…and the fire that you light…' (Qur'an, 56/63-71).

And watching is the true beginning of the first science. Jean Fourastie writes in the *Civilisation of Tomorrow*: 'Watching nature, society, people, is the first stage of main education of children from the West... Interest for the outer world is contrary to the interest of a Brahman philosopher who turns from the outside world to the inside one'.

Why did this 'watching' in the Muslim world stop and what are its consequences?

An unhappy and unjustified percentage of illiterate population is very high among some Muslim nations. I am reading UNESCO's report on the percentage of illiterate persons from 1995. Muslim countries (I will not name them): 38, 24, 48, 56, 54, 33, 56, 28, 21, 18, 21, even 68% of the population is illiterate. The average is 40%, but 60% among our women. This state was present in Europe in the second half of the 19th century, which means that we are dangerously and alarmingly late. Other comparisons with the Western world are also defeating and worrying.

The average number of students in Islamic countries is about 1,000 to 100,000 citizens, while that number is 3,500 in the countries of the West, which means that it is more than three and a half times bigger. The average number of daily papers is 40 to 1,000 citizens in Islamic countries and more than 300 in the West. The number of TV sets in Muslim countries is 100 to 1,000 citizens, and over 500 in Western countries.

Public funds for education are properly alike in Muslim and countries of the West, they are about 5.5% of gross national income, but this is just a relative relation. Absolute outcomes are little because the national income in Muslim countries is very low in most cases.

Education and the reconstruction of Islamic culture and civilisation are in direct relation with the liberation processes that took place in many Muslim countries during this century. The degree of slavery is in adverse relation with the degree of education. School is the best means to fight against any sort of slavery. The conclusion then? We should strongly increase funds for education and do so without delay.

One of the latest books that found its way into my hands is *Islam and Democracy* by John Esposito. He states the fact that the end of this century is passing under the mark of two processes in Islamic countries: a return to Islam and a demand for democracy. In front of all wise Muslims stands the task to harmonise these two processes in the best way. In the era of this technological revolution every free Muslim nation can solve the illiteracy problem relatively quickly and successfully. This is a problem of political will and determination, and then organisation, which is usually not our strong side.

But technology, the so-called third wave that has already spread over developed parts of the world carries with it many advantages and many dangers. There is a well-known and mixed feeling of uneasiness and fear at this so-called progress that is not based on belief in God. But there is also learn, read, and research, in the name of your Lord – this Islamic concept of education is facing great challenges and I want to say a couple of words concerning this today.

In a book I published a long time ago, I proposed making a difference between culture and civilisation, where it is commonly interweaved. A similar thought was presented by much more important authors before me. Culture and civilisation reflect two worlds that are apart. The bearer of culture is man as an individual, the bearer of civilisation is society. Culture's goal is power over oneself through raising one's standards, civilisation's goal is power over nature through science. Culture is turning to a man's inner world and civilisation to the outer world, etc.

When I think of these matters today, I inevitably remind myself that the first received verse of the Qur'an covers both aspects of meaning, both relations, both actions. In the first word of *ikra*, there is a strong call, an emphasis upon man to explore the outside world, but this exploring is not the pure accumulation of knowledge, it is not indifferent, without wish and striving, it is religious in the best meaning of that word, because the verse continues: '…in the name of your Lord', 'Read in the name of God', which makes this learning a noble meditation, reading of God's signs in the physical world. This is the specific thing for Islamic culture, past and future. The object of study is not an 'indifferent nature' but the world that is God's work of art. This approach was never lost, regardless of the numerous attacks on Islamic culture especially on the margins of the Islamic world, regardless of the stagnation of scientific, technical and technological civilisation. Just a light breath of freedom is sufficient for our people to start returning to the sources of their own culture. These are the values that we must be aware of. They can help avoid bad products of civilisational growth that we see in the West and that the West is aware of too.

This takes us to the inevitable matter of the relation between Islamic and Western culture and civilisation. Different studies and books have been written on this subject. One of the authors so occupied with this question, a writer who had both Islamic and Western experiences, Muhammed Asad, described the Western spirit in his well-known book of essays *Islam at the Crossroads*: 'Contemporary Western civilisation does not recognise the necessity of a man serving anything but economic, social or national demands. Its true value is not spiritual: it is comfort.

And its true, life philosophy is expressed in the will for power because of power itself. Both were inherited from the old Roman civilization.'

Muhammed Asad is maybe too critical towards Europe and America and we have to be cautious about his too strict remarks. I personally think that a relatively thin layer of Western society is corrupted and degenerated. The great majority of common people study and work hard and live for their families. The West is strong and a corrupted society cannot be strong.

The truth is that contemporary Western philosophers and futurologists are pointing to the danger of spiritual desertion and deformation, when describing the metropolises of this civilisation. They bring out convincing facts about the so-called mass culture with its serial production of 'spiritual goods', copies, shoddily executed and with no sense for individuality.

Speaking of relations between the Islamic and the West-European culture of civilisation, Muslims are facing a choice where they have to avoid two extremes: the general refusal of Western civilisation and blind following of it. Both are equally dangerous. If we do not cooperate, our weakness will extend infinitely. If we accept this civilisation unselectively, we will lose our identity and stop being who we are.

But we cannot cut ourselves off from the world. Here we must remember what our Prophet said, that knowledge should be looked for 'even in China'. Western civilisation is some sort of international result, contributed by numerous scientists of different religions and nationalities. The power of the West lies not in its economy and military power. That is the external aspect. The permanent source of this power is critical thought, that Europe has maintained since Bacon, who probably got it from the Arabs. This is the second thing that is essential for us.

Muslim wise men are warning of the so-called children's disease of copying Western culture. Asad even dared to say that the harmful consequences of this copying are much greater than the material advantage that it could give Muslims! It is impossible to copy a civilisation in its external dimension without at the same time being under the influence of the spirit that produced that civilisation. Even more because Western civilisation is egocentric, it imposes its own world history picture and because hatred for Islam often sparks from its spirit – under the unremovable shadow of the Crusades. Absorbing this spirit creates an inferiority complex in young generations of Muslims, which includes rejection of their own culture. If we study conflict today in our Muslim populations who had direct contact with Western civilisation, we will notice they are about conflicts of 'progressive' pro-Westerner and 'conservative' traditionalists. This conflict has torn apart Muslim society with sad and catastrophic consequences.

I would like to pick out two large and contemporary ideas that circulate through the European mind now and suggest that we think about them. The first is the one about an open society advocated by Karl Popper in his book *Open Society and its Enemies*. Such (open) society includes the freedom of the individual, personality development, free thought, the right to criticise political establishments, the free exchange of ideas, etc. Why don't Muslims take part in this? Furthermore, Popper's ideas urge tolerance and a stand against the barbaric acts in Europe that are very often used against Muslims on the Continent.

The second idea is the New European Renaissance advocated by German philosopher Weizsacker. This idea differs from the first European Renaissance in turning to worlds and cultures out of Europe, so, according to this philosopher, it will also turn to Islam, its culture and civilisation. I think that we have to enter this game. Didn't the Qur'an call upon us to 'Strive to achieve the virtue of deeds'? (Qur'an 5/48). But we can strive only when we strengthen the consciousness of our identity. Conscious Muslims are ready to give and receive, without throwing their authentic values into oblivion.

To end, a few words on our Bosnian experience. We have participated in the Islamic culture for centuries and in the last century in Western-European civilisation too. Many think that we are one of the most educated Muslim nations. Our encounter with West-European civilisation is direct, daily and inevitable. The regimes under which we have lived in the past hundred years or more, were not Islamic each in their own way. In spite of the unseen devastation of traces of our Islamic culture, we were never assimilated, we kept our strong feeling of belonging to our religion and culture. During this last aggression against Bosnia and Herzegovina, more than 1,000 mosques and 334 Islamic cultural objects were destroyed. Numerous schools, institutes and libraries were devastated. One Turkish historian compared the culturocide in Bosnia – of course, minding the proportions – to the Mongolians tearing apart of Baghdad in the 13th century! The conclusions are clear: attackers, one and the other, wanted to destroy the traces of our Islamic culture and our historical memories. This was their goal. However, the result was contrary: pure *es-sahwa* happened in Bosnia, we returned to our roots.

Out of the many impressive data, it seems illustrative to state the following. In the city of Bihać, located in the very northwest of Bosnia, the furthest western point of Islam, that you are probably familiar with for its brave resistance, a young student of the Theology Faculty in Sarajevo, chose Bihać *medresa* for his graduation paper. He did not know that the *medresa* had previously existed in his city. There was no trace of it in Bihać. After Dayton, the young man began his research and revived the memory of that oldest institution for high education in this part of Bosnia. In these years, even during the war, we opened a new *medresa* in that city. The war could not stop us.

So, we have neither the reason nor the right to look upon the future with pessimism. We, the people of Bosnia want to say that the aggression against us was a punishment from God. There was sin, wandering and oblivion, but also a strong striving for freedom. God rewarded us for our striving. We believe that only strong nations face huge temptations. And the strong nations are those who, holding onto moral principles, remain true to themselves and open up to the world in the most difficult of circumstances.

This is what I wish for my people and the Muslim world.

Appendix 7

SOME MORE IMPORTANT OPINIONS AND STATEMENTS

About democracy:
'Rarely was a word subject to such contradictory ideas, and misuse, as the word democracy. I think that only religion has had a similar fate through history. Absolute leaders rarely admitted they were dictators, they called themselves democrats and asked others to consider them as such and call them so. Because of such controversies the United Nations, as far as I remember, issued the book *Democracy in the World of Tension* in the 1950s, which very plastically depicts this worldly misunderstanding about democracy. Maybe this is why I need to express my personal opinion on this matter.

I believe that God has created people free and equal, that there are no higher or lower races nor good and evil nations. I believe that people carry a certain number of inalienable rights with them, that authority does not have the right to deprive them of those rights, just like I do not believe in the unlimited power of the majority, because tyranny of the majority is tyranny like any other. I believe that the measure for freedom is treatment of the minorities, and freedom of thought is before all the freedom to think differently. This was the short version of my idea of democracy.' (Speech at the American Center for Democracy Award ceremony, New York, UN Palace, 27 March, 1997.)

'Since the first man by definition plays the main part in a dictatory system, the question is: can he, if he is a positive personality turn dictatorship into something similar to democracy? In my opinion, the answer is negative. Maybe there are some good dictators, but there are no good dictatorships. All of them are humiliating and unproductive. Even when they are formally in favour of positive things: economic development, education, the health system, so-called free social insurance, etc. in the final analysis they all produce negative results. They do not promote human rights, and consequentially neither safety nor prosperity, even if they want to. Suppressing freedom and healthy concurrence, introducing ideological criteria (known as aptness), they push rebel and capable people from social work into the second plan and introduce measures of mediocrity. The final result is losing the game to free countries (the classic example is: the USA-USSR race during the Cold War and its inevitable outcome).

Tito's Yugoslavia is a good example of this. According to the many who knew him, Tito was a positive character, and it seems that their judgement is not incorrect, but he could not have changed the essence nor fate of the system. He just made one dictatory system bearable, but he did not cut it down. Yugoslavia could not have reached true prosperity. Even in its best days, Yugoslavia exported workers (over 700,000 of its best workers had to look for bread and employment out of the country), and the apparent well-being of the 1970s was maintained by constantly taking loans from abroad. The external debt of Yugoslavia before its collapse was US$20 billion, almost US$1,000 per citizen. A rigid one-party system shrinked from the problem of freedom and human and national rights or it solved them by using force and imprisonment. Tensions that would have been relieved in political freedom, just kept on growing and inevitably led to an explosion. You are familiar with the result.' (Speech at the Crans Montana meeting, Switzerland, 25 June, 1999.)

About tolerance:
'The century that ends righteously is named the century of violence. Before us are the new century and the new millennium and of course new possibilities and risks.

How this new century will look depends on us to some extent, on what we teach and what example we leave for the next generation. They will, I believe, be less pressured by the past and more dedicated to the future than us. They will, I hope, with new will and in a new way accomplish the ideals we believed in.

The best message and wisdom we can leave for them is tolerance. If God had wanted all of us to be one nation, we would have been so. But, He obviously did not want that. He divided us into tribes and nations, ordered mutual respect and forbade us from doing harm to each other. This, God's message, about the tolerance and mutual respect of the other who is different, has become the greatest human message followed by the civilised world. It also needs to be the highest law in Bosnia, because without it there is no Bosnia and no life in it.

I wish to send such a message to our nations and the world and for us to encourage each other on this path, I regard you all once again and wish you every good.' (From a speech in the Forum of Parliament B&H, Sarajevo, 24 April, 1999.)

About the national question:
'These days I have followed the ongoing presentation of political parties from the Federation through the media.

They are all speaking of an integral Bosnia and democracy. They all say that they want a lawful state, market economy and education. They all want the evicted to return and emphasise their concern for invalids and Šehids' families. They all express their choice of a civic society and entering Bosnia into European integration, etc. Their programmes look as similar as eggs.

This brings about the question: what is the difference, then? What is the specific position of the SDA? Well, there are many differences but the main one is its approach to the national matter in Bosnia and Herzegovina.

There are two contrary theses. First: the stronger the Bosniac people, the stronger the Bosnia. Second: the weaker the Bosniac people, the stronger the Bosnia. Those two contradicting theses reflect different visions and even different destinies for Bosnia.

Parties from the left are asking the Bosniac people to give up their nationality. They do not do this openly or directly, but everything they say and do, even the things they don't say, are pulling in that direction. One form of this message without moral and historical grounds, is the stubborn placing of the SDA in the same basket with the HDZ and SDS. This message repeats itself daily, in one way or the other.

The Bosniac people are under constant pressure from this confusing propaganda. The constant equalling of those two national parties and the SDA is imposing upon the Bosniac people a complex of co-responsibility for the war. In order to get rid of this fabricated 'blame' Bosniac people would have to give up their identity. This leads us to the question: what for and why?

All this is done in spite of clear historical facts. It is undeniable that the SDS was devastating and the SDA defending Bosnia. Isn't it also undeniable that these two parties had an absolutely different approach to man and democracy? How can they be equal when they are completely different?

We have to remind gentlemen from the opposition that what happened in Bosnia was not a conflict of political parties but a conflict of democracy and fascism. In Bosnia, freedom was defended from aggression. We are no third side in Bosnia (nor a 'first' nor a 'third'). We are a part of a defended and free Bosnia that gave out a spark of hope and light in the darkest days of aggression.

This makes it right to ask the question: why are you training democracy only on the Bosniac people, and why only here where democracy has been defended? Why don't you go into the Serbian entity and try your luck there? It is obvious that democracy has bigger problems there.

We do not equate the SDA with the Bosniac people, because the people always are more than one party, but, considering historical facts, we must say that anyone who says the SDA and the SDS are the same, consciously brings confusion to the Bosniac people. And not only this. In the end they put a mark of equality between our fighters and Chetnik butchers. And our people should know this.

Since the forming of a Croatian and Serbian nation in Bosnia is finished, your call for the rejection of nationality is obviously meant only for Bosniacs. If this invitation was to be accepted, that would not be the way to a 'peaceful Bosnia' as you believe. In history, good intentions do not always make good consequences. The 'one-sided national disarming' of the Bosniac people – to call it this – would not weaken but strengthen the other two nationalisms and their known appetites for Bosnia. The Bosniac nation needs its authentic party. If that is not us, someone else will be. The SDA, as a moderate party with strong civic accent, turns the national feelings of the Bosniac people into positive energy. Moving it from its position would create space for radical, even extremist streams in the Bosniac people, which would lead to instability and to a new whirl of nationalism.

In the SDA, we consider that 'the Rubicon has been crossed' and that there is no turning back to a colourless non-national Bosnia. After becoming aware of itself and its name and after the unmeasurable sufferings it has gone through, the Bosniacs will never again give up their nationality and Islam as its component. This feeling cannot be put out, nor is it known that any nation, after becoming aware of itself, agreed to oblivion. A multiethnic Bosnia is possible, a non-national one is no longer possible.

What is real and possible is to lead our nations, Croats, Serbs and Bosniacs forward, towards civilisation, to coordinate this inevitable fact of nationality with the imperatives of the new age. We will be content if we have Croats instead of great-Croats and normal Serbs instead of great-Serbs.

There are no one-way, simple solutions in Bosnia. The SDA is both Bosniac and a civic party: Bosniac according to its member structure, civic according to its programme. This is, above all, a strong invitation to people to maintain an integral Bosnia on the basis of difference and tolerance, it is opposing about radicalism and extremism in our own lines, it is about being open to the world and Western civilisation, and, finally, it is a practical invitation to cooperation to all those who have similar goals. We do not claim that we have defended Bosnia by ourselves. Both here and in the world, there were many others who fought and worked for the same ideal, thank God. We do not reject nor forget our comrades of other nations and religions and political persuasion. Whoever wants to go along with us is welcome, we will greet him. This is the true meaning of the Coalition for Integral and Democratic Bosnia and Herzegovina, its title speaks for itself.

This is the path that will lead to all Bosniacs saying that they are Bosnians and the Croats and Serbs remaining so, saying the same. To see this day come, Bosnia has to become the object of pride for all of us, and to be this, it has to become a land of freedom and prosperity. The aura of suffering we have now is not enough. Only then will a citizen of Bosnia say with pride that he is also a Bosnian. But this is a process that will take decades.

In the meantime, going towards this far and great goal, we will educate our people, teach our men and women love for Bosnia and raise them in the spirit of respect for their own tradition and human values, freedom and tolerance first of all.' (Closing part of the paper to the Second SDA Congress, 7 September, 1997.)

About nationalism:
'The first and the most important way in which permanent confusion is created in the minds of under-informed people is erasing the difference between the national and the nationalistic. However, the difference is sometimes as large as the difference between love and hate.

A man with national feelings loves his people, shares their flaws and virtues, in other words, belongs to them. A nationalist hates others more than he loves his own, and, importantly in practice, wants the property of others. He suffocates the ways of others that are different, he is intolerant and uses physical repression. He is not defending his own, he wants what is not his. Ultranationalism is Godless in its essence. All great religions of the world taught one simple truth (and all great truths are simple): do not do unto others what you do not want to be done unto yourself or: act so that your behaviour could be a universal law, so that it is the same for both you and others.' (*Dnevni Avaz*, 8 April, 1999.)

About false faith:
'Now someone will say that our time of nationalism is marked by the awakening of religious feelings. He will cite pompous religious ceremonies, mass processions, big crosses over Počitelj and Žepče, religious lectures, etc., as evidence.

And I will say that this is mostly false religion that puts up an exaggerated and screaming form instead of a true faith that is lacking.

There is also no true faith when our *muezins* (callers to prayer) compete in turning up the volume on a usually broken loudspeaker. They think that their hollering instead of beautiful human voice will 'bring people into faith'. Nobody ever succeeded in this and neither will they. They can only cause blasphemy and contrary effect. Faith is either in the soul or not. If it is true, it is discreet.

However, there is another side of the coin. We are this way or that, sometimes openly sometimes not, being persuaded that we should not induce the consciousness of belonging to Islam among our people, or at least not talk too much about it. Sometimes the persuasion becomes aggressive. Everything Islamic is equated with fundamentalism, which is then said to be terrorism. Or they talk about the danger of Muslim domination in Bosnia and Herzegovina. We who make up half the population of Bosnia and Herzegovina, really control 32% of the territory (less than a third) and we are said to be the ones who dominate. The goal of this is to make us give up this 'rump third' that we have. There is also this opposition to the principle of two-way returns. You have to take back Serbian and Croatian refugees even if they do not allow your people to return. The international community accepts no conditioning, etc. If this process (one-way returns) continues, the final result for Bosnia and Herzegovina is known.' (*Dnevni Avaz*, Sarajevo, 8 April, 1999.)

About the relation between morals and religion:
Ljiljan: One of your statements caused loud reactions, which often happens with your statements. Maybe you will remember, this was

when you were in the *Black Book of Communism* promotion and you said that atheism includes an absence of any sort of morals. Could you please explain this statement since the number of atheists in Bosnia is not so small. So, is there morality anywhere except in religion or 'devotion to God' as you would put it?

Izetbegović: You will have to admit that an interview is not the best opportunity for such a complex question. It is hard to answer it in a couple of sentences. I have dedicated a part of the book *Between the East and the West* to this question. The essence of the answer, actually the attempt to reply, would be: since morality is our act out of duty, not interest, there is a question why would a man act against his interest if there is only this life and nothing above or out of it? The idea of good cannot at all be defined logically. Kant proved mathematically that no duty can be derived from pure mind. Nobody, as far as I know, managed to successfully challenge this theory. Because doing good often does not pay off. If it did, selfish ones and scum would rush to be examples of virtue. Remember how the people we admire, real or characters from literature, were all sufferers, Socrates, Antigone, Jesus, etc. So, if there is only this life, if there is no God, those sufferers are not heroes, but plain losers and their sacrifice is of no meaning or use.

As a young man I saw a film in which a man loses his life because he refuses to betray his fellow fighters. Then I thought about the controversy in my soul. All the time I was on this hero's side, which practically meant that I wanted him to face the firing squad. Between death and betrayal, betrayal seemed worse. Why? There is only one reasonable answer: because there is something greater than life. In a universe without God, this man's sacrifice is deprived of any sense. And obviously it is not, we all feel it.

The problem is consistency, actually inconsistency. Believers should be led by duty, those who don't believe by interest. This is the only logical thing. But it does not always happen like this. People say one thing, do another, so we have many immoral believers and moral atheists. Nevertheless, one thing is for sure: no moral system can be founded without God. You have to call upon something above life and interest, and every calling upon something above life is some sort of theism or faith. Even human rights, that are becoming the greatest dogma in the West, have their roots, not in revolution as it is commonly thought, but in Christian teaching. The equality of people is a religious category. People are equal and represent value only if they are created by God. As a product of nature, the way they are, they would be completely unequal and there is no room for the 'holiness of human life', so Stalin's 'čistka' are absolutely 'logical' etc. Anyway, Engels rejects morals as a bunch of bourgeois tricks for workers (in the *Communist Manifesto*). Engels is a consistent thinker. 'Morality is what is in the interests of the labour class,' he writes. The result of this morality is known to us. My answer has grown pretty long. I could conclude: there are moral atheists, but atheism as a teaching, a view of life, has nothing to do with morality. Of course, this is my opinion, you ask me and I tell you what I think.' (Interview for *Ljiljan*, Sarajevo, July 1999.)

About the most important question for Bosnia and Herzegovina:
The most important question is the survival of Bosnia and Herzegovina as an integral state. The struggle for this continues daily, for there are different tendencies. Although it has defined Bosnia and Herzegovina as an integral state, Dayton did not exclude factors that can act in a disintegrating way. When it comes to the matter of me being an optimist or not I will tell you this: if I wasn't an optimist, I could not do this job. I believe in the survival of Bosnia and Herzegovina in spite of everything. I will tell you what I found my optimism on. First of all it is the guarantee of Dayton that Bosnia should stay whole. Although this guarantee is not absolute but relative, we can turn it into reality. What makes this vision real is the context in which the process is happening, actually in the surrounding of Bosnia and Herzegovina that is of crucial importance. In the east I see a relatively weaker Serbia for a long period which will thus be incapable of implementing the great-Serbian concept here. I see inevitable democratic development in Croatia. Croatia is on its way to democracy never mind all the difficulties. Croatia will stop interfering with Bosnian matters in perspective. The existing government group is brutally interfering, and we can see this, we are not blind. We are not making a great deal out of this because we think it is a temporary thing. So the great-Croatian plan cannot be either because there is nobody who would dare to declare secession in Bosnia and Herzegovina today. Croatia cannot do it and neither can Serbia without huge consequences. Those are the facts that are slowly taking over. I am speaking about some long-term visions here. So, on the one side a relatively weak Serbia and on the other the democratic development of Croatia make the 'great state' concepts that are the main danger for Bosnia and Herzegovina impossible. The third fact I count on is our Federation. Strong political, economic and social development is about to happen here. Democracy will make this possible because democracy pulls society forward. If we

make progress here with democratic processes, if we do not stop the process, if we establish a lawful state and everything that goes with that, the world will help that part of Bosnia and Herzegovina and it will defeat the darkness around by means of the power of a social, political and economic model. This is my vision and the basis of my optimism when I speak of maintaining an integral Bosnia and Herzegovina.'
(Interview RTV B&H, 10 July, 1996.)

About the so-called 'third entity' in Bosnia and Herzegovina:
'The Dayton Agreement is a delicate balance of the positive and negative, the acceptable and hardly acceptable elements for each of those who signed it. It is a colossal compromise, in which nothing can change, without changing everything. Better said: nothing that is signed in the Dayton Peace Agreement can be changed without the entire situation returning to the beginning. Anyone who does not believe this should read Chapter 18 of Holbrooke's book *To End a War* ('Day Nineteen' and 'Day Twenty'). Not one side (conditionally speaking) can ask for some positive changes without accepting something they are not happy about. Then we are at the same spot again – the same target the same distance, as people say. We believed in the Federation, we were determined to accomplish this project. After the Agreement on the Federation from 10 November 1995 (during the Dayton negotiations, ten days before the initialising of the General Agreement about peace), we believed that the Croats frankly wanted this as well. This is why we did not make problems about the HVO controlling 19% of the territory and the Bosnian Army 32% (not 24% as some like to say). We thought: it is all Federation (now or in the future), in some time it will be one army and it is not important who controls what now. Our eventual request for the HVO to withdraw to their 17.7% would implicitly mean accepting some sort of secession so we rather kept silent about this, hoping that everything would go towards integration. We do not like to make problems in this 51-49 relation, because we are turned towards the future, we believe and work for an integral Bosnia and Herzegovina. We do not like to mention these numbers much, but this is history, Bosnia has passed through all this, and we cannot flee from that.

I listened carefully to speeches at the recent gathering in Mostar. Human rights and the rights of Croats in general were mentioned. I did not notice that any of the many speakers mentioned the position of the Bosniacs in some parts of the Federation (Posavina, Žepče, Stolac, Livno), for comparison if nothing else. In the Federation (need I say under our control) a number of Catholic educational centres are active, two Catholic universities in Sarajevo itself, 'Napredak' the biggest Croatian cultural association in this part of the world, Croatian magazines, etc. and I am happy that this is so, I would be ashamed if it were otherwise, but I am unhappy that there is nothing like this, actually it is not allowed in the area under political control of the round table of Mostar organisers. Does someone think that this duality in human rights can last, and why do these 'fighters for human rights' keep silent about it?

What should be done? The Dayton Agreement cannot be changed, but the spirit of it can. A more loyal approach is also possible, a new practice that will not be based on 'I will totally use all that is convenient for me in the Dayton Agreement and obstruct everything that I do not like in it'. Some inside evolution is possible as well. Democratic forces in Bosnia and Herzegovina can develop, so everything that is written in the Dayton Agreement will have a different, more positive meaning for all the nations and citizens of Bosnia and Herzegovina. If the current nationalistic (chauvinistic) parties undergo evolution to national parties and those into moderate national ones – and I believe that all development in Bosnia and Herzegovina will go that way – then the Dayton Agreement will not be the 'same' again. The Government in Zagreb, this or a future one (I believe the future), will some day when the Bosnian Croats visit them to pick up instructions (and money), say to them: go to Sarajevo, try to find a common language with the people there, they are reasonable people, you can agree on everything with them. When this happens, a new day will dawn in Bosnia.

We are ready to make agreements about everything, absolutely everything with the Croats, of course within the Dayton Agreement, not outside it. Then, no 'third entity' will be required. With different people, the Dayton Agreement will be different as well.' (*Dnevni Avaz*, Sarajevo, 11 March, 1999.)

About Bosnianity:
'It seems that creating the Bosnian nation as a sort of amalgam of Bosniac, Croatian, and Serbian national feelings, is unfortunately late, because the process of forming a Serbian and Croatian nation in Bosnia is finished. Now we can still talk about Bosnia as a common state, about Bosnian patriotism or some feeling like that, but it all depends on the fact of whether Bosnia will become a prosperous and democratic country, if it will become a land for our pride. For now all that Bosnia has is suffering and a resistance that can be a certain reason for our pride, but the aura of

suffering is not enough. Bosnianity can become a certain form of over-nationality for all citizens of Bosnia and Herzegovina and it is possible.' (Answer for *Tjednik*, Zagreb, 28 July 1998.)

About Slavenity:
Ljiljan: Did you ever think about your Slavenian roots, what is your opinion on Panslavenity? What does being a Slaven mean to you?

Izetbegović: I feel Bosniac first, then European, and Slavenian in third place. I think that my Slavenity reflects itself most in my great passion for Russian literature. My favourite writer is Dostoevsky. (*Ljiljan* interview, Sarajevo, July of 1999.)

About so-called 'Bosniac domination' in Bosnia and Herzegovina:
'What Bosniac domination can we talk about? Look at the map of Bosnia and Herzegovina: there are no Bosniacs on almost half the territory called Republika Srpska, let alone authority. If not completely the same, the situation is very similar in the part of the Federation under the control of the HVO, and the sum of these territories is about 68% of Bosnia and Herzegovina territory. Of the remaining 32% of the territory Bosniacs have a certain advantage, this is true, but can this be regarded as Bosniac domination? This reminds me of: what is mine is only mine, and what is yours is both yours and mine. But this cannot be. We resisted this concept from the beginning, first politically, then with arms, then again politically. We want an integral and democratic Bosnia. Fortunately, this is what the world wants as well, for their reasons not for ours. Authority in parts of Bosnia under Croatian and Serbian control are not democratic because they are uni-national. But, as you can see, some processes are going on and this is changing. Sooner or later, uni-national and non-democratic concepts will be defeated. We insist on returns of banished people and we will continue to insist on this every day, every year. They will return and this will considerably change many things. There are also some changes that are not too noticeable. Where are Boban and Karadžić now? Don't the destinies of the two of them show clearly enough in what direction the arrow of time and history is pointing?' (Statement for *Novi List*, Rijeka, 7 February, 1998.)

About the so-called 'change of authority concept':
'This so frequently mentioned 'concept of authority' in Bosnia and Herzegovina is such as it is because Bosnia is such as it is – tri-national, and closing one's eyes to this fact is pointless. Besides this reality, the

'change of authority concept' needs one more 'little thing' and this is a change of Dayton, the SDP should openly tell the people how they are going to do this. Without this, the story about a change of authority concept is a gag for uninformed people. This is why I said that I can see only one realistic path for Bosnia, not the SDP's nationalism, be it good or not, but a gradual lowering of national tensions to a bearable level, and turning nationalistic into national and then moderate national parties. These moderate national parties will agree, they will have to and want to agree on the minimum for the existence of the Bosnian State, and this means a consistent implementation of the Dayton Peace Agreement. Less than this is unacceptable, more than this is unrealistic. Violent reacting, or deterring of national ways, especially the Serbs and Croats in Bosnia and Herzegovina, causes a contrary effect – it adds to national mistrust and national compactness. My view of the possible development in Bosnia and Herzegovina is something that the SDP cannot deny with a plain statement about a 'change of authority concept' or a constant repetition of this saying, but only with one experiment: election results in the Serbian and Croatian corpus of Bosnia and Herzegovina. I do not see this happening for a long time, but the SDP should definitely try it. I wish them a lot of success in this as well as in 'life and work'.' (*Dnevni Avaz*, Sarajevo, 25 March, 1999.)

Once again about the so-called 'change of authority concept':
'All political room is covered by the coalition, not much is left for the opposition. We are for an integral Bosnia and Herzegovina, the return of refugees, freedom of the media and political parties, we are against Chetniks and Ustashas and any form of extremism in general, we have initiated the process with the Constitutional Court of Bosnia and Herzegovina for the constituency of nations, we're fighting for the integrity of Mostar, etc. What does the opposition specifically offer that we do not? Is there something? I don't think so, but I think there is something they should try. If they succeed, I will admit that a new page has been turned in the history of Bosnia. The trouble is that Mr. Lagumdžija instead of doing this constantly repeats the same thing: the authority concept needs changing. He has just one more 'little thing' to do: to tell us exactly what this means and how he plans to accomplish it.' (*Dnevni Avaz*, Sarajevo, 29 April, 1999.)

About justice, injustice and merits in war:
'In the war there were some nice and some very difficult moments, of

course many more of the difficult ones. Memories are fading. Still, we will remember the difficulties for a long time. There are two events that I remember the most. The first one happened somewhere in the middle of 1993. It was a meeting with a unit near Olovo, known for its poverty and courage. After the usual speeches, one soldier walked in front of the troop and asked me: 'President, will there be injustice when freedom comes?' I was surprised by the question, but I answered: 'Yes, unfortunately there will be injustice and you will have to fight against it just like you do now against your enemies.' The other incident that has stayed in my mind concerns a visit to a front line above Vozuca. It was a cold day, and a cold rain was pouring down. It was the late autumn of 1994. At sunset we came to our trenches in some forest. Mud was all around and a few soil-barracks. From time to time, close shots were heard. After the visit, my escort and I sat in the car returning to Kakanj through roundabout routes. We were all covered with mud and tired, but we entered a warm room and had dinner. The soldiers stayed in that forest, but as night fell, the rain was only stronger. And now, when we talk about war deserts, I have this picture in my mind. I will leave it for you to conclude by yourself what I think about the justice and the injustice, and especially about the merits of war. I always ask myself why it is like that and is there anything I can do to make it different.' (Extract from an interview for *The First Line*, 6 April, 1999.)

About Sandžak:
Ljiljan: Officials in Belgrade never answered the request to establish a special status for Sandžak. This request was ignored by the Milošević regime. What do you think about the status of Sandžak?

Izetbegović: I support every legitimate request of our people in Sandžak. I would like to remind you that, with the SDA Declaration from 1990, the autonomy of Sandžak was required. But, before anything else the Milošević regime should give them back local control, cancelled by force two years ago.

Ljiljan: The government of Montenegro, nevertheless, announced a written document about its special status – as a separatist act. A similar attitude is held by opposition parties in Serbia and Montenegro. In what way is Sandžak a regional or ethnic question?

Izetbegović: That story about separatism does not have firm ground. In asking for special status, Sandžak does not require separation from Yugoslavia, or a change of state borders. The story about separatism is obviously made for political disqualification and pressure.

Ljiljan: Belgrade absolutely refuses to define the Sandžak question as a political one. What do you think about that?

Izetbegović: The problem of Sandžak is eminently a political question. Is there a need to prove that?

Ljiljan: How much do the 'closer' relations of Sarajevo and New Pazar hasten a solution on the Sandžak question?

Izetbegović: Well, they certainly could hasten one. But it looks like we are too deep into our own problems. During the following days we will have talks with the representatives of the Bosniac Council of Sandžak, headed by Dr. Ugljanin, and with the circle around Dr. Rasim Ljajic, so we will see what we can do. A little bit more harmony wouldn't hurt.

Ljiljan: Do you think that with the politics of fear and distrust Milošević, in Sandžak, made a reserved base which he could activate according to circumstances?

Izetbegović: That base certainly exists, I don't know if it is in the interests of Milošević. It is a double-edged sword.

Ljiljan: According to you, is an 'exchange of territory' possible in respect of solutions to regional problems in the Balkans?

Izetbegović: I do not find the option of an exchange of territories realistic nor is it acceptable.

Ljiljan: In the end, it is about the people from Sandžak and whether they are in Bosnia and Sarajevo.

Izetbegović: Wise people do not make and do not like differentiations of this kind. I think the situation is good. True, since the peace here, some people are trying to ruffle clear waters. You know, it is good fishing in muddy waters. We will do everything to disturb their plans.

Why we negotiated with the SDS and the HDZ:
Novi List: Can we go back now to the war days and can you answer some of my questions from that time. Why did your party not react more clearly after the Stjepan Kljuić retreat (20 December, 1992) from the top of the HDZ and after clear signs that his party was going to leave Sarajevo?

Izetbegović: There was nothing we could do about this, except take responsibility for all future misunderstandings and conflicts with the HDZ. Kljuić is a good man, but too temperamental and hasty for politics, especially politics in such hellish times. It is a wonder to me, he has a pipe that could help him think and restrain himself. Do you know how Tito used to do that? I watched him giving some interviews, especially to foreigners, during the conflict with the Russians. A journalist would ask him a question, often a very provocative one, and he slowly took his pipe, brought it to his mouth with equal temper, then drew a long, long smoke, returned and emptied it, and then answered the question. And he did this every time. We are not such a genius so we react both quickly and accurately. If I hadn't given up smoking, I would use a pipe. Kljuić sent me a short letter one morning informing the Bosnia and Herzegovina Presidency of his irrevocable resignation from the position of Presidency member. This letter is stored in the Presidency archives. Within an hour I scheduled an emergency meeting, but Kljuić did not show up. This due to the constant shelling, he lived in the Presidency building at that time. So we sent the secretary for him. He wasn't to be found in his office, nor the room he occupied, but a guard told us that he had left the same morning taking all his private belongings with him. As you know, later, much later, on my request he returned and continued his office in the Presidency, until the elections in 1996. But in the meantime, we in the Presidency endured very difficult days with some extreme people from the HDZ. Those were crazy times. Still, the peace could be stipulated only with the HDZ. You negotiate and make peace with those you are fighting with, not those you are at peace with. Only the HDZ could order the cease-fire in Herzegovina in the name of the Croats. Kljuić could not do this, actually, if it was up to him, there would be no war. But neither war nor peace was up to him, and this fact did not depend on me but on Kljuić and the Croatian people.

Novi List: In Split on 12 December, 1992 you made a statement in which you accepted Radovan Karadžić as the negotiating side in war. Why did you do this?

Izetbegović: That was one of the toughest decisions of my life, and I think that I already told you why. There was a choice: either negotiate with the Chetniks or continue the war. The world told me through Lord Owen very clearly that it was not prepared to intervene in Bosnia no matter what happened and that the only way out was through negotiations. Europe was prepared to offer its services only in this way. I do not think that this happened in Split. What I am telling you took place in Tuđman's office in December 1993 or January 1994. Of course, after the battle everyone is a general. I think that I did the only thing that could have been done to prolong the life of Bosnia or at least to postpone the destruction of Bosnia and my people. Time had to be bought. That is why I accepted the negotiations.

Novi List: In preparations for the First Bosniac Congress (September 1993), it is known that there were proposals to put the legal Assembly of the Republic of Bosnia and Herzegovina out of work, and form a Bosniac parliament instead, which is similar to what Karadžić and Boban previously did in their 'republics'. Were you at that time like today 'clear on Bosnia and Herzegovina positions' since you spoke of a percentage arrangement for Bosnia and Herzegovina on the basis of the 'rightful percentage for each nation'?

Izetbegović: My struggle for Bosnia was not a straight-line. Historical facts are known and I do not intend to nor can I change them. It is a snapped, zigzag line, depending on the situation in Bosnia itself and outside, but the general course was always the same: maintaining Bosnia as an integral state within its internationally recognised borders. There were the Carrington, Cutileiro, Vance-Owen, Owen-Stoltenberg plans, and finally Dayton. Many things have changed, but the constant in all these plans was maintaining Bosnia as a state. According to all laws of military and political logic, regarding the relations of forces and the world's behaviour, Bosnia could have been erased from the earth's political map. Remember: in one period, infinitely long for us, from December 1992 to April 1994 we were totally surrounded, on three fronts: Karadžić, Boban, Abdić. But, as you see, Bosnia survived. Negotiations played their part in this because at the same time we both strengthened our defense and ensured some level of presence of the world in Bosnia. I do not know if I have always made the best possible moves, but I always did the best I knew and according to my conscience and was ready to listen to advice from others. I never acted from fear or for some personal reason. A certain historical distance will be necessary for things to be evaluated objectively and righteously. (Answers for Drago Pilsel a journalist of *Novi List*, Rijeka, 7 February, 1998.)

Another answer to a similar question:
Avaz reader: Recently I was reading an article by a poet in which he scolds the SDA for not forming a government with the civilian parties, instead with the SDS and HDZ after the elections in 1990. If the SDA had done this, he claims 'we would have been singing a better song'. Would you comment on this poet's claim?

Izetbegović: Maybe we would be singing a song, but we would have no state. When a poet, instead of poems, writes political articles, something goes wrong. Poets do not like facts, they consider facts 'stupid', so they argue with them. Poets can do this, I must not. And this is what those 'stupid' facts looked like in those unfortunate times: in the parliament of the Republic of Bosnia and Herzegovina, in both houses, there were altogether 240 delegates. The picture, on the basis of free elections, looked like this: the SDA 86, the SDS 73, the HDZ 43, the SDP 19, Reformists 13, the MBO 2, Zeleni 2 and the SPO 1. Since a majority was needed to vote the government in, which means minimally 121 votes, the SDA could not make up a majority in any combination with civilian parties. It could gather 123 votes, but only in theory, that is if Chetnik elements in the SDP and among the Reformists, for instance Kalinić, voted with the SDA. You can judge the reality of this happening for yourself.

Of course, this is one side of the coin. The other side is we could have ignored the choice of the Serbian and Croatian people, no matter what it might have been. If we had done this, the war would not have begun in 1992 but in 1991 and it would have been a civil war. The Communists have defined Bosnia and Herzegovina as a state of three nations. They could not have done differently, nor could anyone in Bosnia. Poets, and those who have a poet's talent for politics, like to make hypotheses. For example: everything would have been different if Milošević hadn't been in Belgrade, and if Tuđman hadn't been in Zagreb, if Marković had stayed, if the Reformists had won the elections, if the JNA wasn't the way it is, if Bosnia had petroleum, etc. A hundred 'ifs'. But Milošević was in Belgrade, Tuđman was in Zagreb, Marković had left, the Reformists didn't win the elections, the JNA was what it was, and Bosnia doesn't have petroleum, etc. Both good and bad presumptions are worth the same here, that is, nothing, because they are only presumptions. For us who were to decide, all mentioned facts were the given quantities that we couldn't change. We could ignore them or take them into account. We, as responsible people, did the second. Unlike your poet, I claim the following: if in 1991 we attempted to make a government without the parties the Serbs and Croats voted for, if we had ignored their choice, Bosnia would not have been recognised, the war would not have happened in 1992 but in 1991, and it would have been a civil war, we would have lost it, and the historical blame for chaos would be ours. Those are the facts, everything else is irresponsible talk. (*Dnevni Avaz*, Sarajevo, 5 August, 1999.)

About freedom of the media in Bosnia and Herzegovina:
'There was no censure even during the war. In my speech in front of the Congress Council of Bosniac Intellectuals at the end of November 1997, I criticised some magazines, saying that they were neither independent nor professional. They were not independent because they were

financed by foreigners, and they were not professional because they did not honour two fundamental rules of the profession: checking the news and hearing both sides. This was my 'dangerous' statement. Never was one journalist persecuted by the state for something he or she wrote nor will they be. Let them do their work. There is no cure for journalists who are prepared to lie in a democratic state, except for raising people and raising the level of general education, so that people themselves can distinguish the truth from a lie, good from bad. But this cannot be done by politics, only by culture. And this is a difficult and time consuming job, but it is the only way. So far, nobody has invented any better idea. Journalists' lies and exaggerations are inevitable products of the freedom of the media. It seems that one does not come without the other. If you want to end the lies, you will end the freedom. These two are connected like smoke and fire. Anyway, you are a journalist, you know this better than I do.' (Interview for *Novi List* from Rijeka, 7 February, 1998.)

About the returning of refugees:
A question put by one refugee: 'I am a refugee from Janja, a rich little city next to Bijeljina where about 20,000 Bosniacs lived before the war. In 1992, they were all banished. Most went abroad via Hungary. My family and I came to Sarajevo. I am an agronomist and I work here as a teacher in high school. I have a wife and two children (14 and 16 years old). I have left a big house and a property of over 100 acres of fertile land. Two Serbian families from Sarajevo have occupied it since 1995. I live in Ilidža in a two-room flat that a Serbian family had tenancy rights on before the war. The flat, when I got it, was completely devastated, the crucial installations were repaired by a German humanitarian organisation, I did the rest myself. Now a member of one of the families who occupied my property in Janja is asking for the flat back. Within two days he got a warrant that claims his right for the return of the flat, so I would have to leave there as well. I know that he is living on my property in Janja, but he denies this. This is the eleventh case I know when a Serb comes, gets a warrant for a property, sells it through a lawyer (or rents the flat, usually for five years), takes the money and returns to Bosniac property. There are also cases where they return to their flats but it never happens that they give back Bosniacs theirs in Republika Srpska. If something like this goes on long enough, the result will be that Serbs will have both flats in Sarajevo (or the money for it) and Bosniac houses in Republika Srpska, and the Bosniacs will have nothing, which scores 2:0 for the cheat. If there are many of those zeroes, and I am afraid there

will be, we will practically lose Bosnia. I wish to know: do you see the danger of this, and if you do, what are you doing to stop this catastrophic outcome? Mr. President, you used to find a way out in war even when it seemed like there wasn't any, will you find a way out of this obvious trap that was set up for our people by some men from the international community? I do not believe that they do not see what is happening, they are just continuing, and we can see what is the result of this. What sort of a law is it that gives everything to one side (in this case the side that committed violence) and takes away everything from the other side? In the moment when official data says that the returning rate of Serbs to the Federation is ten times higher than Bosniacs and Croats to Republika Srpska (in the first two months 425 Serbs, 515 Croats and 85 Bosniacs returned to the Federation, and 90 Bosniacs and 1 Croat to Republika Srpska – UNHCR's data published in *Oslobođenje*, 3 May, 1999), international factors are still calling out to Sarajevo and threatening us with sanctions. Isn't this a politic made for 'neutralising', actually completely marginalising the so-called Muslim element in Bosnia and Herzegovina? So, do you have this threat in mind?'

Izetbegović: Yes I do, but I have to tell you that what you call the 'international community' is a very broad crowd. There are people who do not care much about justice and injustice, but Mr. Westendorp definitely is not one of them. The truth is that around him there are many very different interests that vary from state to state, and person to person. I wish to inform you that I asked the almost identical question (without the last part for understandable reasons) of the High Representative during our meeting yesterday. I told him that for us, minding the situation that you have described, that further returns could only go two ways. I also said that we are ready to make two steps forward and be an example, as they say, not an example of stupidity and blindness but of reasonable people who can take a limited risk, but in no way unlimited. In the last year, according to strict evaluation, 9,430 Serbs and Croats returned to Sarajevo. I said that now it is the turn of Banja Luka and Mostar. I confirmed that we are ready to implement the presidential decision regarding returns on the relation Sarajevo-Mostar-Banja Luka (plan 2000 plus 2000 plus 2000), but this is absolutely a two-way principle. I also mentioned some other issues regarding his decision on property and handed him my opinion in written form (a so-called non-paper).

However, with all this we have to stay committed to the principle of returning 'everyone to their own'. That is the only way to maintain an integral Bosnia and Herzegovina. If the returns are not completed at least at a certain significant level, Bosnia will hardly survive. We must also consider the interest of Bosniacs who want, and can or will really be able to, return to their houses, flats and properties. We must put ourselves in their shoes and try to see the problem through their eyes. Did you, for instance, think of how a Mostar citizen sees this problem, while occupying some temporary housing on the left side of Neretva and looking at his house on the right side for five years? Is he for some limits? I do not think so. It is logical that he must be for unconditional returning, meaning no limits and exceptions. The situation is similar with people from Brčko, Prijedor and many others.

I will have your letter translated into English and forwarded to Mr. Westendorp because it concerns a high number of our banished population. I do not know what his response will be like, but I must say that so far I have no reason to doubt the good intentions of the High Representative when it comes to Bosnia and Herzegovina's long-term interests. The second question is how can he understand all the causes and effects of what is happening and understand all the problems of our very complicated country in a very complicated time.' (Statement for *Dnevni Avaz*, Sarajevo, 6 May, 1999.)

Once again about the return of refugees:
'I greet you on behalf of the highest organs of the SDA who initiated today's meeting.

We have gathered once again, in changed, I hope I can say better, conditions, to argue one of the burning issues of the country: the return of banished persons to their homes. You are the best collocutors for this, because all of you were banished yourselves.

Allow me to give you a few thoughts about the issue of returning.

Our highest and constant goal was and is maintaining the integrity of Bosnia and Herzegovina. This goal cannot be accomplished without returning the refugees to their homes. This is why Annexe 7 remains the crucial part of the Dayton Peace Agreement for us. And this is why questioning of this Agreement is justified if the return of property is not realised.

I cannot emphasise enough the need for these returns to be two-sided: Bosniacs and Croats to Republika Srpska and Serbs to the Federation.

There are many signs of refugees themselves judging that the time has come and, on their own initiative, arranging the return. This mood should be used and given new impulse to the opening process, by providing material and every other support to their local and every other programme. We expect the international community to provide adequate help to this important work.

I wish to remove some doubts that are emerging, concerning the issue. The right to choose the place of living is undeniable. Everyone has the right to choose where they want to live, but this cannot be the excuse for keeping someone else's property. Also, everyone has the right to return to their own. But if it is state (not private) property they can realise this right only with the intent of real return, not a trade with it. A refugee cannot be evicted, unless he is offered the return of his property or given other adequate housing, and he refuses it. I think that those principles should function in the entire territory of Bosnia and Herzegovina, equally in the Federation and Republika Srpska.

Finally, I want to thank the present representatives of embassies of friendly countries and international organisations. Through their presence they express interest for the problem that cannot be successfully solved without their support and help.

Thank you all and I wish you fruitful work. (Address at the SDA meeting 'Everyone to their own property', Sarajevo, 1 July, 1999.)

About 'neutral intellectuals':
'I have a habit of visiting one primary school in Sarajevo from time to time to talk to the children. Comparing children's thoughts with those of some intellectuals, I can tell you that my judgement is often in favour of the children. Some may not agree with this, but that's their problem. Children are very clear about their country Bosnia and the people they belong to. For them, these concepts are clear, there is no confusion in their minds. And I hear intellectuals say: 'I am neutral, war doesn't concern me, I am above all this.' They are always above something, out of something, etc. In this conflict, in which children are killed and women raped, they are neutral, does anyone have the right to be neutral in such a situation? This really is a time of contrast, good and bad have never clashed so clearly, even a blind man could say what is what. But, they are neutral. Shame on them!' (From a speech in Tuzla, 1994, published later on in the *Book of Letters and Interviews*, 1998, page 168.)

Once again about intellectuals:
'The behaviour of some of our intellectuals is a special story. They were never rebels, but they like to act as if they were. How could they be independent if they always found important what others thought of them,

what they would say about them, would they praise them as modern, Europeans, etc. And the Europeans never cared much about what others thought of them, never were toadies, had their own principles, led their people or scolded them, advised them or criticised their flaws, but they were always with them. Ours are always above and out. Even in war, when people are killed and women raped, they are neutral, going in circles around the problem, not ready to clearly say who is shooting, killing and raping. With them, the way they are, we will never get anywhere. Fortunately, not all of them are like this, but, surprisingly, many are.' (*Dnevni Avaz*, Sarajevo, 8 April, 1999.)

There were reactions to this last statement I made about intellectuals. A reader from Tešanj asked me whether my judgement wasn't too harsh. My answer was published in *Avaz* on 15 April, 1999:

'I followed those reactions. The first thing I can say is that I didn't, God forbid, put all intellectuals into the same basket. As if this struggle to create a state and army could have been carried out if there weren't many educated and smart heads on the right side. If our people hadn't had this critical mass of active intelligence in the moment of aggression, resistance would have been impossible. Furthermore, I can make a responsible claim that, regarding the situation, a nation at a lower level of general education would surely have been defeated. In Goražde under siege, our men made little centrals on the River Drina. Without those centrals there would not have been minimal quantities of electricity nor minimal telephone connections, and you know what this would have meant. They were able to do this, because they knew how. Still, a large number of intellectuals, that my objection refers to, even if they shyly said who did the shelling and raping (because it was obvious) never, or always avoided, saying loudly and clearly who defends Bosnia, who organises the resistance to killers and rapists. They still gladly keep silent about this.'

About the so-called conflict of civilisations:
'It is a great honour to greet all the participants of today's panel. Our friends from societies that suffer like ours have a lot to say to us and to hear from us here in Bosnia and Herzegovina. Our panel is taking place in the context of a big programme that we call *The Bridge*. We feel that this is the right name for this programme, because Bosnia and Herzegovina occupies a unique position. It is a bridge between civilisations, cultures and religions. Right across from where we stand is the Serb Orthodox Church, a synagogue is just across the River, the Cathedral is

located less than 100 metres to the east, and 200 metres away is the main mosque. So, in the radius of not more than 200 metres, we can see monuments of Bosnia and Herzegovina's symbolic role as a place where civilisations meet. Facing this picture, we wonder whether our ancestors were wiser and better people than us. Through this interweaving, great civilisations of the past managed to accomplish a high level of mutual understanding. We have to go that way. The conflict of civilisations is not inevitable. On the contrary, civilisations can find common roots and acknowledge common values that outweigh the differences. Bosnia and Herzegovina is a place where this possibility is tested with all risks. Instead of being the conflict site, Bosnia and Herzegovina could be a place where we could build a society in which tolerance and mutual respect will triumph. I believe that our conversations today will contribute to these efforts. Realising that our friends from Northern Ireland and South Africa went through similar troubles and temptations, we see that we are of one kind and that we belong to the same world, with everything this includes.' (From my address to *The Bridge* meeting, Sarajevo, 17 August, 1998.)

About the position of women:
'Dear brothers and sisters,

I said sisters, although I cannot see them here. When I did Hajj two years ago, I saw husbands and wives doing *tawaf* together, and I do not see them together here. I do not know why this is so.

Half the human race consists of women, as well as half of our nation. In the war that has passed, the war for survival and freedom, women carried the burden of war troubles with us. They were killed, suffered and starved with us. We expect them to give birth to and raise the generation of Bosniacs who will maintain what we won and win what we didn't. Such a generation of proud and conscious people cannot be raised by a humiliated and frustrated woman.' (Speech at Ajvatovica, 29 June, 1997.)

Again about the position of women:
'Women, like men, are human beings worthy of respect. They are our mothers, sisters and wives. They raise our children. We cannot allow them to be oppressed and deprived of education. The world we are living in is not perfect, but it can be better than it is today. This depends on the people who are now growing up and on those yet to come. The next generation should be better than this one. Progress lies in this, and the woman's role is irreplaceable here. An oppressed and uneducated

woman cannot raise and bring up a generation that will make our world better. So, let us maintain and protect the dignity of women.' (From a message for the conference about the position of women in the world, Tehran, 17 October, 1997.)

About Tito 1996:
Avaz: Now allow me to ask you a somewhat unexpected question. Lately, there have been many conflicting opinions on the issue of whether Tito helped the Bosniacs or not. You were in jail while he was alive, and during the continuation of socialistic authority, after him. It seems, especially considering your credits and life in this decade, that it would be very interesting, and maybe important, to hear your public judgement about him?

Izetbegović: You have surprised me with this question, which doesn't mean that I haven't given it any thought. On the contrary, a certain sympathy for this man I never tried to hide. It is true that I never liked his ideology, his way of life, his Briunes [island in the Adriatic], villas, houses for hunting, trips, etc. But I had the feeling that he was a good man, and I think that I am not mistaken. Simply, he wasn't a bad guy, as people would say. He was a Communist, but not a Bolshevik. He brought something human and bearable to a system that was wrong. They say he loved life, from which I conclude that he didn't hate people, because these two things are connected. On the other side you have ascetics, who are not ascetics for their beliefs but out of their personal frustrations. They do not know how or cannot live, so they won't let others live either. Those who knew Tito better say that he was not a great strategist, but no one denies his being a big politician, probably one of the biggest on these territories in the 20th century. Maybe this judgement opposes the fact that Yugoslavia fell apart after him, but I do not think that this was his fault. Serbian hegemony that was genetically implanted in the basis of Yugoslavia, carried the seed of decay. Tito truly fought this hegemony, but unfortunately he did not win the battle, he lost it. Still, the good things in Yugoslavia mostly came from his personality, and the bad things came from his ideology or were simply inherited. (*Dnevni Avaz*, Sarajevo, 27 December, 1996.)

Again about Tito:
'Every general judgement on Tito is incorrect: he was good – he was bad. He wasn't either of these things. The truth is: he was both good and bad. Maybe a good man at the head of a bad system. Or bad in the first

part of his rule, but later changed and bettered. Tito ruled for 36 years (1944-1980). In the first 22 years (1944-1966) Tito's Yugoslavia was a pure police state run by the head policeman Aleksandar Ranković. It is a long period that consists of Bleiburg, executions without trials, Dahaus processes, Goli Otok, the persecution of the Young Muslims, a time with-out passports but with press censorship, roll-calling of non grata writers, repressions in Kosovo, ('gun affair'), etc. The 14 year period that followed was better, and, during some time (1975-1980), even good: the growth of standards, more freedom, passports for the great majority of the popu-lation. So, two thirds of Tito's rule were bad, one third was relatively good.

Older people remember the first period whilst the second remains in the memory of the younger ones.

The judgement on Tito's Yugoslavia is a matter of comparison. If you compare it to Austria, it wouldn't pass in life standards nor human rights. But if you take Bulgaria, Romania at that time (or, God forbid, Enver Hodža's Albania), Tito's Yugoslavia seems to be America. For a Czech, whose country Soviet tanks brutally marched into and brought a reign of terror in 1968, Yugoslavia was America.

To summarise: on one side there was Ranković's terror, Goli Otok, media censorship, verbal delict, a $20 billion foreign debt, an inefficient economic system and Serbian hegemony (two main causes of Yugo-slavia's ruin), over 700,000 workers abroad (who couldn't find a job in Yugoslavia), etc. On the other side there was peace, an education system and social security, freedom to travel, etc. Both things about Tito and his Yugoslavia are true. Mix the two, shake well, and you will have Tito.' (*Slobodna Bosna*, May 2000.)

About General Rose and his book Battle for Peace:
'I did not read the whole book, I read parts of it, but I knew General Rose from our numerous meetings when he was the Commander of UNPROFOR for Bosnia and Herzegovina, so I have an idea about the book and the author. The author belongs to the sort of people with prejudice about Muslims and Islam, who are, unfortunately, numerous. Besides, he obviously came here thinking that we provoked the Chetniks to shell and attack us, so that we could secure military intervention. This was permanently in his head. He saw our provocation and cunningness in everything, even when they were constantly shelling the hospital from the hills. It was always our fault. Of course, people have the right to live with a lie if they want to, but it is unacceptable for such people to

come to Bosnia at the worst time for us and determine our fate. Unfortunately, this was the case with General Rose, and he wasn't the only one. Remember Akashi and Janvier and others, you can imagine how much damage they have done to us, how much trouble they could have spared us, but they didn't because of their prejudices. Rose's book is teeming with contradictions and literal incorrectness. He says that we made a drama of the conditions in Goražde and Bihać, and then, a few chapters later, he quotes a report by his officers saying that Serbian tanks are entering the city. He doesn't even know the basic facts. In one place he says: 'Muslims could have prevented war if they had signed the Vance-Owen Plan.' He doesn't know that we signed this plan. We did this in New York at the beginning of 1993, while the Serbian side rejected it. He does not know this because he came here at the beginning of March 1993, and for him, the history of the Bosnian war began with his arrival. We did not only have Chetniks on our necks, but also some people from the international community with their strange and unintelligible aversion, not to say hate. When I remember all these troubles, I think of our survival as a wonder.' (Interview for Radio Sarajevo, 29 December, 1998.)

About the demonising of the SDA:
'A part of this story is the demonising of the SDA. You can see what the press says, but I am not sure that you know the stories in the lobbies. A foreign friend, whom I have all reason to trust, told me about the systematic treatment we receive here among foreigners. He says: 'No meeting, dinner, or any unofficial social gathering goes by without someone finding it necessary to mention the SDA in a negative context. The other night when the SDA was mentioned, one of them made a grimace that he looked as if he had drunk fish oil. Since he noticed that I obviously did not agree, he said that the SDA was a party that gathers primitives, that all sides are the same here, but the Bosniacs did less evil because they were weak. If they had the power...etc. I told him that I knew Izetbegović, Silajdžić, Bičakčić, Ganić, Oručević, Šaćirbej and many others very well and that they do not seem to me as leaders of primitives in the least. And regarding power, during the three years of war they were almighty in Sarajevo, they could have killed off all their opponents, but they didn't. This is the only place where the opposition and independent press could say what they wanted. The Cathedral is whole, orthodox churches also.' He waved this off with his hand. There were about 20 of us, everyone was silent, no one supported my opinion. This

is what you should know, my foreign acquaintance concluded.' (*Dnevni Avaz,* Sarajevo, 8 April, 1999.)

About new Chetniks and Ustashas:
'There is a phenomenon that deserves to be studied: both in this and the previous war there were Chetniks and Ustashas on the scene. It is not important what they were called, but this is what they were. But Chetniks and Ustashas from the end of this century were in every way worse than those in the Second World War. Draža's headquarters were nearby the Aladža Mosque for a long time in 1942, and no one dared to tear it down. These Chetniks of 'ours', from our generation, did this and also destroyed hundreds of mosques and cultural monuments that weren't Serbian. The Ustashas in the Second World War ruled Mostar for almost four years and almost everything remained whole. The Serbian population was killed here and there, but there wasn't a brutal exterminating of roots.

All those terrible things were done by 'our generation' of Chetniks and Ustashas. Why? Of course, the phenomenon deserves to be studied thoroughly, but one observation imposes itself. What happened 50 years ago was nationalism, what is happening now is nationalism combined with atheism. This wave of nationalism came after 40 years of Communist rule. The plant of nationalism was planted in morally and religiously devastated grounds, and then it yielded its most poisonous fruits.' (*Dnevno Avaz,* 8 April, 1999.)

About our 'ruralising' Sarajevo:
Question: When it comes to Sarajevo, the opposition claims that it is not what it used to be, that the SDA has ruralised the city.

Izetbegović: A part of the opposition says so, its heartless part. They are aiming at us letting the refugees enter the city. One oppositionist said in public that if the SDA rules for another year, Sarajevo will no longer exist as a city. This nonsense was published by the press, and, interestingly, did not cause any reaction. It was a message saying that we should banish people from Višegrad, Foča, Srebrenica, who found shelter in the then bombed and hungry Sarajevo. We do not intend to do this and there are no sanctions that could make us. To this 'ruralised' Sarajevo with 70,000 refugees in it came Bono and Milan Scala; Sarajevo Winters are held, Poetry days, Film Festivals and recently MESS. The opposition is talking tittle-tattle, not caring how these stories ring in the ears and souls of those who they call rural.' (In a statement for *Dnevni Avaz*, Sarajevo, 29 October, 1998.)

About military foreign currency books:
'I have talked about this a few times, but it seems like a good idea to repeat it. What is written in the book is not money, it is not cash. It is the written obligation of the state to the soldier who claims that the state, according to the time he served in the army, owes him 10,000, 17,000, 23,000, etc., German Marks. On the other side, although this is not cash, those means are covered. This country has its factories, buildings, flats. So, the state has cover for at least several times more than these books' value. The great majority of soldiers will be able to buy a flat, a shop, or a piece of land in this denationalisation, that is, privatisation. I do have to point out: this is not cash, but is a fixed duty of the state towards a soldier and this duty is covered.' (Interview for RTV B&H, 10 July, 1996.)

About the victory over fascism (The Day of Victory):
Question from an *Avaz* reader: Do you agree that the Day of Victory in Bosnia and Herzegovina was celebrated noticeably humbly?

Izetbegović: Yes, I agree that it is so, but I do not agree that it should be so. This day should have been given more significance. Maybe it is not a day for gatherings, but it is for lectures. Young people in schools and universities should have been given lectures on fascism and the struggle against this evil that always reappears, taking new names and forms.

If we are seeking the reason for, as you said, a humble celebration of this important date in the history of many other, as well as our own people, three reasons come to my mind: first, we are dealing with hot problems daily. We did not feel like celebrating and there is also saturation with holidays in a certain way. There have been many in the last six months. The other reason is that in 1945 fascism was (temporarily) defeated, but it was also a victory of Stalin and his 'gulag system' that inflicted, and continued to do so, as much evil on the people as fascism. There was some bitterness and fear in this victory. Third and the most important reason: the Day of Victory over fascism is celebrated, and fascism obviously was not defeated. After this famous 9th of May 1945, fascism (and other inhumane and anti-human dictatorships) appeared throughout the world in various forms. Still, its worst form showed itself in Bosnia and Herzegovina. Chetniks and Ustashas are in essence fascistic movements for they raise their nations above others and give a free hand to their people, relieving them of any law or principle when it comes to the other and the one who is different. The result of this are the crimes seen in Bosnia and now in Kosovo. This means that the final victory over fascism is postponed for the future, if it ever comes. That is why people say that the quantity of evil in the world is constant, it only changes its shape.' (*Dnevni Avaz*, Sarajevo, 13 May, 1999.)

INDEX

Abdić, Fikret, 84, 85, 91, 107, 163, 183, 191, 258, 524
Abdullah, Prince, 389
Ablakovina, 454
Abraham, 382
Abduladze, Tengiz, 42
Ada, Ciganlija, 456
Adriatic Sea, 117, 258, 300, 381
Adžić, Blagoje, 92, 120, 121
Áerimović, Hilmija, 39
Africa, 281, 408, 453
Agnelli, Susanne, 342, 343, 344
Ahmići, 153, 162, 177
Ajnadžić, Nedžad, 227
Ajvatovica, 531
Akashi, Yasushi, 90, 179, 234, 237, 242, 243, 534
Alagić, Mehmed, 211, 285
Alatović, Haris, 454
Albania, 149, 421, 424, 485, 533
Albright, 348, 432
Alexander, King, 15
Aleksovski, 335
Ali, Abu Hasan, 145
Ali, Mohammad, 295, 296
Alispahić, Bakir, 167, 168, 169, 343
Aljić, Dino, 167
Alps, 408
America, 65, 76, 77, 78, 80, 90, 94, 97, 132, 133, 149, 151, 164, 182, 188, 193, 196, 206, 223, 251, 253, 259, 261, 264, 269, 271, 272, 281, 282, 283, 286, 293, 294, 295, 300, 307, 319, 340, 341, 369, 379, 380, 409, 413, 427, 429, 432, 472, 491, 496, 497, 533
Annan, Kofi, 237
Anđelović, fra Petar, 171
Andrić, Ivo, 386, 448
Ankara, 150, 270, 271
Antigone, 28, 515
Arapčić, Mehmed, 39
Arbour, Louise, 393
Argentina, 386
Arkan, 334
Arkansas, 151, 380
Asad, Muhammed, 505, 506
As-Sufi, Ghalib, 145
Athens, 252, 458

Auschwitz, 476
Australia, 65
Austria, 315, 333, 424, 435, 456, 533
Avdić, Ćamil, 78
Azići, 11, 14, 15
Aziz, Sultan, 456
Azizija, 456

Bacon, 506
Backa, 89
Baghdad, 201, 507
Baker, James, 94
Balinovac, 153, 161
Balkans, 29, 95, 131, 175, 187, 195, 201, 202, 206, 235, 286, 294, 405, 421, 423, 424, 429, 475, 477, 486, 489, 522
Baltak, Nijaz, Daidža, 79, 80
Bangladesh, 201
Banja Luka, 77, 79, 96, 110, 183, 187, 277, 278, 283, 285, 286, 298, 300, 312, 314, 350, 356, 362, 402, 416, 417, 418, 424, 437, 527
Banovići, 285
Bar, 170
Barrio, Jean, 225, 481-490
Barry, Robert, 436, 440, 442, 446
Bašagić, Husref, 16
Baščaršija, 23
Bećirbegović, Edah, 73
Bećirović, Ramiz, 231, 243
Beethoven, 488
Beganović, Mustafa, 122, 169
Begić, Kasim, 110, 113, 218, 296, 352
Behmen, Omer, 31, 32, 35, 43, 46, 47, 73
Behmen, Salih, 31, 35, 46, 47
Behmen, Saliha, 35
Belgium, 111
Belgrade, 11, 16, 25, 45, 53, 56, 60, 62, 66, 74, 77, 78, 86, 89, 91, 92, 94, 97, 98, 99, 105, 117, 131, 136, 174, 248, 262, 264, 269, 282, 299, 316, 321, 331, 333, 357, 386, 421, 456, 459, 470, 521, 522, 525
Beli Manastir, 20, 201
Belje, 20
Bergson, 14, 459, 460
Berisha, Sali, 149
Berjan, Risto, 15
Berković, Eva, 24
Berlin, 44, 303

Berlin Wall, 62, 66, 75, 468, 478
Berne, 147
Bešlagić, 412
Biber, Hasan, 19, 22
Biber, Nusret, 19
Bičakčić, Đula, 31
Bičakčić, Edhem, 31, 32, 376, 425, 418, 496, 534
Bičakčić, Kemal, 73, 493
Biden, 381
Bihać, 80, 92, 125, 191, 192, 193, 196, 197, 199, 204, 205, 206, 208, 215, 217, 218, 221, 222, 263, 334, 384, 424, 507, 508, 534
Bijeli Brijeg, 82
Bijeljina, 116, 183, 187, 229, 278, 330, 356, 424, 439, 526
Bila, 175
Bildt, Carl, 251, 263, 265, 266, 270, 297, 306, 312, 314, 315, 316, 319, 321, 327, 349, 351, 386, 463
Bileća, 78
Bilićar, 15
Bistrik, 118, 119, 168
Bivolje Brdo, 160
Bjelašnica, 151, 155, 254, 255
Blace, 146
Blagaj, 161
Blair, Tony, 90, 434, 448
Bleiberg, 533
Boban, Mate, 114, 116, 139, 144, 146, 171, 175, 354, 496, 519, 524
Bogićević, Bogić, 91, 92
Bojić, Mehmedalija, 63, 116
Bonn, 218, 264, 268, 384, 388, 389, 401, 402, 403, 475
Boras, Franjo, 91
Bosanski Brod, 137, 138, 140, 183, 276
Bosanski, Šamac, 11, 12
Bosanska Krajina, 59, 158, 263
Bosanska Krupa, 227, 276
Bosanski Novi, 283, 284, 285
Bosanski Petrovac, 227
Bosna, river, 11, 137, 456
Boškailo, 160
Bosna, 14, 15, 16, 22, 30, 34, 61, 63, 70, 75, 76, 78, 79, 81, 84, 88, 90, 91, 94, 97, 98, 99, 100, 101, 102, 103, 106, 107, 112, 114, 119, 121, 123, 125, 127, 129, 132, 137, 143, 149, 150, 151, 156, 161, 170, 174, 181, 182, 187, 188, 192, 193, 194, 195, 196, 198, 203, 205, 207, 208, 210, 211, 213, 219, 223, 224, 225, 226,

Bosnia – *cont.*
234, 235, 237, 239, 248, 251, 254, 255, 259, 260, 262, 263, 267, 269, 270, 272, 277, 280, 283, 285, 286, 291, 293, 294, 301, 305, 306, 310, 313, 317, 328, 335, 343, 344, 355, 358, 360, 361, 362, 364, 365, 367, 369, 371, 374, 376, 378, 383, 388, 390, 391, 392, 398, 401, 405, 408, 409, 434, 435, 439, 440, 458, 463, 465, 472, 475, 476, 478, 479, 483, 486, 487, 491, 492, 493, 495, 496, 499, 501, 502, 507, 508, 511, 512, 513, 515, 516, 518, 519, 520, 522, 523, 524, 525, 527, 528, 530, 537
Bosnia and Herzegovina, 15, 17, 19, 29, 40, 45, 59, 60, 61, 62, 63, 64, 65, 68, 69, 74, 76, 78, 80, 81, 84, 85, 86, 91, 92, 93, 94, 95, 96, 98, 99, 103, 104, 105, 108, 110, 111, 112, 113, 114, 116, 120, 122, 123, 128, 136, 138, 139, 140, 141, 142, 143, 145, 147, 148, 152, 153, 154, 157, 165, 167, 171, 172, 173, 176, 177, 178, 184, 185, 190, 197, 199, 200, 201, 204, 206, 209, 212, 214, 215, 216, 217, 218, 229, 231, 238, 240, 241, 242, 243, 244, 245, 249, 252, 253, 256, 261, 264, 268, 273, 274, 276, 278, 279, 281, 283, 290, 292, 297, 311, 316, 326, 329, 331, 335, 340, 349, 351, 353, 354, 357, 359, 366, 368, 370, 372, 377, 380, 382, 384, 385, 394, 396, 402, 403, 406, 407, 414, 417, 418, 420, 423, 425, 426, 429, 433, 441, 442, 445, 447, 448, 452, 453, 455, 462, 464, 468, 473, 475, 482, 484, 485, 486, 487, 488, 490, 491, 495, 498, 499, 507, 511, 513, 514, 516, 517, 518, 519, 520, 523, 524, 525, 527, 528, 529, 530, 531, 533, 536
Bosphorus, 11
Bračković, Ahmed, 73
Bradina, 215
Braunstein, Mathieu, 392
Brčić, Rašid, 39
Brčkanska Malta, 128
Brčko, 128, 137, 140, 183, 242, 264, 276, 291, 304, 309, 311, 312, 319, 321, 324, 326, 330, 351, 352, 368, 374, 375, 376, 377, 384, 403, 407, 409, 410, 411, 412, 413, 414, 415, 421, 422, 438, 457, 495, 496, 528
Breza, 124
Brežnev, 491
Brkić, Milenko, 123, 250

Brodski, Josif, 44
Brozović, Dalibor, 76
Brussels, 100, 112, 114, 115, 126, 316, 320
Buber, Martin, 480
Budapest, 191, 195, 203, 491
Budiša, Dražen, 76
Bugojno, 29, 124, 154, 299, 307, 466, 467
Bukvić, Edib, 169
Bulatović, Momir, 91, 94, 269, 300, 301, 314
Bulgaria, 533
Bush, George, 90, 132
Busovača, 142, 145, 148
Butmir, 180
Bužim, 263

Camp David, 297
Campanella, 27
Campara, Ešref, 23
Canada, 25, 77, 282
Carrington, 113, 247, 248, 249, 250, 476, 488, 524
Carter, Jimmy, 208, 215, 216, 241
Casablanca, 201, 203
Čauševič, Mirsad, 453
Cazin, 64, 78, 137, 192, 197, 220, 263
Ceaucescu, 29
Cerić, Mustafa, 73
Cerović, Stojan, 98
Cerska, 230, 240
Chamberlain, 255
Charlton, Alan, 310
Chicago, 77, 179
China, 23, 480, 506
Chirac, Jacques, 90, 223, 224, 225, 231, 235, 237, 262, 269, 277, 298, 314, 391, 392, 393, 434, 483, 484
Christopher, Warren, 208, 226, 272, 283, 296, 297, 305, 306, 307, 308, 309, 313, 314, 318, 319, 321, 322, 324, 325, 326, 327, 342, 381
Churchill, Winston, 408
Clages, Christian, 312,
Clark, Wesley, 304, 305, 322, 325, 416, 417, 425
Cleas, Willy, 191
Clinton, Bill, 90, 126, 151, 159, 199, 233, 269, 272, 283, 295, 296, 297, 298, 305, 313, 316, 318, 324, 326, 327, 335, 348, 356, 380, 381, 434, 448, 491
Cook, Robin, 496
Cooperman, Alan, 98, 99, 100, 101, 102
Cot, Jean, 234
Crni vrh, 211

Croatia, 63, 79, 81, 83, 91, 92, 94, 95, 96, 97, 98, 99, 102, 105, 107, 110, 111, 116, 121, 123, 128, 140, 142, 146, 154, 170, 184, 189, 191, 192, 196, 201, 205, 207, 210, 211, 223, 229, 251, 263, 265, 270, 274, 285, 292, 307, 308, 316, 335, 356, 363, 371, 372, 383, 397, 400, 401, 403, 405, 406, 426, 427, 436, 437, 438, 440, 465, 470, 471, 472, 483, 484, 487, 488, 516
Cutileiro, 99, 100, 113, 116, 249, 250, 414, 524
Cvetković-Maček, 16, 64, 76, 307
Cyprus, 423
Czechoslovakia, 45

Ćatović, Safet, 78
Ćopić, Branko, 386
Ćoralići, 221
Ćosić, 334

Čamdžić, Sulejman, 73
Čampara, Esref, 23
Čancar, Nusret, 36
Čapljina, 154, 160, 161, 172, 176, 212, 356
Čauševič, Halid, 73, 498
Čeljevo, 161
Čengić, Hasan, 31, 32, 36, 39, 41, 46, 47, 499, 500
Čengić, Muhamed, 73
Čengić, Šačir, 73
Čengic-Vila, 24
Čerimović, Šačir, 73
Čukle, 258

Dahić, Ismet, 428, 429
Dante, 388
Danube, 87
Darwin, 26, 28
Davidović, Ljuba, 15
Dayton, 77, 80, 226, 242, 244, 268, 271, 290, 296, 299, 301, 302, 309, 313, 314, 317, 322, 323, 325, 328, 338, 339, 342, 343, 347, 350, 351, 352, 353, 361, 362, 363, 365, 367, 369, 371, 374, 378, 379, 384, 385, 398, 399, 406, 410, 413, 421, 435, 458, 498, 508, 516, 517, 518, 520, 524, 528
De Charrette, Hervé, 262, 263
De Gaulle, Charles, 434
Dečani, 174
Dejčić, 155

Delalić, Ramiz, Ćelo, 167, 168
DeLaney, Edward, 411
Delić, Rasim, 127, 162, 163, 166, 167, 170, 220, 222, 236, 286, 287, 359
Delić, Sead, 226
Delimustafić, Alija, 122
Demirel, Suleman, 233, 314, 395, 434, 448
Demirović, Zijad, 160
Derventa, 276
Divjak, Jovan, 166, 452, 455
Dizdarević, Raif, 29
Doboj, 276, 285, 313
Dobrinja, 166, 179, 453, 455
Dodik, Milorad, 412, 413, 415, 426, 438, 497, 500
Doko, Jerko, 122
Dole, Bob, 89
Doljani, 162, 163
Domljan, Žarko, 91
Donji Vakuf, 276, 466
Dostoevsky, 459, 519
Dragan, 454
Drašković, Vuk, 97
Drew, Nelson, 266, 310
Drina, river, 76, 79, 105, 128, 187, 217, 230, 266, 313, 319, 323, 530
Drnovšek, Janez, 93
Dubica, 439
Dubrave, 160
Dubrovnik, 95, 102, 210, 219, 334
Dučić, Jovan, 386
Dudaković, General, 222, 285, 360
Dugalija, Sulejman, 442, 443
Duraković, Enes, 169
Duraković, Nijaz, 178, 366
Duvno, 76

Džumhur, Nedžad, 73

Đikovina, 161
Đilas, Milovan, 97
Đozo, Husein, 29, 30, 32
Đurđević, Derviš, 31
Đuricić, Zdravko, 57, 468

Eagleburger, Lawrence, 89
Egypt, 150, 213
Einstein, 18, 485, 488
El Alamein, 14
Engels, 516
Esposito, John, 504
Europe, 13, 65, 83, 93, 100, 103, 112, 125, 129, 130, 131, 132, 136, 156, 162, 164,

Europe – *cont.*
174, 175, 184, 185, 193, 223, 224, 234, 248, 257, 260, 270, 280, 281, 302, 307, 316, 318, 328, 330, 340, 343, 345, 352, 369, 381, 390, 394, 403, 405, 413, 423, 434, 440, 441, 464, 472, 476, 478, 485, 486, 493, 504, 506, 507, 523

Fahd, King, 149, 388, 503
Farrand, Robert, 411
Fejzić, Farhia, 73
Ferdinand, 19
Filali, Abdellatif, 408
Filipović, Muhamed, 65, 77, 83, 97, 99, 258, 496
Finci, 419
Firenca, 381
Fischer, Joschka, 93, 434
Foča, 25, 48, 51, 52, 62, 76, 80, 81, 229, 313, 314, 320, 351, 424, 461, 465, 535
Fojnica, 173, 214
Fourastie, Jean, 503
France, 11, 90, 111, 187, 206, 223, 224, 225, 235, 252, 255, 260, 261, 262, 263, 277, 280, 282, 299, 312, 314, 316, 328, 333, 375, 392, 393, 395, 411, 412, 434, 482, 484, 485, 490
Frankfurt, 259
Frasure, Robert, 266, 310
Frazer, 296
Frewer, Barry, 254
Frowick, Robert, 433

Galica, 211
Gandhi, 500
Ganić, Ejup, 91, 218, 291, 316, 366, 376, 401, 408, 410, 412, 429, 493, 534
Garašanin, Ilija, 127
Gavrić, Svjetlana, 134
Gelbard, Robert, 348, 349, 385, 386, 387, 426
Gelsenkirchen, 360
Geneva, 106, 141, 142, 144, 156, 159, 170, 194, 195, 250, 255, 256, 257, 270, 271, 272, 274, 276, 280, 282, 285, 303, 353, 422, 481
Georgia, 42, 293
Germany, 17, 111, 187, 206, 254, 260, 261, 299, 310, 312, 314, 315, 316, 360, 361, 375, 398, 399, 411, 412, 480, 481, 492
Ghali, Boutros, 90, 136, 234, 284
Gibraltar, 408
Glava Zete, 25

Gligorov, Kiro, 87, 92, 93, 94, 101, 120, 471
Goethe, 488
Goli Otok, 219, 533
Goražde, 80, 124, 126, 135, 136, 137, 140, 151, 155, 158, 180, 181, 229, 230, 232, 238, 241, 242, 245, 259, 264, 276, 284, 286, 291, 303, 304, 314, 316, 317, 318, 319, 320, 322, 364, 436, 530, 534
Gorbachev (Gorbačov), 468
Gore, Al, 151, 264, 265, 270
Gornji Vakuf, 143, 146, 172, 175, 254
Goytisolo, Juan, 135, 156
Grabovica, 163
Gračanica, 174, 386
Gradačac, 139, 140, 360, 457, 492, 493
Granić, Mate, 176, 300, 304
Graz, 139
Grbavica, 132, 133, 317, 318, 322, 323, 347, 348, 349
Grdonj, 167, 169
Great Britain, 90, 126, 129, 187, 252, 255, 259, 261, 299, 311, 312, 314, 316, 333, 375, 386, 411, 490
Grebak, 155, 364, 365
Greece, 29, 260, 282, 485
Grozdanić, Sulejman, 61
Grude, 141, 145, 147, 148, 249
Gubavica, 160
Gutman, Roy, 89

Hadžić, Mehmedalija, 32
Hadžić, Rizah, 31, 33, 36
Hadžići, 226, 349
Hadžifejzović, Senad, 118, 445
Hadžihasanović, Hamdija, 169
Hadžihasanović, Safet, 454
Hadžiomeragić, Maid, 73
Hadžiosmanović, Lamija, 73
Hafizović, Rešid, 39
Hague, the, 103, 104, 162, 163, 239, 293, 298, 334, 347, 369, 393, 402, 420
Hajrić, Mehmed, 239
Hajro, 166, 454
Hajrulahović, Mustafa, 502
Halilović, Sefer, 163, 165, 166, 230, 500
Harriman, Averell, 225
Harriman, Pamela, 225, 226
Harland, David, 239, 240, 241, 242, 243, 244
Hasan, King, 408, 409
Hasića Glavica, 160
Hadšijska, 12

Hays, 254
Haznadar, Medo, 453
Hedges, Chris, 429, 430-433
Hegel, 14, 488
Helsinki, 129, 130, 132, 333
Herzegovina, 62, 110, 140, 144, 145, 146, 152, 155, 160, 171, 176, 251
Herzog, Gilles, 394
Hill, Cris, 282, 322, 323
Hiroshima, 299, 342
Hitler, 17, 116, 408
Hodža, Enver, 29, 149, 424, 533
Hodžić, Nedžad, 116
Hodžić, Šefko, 132, 134
Holland, 435
Holbrooke, Richard, 156, 225, 226, 264, 266, 267, 270, 271, 282, 283, 284, 285, 296, 299, 300, 301, 302, 303, 304, 305, 306, 308, 309, 310, 313, 316, 317, 319, 324, 325, 326, 327, 342, 347, 381, 386, 436, 517
Hrasnica, 166, 453
Hrelja, 436
Hudolin, 412
Hujdur, Hamzalija, 39
Huković, Muhamed, 73
Humo, 360
Hungary, 20, 21, 23, 333, 435, 526
Huntington, S., 200, 307, 501
Hurd, Douglas, 126, 259
Huseinović, Emira, 134
Huskić, Husein, 73

Ibro, 359
Ibsen, 51, 56
Igman, 80, 126, 151, 155, 156, 158, 159, 233, 245, 254, 255, 269, 310, 391, 453, 483
Igrić, Gordana, 383
Ilidža, 83, 339, 348, 349, 526
Ilijaš, 304, 349
Imamović, Munever, 169
Imamović, Nurudin, 117
Indonesia, 33, 201
Iran, 88, 150, 200, 204, 223, 389, 390, 491, 492
Iraq, 204
Irinej, Bishop, 89
Ishinger, 306, 316
Iskjudar, 11
Isović, Safet, 73, 470
Istanbul, 11, 127, 181, 395, 397

Italy, 14, 21, 111, 117, 127, 234, 411, 423, 435
Ivo, 454
Izetbegović, Alija, 31, 32, 33, 43, 46, 47, 73,
    79, 80, 81, 84, 88, 94, 97, 118, 121,
    170-172, 174, 190, 195, 196, 197, 218,
    240-245, 257, 258, 263-266, 271, 272,
    273-274, 280-281, 326, 330, 338, 343,
    349, 352-353, 365, 366, 373-375, 383,
    384, 386, 392, 397, 398-400, 401, 407,
    409-410, 412-413, 416, 418, 427-429,
    430, 432, 436-438, 440, 444, 452, 456-
    474, 481-489, 490-502, 515, 519, 521,
    522, 523, 524, 527, 532, 534, 536
Izetbegović, Bakir, 30, 35, 44, 56, 119, 135,
    223, 427, 428, 430, 446, 465, 466
Izetbegović, Halida, 21, 22
Izetbegović, Lejla, 22, 29, 56, 57, 465, 466
Izetbegović, Sabina, 22, 35, 50, 55, 56, 57,
    117, 118, 119, 326, 327, 465, 466

Jablanica, 162, 163, 223, 362, 364, 453
Jahić, Munir, 122
Jajce, 137, 140, 276, 299, 307
Jamakosmanović, 412
Janja, 187, 526
Janowski, Kris, 348, 349
Janvier, 90, 231, 234, 237, 238, 242, 243,
    270, 534
Japan, 313
Jašarević, Nermina, 36, 37
Jasmina, 44, 465
Jean Paul II, Pope, 382
Jeddah, 149, 150, 151
Jelavić, Ante, 416
Jesus Christ, 27, 28, 190, 382, 439, 489,
    500, 515
Johnston, 424
Joulwan, 180, 234, 235, 317, 318, 342
Jović, Borislav, 92, 334
Juppé, 258, 260
Jusić, Džemo, 116

Kadić, Naim, 113
Kadić, Rasim, 76
Kadijević, Veljko, 87
Kajtaz, Halid, 20
Kakanj, 167, 232, 285, 521
Kalesija, 360
Kalinic, 525
Kanlić, Asim, 31
Kant, 14, 459, 480, 515

Karačić, Hasan, 77
Karađorđevo, 93, 128, 307, 471, 472
Karađozović, Esad, 16
Karadžić, Radovan, 84, 90, 92, 95, 97, 101,
    102, 107, 114, 116, 117, 123, 126, 139,
    156, 158, 159, 179, 182, 187, 190, 191,
    193, 206, 208, 215, 216, 217, 218, 223,
    225, 239, 250, 252, 266, 271, 274, 281,
    284, 285, 287, 299, 300, 301, 314, 316,
    339, 351, 369, 381, 384, 392, 405, 440,
    484, 487, 496, 519, 523, 524
Karahodžić, Indira, 443
Karamehmedović, Belmin, 263, 280, 281
Karavdić, Salih, 73
Karić, Enes, 38, 39
Karisik, Milenko, 347
Karlo Veliki, 418
Karuse, 151
Kasumagić, Ismet, 31, 32, 46, 47
Kati, 326
Kauzlarich, 427
Kečo, Junuz, 51, 461
Kečo, Kuduz, 461
Keraterm, 129, 393
Kerrick, General, 319
Keserović, 457
Kinkel, 258, 260
Kiseljak, 147, 266, 269, 391
Kissinger, Henry, 89
Kladanj, 236, 245
Kladuša, 192
Klauzević, 486
Klein, Jacques, 387, 426, 427
Kličković, Gojko, 348
Ključ, 227, 284, 285
Kljuić, Stjepan, 91, 97, 178, 311, 360, 366,
    522, 523
Knez, Željko, 230
Knezević, Ivo, 169
Kobiljača, 171, 266
Kočić, Petar, 386
Kohl, 298, 356
Koljević, Nikola, 91, 97, 299, 300
Komšić, Ivo, 98, 177, 218, 258, 296, 303,
    309, 360, 366, 377, 412
Konjević-Polje, 230, 240
Konjić, 140, 155, 177, 453
Konjicija, Abdulah, 214
Kopači, 436
Korkut, Edib, 78, 380
Kornblum, John, 325, 385

Koroman, Malko, 58
Koschnik, Hans, 342, 343, 344, 345, 346, 352
Koševo, 168, 383
Kosovo, 30, 52, 62, 63, 65, 69, 78, 79, 101, 201, 210, 307, 335, 421, 422, 423, 470, 533, 537
Kostić, Branko, 92, 120, 121
Kotor-Varoš, 350
Kovač, Nikola, 123, 225, 487
Kovaći, 135, 345
Kozarac, 128, 183
Kozarić, Vahid, 39
Koziriev, Andrei, 286
Krajina, 78, 107, 110, 151, 183, 191, 196, 198, 209, 211, 220, 263, 284, 285, 286, 287, 364
Krajišnik, Momčilo, 91, 97, 252, 299, 302, 304, 354, 374, 385, 386, 387, 388
Kraljević, Marko, 386
Kramarić, Zlatko, 412
Kranj, 93
Kremen, 222
Kreso, Sead, 169
Krka, 386
Krstić, 15
Krstičević, Tomislav, 122
Krupa, 192
Kruzel, Joe, 266, 310
Kučan, Milan, 91, 93
Kukanjac, 118, 119
Kula-Grad, 128
Kulen-Vakuf, 227
Kupres, 125, 191
Kupreška Vrata, 191
Kupusović, Muhamed, 32
Kurski, Dmitri, 54

Lačević, Azra, Dalila and Asim, 179
Lagumdžija, Zlatko, 117, 119, 122, 520
Lake, Antony, 264, 316, 317, 319
Lašvanska Valley, 140
Latić, Džemal/Džemaludin, 31, 36, 73, 74, 77, 79, 408
Latić, Nedžad, 36
Lazović, Miro, 214, 225, 258, 296, 309, 377, 487
Lenin, 54, 464
Levý, Bernard Henry, 391, 393, 394, 395, 485
Lewis, Antony, 273
Libya, 22

Lipton, David, 321, 385
Lisbon, 100, 114, 116, 117, 118, 120, 372
Livno, 111, 114, 172, 176, 356, 517
Ljajić, Rasim, 522
Ljubić, 250
Ljubijankić, Irfan, 169, 218, 220, 222, 258
Ljubljana, 60, 90
Ljubuški, 160, 161, 172
Ljujić-Mijatović, Tatjana, 366
Lokve, 160
London, 141, 164, 190, 193, 238, 249, 257, 261, 264, 316, 484
Lovac, 360
Lučić, Slobodan, 454
Lukav, Haris, 169
Lukavac, 148
Lukavica, 117, 118, 119, 241, 386
Luxembourg, 402, 403

Macedonia, 63, 65, 93, 95, 99, 111, 171, 421, 470
Madrid, 264, 402, 403, 404, 421, 426
Maglaj, 140, 151, 175, 259
Mahmuljin, Sakib, 226
Mahmutćehaić, Rusmir, 32, 113, 122, 169, 170, 500
Major, John, 90, 136, 139, 238, 298, 314
Makkah, 150, 501
Malaga, 408
Malaysia, 200, 201, 491
Malcolm, Noel, 161, 252, 258
Markale, 179, 223, 239
Marković, Ante, 78, 87, 92, 93, 94, 525
Marković, Branko, 147
Marović, Svetozar, 91
Marrakech, 408
Marseille, 15
Martić, 191, 196, 221
Mašović, Sulejman, 73
Mazowiecki, Tadeusz, 194, 237, 478
McKenzie, Lewis, 129, 392
Mehić, Rećo, 453
Mehmedagić, Osman, 169
Mehmedović, Meho, 166, 454
Meigs, 417, 423
Memići, 146
Memija, Mufid, 170
Menzies, John, 277, 286, 287, 305, 314, 319, 324
Merdan, Džemo, 175
Mesić, Stipe, 83, 84, 91, 93
Metković, 148, 258

Michelangelo, 26
Mihajlov, Mihajlo, 79
Mihailović, Dražo, 62
Mikulić, Branko, 29, 61, 62, 497
Miljacka, river, 119, 167
Milošević, Slobodan, 79, 87, 90, 91, 93, 94,
   95, 97, 98, 101, 107, 116, 123, 127, 128,
   139, 173, 216, 252, 256, 263, 266, 268,
   282, 287, 296, 297, 298, 299, 302, 309,
   310, 311, 312, 314, 317, 325, 334, 355,
   381, 405, 423, 440, 441, 468, 471, 486,
   487, 521, 522, 525
Milutinović, 301
Mirković, Radovan, 122
Mitrović, Ljubiša, 94
Mitsotakis, 252
Mitterrand, Francois, 90, 225, 392, 484
Mladić, Ratko, 85, 134, 156, 157, 158, 159,
   234, 235, 238, 239, 242, 254, 270, 277,
   281, 284, 287, 298, 314, 369, 392, 487,
   496
Mock, Alois, 87
Modriča, 457
Montenegro, 25, 62, 63, 92, 93, 99, 101,
   102, 116, 127, 128, 130, 136, 185, 189,
   217, 263, 268, 298, 301, 331, 332, 333,
   363, 421, 440, 466, 470, 521
Morillon, 240
Morocco, 33, 200, 201, 202, 382, 408
Moscow, 34, 44
Moses, 27
Mostanica, 386
Mostar, 22, 82, 128, 144, 145, 148, 151,
   152, 153, 154, 160, 161, 172, 175, 176,
   212, 223, 224, 259, 260, 281, 284, 301,
   308, 330, 342, 343, 344, 345, 346, 352,
   356, 375, 416, 417, 418, 436, 482, 517,
   518, 520, 527, 528, 535
Mrkovići, 179
Muderis, 360
Muftić, Kemal, 156, 387
Muftić, Tarik, 16, 73
Muhamedagić, Izet, 220
Muhić, Fuad, 15, 76
Mujagić, Hamza, 77
Mujezinović, Dževad, 12, 78
Muratović, Hasan, 122, 376
Musa, Amr, 150
Muslim, Nikola, 83
Mutevelija, 360

Naletilić, Mladen, Tuta, 151

Nametak, Fehim, 73
Nanica, 227
Nanić, Faris, 73
Nanić, Izet, 263
Nanić, Kemal, 73
Neretva, river, 137, 155, 163, 342, 346, 528
Neum, 60, 171, 258, 384, 468
Nevesinje, 128
Neville-Jones, Paulina, 310, 311, 315, 316
Newton, 18
New York, 164, 184, 251, 252, 280, 282,
   283, 293, 295, 366, 377, 436, 437, 453,
   510, 534
Nicol, 387
Nikola, 467
Nikolaj, Vladika, 419
Nikolić, Ranko, 122
Nikolić, Slobodan, Nidžo, 458
Nikšić, 25, 466
Njegoš, 386
Northern Ireland, 531
Nova Bila, 175
Novi Pazar, 64, 80, 523
Novi Travnik, 124, 140
Novo Sarajevo, 303
Nuhbegović, Fehim, 73

O'Connor, 341
Odabašić, Jasmin, 443
Odžak, 276
Ogata, Mrs., 255
Ohio, 296, 324
Ohrid, 93
Olovo, 151, 521
Omarska, 129, 393
Omerbašić, Šefko, 73
Omersoftić, Amila, 169
Orić, Naser, 231, 232
Orošolić, 412
Oručević, Safet, 152, 223, 344, 359, 360, 534
Osijek, 412
Ostrog, 386, 466
Otoka, 227, 285
Owen, David, 125, 150, 156, 157, 158, 162,
   163, 164, 165, 231, 244, 250, 251, 252,
   253, 254, 255, 258, 259, 280, 334, 414,
   482, 523, 524, 534
Owen, Robert, 270, 282, 304, 305, 309,
   310, 313, 323, 368, 377, 409, 410, 411,
   413, 415, 416
Özal, Turgut, 88, 150
Ozren, 220, 386

Pakistan, 150, 201, 491
Pale, 158, 224, 252, 264, 267, 277, 339,
    340, 347, 348, 350, 351, 375, 379, 384,
    385, 392, 393, 413, 443
Palić, Avdo, 239
Paljenik, 211
Panama, 386
Papoulias, 260
Pardew, 282
Paris, 130, 132, 181, 193, 214, 223, 224,
    225, 231, 264, 280, 316, 317, 328, 330,
    338, 391, 392, 393, 482, 487
Pašalić, Enver, 37, 38, 41
Pavle, Patriarch, 89, 90, 269
Pećanin, Senad, 490, 499, 501
Pejanović, Mirko, 178, 218, 366
Pekić, Fadil, 221
Pelivan, Jure, 91, 122
Perry, William, 191, 317, 319, 324
Perućica, 25, 466
Pešelj, Branko, 79
Petritsch, Wolfgang, 431, 436, 440, 442, 443
Piava, 12
Pijade, Moša, 19
Pijesak, 153
Pijesci, 160
Pilsel, Drago, 524
Plana, 78
Plavšić, Biljana, 91, 393, 497
Ploče, 401, 438
Pobrić, Omer, 73
Počitelj, 514
Počiteljsko Polje, 161
Podgorica, 94, 116
Podhum, 153
Podrinje, 116, 126, 128, 158, 229, 232,
    242, 244, 355, 442
Pogorelica, 342, 343
Poland, 16, 45, 116
Polog, 224
Poplašen, 407, 415, 416
Popović, Velimir, 15
Popper, Karl, 507
Posavina, 14, 139, 230, 287, 311, 316, 517
Pozderac, Hamdija, 468, 496, 497
Prazina, Juka, 151, 165
Prelić, Vlastimir, 443
Prenj, 128
Prevljak, Fikret, 155, 360
Prguda, Rušid, 31, 34
Prijedor, 128, 131, 183, 283, 284, 285, 528

Primorac, Žarko, 122
Princip, Gavrilo, 19
Prlić, Jadranko, 296, 308, 496
Prozor, 140, 145, 146, 151, 153, 160, 212,
    254
Pučnik, Jože, 76
Pula, 223
Puljić, Vinko, 171
Pušina, Jusuf, 122, 169

Qasim, Shaikh, 149

Rabin, 500
Radišić, Živko, 425
Radončić, 410
Rafsanjani, 233
Raguž, Martin, 123
Raić, Božo, 143
Ranković, Aleksandar, 24, 533
Ravno, 116
Ražnjatović, Željko, Arkan, 285
Reagan, Ronald, 89
Rehn, Elizabeth, 300
Republika Srpska, 242, 270, 271, 273, 278,
    279, 303, 304, 305, 309, 310, 311, 318,
    348, 367, 368, 371, 375, 384, 385, 386,
    393, 402, 403, 407, 412, 413, 414, 415,
    416, 418, 426, 442, 497, 526, 528, 529
Rešidović, Edina, 31, 33, 34, 36, 42, 43
Richardson, Bill, 377
Riyadh, 388, 389
Rogatica, 303, 320
Rogoj, 155
Romania, 45, 533
Romanija, 110
Rome, 89, 117, 342, 343, 344, 345, 346,
    352, 353, 347, 410
Rose, General, 158, 533, 534
Rosetti, Giorgi, 248
Ruez, Jean-René, 232
Ruhe, Folker, 254
Russia, 30, 187, 193, 200, 206, 252, 255,
    261, 275, 286, 292, 299, 318, 333, 375,
    411, 472, 485, 490

Sabrihafizović, Džemil, 218, 296
Sadović, Bakir, 73, 214
Salihbegović, Melika, 31, 32, 458
Salman, Prince, 149, 151
Sandžak, 62, 210, 317, 321, 322, 422, 470,
    521, 522
Sanica, 227, 285

Sanski Most, 183, 227, 276, 287, 314
Saračević, Arijana, 214
Sarajevo, 11, 12, 14, 15, 16, 18, 19, 20, 21,
    22, 23, 24, 25, 29, 31, 36, 38, 40, 44,
    45, 46, 50, 56, 60, 62, 66, 73, 75, 76,
    79, 90, 91, 92, 93, 94, 96, 97, 103, 107,
    108, 110, 114, 116, 117, 118, 119, 120,
    121, 124, 125, 126, 128, 129, 131, 134,
    135, 137, 140, 141, 145, 149, 155, 156,
    158, 163, 165, 166, 167, 168, 170, 173,
    175, 179, 180, 182, 186, 187, 188, 189,
    199, 212, 214, 217, 218, 219, 222, 223,
    224, 226, 227, 231, 233, 234, 237, 239,
    244, 249, 251, 255, 259, 264, 266, 267,
    269, 271, 274, 276, 277, 282, 286, 291,
    296, 297, 299, 301, 303, 304, 309, 312,
    316, 322, 329, 334, 338, 339, 342, 346,
    347, 348, 349, 350, 356, 357, 358, 364,
    373, 381, 382, 383, 391, 392, 397, 404,
    413, 416, 417, 418, 419, 424, 425, 426,
    427, 431, 434, 435, 436, 442, 452, 453,
    454, 456, 457, 462, 466, 471, 473, 476,
    477, 478, 479, 480, 481, 482, 483, 485,
    493, 498, 501, 511, 514, 516, 518, 520,
    522, 525, 527, 528, 529, 530, 531, 532,
    534, 535, 536, 537
Sattar, Muhammed, 150
Saudi Arabia, 149, 388, 390, 422, 503
Sava, river, 11, 128, 171, 325, 456
Scala, Bono and Milan, 535
Schilling, Schwarz Christian, 309, 311
Schroeder, 434
Scowcroft, Brent, 89
Selimović, Meša, 386
Seljubac, Sead, 35, 36
Selma, 22, 466
Serbia, 14, 15, 16, 62, 63, 65, 81, 92, 98,
    99, 102, 105, 116, 127, 128, 130, 136,
    138, 170, 173, 182, 185, 189, 197, 198,
    199, 201, 205, 206, 210, 216, 217, 235,
    237, 252, 263, 267, 268, 270, 274, 283,
    287, 298, 321, 331, 335, 355, 363, 381,
    383, 392, 397, 405, 406, 423, 427, 438,
    440, 445, 465, 470, 471, 472, 484, 487,
    516, 521
Serdarević, Asaf, 16
Šerge, Robert, 386
Server, Daniel, 304
Shattuck, John, 312, 314
Sicily, 14
Sidran, Abdulah, 51, 323, 456-474
Silajdžić, Haris, 114, 122, 150, 168, 169,

Silajdžić, Haris – *cont.*
    170, 176, 180, 218, 222, 258, 259, 261,
    267, 296, 299, 300, 302, 303, 305, 306,
    308, 309, 310, 311, 313, 316, 321, 323,
    324, 331, 376, 408, 410, 418, 425, 426,
    493, 534
Simović, Miodrag, 122
Siniša, 454
Sintra, 401, 402
Skaka, Abdulah, 73
Skenderrija, 118, 119, 135, 167, 539
Sklar, 427
Skopje, 120, 121, 171
Slavonia, 222, 263, 487
Slavonski Brod, 139
Slišković, 499
Slovenia, 60, 62, 81, 91, 92, 93, 94, 95, 99,
    111, 116, 123, 184, 210, 222, 363, 400,
    405, 423, 440, 470, 488
Smailbegović, Faruk, 169
Smajkić, Arif, 169
Smajlović, Nordin, 73
Smith, Admiral, 338, 351
Smith, Rupert, 233, 234, 238, 239, 243, 284
Socrates, 28, 515
Solaković, Adnan, 453, 454
Solana, Javijer, 416, 425
Somalia, 306
Sophia, 19
Sopočani, 174
Soros, 463
South Africa, 126, 531
Soviet Union / USSR, 45, 113, 149, 219,
    275, 491
Spahić, Mirza and Selma, 179
Spahić, Mustafa, 31, 36, 39, 47
Spaho, Mehmed, 64, 470
Spain, 111, 252, 282, 408
Spengler, Oswald (Osvald), 14, 459, 485
Split, 93, 94, 139, 147, 222, 223, 233, 471, 523
Srebrenica, 126, 137, 158, 187, 227, 229-245,
    259, 266, 267, 277, 313, 314, 330, 341, 371,
    376, 381, 393, 403, 439, 485, 487, 535
Srebreniković, Mirsad, 73
Srebrov, Vladimir, 76
St. Augustine, 27
St. Nicolas, 341
St. Sava, 16, 386
Stalin, 17, 19, 34, 42, 116, 219, 516
Stalingrad, 14
Stanić, Peko, 133
Stanojevići, 160

Index

Steiner, Michael, 300, 304, 305, 312, 348, 350
Stiegelmayer, Alexandra, 433
Stipetić, Petar, 139
Stojanov, Dragoljub, 169
Stojanović, Nikola, 57, 468
Stojčevac, 93, 94
Stolac, 20, 154, 160, 161, 171, 172, 176, 212, 299, 307, 362, 517
Stoltenberg, Thorvald, 156, 157, 162, 163, 165, 254, 255, 256, 258, 259, 280, 414, 524
Strasbourg, 423
Stupni Do, 177
Sudar, Pero, 419
Suel, General, 300
Sukno, Nikola, 34
Sulejman, Dugalija, 442, 443
Sultan of Sharjah, 149
Switzerland, 75, 147, 315, 510

Šabić, Jasmina, 438
Šabić, Salem, 65, 73
Šabolić, Mensur, 221
Šaćirbej, 534
Šaćirbegović, Almasa, 73, 77
Šaćirbegović, Muhamed, 150, 238, 267, 282, 283, 296, 304, 308, 310, 311, 312, 315, 316, 323, 325, 331, 376
Šaćirbegović, Nedžib, 77, 78, 81
Šahinpašić, 499
Šamac, 276, 456, 457
Šantić, 211
Šarac, Džemail, 166
Šarinić, Hrvoje, 91
Šarlija, Mate, 80
Šešelj, 334, 416
Šestić, Sead, 73
Ševaš-Polje, 160
Škaljevina, 160
Špegelj, Martin, 92
Šukrija, uncle, 18
Šušak, Gojko, 300, 304
Šusljić, 15

Tadić, 334
Talbott, Strobe, 226
Tanković, Šemso, 65, 73
Tarčin, 214, 215
Tarik, 408
Tarschys, Daniel, 424
Tasovčići, 161
Tbilisi, 42
Tehran, 88, 388, 389, 390, 532

Terazije, 62
Tešanj, 124, 151, 530
Tesla, Nikola, 386
Teslić, 181
Tetovo, 80
Thatcher, Margaret, 129
Tiho, 454
Tirana, 149
Titograd, 116
Tito, Josip Broz, 20, 29, 30, 31, 248, 272, 439, 466, 489, 491, 492, 510, 522, 532, 533
Tokić, 418
Tokyo, 400
Tolstoy, 459, 480, 488
Tomić, Neven, 496
Tomislavgrad, 76, 147
Topalsvić, Mušana-Cace, 166, 168, 169, 452
Topić, Hakija, 214
Toronto, 77
Traljić, Edhem, 73
Travnik, 124, 144, 147, 154, 299, 307
Trebević, 163, 166, 169, 179, 278
Trebinje, 183, 362
Treskavica, 151, 181
Trnka, Kasim, 169, 258, 296, 323, 408
Trnovo, 155, 276
Tuđman, Franjo, 83, 84, 87, 90, 91, 93, 94, 95, 102, 107, 111, 116, 128, 139, 140, 141, 142, 146, 153, 154, 172, 173, 175, 176, 177, 191, 196, 222, 256, 258, 260, 265, 280, 281, 283, 285, 297, 299, 304, 306, 307, 308, 311, 313, 316, 325, 326, 396, 397, 402, 437, 441, 471, 484, 498, 523, 525
Turajlić, Hakija, 122
Turkey, 39, 88, 156, 200, 270, 395, 422, 456, 491, 492
Tursumović, Husein, 215
Tuzla, 80, 120, 128, 181, 218, 220, 223, 230, 232, 236, 245, 283, 285, 304, 418, 423, 424, 426, 430, 431, 442, 462, 529

Udbina, 191, 197
Ugljanin, 522
Una, river, 105, 128, 283
United Arab Emirates (UAE), 149
United States of America (USA), 89, 111, 112, 159, 187, 199, 208, 261, 268, 297, 304, 305, 306, 312, 314, 316, 318, 324, 327, 333, 367, 375, 380, 381, 398, 411, 412, 427, 434, 472, 483, 490, 491, 510

Uzelac, Nikola, 96
Uzelac, Uglješa, 122
Užice, 116, 456

Vance, Cyrus, 103, 107, 110, 164, 244, 250, 251, 252, 253, 254, 414, 482, 524, 534
Vareš, 146, 170, 171, 172
Vasiljević, 81
Veladžić, Mirsad, 73
Velagić, Teufik, 32, 75
Velayati, Ali Akbar, 88, 150
Velešici, 134, 135
Velež, 128
Velika Kladuša, 80, 81, 82, 83, 183, 191, 197, 263
Venezuela, 333
Verbal delict, 31, 42, 43, 54, 65, 79, 467
Vienna, 32, 75, 87, 380, 412, 413, 415
Vietnam, 306
Vidgorova, Frida, 44
Vijaka, 146
Vijenac, 181
Višegrad, 140, 229, 314, 384, 424, 535
Višići, 160, 161
Visoko, 134, 285
Vitez, 140, 177, 260
Vitina, 160
Vladivostok, 44
Vlašić, 211, 215, 218
Vlasić, Ferdo, 76
Vogošća, 347, 349
Vojvodina, 62
Vozuća, 226, 334, 521
Vraca, 128
Vranica, 214
Vujović, Željko, 454
Vukovar, 95, 96, 102, 210, 219

Waldheim, Kurt, 87
Walker, Michael, 348
Wallich, Christine, 300, 312
Washington, 77, 79, 176, 177, 207, 259, 260, 306, 316, 317
Weinstein, 377
Weizsacker, 507
Werner, Manfred, 179
Wernle-Matić, Marija, 145, 146, 148
Westendorp, 386, 387, 398, 401, 417, 431, 495, 496, 527, 528

Williams, Paul, 433

Yeltsin, 286, 298
Yugoslavia, 13, 16, 17, 19, 20, 23, 24, 25, 30, 32, 33, 34, 37, 43, 45, 46, 48, 58, 59, 60, 63, 64, 65, 66, 68, 70, 72, 73, 74, 76, 77, 81, 86, 87, 89, 90, 91, 92, 93, 94, 95, 98, 99, 101, 104, 105, 111, 112, 113, 115, 116, 125, 128, 146, 184, 186, 197, 201, 210, 218, 219, 245, 247, 248, 249, 250, 263, 265, 267, 286, 292, 296, 335, 341, 347, 355, 363, 371, 372, 383, 400, 402, 405, 419, 420, 422, 439, 440, 457, 468, 469, 470, 471, 475, 485, 488, 489, 491, 498, 510, 521, 532, 533

Zadar, 79
Zagreb, 16, 17, 22, 23, 60, 62, 65, 80, 83, 84, 90, 117, 129, 138, 139, 141, 143, 149, 175, 179, 221, 250, 256, 263, 396, 401, 438, 469, 470, 478, 518, 519, 525
Zavidovići, 474
Zedong, Mao, 272
Zekulić, Jak, 314, 315
Zenica, 20, 52, 124, 126, 127, 148, 170, 175, 214, 233, 234, 236, 262, 304, 354, 424
Zenkić, Ilijas, 78
Zeta, 25
Zimmermann, 101
Zubak, 218, 225, 296, 302, 303, 304, 306, 310, 313, 316, 319, 321, 323, 324, 353, 483
Zulfikarpašić, Adil, 75, 77, 82, 83, 97, 98, 470
Zunić, Đulko, 73
Zurich, 75, 145
Zvornik, 80, 128, 229, 278, 330, 351, 362, 375, 376

Žepa, 126, 140, 158, 229, 230, 231, 232, 233, 234, 237, 238, 239, 242, 243, 244, 245, 262, 267, 277, 302, 303, 313, 330, 487
Žepče, 147, 153, 175, 514, 517
Žitomislić, 386
Živalj, Husein, 31, 32
Živkov, 29
Žuč, 357, 358, 359